Family, Law, and Society: From Roman Law to the Present Day

Ius, Lex et Res Publica
Studies in Law, Philosophy and Political Cultures

Edited by Barbara Janusz-Pohl and Anna Jaron

Volume 28

Ewa Dawidziuk / Patricia Panero / Anna Tarwacka (eds.)

Family, Law, and Society: From Roman Law to the Present Day

PETER LANG

Berlin · Lausanne · Bruxelles · Chennai · New York · Oxford

Bibliographic Information published by the Deutsche Nationalbibliothek
The Deutsche Nationalbibliothek lists this publication in the Deutsche Nationalbibliografie; detailed bibliographic data is available online at http://dnb.d-nb.de.

Library of Congress Cataloging-in-Publication Data
A CIP catalog record for this book has been applied for at the Library of Congress.

Cover illustration: Courtesy of Benjamin Ben Chaim.

This publication was financially supported by the Cardinal Stefan Wyszyński University in Warsaw.

This publication has been financially supported by SWPS University.

SWPS University

ISSN 2191-3250
ISBN 978-3-631-91010-8 (Print)
E-ISBN 978-3-631-91068-9 (E-Book)
E-ISBN 978-3-631-91069-6 (E-PUB)
DOI 10.3726/b21356

Published by Peter Lang GmbH, Berlin, Deutschland

info@peterlang.com - www.peterlang.com

This publication has been peer reviewed.

Contents

Introduction

It is an honor and a satisfaction for me to introduce this monograph which incorporates a complex and interdisciplinary vision of a subject that, although it is constantly present in our positive law, it still is the result of the impact that Roman Law has had on our European legal tradition.

Indeed, the greatness, meaning and usefulness of this law does not suffer a substantial decline with the end of its practical application. It is well-known, the unique ability of the Roman Law to develop equitable fair principles, which exceed its own space-time coordinates and adapts to the new realities of many years in which in one way or another will continue in force, providing solutions to various social interactions. These concepts postulated by Roman Law are the axis of the juridical history of the European continent.

Despite the scientific value that everything historical entails, the work we present here is a proof of this, and as its title indicates, it is not limited to showing a historical vision of some institutions of family law. This work shows precisely how Roman Law has adapted to a rapidly changing world, especially in the field of the family, an institution considered one of the three basic pillars of law and society.

In the vast legal system framework, few areas are as fundamental and complex as those involving family and its relationship with society. Throughout history, the family has been considered the primary nucleus of social organization, and the law has played a crucial role in the regulation and protection of its member's rights and obligations.

In this book, this intricate relationship is discussed throughout time, from the beginnings of Roman Law to nowadays. Through an in-depth and rigorous analysis, we examine how family conceptions and its legal rules and regulations have evolved, adapted to social, cultural and political changes.

We can't ignore the challenges facing Family Law in Europe. Demographic transformations, technological advances, changes in family patterns and social inequalities raise questions and ethical dilemmas that require a constant adaptation and updating of family laws. It is imperative that legislators, academics, legal practitioners and society as a whole, actively collaborate to address these challenges and ensure that family law remains a driver of justice and fairness in Europe.

In this context, this book seeks to explore and analyze the importance of family law from multiple perspectives. Changes in the forms of cohabitation, new family conceptions, new reproductive technologies and gender equality are current unresolved legal challenges, where a historical view has much to offer.

Through a careful reflection, this work is structured in five topics: the first one deals with the origin of family and its historical evolution. It studies traditional institutions such as adoption, marriage and its patrimonial effects, divorce and certain institutions of inheritance law reviewed from the Roman legal experience, and through intermediate law and civil codifications.

The second part is entitled: *The Family as the Foundation of Society*, and it includes papers dealing with the role of the family in civil society in its material aspect, or the family as a method or alternative system of social control as opposed to criminal law, to current issues such as the protection of minors in an absolutely digitalized society, or the role of the family in the education of children, in the light of the new social transformations.

In the third part, we find papers related to the *constitution and fundamental rights*: Thus, the family is studied as the fundamental nucleus of society, reflected in the various constitutions throughout history, and there are papers referring to the changes in the labor market in the European context, motivated by the dramatic demographic situation in Europe that aim to support families; the procedural importance of vetting in family matters, an extremely important issue from the perspective of the values protected by the court, such as the welfare of children, or the protection of the family, and there is also talk of such a current issue as surrogate motherhood, and the filiation problems arising from it in Spain. A paper on the problems derived from the obligation of the parents to administer with due diligence the assets of the minor under their parental authority closes this section.

Another section, referred to *The Family in an Inclusive and Global Society: Changes in the Family Structures*, focuses on conceptualizing and contextualizing some figures as current as digital assets, presenting the basic dilemmas they pose, their possible concept and some proposals for necessary solutions, or the maintenance of such Roman terms as "half-siblings," present in some Civil Codes. There are also references to the new modern families, in which animals are treated as members of the family, or to the problems posed by Polish prison law and practice in relation to contact between prisoners and their families, or such current works as those referring to the risks derived from the circulation of data of minors on the Internet, or proposals for possible new tax systems more favorable to the new family models, specifically in Italy.

A fifth and final section, entitled: *The Family of the 21st Century and the Crisis of Values*, closes the work we are presenting and includes aspects of great interest related to the new challenges faced by families in the digital era. Thus, it seems necessary to protect the members of the family nucleus from the new aggressions generated by virtual environments, while at the same time a reflection on whether family and inheritance legislation should be adapted to address the protection and distribution of these assets in cases of inheritance, divorce, or death. Thus, in the case of alimony, it must adapt to contemporary challenges and provide effective responses to the needs of families as reflected in the proposed changes to the Family and Guardianship Code in Poland.

Ultimately, this book seeks to shed light on the interactions between family, law, and society over the centuries, exploring the tensions, contradictions and changes that have defined this complex relationship. In doing so, we hope to contribute to the current debate on the legal challenges and dilemmas facing the family institution in the 21st century.

This book, is a thought-provoking and critical analysis, offering a panoramic look at the evolution of family law and its impact on today's society.

Patricia Panero Oria

Chapter I. Family: Origin and historical evolution

Aleksandra Szymańska

Protection of a wife's assets in the event of her husband's financial problems in Paulus de Castro's printed commentaries and collections of *consilia*

Abstract: Since much of the wife's property passed into the husband's management upon marriage, the law should provide for measures to prevent the loss or diminution of that property. These measures should effectively protect her both against risky or irresponsible actions of her husband and against the resulting claims of his creditors. However, resorting to such measures constituted an extraordinary situation, since the wife, as *socia domi mariti*, should in principle share not only the auspicious moments with him, but also any adversity. Temporary failures in the management of the family's assets, arguably not uncommon in the merchant societies of Italian cities, were certainly not a pretext for taking extraordinary precautions. However, if a husband was on the brink of insolvency, a wife could demand that her husband be deprived of control over her dowry property and also her non-dowry property if she had also entrusted it to him. This paper concerns the protection of a wife's assets against her husband's insolvency in the commentaries and *consilia* by Paulus de Castro.

Keywords: Paulus de Castro, *consilia*, commentary, bankruptcy, dowry, *dos*, *Paraphernalia*, *bona non dotalia*, married woman, matrimonial property regimes, *ius commune*

1. Introduction

The subject of this paper is the protection of a wife's assets in the event of her husband's financial problems in light of the commentaries and *consilia* found in the collection of Paulus de Castro,[1] one of the most prominent jurists of the so-called

1 On the life and work of Paulus de Castro see: G. Panciroli, *De claris legum interpretibus*, Lipsiae 1721, pp. 186–189; F. C. von Savigny, *Geschichte des Römischen Rechts im Mittelalters*, t. VI, Heidelberg 1850, pp. 281–293; N. Del Re, *Sei consigli inediti di Paolo di Castro nei codici vaticani latini 8068, 8069, 11605 e Urbinate latino 1132*, Roma 1945; H. Lange, "Die Rechtsquellenlehre in den Consilien Paul de Castros," in *Aktuelle Fragen aus modernen Recht und Rechtsgeschichte. Gedächtnisschrift für Rudolf Schmidt*, ed. E. Seidl, Berlin 1966, pp. 421–440; N. Del Re, "*Paolo di Castro*, dottore della verità," *Studi senesi* 82 (1970), pp. 193–236; J. Kirshner, "Paolo di Castro on Cives ex privilegio: A Controversy over the Legal Qualifications for Public Office in early Fifteenth-Century

school of commentators. The source, therefore, is legal literature related to academic activities, namely his commentaries on the *Corpus iuris civilis*, as well as legal advice resulting from his advisory work, taking into account both the statutes of the Italian communes and Roman law in its Justinian form. Legal advice was sought from legal experts to clarify legal issues including concerns arising from ambiguities in statutes, gaps in them, as well as contradictions between statutory norms. In order to resolve the problems and disputes arising from the poor financial situation of the husband, lawyers analyzed dowry contracts and other contracts between spouses, city statutes, as well as *ius commune*, that is, earlier legal literature concerning mainly the texts of the Justinian compilation—above all the summa to the Code of Justinian by Azo, the Gloss of Accursius and various commentaries of their predecessors. Both the commentaries and the *consilia* of many lawyers have been published in print. The problem of wives' claims against insolvent husbands in late-medieval Italy has been generally analyzed based on the sources mentioned above by Julius Kirshner in his inspiring

---

Florence," in *Renaissance Studies in Honour of Hans Baron*, ed. A. Molho, J. A. Tedeschi, Dekalb 1971, pp. 227–264; G. d'Amelio, "Castro, Paolo di," in *Dizionario Biografico degli Italiani*, t. XXII, Roma 1979, pp. 227–233; A. Romano, "La giurisprudenza consulente e Paolo di Castro. Alcuni consilia inediti del ms. Venezia, Bibl. Marciana, lat. 2324," *Rivista di storia del diritto italiano* 61 (1988), pp. 141–170; D. Maffei, "Un commentario dimenticato di Paolo di Castro sul Digesto Vecchio," *Rivista internazionale di diritto comune* 14 (2003), pp. 9–13; H. Lange, M. Kriechbaum, *Römisches Recht im Mittelalter*, t. II: *Die Kommentatoren*, Munich 2007, pp. 813–825; S. Lepsius, "Paolo di Castro as consultant: Applying and Interpreting Florence's Statutes," in *The Politics of the Law in Late Medieval and Renaissance Italy*, ed. L. Armstrong, J. Kirshner, Toronto Studies in Medieval Law, t. I, Toronto 2011, pp. 77–105; G. Murano, "Paolo da Castro," in *Autographa*, t. I. 1: *Giuristi, giudici e notai (sec. XII–XV)*, ed. G. Murano, Imola 2012, pp. 129–135; E. Cortese, "Paolo di (da) Castro (Castro)," in *Dizionario biografico dei giuristi italiani*, ed. I. Birocchi, E. Cortese, A. Mattone, M. N. Miletti, t. II, Bologna 2013, pp. 1505–1507; S. Lepsius, "Paulus de Castro als Konsiliator: Anwendung, Interpretation und Fortbildung der Florentiner Statuten," *Rivista internazionale di diritto comune* 25 (2014), pp. 61–122; B. Pieri, *Usurai, ebrei e poteri della Chiesa nei consilia di Paolo da Castro. Le competenze canonistiche di un civilista*, Bologna 2016; R. Sorice, "Il diritto del nemico alla difesa. Ius belli e ius gentium in un Consilium di Paolo di Castro," in *Der Einfluss der Kanonistik auf die europäische Rechtskulturs*, ed. O. Condorelli, F. Roumy, M. Schmoeckel, Wien-Köln-Weimar 2020, pp. 180–189; S. Lepsius, "Paolo di Castro (1360/62–1441)," in *Law and the Christian Tradition in Italy: The Legacy of the Great Jurists*, ed. O. Condorelli, R. Domingo, London-New York 2021, pp. 198–215.

article.[2] In this paper, the works of one of the outstanding commentators of the 15th century—Paulus de Castro—will be subjected to a detailed analysis in this regard.

Paulus de Castro's considerations on the possibility of recovering the dowry due to the husband's impoverishment can be found in his commentary on *l. si constante* (D. 24, 3, 24 pr[3]) and in *consilia*.[4]

As the commentator has written, *lex si constante* states the well-known principle that, if the husband has become so poor that, after deducting his debts, he does not have enough property left to repay the dowry, the woman may also claim it back during the marriage by instituting a personal action (*actio personalis de dote*).[5] The passage provides an opportunity for him to consider more broadly the issue of a wife taking control of her property due to her husband's financial problems and to take into account other passages in the Justinian compilation regarding this matter. As he noticed, there are few of them—besides the abovementioned passage from the Digest, there is the passage from Justinian's Code *l. ubi adhuc* (C. 5, 12, 29[6]) and the passage from the Justinianic novella *l.*

---

2 J. Kirshner, "Wives' Claims against Insolvent Husbands in Late Medieval Italy," in *Women of the Medieval World: Essays in Honor of John H. Mundy*, ed. J. Kirshner, S. F. Wemple, Oxford 1985, pp. 256–303 and in an updated version in: J. Kirshner, *Marriage, Dowry, and Citizenship in Late Medieval and Renaissance Italy*, Toronto-Buffalo-London 2015, pp. 131–160.

3 *Ulpianus libro 33 ad edictum*. Si constante matrimonio propter inopiam mariti mulier agere volet, unde exactionem dotis initium accipere ponamus? Et constat exinde dotis exactionem competere, ex quo evidentissime apparuerit mariti facultates ad dotis exactionem non sufficere.

4 As Susanne Lepsius wrote, the question of which of the printed *consilia* were actually written by Paulus himself requires careful investigation. See S. Lepsius, "Paolo di Castro (1360/62–1441)," p. 200.

5 Si maritus pervenit ad tantam paupertatem, quod deductis debitis non superest tantum de bonis suis, quod sufficiat ad restitutionem dotis, potest mulier etiam constante matrimonio dotem exigere per actionem personalem de dote h[oc] d[dicit] et est famosum principium huius l[egis].—Paulus de Castro, *In Primam Infortiati partem Commentaria*, Lugduni 1585, p. 20, n. 1.

6 Imperator Justinianus. Ubi adhuc matrimonio constituto maritus ad inopiam sit deductus et mulier sibi prospicere velit resque sibi suppositas pro dote et ante nuptias donatione rebusque extra dotem constitutis tenere, non tantum mariti res ei tenenti et super his ad iudicium vocatae exceptionis praesidium ad expellendum ab hypotheca creditorem secundum praestamus, sed etiam si ipsa contra detentatores rerum ad maritum suum pertinentium super isdem hypothecis aliquam actionem secundum legum distinctionem moveat, non obesse ei matrimonium adhuc constitutum sancimus, sed

illud quoque sancire (Auth. 7, 8 = N. 97, 6[7])—but this issue raises many questions.[8] Paulus, aware that many of his predecessors had considered the issues involved, decided to limit himself to only the five main issues raised by the Gloss of Accursius. He found it unnecessary to dwell on the secondary issues, since they had been thoroughly investigated by Bartolus de Saxoferrato and other scholars.[9] Indeed, Bartolus, being the master of Baldus de Ubaldis, who in turn was the teacher of Paulus de Castro, left an extensive commentary on which others who analyzed the issue of the possible actions of a wife in the case of her husband's financial problems were based, including Paulus de Castro.[10]

---

ita eam posse easdem res vindicare vel a creditoribus posterioribus vel ab aliis, qui non potiora iura legibus habere noscuntur, ut potuisset, si matrimonium eo modo esset dissolutum, quo dotis et ante nuptias donationis exactio ei competere poterat: ita tamen, ut eadem mulier nullam habeat licentiam eas res alienandi vivente marito et matrimonio inter eos constituto, sed fructibus earum ad sustentationem tam sui quam mariti filiorumque, si quos habeant, abutatur.

7 Illud quoque sancire necessarium aestimavimus in plurimis videlicet et innumeris rebus quaesitum. Obtulit enim pater dotem aut mater forte pro filia sua, hanc autem illa obtulit marito, et defunctus est vir inops; deinde patre aut matre mortuis exigitur et quae nupsit conferre suam dotem aut minus tantum accipere. Si quidem vir idoneus est, causa undique absoluta est; si vero nullius alterius domina consistit illa nisi actionum quae contra maritum sunt, at ille minus idoneus est, et obiciatur mulieri quod iam data sit dos pro ea, illa vero actionem conferat nullum habentem penitus effectum, legis causa nobis digna putata est. Et novimus quidem iam in plurimis iudiciis duritiam postea sic iudicatam, et mulierem coactam conferre dotem aut certe reputare pro se datam, ex qua nullum ei omnino contigit effectum in ipsis rebus recipere: nos autem ex aliis nostris legibus iuvamus causam. Quia enim dedimus mulieribus electionem et constante matrimonio, si male res maritus gubernet, et accipere eas et gubernare et secundum decentem modum et siculi nostra constitutio dixit, si quidem suae potestatis et perfectas aetatis mulier est, sibimet culpam inferat, cur mox viro incohante male substantia uti non percepit et auxiliata est sibi: sic enim habitura erat in collationis ratione proprias res undique sine diminutione, et in ea minus tantum collationem facere.

8 [...] et in ista materia habemus paucos tex[tus] s[cilicet] istum et l. ubi adhuc, C. de iur[e] do[tium] et auth. de aequa[litate] do[tis] § illud, tamen multae insurgunt quaestiones circa istam materiam—Paulus de Castro, *loc. cit.*

9 Ego autem insistam in istis quinque quae tanguntur hic per gl[ossam] quia superfluum esset insistere in aliis etiam plene examinatis et per eum et alios.—Ibid.

10 Paulus de Castro informs us that Bartolus conducted repetitions on the subject in his youth, before writing a commentary on the Justinian compilation. This took place in Pisa, where he began teaching from 1339 before moving to Perugia. As Paulus expressed it, Bartolus did not want to change anything in this regard in his old age so that it would be apparent to posterity what excellence he had already achieved at the

As mentioned above, Paulus de Castro based his commentary on *l. si constante* on the Gloss of Accursius, which raised five issues, three of which relate to from whom the dowry is to be received and two of which relate to the persons who may demand its return.[11] In the first respect, the husband himself and his *pater familias*, that is, most often the woman's father-in-law, and generally those jointly and severally obligated to return the dowry are considered, while in the second, the wife herself, her *pater familias* and another person who established the dowry without being obligated to do so (*extraneus*). The subject of

beginning of his scholarly career, although he changed his views in many places during his life: *Et Bar[tolus] repetiit in iuventute sua antequam scriberat in iure civili in civitate Pisarum, ubi legebat: et noluit in senectute aliquid de ipsa immutare, ut appareret posteris a quanta perfectione ipse incaepit ut dicit Greg[orius] in dialogo de sancto Benedicto, sed intelligentibus bene apparet iuveniliter in multis fuit locutus, et contrarium in compluribus ipse dixit in aliis locis, licet plura bona ipse dicat*—Ibid. Here, Paulus invoked the words of Gregory the Great in his dialogue on St. Benedict, referring to the story of the miraculous repair, thanks to fervent prayer, of the tray for cleaning wheat (*capisterium*), borrowed by Benedict's nurse. The passage of interest to us in the translation reads as follows: "News of the miracle spread to all the country around Affile and stirred up so much admiration among the people that they hung the tray at the entrance of their church. Ever since then it has been a reminder to all of the great holiness Benedict had acquired at the very outset of his monastic life. The tray remained there many years for everyone to see and it is still hanging of the church in these days of Lombard rule."—Saint Gregory the Great, *Dialogues*, trans. J. Zimmerman, New York 1959, p. 57, book 2, chapter I. In the case of Bartolus de Saxoferrato, it is difficult to talk about old age, because he died at the age of 43. He was, however, an extremely creative and prolific scholar and if he had wanted to change the analysis of the passages on dowry return, which, according to Paulus, he had done in his youth, he would certainly have done so. In his commentary, Paulus de Castro cites Bartolus' opinions, which he critically analyses, not hesitating to point out the mistakes of his eminent predecessor, sometimes explaining them by the fact that they were expressed at a young age.

11 [...] et gl[ossa] hic formavit quinque, quarum tres s[cilicet] prima et secunda et ultima concernunt personas eorum a quibus fit repetitio aliae duae personas repetentium. Sed in l. ubi adhuc [C. 5, 12, 29] format 20. Bart[olus] vero format 40. quarum 10 respiciunt personas illorum a quibus repetitur: aliae decem personas illorum qui repetunt: aliae decem formam repetendi, et etiam modum, aliae X repetitionis effectum, et satis sunt clarae et faciles bene intuenti.—Paulus de Castro, *In Primam Infortiati*, p. 20, n. 1. Accursius' commentary on l. ubi ad huc (C. 5, 12, 29) is more elaborate, as it contains 20 issues, while Bartolus de Saxoferrato's commentary contains twice as many: ten of them concern the persons from whom the dowry can be claimed, ten the persons who can claim it, ten the form and manner of claiming it and ten the consequences of doing so.

consideration in this paper will also be the actions that the wife may have instituted, the determination of the husband's financial situation and the moment when the wife could make efforts to return the property, the consequences of returning the dowry and other property of the wife.

2. Types of wife's assets

According to customs in Italy at the time of the commentators, a wife marrying would bring a dowry to the newly established family. Since the purpose of the dowry estate was to assist the husband in bearing *onera matrimonii*, the income should be used to support the family and run the household. For this purpose, the husband was in charge of administering the dowry. While the dowry was the most important asset a wife brought into the marriage, it was not the only asset. In addition to the dowry, the wife could also have nondotal property, which, according to commentators, was divided into two types: *paraphernalia*,[12] that is, things brought into the husband's home apart from the dowry, and nondotal things (*bona non dotalia*), which were not brought into the husband's house.[13]

Things constituting paraphernalia, like the dowry, were brought into marriage. According to these jurists, the primary difference between a dowry and nondotal assets concerned the issue of ownership, which in the case of the dowry during the marriage passed to the husband. The owner of the *paraphernalia* was his wife. Unlike the dowry, however, the husband's use of paraphernalia depended on his wife's consent. The husband should not interfere in matters related to the wife's *paraphernalia* if she objected to it. However, wives customarily gave their husbands this type of property or entrusted it to their management, hence the presumption that the husband was the wife's *procurator* in the field of paraphernalia. In managing his wife's affairs, the husband should exercise even higher diligence than in his own affairs. A wife who allowed her husband to manage *parafernalia* could demand that he stop dealing with her property at any

---

12 There are various spelling variants in the sources: *parafernalia, paraphernalia* and *paraphrenalia*.

13 See J. Kirshner, "Materials for a Gilded Cage: Nondotal Assets in Florence, 1300–1500," in *Marriage, Dowry, and Citizenship*, pp. 74–93; A. Szymańska, "Prawne regulacje majątku parafernalnego w twórczości glosatorów," in *Regulacje prawne dotyczące małżeństwa w rozwoju historycznym*, ed. Tomasz Dolata, Wrocław 2018, pp. 53–63. Further literature there.

time.[14] The husband handled the management of *paraphernalia* at his own risk. If these assets were diminished, he was obliged to compensate, guaranteed by his own belongings.

The second type of nondotal assets, called *res extra dotem*, differed from the first in that they were not contributed to the husband's household. The wife retained both ownership and the ability to administer this category of property. Like *paraphernalia*, it could include both movable and immovable goods. In principle, the benefits of this property were to be enjoyed by the wife, but with her explicit consent. These benefits, it should be emphasized, could also accrue to the husband. Thus, in the case of the third type of wife's property, which was neither dowry nor *paraphernalia*, there was no presumption that the husband was entitled to management of it. The jurists assumed in this respect that there was no consent for management and use. If it was not known whether the wife had consented, it was assumed that she had not.

If the husband had sufficient resources to support the family, the wife was not obliged to support him financially from her own nondotal assets. The husband's plight was a special situation. The source of his sustenance, when he fell into poverty, should be the benefits of dowry property and *donatio propter nuptias*, not the benefits of nondotal property. According to *communis opinio*, if the benefits from the dowry were not sufficient, were consumed or were lost in some way, the poor husband should be supported from *paraphernalia* or other property of the wife.

Paulus de Castro mentions that in the case of the husband's poverty, the wife, in addition to the possibility of regaining her dowry or securing it, also has the possibility of obtaining a marital donation, which she hopes to obtain, and *paraphernalia* entrusted to her husband. The *donatio propter nuptias* and the *paraphernalia* are secured by a privileged hypothec on the husband's property, as is the dowry.[15]

---

14 Baldus de Ubaldis argued in favor of this possibility, noting, however, that the possibility of claiming restitution may be limited to situations where the husband was driven into poverty. *Item queritur de rebus parafernalibus, utrum constante matrimonio res consignate viro tanquam parafernales ad utendum et custodiendum possint per uxorem libere vendicare, et videtur quod non nisi in casu inopie, ut hic. Contrarium est verum quia possunt libere vendicare, cum sint ipsius mulieris, infra de pac. conven. l. fi.* [C. 5, 14, 11], *non ob[stante] hec l.*—Baldus de Ubaldis, *In quartum et quintum codicis libros commentaria*, Venetiis 1577, comm. ad C., 5, 12, 29 (*ubi adhuc*), p. 187 v, n. 56.

15 Tertium est, quia non solum pro dote, et eius securitate, ut hic, sed etiam pro donatione propter nuptias quam sperabat posse lucrari, et etiam pro rebus paraphernalibus donatis marito, pro qua donatione, et rebus cetera bona mariti sunt tacite obligata, sicut

3. Determining the financial situation of the husband and the moment when the wife can try to recover the assets

There could be many reasons for insolvency, from reprehensible actions of husbands to unfortunate coincidence. Bankruptcy was a constant feature of life in Italian cities, not only because of the instability of the economy, but also because of onerous taxes.[16] Add to this numerous armed conflicts that destabilize the situation, as well as the specter of confiscation of property due to taking the wrong political side.

One of the basic issues in the matter of interest is to determine the financial condition of the husband and when the wife can claim the dowry during the marriage. Although the passage of the Digest under review says that it refers to a husband's falling into such financial difficulties when, after deducting all debts, there is not enough money to repay the dowry, Paulus de Castro, taking into account other passages of the Justinian compilation, stated that the transfer of a dowry to a wife is justified when, although the goods are sufficient to satisfy creditors and guarantee a livelihood and even the return of the dowry, they do not leave sufficient funds for a life adequate to his personal status.[17] Paulus also discussed the provisions in the Justinian novella, which extend the possibility of action to a situation where the husband, while still actually rich (because, after paying off all debts and dowry, he would be left with assets from which he could live with dignity), nevertheless began to misuse his assets. The misuse of his wealth may have involved gambling or incurring more expenses than his financial situation would allow, for example, when, having no experience, he took up seafaring and, although he was losing out on this business, he still stubbornly stuck to it.[18]

---

pro dote, ut est ibi tex. not. et singularis.—Paulus de Castro, *In Primam Infortiati*, p. 20, n. 2.

16 See Kirshner, "Wives' Claims," p. 135.

17 Quia non expedit quod maritus pervenerit ad tantam paupertatem, quod deductis debitis omnibus et alimentis per se eius bona non sufficiant ad restitutionem dotis: sed sufficit si ad paupertatem pervenit ut ibi habetur et hoc non potest contingere, etiam si bona ista sufficiant ad satisfaciendum creditoribus, et etiam doti, tamen non remanet tantum, quod sufficiat sibi ad vitam inspecto conditione personae suae.—Paulus de Castro, *In Primam Infortiati*, n. 2.

18 Postea per auth. de aequalit[ate] dotis § illud. [Auth. 7. 8] additur aliud, quod licet maritus non pervenerit ad paupertatem immo etiam sit adhuc dives, quia solutis omnibus debitis et dote superset sibi tantum de quo potest honeste vivere: si tamen incipit uti male substantia sua, quia effectus est lusor vel iocator, vel incipit facere impensas

The question of sea voyages was raised in one of the *consilia*,[19] in which a consultant considered the case of a certain Andriola, daughter of Bonaguita of Pesaro, and her husband Franciscus Viti, who moved to Venice, taking his wife's dowry while she stayed in her homeland. This matter is multi-faceted, but we will be interested in the topic of maritime investments here. The wife wanted her dowry back, referring to a fragment of the Code of Justinian—*ubi adhuc* and the fact that her husband was a sea merchant. The author of the *consilium* stated that it is not enough that the husband has transported the dowry from Pesaro to Venice and is at sea, so there is a risk of losing his fortune, because he must actually start losing something in this situation.[20] It is not enough that the husband's belongings are in a dangerous place, which is the sea. Moreover, the transfer of the dowry under *l. ubi adhuc* cannot take place, since it has not been proved that Franciscus began to misuse his property after the marriage. Mere trade by sea does not justify the return of the dowry, unless the husband's property is diminished.[21]

4. Actions that can be brought by the wife and the limitations associated with them

The sources analyzed by J. Kirshner show that the right included in Roman law, which allows a wife to act against her husband in the event of imminent insolvency, has not been fundamentally questioned by medieval lawyers. As J. Kirshner writes, all leading medieval civilists such as Accursius, Odofredus, Jacobus de Arena, Dinus Mugellanus, Cinus Pistoriensis, Bartolus de Saxoferrato, Jacobus Butrigarius and Albericus de Rosate accepted the possibility of a

---

maiores quae supppetant facultates, puta traficare per mare, cum esset inexperitus, et perdere persistebat in suo proposito, et sic est timor, quod pervenit ad paupertatem, providetur mulieri, ut possit petere consignationem dotis per illam auth.—Ibid., n. 4.

19 Paulus de Castro, *Consilia*, t. I, Venetiis 1581, pp. 31 v–32 v, cons. 65.

20 Nam non sufficiat narrare quod dictus maritus dotem praefatam transtulerit de Pesaro, Venetias, et quod ipse mercatus est in mari, et potest perdere, sed requirebatur ut dicerat, quod iam incaeperat aliquid perdere in mari, secundum ea quae no. Bar[tolus] in l. si constante sol. mat. in I q. princ. q. 4 [...]—Ibid., p. 32 r, n. 3.

21 Similiter id quod pertinet ad restitutionem non totalem, sed ad consignationem dotis virtute l. ubi adhuc non est probatum, scilicet, quod Franciscus post contractum matrimonium incaeperit male uti sua substantia, posito quod esset probatum, quod traficat per mare, nam hoc non sufficit, nisi incaeperit ibi perdere ut supra dictum est.—Ibid., n. 4.

woman taking legal action against her husband, who was on the brink of bankruptcy, in order to recover her dowry, nondotal property and prenuptial donation.[22] From a practical point of view, the question of the means by which the wife was able to take over her property is important. Kirshner also noted that "By the mid-fourteenth century, a consensus had been reached on the series of legal actions a wife could institute against a husband squandering the dowry and simultaneously approaching insolvency."[23] Among the actions that could be used by a wife in such a situation was a personal action for the return of the dowry (*actio personalis de dote*), if the dowry, as Bartolus wants, consisted of things designated as to species characteristics.[24] If the husband acquired some things with the dowry money or the dowry was estimated, the wife could use *actio utilis in rem* and *rei vindicatio utilis*. The wife could also bring the *rei vindicatio*. In the case of *dos inestimata*, it was possible to put the dowry in a sequestration deposit (*remedium sequestrationis*). The wife was also entitled to a hypothecary action (*actio hypothecaria*), which could, as J. Kirshner noted, prove to be the most effective remedy, since in Italian cities such as Florence, Siena, Pisa and Bologna in the time of Paulus de Castro, dowries consisted largely of money. A wife was entitled to an implied and privileged hypothec on her husband's property, proportional to her marital contributions, thus a dowry, trousseau, as well as *donatio propter nuptias*.[25]

The issue of the type of action a wife can bring was also raised by Paulus de Castro, who stated that in addition to a personal action, she was also entitled to a hypothecary action to recover her husband's property from any possessor.[26] It may be doubted whether in this case using a hypothecary action the wife has the privilege of priority (*privilegium prioritatis*), as in the case of actions taken after the dissolution of marriage. Paulus held that she could make a claim unless it was

22 Kirshner, "Wives' Claims," pp. 137–138.

23 Ibid., p. 150.

24 Primo ergo quaero, qua actione aget mulier ad illam dotem. Resp. aut mulier dedit in dotem res quae pondere, numero, vel mensura continentur, et tunc mulier poterit agere actione personali de dote, ut hic, ibi, dotis exactionem, et cetera de manumiss[ionibus] l. servum dotalem. [D. 40, 1, 21] de dote praele[gata] l. pater [D. 33, 4, 7].—Bartolus de Saxoferrato, *In secundum tomum pandectarum, Infortiatum Commentaria*, Basileae 1562, comm. ad D. 24, 3, 24, p. 53, n. 70.

25 See Kirshner, "Wives' Claims," p. 150.

26 Aliud est quia potest agere non solum actione personali pro dote, ut hic, sed hypothecaria pro reb[us] mariti contra quoscunque possessores, et ipse posset adversus eos se tueri exceptione.—Paulus de Castro, *In Primam Infortiati*, p. 20, n. 2.

for creditors who had a prior and express hypothec on her husband's property.[27] This problem was also raised in advice 6, included in the third volume of Paulus de Castro's *consilia*, which is discussed in more detail later in this work.

The commentator also wondered about the scope of the property obtained from the husband on the basis of the mortgage claim, since all the husband's goods were pledged to secure the dowry. His deliberations went along the following lines: it follows from the nature of a hypotheca that, by bringing an action, one can obtain all the pledged property, no matter how much more it is worth than the debt. So if the husband's fortune is worth 40, and the dowry is 10, then the woman should be able to claim all his pledged goods.[28] He referred here to C. 8, 27, 6.[29] He combined this thought with his consideration of whether other creditors could offer a dowry to the wife. According to Cinus Pistoriensis, who followed the views of Jacobus de Arena, creditors would not be able to offer a dowry to a woman as long as the marriage still existed. On the other hand, there was a risk that the husband's creditors would be cheated, because as soon as the husband began to abuse his wealth, no matter how rich and solvent he might be, the woman would be able to seize all his assets.[30] As a solution to this dilemma, Paulus gave the opinion of the Doctors, according to which, although the mortgage in the light of the *ius commune* has just such a character, as stated above, in this case, since it is a special right, the woman will be able to obtain

27 Quartum est quia in ista hypothecaria habet privilegium prioritatis, sicut quando agit soluto matrimonio, de quo poterat esse dubium: quoniam/quam agendo constante matrimonio, agit ex quodam privilegio contra regula: unum/utrum videbatur sufficere, quod agere possit, et tunc contrarium est, ibi patet, nisi sint creditores habentes expressam hypothecam anteriorem tempore.—Ibid.

28 Item adhuc opp. et ista oppositio concernit l. ubi adhuc in quantum dicit quod potest agit hypothecaria pro rebus mariti: nam omnia bona mariti sunt obligata pro dote: ergo si bona mariti valent XL et dos ascendebat ad X, tamen, certe poterit agere mulier pro omnibus bonis, quia ista est natura hypothecaria, quod per eam advocantur omnia bona hypothecata, quantuncunque plus valeant quam sit debitum, ut l. quamdiu C. de distract[ione] pig[norum] [C. 8, 27, 6] nec poterunt creditores offere dotem mulieri cum matrimonium adhuc consistat, ut no. Cy[nus] secundum Ja[cobum] de Ar[ena] in l. cum tibi C. qui po[tiores] in pig[nore] ha[beantur] [C. 8, 17, 10]—Ibid., n. 5.

29 Imperator Gordianus. Quamdiu non est integra pecunia creditori numerata, etiamsi pro parte maiore eam consecutus sit, distrahendi rem obligatam non amittit facultatem.

30 Si creditores remanebunt fraudati, quia statim quod maritus incipiet male uti substantia sua quatumcunque sit dives et solvendo, mulier poterit reducere ad manus suas omnia bona eius, ut ponantur in sequestro, et creditores mariti remanebunt delusi.—Paulus de Castro, *In Primam Infortiati*, n. 5.

through the hypothecary action only enough for the dowry, while the rest must be returned to the creditors.[31]

Paulus eventually accepted, following Baldus and Angelus de Ubaldis, that the husband's creditors could offer the woman a dowry. If this is done, she will be obliged to give them her husband's property in her possession, if the dowry's benefits are sufficient to feed her family. Indeed, a woman should be content with her dowry. Otherwise, if the fruits from the dowry were not enough, she will be able to receive from her husband's estate as much as she needs to support herself.[32] This solution made it possible to protect the wife's rights while taking into account the interests of creditors.

5. Who could demand a dowry for the wife

Paulus devoted a relatively large amount of space in his commentary on the *si constante* passage to entities that could potentially claim the return of the dowry. Thus, he wondered if and when a woman, being a *filia familias*, for whom her father had established a dowry, could claim it without her father's consent (*sine voluntate patris*). The commentator concluded, that based on a fragment of Justinian's novella, *Illud quoque sancire*, the possibility of action depends on the size of the dowry. A dowry of considerable size enables a daughter who is under her father's authority to act independently. Paulus, however, referring to another fragment of Justinian's compilation, namely D. 3, 3, 8 pr.,[33] decided that the

---

31 So[lutio]: do[ctores] dicunt in ista materia quod licet hypothecaria quando intentatur de iure communi sit illius naturae de qua supra. In casu tamen isto quia intentatur de iure speciali, non poterit mulier per hypothecariam consequi nisi tantum, quantum sufficit pro dote, et illud sequestrabitur, residuum tenetur remittere creditoribus quinimmo quicquid dicat Cyn[us] in l. cum tibi [C. 8, 17, 10].—Ibid.

32 Bald[us] et Ang[elus] in auth. quod locum, C. de col[lationibus] tenant quod etiam pro rebus quae remanent apud uxorem usque ad quantitatem dotis, si creditores offerant sibi dotem, tenetur mulier illas res eis relaxare, quia si maritus offerat hoc idem facere teneatur. Idem ergo si faciunt creditors habentes causam a marito, quia possunt uti facultate, competente marito, ut l. si cui C. de non num[erata] pec[unia] [C. 4, 30, 15], quod mihi videtur verius per id quod no. Cy[nus] qui fundat se in illa l[ex] ad quam poterit responderi de facili. Debet enim sufficere mulieri, quod habeat dotem suam. Hoc tamen verum, si fructus dotis sufficient ad alendum familiam, alias debebit sequestrari da bonis mariti tantum quod sufficiat ad alimenta, cum ad ipsa teneatur, ut in l. si cum dotem § sin autem in saevissimo [D. 24, 3, 22, 8].—Ibid., n. 6.

33 Ulpianus libro octavo ad edictum. Filius familias et ad agendum dare procuratorem potest, si qua sit actio, qua ipse experiri potest: non solum si castrense peculium habeat, sed et quivis filius familias: ut puta iniuriam passus dabit ad iniuriarum actionem, si

daughter could act independently also in the case of a small dowry.[34] This was in line with Bartolus' view, according to which a daughter could demand the return of a small dowry without her father's consent, if he could not afford to give her a dowry if she wanted to enter a second marriage. This also applied to the situation when the father was not a man who behaved shamefully (*persona turpis*).[35]

He also considered the opposite situation, namely the possibility of the father demanding a dowry without the daughter's consent. According to the Glossa, the father has this possibility, as it is in his interest that the dowry is not lost, since it is incumbent on him to establish a dowry for his daughter in the event of remarriage.[36] Besides, as Bartolus rightly pointed out, the dowry will not be returned to the father himself, nor will it end up in his hands, but will be transferred and deposited to serve the good of the marriage.[37] Paulus here refutes Bartolus' arguments that a father cannot act against his daughter's will and apply for the return of the dowry himself. The return of the dowry does not harm the daughter, but works in her favor. Therefore, it should always be assumed that the daughter

---

forte neque pater praesens sit nec patris procurator velit experiri, et erit iure ab ipso filio familias procurator datus. Hoc amplius Iulianus scribit et si filio familias patri per filium eius in eadem potestate manentem fiat iniuria neque avus praesens sit, posse patrem procuratorem dare ad ulciscendam iniuriam, quam nepos absentis passus est. Ad defendendum quoque poterit filius familias procuratorem dare. Sed et filia familias poterit dare procuratorem ad iniuriarum actionem. Nam quod ad dotis exactionem cum patre dat procuratorem, supervacuum esse Valerius Severus scribit, cum sufficiat patrem dare ex filiae voluntate. Sed puto, si forte pater absens sit vel suspectae vitae, quo casu solet filiae competere de dote actio, posse eam procuratorem dare. Ipse quoque filius procurator dari poterit et ad agendum et ad defendendum.

34 Additur etiam, quid iuris, si mulier erat filiaf[amilias] pro qua pater dederit dotem, an ipsa mulier possit petere hanc consignationem sine voluntate patris? et distinguitur ibi, an erat dos magna an parva et tunc secus, quod intelige patre praesente, alias etiam pro parva posset agere, ut in l. filius fam[ilias] § sed et filia. de procura[toribus et defensoribus] [D. 3, 3, 8 pr].—Paulus de Castro, *In Primam Infortiati*, n. 4.

35 […] tamen Bar[tolus] tenet quod si erat parva, si tamen pater non erat sufficiens ad iterum ipsam dotandam in secundo matrimonio, adhuc possit, per id quod not. gl[ossa] in l. 2 § quod si in patris que incipit morte, .s. eod. [D. 24, 3, 2, 2] etiam sine patris voluntate et licet patris non sit turpis persona.—Ibid., n. 9.

36 Secundum dubium, an ipse pater hoc possit? et hic determinat ista gl. quod hoc potest propter suum interesse, ne dos perdatur, cum habeat necesse eam dotare in secundo matrimonio.—Ibid.

37 Bar[tolus] addit hic duo et bene, quod non fiet restitutio ipsi patri, nec ad eius manus pervenit, sed consignabitur et deponetur ad commodum matrimonii.—Ibid., n. 10.

consents to the father's action to take the dowry out of her husband's hands, even if the daughter opposes it and the father is a despicable person (*turpis persona*) because the dowry does not end up in his hands. It is in the daughter's interest for someone else to demand the return of the dowry on her behalf. Paulus also used the argument that, since the daughter can demand the return of the dowry without the father's consent, the father can also demand it without her will.[38]

The case is different from that of a dowry established by the *pater familias* when the dowry was established by someone else. In the case where the dowry was established by someone outside the family (*extraneus*), who stipulated that it was to be returned to him after the dissolution of the marriage, according to the view expressed in Glossa, he cannot claim its return due to the husband's poverty during the marriage. The rationale for this, according to Paulus de Castro, is that there is no obligation for an outsider of the family to establish a dowry in the event of a woman's remarriage. The *extraneus*, however, has the option of claiming security for the return of the dowry in the event of the dissolution of the marriage.[39]

Paulus de Castro also questioned whether, in turn, a woman for whom an *extraneus* has established a dowry has the ability to demand its return during the marriage because of her husband's poverty. This may seem doubtful, since after the dissolution of the marriage, an action for the return of a dowry established by an extraneous person who has reserved the return is vested in that person, not the woman. The author of the *Glossa ordinaria* took a different position, holding that a woman cannot be allowed to starve to death or be left without a dowry. Paulus' contribution to this issue is to clarify the legal remedy that a woman can use, which is not mentioned in the *Glossa* or in the writings of the doctors. She

---

38 Dicit tamen Bar[tolus] hic alia tria et non bene, quod pater non poterit petere hanc consignationem sine voluntate filiae, quod non placet, quia hoc non tendit in praeiudicium filiae sed ad suam utilitatem. Unde semper praesumitur consentire, etiam si contradicat, et pater sit turpis persona, quia dos non habet pervenire ad eius manus. Unde interest filiae quod alius possit pro ea hoc petere. Preterea si filia potest sine voluntate patris, ut supra dixi, idem esse econverso.—Ibid., n. 10.

39 Circam quartam quaestio quando extraneus dedit dotem pro muliere, et pactus est sibi reddi soluto matrimonio glossa ponit pro constanti, quod constante matri[monio] non possit petere hanc consigantionem fieri propter paupertatem, et in hoc differt extraneus a patre: quoniam extraneus non tenetur illam dotare in secundo matr[imonio]. Videtur tamen quod possit petere sibi caveri de dote restituenda sol. matr. ex causa superveniente de novo, per l. in omnib[us] s. de iudi[ciis: ubi quisque agere vel conveniri debeat] [D. 5, 1, 41].—Ibid., n. 12.

can ask for help from a judge to decide the case taking into account the principles of equity.[40]

6. Persons from whom the dowry can be claimed back

The primary subject from whom a wife could demand the return of her dowry in the event of her husband's financial problems is precisely the husband, as emphasized in *consilium* No. 8 found in Volume II of Paulus de Castro's legal advice.[41] There we read that the wife must first file a complaint against her husband and demand the transfer of her dowry, citing the fact that the husband is approaching insolvency or beginning to misuse his property. If she fails to do so, she cannot stop creditors who want to seize her husband's assets.[42]

Paulus de Castro also considered who, besides the husband, could be considered as a defendant in a lawsuit to recover a dowry during the marriage. The first place to be mentioned here is his *pater familias*, which is usually the father, and therefore the woman's father-in-law. This is because under his control comes the dowry in the event that the son is under his authority. In such a situation, one would expect that when the father-in-law, in possession of his daughter-in-law's dowry, was approaching insolvency, she could seek the return of the dowry through the courts. Paulus here cited the position in the *Glossa Ordinaria*. The general rule is that the return of the dowry can be sought after the dissolution of the marriage, and the passage in the Digest in question constituting an exception to this rule only mentions the husband approaching insolvency, and therefore does not seem to apply to the father-in-law. However, the *Glossa* took the

40 Sed dubium est, an ipsa mulier possit petere hanc consignationem fieri et facit dubium, quia si matrimonium esset solutum, mulier ista non haberet actionem ad dotem repetendam, sed ipse extraneus, qui pactus est vel stipulatus sibi reddi: ergo nec ipso constante quoniam in casu huius legis eo constante, intentat illam actionem quam posset intentare ipso soluto. Glo[ssa] hic determinat contrarium ne fame pereat, et remaneat indotata, non tamen declarat quam actionem habebit, nec etiam doct[ores]. Ego putto, quod solum poterit implorare iudicis officium ex aequitate.—Ibid., n. 13.

41 In the Nuremberg edition of 1485 *Pauli castrensis… consilia… Bartholomeus cepolla verone[n]sis… colligere elaborauit…*, in which there is no division into volumes, this consilium bears the number CCXX.

42 Nam primo debet agere contra virum, et petere sibi dotem consignari, quia vergat ad inopiam, vel incipiat male uti substantia sua. Et antequam hoc faciat, non potest impedire creditores petentes se immitti in tenutam bonorum viri.—Paulus de Castro, *Consilia*, Venetiis 1581, vol. II, p. 5, n. 3.

opposite position and allowed action also against the father-in-law.[43] Paulus also mentioned Bartolus' extensive deliberations on the subject,[44] but chose not to summarize them. Paulus allowed the possibility of suing the father-in-law for the return of the dowry, writing that when the provision is just and useful, it should be extended from person to person or from case to similar case, even if there are specific words in the text, precisely specifying something.[45] As is the case in the passage *si constante*, where only the husband is mentioned. So what applies to a husband on the brink of poverty also applies to a father-in-law.

According to what J. Kirshner stated, in cities such as Florence it was customary for a son to accept a dowry with the consent of his father, as long as the latter was alive. In the Florence mentioned above, this accounted for nearly 1/3 of marriages.[46] This resulted in their joint and several liability for the return of the dowry in all situations in which the dowry should be returned. Paulus wondered how to claim the transfer of the dowry in a situation where two people were jointly and severally liable to return the dowry and only one of them was approaching insolvency. Traditionally, he began by referring to the views expressed in the *Glossa Ordinaria*, according to which such a possibility is provided by the *illud quoque sancire* fragment, although neither the Codex of Justinian nor the Digests provide it.[47] On the other hand, according to Cinus, expressed in the commentary on *l. ubi adhuc* (C. 5, 12, 29), he can demand in any case, because it is advantageous for a woman to have more debtors.[48] Referring to Bartolus' view, Paulus said that in his opinion he could undoubtedly demand the return of the dowry from one who stood on the brink of poverty or began to misuse his property. As for the possibility of claiming repayment from a person who is not burdened by the abovementioned situations, Bartolus mentions two cases: if he is a partner, because the act of one partner harms the other,

---

43 Paulus de Castro, *In Primam Infortiati*, n. 7.

44 Ibid.

45 Cum igitur provisio sit pia et utilis, debet fieri extensio de persona ad personam, vel de casu ad casum similem, etiam si esset apposita dictio taxativa ut in l. illud circa fin. cum ibi not. C. de sacrosan. eccle. [C. 1, 2, 19]—Ibid.

46 Kirshner, "Wives' Claims," p. 146.

47 Cum duo sunt obligati insolidum ad restitutionem dotis et alter ipsorum vergit ad inopiam, alter non gl[ossa] tenet hic quod isto iure non poterat peti ista consignatio, nec etiam iure C. sed hodie per auth. de aequa. [Auth. 7, 8; Nov. 97, 6].—Paulus de Castro, *In Primam Infortiati*, n. 8.

48 Cy[nus] in l. ubi adhuc [C. 5, 12, 29], tenet, quod indistincte poterit peti quia intererat mulierit habere plures debitores.—Ibid.

and if he is a co-debtor, because the poverty of one harms the other, as he loses the *beneficum divisionis*, and therefore the power to distribute the debt to all. This, however, has not gained the approval of the jurist, because the action of a partner harms the other partner in the case of acquisition, not in the loss of acquisitions.[49]

Paulus de Castro made the possibility of action dependent on two elements. The first is falling into poverty or starting to squander his property, and the second is bearing the burdens of marriage. If these two elements are met, a woman can demand to be entrusted with things from his property, and if that is not enough, also from the other person's property. This is done for two reasons, so that she can support herself and her family, and so that she can be sure of her dowry. The condition, however, is that neither of them is cheated.[50] If, on the other hand, it is not the one who bears the burdens of marriage but the other who falls into poverty, then there is no need to demand the return of the dowry, since the woman is not cheated by either of them. It should not be assumed that he too can fall into poverty one must take into account the case of both chance and unfavorable and favorable fate.[51]

The problem of co-responsibility for the return of the dowry during the marriage is dealt with in advice 6 in the third volume of Paulus de Castro's *consilia*.[52] In the time of Paulus, the groom and someone in his family made a promise that the dowry would be returned to the woman whenever it should be returned. Such a promise to return the dowry in all cases in which it should be returned both after the dissolution of the marriage and during the marriage was made by Antonia together with her sons Andrea and Laurentius to the wife of the former, Matthia. The question is whether, as Andrea approached poverty and began to

49 Ibid.

50 Puto dicendum in hoc articulo, reiectis dictis per doct[ores] quod si perveniat ad paupertatem, vel incipit uti male substantia sua ille, qui subiit onera matrimonii, petit possit ista consignatio in bonis eius, et si illa non sufficerent etiam in bonis alterius, quoniam fit propter duo scilicet ut mulier cum sua familia alatur, et ut sit secura de dote, et nisi hoc fieret fraudaretur alter ipsorum.—Ibid.

51 Si autem alter, qui non sustinet onera matrimonii devenit ad paupertatem, ille vero qui sustinet, non, tunc esset remedium harum legum, quia mulier non fraudatur aliquo istorum, nec debet considerari quod etiam ipse poterit ad paupertatem devenire, quia hoc non praesumitur, et casum, adversamque fortunam considerare debemus l. inter stipulantem § sacram in de verbo obliga [D. 45, 1, 83, 5].—Ibid.

52 Paulus de Castro, *Consilia*, Venetiis 1581, vol. III, pp. 6 v–7 v. In the Nuremberg edition of 1485, this *consilium* is numbered CXXVII.

misuse his property, which is presumed to have squandered the dowry he received, his wife could institute a hypothecary action against his mother Antonia? There were three estates at stake, from which the assets corresponding to the dowry could go to the wife. Firstly, the property belonging to Antonia's sons, which they received from their father, and which she currently held on their behalf, secondly, her dowry goods, secured by her husband's belongings, for which her sons were now responsible as his heirs, and thirdly, Antonia's own property, that is, nondotal possessions. The basis for this was supposed to be a fragment of Justinian's Code *ubi adhuc* [C. 5, 12, 29]. Paulus responded positively as to the share of the plaintiff's husband in the first of the abovementioned estates, insofar as his mother held them without just cause. Hypothecary action is generally brought against any possessor of property, unless it is someone who has an earlier and better lien on it, insofar as he is not personally obligated. Antonia had a prior and better right to the property that her sons inherited from their father, her husband, as he secured the return of her dowry. The question to be decided was whether Antonia had a personal obligation to her daughter-in-law under the promise of *restitutio dotis* made to her. If so, a hypothecary action may be brought against her for delivery of her property, as well as the property of her sons, for which she is entitled to a *hypotheca* on the same basis as her daughter-in-law. At this point, Paulus analyzed what is implied by the phrase *restitutio dotis*, since this is the only thing that Antonia's commitment refers to. During the marriage there can be no real restitution because of poverty because the dowry should continue to support the burdens of the marriage. Real restitution may sometimes occur during marriage when there is a separation between the spouses for some just cause or when dowry is returned for a reason other than poverty. Paulus de Castro held that if the mother-in-law obligated *in casu restituenda dotis*, this does not include restitution due to her husband's falling into poverty, since *restitutio dotis* cannot be extended to the case of poverty due to the meaning of the word restitutio. The proper meaning of the word *restitutio* does not extend to the case of poverty, for which *consignatio* is a more appropriate word. In this case, it also does not seem that the parties had the opposite intention, that is, that they included in the promise of the return of the dowry also the case of the husband's poverty.[53]

53 Nec apparet hic de contraria intentione partium, et potest satis operari secundum dictam intentionem, secundum Bar. in praellegata l. si quis ita stipulatus, ergo et c[etera].—Paulus de Castro, *Consilia*, vol. III, p. 7 r, n. 10.

In addition, a promise to return a dowry made by one to whom it did not accrue can be extended only to the extent permitted by the words of the promise. Since the dowry fell to Anthony's son and not to her, an extensional interpretation cannot be applied.[54] Recognition of the guarantee of return applies only in the case in which she undertook to return the dowry.[55]

In his conclusion, Paulus de Castro stated that in the case under review, the daughter-in-law cannot bring a hypothecary action against her mother-in-law to hand over her own belongings or the property of her sons, mortgaged for dowry, since she herself is entitled to a hypothec of a prior and better kind against these things. And her promise, which she gave in connection with her son receiving a dowry, does not cover the case of returning the dowry during the marriage due to poverty. Nor is she harmed by her son's obligations in relation to the things indicated, and the fact that her daughter-in-law may take legal action against him.[56]

It is not known whether, in the above-described case, the wife acted in concert with her husband, who had run out of funds and wanted to take over the property, which was his father's inheritance and which was inaccessible to him and his brother due to the fact that their mother had a hypothec on it to secure the return of her dowry.

In a similar vein is brief advice 230 found in Volume I of Paulus de Castro's legal advice. The case analyzed there was commented on by another legal adviser, Ardignius, and concerned the possibility of a certain woman suing Michael and Johannes for the equivalent of her dowry, as these men had promised to return it (*restitutio*). The author of the *consilium* referred here to the considerations of Bartolus, who stated that the promise to return the dowry in any case in which it should be returned does not include the case in which it should be given because

54 Quia illi non tenetur nisi quatenus verba promissionis eorum patiuntur ff. de fideiuss [oribus et mandatoribus] l. si fideiussores magistratuum § pro Aurelio [D. 46, 1, 68, 1], et ista domina Antonia est huiusmodi, quia ad eam dos non pervenit, sed ad dictum Andream, ergo et c[etera].—Ibid., p. 7 r, n. 14.

55 Et sic dicta confessio de recepto solum operatur in illo casu in quo se oblogavit, et ad illum tantum restringitur non in alio [...].—Ibid., p. 7 r, n. 17.

56 Concludo igitur contra dictam dominam Antoniam agi non posse in casu praedicto hypothecaria pro rebus propriis ipsius mulieris, aut pro rebus filiorum suorum obligatis pro dicta dote cum ipsa in eis habeat priorem et potiorem hypothecam quia sua promissio et obligatio tam quod obligationem personalem pro bonis suis, et iuribus quae habet in bonis filiorum, casum istum non comprehendit, obligatio autem viri, et quod contra eum agi possit non debet dictae dominae in bonis praedictis nocere, secundum iam dicta.—Ibid., p. 7 v, n. 26.

of the husband's poverty.[57] Michael and Johannes are only responsible for what the words of their promise contained, regardless of whether we say they are guarantors or co-debtors. Michael and Johannes are only responsible for what is contained in the words of their promise, whether we say they are guarantors or co-debtors. Since the promise concerned only the restitution of the dowry in the event of dissolution of the marriage, the author of the *consilium* stated in the conclusion that the woman could not demand that the abovementioned men transfer her dowry.[58]

7. Consequences of returning a dowry

During the marriage, the wife's dowry assets, and generally the wife's nondotal assets as well, while remaining in the husband's possession, provided support for the obligation to bear the burdens of marriage. The husband was responsible for the proper administration of this property and used the benefits derived from it to maintain a common household. Since the basic function of *bona mulieris* was to facilitate the burden of marriage, which rested on the shoulders of the man, their return took place after the dissolution of the marriage bond. Their earlier return made this function impossible to fulfill. Temporary failures in managing the family's property, probably not uncommon in the merchant societies of Italian cities, certainly did not constitute a pretext for taking extraordinary precautions. However, if the husband was on the brink of insolvency, the wife could demand that control of her dowry and non-dowry property be taken away from him, if she also entrusted it to him. The wife was obliged to use the fruits from the dowry taken from her husband to support herself, her husband, and her children. Since the purpose of the dowry was to support the burdens of marriage, the wife was forbidden to alienate the returned property.

This was also the position of Glossa, according to which, having regained her dowry, a woman cannot do with it freely, for example, make some alienation. After regaining the dowry, the fruits from it should serve the burdens of the marriage. Not only should she be supported by them, but also her husband and

---

57 Ultra ea quae superius scripta sunt per eximium consultorem dominum Ardignium quaestio ista determinatur ex no. per Barto. in l. si quis hic stipuletur ff. de solut. matrim. [D. 24, 3, 56] ubi Bart[olus] determinat quod stipulatio de restituenda dote in omnem casum dotis restituendae non extenditur casum dotis consignandae propter inopiam viri, nec ipsum casum comprehendit: quia consignatio non est restitutio.— Paulus de Castro, *Consilia*, vol. I, Venetiis 1617, p. 111.

58 Ibid.

the whole family. Paulus noted, however, that from the passage under scrutiny it appears that this is a judicial assertion of the dowry due, which should be given to the woman to do with it what she wants, as can be inferred from the word *exactione*. And this provision seemed more just and reasonable to Paulus.[59]

The protective measures taken into account by the commentator, which consisted of the possibility to sue for the return of the dowry during the marriage due to the impending insolvency of the husband, were aimed at safeguarding the livelihood of the spouses and their offspring. It was also about securing another function of the dowry, namely, to provide for the wife's livelihood after the husband's death.

8. Conclusion

Since much of the wife's property passed into the husband's management upon marriage, the law should provide for measures to prevent the loss or diminution of that property. These measures should effectively protect her both against risky or irresponsible actions of her husband and against the resulting claims of his creditors. However, resorting to such measures constituted an extraordinary situation, since the wife, as *socia domi mariti*, should in principle share not only the auspicious moments with him, but also any adversity.

Since Paulus de Castro was one of the highest-paid law professors of his time, as well as a sought-after legal consultant, his wife, who was the granddaughter of canon law professor Petrus Ancharanus, was unlikely to have to face the need to reclaim her dowry *propter inopia mariti*. In turn, the problems of insolvency and bankruptcy were encountered by Paulus in his legal practice. He also encountered them in theory, analyzing the provisions of Roman law contained in the *Corpus iuris civilis*. Three passages from the Digests, the Codex and the Novels of Justinian are of key importance for the possibility of the wife demanding the return of her property. Unfortunately, we do not have Paulus de Castro's commentary on Book 5 of the Code of Justinian or Novels, in which the fragments of interest to us are found.

---

59 Quintum, et ultimum additur per illam l[ex] quod ista exactio dotis non sit omnino exactio, quia non ponitur in manibus mulieris, pro libito voluntatis: immo consignatur, et deponitur, ut fructus eius deserviant oneribus matrimonii non solum mulieris, sed etiam viri et totius familiae nec potest mulier aliquid alienare de rebus consignatis, sed per istam legem videbatur, quod esset dotalis exactio, et quod traderetur ipsi mulieri ut faceret quicquid vellet, ut colligitur in ver. exactionem, et illa provisio fuit magis aequa, et rationabilis.—Paulus de Castro, *In Primam Infortiati*, n. 3.

The commentary on l. *si constante* from Digest and *consilia* in Paulus de Castro's collection of legal advice contain considerations about who might have been involved in the recovery of his wife's property. A wife whose husband mismanaged his affairs and wasted his fortune could, in order to regain her dowry, act alone or jointly with her father, if she was under his authority. Appropriate legal steps could also be taken by her *pater familias*. Failure to take any steps could have unpleasant consequences in the future. On the other hand, as entities from which a woman could demand the surrender of her property, her father-in-law, his brothers and creditors, and even her mother-in-law were also taken into account. The commentator saw the need to protect the property interests of the wife, but he also had to take into account the interests of the husband's creditors and members of his family.

The commentaries and *consilia*, found in the collection of Paulus de Castro, have been published in print several times in various places in Europe. His work was invoked by later jurists, referring to his views in their commentaries and legal advice, which, through the medium of print, were increasingly disseminated, influencing European judicature and legal thought in the early modern era.

Bibliography

Sources

Baldus de Ubaldis, In quartum et quintum codicis libros commentaria, Venetiis 1577.

Bartolus de Saxoferrato, *In secundum tomum pandectarum, Infortiatum Commentaria*, Basileae 1562.

Paulus de Castro, *Consilia*, Venetiis 1581.

Paulus de Castro, *Consilia*, Venetiis 1617.

Paulus de Castro, *In Primam Infortiati partem Commentaria*, Lugduni 1585.

Saint Gregory the Great, *Dialogues*, trans. J. Zimmerman, New York 1959.

Literatures

Cortese, E., "Paolo di (da) Castro (Castro)," in *Dizionario biografico dei giuristi italiani*, ed. I. Birocchi, E. Cortese, A. Mattone, M. N. Miletti, vol. II, Bologna 2013.

d'Amelio, G., "Castro, Paolo di," in *Dizionario Biografico degli Italiani*, vol. XXII, Roma 1979.

Del Re, N., *Sei consigli inediti di Paolo di Castro nei codici vaticani latini 8068, 8069, 11605 e Urbinate latino 1132*, Roma 1945.

Del Re, N., "*Paolo di Castro*, dottore della verità," *Studi senesi* 82 (1970).

Kirshner, J., "Paolo di Castro on Cives ex privilegio: A Controversy over the Legal Qualifications for Public Office in early Fifteenth-Century Florence," in *Renaissance Studies in Honour of Hans Baron*, ed. A. Molho, J. A. Tedeschi, Dekalb 1971.

Kirshner, J., "Materials for a Gilded Cage: Nondotal Assets in Florence, 1300–1500," in *Marriage, Dowry, and Citizenship in Late Medieval and Renaissance Italy*, Toronto-Buffalo-London 2015.

Kirshner, J., "Wives' Claims against Insolvent Husbands in Late Medieval Italy," in *Women of the Medieval World: Essays in Honor of John H. Mundy*, ed. J. Kirshner, S. F. Wemple, Oxford 1985.

Kirshner, J., "Wives' Claims against Insolvent Husbands in Late Medieval Italy," in *Marriage, Dowry, and Citizenship in Late Medieval and Renaissance Italy*, Toronto-Buffalo-London 2015.

Lange, H., "Die Rechtsquellenlehre in den Consilien Paul de Castros," in *Aktuelle Fragen aus modernen Recht und Rechtsgeschichte. Gedächtnisschrift für Rudolf Schmidt*, ed. E. Seidl, Berlin 1966.

Lange, H., and Kriechbaum, M., *Römisches Recht im Mittelalter*, vol. II: *Die Kommentatoren*, Munich 2007.

Lepsius, S., "Paolo di Castro (1360/62–1441)," in *Law and the Christian Tradition in Italy: The Legacy of the Great Jurists*, ed. O. Condorelli, R. Domingo, London-New York 2021.

Lepsius, S., "Paolo di Castro as consultant: Applying and Interpreting Florence's Statutes," in *The Politics of the Law in Late Medieval and Renaissance Italy*, ed. L. Armstrong, J. Kirshner, Toronto Studies in Medieval Law, vol. I, Toronto 2011.

Lepsius, S., "Paulus de Castro als Konsiliator: Anwendung, Interpretation und Fortbildung der Florentiner Statuten," *Rivista internazionale di diritto comune* 25 (2014).

Maffei, D., "Un commentario dimenticato di Paolo di Castro sul Digesto Vecchio," *Rivista internazionale di diritto comune* 14 (2003).

Murano, G., "Paolo da Castro," in *Autographa*, vol. I. 1: *Giuristi, giudici e notai (sec. XII–XV)*, ed. G. Murano, Imola 2012.

Panciroli, G., *De claris legum interpretibus*, Lipsiae 1721.

Pieri, B., *Usurai, ebrei e poteri della Chiesa nei consilia di Paolo da Castro. Le competenze canonistiche di un civilista*, Bologna 2016.

Romano, A., "La giurisprudenza consulente e Paolo di Castro. Alcuni consilia inediti del ms. Venezia, Bibl. Marciana, lat. 2324," *Rivista di storia del diritto italiano* 61 (1988).

Sorice, R., "Il diritto del nemico alla difesa. Ius belli e ius gentium in un Consilium di Paolo di Castro," in *Der Einfluss der Kanonistik auf die europäische Rechtskulturs*, ed. O. Condorelli, F. Roumy, M. Schmoeckel, Wien-Köln-Weimar 2020.

Szymańska, A., "Prawne regulacje majątku parafernalnego w twórczości glosatorów," in *Regulacje prawne dotyczące małżeństwa w rozwoju historycznym*, ed. Tomasz Dolata, Wrocław 2018.

Von Savigny, F. C., *Geschichte des Römischen Rechts im Mittelalters*, vol. VI, Heidelberg 1850.

Belén Fernández Vizcaíno

Some assumptions of *ius adscrescendi* in the material necessary succession of *ius civile*

Abstract: In the study of the regulation of inheritance in the *ius civile*, the fact of the lack of equality of the sexes in the case of preterition of a legitimate heir cannot be ignored, but this situation evolves in the same way that Roman society does from forgetfulness in the case of disinheriting a daughter, thus revealing the worst condition of women in Roman Law, to the granting of *ius adcrescendi in partem* as a general rule to excluded daughters and grandchildren. The nature of this appeal configures the nucleus of a doctrinal controversy, as it is considered as an exception to the principle *nemo pro parte testatus pro parte intestatus decedere potest*, or as an appeal completing the testament through a legal fiction, until Justinian in C. 6, 28, 4, orders the increase of the *ceteri sui* in what meant a further reinforcement of the right of legitimaries that compressed the effectiveness of the *wills testatoris*, thus, this appeal to the forgotten would form part of the *successio ex testamento*, and the use of the term *ius adcrescendi* by the improper emperor.

Keywords: inheritance, women, ius adcrescendi, legitimaries, disinheritance

1. Background

The situation of inferiority of women with respect to men finds its reflection in Roman Law recognized by jurists, highlighting the opinion of Papinian collected in D. 1, 5, 9.—"*In multis iuris nostri articulis deterior est condicio feminarum quam masculorum*," in the same sense, Ulpian in D. 1, 9, 1.—"*Consulari feminae utique consularem virum praeferendum nemo ambigit. Sed vir praefectorius an consulari feminae praeferatur, videndum. putem praeferri, quia maior dignitas est in sexu virili*."

Thus, for Roman Law, this position was based on the supposed physical and mental weakness of women, which in principle forced all women to be subject to family authority or under perpetual guardianship.[1] To affirm this idea, terms

1 The Roman family, the nucleus of Law and society, was made up of a group of people who were subjected in *nature aut iure* to the same power, that of the *paterfamilias*, the only subject with full rights, among those people were women, subjected to in the Old, the right to it, being this subjection the link that determined the integration of women in the family, without participation in public life, in its political and legal aspects, without being able to have successors or anyone under their power. The *sui*

such as *levitas* or *fragilitas animi* were used, the *imbecilitas mentis* or you *infirm it consilii*, as can be seen in the passage by Ulpian collected in D. 16, 1, 2, 2, in a constitution by Justin I on actresses, promulgated between 520 and 523 in C. 5, 4, 23 pr., as well as in C. 5, 17, 10; likewise, references to the term *imbecilitas* can be found in literary sources such as the *Controversiae* 1, 6 and 2, 7, and in the *Dialogues* 12, 19, 5, of Seneca; in the "Memorable sayings and facts" of Valerius Maximus, or in the "Tusculanae disputationes" of Cicero 3, 16, 34, thus signifying the weakness and fragility of the feminine condition, which in Law was equivalent to an incapacity, which constrained its scope of action exclusively the *domus* and her role as caretaker of the home and its members.[2]

Despite this statement, Roman society and in turn the law evolved, so the legal capacity of women in Rome has been changing since the 2nd century BC, going from total submission to the father, husband, or guardian, to increasingly acquire a greater status of personal freedom and less legal inequality, both privately and

iuris condition of the woman implied an improvement in her situation despite the submission to *mulierum guardianship*, which with the evolution of the Law was eliminated in some cases according to the norms of the *ius liberorum* that allowed the succession of the woman, as well as the *testamenti factio* active, although it did not mean the free capacity of the woman. However, it can be affirmed that, despite the limitations, Roman women were in a better situation than in other communities, since their role as educators of future Roman citizens gave them a privileged position as midwives, a role that had high social esteem, *vid.* E. Volterra, *Instituciones de Derecho privado romano*, Madrid 1986, p. 133ff.; C. Pereira Porto, "La representación del concepto de mujer en Roma," *Revista de Filosofía del Derecho y derechos humanos* 5 (1995), p. 292ff.; S. Pomeroy, *Diosas, rameras, esposas y esclavas*, Madrid 1999, p. 173; R. Herrera Bravo, A. Salazar Revuelta, and M. Salazar Revuelta, "La condición de la mujer en la represión del adulterio en derecho romano y su recepción histórica," *Experiencias jurídicas e identidades femeninas* (2011), p. 186ff.; B. Fernández Vizcaíno, "El *ius adcrescendi* en los senadoconsultos Tertuliano y Orficiano," in *RIDROM*, 2011, p. 455ff.; J. A. González Ares Fernández, *Mujer, Política e Igualdad. De las Palabras a los Hechos*, Valencia 2017, p. 61; V. Pérez Pérez, "Capacidad de la mujer en derecho privado romano," *Revista Clepsidra* 16 (2017), pp. 191–217; A. López Güeto, *Madres e hijos en el Derecho romano de sucesiones. Los senadoconsultos Tertuliano y Orficiano*, Madrid 2017, p. 27ff.

2 D. Espín Cánovas, "Capacidad jurídica de la mujer casada," in *Revista Gráficas Europa*, Salamanca 1969, p. 7; R. P. Rodríguez Montero, "Hilvanando 'atributos' femeninos en la antigua Roma," in *Fundamentos romanísticos del Derecho contemporáneo, BOE*, 2012, pp. 897–903; M. Salazar Revuelta, "Estatus jurídico y social de la *materfamilias* en el marco de la ciudadanía romana," in *Mulier: algunas historias e instituciones de Derecho Romano*, 2013, p. 200ff.; M. J. Bravo Boch, *No tan lejano, una visión de la mujer romana a través de temas de actualidad*, Valencia 2018, p. 15.

publicly. In this sense, the situation of the Roman woman was favored by the war and the masculine mortality, passing from obscurity to a prominent social plane when assuming the administration and management of the family patrimony in the absence of a man, in some occasions of large sums of money. The law allowed women to take an oath and testify, act in court or appoint a solicitor, although in the Republican era they were not entitled to file a *iudicium legitimum* before the *quaestiones*, and they continued to be vetoed in trades proper to men, thus, at the legal level they could not be judges, exercise magistracies or be attorneys, and in other aspects the exercise of banking and exchange was excepted, from which they were excluded. This evolution had circumstances that favored it, thus it has an aspect of geographical influence, since urban centers offered greater opportunities to women in the world of work, just as a clear distinction was established by social class, since women of lower class high they carried out large economic operations, being medium or large owners who ran land, mines or factories, and on the other hand, the freedwomen formed the great mass of working women, applying to their lives the trade learned as slaves; likewise, it began to be normal for women to manage businesses, or small workshops in the event that the father or husband died, which led to the fact that with the passage of time, society and morality accepted women as subjects of the labor market, although the equivalence between man and woman was not totally accepted socially.[3]

In this regard, this ability to evolve throughout its history meant that women were gaining levels of power and independence compared to men. Already at the end of the Republic there were demonstrations of women, and despite their limited capacity their participation in public life became more and more present, despite the fact that political life and family government was in the hands of men, limiting the female role as we can see in D. 50, 17, 2 pr.,[4] especially due to

3 C. Pereira Porto, "La representación del concepto de mujer en Roma," *Revista de Filosofía del Derecho y derechos humanos* 5, cit., p. 292; R. P. Rodríguez Montero, "Hilvanando 'atributos' femeninos en la antigua Roma," in *Fundamentos romanísticos del Derecho contemporáneo, BOE*, cit., p. 899; R. Rodríguez, "La mujer en el mundo laboral de la Roma antigua," in *Mulier: algunas historias e instituciones de Derecho Romano*, 2013, p. 242ff.; Mª E. Ortuño, "Una limitación de la capacidad patrimonial de la mujer en el ámbito sucesorio: la *Lex Vocconia*," in *Mulier: algunas historias e instituciones de Derecho Romano*, 2013, p. 452ff.; J. A. González Ares Fernández, *Mujer, Política e Igualdad. De las Palabras a los Hechos*, cit., p. 62.

4 D. 50, 17. 2 pr.- Ulpianus 1 ad sab. Feminae ab omnibus officiis civilibus vel publicis remotae sunt et ideo nec iudices esse possunt nec magistratum gerere nec postulare nec pro alio intervenire nec procuratores existere. In the same sense, D. 3, 1, 1, 5 and D. 5, 1, 12, 2.

the impossibility or difficulty of communicating in public and with an audience that is masculine since any activity or business in that area was prohibited, but in the 1st century BC, partly because of the activity carried out by upper-class women that they had received a good education, sometimes women took public spaces to express their ideas, which previously would have been unimaginable and all this despite the contrary opinions expressed by the masculine society represented by Cato regarding a feared and possible equality between men and women.[5]

This process favorable to women had its legislative reply in an attempt to control female attitudes or behaviors, putting obstacles to this evolution in the *lex Oppia*, from 215 BC, abrogated in 195 BC, by the *lex Valeria Fundania,* or the *lex Vocconia de mulierum hereditatis* of 169 BC, established with the aim of limiting the inheritance capacity of women, to curb the autonomy they had achieved, thus maintaining Roman customs, as previously stated, prohibiting their performance as lawyers, or in some trades civil and public, such as judges, magistrates, postulate, intervene for another, or be attorneys, which were considered masculine trades, and later, with the coming to power of Augustus and the beginning of the Principate promulgating different laws, *Lex Iulia de maritandis ordinibus*, 18 BC; *Lex Iulia sumptuaria*, 18 BC plebiscite; *Lex Iulia de adulteriis coercendis*, 17–16 BC; *Lex Papia Poppaea*, 9 AD,[6] which tried to stop the process of emancipation of women, and with which it was intended to return to a restrictive legal situation for women, since said legislation tried to recover the image of a Roman matron dedicated to the *domus* and to the family, which shows that their need arose from a reality, from women who violated their traditional role, carrying out behaviors that went beyond what was accepted by the morality of the time.

However, and despite this control of female emancipation carried out in different legal stages, it can be observed from legal and literary sources a long social and regulatory development that made this process of evolution unstoppable.

Among the consequences of this idea of women as the weaker sex, light of judgment and ignorant of the things of the forum, the perpetual guardianship of women with the institution of the *tutela mulierum*[7] stands out, which in the

5 In this sense, Cato maintains "*Extemplo simul pares esse coeperunt, superiores erunt*," collected in *Livio, Ab urbe condita*, XXXIV, 3. *Vid*. López Güeto, A., "Mujer, poder y derecho en Roma," en *Revista jurídica Piélagus*, 17, 2018, 12–13.

6 Regarding the Augustan laws in matters of sexual morality and the failure in their objectives, E. Cantarella, *Pasado próximo. Mujeres romanas de Tácita a Sulpicia*, trans. M. M. Núñez, Madrid 1997, p. 197ff.

7 Cicero, *Pro Murena* 12, 27; *Tit. Ulp.* 11, 1; *Tit. Ulp.* 11, 27.

oldest Roman Law was justified because at the death of the *pater* the woman continued to be considered a *filia familias*, being then subject to the authority of the heirs understood as an extension of the parental authority of the deceased.

Later, with the admission of the woman as *sui iuris*, the *potestas* changes to be a testamentary or legitimate guardianship, but not based on the woman's own incapacity, even more so when the *ius liberorum* is established,[8] which releases the woman from guardianship, since the fact of having a certain number of children could not lead to a disability that was intrinsic to be a woman.[9]

Regarding guardianship, it is worth noting, as López Güeto affirms,[10] that although the majority discourse based it on issues of feminine weakness and fragility, the reality of *tutela mulierum* was mostly economic, since in most cases the guardian was a relative and heir of the woman, for which reason one can speak of an interested management of the goods and life of the women. However, in this aspect, the evolution of Roman Law can also be observed, dictating the *ius civile* different norms that allowed, even slowly, women to have a presence in the management of their assets and their own lives.

In this sense, in classical Roman Law Gaius exposes in his Institutes the relevance of the guardianship of prepubescents, raising doubts about the reasons that support the guardianship of women, since in his opinion these were more apparent than true, since he was able to observe that in his time women of full age carried out business by themselves, with cases in which the tutor imposed his authority by pure formalism, even though it is not strange that the Praetor was the one who authorized acts against the will of the tutor. This is how Gaius expresses it 1, 190:

> Gaius 1, 190. *Feminas vero perfectae aetatis in tutela esse fere nulla pretiosa ratio suasisse videtur: Nam quae vulgo creditur, quin levitate animi plerumque decipiuntur et aequum erat eas tutorum auctoritate regi, magis speciosa videtur quam vera; mulieres enim, quae*

---

8 H. Campos Vargas, "La mujer en la literatura jurídica romana: una aproximación de género a las 'Instituciones' de Gayo," *Revista de Ciencias Jurídica* 107 (2005), p. 151ff.; A. López Güeto, *Madres e hijos en el Derecho romano de sucesiones. Los senadoconsultos Tertuliano y Orficiano*, cit., p. 20ff.; B. Fernández Vizcaíno, "El *ius adcrescendi* en los senadoconsultos Tertuliano y Orficiano," in *RIDROM*, cit., p. 455ff.; A. López Güeto, "Mujer, poder y derecho en Roma," *Revista jurídica Piélagus* 17, cit., p. 19.

9 P. Resina Sola, "La condición jurídica de la mujer en Roma," in *La Mujer en el mundo mediterráneo antiguo*, Granada 1990, p. 105ff.; V. Pérez Pérez, "Capacidad de la mujer en Derecho privado romano," in *Revista Clepsydra*, cit., p. 13ff.

10 A. López Güeto, "Mujer, poder y derecho en Roma," *Revista jurídica Piélagus* 17, cit., p. 15.

perfectae aetatis sunt, ipsae sibi negotia tractant, et in quibusdam causis dicis gratia tutor interponit auctoritatem suam; saepe etiam invitus auctor fieri a praetore cogitur.

Thus, the distinguished jurist states in this text that those who believe that women are weaker than men do not know women, because "in our time," he continues, "they trade and carry out all kinds of legal acts just like us." This statement in Gaius' text seems to imply that the Romans began to change their perception of feminine nature and its role in society, understanding that an adult woman is a free and independent human being without the need for guardianship, although this idea exposed is a digression in the work of Gaius and in Roman culture, since in all his work he constantly distinguishes the capacity of men and women as different,[11] but it is configured as an argument for the normative progress that goes from the text of Gaius who was already contemplating a different era, more favorable to women, until Diocletian AD 284–305 no longer refers to the guardianship of women.

This idea of women's lesser capacity was reflected in all family, social and legal spheres of Roman life throughout its history since, although there were some corrective measures favorable to women, especially from the Law Postclassical and Justinian, discrimination based on sex was a continuum in Rome.

2. Conceptual details

Taking this idea of female inequality in Roman Law as a starting point, we will focus our attention on hereditary law and more specifically on testamentary succession in which there is a legal situation of women of clear inferiority in a singular case of improper use from the expression *ius adscrescendi.*

We refer to the text of Gaius collected in his Institutions, in Gaius 2, 124, in which the consequences of the preterition of the descendants of de *cuius are affirmed*:

Gaius 2, 124.—*Ceteras uero liberorum personas si praeterierit testator, ualet testamentum: sed praeteritae istae personae scriptis heredibus in partem adcrescunt, si sui heredes sint, in uirilem, si extranei, in dimidiam: id est, si quis tres uerbi gratia filios heredes instituerit et filiam praeterierit, filia adcrescendo pro quarta parte fit heres et ea ratione id consequitur, quod ab intestato patre mortuo habitura esset; at si extraneos ille heredes*

11 L. Friedlander, *La sociedad romana. Historia de las costumbres en Roma, desde Augusto hasta los Antoninos*, México 1947, p. 301; J. Iglesias, *Derecho romano*, Madrid 2010, 383; V. Pérez Pérez, "Capacidad de la mujer en Derecho privado romano," in *Revista Clepsydra*, cit., p. 13.

instituerit et filiam praeterierit, filia adcrescendo ex dimidia parte fit heres. quae de filia diximus, eadem et de nepote deque omnibus ceteris liberorum personis seu masculini seu feminini sexus dicta intellegemus.

This passage affirms that if the testator had deferred to other descendants who were not male under authority, that is, daughters and grandsons *ex filio*, of either sex,[12] the will was valid,[13] although for the quota that these people will later be called legitimate, validly omitted by the old law were partially admitted to the inheritance, together with the instituted heirs, in a part equal to that of the others if they were heirs in their own right, and in half if they were strangers,[14] using the term *in partem adcrescunt.*

On this issue, and despite the terminological identity, we can affirm that this situation does not correspond to the *ius adscrescendi* that was widely applied in Roman inheritance law, which formed an institute that was verified regardless of the field of law in which the circumstance that made the increase necessary arose, therefore, consequently, it had absolute legal autonomy both from the rest of the hereditary institutes with which it was interrelated, and from the practical situation that made it display its effectiveness, as well as its own nature and

12 Gaius 2, 128; Gaius *Ep.* 2, 3, 1; *Tit.Ulp.* 22, 20; *Nov. Maior* 6, 3; *Lex Romana Burgundionum, XLV.*

13 In relation to the validity of the will when they had been forgotten *sui by* the testator, it must be affirmed that these subjects were also granted the possibility of invalidating the succession arrangement by filing a *querela inofficiosi testamenti*, emerged around the first century BC in the Court of the *Centumviri* as an action for rescission of the testament due to the unjust omission of close relatives of the testator. Pérez Simeón, M., *Nemo pro parte testatus pro parte intestatus decedere potest*, Barcelona 2001, p. 243ff.

14 Tit. Ulp. 22, 17.—Reliquae vero personae liberorum, velut filia, nepos, neptis, si praeteritae sint, valet testamentum, scriptis heredibus adcrescunt, suis quidem heredibus in partem virilem, extraneis autem in partem dimidiam.

Pauli Sent. 3, 4b, 8.—Filio et extraneo aequis partibus heredibus institutis si praeterita adcrescat, tantum suo avocabit, quantum extraneo: si vero duo sint filii instituti, suis tertiam, extraneis dimidiam tollet.

Vid. F. Glück, *Comentario alle Pandette*, XXXVI, Milano, 1907, p. 338ff.; E. Cuq, *Manuel des institutions juridiques des Romains*, Paris 1928, p. 707; U. Robbe, *Il diritto di accrescimento e la sostituzione volgare nel diritto romano classico*, Milano 1953, pp. 191–192; U. Robbe, voz: "accrescimento," NNDI, vol. I, p. 159; L. Di Lella, *Querela inofficiosi testamenti. Contributo allo studio della sucessione testamentaria*, Napoli 1972, p. 104ff.; M. Talamanca, *Istituzioni di Diritto Romano*, Milano 1990, pp. 766–767; G. Impallomeni, *Scritti di diritto romano e tradizione romanistica*, Padova 1996, p. 323; M. Pérez Simeón, *Nemo pro parte testatus pro parte intestatus decedere potest*, cit., p. 255ff.

structure to respond to a function and purpose precisely defined by the *ius civile* since the earliest stage of Roman law.[15]

Thus, it can be observed in the doctrine the difference established between the general *ius adscrescendi* of application in all Roman succession law and that which took place before the preterition of daughters and grandsons called *ius adscrescendi in partem*, configured the latter in the opinion of Arias Ramos-Arias Bonet[16] in a situation of preterition by the testator of daughters and grandchildren by the Roman civil regulations that had as a consequence the increase in the number of instituted, for which reason it was essentially different from that used in general inheritance law, since the expression *ius adscrescendi* in inheritance law concerns only two well-defined cases, on the one hand when a share of the inheritance remained vacant joining the portion of the other co-heirs, and on the other, when a thing or right bequeathed *per vindicationem or per* praeceptionem to several persons it was not acquired by one of them and it was joined to the part of the others[17]; and on the other hand, there were other cases in which the expression right to accretion was used without having the essential meaning of general accretion to which reference is made in matters of inheritance and legacies, as was the case with the qualification of right to accretion when the quota from the distributing co-owner it was returned to the other co-owners,[18] as can

15 U. Robbe, *Il diritto di accrescimento e la sostituzione volgare nel diritto romano classico*, cit., pp. 191–192; U. Robbe, voz: "accrescimento," in *NNDI*, vol. I, p. 159.

16 J. Arias Ramos, and J. Arias Bonet, *Derecho Romano II, Obligaciones-Familia-Sucesiones*, Madrid 1981, p. 841.

17 G. Pugliese, voz: "accrescimento," in *Enciclopedia del diritto*, vol. I, cit., p. 313. En el mismo sentido S. Perozzi, *Istituzioni di diritto romano, II*, Roma 1928, p. 558, n. 1.

18 The return or not of the quota of a slave manumitted by one of the community members is highly complex and worthy of a unitary study, since the legal regime that ordered the issue changes over time, in such a way that, in the oldest stage the emancipation of a common slave carried out by one among several owners was effective before all, later in classical times the emancipation of the common slave caused the manumission to lose his quota that increased the rest, and finally in Justinian law the emancipation was valid although the manumitant or the freed slave had to buy the freedom of the rest of the commoners, these changes were closely related to the different currents of ethical thought in Rome that modified the Law over the centuries, however, it is not the study This matter is the object of this work, so for in-depth knowledge it is recommended to consult the following doctrinal works as well as the bibliography contained in them, *vid.* M. Bretone, *Servus communis: contributo alla storia de la comproprietà romana in età clásica*, Napoli 1958, p. 140ff.; P. Bonfante, *Corso di Diritto Romano, II "La Proprietà,"* Milano 1968, p. 21ff.; A. Torrent, "Notas sobre la relación entre *communio* y copropiedad," in *Studi Grosso, II*, Torino 1968, p. 111ff.

be observed in *Fr. Dositheanum*, 10,[19] in D. 29, 2, 59, where the *iure adscrescendi* acquisition of the inheritance returned to the substitute pupil is upheld, and finally, the case that interests us in Gaius 2, 124 that refers to the *ius adscrescendi* regarding the legal call to the inheritance of the daughter and grandchildren *praeteriti* who were added to the other instituted heirs.

The preterition of heirs had a different legal response depending on whether the preterite was a man *in potestate* or if it was a woman or the grandchildren of the testator, in this sense, in the first case the paternal will was rescinded,[20] while in the case of the daughters and grandsons were resolved by assigning a part of the inheritance to those affected by the paternal will, that is, a virile quota to the preterite if the instituted were *sui* and, half of the *hereditary* ace if they were strangers, the right of these *ceterae liberorum personae, praeteritae* by the *paterfamilias* is referred to in the sources as *ius adscrescendi in partem*; this same legal situation is also defined as *ius adscrescendi ad certam portionem* by Justinian in I. 2, 13, pr.[21]:

> I. 2, 13, pr.—... *sed si non fuerant heredes scripti scriptaeve vel exheredati exheredataeve, testamentum quidem non infirmabatur, ius autem adcrescendi eis ad certam portionem praestabatur. sed nec nominatim eas personas exheredare parentibus necesse erat, sed licebat et inter ceteros hoc facere.*

Likewise, in Gaius 1, 126 it is called *iure adcrescendi*:

> Gaius 1, 126.—*Et hoc iure utebamur, quasi nihil inter feminas et masculos interesset; sed nuper imperator Antoninus significauit rescripto suas non plus nancisci feminas per bonorum possessionem, quam quod iure adcrescendi consequerentur. quod in emancipatarum*

19 Tit.Ulp. 1, 18; Pauli Sent. 4, 12, 1.

20 *Cicero, De Oratore*, I, 38, 175; *Cicero, De Oratore*, I, 57, 245; Valerio Maximo 7, 7, 1; *Tit.Ulp.* 22, 16; *Ep.Gayo* 2, 3 pr.; D. 28, 2, 7; D. 28, 3, 1; D. 28, 3, 17; C. 6, 28, 4 pr; C. 6, 28, 4, 1; I. 2, 13, pr.
Vid. A. Dernburg, *Pandette, III* (traducción italiana de Cicala), Torino 1905, p. 540ff.; G. Pacchioni, *Corso di diritto romano, II*, Torino 1910, p. 778; S. Perozzi, *Istituzioni di diritto romano, II*, cit., p. 606ff.; G. La Pira, *Successione ereditaria intestata e contro il testamento in diritto romano*, Firenze 1930, p. 347; P. Voci, *Istituzioni di diritto romano*, Milano 1954, p. 576ff.; P. Voci, *Diritto ereditario romano, II*, Milano 1963, p. 634ff.; M. Talamanca, *Istituzioni di Diritto Romano*, cit., p. 766; J. Arias Ramos and J. Arias Bonet, *Derecho Romano II, Obligaciones-Familia-Sucesiones*, cit., pp. 798ff.–840ff.; A. Sanguinetti, "Considerazioni sull'origine del principio '*sui heredes instituendi sunt vel exheredandi*,'" in *SDHI, LIX*, 1993, p. 262ff.; M. Pérez Simeón, *Nemo pro parte testatus pro parte intestatus decedere potest*, cit., pp. 244ff.–254, n. 25.

21 S. Solazzi, *Diritto ereditario romano I*, Napoli 1932, p. 227ff.

quoque personis obseruandum est, ut nimirum hae quoque, quod adcrescendi iure habiturae essent, si in potestate fuissent, id ipsum etiam per bonorum possessionem habeant.

3. Dual responses of Roman Law to the assumption of preterition of daughters and grandchildren from the perspective of civil law

In order to explain the solution given by the *ius civile*, we will refer to the circumstances of the aforementioned text from the sources Gaius 2, 124, that is, if a person instituted heirs, for example, to three sons and had preteritated a daughter, through the increase made her heir to a quarter, since she had a virile quota, as if her father had died intestate, but in the same situation, if the institution belonged to strangers, the growing daughter became heir to half from his father's estate. This same right of the daughter corresponded to the grandson and other descendants, both male and female, thus making the civil regulations clear in favor of the verification of a *ius adscrescendi in partem*.

This rule has its origin in the opinion of Di Lella[22] in the court of the *centumviri* and not in Roman jurisprudence, stating that the omission in the paternal will of the daughter and grandchildren of either sex and its consequence in the application of the *ius adscrescendi in partem* "has charactere cosí positive che non è certo venuta dalla giurisprudenza"; in this way, by means of fiction the daughter was considered established in the will and a part of the inheritance was granted to her in equality with the testamentary heir, even in her obligation to the legacies, for which reason it can be granted to the[23] court an important role in determining the concept of necessary succession.

Another issue that is part of Di Lella's study in relation to this rule of *ius civile* is the fact of its recent creation throughout the history of Roman Law, since as demonstrated in *Cicero, de finibus* 2, 55—*…nemo nostrum credebat, eratque veri similius hunc mentiri, cuius interesset, quam illum, qui id se rogasse scripsisset, quod debuisset rogare. addebat etiam se in legem Voconiam iuratum contra eam facere non audere, nisi aliter amicis videretur. aderamus nos quidem adolescentes,*

22 L. Di Lella, *Querela inofficiosi testamenti. Contributo allo studio della sucessione testamentaria*, cit., p. 104ff. Regarding this thesis, vid. C. Appleton, *Le testament romain. La méthode du droit comparé et authenticité des XII tables*, Paris 1903, p. 100ff.; S. Solazzi, *Diritto ereditario romano I*, cit., 103, 154ff., 173 (n. 2), 174ff., 222ff.; C. Sanfilippo, *Corso di diritto romano. Evoluzione storica della hereditas*, Napoli 1946, p. 64ff.

23 S. Perozzi, *Istituzioni di diritto romano, II*, cit., p. 607 affirms that the heirs that accrued found their quota taxed with the legacies imposed on the instituted.

sed multi amplissimi viri, quorum nemo censuit plus Fadiae dandum, quam posset ad eam lege Voconia pervenire. tenuit permagnam Sextilius hereditatem…, at the time it was not known, since from the study of this text it can be extracted that if at that time the preterition had given rise to the right of the daughter to ask for half of the hereditary ace with a stranger established in the will It would be inexplicable that Sextilius could have retained the entire inheritance if the daughter had asserted her right; complementary to this assumption is found in *Cicero, in Verrem*, II, 1, 105, a case of annulment of the institution of a daughter granting the inheritance to the substitute heir following the guidelines of the lex *Voconia,* which leads Di Lella to affirm the difficulty of reconciling the *lex Voconia* and the *ius adcrescendi in partem*, as well as concluding that the granting of a virile quota or half of the inheritance in case of preterition must correspond to a moment after the event that the two fragments of Cicero collect and, therefore, to the *lex Voconia*, since at that time the consequences of the omission of a daughter or grandson had not yet been established by the[24] *centumviri.*

Despite the exposed texts, Kübler manifests himself against these affirmations[25] since he affirms that it cannot be established with certainty that the right of growth in this case is before or after the *lex Voconia.* In the same order of ideas, Solazzi,[26] who is in favor of the centunviral origin of the *ius adscrescendi in partem,* takes as a reference the modality of the disinheritance of the posthumous and their difference with the men fixed by the *lex Iunia Vellaea* to affirm, on the one hand, that this situation would have prevented any court from granting the preterition of the posthumous consequences other than the legal ones, and, on the other, to reject the theory according to which the recognition of the necessary succession of the daughter belonged to an age recent, always after the *lex Voconia.*

However, according to the cited literature on this matter, it seems more plausible that the beginnings of this rule were after the *lex Voconia*, since if that were the case, Cicero would undoubtedly have contemplated it in his work, also regarding its origin. In the work of the courts, it seems to be deduced from the wording of the different fragments that expose this norm its character of positive law as Di Lella affirms, since from the state of the sources it is impossible for us to specify this reform more.

---

24 This same theory is followed by E. Costa, *Cicerone giureconsulto, I*, Roma 1964, p. 228ff.; S. Brassloff, *Studien zur romischen Rechtsgeschichte, I*, 1925, pp. 85ff., 93.

25 B. Kübler, "Das Intestaterbrecht der Frauen im alten Rom," in *ZSS, XLI*, 1920, p. 29ff.

26 S. Solazzi, *Diritto ereditario romano I*, cit., p. 223, n. 1.

Another issue to be taken into consideration related to the regulations applicable according to the sources to the *ius adcrescendi in partem* daughter and grandchildren is the legal nature that the heirs assumed, a point on which there is doctrinal controversy since various theses framed within Roman civil law can be observed.

Thus, in this aspect of inheritance regulations, some authors maintain that the daughter or grandchildren excluded from the inheritance came to be treated as if they had been instituted together with the testamentary heirs, granting said meaning to the term *adcrescunt* used in the sources, so as has been established, the preterite received either a virile share of the inheritance if the testamentary heir was *suus*, or half of it in the event of being a stranger.

In this order of ideas, Perozzi[27] maintains that in the event of the preterition of a daughter or grandchildren, the will remained in force although the preteritors were considered instituted, that is, *scriptis heredibus adcrescunt*, each subject receiving a virile quota if they concurred with other instituted *sui heirs* and, in the case of instituted strangers, they all jointly became owners of half of the hereditary case,[28] which was distributed among them in equal parts, leaving the other half to the strangers instituted, until Justinian at the time of writing the Digest became aware of the discrimination against women in the event of preterition in the will, giving as a solution his constitution C. 6, 28, 4, 3 in which he equated men and women, children and grandchildren, granting the same rights to all of them, that is, from the aforementioned constitution, all *sui* disinheritances had to be nominal, even in the event of posthumous.[29]

A fortiori, in relation to Justinian's aforementioned constitution and by virtue of what Dernburg[30] calls "the emperor's favorite concept" which is related to the

27 S. Perozzi, *Istituzioni di diritto romano, II*, cit., p. 607. Otros autores que siguen esta tesis son A. Dernburg, *Pandette, III* (traducción italiana de Cicala), cit., p. 542; J. Arias Ramos, and J. Arias Bonet, *Derecho Romano II, Obligaciones-Familia-Sucesiones*, cit., p. 841.

28 M. Pérez Simeón, in *Nemo pro parte testatus pro parte intestatus decedere potest*, cit., p. 255 maintains in the same sense that, despite the absence of sources that justify them, in the event of institution of a stranger and preterition of daughters or grandsons, the latter were jointly entitled to half of the inheritance. To the same effect, O. Karlowa, in *Römisches Rechtsgeschichte Privatrecht, II*, Leipzig 1901, p. 890ff. maintains that the preterite ones that increased received a single virile portion as a whole.

29 M. Pérez Simeón, *Nemo pro parte testatus pro parte intestatus decedere potest*, cit., pp. 262–263.

30 A. Dernburg, *Pandette, III* (traducción italiana de Cicala), cit., p. 542ff.

idea that women should be esteemed just as men ordered that the preterition of a daughter or a grandson had the same effect as the omission of a *filius sus*, thus abolishing the particular *ius adcrescendi* declared by civil law in the case at hand, in the same provision the emperor ruled the need to use the term *exheres* to disinherit, as well as that the disinheritance should always be nominative and made anywhere in the will.[31]

This idea can be framed in the Roman rule *nemo pro parte testatus pro parte intestatus decedere potest*, since taking as a reference the idea of incompatibility between the two causes of denunciation, testamentary and intestate, as well as the impossibility of accumulating the rights granted by them, it can be affirmed that if there was an heir named by will, the successors in *intestate* they could be called absolutely to the inheritance, having to resort then to the fiction that a single testamentary heir, even instituted *pro parte*, had the right to the total of the hereditary ass, and the successors could not be called intestate or in the residual part.[32]

This Roman principle had as an exception in Roman Law, considered by Bonfante as the only real one, the one recognized in the testament of the military[33] in

31 C. 6, 28, 4. *Vid.* C. Fadda, *Concetti fondamentali del diritto ereditario romano*, parte prima, Napoli 1900, p. 335; P. Voci, "Il diritto ereditario romano dalle origini ai Severi," in *Studi di diritto romano, II*, Padova 1985, p. 28 (n. 97) (=en *Ausfstieg und Niedergang der römischen Welt, II*, 14, Berlin 1982, p. 392ff.); J. Arias Ramos, and J. Arias Bonet, *Derecho Romano II, Obligaciones-Familia-Sucesiones*, cit., p. 785ff.; M. Pérez Simeón, *Nemo pro parte testatus pro parte intestatus decedere potest*, cit., p. 249ff.

32 P. Bonfante, *Corso di Diritto Romano, VI "Le successioni,"* Milano 1930 (reprint 1974), p. 216ff. Regarding the different theories that serve as the basis for the rule *nemo pro parte testatus pro parte intestatus decedere*, may consult the aforementioned work by Bonfante and the authors listed therein, as well as his work "L'origine dell'*Hereditas* e dei *Legata* nel diritto successorio romano. A proposito della regola *Nemo pro parte testatus pro parte intestatus decedere potest,*" in *BIDR, IV*, 1891, pp. 97ff. (=en *Scritti Giuridici Varii, I "Famiglia e successione,"* Torino 1916, pp. 101ff.). Likewise, regarding the origin and scope of the Roman rule, it is recommended to consult two very interesting current monographs both regarding their content and the quantity and quality of citations that they collect, thus, *vid.* M. Pérez Simeón, *Nemo pro parte testatus pro parte intestatus decedere potest*, cit., 43ff.; E. Bosch Capdevila, *El principio nemo pro parte testatus pro parte intestatus decedere potest. Evolución y significado*, Madrid 2006, p. 19ff.

33 D. 29, 1, 6; D. 29, 1, 37.; D. 49, 17, 19, 2. *Vid.* A. Dernburg, *Pandette, III* (traducción italiana de Cicala), cit., p. 537, n. 4; Windscheid, B., *Diritto delle Pandette*, III, Torino 1930, p. 333ff.; V. Arangio Ruiz, "L'origine del *testamentum militis* e la sue porzione nel diritto romano classico," in *BIDR, XVIII*, 1906, p. 157ff.; A. Hernández-Gil, *El testamento*

which the Romans allowed the military to be able to test validly on a part of his assets and on the rest to admit to the legitimate successors; likewise, other unrecognized exceptions are exposed[34] that derive mainly from the conflict between the will and the late legitimate succession against it developed from the imperial stage, among them is the exception that interests us, the object of this work.

Thus, and in relation to this question, Bonfante[35] maintains that if the testator had preterited legitimaries other than male children until Justinian, the will remained in force, corresponding to daughters and grandsons only the

---

militar(en torno a un sistema hereditario militar romano), Madrid 1946, p. 102ff.; G. Sciascia, "*Miles pro parte testatus pro parte intestatus decedere potest*," in *Seminar, V*, 1947, p. 31ff.; S. Von Bolla, *Aus römischem und bürgerlichem Erbrecht*, Wien 1950, p. 1ff.; S. Von Bolla, "Zum römischem Militärtestament," in *Studi Arangio-Ruiz*, I, 273ff.; P. Bonfante, *Corso di Diritto Romano, VI "Le successioni*," cit., p. 223ff.; S. Solazzi, "Diritto di accresciment e testamento dei militari," in *Scritti Giuridici-Raccolti per il Centenario della Casa Editrice Jovene*, Napoli 1954, p. 95ff.; B. Biondi, *Diritto ereditario romano*, Milano 1954, p. 162ff.; L. Chevalier, "Notes sur le testament militaire," in *Varia, II*, 1956, p. 1ff.; V. Ferrari, "Un volume di 'Varia,'" recensión a Varia, Études de droit romain, 2, 1957, in *LABEO, III*, 1957, p. 395ff.; Niederländer, "Zur Herkunft der römischen Impensendreiteilung," in *ZSS, LXXV*, 1958, p. 201ff.; M. Amelotti, *Il testamento romano attraverso la prassi documentales. I. Le forma classiche di testamento*, Firenze 1966, 81ff.; P. Voci, *Diritto ereditario romano, I*, Milano 1967, p. 497; G. Scherillo, "D. 1, 4, 3 (Giavoleno, L.13 'EP') e il testamento militare," in *Studi in onore di Edoardo Volterra, III*, Milano 1971, p. 613ff.; M. Kaser, *Das römische Privatech*, München 1971, I, p. 569, II, p. 345; G. Ermini, "La regola *nemo pro parte testatus pro parte intestatus decedere potest* nella glossa ordinaria al *Corpus iuris*," in *Scritti di diritto comune*, Padova 1976, p. 320ff. (=*Rivista Italiana per le Scienze Giuridiche, I*, Roma 1937); J. Arias Ramos, and J. Arias Bonet, *Derecho Romano II, Obligaciones-Familia-Sucesiones*, cit., p. 785ff.; M. Pérez Simeón, *Nemo pro parte testatus pro parte intestatus decedere potest*, cit., p. 219ff.; E. Bosch Capdevila, *El principio nemo pro parte testatus pro parte intestatus decedere potest. Evolución y significado*, cit., p. 22ff.

34 Regarding the various exceptions to the Roman principle of incompatibility between the two causes of succession, as well as the causes and meaning of the rise of the same *vid.* P. Bonfante, *Corso di Diritto Romano, VI "Le successioni*," cit., p. 224ff.

35 P. Bonfante, *Corso di Diritto Romano, VI "Le successioni*," cit., p. 225, n. 2. In the same sense of denying the breach of the prohibition of incompatibility between testamentary and intestate succession. O. Karlowa, in *Römisches Rechtsgeschichte. Privatrecht, II*, cit., p. 891ff.; S. Solazzi, in *Diritto ereditario romano I*, cit., p. 221ff.; M. Kaser, *Das römische Privatech*, cit., I, p. 706; P. Jörs, W. Kunkel, and L. Wenger, *Römisches Recht: römisches privatrecht, abriss des römischen zivilprozessrechts*, Berlin-Heidelberg-New York 1978, p. 328; L. Di Lella, *Querela inofficiosi testamenti. Contributo allo studio della sucessione testamentaria*, cit., p. 105 (n. 132); J. Iglesias, *Derecho Romano*, cit., pp. 424–425.

ius adcrescendi ad certam portionem, receiving the corresponding fee as stated depending on whether the institution of the testamentary disposition went to a stranger or to other *heredes sui*, however, regarding the nature of the aforementioned right, the Italian author clearly states that the omitted were specifically joined to the *heredes scripti* without being considered in any way as intestate heirs.

In favor of this theory regarding an alleged unrecognized exception to the principle *nemo pro parte testatus pro parte intestatus decedere* Biondi, who also considers that the Roman principle of incompatibility of successions has as its only breach the military will, considering[36] *that* the preterition of daughters and grandsons, which Gaius defines as *adscrescere*, is not such, since by virtue of the *ius* In no case *adcrescendi* next to a testamentary heir was succeeded by an heir named by law, configuring the case at hand as a formula to admit a legitimary to the inheritance without overturning the will.

Thus, from the study of the doctrine and the sources, it cannot be established that this assumption was an intestate call to the inheritance of the preterite.

On this issue, it is worth noting the etymological reasons used by Pérez Simeón[37] to affirm that the addition of the *ceteri sui* preferred to the father's will did not mean the partial opening of the intestate succession, but that the omission of these subjects was solved by completing the will, since that the use by Gaius in his Institutions 2, 124 of the imperfect past of the subjunctive *habitura esset* shows that the estranged daughter did not get her due *intestate*.

On the other hand, this thesis is also based on the sources, from which no other idea can be extracted, since in no text is it stated that this increase in the number of heirs resulted in the opening of the intestate succession, as can be observed in the passages collected in *Tit. Ulp*. 22, 17 and in C. 6, 28, 4, 1, which serve as an example of said assertion, thus, in the first the validity of the testament is clearly manifested with the expression "valet testamentum," in the same sense, Justinian maintains in the aforementioned text of its *Codex* that "… *filia autem praeterita ius adcrescendi ex iure vetere accipiebat, ut eodem momento et testamentum country quodammodo ex parte iure adcrescendi evertat et ipsa almost scripta legatis supposeretur, …*" this fragment of the *Codex*, due to the practical repercussion of the assumption it raises, actually has more than the meaning of *ius adscrescendi* that of *ius delationis ex iure vetere accipiebat*, since the daughter or grandchildren had at that time an appeal to a certain share of their father's

36 B. Biondi, *Diritto ereditario romano*, cit., p. 164.

37 M. Pérez Simeón, *Nemo pro parte testatus pro parte intestatus decedere potest*, cit., p. 258ff.

inheritance dictated by law, which they lacked by virtue of the mortis causa provision, which, although it has a different origin, maintains the same structure and meaning than that granted by will.

Regarding these texts, Pérez Simeón affirms that with the right to increase granted to the *ceteri sui* an effect similar to the rupture of the will was obtained, however, with the inclusion of the term *quodammodo* the non-existence of a real rupture of the will was made clear; another issue that supports his thesis is that when the person named in the will was a stranger, the person who was rejected had the right to half of the inheritance, which meant an amount greater than his intestate share, which leads the author to wonder how the rejected could obtain more than the virile quota that corresponded to him in the intestate succession.

Thus, following the thesis Pérez Simeón serves as a reinforcement of the reasons to which he resorts to deny the partial opening of the intestate succession, the constitution of Justiniano already mentioned where the modification of the classic regime of the preterition of the *sui* is externalized, also presenting the norm that ruled in the classical and postclassical stages, thus, in the broad development of C. 6, 28, 4, from its beginning reference is made to a *successio ex testamento*, appreciating in the first paragraph *quasi scripta,* which serves as the basis for the opinion that we are dealing with a fiction that considers a subject not established in the will as a testamentary heir, which is confirmed by the insertion in this Justinian provision of two words: *legatis supposeretur*, that is, the daughter or grandchildren must pay the legacies that corresponded to the quota received, which would have been completely unnecessary if the succession were intestate.

This last statement regarding the payment of legacies leads Di Lella to argue[38] that it is clear that *adscrescere* should be interpreted as that the preterite ones were added to the established heirs, as if they had been mentioned in the will, never as intestate heirs, since as recalls Justiniano,[39] they were taken into account to pay the legacies established in the succession provision.

A sensu contrario, part of the doctrine maintains a different position to the one presented, thus, against this theory shared by authors such as Biondi or Bonfante, Volterra positions himself[40] by stating that one of the exceptions to the principle of the incompatibility of successions is the assumption of a testator who has left

---

38 L. Di Lella, *Querela inofficiosi testamenti. Contributo allo studio della sucessione testamentaria*, cit., p. 104ff.

39 C. 6, 28, 4, 1.

40 E. Volterra, *Instituciones de Derecho privado romano*, cit., p. 704ff.

daughters or grandchildren *ex filio*, male or female, these omitted subjects had the right to concur with the testamentary by the *ius adscrescendi ad certam portionem.*

Fadda[41] manifests itself since when citing the situation collected in Gaius 2, 124, he considers it as an exception to the rule *nemo pro parte testatus pro parte intestatus decedere potest,* that is, his thesis is the opposite of Bonfante, affirming that in this case when certain people were omitted from the will, an objective law norm attributed to these subjects a right of succession over a share of the deceased's assets, as well in his opinion, such action is justified not as affirmed by the majority of the doctrine[42] in which the rule *nemo pro parte testatus pro parte intestatus decedere potest* tried to prevent the concurrence of the two calls only if it had its origin in the will of the testator, so that when the situation had its origin in the intervention of a stranger, the rule was not broken, on the contrary, it maintains that the preterition of these subjects should represent the total ineffectiveness of the will as it happened with male children *in potestate*, however, due to the lesser importance of these *ceteri sui* in the Roman family organization, good sense leads us to accept the validity of the will, attributing to them a share of the inheritance, so that, on the one hand, the *favor testamenti* tried as far as possible to keep the succession within the limits of the will of the testator, but on the other hand, the new concept of family as well as the tendency to favor relatives had as transcendental consequence in this case an exception to the well-known Roman rule of incompatibility between denunciations.

In this order of ideas, contrary to the opinion that the preterition of daughters and grandchildren, without distinction of sex, should be resolved by assuming the fiction of a call made by the testator to the *ceterae liberorum personae* together with the instituted heirs to whom it accretes, Robbe[43] is shown stating that, logically, it does

41 C. Fadda, *Concetti fondamentali del diritto ereditario romano*, parte prima, cit., p. 344ff. Likewise, they follow this thesis that affirms the existence of a breach of the principle *nemo pro parte testatus pro parte intestatus decedere potest.* C. F. Mülenbruch, *Commentario alle Pandette, XL*, Erlangen 1838, p. 166; E. Costa, *Storia del diritto romano privato*, Torino 1925, p. 492; E. Rabel, "Die Erbrechtstheorie Bonfantes," in *ZSS, L*, 1930, p. 306ff.; L. Chevalier, "Notes sur le testament militaire," in *Varia, II*, cit., p. 31; A. Guarino, *Diritto privato romano*, Napoli 1981, p. 471; G. Scherillo, *Corso di diritto romano: il testamento*, Milano 1995, p. 180 (n. 1).

42 C. F. Mülenbruch, *Commentario alle Pandette, XL*, cit., p. 146ff.; B. Windscheid, *Diritto delle Pandette*, III, cit., p. 232ff.; T. Schirmer, *Handbuch des Römischen Erbrechtes*, Leipzig 1863 (reproducción facsimil de 1970), p. 58ff.; K. Köppen, *Lehrbuch des heutigen römischen Erbrechts*, Würzburg 1895, p. 91; K. Vangerow, *Lehrbuch der Pandekten, II*, Marburg-Leipzig 1863–1869, p. 9ff.

43 Robbe, U., Il diritto di accrescimento e la sostituzione volgare nel diritto romano classico, cit., 194 (nota 1).

not seem possible to imagine that the deferred and the *scripti heirs* were mentioned together in the paternal will, that is, a situation could not be feigned in which the *paterfamilias*, even due to a single distraction, had not acted and, even more, simulated the effect of a declaration of will that had not taken place, therefore, since what had happened was the preterition, the legal remedy of acting against the express will of the *de cuius* was resorted to, thus, in this case, even using the term *adcrescere*, the premise according to which it can only increase between equals[44] should be demonstrated and said circumstance cannot be verified in this case.

A fortiori, in relation to the requirement of the obligation to the legacies that serves as a basis in the theory of various authors to consider the preterite as instituted in the testamentary disposition when affirming that the preterite daughter, once claimed her right to the *ius adcrescendi in partem*, was obliged to the legacies ordered by the paternal[45] will as Justinian tells us in C. 6, 28, 4, 1 and C. 6, 28, 4, 4,[46] in Robbe's opinion[47] it only had support due to justice and equity, since the testamentary heirs could not be forced to respond for the legacies to the same extent wanted by the testator when they due to the increase *in partem* to theirs of the *ceterae liberorum personae praeteritae*, received less than what had been allocated to them in the will of the *paterfamilias*.[48]

---

44 M. Pérez Simeón, in *Nemo pro parte testatus pro parte intestatus decedere potest*, cit., p. 37 (n. 62), affirms in his thesis on the origins of the incompatibility between testate and intestate denunciation and, specifically in reference to the will per aes et libram that "the increase occurs only between *persons who* occupy a similar legal position."

45 In the general hereditary accretion, it was also stated that, if some charges were imposed on the accretive quota, the subject that accrued in it should be responsible for them, except in the case that they were personal obligations, since in this case the charge should be levied to the person and not to the portion, in this sense *vid.* S. Perozzi, *Istituzioni di diritto romano, II*, cit., p. 557.

46 C. 6, 28, 4, 1.—... et ipsa quasi scripta legatis supponeretur, ex praetore autem habebat contra tabulas bonorum possessionem in totum...
C. 6, 28, 4, 4.—...Cum enim per contra tabulas bonorum possessionem vel ius adcrescendi semissem substantiae filia praeterita accipiebat et omnibus legata praestare compellebatur, scilicet usque ad dodrantem suae portionis, remanebat ei sescuncia tantummodo in sua successione.

47 U. Robbe, *Il diritto di accrescimento e la sostituzione volgare nel diritto romano classico*, cit., p. 194, n. 1.

48 Regarding the recognition of legacies arranged in a will when the bonorum was granted by the praetor possessio against tabulas we must resort to the edictum de legatis praestandis contra tabulas bonorum possessione petita, in this sense it is recommended to consult the exposition that G. La Pira, in *Successione ereditaria intestata e contro il testamento in diritto romano*, cit., p. 352ff. Vid. A. Dernburg, *Pandette*, III (traducción

Regarding the nature of the right of the omitted, in Robbe's opinion,[49] once the existence of the substantial exception was admitted in this matter and that the incompatibility between the testamentary and intestate calls in this case was not violated, the equality of the missing daughter with the children *you inherit scripti* regarding the obligations of the legacies, it is not enough to reach the conclusion that the daughter did not *intestate.*

He maintains an eclectic position, limiting himself to assuming the texts of the sources without assessing or interpreting them regarding the right to call the daughter and grandchildren neglected by him of *cuius* as well as its nature, Voci[50] when affirming the coexistence between testamentary and *intestate heirs* in the event of preterition of *ceteri sui iam nati,*[51] and thus the existence of an exception to the rule *nemo pro parte testatus pro parte intestatus decedere potest* in the omission of these subjects that granted them the right to concur with the *scripti heirs,* according to the circumstances, in a virile quota or in half of the hereditary ace; likewise, Voci[52] affirms that the *ceteri sui*, by virtue of the exception to the rule of incompatibility of successions, received their quota as intestate successors, although they were considered as if the testator had contemplated them in his disposition, taking as a basis for such assertion. Justinian's regulations as well as the same reasons that Robbe uses, and which affirm that in this case the burdens of the legacies subsisted in terms of these subjects.

Lastly, regarding the doctrinal theses, Talamanca's opinion shows special interest[53] when he argues that the fact that in this case of concurrence between the heirs established in the paternal will and those other preterite descendants did not result in the nullity of the will constitutes an exception to the rule *nemo pro parte testatus pro parte intestatus decedere potest*, since in this case it is not necessary to comply with the formalism required by the aforementioned norm when we are faced with a contest between the legitimate succession and the testamentary one, although such affirmation does not have a rational explanation; in addition, Talamanca continues his thesis stating that, even if there is an exceptional contest between the two types of calls, this circumstance does not affect in any way the effectiveness of

---

italiana de Cicala), cit., p. 547; S. Perozzi, *Istituzioni di diritto romano*, II, cit., pp. 609–610.

49 U. Robbe, *Il diritto di accrescimento e la sostituzione volgare nel diritto romano classico*, cit., p. 194, n. 1.

50 P. Voci, *Diritto ereditario romano*, I, cit., p. 497ff.

51 P. Voci, *Diritto ereditario romano*, II, cit., p. 640ff.

52 P. Voci, *Diritto ereditario romano, I,* cit., p. 498, n. 9.

53 M. Talamanca, *Istituzioni di Diritto Romano*, cit., pp. 678–766.

testamentary provisions in a private capacity, as stated by the sources as well as the majority doctrine.

Once the right and its nature corresponding to the estranged daughter have been established, as well as to the grandchildren of either sex in the same situation, it is worth clarifying the influence of Roman inheritance law that orders the *ius adcrescendi in partem* with respect to the figure of the instituted in the will, since it can be determined that in a certain way we are facing a partial disinheritance of those instituted in the will, since in practice the latter saw the amount of their appeal compressed, the development of this last argument is undoubtedly worthy of a careful job that we reserve for the future.

In conclusion, as can be extracted from everything exposed to the injustice that the null consequence of the preterition of a daughter or grandchildren, of either sex, represented, the ius civile responded by ordering that these subjects not be left helpless by reason of their belonging to the Roman family, understood as that formed by blood ties, for this purpose granted them either a virile share of the inheritance in concurrence with other *sui*, or half when the person established in the will was a stranger to the family, civil law Roman called this right as accretion in its technical sense of the term, although this was not equivalent to the general *ius adscrescendi* applicable in succession law to perfectly identified cases that do not coincide with the *ius adscrescendi in partem*.

Thus, based on the etymological character of the texts of the sources, as well as the fact that no text maintains that this increase in the number of heirs was the result of a partial opening of the intestate succession and, above all, that it denies this possible solution to our problem the normative assumed by Justinian regarding this question collected in C. 6, 28, 4, premises all of them used in the different theses presented regarding the right and nature of the call made to the daughter and grandchildren, of any sex, omitted in the will of the *paterfamilias*, it can be extracted that the *ius civile* considered, by means of a fiction, the daughter and other *ceteri sui* as instituted in the will, granting them a part of the inheritance together with the testamentary heir, even affirming their obligation to the legacies established by the testator, which was done by adding the deceased subjects to the instituted heirs as if they were mentioned in the will, but never as *intestate heirs*, thus, this is the meaning that should be given to the term *adcrescunt* used to define this situation in the sources, so that until Justinian the will remained in force and the preterite received, or a virile share of the inheritance if the instituted heir was *suus*, or half of being a stranger leaving the will in force and the preterited *scriptis heredibus adcrescunt*, without being able to be considered in any way as intestate heirs.

Bibliography

Roman legal sources

Gaius 1, 190.

Gaius 2, 124.

Gaius 1, 126.

Gaius 2, 128.

Ep. Gai 2, 3 pr.

Ep. Gai 2, 3, 1.

Tit. Ulp. 1, 18.

Tit. Ulp. 11, 1.

Tit. Ulp. 11, 27.

Tit. Ulp. 22, 16.

Tit. Ulp. 22, 17.

Tit. Ulp. 22, 20.

Pauli Sent. 3, 4b, 8.

Pauli Sent. 4, 12, 1.

C. 6, 28, 4.

C. 6, 28, 4 pr.

C. 6, 28, 4, 1.

C. 6, 28, 4, 4.

D. 3, 1, 1, 5.

D. 5, 1, 12, 2.

D. 28, 2, 7.

D. 28, 3, 1.

D. 28, 3, 17.

D. 29, 1, 6.

D. 29, 1, 37.

D. 49, 17, 19, 2.

D. 50, 17.2 pr.

I. 2, 13, pr.

Roman Literaty sources

Livius, Ab urbe condita, XXXIV, 3.

Cicero, Pro Murena 12, 27.

Cicero, De Oratore, I, 38, 175.

Cicero, De Oratore, I, 57, 245.

Valerius Maximus 7, 7, 1.

Nov. Maior 6, 3.

Lex Romana Burgundionum, XLV.

Literature

Amelotti, M., *Il testamento romano attraverso la prassi documentales. I. Le forma classiche di testamento*, Firenze 1966.

Appleton, C., *Le testament romain. La méthode du droit comparé et authenticité des XII tables*, Paris 1903.

Arangio Ruiz, V., "L'origine del *testamentum militis* e la sue porzione nel diritto romano classico," in *BIDR, XVIII*, 1906.

Arias Ramos, J., and Arias Bonet, J., *Derecho Romano II, Obligaciones-Familia-Sucesiones*, Madrid 1981.

Biondi, B., *Diritto ereditario romano*, Milano 1954.

Bonfante, P., "L'origine dell'*Hereditas* e dei *Legata* nel diritto successorio romano. A proposito della regola *Nemo pro parte testatus pro parte intestatus decedere potest*," in *BIDR, IV*, 1891 (=en *Scritti Giuridici Varii, I "Famiglia e successione*," Torino 1916).

Bonfante, P., *Corso di Diritto Romano, VI "Le successioni*," Milano 1930 (reprint 1974).

Bonfante, P., *Corso di Diritto Romano, II "La Proprietà*," Milano 1968.

Bosch Capdevila, E., *El principio nemo pro parte testatus pro parte intestatus decedere potest. Evolución y significado*, Madrid 2006.

Brassloff, S., *Studien zur romischen Rechtsgeschichte, I*, 1925.

Bravo Boch, M. J., *No tan lejano, una visión de la mujer romana a través de temas de actualidad*, Valencia 2018.

Bretone, M., *Servus communis: contributo alla storia de la comproprietà romana in età clásica*, Napoli 1958.

Campos Vargas, H., "La mujer en la literatura jurídica romana: una aproximación de género a las 'Instituciones' de Gaius," *Revista de Ciencias Jurídica* 107 (2005).

Cantarella, E., *Pasado próximo. Mujeres romanas de Tácita a Sulpicia*, trans. M. M. Núñez, Madrid 1997.

Chevalier, L., "Notes sur le testament militaire," in *Varia, II*, 1956.

Costa, E., *Storia del diritto romano privato*, Torino 1925.

Costa, E., *Cicerone giureconsulto, I*, Roma 1964.

Cuq, E., *Manuel des institutions juridiques des Romains*, Paris 1928.

Dernburg, A., *Pandette, III*, (traducción italiana de Cicala), Torino 1905.

Di Lella, L., *Querela inofficiosi testamenti. Contributo allo studio della sucessione testamentaria*, Napoli 1972.

Ermini, G., "La regola *nemo pro parte testatus pro parte intestatus decedere potest* nella glossa ordinaria al *Corpus iuris*," in *Scritti di diritto comune*, Padova 1976 (=*Rivista Italiana per le Scienze Giuridiche, I*, Roma 1937).

Espín Cánovas, D., "Capacidad jurídica de la mujer casada," *Revista Gráficas Europa*, Salamanca 1969.

Fadda, C., *Concetti fondamentali del diritto ereditario romano*, parte prima, Napoli 1900.

Fernández Vizcaíno, B., "El *ius adcrescendi* en los senadoconsultos Tertuliano y Orficiano," in *RIDROM*, 2011.

Ferrari, V., "Un volume di 'Varia,'" recensión a Varia, Études de droit romain, 2, 1957, en *LABEO, III*, 1957.

Friedlander, L., *La sociedad romana. Historia de las costumbres en Roma, desde Augusto hasta los Antoninos*, México 1947.

Glück, F., *Comentario alle Pandette, XXXVI*, Milano 1907.

González Ares Fernández, J. A., *Mujer, Política e Igualdad. De las Palabras a los Hechos*, Valencia 2017.

Guarino, A., *Diritto privato romano*, Napoli 1981.

Hernández-Gil, A., *El testamento militar (en torno a un sistema hereditario militar romano)*, Madrid 1946.

Herrera Bravo, R., Salazar Revuelta, A., and Salazar Revuelta, M., "La condición de la mujer en la represión del adulterio en derecho romano y su recepción histórica," *Experiencias jurídicas e identidades femeninas* (2011).

Iglesias, J., *Derecho romano*, Madrid 2010.

Impallomeni, G., *Scritti di diritto romano e tradizione romanistica*, Padova 1996.

Jörs, P., Kunkel, W., and Wenger, L., *Römisches Recht: römisches privatrecht, abriss des römischen zivilprozessrechts*, Berlin-Heidelberg-New York 1978.

Karlowa, O., in *Römisches Rechtsgeschichte Privatrecht, II*, Leipzig 1901.

Kaser, M., *Das römische Privatech*, München 1971.

Köppen, K., *Lehrbuch des heutigen römischen Erbrechts*, Würzburg 1895.

Kübler, B., "Das Intestaterbrecht der Frauen im alten Rom," in *ZSS, XLI*, 1920.

La Pira, G., *Successione ereditaria intestata e contro il testamento in diritto romano*, Firenze 1930.

López Güeto, A., *Madres e hijos en el Derecho romano de sucesiones. Los senadoconsultos Tertuliano y Orficiano*, Madrid 2017.

López Güeto, A., "Mujer, poder y derecho en Roma," *Revista jurídica Piélagus* 17 (2018).

Mülenbruch, C. F., *Commentario alle Pandette, XL*, Erlangen 1838.

Niederländer, "Zur Herkunft der römischen Impensendreiteilung," in *ZSS*, LXXV, 1958.

Ortuño, Mª E., "Una limitación de la capacidad patrimonial de la mujer en el ámbito sucesorio: la *Lex Vocconia*," in *Mulier: algunas historias e instituciones de Derecho Romano*, 2013.

Pacchioni, G., *Corso di diritto romano, II*, Torino 1910.

Pereira Porto, C., "La representación del concepto de mujer en Roma," *Revista de Filosofía del Derecho y derechos humanos* 5 (1995).

Pérez Pérez, V., "Capacidad de la mujer en derecho privado romano," *Revista Clepsidra* 16 (2017).

Pérez Simeón, M., *Nemo pro parte testatus pro parte intestatus decedere potest*, Barcelona 2001.

Perozzi, S., *Istituzioni di diritto romano, II*, Roma 1928.

Pomeroy, S., *Diosas, rameras, esposas y esclavas*, Madrid 1999.

Rabel, E., "Die Erbrechtstheorie Bonfantes," in *ZSS, L*, 1930.

Resina Sola, P., "La condición jurídica de la mujer en Roma," in *La Mujer en el mundo mediterráneo antiguo*, Granada 1990.

Robbe, U., *Il diritto di accrescimento e la sostituzione volgare nel diritto romano classico*, Milano 1953.

Robbe, U., voz: "accrescimento," *NNDI*, vol. I, p. 159.

Rodríguez Montero, R. P., "Hilvanando 'atributos' femeninos en la antigua Roma," in *Fundamentos romanísticos del Derecho contemporáneo, BOE*, 2012.

Rodríguez, R., "La mujer en el mundo laboral de la Roma antigua," in *Mulier: algunas historias e instituciones de Derecho Romano*, 2013.

Salazar Revuelta, M., "Estatus jurídico y social de la *materfamilias* en el marco de la ciudadanía romana," in *Mulier: algunas historias e instituciones de Derecho Romano*, 2013.

Sanfilippo, C., *Corso di diritto romano. Evoluzione storica della hereditas*, Napoli 1946.

Sanguinetti, A., "Considerazioni sull'origine del principio '*sui heredes instituendi sunt vel exheredandi*,'" in *SDHI, LIX*, 1993.

Scherillo, G., "D. 1, 4, 3, (Giavoleno, L.13 'EP') e il testamento militare," in *Studi in onore di Edoardo Volterra, III*, Milano 1971.

Scherillo, G., *Corso di diritto romano: il testamento*, Milano 1995.

Schirmer, T., *Handbuch des Römischen Erbrechtes*, Leipzig 1863 (reproducción facsimil de 1970).

Sciascia, G., "*Miles pro parte testatus pro parte intestatus decedere potest*," in *Seminar, V*, 1947.

Solazzi, S., *Diritto ereditario romano I*, Napoli 1932.

Solazzi, S., "Diritto di accresciment e testamento dei militari," in *Scritti Giuridici-Raccolti per il Centenario della Casa Editrice Jovene*, Napoli 1954.

Talamanca, M., *Istituzioni di Diritto Romano*, Milano 1990.

Torrent, A., "Notas sobre la relación entre *communio* y copropiedad," in *Studi Grosso, II*, Torino 1968.

Vangerow, K., *Lehrbuch der Pandekten, II*, Marburg-Leipzig 1863–1869.

Voci, P., *Istituzioni di diritto romano*, Milano 1954.

Voci, P., *Diritto ereditario romano, II*, Milano 1963.

Voci, P., *Diritto ereditario romano, I*, Milano 1967.

Voci, P., "Il diritto ereditario romano dalle origini ai Severi," in *Studi di diritto romano, II*, Padova 1985 (=en *Ausfstieg und Niedergang der römischen Welt, II*, 14, Berlin 1982).

Volterra, E., *Instituciones de Derecho privado romano*, Madrid 1986.

Von Bolla, S., "Zum römischem Militärtestament," in *Studi Arangio-Ruiz*, I.

Von Bolla, S., *Aus römischem und bürgerlichem Erbrecht*, Wien 1950.

Windscheid, B., *Diritto delle Pandette*, III, Torino 1930.

Bronisław Sitek

"Hominis" appellatione tam feminam quam masculum contineri non dubitatur. Interpretation of Gai. D. 50.16.152

Abstract: The subject of this study is the analysis of the meaning of the term homo, hominis defined in the fragment D. 50.16.152 by Gaius. The analysis was performed using O. Lenel's Palingenesia. The author of the text analyzed fragment D. 50.16.152 in terms of its original location. Then, an analysis of the meaning of the definition of homo given to it by the compilers was carried out by placing it in the book of 50 Digests under the title 16: De diversis regulis antiqui. The analysis of the sources of law showed that the definition of homo, hominis included both men and women. However, this legal rule is not a prototype for the constitutional principle of gender equality in the modern sense.

Keywords: males and females, inheritance law, Roman law, D. 50.16.152, rules of law

1. Introduction

In the source texts of Roman law, one can find diverse types of definitions having the character of legal principles, and even from the point of view of modern constitutional law, constitutional principles. Undoubtedly, one of them is the definition of Gaius, according to which "'Hominis' appellatione tam feminam quam masculum contineri non dubitatur."[1]

The definition of the term *homo, hominis* was based by Gaius on the indication of the components included in the content of this term and the relationship that connects these elements with each other. According to Gaius, the elements constituting the term *homo* are two subjects of different sexes, it means—a man and a woman. The relationship between them is based on equality. *Prima facie*, such a definition of the term *homo* can take the reader to contemporary considerations, and even to international legal regulations regarding gender equality,[2]

---

1 G. l. 10 *ad leg. Iul. et Pap.* (D. 50.16.152).

2 The preamble to the Universal Declaration of Human Rights of 1948 already mentions the equality of men and women. In turn, in the article 23 of the Charter of Fundamental Rights of the European Union from 2000, it was decided: *Equality between women and men must be ensured in all areas, including employment, work and pay.* For more on contemporary concepts of equality between men and women, see E. O'Neill, "The

or the concept of the social and historically shaped gender role.[3] For representatives of the so-called "progressive ideologies," the quote from Gaius can be the basis for claiming that there are already examples in Roman law in support of contemporary feminist views.[4] Is this how we can really understand Gaius' definition of the term *homo*?

The purpose of this study is to explain the original meaning of the phrase "'Hominis' appellatione tam feminam quam masculum contineri non dubitatur" by Gaius, as well as to determine the meaning given to this definition by the Justinian compilers. Only later, it will be possible to look for an answer to the question of the usefulness of Gaius' statement for contemporary considerations about human being, especially gender equality.

2. Original location of the Gaius text

Gaius' definition of the term "*Homo*" was placed by the Justinian compilers in the last book of the Digest, *De diversis regulis iuris antiqui*. The role of this title in the Digest and the positioning of the fragment by Gaius by the compilers will be discussed in the next section. At this point, it is important to state that originally this fragment was in a different substantive context than it is now. From reading the preserved fragment, it appears that the definition in question was taken by the compilers from the 10th book of Gaius's commentary to the act *lex Iulia et Papia Poppaea* from AD 9.

The purpose of the *lex Iulia et Papia Poppaea* was to oblige the Romans to increase the fertility rate and restore the former concept of marriage. An instrument of encouragement or maybe coercion to adopt the model of marriage

---

Equality of Men and Women," in *The Oxford Handbook of Philosophy in Early Modern Europe*, ed. C. M. Desmond and C. Wilson, Oxford 2011, pp. 445–475.

3 B. Cislaghi and H. Lori Heise, "Gender Norms and Social Norms: Differences, Similarities and Why They Matter in Prevention Science," *Sociology of Health & Illness* 42/2 (2020), pp. 407–422; B. Laslett and J. Brenner, "Gender and Social Reproduction: Historical Perspectives," *Annual Review of Sociology* 15/1 (1989), pp. 381–404.

4 In contemporary Roman studies, one can find numerous examples of publications whose authors look for examples to support contemporary innovative views or examples to negate the traditional concept of human being based on a culture consisting of Greek philosophy, Roman law and Christianity. Examples of such publications include R. Bauman, *Human Rights in Ancient Rome*, London-New York 2012; P. G. Lauren, "History and Human Rights: People and Forces in Paradoxical Interaction," *Journal of Human Rights* 7/2 (2008), pp. 91–103.

outlined in the Augustan legislation by the citizens was, among others, limitations to the inheritance rights for the childless (*orbi*) and for the unmarried (*caelibes*). The *orbi* could inherit only half of the inheritance that fell to them in the will, while the *caelibes* could not inherit at all. It can therefore be concluded that Augustus, in *lex Iulia et Papia Poppaea*, largely linked the issue of shaping the correct model of marriage with the law of inheritance.

Describing the substantive context for the original location of Gaius' definition is possible thanks to O. Lenel. This well-known and respected historian of law performed an extremely significant work consisting in restoring the original arrangement of fragments of Roman jurists' texts found in the Digest according to their original position in the works of *prudentes*. The result of this work is a study published in two volumes, and briefly referred to as *Palingenesia*.[5]

This definition of Gaius comes from the 10th book of his commentary on the act *lex Iulia et Papia Poppaea*. This book was entitled *De bonis libertorum*, it means—about the inheritance belongs to people in the first inheritance group according to the praetor's edict.[6] In total, three fragments from this book have been preserved. The fragment in question was placed by O. Lenel as the last of the three surviving fragments of Book X. Let us therefore proceed to the analysis of particular fragments from Book X.

> G. l. 10 *ad leg. Iul. et Pap.* (D. 38.16.13). *Nulla femina aut habet suos heredes aut desinere habere potest propter capitis deminutionem. [No woman either has proper heirs, or can cease to have them, on account of her loss of civil rights.]*[7]

Two issues are raised in this passage. The first concerns the determination of the circle of people entitled to statutory succession (*ab intestato*) after a deceased woman. According to the The Laws of the Twelve Tables, the first group of people entitled to intestate inheritance were *sui heredes*, which means people being a

5 O. Lenel, *Palingenesia Iuris Civilis*, Lipsiae 1889.

6 In the edict, the praetor introduced significant changes in the inheritance system in relation to the existing one, which had its source in the Act XII Tab. All children of the testator were included in the first inheritance group (*unde liberi*). This system was later supplemented on the basis of *senatus consultum Tertullianum* and *senatus consultum Orfitianum*. See F. Longchamps de Berier, *Law of Succession. Roman Legal Framework and Comparative Law Perspective*, Warszawa 2011, p. 96; M. Kuryłowicz, "Zum Noterbrecht der Adoptierten im römischen Recht," in *Leges sapere. Studia i prace dedykowane J. Sondlowi*, Kraków 2008, pp. 243–244; F. Samper, "De bonis libertorum." *Anuario de historia del derecho español* 41 (1971), pp. 149–236.

7 Translations of Latin texts into English are given after S. P. Scott.

subject to paternal authority. Gaius states that the woman has no such group of heirs. However, we must realize that this is a situation in which the woman was not under the authority of her husband (*matrimonium cum manu*) or under the authority of the head of the family (*pater familias*). It is therefore a case of a woman with the status of a *sui iuris* person. In Gaius' time such a woman could make a will. The exclusion of *sui heredes* from inheritance from a woman resulted from the structure of the Roman family. A man was always the head of the family—*pater familias*. A woman did not have such power, so she could not have a group of heirs known as *sui heredes*.[8]

The second element of the quoted fragment concerns the change of the woman's marital status, for example—the loss of an independent position (*sui iuris*) in the family due to the woman coming under the authority of her husband (*alieni iuris*). Such a change in marital status could not result in a change in the scope of persons entitled to inherit from it.

The second analyzed text from Book X reads as follows:

> G. l. 10 *ad leg. Iul. et Pap.* (D. 50.16.149). *Nam quem sine liberis esse dicere non possumus, hunc necesse est dicamus liberos habere. [For we cannot say of such a person that he is childless, and we must necessarily say that he has children.]*

This fragment is not directly correlated with the other two from the book X of Gaius, although it belongs to the issues of inheritance law. In this passage, the issue of the presumption of having a child was resolved. This problem had legal significance in the case of inheritance by *orbi* or *caelibes*, which was mentioned earlier. Therefore, if there was a doubt as to whether the heir had a child or not, then it was to be resolved in favor of the heir. However, it was assumed that she had a child.[9] Such doubts could arise if the child died before the opening of the inheritance.

Finally, we have to discuss the last fragment by Gaius from book 10 of the commentary on lex Iulia Papia et Popea, and which fragment is the main theme of this study.

> G. l. 10 *ad leg. Iul. et Pap.* (D. 50.16.152) *"Hominis" appellatione tam feminam quam masculum contineri non dubitatur. [There is no doubt that both males and females are included under the term "man."]*

---

8 The legal position of a woman in Roman law was constantly evolving. An example of this is the passage from Gaius. See D. Spano, *Pater famlias reg matrimoniale*.

9 G. Astolfi, *La Lex Iulia et Papia*, Padova 1995, p. 153.

The above text is relatively poorly commented on by Romanists or legal historians. A small commentary on this text is provided in a study by R. Quandrato.[10] Undoubtedly, this text should be seen in the perspective of the growing social position of women toward the end of the republic, especially in the field of private law. An important contribution to the discussion on the explanation of the definition of *hominis* according to Gaius is made by H. Capos Vargas. According to the Spanish Romanist, the masculine gender was very often used in Latin to denote the masculine and feminine at the same time.[11]

On the basis of public law, the position of a woman was significantly impaired in relation to the position of a man for a long time. Much later, Ulpian wrote:

> Ulp. l. *1 ad Sab*. (D. 50.17.2 pr.): *Feminae ab omnibus officiis civilibus vel publicis remotae sunt et ideo nec iudices esse possunt nec magistratum gerere nec postulare nec pro alio intervenire nec procuratores existere. [Women are excluded from all civil or public employments; therefore, they cannot be judges, or perform the duties of magistrates, or bring suits in court, or become sureties for others, or act as attorneys.]*

According to Ulpian, women are excluded from all civil and public duties, and therefore cannot be either judges or be in offices, or set the petitions in court, or act on behalf of someone else, or act as attorneys. This was the case with both *sui iuris* and *alieni iuris* women.

Returning, however, to the basic text of Gaius (D. 50.16.152), it should be noted that he served to define the term *homo*—"human being." According to Gaius, the term includes both male and female. So why did Gaius specify the meaning of the term *homo*? From the context of the location of this text, it follows that this action was performed solely for the purpose of dispelling doubts as to the heir. In the times of Gaius, women could inherit both in the case of inheritance *ab intesato* and testamentary inheritance. Perhaps at that time there was still doubt as to whether a woman could really inherit.

Such an explanation of the meaning of the term *homo* was not unusual. It is possible to quote similar later texts by other jurists, especially by Ulpian and Paulus. Three sample texts will be discussed below, two of which are by Ulpian and one by Paulus.

---

10 R. Quadrato, "Hominis appellatio e gerarchia dei sessi in Gaio," *BIDR* 94–95 (1991–1992), pp. 309–348.

11 H. Campos Vargas, "La mujer y la economía romana: una aproximación desde del lacio," *Ciencias Económicas* 28/2 (2010), p. 293 (289–294); C. Lázaro Guillamón, "Mujer, comercio y empresa en algunas fuentes jurídicas literarias y epigráficas," *Revue internationales des droits de l´ ántiquité* 50 (2003), pp. 155–194.

Ulp. l. *1 ad ed.* (D. 50.16.1.): *Verbum hoc "si quis" tam masculos quam feminas complectitur. [The following words, "If anyone," include males as well as females.]*

The above passage by Ulpian is evidence that the phrase "*si quis*" often used in legal texts meant a woman and a man. From the point of view of today's legislative technique, Ulpian's statement can be described as a legal definition, which is called equality definition.[12] Thus, we have a word defined "*si quis*," then there is a phrase defining "males" and "females" and a link between these two words stating their identity.

Ulp. *L.* 62 *ad ed.* (D. 50.16.56.1): *"Liberorum" appellatione continentur non tantum qui sunt in potestate, sed omnes qui sui iuris sunt, sive virilis sive feminini sexus sunt exve feminini sexus descendentes. [Under the term "children" are included not only those who are under paternal control, but also all those who are their own masters, whether they are of the male or female sex, or descendants from females.]*

In this fragment by Ulpian, it was also about defining the material scope of persons entitled to inheritance. The subjective scope of persons entitled to inheritance in the case of intestate inheritance within the *unde liberi* group was subject to evolution.[13] According to Ulpian, the notion of *liberii* should be understood not only of those descendants who were under paternal authority at the time of the death of *pater familias*, but also of those who have already become persons *sui iuris*, regardless of whether they were male or female, and also whether they were male or female descendants.[14]

Paul. l. 2 *ad Sab.* (D. 50.16.163.1): *"Pueri" appellatione etiam puella significatur: nam et feminas puerperas appellant recentes ex partu et Graece paidion communiter appellatur. [Under the term "child" a girl also is included, for women who have recently brought forth children are called puerperse, and are generally styled by the Greeks.]*

This passage comes from book 2 of Paulus' commentary on Sabinianus's work. O. Lenel entitled this part of the book *De legitima hereditate*, so the texts contained under this title concerned statutory inheritance.[15] In this context, Paulus clarified the meaning of the term *pueri*—the plural of the word *puer* According to Paulus, the term includes both boys and girls. And here is quite an interesting

12 M. Zieliński, *Wykładnia prawa. Zasady. Reguły. Wskazówki*, Warszawa 2002, p. 195.

13 S. Kursa, *Testator i formy testamentu w rzymskim prawie justyniańskim*, Warszawa 2017, p. 243.

14 H. Kaufmann, *op. cit.*, p. 46.

15 A. Stępkowska, "Dziedzicznie beztestamentowe krewnych kognicyjnych w świetle nowel 118 i 127 Justyniana," *Czasopismo Prawno-Historyczne* 54 (2002), pp. 57–80.

discourse of Paulus because of his reference to the example of a woman who gave birth to a child. At that time, the term *puerpera* was used for such a child, which included both boys and girls. Also in Greek, a child "paidion" is called both a boy and a girl.

3. The meaning of text D. 50.16.152 given to it by Justinian compilers

After clarifying the original placement and meaning of the passage by Gaius (D. 50.16.152), it is necessary to clarify the meaning given by the Justinian compilers to the definition of the word *homo*. The constitution of Justinian of 16th December 533, *Tanta, De confirmatione Digestorum*, which means—the constitution on the approval of the publication of the Digests, is of key importance for explaining the above issue. Already at the beginning of this constitution (Tanta 1), the emperor explains that the entire Digest is divided into 50 books, which are grouped into 7 thematic sections. The last seven sections include the last six books (Tanta 6). There are issues related to stipulation—which means verbal obligations (two books). The next two books contain provisions on criminal matters. In accordance with the provisions of Tanta's constitution, the last 50th book of the Digest included dispositions on municipia, decurions, public duties, *pollicitationes*, census, and finally the compilers included passages containing definitions explaining the meaning of words used in legal texts.[16]

According to Justinian's will, therefore, the compilers were given the power to select timely and useful passages from the writings of Roman jurists from earlier periods, especially from the classical period. The rules for the selection of these fragments should be seen in the constitution Tanta. Justinian writes in it that all the most useful fragments were included in the Digest (*…quod utilissimum errat…*). Moreover, all pre-existing doubts in the legal doctrine were removed by the compilers (*… omnes ambiguitates decisae nullo seditioso relicto.*).[17] Anyway, similar assumptions for the entire compilation were adopted by Justinian in the constitution *Deo auctore* 2 pr. of 15th December 15, 530.[18]

---

16 M. Bianchini, *Appunti su Giustiniano e la sua compilazione*, Torino 1983, p. 117.

17 Tanta, 1. B. Sitek, "Założenia metodologiczne pracy kompilatorów justyniańskich," in *Justynian i prawo rzymskie*, ed. K. Szczygielski, Białystok 2015, pp. 15–32.

18 Deo auctore 2 pr.: Hocque opere consummato et in uno uolumine nostro nomine praefulgente coadunato, cum ex paucis et tenuioribus releuati ad summam et plenissimam iuris emendationem peruenire properaremus et omnem Romanam sanctionem et colligere et emendare et tot auctorum dispersa uolumina uno codice indita ostendere,

The scope of tasks performed by the compilers and the assumptions made regarding the works designed under the direction of Justinian show that they were aware that explaining the meaning of various legal terms used by *prudentes*, in isolation from their original context, often resulted in a change in their meaning.

Originally, the formulations or definitions built by lawyers, including the definition of the term *homo* analyzed in our study, were only significant for a specific case.[19] The compilation of definitions of individual terms by the compilers in Title 16 of the 50th Book of Digests meant that they could also be used in cases other than in their original meaning, when there were doubts as to the subjective scope of a given term. Thus, Gaius's definition of the term *hominis* became a legal rule of a general nature. In the case of its application, however, each time it was necessary to clarify whether this definition can be applied in a particular case.

At the end of this study, it is necessary to clarify the meaning of the term "regula." Helpful in this thought process is the text of Paulus, which defines and explains the meaning of the term "regula."

> Paul. l. 16 *ad Plaut.* (D. 50.17.1): *Regula est, quae rem quae est breviter enarrat. Non ex regula ius sumatur, sed ex iure quod est regula fiat. Per regulam igitur brevis rerum narratio traditur, et, ut ait Sabinus, quasi causae coniectio est, quae simul cum in aliquo vitiata est, perdit officium suum. (A rule is a statement, in a few words, of the course to be followed in the matter under discussion. The law, however, is not derived from the rule, but the rule is established by the law. Hence, a short decision of the point in question is made by the rule; or, as Sabinus says, a concise explanation of the case is given, which, however, in other instances to which it is not applicable loses its force).*

According to Paulus, a rule is a short description of the object being defined. However, a rule is not a source of law. On the contrary, it is the legal norms that create the rule of specific conduct. Paulus, referring to the opinion of Sabinus, stated that a rule is a short explanation of a term addressed to a specific addressee of a legal norm. A legal rule, as it is not a legal norm, should be decided on its application in each case.[20]

---

quod nemo neque sperare neque optare ausus est, res quidem nobis difficillima, immo magis impossibilis uidebatur.

19 G. Ostrogorsky, *Storia dell'impero bizantino*, Torino 1993, pp. 29–31; M. Bretone, *Tecniche e ideologie dei giuristi romani*, Napoli 1984; A. Watson, *Law Making in the later Roman Republic*, Oxford 1974; F. Horak, *Rationes decidendi, Entscheidungsgründe bei den Älteren Römischen Juristen bis Labeo*. I. Band, Aalen 1969; F. Schulz, *Geschichte der römischen Rechtswissenschaft*, Weimar 1961.

20 S. Alicic, "Diversis Regulis Iuris Antiqui (D. 50.17)," *De. Zbornik Radova* 40 (2006), pp. 433–452.

4. Final conclusions

The definition of "'Hominis' appellatione tam feminam quam masculum contineri non dubitatur" by Gaius, may seem to resemble contemporary slogans of the so-called progressive feminist ideologies. Meanwhile, the analysis of the original location of this text indicates its exclusive relationship with the law of inheritance, and more specifically with the woman's right to inheritance, which has undergone a far-reaching evolution since August's family legislation. Women gained a fairly equal position with men in this area of the law. Proof of this is the text by Gaius and other analyzed texts by Ulpian and Paulus.

The compilers removed fragment D. 50.16.152 from its original location and moved it to the last book of the Digest to title 16 entitled *De diversis regulis iuris antiqui*. The very title suggests that the definitions of equal concepts contained therein are in the nature of legal rules. The analysis of the text of D. 50.17.1 shows that a legal rule must result only from the provisions of law and does not apply in every case.

In conclusion, it should be stated that fragment D. 50.16.152 cannot be perceived as a systemic principle in the modern sense. Its main goal was to define the circle of intestate heirs, regardless of gender. Therefore, the text of D. 50.16.152 cannot be the basis for contemporary considerations about gender equality.

Bibliography

Alicic, S., "Diversis Regulis Iuris Antiqui (D. 50.17)," *Zbornik Radova* 40 (2006), pp. 433–452.

Astolfi, G., *La Lex Iulia et Papia*, Padova 1995.

Bauman, R., *Human Rights in Ancient Rome*, London-New York 2012.

Bianchini, M., *Appunti su Giustiniano e la sua compilazione*, Torino 1983.

Bretone, M., *Tecniche e ideologie dei giuristi romani*, Napoli 1984.

Campos Vargas, H., "La mujer y la economía romana: una aproximación desde del lacio," *Ciencias Económicas* 28/2 (2010), pp. 289–294.

Ciccotti, E., *Profilo di Augusto*, Torino 1938.

Cislaghi, B., and Lori Heise, H., "Gender Norms and Social Norms: Differences, Similarities and Why They Matter in Prevention Science," *Sociology of Health & Illness* 42/2 (2020), pp. 407–422.

Horak, F., *Rationes decidendi, Entscheidungsgründe bei den Älteren Römischen Juristen bis Labeo*. I. Band, Aalen 1969.

Kaufmann, H., *Die altrömische Miete. Ihre Zusammenhänge mit Gesellschaft, Wirtschaft und staatlicher Vermögensverwaltung*, Köln 1964.

Koch, E., "Vom Versuch, die Frage, ob Weiber Menschens sein oder nicht', aus den Digesten zu beantworten," *Rechtshistorisches Journal* 1 (1982), pp. 171–179.

Kursa, S., *Testator i formy testamentu w rzymskim prawie justyniańskim*, Warszawa 2017.

Kuryłowicz, M., *Zum Noterbrecht der Adoptierten im römischen Recht*, In: *Leges sapere. Studia i prace dedykowane J. Sondlowi*, Kraków 2008, pp. 239–253.

Laslett, B., and Brenner, J., "Gender and social reproduction: Historical perspectives," *Annual Review of Sociology* 15/1 (1989), pp. 381–404.

Lauren, P. G., "History and Human Rights: People and Forces in Paradoxical Interaction," *Journal of Human Rights* 7/2 (2008), pp. 91–103.

Lázaro Guillamón, C., "Mujer, comercio y empresa en algunas fuentes jurídicas literarias y epigráficas," *Revue internationales des droits de l'ántiquité* 50 (2003), pp. 155–194.

Lenel, O., *Palingenesia Iuris Civilis*, Lipsiae 1889.

Longchamps de Berier, F., *Law of Succession. Roman Legal Framework and Comparative Law Perspective*, Warszawa 2011.

O'Neill, E., "The Equality of Men and Women," in *The Oxford Handbook of Philosophy in Early Modern Europe*, ed. C. M. Desmond, and C. Wilson, Oxford 2011, pp. 445–475.

Ostrogorsky, G., *Storia dell'impero bizantino*, Torino 1993.

Quadrato, R., "Hominis appellatio e gerarchia dei sessi in Gaio," *BIDR* 94–95 (1991–1992), pp. 309–348.

Robleda, O., *El matrimonio en derecho Romano. Esencia, requisitos de validez, efectos, disolubilidad*, Roma 1970.

Samper, F., "De bonis libertorum," *Anuario de historia del derecho español* 41 (1971), pp. 149–236.

Schulz, F., *Geschichte der römischen Rechtswissenschaft*, Weimar 1961.

Sitek, B., "Założenia metodologiczne pracy kompilatorów justyniańskich," in *Justynian i prawo rzymskie*, ed. K. Szczygielski, Białystok 2015, pp. 15–32.

Stępkowska, A., "Dziedziczenie beztestamentowe krewnych kognicyjnych w świetle nowel 118 i 127 Justyniana," *Czasopismo Prawno-Historyczne* 54/1 (2002), pp. 57–80.

Tarnacka, A., "Zbiór ustaw Lex Iulia et Papia jako próba wyjścia z kryzysu obyczajowo-społecznego zapoczątkowanego u schyłku Republiki Rzymskiej," *Kultura Prawna* 1/2 (2018), pp. 132–142.

Watson, A., *Law Making in the Later Roman Republic*, Oxford 1974.

Zabłocka, M., "Zmiany w ustawach małżeńskich Augusta za panowania dynastii julijsko-klaudyjskiej," *Prawo Kanonicze: kwartalnik prawo-historyczny* 30/1–2 (1987), pp. 151–178.

Zieliński, M., *Wykładnia prawa. Zasady. Reguły. Wskazówki*, Warszawa 2002.

Anna Tarwacka

Adoption under the scrutiny of the censors in Republican Rome*

Abstract: The influence of the censors on the family in republican Rome was twofold: on the one hand, the officials had powers of control and had sanctions at their disposal to punish *patres familiarum* abusing their authority, but on the other hand, their task was to protect family members who were subject to this authority. The institution of adoption allowed to acquire a new family member. This could take place for persons both *sui iuris* (*adrogatio*) and *alieni iuris* (*adoptio*) and entailed significant consequences. The censors were able to control cases of adoption, in particular, to sanction abuses leading to the enjoyment of the privileges attributed to fathers without having to bear the hardship of exercising *patria potestas*.

Keywords: Roman law, censorship, nota censoria, patria potesas, adoptio, adrogatio, pater familias

The office of censor was extremely important for the Roman Republican system due to its specific powers related to conducting the census. The censors were controlling the social structure, as they could assign citizens to specific units (*centuriae* and *tribus*), as well as select the composition of the senate and the elite *centuriae* of the knights. The activity of compiling lists of citizens had an additional aspect, namely the exercise of guardianship over good morals (*regimen morum*). The censors could punish citizens with a *nota* for breaking the norms of morality. The authority of the censors was, however, much broader, and also included the custody of public places, in particular leasing the construction and repair of public buildings on behalf of the state, as well as preventing the occupation of public places by private parties. Furthermore, it was the censors who managed the collection of taxes, leasing these functions to the companies of the *publicani*. At the end of their term of office, the censors also performed a state purification ritual—*lustratio*—which ensured prosperity for the next five years.[1]

* The article is a result of the project 2018/29/B/HS5/00949 financed by the National Science Centre, Poland.

1 On the office of censor see A. Tarwacka, *Prawne aspekty urzędu cenzora w starożytnym Rzymie*, Warszawa 2012; Eadem, *Cenzor w sypialni. Urzędnicza kontrola moralności w życiu rodzinnym Rzymian okresu republiki*, Warszawa 2021 with extensive overview of the literature.

The use of the censorial *nota* is the most picturesque and anecdotal aspect of censors' activity. Originally, censors seem to have been able to manipulate the value of property reported at the moment of the census, and only over time did they acquire the competence to control the customs of their fellow citizens and punish them with a censorial *nota*. This happened gradually, but the turning point, arguably the beginning of a true *regimen morum*, was the *plebiscitum Ovinium*.[2]

The term "censorial nota" itself (*nota censoria*, *notatio censoria*, *animadversio censoria*) is the general term for the sanction applied by the censors. Its effects could, however, vary depending on the status of a punished citizen and the intent of the officials themselves.

In a commentary on one of Cicero's speeches (*divinatio in Caecilium*) attributed to Asconius, there is a description of the penalties used by the censors within the *regimen morum*.[3] The commentator noted that senators were removed from the senate, knights were removed from the equestrian *centuriae*, and plebeians were transferred to the *tabulae Caeritum* and to the ranks of the *aerarii*, so that they were not listed in their original *centuria*. Although this text does not offer the full picture of the sanctions imposed by the censors, it can nevertheless be considered as a starting point.

The censors' interest was certainly, though not exclusively, focused on the upper strata of society. As far as senators were concerned, the basic and very severe punishment was removing their names from the senate list. However, in

2 Cf. T. J. Cornell, "The 'Lex Ovinia' and the Emancipation of the Senate," in *The Roman Middle Republic. Politics, Religion and Historiography*, ed. Ch. Bruun, Rome 2000, pp. 69–89; Tarwacka, *Prawne aspekty*, pp. 221ff.; C. Busacca, "Sulla datazione del 'plebiscitum Ovinium,'" in *Scritti per Alessandro Corbino*, I, ed. I. Piro, Tricase 2016, pp. 429–452.

3 Ps.-Ascon., In. Cic. div. in Caec., p. 103 ed. Orelli: Regendis moribus civitatis censores quinto quoque anno creari solebant. Hi prorsus cives sic notabant: ut, qui senator esset, eiiceretve senatu; qui eques Romanus, equum publicum perderet; qui plebeius, in Caeritum tabulas referretur et aerarius fieret, ac per hoc [non] esset in albo centuriae suae, sed ad hoc non esset civis, tantummodo ut pro capite suo tributi nomine aera praeberet. There are doubts as to whether there should be a non after the words per hoc in the text of Pseudo-Asconius. However, it seems that the author did not have in mind the loss of citizenship in general, but only the inclusion in the category of paying tributum, from which citizens residing in Italy were exempted since 167 BCE. Cf. E. Lo Cascio, "Il census a Roma e la sua evoluzione dall'età "serviana" alla prima età imperiale," *MEFRA* 113/2 (2001), p. 583.

other source texts, in addition to the phrase *senatu eicere* or *senatu movere*, that is, "to expel from the senate," there is also the phrase *praeterire*, that is, "to omit."

According to Festus' text, which constitutes incidentally, the primary source of information on the *lex Ovinia*, the overlooked senators—*praeteriti*—did not suffer disgrace in earlier times.[4] Indeed, the selection of senators was then the prerogative of the king or the highest officials, who had absolute discretion as to the criteria used. The situation has only changed after the *lex Ovinia*, a plebiscite on compilation of a list of senators by the censors. In Festus' text on the *lex Ovinia*, which gave the censors the power to determine the composition of the senate, *praeteriti* appeared alongside *loco moti*, that is, senators removed from the list. It does not appear that these terms could be treated as synonymous.

Those citizens who held offices customarily associated with the right to enter the senate had to wait for the next *lectio* to actually sit in the curia.[5] However, it did happen that the censors, who were after all not absolutely obliged to include someone on the list, considered the person unworthy of such a dignity and simply omitted him when compiling the list of senators. It seems, therefore, that the verb *movere* or *eicere* denotes the removal/expulsion of an existing member from the senate, while *praeterire* denotes the omission of one who, according to the *lex Ovinia*, could expect to be included in the list of senators.

Another category of people mentioned by Pseudo-Asconius who could be the subject to a censorial *nota* were the *equites*, who had the right to a public horse, fed and maintained at state expense. The horse was taken away from the punished knight (*equum adimere*) with the consequence of excluding him from the elite *centuria*. It is worth mentioning that the catalog of acts for which the censors punished the knights with a *nota* was extended to include specific behaviors

---

4 Fest. 290 L., s.v. praeteriti senatores: Praeteriti senatores quondam in opprobrio non erant, quod, ut reges sibi legebant, sublegebantque, quos in consilio publico haberent, ita post exactos eos consules quoque et tribuni militum consulari potestate coniunctissimos sibi quosque patriciorum, et deinde plebeiorum legebant; donec Ovinia tribunicia intervenit, qua sanctum est, ut censores ex omni ordine optimum quemque curiatim in senatum legerent. Quo factum est, ut qui praeteriti essent et loco moti, haberentur ignominiosi.

5 An example is the story of P. Crassus, to whom Q. Fabius Maximus Servilianus divulged the secret of the Senate's deliberations, because he remembered that Crassus had recently held the office of quaestor, which entitled him to become a senator. However, as the *lectio* had not yet taken place in the meantime, the young politician was still not included in the list. Cf. Val. Max. 2, 2, 1; J. Zabłocki, "Il segreto nel diritto romano," in *Scritti per Alessandro Corbino*, VII, ed. I. Piro, Tricase 2016, pp. 589–599.

toward the state: the basic charge was failure to take care for his horse. Excessive obesity, on the other hand, did lead to expulsion from the equestrian *centuria*, but was not associated with loss of good name.[6]

Finally, the commentator mentioned plebeians, a term to be understood as citizens who were neither senators nor *equites*, and not necessarily those who came from plebeian families. Although the distinction between patricians and plebeians had political significance for quite a long time (if only in the context of having a right to be elected to the office of plebeian tribune), the colloquial language of the late republican period developed a connotation of the word "plebs" with a group of citizens of low social status. In any case, anyone who was neither a senator nor a knight was, according to the source account, subject to two parallel sanctions: entry on the *tabulae Caeritum* and transfer to the ranks of the *aerarii*.

As Gellius noted,[7] the term *tabulae Caeritum*[8] derived from the city of Caere, whose inhabitants were the first to receive *civitas sine suffragio*.[9] The antiquarian added that on these tabulae the censors inscribed those whom they punished with a *nota*, thus depriving them of the right to vote. Inscription on the *tabulae Caeritum* therefore meant in practice depriving the citizen of the *ius suffragii*.

As for the term *aerarium facere*, it was linked to the removal of a citizen from the list of his *centuria*[10] and the necessity to pay a *tributum*,[11] an obligation from which citizens enjoying full rights were exempted from 167 BCE. Prior to that date, the punished citizens probably had to pay more than the rest of

6 Cf. Tarwacka, *Prawne aspekty*, pp. 215ff.

7 Gell. 16,13,7: Primos autem municipes sine suffragii iure Caerites esse factos accepimus concessumque illis, ut civitatis Romanae honorem quidem caperent, sed negotiis tamen atque oneribus vacarent pro sacris bello Gallico receptis custoditisque. Hinc "tabulae Caerites" appellatae versa vice, in quas censores referri iubebant, quos notae causa suffragiis privabant.

8 Cf. Strab. 5, 2, 3; Hor., *Ep.* 1, 2, 62–63.

9 In 353 or as late as 270 BC. Cf. P. A. Brunt, *Italian Manpower 225 B.C.–A.D. 14*, Oxford 1971, pp. 515 ff.

10 They may have been enrolled in a special *centuria*, which C. Nicolet, "Les listes des centuries: La prétendue centurie 'Niquis scivit,'" *MEFRA* 113/2 (2001), pp. 723–734, identifies it with the centuria *niquis scivit* mentioned by Festus (184 L.).

11 Cf. M. Humm, "Il 'regimen morum' dei censori e le identità dei cittadini," in *"Homo, caput, persona." La costruzione giuridica dell'identità nell'esperienza romana*, ed. A. Corbino, M. Humbert, and G. Negri, Pavia 2010, pp. 301–302.

the citizens.[12] This is probably why, after the census was completed, the censors deposited the list of *aerarii* in the temple of Saturn, where the treasury (*aerarium*) was located,[13] and gave it to the quaestors.

Interestingly, while the term *aerarium facere* appears in other source texts, it is in principle never accompanied by information about entry on the *tabulae Caeritum*. Instead, many authors mentioned a different sanction: *tribu movere*, that is, change of *tribus* affiliation. Are these two different sanctions? First of all, it should be noted that the city of Caere, located in Etruria, became part of the *tribus Arniensis*. It is therefore possible that the sanction resulted in being transferred to another *tribus*, although initially those punished by the *nota* were listed as Caere residents in order to deprive them of the *ius suffragii*: later this sanction acquired more general meaning also including transfer to an "inferior" *tribus*, rather than just the *tabulae Caeritum*. It should be pointed out at this point that the category of *cives sine suffragio* seems to have disappeared by the end of the 2nd century BCE. Therefore, the term *tabulae Caeritum* is rarely present in the sources. The change of *tribus*, on the other hand, began to involve the transfer of the citizen from a rural *tribus* to an urban one, where the number of citizens was much higher and therefore their votes in the assembly were of negligible value.

The listed sanctions could also be applied cumulatively: a citizen expelled from the senate or from the equestrian *centuria* could additionally be enrolled as an *aerarius* or transferred to another *tribus*, which in practice led to a significant reduction in his political participation.

In addition, the imposition of a censorial *nota* also entailed a loss of good name—*ignominia*. According to Cicero[14] the *nota* brought the punished person into disrepute[15]: a blush, as he put it.[16] The subject of *ignominia* was not deprived

12 Cf. P. Fraccaro, "'Tribules' ed'aerarii'. Una ricerca di diritto pubblico romano," in *Opuscula*, II, Pavia 1957, passim, especially pp. 168–170.

13 Cf. Liv. 29, 37; F. Millar, "The 'Aerarium' and Its Officials under the Empire," *JRS* 54 (1964), pp. 35–36.

14 Cic., De rep. 4,6: Censoris iudicium nihil fere damnato nisi ruborem adfert: itaque, ut omnis ea iudicatio versatur tantum modo in nomine, animadversio illa ignominia dicta est.

15 Cf. M. Ducos, *Les Romains et la loi. Recherches sur les rapports de la philosophie grecque et de la tradition romaine à la fin de la République*, Paris 1984, p. 385.

16 Cf. A. Wlosok, "'Nihil nisi ruborem'—über die Rolle der Scham in der römischen Rechtskultur," *Grazer Beiträge* 9 (1980), pp. 158–166; H. I. Flower, *Disgrace and Oblivion in Roman Political Culture*, Chapel Hill 2006, p. 52.

of political rights: he could still run for office,[17] although, as expelled from the senate, he had to attain a position associated with the right to sit in the senate again.[18] Such sanction could even provide the impetus for a brilliant career, as exemplified by the two cases described by Valerius Maximus[19] of senators removed from the curia who later became censors themselves: Geta and Valerius Messala were so ashamed of their notes that subsequently they did their best to show their fellow citizens that they were worthy to perform censorial duties.[20]

The imposition of the *nota* was purely discretionary. The decision could be taken by only one of the censors, but his colleague could block it by applying *intercessio*. There was no catalog of acts subject to the *nota*,[21] and the determinant of its application was ancestral customs—*mores maiorum*. One of the spheres covered by censor control was family life.

Dionysius of Halicarnassus vividly described Roman censors as officials looking into the bedrooms of fellow citizens and controlling every aspect of private life.[22] Similarly, Plutarch emphasized that among Romans neither marriage,

---

17 Cic., Pro Cluent. 120: quapropter in omnibus legibus quibus exceptum est de quibus causis aut magistratum capere non liceat aut iudicem legi aut alterum accusare, haec ignominiae causa praetermissa est. It should be added, however, that the penalty of placing a citizen on the tabulae Caeritum resulted, as mentioned above, in the loss of ius suffragii.

18 P. Cornelius Lentulus Sura, a consul in 71 BC, was expelled from the senate by the censors in 70 BC. Later he managed to win election as praetor in 63 BC and thus regain his seat in the senate.

19 Val. Max. 2, 9, 9: Secuntur duo eiusdem generis exempla, eaque adiecisse satis erit. "C." Geta, cum a L. Metello et Cn. Domitio censoribus senatu motus esset, postea censor factus est. item M. Valerius Messala censoria nota perstrictus censoriam postmodum potestatem impetravit. quorum ignominia virtutem acuit: rubore enim eius excitati omnibus viribus incubuerunt, ut digni civibus viderentur, quibus dari potius quam obici censura deberet.

20 Cf. Cic., *Pro Cluent.* 119.

21 Such a catalog was crafted by Th. Mommsen, *Römisches Staatsrecht*^{3}, II.1, Graz 1952 (reprint), pp. 377–382. Cf. C. E. Jarcke, Versuch einer Darstellung des censorischen Strafrechts der Römer: ein Beytrag zur Geschichte des Criminalrechts, Bonn 1824, pp. 14–45; E. De Ruggiero, *Dizionario epigrafico di antichità romane*, Roma 1900, s.v. censor; M. Nowak, *Die Strafverhängungen der Censoren*, Breslau 1909, pp. 58–71.

22 Dion. Hal. 20, 13, 3: Ῥωμαῖοι δὲ πᾶσαν ἀναπετάσαντες οἰκίαν καὶ μέχρι τοῦ δωματίου τὴν ἀρχὴν τῶν τιμητῶν προαγαγόντες ἁπάντων ἐποίησαν ἐπίσκοπον καὶ φύλακα τῶν ἐν αὐταῖς γινομένων. Cf. Dion. Hal. 19, 16, 5; M. Coudry, "Denys d'Halicarnasse, Plutarque, Dion Cassius: trois visions grecques de la censure?," in *Visions grecques*

the upbringing of children, daily life nor feasts could remain outside the control and judgment exercised by the censors.[23] These opinions prove that it seemed something odd and strange to foreigners that magistrates could intervene in family affairs, which in their understanding should be a private sphere of life. However, such an arrangement had specific reasons.

In Republican Rome the family had not only social or economic importance, but also political one.[24] It was headed by the *pater familias*, who held the cult (*sacra*), owned the property, and exercised discretional power over all the members of the family: descendants (*patria potestas*) and in some cases the wife (*manus*), as well as slaves (*dominica potestas*) and those in a position similar to slaves. His actions could have a serious impact on the functioning of the state: the presence of sons in political and military structures, the payment of taxes and even the balance between the world of humans and the world of deities (*pax deorum*). Therefore, the family could not remain completely outside the control of the state. The influence of the censors on the family in Republican Rome was twofold: on the one hand, the magistrates had controlling powers and could sanction *patres familiarum* abusing their rights, but on the other hand, they also protected family members who were subject to this authority.

Among the children under *patria potestas* were not only those born of *iustum matrimonium*, but also those adopted. Roman law knew two forms of adoption: *adrogatio* and *adoptio*.[25] The first consisted of the entering of a mature male

---

de Rome. Griechische Blicke auf Rom, ed. M. L. Freyburger, and D. Meyer, Paris 2007, pp. 36–46.

23 Plut., *Cat. Mai.* 16 Cf. M. Coudry, *op. cit.* pp. 46–50.

24 Cf. J. Zabłocki, "The Image of a Roman Family in "Noctes Atticae" by Aulus Gellius," *Pomoerium* 2 (1996), p. 36.

25 Cf. Gell. 10, 20; G. 1, 97–107; D. 1, 7, 1 (Modest. 2 *reg.*); D. 1, 7, 2 (Gai. 1 *inst.*); M. Kuryłowicz, *Die "adoptio" im klassischen römischen Recht*, Warszawa 1981; M. Zabłocka, "'Adrogatio' Nerona przez Klaudiusza w świetle ówczesnego ustawodawstwa," *Prawo Kanoniczne* 28/1–2 (1985), pp. 209–215; C. Russo Ruggeri, *La "datio in adoptionem," I: Origine, regime giuridico e riflessioni politico-sociali in età repubblicana ed imperiale, II: Dalla pretesa influenza elleno-cristiana alla riforma giustinianea*, Milano 1990–1995; M. Migliorini, *L'adozione tra prassi documentale e legislazione imperiale nel diritto del tardo impero romano*, Milano 2001; J. Zabłocki, "'*Adrogatio*' *nel dirito romano*," in "*Leges Sapere.*" *Studia i prace dedykowane Profesorowi Januszowi Sondlowi w pięćdziesiątą rocznicę pracy naukowej*, ed. by W. Uruszczak, P. Święcicka, and A. Kremer, Kraków 2008, pp. 719–732; Idem, "'Adrogatio" in Roman Law," in *Scripta Gelliana*, Warsaw 2020, pp. 71–92; A. M. Seelentag, "*Ius pontificium cum iure civili coniunctum.*" *Das Recht der Arrogation in klassischer Zeit*, Tübingen 2014.

sui iuris under someone else's power (*patria potestas*). As a result of the formal act of *adrogatio* one *pater familias* entered under the *patria potestas* of another, thus suffering *capitis deminutio minima*, that is, becoming a person *alieni iuris*. Therefore, *adrogatio* had a public law character in Roman law. The adoptive father presented to the *comitia curiata* the man he wished to adopt, and the assembly gave its consent, perhaps by acclamation or even in the form of a *lex curiata*.[26] As the purpose of *adrogatio* was to prolong an expiring lineage, the adoptive father had to meet certain criteria: he should be childless and unlikely to expect any offspring in the future.[27] In practice, the requirement was that he should be at least 60 years old and unmarried. The control of the assembly was necessary in order to prevent abuses—the adoptee was, after all, entering a new family and his *sacra familiaria* would expire. Therefore, the adoptive father had to take an oath assuring his pure intentions. The controlling function in *adrogatio* was performed by the priestly college of pontiffs. The priests conducted a *cognitio* to investigate the validity of the *adrogatio* and then recommended the case to the *comitia curiata*.

Adoptio, on the other hand, was developed on the basis the interpretation of provision 4,2b of the Law of the Twelve Tables.[28] It consisted in the transfer of power over an *alieni iuris* person from one *pater familias* to another. The first step of the procedure was the fiduciary mancipation of a child (a son had to be mancipated three times, while a daughter or grandchild had to be mancipated only once, according to the provision of the Law). The second part took place before a magistrate (e.g., praetor) in the form of fictitious trial (*in iure cessio*). The adoptive *pater familias* declared to have power over the adoptee, and the original *pater familias* did not question it. Next, the praetor made an adjudication (*addictio*) in favor of the new *pater familias*. The *praetor* could make a decision *in iure* since the whole trial was only fictitious and the parties acted together in order to transfer the power over the adoptee. Thus, there was no real dispute among parties and no reason to grant any action or to submit the case to a private judge.

Of the two forms of adoption, *adrogatio* was much more momentous, as it resulted in universal succession of rights and duties and the disappearance of the adoptee's family *sacra*. *Adoptio*, on the other hand, did not change a legal

26 The *lex curiata* was mentioned by Cicero in the context of Clodius' *adrogatio*, cf. Cic., *De dom*. 39.

27 Cf. Cic., *De dom*. 34–38; A. Watson, *The Law of Persons in the Later Roman Republic*, Oxford 1967, pp. 82–88.

28 Tab. 4,2b: Si pater filium ter venum du[uit] filius a patre liber esto (FIRA I, p. 35).

status of the adoptee, but could influence his social standing, especially if he was adopted by the eminent family.[29] Therefore, it can be assumed that censors were also interested in cases of adoption, especially among the members of the *nobilitas*.

In 142 BCE, the censor Publius Scipio Africanus delivered a speech in which he strongly condemned as contrary to *mores maiorum* treating adopted sons as natural ones for the purpose of granting certain privileges to citizens having a numerous offspring[30] (*praemia patrum*).

Scipio was disgusted that an adopted son, not even enrolled in the *tribus* of his new *pater familias*, was treated as a natural son and provided the privileges to his *pater familias*. It does not appear that the mere fact of adoption as such has caused the censors' objections. However, it is possible that the magistrates were especially suspicious toward adoptions which the only motive consisted in obtaining privileges from having offspring. In those cases, it cannot be ruled out that family ties created with the adoptee were later dissolved by emancipation. This would give the censors a good reason to intervene with a *nota*. The fact, mentioned by Scipio, that father and son by adoption voted in different *tribus* precisely indicates the fictitious nature of the legal procedure.

Scipio also stressed that adoptive fathers enjoyed certain privileges because of having offspring, which he called *praemia patrum*. Indeed, in the republican order multi-children *patres familiarum* were favored. For example, Livius[31] described the decision of the censors in 169 BCE, who decided to enroll all freedmen in one of the four urban *tribus* but made an exception for fathers with at least one five-year-old son, enrolling them where their names were listed in the previous census. Gellius referred to Ateius Capito, according to whom a father of at least three children was exempt from presenting his daughter as a candidate

---

29 However, adoption could not affect *dignitas*, so that a senator or his son continued to belong to the senatorial order after adoption. Cf. D. 1,7,35 (Paul. 1 *resp.*).

30 Gell. 5, 19, 15–16: Animadvertimus in oratione P. Scipionis, quam censor habuit ad populum de moribus, inter ea, quae reprehendebat, quod contra maiorum instituta fierent, id etiam eum culpavisse, quod filius adoptivos patri adoptatori inter praemia patrum prodesset. Verba ex ea oratione haec sunt: "In alia tribu patrem, in alia filium suffragium ferre, filium adoptivum tam procedere, quam si se natum habeat; absentis censeri iubere, ut ad censum nemini necessus sit venire." Scipio was a very strict censor (cf. Val. Max. 6,4,2) and hence his emphasis on regimen morum.

31 Liv. 45, 15.

for a Vestal virgin.[32] Caesar's agrarian law, on the other hand, provided for the allocation of land to twenty thousand citizens who had three or more children.[33] In addition, it can also be mentioned that at least once during the Republic the censors punished childless citizens by imposing a tax on them. Their arguments were highly convincing[34]: for the nature not only gives to a man a possibility of having offspring but also obliges them to have it, therefore childless bachelors as not performing their natural duty to raise a child should contribute in money in order to be released from such debt. This social perception of fatherhood may also encourage to adopt.

It can therefore be assumed that some citizens adopted precisely only to obtain certain privileges or avoid penalties, and then dissolved this legal relationship by emancipation.

The fragment of Scipio's speech is unfortunately the only source text directly indicating the censors' interest in adoption. However, some light may be shed on the matter by the very famous and controversial case of Publius Clodius' *adrogatio* in 59 BCE.[35] Clodius wanted to be transferred to the plebeian order, since his affiliation to a patrician family prevented him from running for the office of plebeian tribune. The legality of the whole procedure was challenged by Cicero. The Arpinate thought that proving the illegitimacy of the *adrogatio* would put in question the entire tribunate of Clodius, including the plebiscites he applied for, above all those related to Cicero's exile and the demolition of his house. The orator focused primarily on the sacral aspects of *adrogatio* and argued that Clodius' adoption was contrary to pontifical law. He stressed that the adoptive father should be of an age that precluded begetting offspring, yet Fonteius, who was younger than Clodius and only 20 years old, was married and was able to procreate.[36] The pontiffs should have therefore ensured that the *adrogatio* was

32 Gell. 1, 12, 8: Praeterea Capito Ateius scriptum reliquit, neque eius legendam filiam qui domicilium in Italia non haberet, et excusandam eius qui liberos tres haberet.

33 Suet., *Iul.* 20, 3.

34 Cf. Val. Max. 2.9,1; Plut., *Camill.* 2, 2; A. Tarwacka, "The Censors' Influence on Marriage in Republican Rome," *Zeszyty Prawnicze* 18/1 (2018), pp. 182–184.

35 Initially, Clodius simply renounced his patrician status, came to the *concilia plebis* and declared his candidacy for the tribunate, but Metellus objected to this on the grounds that a patrician could only become a plebeian by the virtue of the *lex curiata*, i.e., by *adrogatio* (Dio Cass. 37, 51,1-2). Consequently, *adrogatio* was brought about with the help of Caesar and Pompey (Dio Cass. 38, 12, 2; Cic., *De dom.* 33–38). Cf. W. J. Tatum, *The Patrician Tribune Publius Clodius Pulcher*, Chapel Hill 1999, p. 87ff.; H. Lindsay, *Adoption in the Roman World*, Cambridge 2009, pp. 174–181.

36 Cic., *De dom.* 35–37.

made for the sole purpose of adopting a descendant and heir and prolonging a lineage which, if the adoptive father died childless, would have expired along with his *sacra*.

However, Cicero also raised arguments that were not directly related to the defective *cognitio* of the pontiffs, but also referred to the *ius civile*. Namely, he reported that Clodius did not take the name of the adoptive father,[37] nor did he become his heir, and, in addition, was emancipated shortly after the *adrogatio*.[38] This information is very consistent with Scipio's speech. The adoption of Clodius did not have the effect of bringing him under the *patria potestas* and assuming the name,[39] and therefore could not have caused the adoptee to be transferred to another *tribus* either.

Of course, one can ask why the case of Clodius did not attract the interest of the censors. The closest in time is the censorship of 61 BCE,[40] exercised by G. Scribonius and his colleague, who may have been Curio Burbuleius or L. Iulius Caesar. We know that these censors carried out a very mild *lectio senatus*, which resulted in exceeding the maximum number of senators. They also probably concluded *locationes censoriae*. However, they did not carry out a census or a lustral ceremony and resigned from the office earlier, probably before the *adrogatio* of Clodius, which took place in March 59 BCE. The next couple of censors were not elected until 55 BCE. This was after Clodius himself limited the powers of these officials by putting the plebiscite, *lex Clodia de censoria notione*, to a vote. This

---

37 On the subject of name changes in cases of adoption, cf. O. Salomies, "Names and Adoptions in Ancient Rome," in *Adoption and Fosterage*, ed. M. Corbier, Paris 1999, pp. 141–156.

38 Cic., De dom. 35: Tu neque Fonteius es, qui esse debebas, neque patris heres, neque amissis sacris paternis in haec adoptiva venisti. (…) 37: nam adoptatum emancipari statim, ne sit eius filius qui adoptarit.

39 The property aspect is worth considering on this occasion. Since Clodius did not take the name of Fonteius, it also does not appear that the latter could become the universal successor. Formally, however, this is what *adrogatio* resulted in. It is possible that Clodius fiduciarily transferred the property to another person and then recovered it after emancipation. There is also a possibility that he remancipated his property from Fonteius himself.

40 Cf. C. De Boor, *"Fasti censorii,"* Berolini 1873, p. 28; T. R. S. Broughton, *The Magistrates of the Roman Republic*, II, New York 1952, p. 179; J. Suolahti, *The Roman Censors. A Study on Social Structure*, Helsinki 1963, pp. 475–477; E. Reigadas Lavandero, *Censura y "res publica": aportación constitucional y protagonismo político*, Madrid 2000, pp. 465–470.

may indicate that Clodius was afraid of censors. There could be many reasons for this, a fictitious adoption among them.

It is worth recalling that Cicero strongly wished to become a censor himself.[41] It was the only dignity he missed for his political career to be complete and crowned with the office sometimes even called *sanctissimus magistratus*.[42] Once he attained this honor, it is not difficult to guess that he would have sanctioned with a *nota* all cases where, in his opinion, *mores maiorum* were violated, such as in the case of fictitious adoptions.

In these circumstances, it must be assumed that, while the pontifical *cognitio* was intended to avoid *adrogationes* harmful for either party, as well as those not justified by the necessity to prevent a family lineage to extinct, the censorial control may have also occurred *post factum*. Scipio's speech probably foreshadowed the application of the censorial *nota* in the case of a fictitious adoption followed by a rapid emancipation.

The fact that fictitious adoptions constituted a serious social problem is further evidenced by Tacitus,[43] who writing about the year 62 CE reported a disgraceful custom to have emerged. In front of the forthcoming elections or provincial draw, childless people performed fictitious adoptions and then, once obtaining the office in the city or province governorship, terminated them by emancipation. Over the protests of fathers, who argued that parenthood entailed great hardships, as well as the threat of losing their offspring, the senate passed a resolution that fictitious adoptions could in no way give the right to hold a public office or the right to inherit. This resolution is known as the *senatus consultum Memmianum* and it referred to the previous legislation *lex Iulia de maritandis ordinibus*, which excluded or restricted unmarried and childless persons in the testamentary succession (except in the case of inheritances from the closest relatives). In the seventh chapter, the priority to take the *fasces* was given to that of the two consuls who had more children (including those lost in war). In case they had the same number of children, the one who was married was submitted.[44] From the age of Augustus, numerous offspring began to be a necessary condition for obtaining certain rights, which probably encouraged many citizens

---

41 Cf. Cic., *Ad Att.* 4, 2, 6.

42 Cic., *Pro Sest.* 55; Quint., *Inst. or.* 4, pr. 3; *Nov. Mar.* 4, 2; cf. also Plut., *Aem. Paul.* 38, 7; *Camill.* 14, 1; *Flam.* 18, 1. More extensively Tarwacka, *Prawne aspekty*, pp. 70ff.

43 Tac., *Ann.* 15, 19.

44 Gell. 2, 15, 4–5.

to conduct fictitious adoptions.[45] The disappearance of the office of the censor made it necessary to the state to impose certain sanctions.

The control exercised by the pontiffs at the *adrogatio* constituted some kind of security for the parties, since the priests would supervise if it was not made with malicious intent only for financial benefit (both against the interests of the adoptee, whose property was transferred to a new *pater familias* in result of universal succession, and of the adoptive father, who was making a *de facto* decision regarding his inheritance), but also to the state, since it was in its interest to ensure the continuation of the family, the name and the *sacra*. However, the role of the pontiffs ended once the *adrogatio* had been completed and they had no power to act in case of subsequent irregularities. This is why the role of the censors, who had the possibility to apply the nota, must have been extremely important. It can be assumed that the adoptive father would be sanctioned in the case of acting against the interests of the adoptee or his descendants, while in the case of a fraudulent termination of the *adrogatio* relationship the party who benefited would be sanctioned. In addition, the censors could probably also take some measures in cases where it was the *adoptio* and not the *adrogatio* that was of a fictitious nature and the adoptee either came back under the natural father's authority or was emancipated shortly afterward.

Bibliography:

Broughton T. R. S., *The Magistrates of the Roman Republic*, II, New York 1952

Brunt P. A., *Italian Manpower 225 B.C.– A.D. 14*, Oxford 1971

Busacca C., "Sulla datazione del 'plebiscitum Ovinium,'" in *Scritti per Alessandro Corbino*, I, ed. I. Piro, Tricase 2016, pp. 429– 452

Cornell T. J., "The 'Lex Ovinia' and the Emancipation of the Senate," in *The Roman Middle Republic. Politics, Religion and Historiography*, ed. Ch. Bruun, Rome 2000, pp. 69– 89

Coudry M., "Denys d'Halicarnasse, Plutarque, Dion Cassius: trois visions grecques de la censure?," in *Visions grecques de Rome. Griechische Blicke auf Rom*, ed. M.L. Freyburger, D. Meyer, Paris 2007, pp. 31-72

45 Although Augustus himself placed emphasis on children born out of wedlock, the text of Tacitus seems to confirm that adopted offspring were treated as one's own as long as they remained under *patria potestas*. Cf. M. Zabłocka, "Le modifiche introdotte nelle leggi matrimoniali augustee sotto la dinastia giulio-claudia," *BIDR* 89 (1986), pp. 379ff.; Eadem, "Il 'ius trium liberorum' nel diritto romano," *BIDR* 91 (1988), pp. 361ff.

De Boor C., *"Fasti censorii,"* Berolini 1873

De Ruggiero E., *Dizionario epigrafico di antichità romane*, Roma 1900

Ducos M., *Les Romains et la loi. Recherches sur les rapports de la philosophie grecque et de la tradition romaine à la fin de la République*, Paris 1984

Flower H. I., *Disgrace and Oblivion in Roman Political Culture*, Chapel Hill 2006

Fraccaro P., "'Tribules' ed'aerarii'. Una ricerca di diritto pubblico romano," in *Opuscula*, II, Pavia 1957, pp. 149-170

Humm M., "Il 'regimen morum' dei censori e le identità dei cittadini," in *"Homo, caput, persona." La costruzione giuridica dell'identità nell'esperienza romana*, ed. A. Corbino, M. Humbert, and G. Negri, Pavia 2010, pp. 283-314

Jarcke C.E., *Versuch einer Darstellung des censorischen Strafrechts der Römer: ein Beytrag zur Geschichte des Criminalrechts*, Bonn 1824

Kuryłowicz M., *Die "adoptio" im klassischen römischen Recht*, Warszawa 1981

Lindsay H., *Adoption in the Roman World*, Cambridge 2009

Lo Cascio E., "Il census a Roma e la sua evoluzione dall'età "serviana" alla prima età imperiale," *MEFRA* 113/ 2 (2001), pp. 565-603

Migliorini M., *L'adozione tra prassi documentale e legislazione imperiale nel diritto del tardo impero romano*, Milano 2001

Mommsen Th., *Römisches Staatsrecht*[3], II.1, Graz 1952

Nicolet C., "Les listes des centuries: La prétendue centurie 'Niquis scivit,'" *MEFRA* 113/ 2 (2001), pp. 723- 734

Nowak M., *Die Strafverhängungen der Censoren*, Breslau 1909

Reigadas Lavandero E., *Censura y "res publica": aportación constitucional y protagonismo político*, Madrid 2000

Russo Ruggeri C., *La "datio in adoptionem," I: Origine, regime giuridico e riflessioni politico- sociali in età repubblicana ed imperiale, II: Dalla pretesa influenza elleno- cristiana alla riforma giustinianea*, Milano 1990- 1995

Salomies O., "Names and Adoptions in Ancient Rome," in *Adoption and Fosterage*, ed. M. Corbier, Paris 1999, pp. 141- 156

Seelentag A. M., *"Ius pontificium cum iure civili coniunctum." Das Recht der Arrogation in klassischer Zeit*, Tübingen 2014

Suolahti J., *The Roman Censors. A Study on Social Structure*, Helsinki 1963

Tarwacka A., *Cenzor w sypialni. Urzędnicza kontrola moralności w życiu rodzinnym Rzymian okresu republiki*, Warszawa 2021

Tarwacka A., *Prawne aspekty urzędu cenzora w starożytnym Rzymie*, Warszawa 2012

Tarwacka A., "The Censors' Influence on Marriage in Republican Rome," *Zeszyty Prawnicze* 18/ 1 (2018), pp. 173-191

Tatum W. J., *The Patrician Tribune Publius Clodius Pulcher*, Chapel Hill 1999

Watson A., *The Law of Persons in the Later Roman Republic*, Oxford 1967

Wlosok A., "'Nihil nisi ruborem'— über die Rolle der Scham in der römischen Rechtskultur," *Grazer Beiträge* 9 (1980), pp. 155-172

Zabłocka M., "'Adrogatio' Nerona przez Klaudiusza w świetle ówczesnego ustawodawstwa," *Prawo Kanoniczne* 28/ 1- 2 (1985), pp. 209- 215

Zabłocka M., "II 'ius trium liberorum' nel diritto romano," *BIDR* 91 (1988), pp. 361-390

Zabłocka M., "Le modifiche introdotte nelle leggi matrimoniali augustee sotto la dinastia giulio- claudia," *BIDR* 89 (1986), pp. 379-410

Zabłocki J., "'Adrogatio" in Roman Law," in *Scripta Gelliana*, Warsaw 2020, pp. 71- 92

Zabłocki J., "'*Adrogatio' nel dirito romano*," in "*Leges Sapere." Studia i prace dedykowane Profesorowi Januszowi Sondlowi w pięćdziesiątą rocznicę pracy naukowej*, ed. by W. Uruszczak, P. Święcicka, and A. Kremer, Kraków 2008, pp. 719- 732

Zabłocki J., "Il segreto nel diritto romano," in *Scritti per Alessandro Corbino*, VII, ed. I. Piro, Tricase 2016, pp. 589- 599

Zabłocki J., "The Image of a Roman Family in "Noctes Atticae" by Aulus Gellius," *Pomoerium* 2 (1996), pp. 35-44

Maria Casola

Family: A brief legal historical reflection

Abstract: There is no doubt that from ancient times until now, the family has represented an institution, whose social function has been constantly recognized and never questioned. From this circumstance, however, arose the question, which involved scholars of the subject, whether Roman law has shown a tendency to recognize juridical consequences (and possibly within what limits) even to unions that did not constitute *matrimonium iustum*. The contribution aims to highlight how, in reality, the answer must be sought in facts, in individual concrete cases, confirming the absolute inclination of Roman law toward a casuistic approach, which however does not want to feed uncertainty rather aims to identify the most suitable response to the concrete case, inspired by canons of justice and reasonableness or to use the now well-known words of Celsus to the bonum ed.

Keywords:*Familia, societas*, models of different family, Roman Law

1. Growth in the *familia* and in the *societas*

One of the common denominators both of ancient and modern contemporary experience has been the *familia*, within which there was also the man-*persona*, the reference was not to man-value, as it was in the Christian theological speculation and in the visions of ethical States but the "historical man" which was identified with the legal concept of person.

This man-*persona* was seen within real life and within the familia, of the *Civitas*, according to a structure with concentric circles designed by Cicero.

Cicero's statements are very important. He spoke of the existence of a society organized in several *gradus* founded on nature[1] the individual one, the

1 Cic., *De off.* 1.17.53–54: *Gradus autem plures sunt societatis hominum. Ut enim ab illa infinita discedatur, proprior est eiusdem gentis, nationis, linguae, qua maxime homines coniunguntur. Interius etiam est eiusdem esse civitatis; multa enim sunt civibus inter se communia, forum, fana, porticus, viae, leges, iura, iudicia, suffragia, consuetudines praeterea et familiaritates multisque cum multis res rationesque contractae. Artior vero colligatio est societatis propinquorum; ab illa enim inmensa societate humani generis in exiguum angustumque concluditur.* 54. *Nam cum sit hoc natura commune animantium, ut habeant libidinem procreandi, prima societas in ipso coniugio est, proxima in liberis, deinde una domus, communia omnia; id autem est principium urbis et quasi seminarium*

family's one and the society's one. Each one is autonomous both historically and chronologically, so that like spheres intersecting themselves without a mutual cancellation.[2] It was not conceivable one might limit or cancel one another.

There were several structured close links the base of which was the family *principium urbis et quasi seminarium rei publicae.*[3]

According to Cicero, the social aim of the *familia* was the foundation of civil society that is the procreation for themselves and for the *Civitas*.[4] The family was the basis of the formation process of the city, ensuring its survival.

When Cicero, at the beginning, made reference to *urbs* and to *res publica*, he probably wanted to emphasize two complementary but not identical aspects. On one hand the formation of the city had been the work of the families, on the other the life and the continuation of the community couldn't take place without the families since without the latter the community couldn't reach any aim. There was, consequently, a concept of "nature" at the basis of the family. Such a concept aimed at the creation of links with marriage and with procreation and consequently with the expansion of groups moving into the city.

The *Civitas* in their turn grew[5] and could support themselves thanks to the ties developed with marriages and the resulting offspring. The idea expressed in the Cicero's words was not only typical of an author or of a period.

---

rei publicae. Sequuntur fratrum coniunctiones, post consobrinorum sobrinorumque, qui cum una domo iam capi non possint, in alias domos tamquam in colonias exeunt. Sequuntur conubia et affinitates ex quibus etiam plures propinqui; quae propagatio et suboles origo est rerum publicarum. Sanguinis autem coniunctio et benivolentia devincit homines [et] caritate.

2 It has been observed (S. Tafaro, *Ius hominum causa constitutum. Un diritto a misura d'uomo*, Napoli, 2009, p. 50, where we remember M. Bretone, *Storia del diritto romano*, Roma-Bari, 2001, p. 38f.) "che la visione romana della realtà era quella di cerchi concentrici, nei quali i due estremi sono l'umanità e la famiglia, la cellula minima di cui il singolo individuo fa parte; fra questi estremi si situa lo stato, un'istituzione insieme naturale e storica."

3 Cic., *De off.* 1.17.54.

4 On this point, see M. Casola, "Dote tra Familia e Civitas," *GLOSSAE. European Journal of Legal History* 14 (2017), p. 232, ivi bibliography.

5 The history of Rome itself was taken into consideration with reference to the stages of its growth. Witness to the latter is the incisive picture drawn by Sesto Pomponio (II cent. d.C) in D1.2.2.2 of the growth and evolution of the law and of the structure of Rome. Such statement has been subject of in-depth analysis by M. P. Baccari, "Il

It's the ideal of procreation and, through it, of the *familia* and the *civitas* at the basis of a trend which, starting from Greek speculation, spread in Rome[6] and was linked to *ius naturale* above all by Severian jurists as a right pre-existent at *Civitas* and subject to any form of society.

All this is proved by a passage of Ulpian which was worthy of criticism,[7] for that reference to *coniuctio*, *procreatio* and *educatio liberorum*, a parallel with Cicero's reflection in terms of *coniugium* and *societas liberorum*[8]:

> D. 1.1.1.3 (Ulp. *l* 1 *inst.*): *Ius naturale est, quod natura omnia animalia docuit: nam ius istud non humani generis proprium, sed omnium animalium, quae in terra, quae in mari nascuntur, avium quoque commune est. Hinc descendit maris atque feminae coniuctio, quam nos matrimonium appellamus, hinc liberorum procreatio, hinc educatio: videmus etenim cetera quoque animalia, feras etiam istius peritia censeri.*

The Roman conception of a married couple as a primordial cell of civil society emphasized marriage as *consortium*,[9] focused on the solidarity of the family in face of which individual choice was not important.

---

concetto di civitas augescens: origine e continuità," *SDHI* LXI (1996), p. 759f.; M. P. Baccari, *Cittadini popoli e comunione nella legislazione dei secoli IV–VI*, Torino, 1996, partic. 57f.), who developing Catalano's suggestion, several times over paid particular attention to the noun-phrase *civitas augescens*.

6 The jurist's idea was influenced by Pitagora's and Empedocle's thinking and matched the concepts of nature outlined by Cicero. The states, S. Tafaro, *Ius hominun causa constitutum*, cit., p. 56, that: "idee forse originatesi in India, circolanti nel Mediterraneo, dove si erano diffuse per la diffusione delle correnti pitagoriche, le quali avevano suscitato nuove aspettative, anche a seguito della divulgazione fattane da Apollonio di Tiane, e dal suo agiografo Flavio Filostrato."

7 See R. Quadrato, "'Maris atque feminae coniuctio': 'matrimonium' e unioni di fatto," *Index* 38 (2010), p. 223f., where bibliography.

8 P. P. Onida, *Studi sulla condizione degli animali non umani nel sistema giuridico romano*, Torino 2002, p. 111 and ivi nt. 20.

9 As to definition of *matrimonium* as *consortium* and *societas* see G. Lobrano, "Uxor quodammodo domina. Riflessioni sul Paul. D. 25.2.1," in *Univ. di Sassari-Fac. Di Giur.-Pubbl. Del Seminario di Diritto Romano*, 6, Sassari 1989, cap. II, pp. 48–54 (ora online al sito web http://dirittoestoria.it/dirittoromano/.Lobrano-Uxor.htm); R. Quadrato, "Maris atque feminae coniuctio," cit., pp. 250–251, cui *adde*, F. Lamberti, "Convivenze e unioni di fatto nell'esperienza romana: l'esempio del concubinato," in *Unioni di fatto. Dal diritto romano ai diritti attuali. Atti dell'incontro italo-tedesco (Imperia, 27–28 novembre 2015)*, ed. G. Viarengo, Torino 2016, pp. 1–26.

The famous definitions of Modestinus[10] and Ulpian,[11] according to which weddings are *coniuctio maris et feminae* and are still very relevant.

We find the same concepts in Latin writers as Quintilian[12] who describes a wife as *femina viro nuptiis collocata in societatem vitae* e *socia tori, vitae consors,*[13] or as oppure Tacitus, who defines marriages as *consortia rerum secundarum adversarumque.*[14]

10 D. 23.2.1 (Modest. 1 *reg.*): *Nuptiae sun coniuctio maris et feminae et consortium omnis vitae, divini et humani iuris communicatio.* Some authors have doubted the authenticity and juridical relevance of the ancient definitions of marriage. See, in particular, even with different readings: S. Perozzi, *Istituzioni di diritto romano*, I, Roma 1928², p. 316; S. Solazzi, *Scritti di diritto romano*, III, Napoli 1960, p. 313f.; F. Schulz, *I principi di diritto romano*, trad. It., Firenze 1995 (rist. Anast. 1946), p. 40; A. Carcaterra, *Le definizioni dei giuristi romani. Metodo mezzi e fini*, Napoli 1966, p. 167; P. Bonfante, *Corso di diritto romano*, I, Milano 1963², p. 263; E. Albertario, "La definizione del matrimonio secondo Modestino," in *Studi di diritto romano*, I, Milano 1933, p. 181ff.; P. Lanfranchi, "Le definizioni e il concetto del matrimonio nei retori romani," *SDHI* 2 (1936), p. 148ff.; J. Gaudemet, "Justum matrimonium," *RIDA* 2 (1949), p. 310f.; O. Robleda, *El matrimonio en derecho romano. Esencia, requisitos de validez, efectos, disolubilidad*, Roma 1970, p. 59ff.; M. Humbert, *Le remariage à Rome. Etude d'historie juridique et sociale*, Milano 1972, p. 28; E. Volterra, "voce *Matrimonio* (diritto romano)," *Enc. Dir.* XXV (1975), p. 754f.; K. Visky, "*Le divorce dans la législation de Justinien*," *RIDA* 23 (1976), p. 249; C. Castello, *Scritti scelti di diritto romano. Servi filii nuptiae*, Genova 2002, p. 411ff.; R. Astolfi, *Il matrimonio nel diritto romano preclassico*, Padova 2000, p. 99ff.; G. Eisenring, *Die römische Ehe als Rechtsverhältnis*, Böhlau-Wien-Köln-Wiemar 2002, p. 240.

11 D. 1.1.3 (Ulp. 1 *inst.*): ... *hinc descendit maris atque feminae coniuctio, quam nos matrimonium appellamus...;* See, also I. 1.9.1: *Nuptiae autem sive matrimonium est viri et mulieris coniuctio, individuam consuetudinem vitae continens.*

12 Quint., *decl.* 247.

13 Quint., *decl.* 376.

14 Tac., *ann.* 3.34; 12.5.

In his turn as well as in D. 50.16.195.2,[15] Justinian availing himself of Ulpian's passage, considered the *familia* as *corpus*[16] (united, cohesive, homogeneous).

The choice of *corpus* is very important since, as Catalano[17] has emphasized, it reminds of a concept of collectivity, so that the family is proved to be a body modeled under the power of a leader (*pater familias*), without excluding that its members, free and bond, might have important autonomous roles and positions.

---

15 D. 50.16.195.2 (Ulp. 46 *ad ed.*): *Familiae appellatio refertur et ad corporis cuiusdam significationem, quod aut iure proprio ipsorum aut communi universae cognationis continetur. Iure proprio familiam dicimus plures personas, quae sunt sub unius potestate aut natura aut iure subiectae, ut puta patrem familias, matrem familias, filium familias, filiam familias quique deinceps vicem eorum sequuntur, ut puta nepotes et neptes et deinceps. Pater autem familias appellatur, qui in domo dominium habet, recteque hoc nomine appellatur, quamvis filium non habeat: non enim solam personam eius, sed et ius demonstramus: denique et pupillum patrem familias appellamus. Et cum pater familias moritur, quotquot capita ei subiecta fuerint, singulas familias incipiunt habere: singuli enim patrum familiarum nomen subeunt. Idemque eveniet et in eo qui emancipatus est: nam et hic sui iuris effectus propriam familiam habet. Communi iure familiam dicimus omnium adgnatorum: nam etsi patre familias mortuo singuli singulas familias habent, tamen omnes, qui sub unius potestate fuerunt, recte eiusdem familiae appellabuntur, qui ex eadem domo et gente proditi sunt.*

16 The word *corpus* indicates all the organizations recognized by the law since they were a single body which absorbed all individuals. I recall by way of explanation, two passages in which the word corpus indicated an assembly. The first is by Gaius who linked corpus to society and to a college: D. 3.4.1. *pr.* (Gai 3 *ad ed. provinc.*): *Neque societas neque collegium neque huiusmodi corpus passim omnibus habere conceditur: nam et legibus et senatus consultis et principalibus constitutionibus ea res coercetur. Paucis admodum in causis concessa sunt huiusmodi corpora: ut ecce vectigalium publicorum sociis permissum est corpus habere vel aurifodinarum vel argentifodinarum et salinarum. Item collegia romae certa sunt, quorum corpus senatus consultis atque constitutionibus principalibus confirmatum est, veluti pistorum et quorundam aliorum, et naviculariorum, qui et in provinciis sunt.* The second is by Ulpian: D. 4.2.9.1 (Ulp. 11 *ad ed.*): *Animadvertendum autem, quod praetor hoc edicto generaliter et in rem loquitur nec adicit a quo gestum: et ideo sive singularis sit persona, quae metum intulit, vel populus vel curia vel collegium vel corpus, huic edicto locus erit. Sed licet vim factam a quocumque praetor complectatur, eleganter tamen pomponius ait, si quo magis te de vi hostium vel latronum vel populi tuerer vel liberarem, aliquid a te accepero vel te obligavero, non debere me hoc edicto teneri, nisi ipse hanc tibi vim summisi: ceterum si alienus sum a vi, teneri me non debere, ego enim operae potius meae mercedem accepisse videor.*

17 As to this point I redirect the reader to the discerning and persuasive observations which are contained in P. Catalano, *Diritto e persone, Studi su origine e attualità del sistema romano*, I, Torino 1990, p. 173.

It was, however a community that was projected into its own growth, which also finalized the power of the head of a family. All this meant that they might be arbitrary but they had at the same time to help the members of the family from conception even of the vulnerable ones.

In this context we can place all the protective measures for the weaker members such as the unborn,[18] children[19] and women,[20] respectful of

---

18 Frequent studies state that in the Roman law the conceived was considered *persona* and an autonomous legal value from the moment of conception: from this we can deduct the right to be born. I recall the most recent literature: M. P. Baccari, *Concepito: l'antico diritto per il nuovo millennio*, Torino 2004; M. P. Baccari, *La difesa del concepito nel diritto romano dai Digesta dell'Imperatore Giustiniano*, Torino 2006; M. P. Baccari, *Curator ventris. Il concepito, la donna e la res publica tra storia e attualità*, Torino 2012; P. Ferretti, *In rerum natura esse. In rebus humanis non esse. L'identità del concepito nel pensiero giurisprudenziale classico*, Milano 2008; P. Catalano, *Diritto e persone*, cit., p. 216f.; G. Fontana, *Quin in utero sunt. Concetti e condizione giuridica del nascituro nella codificazione di Giustiniano*, Torino 1994; M. Lubrano, *Persona e homo nell'opera di Gaio. Elementi concettuali del sistema giuridico romano*, Torino 2002, p. 3f.; M. Gayosso y Navarrete, *Persona: naturaleza original del concepto en los derechos romano y náhuatl*, Veracruz 1992: M. G. Petrucci, "Quale status per il nascituro?," in *Rassegna di diritto civile*, 1998, p. 462f.; P. Ferretti, "Diritto romano e diritto europeo: alcune considerazioni in tema di qui in utero sunt," *Ann. Univ. Ferrara- Sc. Giur. Nuova serie* XIII (1999), p. 96ff.; T. Mayer-Maly, "Das Menschenbild des Rechts," in *Giovanni Paolo II. Le vie della giustizia*, ed. A. Loiodice and M. Vari, Roma 2003, p. 35 and lastly A. Palma, "Il nascituro come problema 'continuo': Diritto Romano e Diritto Privato italiano alla luce di recenti asserti giurisprudenziali," *Revista Europea de Historia de las Ideas Políticas y de las Instituciones Públicas* (2014), pp. 45–78.

19 Cfr. S. Tafaro, "I diritti dei fanciulli," in *Scritti in onore di G. Melillo*, vol. III, ed. A. Palma, Napoli 2009, p. 1281f.

20 In particular such protection seems to be the result of a profound reflection and of an awareness that women, since they were essential to the growth of the city should be protected even through the safeguard of their dowries. These ideas were the fruit of deep change in the Roman law from the end of the Republic, brought to maturity with the principality when all institutions were embedded with new ideas which allowed to overcome the atavistic definitions of familia to give more importance to the needs of the *Res publica* even as compared to questions previously considered private such as in the case of dowries. The dowry, actually, was an essential instrument of the policy of promoting marriages; thanks to the latter, according to the juristconsult Pomponius (D. 24. 3. 1, Pomp. 15 *ad Sab.*) "procreare prole e riempire la città di figli." There was a copious literature. Here I only mention M. Bretone, *Storia*, cit., cap XII. On the role of

general principles, deduced or recognized, involving the perception of all men's dignity.[21]

As a consequence of these considerations, more than once, scholars have wondered if Roman law acknowledged one type of marriage or a multiplicity of marital unions.

I am aware, I cannot deal with this subject in this context, anyhow I will try to deal with two points. First of all I will try to verify if the sources of information bring out the coexistence of more models of legally acknowledged couples, on the basis of which it should be possible to draw a distinction according to the most recent studies[22]; I will also try to verify if the conclusion is different according to traditional theories,[23] which exclude such multiplicity and leave the whole marital landscape a good alternative between *matrimonium iustum* (existing) and *matrimonium iniustum* (non-existing).

---

the woman, belonging to that unity, in the *societas vitae* of the *matrimonium*, which made her *quodammodo domina*, see G. Lobrano, *Uxor quodammodo domina*, cit.

21 T. Honoré, "Les droits de l'homme chez Ulpien," in *Le monde Antique et les Droits de l'Homme: actes de la 50e session de la Societé Internationale Fernard De Visscher pour l'Histoire des Droits de l'Antiquité (Bruxelles, 16–19 septembre 1996)*, ed. H. Jones, Bruxelles 1998, pp. 235–253.

22 G. Rizzelli, "Alcuni aspetti dell'accusa privilegiata in materia di adulterio," *BIDR* 89 (1986), pp. 411–441; G. Rizzelli, *La lex Iulia de adulteriis. Studi sulla disciplina di adulterium, lenocinum, stuprum*, Lecce 1997. See, also, F. Lamberti, "La storiografia sulla familia rmana fra inquadramenti tradizionali e nuove tendenze di ricerca," in *La famiglia tardoantica. Società, diritto, religione*, ed. V. Neri and B. Giratti, Milano 2016, https://www.ledonline.it/index.php/Erga-Logoi/pages/view/qel-5-famiglia-tardoantica.

23 E. Volterra, "Iniustum matrimonium," in *Studi in onore di Gaetano Scherillo*, vol. 2, Milano 1972, pp. 441–470; E. Volterra, "Precisazioni in matria di matrimonio classico," *BIDR* 17 (1975), pp. 245–270; E. Volterra, s.v. *Matrimonio* (diritto romano), in *Enc. Dir.*, vol 25, Milano 1975, pp. 727–807 (= *Scritti giuridici*, vol. 3, *Famiglia e successioni*, Napoli 1991, pp. 223–304). E. Volterra, "Per lo studio del reato di bigamia," in *Studi in memoria di Umberto Ratti*, ed. E. Albertario, Milano 1934, pp. 387–447; E. Volterra, "Ancora sulla manus e sul matrimonium," in *Studi in onore di Siro Solazzi*, Napoli 1948, pp. 676–688; E. Volterra, "Quelques observations sur le mariage des filiifamilias," *RIDA* 1 (1948), pp. 213–242; E. Volterra, "La nozione giuridica del conubium," in *Studi in memoria di Emilio Albertario*, vol. 2, Milano 1950, pp. 347–384 (= *Scritti giuridici*, vol. 2, *Famiglia e successioni*, Napoli 1991, pp. 283–320).

2. De facto relationships in the Roman legal experience

In the Roman experience, it was possible for a man and a woman to have a long-term partnership with the birth of children without being married.

There wasn't actually only one type of union[24] and there might be several reasons for this. They were actually stable relations, which were different from marriage owing to either lack of one or more requirements or they started in the violation of specific prohibitions for certain categories of subjects (*matrimonium iniustum*[25]) or to the absence of constitutive or structural elements (*concubinatus*[26]).

---

24 Ulpiano in D. 48.5.14 (13).1, Ulp. 2 *de adult.*, commenting on the Augustan matrimonial legislation asserts that the latter was about ad omnia matrimonium pertinet. Among all the scholars who have studied all the categories of well-known married couples in ancient Rome, we can mention M. V. Sanna, *Matrimonio e altre situazioni matrimoniali nel diritto romano classico: matrimonium iustum, matrimonium iniustum*, Napoli 2012; R. Quadrato, *Maris atque feminae coniuctio: matrimonium e unioni di fatto*, cit., pp. 223–252. In our legal mind, until a few years ago, we had a monolithic vision of marriage. In Roman law such a vision was in contrast with multiple realities which reflected the several facets of couple relations in everyday life. Whatever the model of the latter was, they should be unions of two different sexes since Roman law disapproved of homosexual ones. On the subject see E. Cantarella, "Secondo natura. La biosessualità nel mondo antico," *BUR*, Milano 2008; D. Dalla, "*Ubi Venus mutatur.*" *Omosessualità e diritto nel mondo romano*, Milano 1987; G. Giulina, "Unioni omosessuali e diritto romano," *APG* 5 (2016), pp. 111–127.

25 Cfr. F. Rossi, *Apparenza del diritto e rapporti di fatto nell'esperienza giuridica di Roma antica*, Firenze 2020, where bibliography.

26 Concubinage was a widespread practice in the Roman and Greek world. In particular, in ancient law, the concubine had a precise social role, which made her different both from the hetaera and from the wife. Unlike the former, the concubine lived in her partner's house like a wife; unlike the latter however, the concubine did not generate legitimate offspring and did not share the social *status* of her husband since she was not bound by a valid legal restriction with him. Not all stable partnerships were qualified as matrimonium and, at the same time, not every woman who lived with a man was considered his *uxor*: "*non omnis mulier iuncta viro uxor est viri.*" Such situations, foreign to our mentality might lead us to think that Roman society allowed bigamy, but all the studies about the legal history of bigamy have proved that "il secondo matrimonio dell'uomo sposato era nullo e la donna che lo contraeva non ne diveniva moglie, ma era considerata soltanto e con proprietà la sua concubina." V. R. Astolfi, "Sintesi della storia della bigamia in Roma," *SDHI* 76 (2010), p. 281. Del resto, si veda D. 50.16.144 (Paul. 10 *ad l. Iul. Et Pap.*): *Libro memorialium Massurius scribit "pellicem" apud antiquos eam habitam, quae, cum uxor non esset, cum aliquo tamen vivebat: quam*

For example, in the age of the principate, unions between a free man and a slave as well as between a free woman and a slave were subject to repeated sanctions, whereas the unions between slaves were considered without binding legal effects (*contubernia*).[27] The unions between a *civis romanus* (or a Roman free-born woman) and a *peregrinus* (or *a Latinus*) might be considered *nuptiae* only after a special concession.[28]

Unions between relatives in the same ascending and descending line were also forbidden, as well as between collateral relatives within the third degree of consanguinity.[29]

Moreover, both the "paramarital" union between a married man and a woman different from the *uxor* (defined *paelex*) and the union where the previous marriage was not yet dissolved, were also considered forbidden.

On the subject there might be several examples, but I cannot comment here on their multiple and complex implications. I can approximately underline that the *matrimonium iustum* did not represent the whole universe of the relationship between a man and a woman even though it was the main model. It is necessary, however, to verify if some consequences, typical of the main model, that is the *iustum matrimonium* could be extended to the unions differentiated,[30] by this

---

nunc vero nomine amicam, paulo honestiore concubinam appellari. Granius Flaccus in libro de iure Papiriano scribit pellicem nunc volgo vocari, quae cum eo, cui uxor sit, corpus misceat: quosdam eam, quae uxoris loco sine nuptiis in domo sit, quam παλλακὴν Graeci vocant. What is relevant is the lack of *affectio maritalis* and consequently of *honor matrimonii*. Cfr. C. Fayer, *La familia romana: aspetti giuridici ed antiquari*, vol. 3, *Concubinato Divorzio, Adulterio*, Roma 2005, p. 11.

27 V. *Tit. Ulp*. 5.5 ... *Cum servis nullum est conubium*; PS. 2.19.6: ... *Inter servos et liberos matrimonium contrahi non potest, contubernium potest*; D. 16.3.27 (Paul. 7 *resp*.).

28 *Tit. Ulp*. 5.4: *Conubium habent cives Romani cum civibus Romanis; cum Latinis autem et peregrinis ita, si concessum sit.*

29 Gai 1.59–64: *Inter eas enim personas, quae parentum liberorumve locum inter se optinent, nuptiae contrahi non possunt, nec inter eas conubium est, velut inter patrem et filiam vel inter matrem et filium vel inter avum et neptem; et si tales personae inter se coierint, nefarias et incestas nuptias contraxisse dicuntur. Et haec adeo ita sunt, ut quamvis per adoptionem parentum liberorumve loco sibi esse coeperint, non possint inter se matrimonio coniungi, in tantum, ut etiam dissoluta adoptione idem iuris maneat; itaque eam, quae mihi per adoptionem filiae seu neptis loco esse coeperit, non potero uxorem ducere, quamvis eam emancipaverim.*

30 On the subject it has been stressed (F. Lamberti, *Convivenze e unioni di fatto nell'esperienza romana: l'esempio del concubinato*, cit., p. 15) that, starting with the principate, the legitimacy of such unions, in particular of concubinage, found its own way in the

form of *matrimonium*, assuming that the foundation of marriage was procreation.[31] In a number of respects, jurists, in the course of their interpretation work have highlighted similarities, as between marriage and concubinage, ending up extending the effects of the former.

They were, however, cases which were not considered with a view to "*favor familiae*" that is to ensure legal safeguard to unmarried couples. Far from it: actually, even when it is possible to record the effects on different forms of union, we cannot assert that they favored the latter.

On the subject it is very interesting a passage from Ulpiano which we can read in Giustiniano's *Digesta*, more exactly:

> D. 25.7.1 *pr.* (Ulp. 2 *ad leg. Iul. et Pap.*): *Quae in concubinatu est, ab invito patrono poterit discedere et alteri se aut in matrimonium aut in concubinatum dare? ego quidem probo in concubina adimendum ei conubium, si patronum invitum deserat, [quippe cum honestius sit patrono libertam concubinam quam matrem familias habere].*

Both the issue dealt with, and above all, the solution found, confirm the theory of the extension of the legal rule, which forbade a freedwoman divorced from her *patrono*, to remarry, also the *patrono* to keep his freedwoman with him as a concubine and not as his wife.

The hypothesis of the *accusatio adulterii*[32] of the *uxor iniusta* and of the concubine allows us to identify the problem more clearly: in this case, equalization

---

Augustan legislation. The latter, excluding its validity as *iustae nuptiae*, implicitly determined the necessary configuration as an alternative form of couple relationship.

31 It followed that the emotional and sentimental side of a couple's life was inevitably relegated in the background. More precisely, it was not absent but it was a consequential effect of marriage and not its premise. As an example, we can mention the happy marriage between Catone the Young and Marzia in F. Cantarella, "Matrimonio e sessualità nella Roma repubblicana: una storia romana di amore coniugale," *BIDR* 39 (1997), pp. 205–219 [= Storia delle donne, 1, 2005, pp. 115–131].

32 The *accusatio adulterii* was the legal act which determined the beginning of a court trial to determine the criminal responsibility of the alleged adulterous woman and of her partner. Such a proceeding, took place in a special court, the quaestio de adulteriis, which had the specific skills in the field of sex crimes. See F. Botta, "Ancora in tema di accusatio adulterii del minor XXV annis," in *Fides Humanitas Ius. Studii in onore di Luigi Labruna*, vol. 1, ed. C. Cascione and C. Masi Doria, Napoli 2007, pp. 439–463; F. Botta, "Legittimazione, interesse ed incapacità all'accusa nei 'publica iudicia,'" in *AV*, Cagliari 1996; D. Daube, "The Accuser under the lex Iulia de adulteriis," in *Collected Studies in Roman Law*, vol. 1, ed. V. Klostermann, Frankfurt am Main 1991, pp. 561–573; M. A. De Dominicis, "Sulle origini romano-cristiane del diritto del marito ad accusare 'constante matrimonio' la moglie adultera (A proposito di Dig. 48, 5, 27 [26]

was to the disadvantage of the *uxor iniusta* and, for some scholars, even of the della concubine,[33] who, while not being a real wife, was criminally treated as such, since both of them might be accused of adultery.

> D. 48.5.14 (13).1 (Ulp. 2 *de adult.*): *Plane sive iusta uxor fuit sive iniusta, accusationem instituere vir poterit: nam et Sextus Caecilius ait, haec lex ad omnia matrimonia pertinet, et illud Homericum adfert: nec enim soli, inquit, Atridae uxores suas amant. Οὐ μόνοι φιλέουσ' ἀλόχους μερόπων ἀνθρώπων Ἀτρεῖδαι.*

On the subject, Ulpiano, comparing *uxori "iusta"* to "*uxor iniusta*," placed legal marriage (*iustae nuptiae or iustum matrimonium*) and illegitimate marriage (specularly, *iniustae nuptiae* or *iniustum matrimonium*) on the same level. Ulpiano assumed that, in both cases, the man, either husband or partner, in order to prosecute the infidelity of his wife or of his partner, might *accusatio instituere.*

The jurist believed that, without any doubt (*plane*) the man could accuse both the *uxor iusta* and the *uxor iniusta.* What is relevant in this passage is that in case of violation of marital fidelity, the man could bring an adultery lawsuit against the *uxor* either *iusta* or *iniusta, sive iusta, sive iniusta.*

In light of this theory,[34] some scholars have gradually expanded the concept of *matrimonium* to stable monogamous relationships even though the latter were unions different from *iustae numptiae.*

---

pr.)," *SDHI* 16 (1950), pp. 221–253; M. Kaser, "Rec. M. A. De Dominicis, Sulle origini romano-cristiane del diritto del marito ad accusare 'constante matrimonio' la moglie adultera (A proposito di Dig. 48, 5, [26] pr.)," *SDHI* 16 (1950), pp. 221–253 [= *Iura*, 2 (1951), pp. 324–325]; G. Rizzelli, "Alcuni aspetti dell'accusa privilegiata in materia di adulterio," *BIDR* 89 (1986), pp. 411–441; J. A. C. Thomas, "Accusatio adulterii," *Iura* 12 (1961), pp. 65–80; C. Venturini, "'Accusatio adulterii' e politica costantiniana (Per un riesame di CTH 9, 7, 2)," *SDHI* 54 (1988), pp. 66–109; C. Venturini, "Innovazioni postclassiche in materia di accusatio adulterii," in *Crimina e delicta nel tardo antico: atti del Seminario di studi, Teramo 19–20 gennaio 2001*, ed. F. Lucrezi e G. Mancini, Milano 2003, pp. 17–37; E. Volterra, "Per la storia dell'accusatio iure mariti vel patri," in *Scritti giuridici*, vol. 1, *Famiglia e successioni*, Napoli 1991, pp. 219–278; E. Volterra, "In tema di 'accusatio adulterii'. I. L'adulterium' della 'sponsa'. II. L'adulterium' dell'uxor in captivitate'," in *Scritti giuridici*, vol. 1, *Famiglia e successioni*, Napoli 1991, pp. 313–328.

33 D. 48.5.14 (13) pr. (Ulp. 2 *de adult.*): *Si uxor non fuerit in adulterio, concubina tamen fuit, iure quidem mariti accusare eam non poterit, quae uxor non fuit, iure tamen extranei accusationem instituere non prohibebitur, si modo ea sit, quae in concubinatum se dando matronae nomen non amisit, ut puta quae patroni concubina fuit.* Cfr. G. Rizzelli, *Lex Iulia de adulteriis*, cit., pp. 195–196.

34 The reference is to G. Rizzelli, *Lex Iulia de adulteriis*, cit., p. 188, who has devoted several exhaustive studies to the theme of *adulterium* and, therefore, we cannot disregard

According to some jurists, some prohibitions could not be extended to concubinage and de facto unions, even if they were admissible in relations between spouses:

> D. 24.1.3 pr. (Ulp. 32 *ad Sab.)*: *Haec ratio et oratione imperatoris nostri Antonini Augusti electa est: nam ita ait: "Maiores nostri inter virum et uxorem donationes prohibuerunt, amorem honestum solis animis aestimantes, famae etiam coniunctorum consulentes, ne concordia pretio conciliari viderentur neve melior in paupertatem incideret deterior ditior fieret". 1. Videamus, inter quos sunt prohibitae donationes. et quidem si matrimonium moribus legibusque nostris constat, donatio non valebit. sed si aliquod impedimentum interveniat, ne sit omnino matrimonium, donatio valebit: ergo si senatoris filia libertino contra senatus consultum nupserit, vel provincialis mulier ei, qui "provinciam regit vel qui" ibi meret, contra mandata, valebit donatio, quia nuptiae non sunt. sed fas non est eas donationes ratas esse, ne melior sit condicio eorum, qui deliquerunt. divus tamen Severus in liberta Pontii Paulini senatoris contra statuit, quia non erat affectione nuxoris habita, sed magis concubinae.*

It followed that the only legally valid union in Rome was the *matrimonium iustum*. When there was an extension of effects to other models, it was due not so much to protect an illegitimate couple (*iniusta*) through the recognition of rights and faculties, but to impose oligations (such as the one of marital fidelity), which once violated were punishable.

What has been asserted so far, does not mean, that all the theories of the cultural sources are less important, but, on the contrary, the former offered valuable elements to confirm our argument.

On the other hand, if the Romans admitted the existence of manifold relationships (*matrimonium iustum, matrimonium iniustum, concubinage*) giving each of the latter a specific place and a specific social function, it is easy to think there were probably no strict boundaries.

In order to understand the complexity of the phenomena briefly dealt with so far, and to grasp and appreciate their essence, it is necessary to observe them from the right perspective. If we try to do that, these phenomena do not appear disorderly any longer but rather the result of a very precise and, by no means,

---

his opinion. L'a. believes that this extension is not due to a variation of the notion of *adulterium* within social consciousness, but to the birth of new types of union which represent the prerequisite of the *adulterium*. Among the former, the adultery committed by the concubine is exemplary, since this hypothesis is not regulated by the *Lex Iulia de adulteriis*. On the contrary, M. V. Sanna, "*Matrimonio e altre situazioni matrimoniali,*" cit., pp. 146–147, excludes the inclusion of concubinage within *omnia matrimonia*.

casual approach. In fact, all doctrinal debates either on the borderline between *matrimonium iustum* and *matrimonium iniustum*, or on the legal implication of the latter compared with the former, or the difficulty to distinguish the *affectio maritalis* from the *affectio concubinae*[35] are potential problems since they are assessed in abstract terms. All this happens when on the basis of legal categories, general matters, which are inside the *factum* are tried to be solved.

If we think that concubinage spread during the principate, when marriage was not allowed, we can consider it an extreme case which means that people resorted to concubinage only when it was not possible or it was highly inadvisable that a bond with a certain person was sealed by a proper *matrimonium.*[36]

The solution for legal issues in Rome was never left to chance, but it was based and forged on individual and concrete cases with their specificity. We can confirm that Roman law aimed at a case study approach, which did not want to foster uncertainty.

On the contrary, it aimed either to find the most suitable reply to a real case inspired by canons of justice and reasonableness, or to use Celso's well-known words *bonum et aequum.*[37]

---

35 Cfr.R. Quadrato, "*Maris atque feminae coniuctio,*" cit., p. 231: "Non è agevole separare *l'affectio uxoris* dall'*affectio concubinae.* Il discrimine è esile: "senza le nozze" la differenza fra la *uxor* e la donna *uxoris loco*, che è considerata "come moglie" vivendo nella stessa casa dell'uomo al quale è unita da un rapporto durevole anche se fattuale, sembra impalpabile: pare risolversi in una mera questione terminologica [...]."

36 Scholars believe that in spite of the lack of interest in the legal recognition of concubinage as *iustum*, its diffusion was partly due to *Lex Julia de adulteriis.* This law, in listing the people it would have been possible to have sex, did not completely forbid extramarital relationships. It was also due to the *Lex Iulia et Papia Pappaea* which, sanctioning a series of matrimonial impediments of social nature, almost tacitly advised to resort to concubinage in these cases. As compared to the women who were forbidden to get married by such bans, further on extended by the imperial legislation of the classical age, the only chance left was the extramarital union which could integrate a hypothesis of concubinage.

37 So M. P. Baccari, "Alcuni principi del diritto romano per la difesa dell'uomo nella globalizzazione," *Teoria del diritto e dello Stato. Rivista europea di cultura e scienza giuridica* 1 (2005), p. 25. She adds that: it's necessary to go back to old certainties: the legal certainly of the law as ars boni et aequi which is starting to re-emerge within International and European Union law (p. 5).

Bibliography

Albertario, E., "La definizione del matrimonio secondo Modestino," in *Studi di diritto romano*, I, Milano 1933.

Astolfi, R., Il *matrimonio nel diritto romano preclassico*, Padova 2000.

Baccari, M. P., *Cittadini popoli e comunione nella legislazione dei secoli IV–VI*, Torino 1996.

Baccari, M. P., "Il concetto di civitas augescens: origine e continuità," *SDHI* LXI (1996).

Baccari, M. P., *Concepito: l'antico diritto per il nuovo millennio*, Torino 2004.

Baccari, M. P., "Alcuni principi del diritto romano per la difesa dell'uomo nella globalizzazione," *Teoria del diritto e dello Stato. Rivista europea di cultura e scienza giuridica* 1 (2005).

Baccari, M. P., *La difesa del concepito nel diritto romano dai Digesta dell'Imperatore Giustiniano*, Torino 2006.

Baccari, M. P., *Curator ventris. Il concepito, la donna e la res publica tra storia e attualità*, Torino 2012.

Botta, F., "Ancora in tema di accusatio adulterii del minor XXV annis," in *Fides Humanitas Ius. Studii in onore di Luigi Labruna*, vol. 1, ed. C. Cascione and C. Masi Doria, Napoli 2007, pp. 439–463.

Botta, F., "Legittimazione, interesse ed incapacità all'accusa nei 'publica iudicia,'" in *AV*, Cagliari 1996.

Bretone, M., *Storia del diritto romano*, Roma-Bari 2001.

Cantarella, F., "Matrimonio e sessualità nella Roma repubblicana: una storia romana di amore coniugale," *BIDR* 39 (1997), pp. 205–219 [= Storia delle donne, 1, 2005, pp. 115–131].

Cantarella, E., "Secondo natura. La biosessualità nel mondo antico," in *BUR*, Milano 2008.

Carcaterra, A., *Le definizioni dei giuristi romani. Metodo mezzi e fini*, Napoli 1966.

Casola, M., "Dote tra Familia e Civitas," *GLOSSAE. European Journal of Legal History* 14 (2017).

Castello, C., *Scritti scelti di diritto romano. Servi filii nuptiae*, Genova 2002.

Catalano, *Diritto e persone, Studi su origine e attualità del sistema romano*, I, Torino 1990.

Dalla, D., "*Ubi Venus mutatur.*" *Omosessualità e diritto nel mondo romano*, Milano 1987.

Daube, D., "The accuser under the lex Iulia de adulteriis," in *Collected Studies in Roman Law*, vol. 1, ed. V. Klostermann, Frankfurt am Main 1991, pp. 561–573.

De Dominicis, M. A., "Sulle origini romano-cristiane del diritto del marito ad accusare 'constante matrimonio' la moglie adultera (A proposito di Dig. 48, 5, 27 [26] pr.)," *SDHI* 16 (1950), pp. 221–253.

Eisenring, G., *Die römische Ehe als Rechtsverhältnis*, Böhlau-Wien-Köln-Wiemar 2002.

Fayer, C., *La familia romana: aspetti giuridici ed antiquari*, vol. 3, *Concubinato Divorzio, Adulterio*, Roma 2005.

Ferretti, P., "Diritto romano e diritto europeo: alcune considerazioni in tema di qui in utero sunt," *Ann. Univ. Ferrara—Sc. Giur. Nuova serie* XIII (1999).

Ferretti, P., *In rerum natura esse. In rebus humanis non esse. L'identità del concepito nel pensiero giurisprudenziale classico*, Milano 2008.

Fontana, G., *Quin in utero sunt. Concetti e condizione giuridica del nascituro nella codificazione di Giustiniano*, Torino 1994.

Gaudemet, J., "Justum matrimonium," *RIDA* 2 (1949).

Gaiussso y Navarrete, M., *Persona: naturaleza original del concepto en los derechos romano y náhuatl*, Xalapa-Veracruz 1992.

Giulina, G., "Unioni omosessuali e diritto romano," *APG* 5 (2016), pp. 111–127.

Honorè, T., "Les droits de l'homme chez Ulpien," in *Le monde Antique et les Droits de l'Homme: actes de la 50e session de la Societé Internationale Fernard De Visscher pour l'Histoire des Droits de l'Antiquité* (Bruxelles, 16–19 septembre 1996), ed. H. Jones, Bruxelles 1998.

Kaser, M., "Rec. M. A. De Dominicis, Sulle origini romano-cristiane del diritto del marito ad accusare 'constante matrimonio' la moglie adultera (A proposito di Dig. 48, 5, [26] pr.)," *SDHI* 16 (1950), pp. 221–253 [= *Iura*, 2 (1951), pp. 324 325].

Lamberti, F., "Convivenze e unioni di fatto nell'esperienza romana: l'esempio del concubinato," in *Unioni di fatto. Dal diritto romano ai diritti attuali*. Atti dell'incontro italo-tedesco (Imperia, 27–28 novembre 2015), ed. G. Viarengo, Torino 2016.

Lamberti, F., "La storiografia sulla familia rmana fra inquadramenti tradizionali e nuove tendenze di ricerca," in *La famiglia tardoantica. Società, diritto, religione*, ed. V. Neri and B. Giratti, Milano, 2016, https://www.ledonline.it/index.php/Erga-Logoi/pages/view/qel-5-famiglia-tardoantica.

Lanfranchi, P., "Le definizioni e il concetto del matrimonio nei retori romani," *SDHI* 2 (1936).

Lobrano, G., "Uxor quodammodo domina. Riflessioni sul Paul. D. 25.2.1," in *Univ. di Sassari-Fac. di Giur.-Pubbl. del Seminario di Diritto Romano*, 6,

Sassari 1989, cap. II, pp. 48–54, ora on-line al sito web http://dirittoestoria.it/dirittoromano/.Lobrano-Uxor.htm.

Lubrano, M., *Persona e homo nell'opera di Gaio. Elementi concettuali del sistema giuridico romano*, Torino 2002.

Mayer-Maly, T., "Das Menschenbild des Rechts," in *Giovanni Paolo II. Le vie della giustizia*, ed. A. Loiodice and M. Vari, Roma 2003.

Onida, P. P., *Studi sulla condizione degli animali non umani nel sistema giuridico romano*, Torino 2002.

Palma, A., "Il nascituro come problema 'continuo': Diritto Romano e Diritto Privato italiano alla luce di recenti asserti giurisprudenziali," *Revista Europea de Historia de las Ideas Políticas y de las Instituciones Públicas* (2014).

Petrucci, M. G., "Quale status per il nascituro?," *Rassegna di diritto civile* (1998).

Quadrato, R., "'Maris atque feminae coniuctio': 'matrimonium' *e unioni di fatto*," *Index* 38 (2010).

Rizzelli, G., "Alcuni aspetti dell'accusa privilegiata in materia di adulterio," *BIDR* 89 (1986), pp. 411–441.

Rizzelli, G., *La lex Iulia de adulteriis. Studi sulla disciplina di adulterium, lenocinum, stuprum*, Lecce 1997.

Rossi, F., *Apparenza del diritto e rapporti di fatto nell'esperienza giuridica di Roma antica*, Firenze 2020.

Sanna, M. V., *Matrimonio e altre situazioni matrimoniali nel diritto romano classico: matrimonium iustum, matrimonium iniustum*, Napoli 2012.

Schulz, F., *I principi di diritto romano*, trad. it., Firenze 1995 (rist. anast. 1946).

Tafaro, S., "I diritti dei fanciulli," in *Scritti in onore di G. Melillo*, vol. III, ed. A. Palma, Napoli 2009.

Tafaro, S., *Ius hominum causa constitutum. Un diritto a misura d'uomo*, Napoli 2009.

Thomas, J. A. C., "Accusatio adulterii," *Iura* 12 (1961), pp. 65–80.

Venturini, C., "'Accusatio adulterii' e politica costantiniana (Per un riesame di CTH 9, 7, 2)," *SDHI* 54 (1988), pp. 66–109.

Venturini, C., "Innovazioni postclassiche in materia di accusatio adulterii," in *Crimina e delicta nel tardo antico: atti del Seminario di studi, Teramo 19–20 gennaio 2001*, ed. F. Lucrezi and G. Mancini, Milano 2003, pp. 17–37.

Visky, K., "Le divorce dans la législation de Justinien," *RIDA* 23 (1976).

Volterra, E., "Iniustum matrimonium," in *Studi in onore di Gaetano Scherillo*, vol. 2, Milano 1972, pp. 441–470.

Volterra, E., "Per lo studio del reato di bigamia," in *Studi in memoria di Umberto Ratti*, ed. E. Albertario, Milano 1934, pp. 387–447.

Volterra, E., "Ancora sulla manus e sul matrimonium," in *Studi in onore di Siro Solazzi*, Napoli 1948, pp. 676–688.

Volterra, E., "La nozione giuridica del conubium," in *Studi in memoria di Emilio Albertario*, vol. 2, Milano 1950, pp. 347–384 (= *Scritti giuridici*, vol. 2, *Famiglia e successioni*, Napoli 1991, pp. 283–320).

Volterra, E., "Quelques observations sur le mariage des filiifamilias," *RIDA* 1 (1948), pp. 213–242.

Volterra, E., "Precisazioni in matria di matrimonio classico," *BIDR* 17 (1975), pp. 245–270.

Volterra, E., "voce *Matrimonio* (diritto romano)," *Enc. dir.* XXV (1975).

Volterra, E., "Per la storia dell'accusatio iure mariti vel patri"," in *Scritti giuridici*, vol. 1, *Famiglia e successioni*, Napoli 1991, pp. 219–278.

Volterra, E., "In tema di 'accusatio adulterii'. I. L'adulterium' della 'sponsa'. II. L'adulterium' dell'uxor in captivitate"," in *Scritti giuridici*, vol. 1, *Famiglia e successioni*, Napoli 1991, pp. 313–328.

Sebastiano Tafaro

Family in historical perspective: Yesterday and today—Rhapsodic peeks between the past and a bit of the present

Abstract: The etymology of Family, contrary to popular belief, derives from Oscan (Faama—famŭli). Imported by the Romans, it meant both goods and people united by a community bond and, over time, passed from a collective meaning (which resulted in class marriage) to a more restricted meaning referring to the patriarchal group (which was born with marriage monogamous). It never had an individualistic value and was linked to the primary need in every community: that of "growth," achieved through gradus societatis, as Cicero illustrated.

Even today we speak of a "wedding," in memory of the fact that the woman who presented herself to her husband was "veiled" (nupta).

As for the meaning of the word used to indicate the union between a man and a woman for procreative purposes, it should be noted that it was indicative of the woman's task: which, precisely, was that of generating; in effect matrimonium was constituted by the fusion of the terms matris and munus, recalling the very purpose of the union, consisting in the duty-office of the woman to give children to the group. It was related to the husband's duty-office of economic support (patris munus).

The spouses (but above all the wife) did not have to love each other but to be faithful, to ensure certainty of filiation, reason and cause of the transition from group marriage to monogamy, as symbolized by the ring that was placed on the finger (the middle finger because from it started a nerve that went straight to the heart, the seat of the feeling of affection and fidelity) and which was therefore called and is still called "faith" (not, for example, love).

Keywords: Familia, matrimonium: sponsalia, nuptiae, nupta, gradus societatis, gens, famuli, monogamy

1. Background

The continuous and assiduous research of new formulations of the contemporary "family" makes it stimulating to revisit the notions of Roman law, which, through the mediation of canon law, reflects many of the legislations of Europe and countries that have been influenced by the tradition deriving from Roman sources.

This, if nothing else, serves to clarify the legal concepts pertaining to the family and to understand what were the anchoring parameters of the constructions elaborated for the family.

The more articulated knowledge of them does not preclude new and different (often deeply different) solutions, as in the case of same-sex unions; it does, however, serve to understand whether they can still fit within the framework of the culture and tradition of legal civilization of European matrix.

Here I focus, essentially, on two aspects: the meaning and purpose of the family in the experience of Roman law and the interactions between family and community.

I am, indeed, convinced that the concept of the family and the legal constructions that characterize it (in our European civilization) had deep roots in Roman law and the legal experience that was the basis of it. This is so even though I do not underestimate (while disagreeing with them to a great extent) the "reasons of those who argue that Roman law is completely outdated and cannot be recalled in the present day, since we have long been faced with the expectations of technological civilization far removed from the *Welthanschauung* of the agrarian-pastoral society, which was the basis of the Roman experience and which deeply permeated Roman law."

This topic is difficult and would require complex and articulate analyses, which have long since been the subject of insightful and lavish doctrine. Therefore, I do not intend to go into the complex issue and numerous literature that has accompanied it, but I would only like to dwell on less highlighted aspects, as a whole and in their connections with each other.

Here, I would only like to focus on the less analyzed aspects, as a whole and in their mutual connections. I think they reveal what and how many contributions certain constructions of Roman law can make to the elaboration of concepts and solutions for the "family of today," giving it profiles of great relevance in the current day-to-day life. The concern that I would like to clarify refer to the importance of the principles of the Roman law that are still relevant in our times and are able to show how far removed from the roots of our civilization are the claims of being able to find the family from individualistic visions and ideas.

It would be useful to revisit points that have long been known to interpreters and have been the subject of reflection and clarification as far back as antiquity.

2. Marriage of "classes"

For a long time Eurocentric prejudice has prevented us from grasping many common features between the ancient civilizations of the Mediterranean area and "primitive" societies.

Where we lose such a prejudicial view and make use of comparative ethnography, we are able to grasp characteristic aspects of human aggregation that are very divergent from today. In them it seems certain the existence of forms of kinship without degrees, which is a consequence of the original equality of siblings of equal sex.

The point was brought out effectively by Lewis H. Morgan, through his investigations of certain groups of North American Indians in the second half of the last century and to the findings of ethno-anthropological research. It is well-known that Morgan, in studying the marriage customs of the Iroquois of North America, noticed a mismatch between the kinship terminology used and the marriage system in place, in America and (more generally) in the geopolitical area of the West, which was that of a couple family.

Among "native" Americans, sons extended the appellation of father to their father's brothers as well and the appellation of mother to their mother's sisters as well. In turn, adult males called children not only their own natural children but also the children of their brothers, while adult females extended the appellation of son also to the children of their sisters. The same appellations did not, however, extend to cross-uncles (mother's brother, father's sister); nor to sisters' children (for men) and brothers' children (for women).

From the above, Morgan hypothesized the existence of a more ancient form of marriage: that of collective unions between groups of brothers and groups of sisters. For this purpose he spoke about a "classificatory" kinship system, originally axed on "matriarchy."

Subsequent research has confirmed the existence, among various populations, of this form of marriage; moreover, it is attested by sources concerning peoples of antiquity, from Indo-European or properly Italic backgrounds, and it is reflected not only in certain aspects of the Roman religion, but also and above all in the Latin names of kinship. It should be emphasized that these practices are dated back to high antiquity, of which there are obviously no more traces in the Rome of the historic age.

Only the principle of equality of siblings and descent from forms of collective marriage can explain the structure of a group such as the gens and its kinship without degrees. It is controversial whether, in fact it was the gens (clan) that was the first form of aggregation of men. In this regard, Franciosi has argued that the familia, as we know, was born and established at a later stage within the gens on the basis of the introduction of monogamous marriage and the privatization of collective wealth. I have recently expressed my doubts on this point, speculating that a very small nucleus, which only by approximation we can refer to the "familia," may have preceded the formation of larger structures having "political" values, such as the gens.

3. Matriarchy?

As long as humans lived by pure gathering (hunting, fishing, spontaneous gathering of the fruits of the soil and subsoil) the aggregating or institutionalizing elements of marriage forms were extremely tenuous. Marriage was exogamic, as Caesar attests for the Britons, who married in groups of 10 or 12 (deni duodenique), mostly through series of brothers (maxime inter se fratres) and series of sisters.

At this stage, wealth and prosperity were created by both sexes, as Tacitus points out when speaking about the Finni. While the fertility necessary to ensure more wealth procurers was the prerogative of women, giving precisely the female sex priority and superiority. Precise evidence of this has been found, revealed by archaeology, corroborated by the few but circumstantial sources relating to early antiquity. All of which seem to converge on one aspect: the exclusion of an actual subordination of the female to the male; indeed, "from a whole frame of reference, which also takes into account aspects of the earliest religiosity, there emerges a greater social importance of the woman. I speak of social importance, not matriarchy or gynecocracy, which represent only institutional projections of patriarchal society in societies that did not know forms of despotic domestic power."

In this regard, great credit must be given to Bachofen, who, albeit perhaps too radically and exaggeratedly, argued for the superiority and prevalence, in the earliest forms of societal organization, of women, hypothesizing the existence of a regulatory and commanding power of women, best defined by the term *Frauenherrschaft* (woman's command/rule), which he preferred to the customary *Mutterrecht* (mother's law); the Swiss jurist and scholar on the basis of much evidence from the sources relating to some ancient peoples such as, Lycians, the Lydians, the inhabitants of the Balearic Islands, hypothesized the pre-eminence of women flowing from the type of unions aimed at procreation. Originally there were not individual marriages, but marriages of a collective nature, and in relation to them there was not a supremacy of man over woman in the sense of the

Roman family, but a social superiority of woman over man, since the first discoveries, are the work of women.

The scholar argued that three periods would follow one another: agamy or promiscuity followed by matriarchy, and finally patriarchy.

This would be matched by the fact that the most ancient deities would also have been women. Throughout the planet, in fact there is a significant flowering of female deities, mostly related to the "primary" function of the birth of life, procreation, fertility. There has, in this regard, been talk of the GREAT DEA, at the origin of the world and/or the universe: certainly of life. After all, the Earth itself was seen as a female deity, Gaia, while the Phrygian Cybele, imported into Rome as Magna Mater, was even regarded as the "Mother of the gods." Next to whom should be mentioned, as deities of birth, the cult of Mater Matuta and the goddess Bona (Goddess of fertility), also called "great mother." She was a pre-Roman Italic Goddess and not from Greece, although there was later assimilation with the Hellenic Leucothea. The Goddess dates back to matriarchy and there are visible traces of her as far back as 1500 BC. But traces of the Great Mother are found in every part of the world, as far back as 30,000 years ago.

A similar path can be found on other continents as well: just remember the goddess of creation Nüwa, in China; the goddess Devi in India, the goddess Mut in ancient Egypt; without omitting Pachamama: the great Mother Goddess, goddess of the earth, agriculture and fertility, of the Latin American continent. We can easily deduce from this, the existence of social arrangements if not centered around women, at least such as to give the female sex relevance and incidence equal to the male; with the knowledge that growth achieved mainly through gestations and consequent births depended on it.

And, on reflection, many reasons led to the recognition of women's superiority:

Medicine. While the man goes hunting and fishing, in packs, the woman stays at her dwelling, the cave, the hut, depending on whether we refer to the Paleolithic or the Neolithic. Later will come the domus, in more recent times, when the woman will stay at home and in addition taking care of household chores, some of which are very important, with a digging stick, an object found at the archaeological level, she will begin to study herbs and tubers. Even the invention of cooking food is a female invention, an embryonic medicine is developed, in the sense that by studying herbs, the woman notices which herb is toxic and which is not, which is edible and which is not. Which one has certain pharmaceutical properties (pharmacos) and which one does not have these properties. In addition, weaving, like pottery, are also female inventions.

Reproduction of the species. In the face of primitive humanity, it acquires a mystical, sacred, inexplicable character. Also, because the time between mating and generation is long enough for primitive peoples to have memories of certain facts.

Then also a number of other activities. For example, MANTICS, that is, the art of prophesying, is peculiar to the female element. The Sibyls, the Pythia and so on. While in Rome the art of prophesying is forbidden because it is believed that women with their prophecies could endanger the rigidly patriarchal structure that Roman society has now assumed. In Greece, however, it is practiced.

Finally, the MESTRUAL CYCLE itself, which is seen among primitive peoples with its LINK WITH THE MOON PHASES, as an almost superhuman character of woman. This connection with the lunar phases is especially important if we keep in mind that at all primitive cosmogonies, the Moon, through an anticipation that scientists today tend to corroborate, is seen as a fragment of the Earth-mother. There is thus a link between the woman-Moon and the early female deities

There is even male envy: expressed in the paradoxical ritual of the couvade.

Even Caesar, to those who (because of his suspected homosexuality) accused him of being a "woman" and, consequently, unfit for noteworthy endeavors, replied in the Senate by recalling that Semiramis had been queen of Syria and the Amazons had ruled Asia, even though they were women; citing this not as a reference to a myth, but as facts that happened and were well known.

It is not surprising, therefore, that with regard to remote antiquity, many sources attest to female offspring for populations of the Mediterranean East or the transition phase toward individual paternity and male supremacy through mechanisms of offspring attribution based on presumptive elements (physical resemblance, priority in female possession, etc.).

On the very level of the earliest economic activities we are not given to glimpsing male supremacy: passim enim comitantur pariterque praedare petunt attests Tacitus; and the same early division of labor (hunting, digging stick research) coupled with female craft activities (spinning, weaving, etc.) do not legitimize a superiority of the male. Add the importance of motherhood and the rearing of offspring in an archaic society and it will be understood how even in the face of religion the first priestesses and soothsayers were women. The magical-religious aspects legitimize on the ideological level the real social importance of women.

4. New configuration of the family

Despite this we know that societies blossomed into patriarchy and a progressive and absorbing predominance of males.

By what such radical change was brought about is perhaps easy to reconstruct.

Hunting, although practiced by both males and women, as Tacitus attested when speaking of the Finns, because of recurrent gestations ended up becoming a predominantly male activity. At a later stage, the desire/need for greater certainty and stability regarding the supply of foodstuffs necessary for subsistence prompted the setting aside of foodstuffs and livestock, giving rise to animal husbandry and production, resulting in the appropriation of a surplus removed from the group's immediate consumption.

Thus, the logic of appropriation took over. It, however, contrasted with the traditional logic of collective consumption (of captured or killed game or of the fruits of the earth caught on the spot), of which Gaius of the Res cottidianae preserved traces. It was ranching, which also entailed the tendency to land appropriation (as a grazing site), that caused the reversal of the initial relations between the sexes. For these specific reasons, the ranching peoples as a rule have patriarchal family structures.

Thus, the mechanism of accumulation was triggered, which pitted the "private" (small nucleus organized around a single individual, which would become the "family" as we still know it today) against the "social" (clan, tribe).

Franciosi highlighted this transition, observing that "the privatization of production vis-à-vis the group postulates the privatization of consumption and the consumers themselves of the wealth produced or accumulated, both in life and in death of the paterfamilias, that is, the privatization of the offspring, formerly reared collectively within the group, as numerous testimonies relating to the ancient world show. But the certainty of paternity is achieved only with the institution of monogamous marriage and the woman's obligation of fidelity, the violation of which is punishable by death."

In other words, if before for the children, collectively reared by the clan, it was not relevant to know paternity now, with the desire to pass on to them (and only to them) how much one has accumulated arises the need to have certainty that they are really one's own children. To which "class marriage" could no longer provide an adequate answer. Instead, it was necessary to introduce a reproductive system that could guarantee with certainty the provenance of each infant. This could only be ensured by the union in which the woman could only unite with one man. Therefore, progressively we saw the disappearance of group marriage and the establishment of MONOGAMIC MATRIMONY.

The ensuing transformation was accompanied by a specific philosophical and conceptual elaboration, from which arose the patrimonial conception of the family, resulting in the exaltation of the role and power of the head of the family (paterfamilias), the obligation of fidelity understood (unilaterally) as the wife's fidelity; meaning that she was not only to think only of her husband but was to follow his fortunes. That is, for example, if she ran for office she had to support him at the polls, if she had enemies she had to side with her husband and not with her enemies. In other words, it was fidelity of life, but profoundly different from how we conceive it now. For us fidelity means affective, exclusive physical relationship, and instead here it means above all social relationship, that is, being on the husband's side, and this makes the woman live her life in function of her husband.

The result was the accentuation of parental ties on the male side (adgnatio) and succession in inheritance (for a long time) only in the male line.

This new formation constituted the *familia* and became progressively detached from the larger original group of the gens, so that "[t]he two structurally and historically different 'familial' formations known to ancient Roman society are thus on the one hand the family—born on the basis of the privatization of wealth and institutionalized monogamy—on the other hand the gens, an older organism that arose in remote times from a different marriage regime of a collective and exogamic character."

5. Familia in Rome

The term familia did not originate either from Rome or, more generally, from the Latins; moreover, it originally had exclusively patrimonial meanings.

On the origin of the word, we have one indisputable testimony, which affirms its origin from the Oscans. Festus stated that the term seems to be subsumed from an Oscan voice indicating servitude:

> Festi (L. 77) v. ***famuli***: *Famuli origo ab Oscis dependit, apud quos servus famel nominabatur, unde et familia vocata*[1].

The term for the Oscans was also connected with *faama*, which denoted the house and, therefore, meant, that is, the whole of the *famŭli* (wife, children, servants and slaves who were in the dwelling of a head of the house).

In Rome *familia*, in the last instance, usually was used to indicate the set of "living people" grouped in a domus and constituting a single, unified organism under the power of the *paterfemilias*, with language normally declined to the masculine. In this meaning, the term referred to both men (*filii*, wives, other

1 (Tr., *famuli trae origine dagli Osci, presso I quali il servo era nominato famel, dal che anche la famiglia prende nome):*

freemen subject in various capacities to the *potestas* of the father, slaves) and animals.

In many contexts *familia* was used also together with pecunia: in this case the endiadi *familia pecuniaque* included "slaves and livestock," but toward the end of the Republic it took on the meaning of patrimony.

The terms of *familia*, in the use of Roman legal language, indicated multiple and less unambiguous realities than those expressed today by "family." In attempting to trace its history and summarize its meanings, the jurisconsult *Ulpianus* attempts to identify two main strands of the meanings attributed to *familia*; in fact, he identified a primary bipartition in the meanings of the term, specifying that they were to be divided into two basic groups (genus): the one in which *familia* concerned things (goods) and the one in which it was intended to look at persons:

> D. 50. 16. 195. 1, Ulp. 46 *ad ed.: "Familiae" appellatio qualiter accipiatur, videamus. et quidem varie accepta est: nam et in res et in personas deducitur. In res, ut puta in lege duodecim tabularum his verbis "adgnatus proximus familiam habeto". Ad personas autem refertur familiae significatio ita, cum de patrono et liberto loquitur lex: "ex ea familia", inquit, "in eam familiam": et hic de singularibus personis legem loqui constat*[2].

---

2 We refer on the term "familia" and how is used. There are different meanings: in fact it is used both with regard to goods and with regard to people. Referred to goods such as, for example, in the law of the XII tables with these words "the neighbor agnate will have the family." On the other hand, the meaning of familia concerns people when the law regarding the relationship between patron and freedman says "from that family" or "in that family": and here it turns out that the law speaks of single persons. It is hardly necessary to observe that the attempt to arrange the "matter" treated using partitions capable of allowing classifications and distinctions was typical of an argumentative technique that penetrated Roman legal thought through the techniques of Greek dialectics, which had great diffusion in the world Roman: suffice it to mention the significant summa divisio of law proposed by Gaius, at the beginning of his commentaries: Gai. 1. 8: *Omne ius quo utimur, vel ad personas pertinet vel ad res vel ad actiones*; sul punto v. R. Quadrato, *Le Institutiones nell'insegnamento di Gaio*, Jovene, Napoli, 1979, 5 ed ivi ntt. 19–20; in general terms on the introduction and adoption of tecniques focused on *diairesis* v. M. Bretone, *Storia del diritto romano*, Laterza, Bari 1987, 184ff. See also M. Talamanca, "*Lo schema 'genus-species' nelle sistematiche dei giuristi romani,*" in *Colloquio Italo-Francese La filosofia greca e il diritto romano (Roma, 14–17 aprile 1973)*, t. II, *Quaderno dell'Accademia nazionale dei Lincei* N. 221, 1977, 3ff. L'A., osserva: "le tecniche divisorie, di cui lo schema genus-species rappresenta—si può dire—il paradigma, costituiscono il momento portante di tutta l'attività sistematica—per usare di questa terminologia—dei giuristi romani."

The concept of familia consisting of the union of persons united by the bond of blood had been the last to be established, as is evident from the jurist's expository order. It had experienced an important bipartition: familia proprio iure, *familia communi iure*. The *familia proprio iure* embraced the nucleus grouped under the power of a father of the family, either by natural bonds or by legal bonds; it included the father of the family himself, the mother of the family, the sons, daughters and their descendants, the subordinates in servile condition. The familia communi iure, according to the jurist, consisted of all those who, although part of families that had become autonomous, had formerly belonged to a single familia.

In the earliest age familia denoted things (i.e., patrimony), as is clear from the XII Tables, which in the prescription adgnatus proximus familiam habeto used the term to denote the inheritance.

There are many contexts in which the term familia referred to people, their conditions, and their aggregations.

The Twelve Tables themselves contained prescriptions, such as ex ea familia or in eam familiam, in which familia denoted persons belonging to a nucleus, which was considered both as a unit and with regard to individual members.

A particular use of the term recorded cases in which familia was used to denote a corpus, recognized by law as unitary although composed of many persons.

One essential point in the concept of familia was the following: its derivation from law; it did not depend exclusively on connotations (which there might have been), such as marriage and filiation, but rather on legal qualification.

Which prefigured as familia also the individual: Ulpianus expressly attests:

> D. 50. 16. 195. 2: … *Pater autem familias appellatur, qui in domo dominium habet, recteque hoc nomine appellatur, quamvis filium non habeat: non enim solam personam eius, sed et ius demonstramus: denique et pupillum patrem familias appellamus. Et cum paterfamilias moritur, quotquot capita ei subiecta fuerint, singulas familias incipiunt habere: singuli enim patrum familiarum nomen subeunt. Idemque eveniet et in eo qui emancipatus est: nam et hic sui iuris effectus propriam familiam habet.*[3]

The jurist made explicit the cases in which the familia was considered to be such even if it consisted of only one person, that is, a single pater familia: those who had no children, the orphan who was still impubescent and under guardianship, and the emancipated (i.e., even though still single). Finally, the jurist recalled

3 See the translation above.

that upon the death of the father all children, subject to him, became autonomous and each with his own family.

In conclusion, the familia was the result of legal creation.

Regarding it, however, it should be clear that it was not the result of arbitrary visions, but was a consequence of the way of considering man in the whole of the place and purpose within the entities to which he belonged: which were the Cosmos and the Civitas.

6. *Familia* and Cosmos. The sacra

In antiquity and, for that matter in Rome, it was believed that "life," including human life, was embedded in a "cycle," not dependent on humans but governed by laws of cosmic value. It was required a profound religiosity, understood as an awareness of belonging to a transcendent order of the universe, which embraced in a single afflatus the seasons of man along with the seasons of the fields, the alternation of day and night, the movements of the sun and stars, and the existence of inescapable moments: birth, childhood, maturity, and old age were held to be universal scans that were valid for both men and cities. They were perceivable and quantifiable through the law of numbers, capable of incorporating and expressing data about the course of the entire universe and the cycle of life.

All this was filtered through the belief that there was in the universe and corresponding to the law of nature a course of birth, growth, decay and death, having general and universal value. This idea was certainly derived from the observation of what happened to men, but it was also applied to their organized collectivity: Civitas, the confluence structure of individuals, was, in fact, considered in terms of physiological development, according to a widespread tendency, which interpreted the history of Rome as the development of a living organism, inserted in the terrestrial cycle, at the center of which was man; which therefore was pre-existent to other forms of aggregation.

In the universal life "cycle" Civitas was not antecedent, but rather the next stage in the organization of men. First there was man, who was born into a familia. To such a conclusion seems to me to be led by consideration of the role and importance played by the sacra, both for individuals and for collectivities.

The sacra were central to the Roman experience. Consequently, one cannot have a satisfactory understanding of Roman reality if one does not take into account the sacra. They were both publica and private; the latter continued to persist even after the establishment of the Civitas, probably because they were pertinent to man regardless of the group to which he belonged:

Festi, L. 284: *Publica sacra quae publico sumptu pro populo fiunt, quaeque pro montibus, pagis, curiis, sacellis; at privata quae pro singulis hominibus, familiis, gentibus fiunt.*[4]

Indeed, the familia had profiles that conceived of it as a single entity, shaped under the power of a head (the paterfamilias), but without excluding that the members, both free and servants, had their own positions and roles, relevant even autonomously, as was certainly the case with regard to the sacra. The term itself, as has been pointed out, referred to a concrete notion of the "collectivity," made up of men with their earthly and supernatural perspectives, which is not easy for us to grasp, because we are frequently used to underestimate the importance and incidence of the sacra in Roman society, not fully perceiving the implications arising from the fact that they scanned every aspect and every moment of Roman life. The sacra privata were an expression of man and his fundamental associative forms. According to Festus the sacra privata, were articulated in several degrees: regarding individuals, regarding families and regarding the people: "pro singulis hominibus, familiis, gentibus fiunt." The order of different spheres of impact of the sacra privata in Festus' passage is not only representative of the existing, but also contains a description of the stages through which human life evolved. It, therefore, expressed the temporal scansion and a hierarchy of values, at the apex of which viera vertexed man, first as an individual then later included in the family and public structure (which had originally been the gens). Consequently, the sacra privata were irrepressible and imperishable: "sacra privata perpetuo manento," said Cicero (De legibus, 2. 9. 22); with respect to them the Civitas could not interfere, having, instead, to leave total autonomy to private individuals, since they were the exclusive prerogative of men and of its essential form of aggregation, which was the family. The sacra privata marked every essential moment of Roman man and the Roman family: they were the religious transposition of the cycle of life, having universal values.

It followed that the paterfamilias was at once the head of the family, but also its priest and the guardian, within it, of custom.

In the Archaic Age and the first phase of the Respublica the "family" was deeply embedded in its gens and, always, was embedded in the Civitas. This made the behavior of its members and especially of the pater subject to the careful and severe assessment of the Censors.

The whole was considered an expression of universal laws of the Cosmos.

---

4 See Festi, L. 298, su *popularia sacra*. V. M. Fiorentini, *Ricerche sui culti gentilizi*, cit., partic. pp. 106f., 251, 293, 355f.

Almost "concentric circles" were considered to exist in which man's journey was realized and in which the family was also a part, as the first basic cell. In them "the two extremes are humanity and the family, the minimal cell of which the individual is a part; between these extremes lies the state, an institution both natural and historical."

Of such a perspective, at the end of the *Respublica*, Cicero gave a lucid testimony, in De officiis.

The Arpinate in his examination of the societas hominum, sketched the succession of models that had historically connoted the organization of society, with the intention of specifying its foundation and justification. His conclusion was that all existing forms were established by nature (before men), through an insoluble web of varied and articulated ties, sometimes even difficult to understand, at the center of which was the family.

The family constituted the knot of every organization and of all humanity.

The conception of the family reflected ideas about the nature-society relationship; which in the work of the Arpinate followed the traces marked by the dispute (raised by Greek thinkers) between those who believed that the only natural order should be the whole of humanity and those who legitimized the division of men on the basis of citizenship. Cicero, believed that the City, with the exclusivity of the relationship of membership reserved for cives, was the model of man's reference and derived from nature, since the principles of nature were not realized through a single agglomeration (such as humanity as a whole would be), but rather through a ladder in a form of aggregation, intersecting with each other, expanding into forms of increasing size, imagined as concentric circles of different widths. In this progression of forms everyone found his or her position, which postulated membership either in a narrower group or in the larger group in which the narrower group fit. It was the range and progressiveness of groupings that gave the motivations and justifications to each group and realized the principles of nature.

In the ideological and cultural context of the time, they were then convinced that no matter how varied the forms of organization might be, there was one that always existed and existed, at all times, among all living things, humans and animals: the family.

It could not be an end in itself, but had to integrate and harmonize with the gradualness and other forms of aggregation of human society.

It followed that:

1. the Roman family realized the principles of "nature" and, therefore, in law, had natural law as its point of reference;

2. the Roman family was functional to the person and to the order (cosmic, human and divine) to which the living person belonged;
3. the Roman family was the first but not the only form of organization of society.

7. Nature

Based on the picture afore described it is essential to underline the importance of the link between family and nature. Therefore, it is worth examining more closely the indication that the family is based on "nature," which is echoed also in contemporary enunciations; such as, the Italian Constitution, where explicitly a juxtaposition between family and nature is made:

> Art. 29 *La Repubblica riconosce i diritti della famiglia come società naturale fondata sul matrimonio.*

Since, therefore, the conviction of the existence of a synapse between family and nature, as a limiting and at the same time inspiring criterion of law, is still alive, it is worth making an effort to go back to the origins and, specifically, to the Roman thought.

Here, again I would like to remind the essential thought of Cicero.

The Roman author affirmed the existence of principles dictated by "nature" for human communities and societies. Among them, the first derives from the *ratio* and the communicative and persuasive capacity of speech. This principle applied to humanity considered as a whole and served to bring men together, unifying them in a "natural society." It was not, however, sufficient by itself: it had to be integrated with the other principle, also an expression of the universal law common, consisting (as the Arpinate specified in § 54 below) in the aspiration/necessity to procreate, which demanded the union of male and female in marriage. Consequently, the essentiality and priority of procreation was declared, which was considered the primary and irrepressible end of human nature and society. It imposed marriage as the pivot of the family and, the Arpinate pointed out, it was the basis for the *Respublica*, which originated from it, so much so that, in this way, the family could be considered "*principium urbis et quasi seminarium rei publicae*."

Cicero, in this way, placed the family at the basis of the city's formation process, guaranteeing its permanence.

Through the references to urbs and res pubblica Cicero intended to emphasize two complementary but not entirely identical aspects. On one hand, the formation of the city: it had been the work of families. On the other hand, the life, the persistence of the community: it could not take place without the families, for without the families the city itself could not pursue its purpose.

Here it is worth reflecting on the expression quasi *seminarium rei publicae*. It is necessary, in this regard, to bear in mind that the Latin meaning of *quasi* did not correspond to our "*quasi*." In the language of the Romans, quasi served to introduce an analogical type of discourse and, therefore, to indicate that one situation was to be considered equal to another. Cicero did not mean that the family only approximately could be considered as the "seedbed" of the Republic. Instead, he was asserting that the family, for the Republic, operated as a "nursery," because it should be considered as the nursery of the Republic.

This, because, as he reiterated the formation and existence of the Res Publica derived from families understood as the center of bond-making and the birth of offspring.

In this regard Cicero, specified the concept of "nature" as the basis of the family. It resided in the creation of bonds based around marriage aimed at procreation, since there was a need to allow the expansion of the groups converging in Civitas; which could not have grown and sustained itself if there were not the unions created through marriages, with the birth of children resulting from them.

Cicero's beliefs did not remain the opinion of an author or of a period, but, partly because of the constructive force and dissemination capacity of the Greek matrix (from which it emanated), it became established and was followed throughout the whole experience of Roman law.

A passage from Ulpian confirms this:

> D. 1. 1. 1. 3, Ulp. 1 *Inst.: Ius naturale est, quod natura omnia animalia docuit: nam ius istud non humani generis proprium, sed omnium animalium, quae in terra, quae in mari nascuntur, avium quoque commune est. Hinc descendit maris atque feminae coniunctio, quam nos matrimonium appellamus, hinc liberorum procreatio, hinc educatio: videmus etenim cetera quoque animalia, feras etiam istius iuris peritia censeri.*[5]

Already *ictu oculi* the Ulpian commentary shows considerable coincidence with Cicero's passages, of which it seems almost a paraphrase. There is an undoubted closeness between Ulpian's passage and those of Cicero, despite the temporal

5 Tr.: Natural law is what nature has taught to all animated beings: as a matter of fact, this right is not proper to mankind, but it is common to all animated beings that are born on land, in the sea, and it is also common to birds. Hence the union of male and female, which union we call marriage; from here comes the procreation of children; hence the education. We see, in fact, that even all animated beings, including wild beasts, are considered in a congruous way in the law.

distance. It is neither unfounded nor ahistorical, for Cicero was read and known by the jurists of the Principate. His references to nature must have found easy reception due to the fact that the notions of "nature" and "natural law" had had great penetration in legal literature and had been the basis for the construction of the concept of ius naturale, current until the age of the Severans. The latest doctrine clarified the Pythagorean and Empedoclean ancestry notion of natural law, moreover already highlighted by Cicero.

These precedents, although obscured by the assertion of the superiority of man advocated by Aristotle, were nevertheless present to many Roman thinkers and, among jurists, to Ulpian, who based on them the statements contained in the fragment of D. 1.1.1.3.

One can, therefore, discern a fundamental continuity of approach between the thought of Cicero and that of Ulpianus, both expressions of conceptions circulating in the Mediterranean, thanks to the power of conviction and diffusion of the Greek matrix and the Pythagorean currents; which had aroused new expectations, not least as a result of the popularization made of them by Apollonius of Tyane, and his hagiographer Flavius Philostratus.

The interactions, perhaps even unconscious, that, in this cultural climate, were created between Cicero's utterances and those of Ulpianus appears clear and rooted in ancient thought and Roman law, with variety of facets and accentuations.

Cicero, as we have seen, affirmed the existence of a society, common to humans and animals, organized in different gradus, based on natural law. Ulpian moved in a similar vein "in his definition of ius naturale as a law common to men and other animate beings, where the parallelism with Cicero's reflections on coniunctio, procreatio and educatio liberorum is evident in that reference to coniunctio, procreatio and educatio liberorum, on the subject of coniugium and societas liberorum."

It does not seem to me far-fetched to generalize to the point of asserting that throughout the experience of Roman law there has been a conviction that on the one hand the family was derived from natural law and as such could not depend on ius civitatis (i.e., we would say today, on the laws of the state), and on the other hand, that it fulfilled a primary purpose constituted by its contribution to the growth of the community and the Respublic.

8. *Augescere*

Antiquity is permeated and dominated by an aspiration/need of growth.

In the Mediterranean area, for example, the promise of "growth" deeply pivots God's covenant with Abraham and Israel. A sign of God's own benevolence, repeatedly in the Bible, growth appears to be seen as the deepest and most constant aspiration and projection of peoples.

Rome and its history denote that "growth" was the purpose, but also as the primary "need", of humanity, human society, Civitas, familia.

A reflection and at the same time, a confirmation can be discerned in a different way of considering what we call "legal capacity."

Today's legal systems, as well known, attribute (so-called) legal capacity to the birth of the natural person and eligibility for the effective exercise of one's rights (legal capacity) upon attainment of intellectual and psychological maturity (presumptively set at an age varying between 18 and 21). In the Roman system, on the other hand, one had as a point of reference the fact of not being subject to the potestas of others and, for the effective exercise of rights the pubertas, which also marked the moment of participation in public life with entry into the centuriate comitium.

The reason for the reference to puberty and not to intellectual maturity, the absence of which in the child who had become pubescent (at just 14 if male, 12 if female) the Romans were aware of the ability to contribute to "growth" (with the acquisition of sexual maturity and thus the possibility of procreation) that was the watershed of people's condition. Moreover, among them it was a common belief that puberty gave rise to a rebirth of the person. It was puberty that was the watershed between childhood and adolescence, discerned not in maturity of thought, but in the ability to contribute or not to the "growth" of the community. Therefore, the pubescent, with the acquired ability to procreate and, consequently, to increase one's community (familia and Res Publica) was recognized as a man fully capable of carrying out political activities and legally relevant negotiations, becoming part of the comitium and acquiring full prominence with regard to public law and the possibility of being part of the army, of participating in the conquest and division of booty.

The attainment of puberty was made known by "fathers" of the children, who, as a testimony to the occurrence of puberty, presented their children in public, on the occasion of the spring festival of Liberalia, highlighting the close link existing BETWEEN THE CYCLES OF LIFE AND NATURE.

The notions presupposed by the reference to puberty thus turn out to refer both to the individual boy and to his status as a civis.

This very important aspect of life and its conception by the Romans also confirms that they conceived of man in a dimension that projected him toward growth and that this, according to natural law, took place in the family based on heterogamic and heterosexual marriage.

Growth also pertained to the terms by which the Community was referred to.

Indeed, the word pop(u)lus, used to refer to the collectivity of the Romans, appears to have been derived from a Mediterranean root imported by the Etruscans and equivalent to "grow." So that the terms "people" and "public" were the projection in language of the idea of growth, and all of Rome's development and its history were conceived in terms of growth.

This is evidenced by the incisive picture outlined by Sextus Pomponius regarding the formation, the evolution of law and the structure of Rome, where the author always used expressions that chiseled the being of the Roman legal experience in terms of growth. Clearly, throughout the legal experience of the Romans, the idea of civitas augescens, never faded in Roman thought and Roman law.

9. *Viripotens*: Age of engagement

With regard to the women, we discover a similar path: they entered society through the familia, which was seen as the analog of the entry of males into the people. For them, therefore, marriage was corresponding to what for males was the public presentation during the Liberalia.

For girls, "the path followed was that of the extension to females of concepts elaborated for male puberty… the tendency was to apply progressively to girls ideas and notions elaborated for males. This was done according to a path traced and guided by jurists." But while for males puberty marked the transition from familia to civitas, for women it was the transition from their own to a new family, through marriage; to which they were destined by their fathers. So that, it was marriage that marked the maiden's (and, more generally, the woman's) entry into social life. For the woman, puberty was not expressed by the term puber, but rather by viripotens: indicative of her sexual capacity and by which it was intended to emphasize that her entry into the community was functional to procreation (and with it the growth of the family and the city), in relation to which she was to assist the male. It was, therefore, marriage that was defined as women's maturity as virum pati capacity. The expression, in fact, did not constitute a simple reference to a woman's fitness for sexual intercourse, but was referred to a woman's ability to unite in marriage, for the realization of the procreative function recognized as primary and prevalent for men.

In this way viripotence was defined not only on the basis of female physiology, but also and perhaps primarily in relation to the complementary capacity of women to enable the realization of the procreative capacity of the pubes, from whose concept we started to identify "viripotens" (in ancient virapatiens).

About this, we retrieved clear testimony once again by Festus:

> *Festi* Th. 330. 6: _ ||*Pubes et qui + pubem generare potest; his + incipit || esse a quattuordecim annis: femina aquodecem + || viri potens, sive patiens ut quidam putant* ||[6]

> *Festi* L. 296. 18: _||*Pubes + et qui pubem + generare potest. Is incipit || esse a quattuordecim annis: femina a duodecim || viri potens, sive patiens, ut quidam putant.*[7]

Paul the Deacon's Epitome also reproduced the definition with some seemingly formal, actually relevant variations from the original festus:

> Festi P. L. 297. 2 = Th. 331: *Pubes puer, qui iam generare potest. Is incipit esse ab annis quattuordecim; femina viripotens a duodecim.*[8]

The result was that maidens were given in marriage too prematurely, as Tacitus denounced, contrasting this (for him deplorable) custom with the Germans one. Who allowed maidens to harden their bodies by living free in the open air (in fields and thickets) before allocating them to marriage, without the excessive haste (which he stigmatized) with which the Romans placed their daughters in marriage; all in the likeness and analogy of NATURE, which in Spring makes fields, trees and men flourish.

The ages of 14 and 12, which seem to have constituted a presumption of puberty, were established, not without resistance, by Roman jurisprudence (in the school of the Proculians), for the sake of certainty and to curb the arbitrariness of the patres. The choice of those dates depended on the desire to anchor such a decisive moment in the universal order of the cosmos expressed by the number 7 (*nodus totius universi*, according to Cicero), because "So many and such were the virtues attributed to 'seven' that the number was taken as a symbol of excellence, in the order of nature …" 14 was a multiple of 7, which by the way was a masculine number, like all odd numbers. A female number, that is, an even, early

6 Th. 330. 6: *Pubes* is who … can generate the pubem (to mean the puberty, for the majority of commentators, the pubes, according to my reading); to these … begins to be (belong?) from 14 years: the female from 10 … viripotente, or virisbearing) according to what some believe.

7 L. 296. 18: _*Pubes* is who … can generate pubem (to be understood the puberty, for most commentators, the pubes, according to my reading). He begins to be such at 14: the female from 12 becomes viripotent or virebearing, as general beliefs.

8 (*Pubes* (è) the child, who can already generate. He begins to be such from the age of 14: while the woman becomes viripotent from the age of 12).

number, was indicated for woman, because it was believed that woman matured earlier than the male.

Although manifestly inadequate, the ages indicated, sometimes rigorously in the Republican age by Servius Sulpicius Rufus, who recognized no consequences to marriages contracted before those ages, clashed with the practice of "early marriages." It appears to have been widespread throughout the Roman experience, including the Christian period, and found understanding among the jurists themselves, during the Principate: witness a passage from Salvius Julianus, who argued that benevolence was needed toward the father who gave his daughter as a wife while still a girl, because, according to him, he would have done so "out of affection":

> D. 27. 6. 11. 3–4, Ulp. *Libro trigesimo quinto ad edictum: Iulianus libro vicesimo primo digestorum tractat, in patrem debeat dari haec actio, qui filiam minorem duodecim annis nuptum dedit. et magis probat patri ignoscendum esse, qui filiam suam maturius in familiam sponsi perducere voluit: affectu enim propensiore magis quam dolo malo id videri fecisse.*[9]

Julian, as well as, earlier Neratius, is reluctant to give any recognition to early marriage having a maiden not yet 12 years old enter her husband's house did not give rise to a marriage, but it was not without effect; for it would, in any case, constitute an engagement. His solution (or his artifice) had no luck, so much so that Ulpianus, in reporting it, was fond of denying that that construction had any foundation and could be accepted:

> D. 24. 1. 32. 27, Ulp. *Libro trigesimo tertio ad Sabinum: Si quis sponsam habuerit, deinde eandem uxorem duxerit cum non liceret, an donationes quasi in sponsalibus factae valeant, videamus. Et Iulianus tractat hanc quaestionem in minore duodecim annis, si in domum quasi mariti immatura sit deducta: ait enim hanc sponsam esse, etsi uxor non sit. Sed est verius, quod Labeoni videtur et a nobis et a Papiniano libro decimo quaestionum probatum est, ut, si quidem praecesserint sponsalia, durent, quamvis iam uxorem esse putet qui duxit, si vero non praecesserint, neque sponsalia esse, quoniam non fuerunt, neque nuptias, quod nuptiae esse non potuerunt.*[10]

---

9 (Tr.: Giuliano, in the 21st book of the Digesti, wonders whether this action should be given against the father, who married a daughter under 12 years of age. And he considers it more acceptable that we should prefer to forgive the father, that prematurely he wanted to give his daughter in marriage by letting her enter the house of his fiancé: it must, in fact, be considered that he acted more out of affection than with malice).

10 (Tr.: If one had a fiancée and then married her even though it was not lawful, we have to see if the donations are worth considering them as if they had been made in the betrothal. Julian deals with this question regarding the twelve-year-old girl who was brought into the house her husband while she was immature: he maintains that she is

Julian's proposed solution based on the consideration that in early marriage, as a rule, betrothal must certainly precede marriage itself; so that it could be taken for granted. The low age of the maiden was no obstacle to it, since it was known that, unlike marriage, in betrothal (which was not already projected to procreation) there was no need to indicate a minimum age; it could even take place from birth. This is confirmed by common examples of betrothals to maidens still in early childhood and then given in marriage prematurely even throughout the Principality: Augustus, for example, concluded the betrothal "between a niece of Attalus vix annicula and Tiberius Claudius Nero."

Still at the end of the "classical" experience Modestine could, therefore, assert that there was no minimum age for engagements and (but perhaps the point was a consequence of a correction made by the compilers of Justinian's Digesta) inferred that the virtues of the "seven" should also be invoked for them, so that the very age of seven should be required:

> D. 23, 1, 14, (Mod. l. 4 *diff.*): *In sponsalibus contrahendis aetas contrahentium definita non est ut in matrimoniis. Quapropter et a primordio aetatis sponsalia effici possunt, si modo id fieri ab utraque persona intellegatur, id est, si non sint minores quam septem annis.*[11]

I would like, then, to mention that betrothal in Rome was called sponsalia, a term whose meaning in the sources has three explanations.

Gellius connects the word to the custom, in use in ancient Latium and until the granting of citizenship (with the Julian law), of committing oneself by verbal contract (the sponsio, to be precise, which was the first form of verbal contract) to give or take a woman as a wife:

> Gell., Noct. att. IV.4: *Sponsalia in ea parte Italiae, quae Latium appellatur, hoc more atque iure solita fieri scripsit Servius Sulpicius in libro, quem scripsit de dotibus: Qui uxorem inquit ducturus erat, ab eo, unde ducenda erat, stipulabatur eam in matrimonium datum iri. Qui ducturus erat, itidem spondebat. Is conctractus stipulationum sponsionumque dicebatur "sponsalia". Tunc, quae promissa erat, "sponsa" appellabatur, qui spoponderat*

---

betrothed, although she is not a wife. But what Labeon and I and Pomponius believed we accepted in the tenth book of the "Questions" is more true, so that the betrothal lasts, if indeed it was contracted earlier, despite whoever married her already considers her a wife; if, on the other hand, the betrothal was not contracted, neither the betrothal itself cannot be considered to exist, because it did not take place, nor the marriage, because it could not be contracted).

11 Tr.: For engagements there is no defined age as for marriages. Consequently, marriage can take place from birth (since early childhood), provided both understand what they are doing, that is, provided they are not less than seven years old).

> *ducturum, "sponsus". Sed si post eas stipulationis uxor non dabatur aut non ducebatur, qui stipulabatur, ex sponsu agebat. Iudices cognoscebant. Iudex, quamobrem data acceptave non esset uxor, quaerebat. Si nihil iustae causae videbatur, litem pecunia aestimabat, quantique interfuerat eam uxorem accipi aut dari, eum, qui spoponderat, "aut" qui stipulatus erat, condemnabat. Hoc ius sponsaliorum observatum dicit Servius ad id tempus, quo civitas universo Latio lege Iulia data est. Haec eadem Neratius scripsit in libro, quem de nuptiis composuit.*[12]

Differently, Gellius, who recalled that Verrius Flaccus himself had given two different explanations: firstly, he had asserted that the use of the verb spondere referred to the fact that these were acts performed spontaneously; then, contradicting himself, he had asserted that it derived from Greek regarding the use of betrothed persons to make libations, which represented a form of invocation and prayer to the gods, using cups, which in Greek were called spondàs:

> Festi, *De verb. signif.* L. 440.1: ***Spondere*** *Verrius putat dictum, quod sponte sua, id est voluntate, promittatur. Deinde oblitus inferiore capite sponsum et sponsam ex Graeco dicta[m] ait, quod i spondàs interpositis rebus divinis faciant.*[13]

It is important also to mention that the sponsalia did not bind to marriage, unless it was stipulated that a sum would be paid in the event of failure to the subsequent marriage.

---

12 (Tr.: Servio Sulpicius, in the book he wrote on dowries, wrote that, in that part of Italy called Lazio, betrothals were made according to the following rules, dictated by custom and law: Who, he writes, was about to take a wife, he made himself promise by the one from whom he was to take it, that the same would be given to him. He in turn undertook to take her in the same way as a wife. This contract of stipulations and "sponsions" was called "sponsali." Consequently, she who had been promised was called "bride," whoever had promised to take her in marriage, "groom." But if after those promises the woman was not given or was not taken in marriage, whoever had the promised acted by virtue of the sponsio. The judges were invested. The judge investigated the reason why the woman had not been given or taken. If there seemed to be no just cause, he proceeded to the pecuniary estimate of the dispute and sentenced, whoever had promised to take or whoever had undertaken to give the woman in marriage, to pay the value corresponding to the interest he had in giving or being given his wife. Servius says that this discipline of nuptials was observed at the time when, with the Giulia law (90 BC), citizenship was given to the whole of Lazio. Nerazio also wrote the same things in his book on weddings).

13 (Tr.: ***Spondere*** Verrio ritiene che sia detto cosí perché si promette sua sponte cioè di propria volontà. Poi, dimentico di ciò, in un capitolo successivo afferma che sposo e sposa derivano dal Greco, in riferimento al fatto che essi, nel rito religioso, fanno libagioni—*spondàs*).

Varro de ling. lat. 70: *"Si"> spondebatur pecunia aut filia nuptiarum causa appellabatur et pecunia et quae desponsa erat sponsa: quae pecunia inter se contra sponsum rogata erat, dicta sponsio; cui desponsa quae erat, sponsus; quo die sponsum erat, sponsalis. §. 71: Qui spoponderat filiam, despondisse dicebant, quod de sponte eius, id est de voluntate, exierat: non enim si volebat, dabat, quod sponsu erat alligatus: nam un in comoediis vides dici: "Sponde'n>' tuam gnatam filio uxorem meo?" Quod tum et praetorium ius ad legem et censorium iudicium ad aequm existimabatur.*[14]

10. Matrimonium

It was within the Weltanschauung that matrimonium was developed.

Evidence of it is the very etymology of the term.

Matrimonium was a term formed from the singular genitive of mater (i.e., matris) combined with the suffix—monium, linked, transparently, to the noun munus (duty, task) to describe the function of the institution; that is the obligation for the woman to have children. It mirrored patrimonium (patris munus), which indicated the man's duty (patris), centered on the obligation to support wife and children; therefore, the term became synonymous with the consistency of property.

It follows that the word matrimonium, with its reference to "the duty of a fruitful mother," emphasized the procreative purposes of the union: the woman joined the man to become a mother and procreate legitimate children.

Dupont observes, "The Romans always said that nothing is worse than marriage, and that if there were no need for children, no one would marry."

It was, therefore, procreation that expressed the motive and function of marriage. According to the views of the ancients, present in Roman law, corresponded to a primary need of society; that, precisely, of growth. The need to have

14 (Tr.: Se si prometteva del denaro o la figlia in matrimonio, "*sponsa*" "promessa" veniva chiamata tanto la somma di denaro quanto la fidanzata; il denaro che, interrogandosi fra di loro, avevano pattuito in contrapposizione "in cambio del" al fidanzamento era detto "*sponsio*"; "*sponsus*" "promesso" era detto colui cui era stata promessa una moglie; "sponsale" era detto il giorno della promessa "il giorno in cui era avvenuto il fidanzamento". Chi aveva impegnato al figlia, dicevano che l'avesse liberata, poiché era uscita dalla sua disponibilità, cioè dalla sua volontà: infatti se voleva non adempiva, a ciò cui era tenuto per forza del fidanzamento: vedi appunto quel che si dice nelle commedie: prometti tua figlia in moglie a mio figlio? Allora si procedeva alla stima dell'accaduto secondo il diritto pretorio facendo riferimento alla legge, secondo il giudizio dei censori facendo riferimento all'equità).

to grow was essential and central to the ancient conception of life and constituted the motive for unions to be realized in the society of men (but also in nature).

Hence marriage, compared to other terms that are currently employed with related meanings, places, at least originally, greater emphasis on the procreative purpose of the union: the etymology itself refers to the "task of mother" rather than of wife, almost believing that the complete realization of the union between a man and a woman takes place with the act of procreation, with the woman becoming a mother and generating, within the marriage bond, legitimate children.

Incisively, the Roman experience in marriage linked the universal dictates of nature with the task of wives to bear children. In this regard, the testimonies are numerous and unambiguous.

Beginning with the aforementioned aventi text of Ulpianus, which placed marriage within the framework of natural law and the consequent requirement of procreation (D. 1. 1. 1. 3: ... *Hinc descendit maris atque feminae coniunctio, quam nos matrimonium appellamus, hinc liberorum procreatio, hinc educatio: videmus etenim cetera quoque animalia, feras etiam istius iuris peritia censeri*).[15]

After all, it was undisputed that the familia should be functional for the preservation of humankind and, therefore, of the Respublica it appeared obvious, in Roman thought, that its task was centered in filiation, according to a tendency common to all animate beings, as Cicero pointed out and also highlighted by other authors:

> Cic., *De finibus* 3. 19. 64: *Cum autem ad tuendos conservandosque homines hominem natum esse videamus, consentaneum est huic naturae, ut sapiens velit gerere et administrare rempublicam atque, ut e natura vivat, uxorem adiungere et velle ex ea liberos.*[16]

> Cicero, *De off.* 1. 4. 11: *Commune item animantium est coniunctionis adpetitus procreandi causa, et cura quaedam eorum quae procreata sunt.*[17]

> Cic., *De off.* 1. 17. 53–54: ... *Nam cum sit hoc natura commune animantium, ut habeant libidinem procreandi, prima societas in ipso coniugio est, proxima in liberis,...*.[18]

---

15 V. *retro*.

16 (Tr.: Poiché l'uomo è nato per la tutela e la conservazione della specie, è conseguente che chi è saggio voglia prendersi cura ed amministrare la repubblica e, per assicurare la sopravvivenza, prendere moglie per avere da lei dei figli).

17 (Tr.: Dunque è comune a tutti gli animali il desiderio di unirsi per procreare e prendersi cura dei figli).

18 (Tr.: *Infatti, poiché per natura è comune a tutti gli animali il desiderio di procreare, l'unione che ne consegue è la prima forma di società*); v. sopra.

Svet., *Caesar* 52: *Helenius Cinna plerisque confessus est habuisse se scriptam paratamque legem quam Caesar ferre iussisset, cum ipse abesset, ut ei uxores liberorum quaerendorum causa, quas… velle ducere liceret.*[19]

Quintil., *Declam.* 247: … *ita illud nuptiis conlocata efficit uxorem: sed non haec solummodo erit uxor. Fingamus enim nuptias fecisse nullas, coisse autem liberorum creandorum gratia: non tamen uxor non erit, quamvis nuptiis non sit collocata.*[20]

D. 50. 16. 220. 3, *Call.* 2 *quaest.*: *Praeter haec omnia natura nos quoque docet parentes pios, qui liberorum procreandorum animo et voto uxores ducunt, filiorum appellatione omnes qui ex nobis descendunt continere: nec enim dulciore nomine possumus nepotes nostros quam filii appellare. Etenim idcirco filios filiasve concipimus atque edimus, ut ex prole eorum earumve diuturnitatis nobis memoriam in aevum relinquamus.*[21]

The finalization of marriage to parenthood was also accentuated by regulatory measures. For example, a Giulia law expressly contemplated it, stipulating that provisions facilitating the acquisition of citizenship applied only to marriages contracted with a commitment to bear children:

Tit. Ulp. 3. 3: *Nam lege Iunia cautum est, ut si civem romnanam vel latinam uxorem duxerit, testatione interposita, quod liberorum quaerendorum causa uxorem duxerit postea filio filiave nato natave et anniculo facto possit apud praetorem vel praesidem provinciae causam probare et fieri civis Romanus tam ipse quam filius filiave eius et uxor, scilicet si et ipsa Latina sit….*[22]

19 (Tr.: Elvio Cinna tribuno della plebe confessò a parecchi di avere avuto tra mano, scritta e pronta, una legge, che Cesare aveva ordinato di pubblicare in sua assenza, per la quale fosse lecito, per avere figli, prendere quali e quante mogli volesse).

20 (Tr.: … pertanto "moglie" è colei che sia stata collocata in nozze: tuttavia non soltanto essa potrà essere considerato "moglie." Facciamo l'esempio di uno che non abbia contratto le nozze, ma ugualmente si sia unito con una donna allo scopo di avere figli: non si può dire che questa non sia "moglie," sebbene non sia stata collocata in nozze).

21 (Tr.: Oltre a tutto ciò, la natura insegna anche a noi pii genitori quali sono coloro che si sposino con l'intenzione e l'**impegno di procreare figli**, di potere chiamare figli tutti coloro che discendono da noi: né infatti possiamo chiamare i nostri nipoti con un nome più dolce di figli. Infatti, concepiamo ed alleviamo i figli e le figlie per questo motivo: affinché possiamo lasciare il ricordo di noi stessi per sempre per mezzo dei figli e delle figlie di loro). V. E. Volterra, *Lezioni di diritto romano. Il matrimonio romano.* Anno accademico 1960–1961, Ricerche, Roma 1961.

22 (Tr.: Invero con una legge Giulia si provvide a che il cittadino che volesse prendere una moglie romana o latina, **dovesse premettere, con giuramento, di sposarsi per avere figli**; solo in tale ipotesi in seguito al compimento dell'anno da parte del figlio o della figlia potrà provare ciò presso il pretore o il preside della provincia e diventeranno cittadini romani sia lui stesso, sia il figlio o la figlia o la moglie, purché sia Latina…).

In conclusion, the marriage, in accordance with nature, was "preordained to the end of the procreation of offspring, liberorum quaerendorum causa." Aim and requirement so commonly recognized that the Censors, forced to divorce from the barren wife, even though she was much loved:

Gellius, Noct. Att. 4. 3. 2: *Atque is Carvilius traditur uxorem, quam dimisit, egregie dilexisse carissimamque morum eius gratia habuisse, sed iurisiurandi religionem animo atque amore praevertisse, quod iurare a censoribus coactus erat uxorem se liberum quaerundum gratia habiturum.*[23]

Filiation was so characterizing and decisive that it defined marriage per se as the union from which children were born:

Quintil., Declam. 247: *ita illud nuptiis conlocata efficit uxorem: sed non haec solummodo erit uxor. Fingamus enim nuptias fecisse nullas, coisse autem liberorum creandorum gratia: non tamen uxor non erit, quamvis nuptiis non sit collocata.*[24]

Christian sources also emphasized the procreative purpose of marriage:

August., *Contra Fausturn Manichaeurn libri XXXIII.* XIX: *Matrimonium quippe ex hoc appellatum est, quod non ob aliud debeat femina nubere, quam ut mater fiat.*[25]

The constant and insistent reference to Nature was undoubtedly meant to remind everyone, lawmakers and jurists included, that the matrimonium belonged to man and his historical-social agglomeration and, therefore, that, although varying in time and configuration, it was men who forged it, dictating its arrangement within the framework of the mos (custom), based on the ius sacrum.

Therefore, the activity of Roman jurists consisted in grasping the social concept and pouring it into the resulting legal relationship. Therefore, statements that declare marriage concluded with the expression of the will and not from the actual beginning of the union of the spouses should not mislead.

Once again it is Ulpianus, whose source may have been the extensive commentaries of Pomponius (who lived about a century earlier) who accounts for this:

---

23 (Tr.: E si ricorda che Carvilio amava molto la moglie che aveva cacciato e di cui aveva care le abitudini, ma all'amore e all'affetto preferí la fedeltà al giuramento, perché era stato costretto dai censori a giurare che avrebbe preso moglie per avere prole).

24 (Tr.: normalmente "moglie" è colei che sia stata collocata in nozze: tuttavia non soltanto essa potrà essere considerato "moglie." Facciamo l'esempio di uno che non abbia contratto le nozze, ma ugualmente si sia unito con una donna allo scopo di avere figli: non si può dire che questa non sia "moglie," sebbene non sia stata collocata in nozze).

25 (Tr.: matrimonio e senza dubbio chiamato cosí perché la donna si deve sposare non per altro motivo che per diventare madre).

D. 50.17.30, Ulp. 36 *ad Sab.*: *Nuptias non concubitus, sed consensus facit.*[26]

D. 35.1.15, Ulp. 35 *ad Sab.*: *Cui fuerit sub hac condicione legatum, "si in familia nupsisset" videtur impleta condicio statim atque ducta est uxor, quamvis nondum in cubiculum mariti venerit. Nuptias enim non concubitus sed consensus facit.*[27]

In reality, these statements were aimed at capturing the constitutive moment of marriage and were not intended to indicate its characterizing purpose.

It has to be emphasized that the matrimonium, which had become monogamous, was projected toward filiation and the transmission of the pater's patrimony, to the point that "one married in only one case: if one decided to transmit one's patrimony to children."

The matrimonium had, therefore, as its primary and almost sole purpose that of increasing and perpetuating the family of the pater; who, moreover, had to be certain that the births of his familia came exclusively from him, so that the family patrimony (which was to be divided among the children) would go to whomever he had planned.

The institutive foundation of marriage, albeit with profound variations among the different forms of marriage (cum manu, sine manu, communi consensu), was the constitutive element of the bond and had to be that of the pater and had the peculiarity of having to be continuous.

This was also responsible for the severe punishment of adultery; which, as the term indicated, consisted in the alteration of the father-son blood bond.

In Rome and for a long time, almost to the threshold of our own day, the punishment was most severe but concerned exclusively the woman, because only the intercourse had by the wife with anyone other than her husband could jeopardize the certainty of the provenance from the latter of any offspring, which resulted.

Love between spouses was not, as a rule, contemplated and, indeed, was not infrequently considered disreputable and a symptom of unacceptable "softness."

Often infertile women were repudiated or they themselves divorced to allow their husbands to find a "fertile womb."

The evolution of this conception, which took place between AD 2 and 3, then formed the basis of Christian marriage, which focused on chastity of life and the permissibility of sexual relations only in marriage and for filiation.

---

26 (Tr.: Le nozze non le fa l'accoppiamento, bensí il consenso).

27 (Tr.: *Per colui cui fu lasciato un legato a condizione che sposasse un membro della famiglia la condizione si deve ritenere avverata al momento della deduzione nella casa del marito e non ha importanza se non sia ancora andata nella camera da letto del marito. Ciò perché è il consenso e non l'accoppiamento a costituire le nozze*).

The Roman view of marriage, family, and society in general was also reflected in the status of women and their right to have a name and to participate in social life. In the Roman patriarchal family, women were not entitled to their own name, unlike Egyptian and Etruscan women. They were not relegated and destined to obscurity like the Greeks because they could also participate in banquets, but only in a first part, when wine was not yet drunk, which was strictly forbidden to them (especially in ancient times); moreover, by sitting not lying down (like males).

In case she had a proper name, it was not known except to the immediate family and was never to be pronounced in public.

At birth, in fact, three names were assigned to the male: praenomen (e.g., Mark; there were about 20 in all), nomen (e.g., Tullius) and cognomen (e.g., Cicero); and only one to the female, that of the gens to which she belonged, used in the feminine. The woman was considered not as an individual but as part of a family unit. Cicero, for example, would call his daughter by the name Tullia. If there were more than one daughter, they bore the generic name Prima, Secunda, etc. next to the gens name. But this was the plebeians to do; the patricians preferred to draw on distinguished ancestors. The adjective senior or junior was used to distinguish two sisters or mother and daughter. Freedmen, male or female, assumed the name of the patron. Sometimes, but only for males, a nickname was added for civil or military merit: for example, the Uticense, the Censor, the Africanus, etc.

On the other hand, having a proper name mattered relatively: in republican Rome, only women who, as heiresses, were obliged to help maintain the army were counted.

11. Dowry

It was therefore in marriage that the woman realized herself and realized her legal-social position within the Roman society. As a result of this, marriage was in the woman's interest, but also in the interest of her familia and the Respublica. But to arrive at marriage the woman needed to have the dowry, which had become essential in the structure of Roman marriage. This need was very old in the Roman experience and was so felt that Plautus emphasized the difficulty of marriage for women without dowries, comparing a marriage without dowry to the concubinage.

In order to ensure that women could effectively contract marriage, the jurists affirmed the need for public intervention, thus removing the protection of women from the sole forms provided by private law, even in cases where the marriage was not yet valid, such as that of the child under 12 years of age, who remained in her husband's house while waiting for her to reach marriageable age:

> D. 23, 3, 2, Paul. 60 *ad ed.: rei publicae interest mulieres dotes salvas habere, propter quas nubere possunt.*[28]

> D. 42. 5. 18 (Paul. 60 *ad ed.*): *interest enim reipublicae et hanc solidum consequi, ut aetate permittente nubere possit.*[29]

For Paul, summing up the thinking of Roman evolution, therefore, dowry is essential to marriage, to the point that without it there could have been no marriages. Then, we might affirm that Romans married "for love," but not necessarily of future wives, but rather of dowries!

The defense of the dowry was strictly connected to the concept of marriage, essential to the growth of the Respublica; a reason why it was really had to be facilitated by safeguarding the integrity of dowries. Which, in any case and peacefully, were considered customary and indispensable, as Sextus Pomponius had reiterated in his extensive commentary:

> D. 24. 3. 1, Pomp. 15 *ad Sab. [612]: Dotium causa semper et ubique praecipua est: nam et publice interest dotes mulieribus conservari cum dotatas esse ferninas ad subolem procreandam replendamque liberis civitatem maxime sit necessarium.*[30]

From other fragments of the Digest we know that the public interest in the preservation of dowries had protection through the granting of a privilegium, that is, a royal action that allowed the woman to regain the dowry property wherever it was located and even if, in the meantime, it had been alienated.

What was the origin of the term dos = dowry?

The most commonly used term for dowry was dos. The sources tell us that it came from a Greek root meaning to give: this is attested by the grammarians Varro and Festus, as evidenced by the origin of do from the verb dare:

---

28 (Tr.: alla Repubblica interessa che le donne abbiano salva la propria dote, perché è per mezzo di essa che possono sposarsi).

29 (Tr.: è infatti di interesse della Repubblica che anche questa (si riferiva alla minore di 12 anni) consegua il patrimonio, in modo che possa sposarsi quando l'età lo consenta).

30 (Tr.: La causa delle doti è sempre ed ovunque particolare: infatti è di pubblico interesse che le donne conservino le doti, essendo oltremodo necessario che le donne siano dotate per procreare e riempire la città di figli). Sul legame tra la dote e l'interesse della Repubblica v. M. Casola, "Interesse *rei publicae* alla salvezza della dote," in *Ionicae disputationes—Umo e ambiente. II incontro ionico-polacco* (Taranto 17–20 settembre 2007), Taranto 2008, p. 187f.

Varro, *De lingua Latina* 5, 175: *Dos, si nuptiarum causa data; haec Graece dwt…nh: ita enim hoc Siculi. Ab eodem donum.*

Festi M. 69, *De verb. signif.: Dotem manifestum est ex Graeco esse. Nam didÒnai dicitur apud eos dare.*

The term dos was not the first but belonged to the time when the influence of Greek culture began to be significant in Roman life and language. We are not able to go back to the words used in archaic Rome to indicate the goods that were then included in the word dos; we know, however, that already in the early days of Rome women brought to their husbands a "dowry."

The purpose of the dowry was to support married life: therefore its purpose consisted in being destined to favor marriage, to which it had to provide help to support the tasks and costs.

The specific destination of the dowry to pay *matrimonii sustinenda* appears specifically presupposed by Paul, when he affirmed that the dowry existed where there were the weights of marriage:

D. 23. 3. 56. 1, Paul. 6 ad Plautium: Ibi dos esset debet, ubi onera matrimonii sunt.[31]

The controversial point in doctrine has been confirmed by the discovery of a fragment extracted from book 32 of the commentary on the edict of Paul, which, for having reached us outside the Digest of Justinian, should have come directly from the work of the Severian jurist, has definitively confirmed the destination of the dowry for matrimony:

Pap. Grenf. 2, 107 recto: [*Quia apud eum esse debet*] *q(u) on[e/ra sustinet: quod si iam dis]soluto / matrimonio [(societas) distrahatu]r, isdem dieb(us) prae/[cipi debet qui]b(us) et solvi debet. [Ha Se]r(vius) et Lab(eo) scribunt.*[32]

---

31 (La dote deve stare dove stanno i pesi del matrimonio). L'affermazione del giurista verosimilmente era inserita in una discussione sull'attribuzione della dote al padre ed ai suoi eredi o al figlio-marito della donna che aveva costituito la dote. Il giurista, al § successivo, precisava che in caso di morte la dote non seguiva la sorte del patrimonio del *pater*, ma passava al figlio-marito, perché aveva propria autonomia dovuta alla destinazione al sostegno del matrimonio e non seguiva la sorte degli altri beni del *pater*: *Post mortem patris statim onera matrimonii filium sequuntur, sicut liberi, sicut uxor.*

32 Esso è stato scoperto in un papiro inserito nella collezione Bodleiana ed è noto come *fragmentum Bodleianum*. L'ipotesi ricostruttiva è in C. Fayer, *La familia romana. Aspetti giuridici ed antiquari. Sponsalia matrimonio dote* 2, Roma 2005, 682. Il frammento corrisponde a D. 17. 2. 65. 16, Paul. 32 *ad ed.*: *Si unus ex sociis, maritus sit et distrahatur societas manente matrimonio, dotem maritum praecipere debet, quia apud*

In conclusion, contemporary doctrine is unanimous in affirming the existence of a necessary and direct link between dowry and the burdens of marriage: dowry was an essential instrument of the policy of encouraging marriages, through which, as the jurisconsult Pomponius pointed out, one had to "procreate offspring and fill the city with children."

In departure the dowry belonged to the husband (or to the father of him if it was not autonomous), but already at the end of the Republic an action was introduced for the restitution of the dowry (actio rei uxoriae) that allowed the wife (or the father of her) to have the goods returned. At the end of this process, the husband appeared more an administrator of the endowments rather than the owner of them and was obliged to a management evaluated very severely: perhaps already at the end of the classical age and certainly with Justinian, He was required to manage it with a "very accurate diligence" (diligentia exactior or exactissima), by reason of which he would have been held responsible for malice and guilt, but, if endowed with particular ability, also the level of attention he reserved to his own things (*diligentiam quam suis*).

Who gave the dowry?

This obligation could derive directly or indirectly from the legislation of Augustus, although it might have been introduced by the Emperors Septimius Severus and Antonius Caracalla, if not only by Justinian.

The basis of the various hypotheses is a fragment of Marciano:

> D. 23. 2. 19, Marcianus 16 *Institutionum: Capite trigesimo quinto legis Iuliae qui liberos quos habent in potestate iniuria prohibuerint ducere uxores vel pubere, vel qui dotem dare non volunt ex constitutione divorum Severi et Antonini, per proconsules praesidiesque provinciarum coguntur in matrimonium collocare et dotare. Prohibere autem videtur et qui condicionem non quaerit.*[33]

---

eum esse debet qui onera sustinet: quod si iam dissoluto matrimonio societas distrahatur, eadem die recipienda est dos, qua et solvi debet. (Se uno dei soci sia marito e la società si sciolga durante il matrimonio, il marito deve prelevare la dote dalla società, perché questa deve essere presso colui che sostiene i pesi del matrimonio; che, se la società si rompe quando già si è sciolto il matrimonio, la dote deve essere prelevata, nel medesimo giorno in cui deve essere pagata (restituita alla moglie).

33 (Secondo il capitolo 35° della legge Giulia, coloro che abbiano proibito senza giusta causa che i figli che hanno in potestà prendano moglie o marito, oppure coloro che non vogliono costituire la dote, in forza di una costituzione dei divinizzati (Settimio) Severo e Antonino (Caracalla), vengono costretti dai proconsoli e dai governatori delle province a provvedere al matrimonio e a costituire la dote. Infatti sembra proibire (il matrimonio) anche colui che non procura un buon partito).

According to the Moriaud, the lex Julia would have allowed recourse to the urban praetor to force his father to consent to the wedding and equip his daughter; subsequently the duties of the praetor were transferred to the proconsuls and the governors of the provinces by the Severi.

The passage presupposes the pre-existence of an obligation to equip the daughters, for the fulfillment of which, perhaps at the time of the Severi, recourse was granted to the magistrates of the provinces. Of this obligation there is trace in a passage of the jurist Celsus, who mentioned a duty of the father to equip his daughter (*et quia pater filiae … dotem dare debet*).

A constitution of Justinian of 531 recalled the obligation to equip the daughters:

> C. I. 5. 11. 7. 2, *Imp. Iustinianus a. Ihoanni praefecto praetorio: Neque enim leges incognitae sunt, quibus cautum est omnimodo paternum esse officium dotes vel ante nuptias donationes pro sua dare progenie (a. 531).*[34]

But who was the final beneficial owner of the dowry?

The ownerrship of the dowry is one of the points that have undergone the greatest variations.

In the Proto-Republican age the dowry belonged to her husband sui iuris or to his pater.

To allow the wife to regain it, in the event of the dissolution of the marriage, a specific contract, through which the husband (or the pater of him, if alive) undertook to return the dowry to the woman; in which case the dowry was called recepticia, except that it was dos profecticia, which, if the wife had died, while she was still united in marriage, returned to her pater still alive; otherwise it remained in the hands of her husband.

In the agnatizia family, having been present by the ius civile vetus, the dowry must necessarily have been the property of the husband or of the having power over him; there are numerous texts from which the ownership of the dowry property in the hands of the husband emerges.

As a result of the acquired property, the husband has the right to pass on the property to the heirs, has the possession on the endowment goods with the possibility of usucapione in the event that the constituent does not have the property, the possibility of tampering with the dowry slaves becoming them. Moreover,

34 (Infatti non si ignorano le leggi che hanno stabilito che ad ogni modo è dovere del padre dare ai propri figli la dote o la donazione nuziale).

the endowed slaves established heirs or gratified to a legate can buy only as a result of the husband's issues and in his interest.

In apparent contrast to these data, there are some sources (not few) in which it is possible to expect the dowry to belong to the wife, so much so that a jurist of the last period of Roman jurisprudence summarized the situation with the statement that the dowry, even in the husband's estate, it actually belonged to the wife:

> D. 23. 3. 75, *Tryph*, 6 *Disputationum: Quamvis in bonis mariti dos sit, mulieris tamen est: et merito placuit, ut si fundum inaestimatum dedit cuius nomine duplae stipulatione cautum habuit, isque marito evictus sit, statim earn ex stipulatione agere posse ...*[35].

The aporia actually reflects the convictions that gradually became rooted also in the law and reflected the duty of the husband to allocate the assets to the exclusive advantage of marriage: duty, moreover, remitted to the assessment of the domestic Court and on whose observance the Censors supervised. With the weakening of the agnatic family, a new discipline emerged, which, through progressive limitations of her husband's powers, transformed him more into an administrator than into the actual and uncontrolled owner, as he had originally been.

The process knew the first effective stage with the introduction (perhaps in the second half of the 2nd century d. C.) of the actio rei uxoriae, the action that allowed his wife (or her father, with his consent) to demand the restitution of the dowry in case of dissolution of the marriage. Already the name of the action alluded to the belonging of the dowry to the woman.

At that point the chances that the wife could regain the dowry, in case of dissolution of the marriage, were two:

if a promise of restitution was set, it could be demanded with the action arising from the promise (actio ex stipulatu). In this case, the husband had to give all he had received, except that fortuitous events or events of force majeure had occurred, which had caused the extinction of part or all the endowments. It was possible that a dowry valuation (aestimatio dotis) would be included in the stipulation: in this case, the full amount of the dowry had to be returned, without taking into account any losses, even if completely independent from the husband.

35 (Nonostante la dote sia tra i beni del marito, tuttavia è della donna: ed a ragione si ritenne che, se diede in dote un fondo senza che ne venisse preventivamente stimato il valore, per il quale si ebbe una cauzione stipulata del doppio, e quel fondo sia stato evitto dal marito, la moglie subito può agire secondo lo stipulato...).

In any case, the return could be claimed with the actio rei uxoriae. This was born as an action to protect the factual situation (actio in factum) and, by the intervention of the jurisconsults, had turned into an action of law (actio in ius), having a particular structure, which brought it closer to the actions of good faith (iudicia bonae fidei) by the fact that the judge had to attribute to the plaintiff not necessarily the amount of the dowry, but what in his opinion seemed fair to him that the instant should achieve (id quod melius equus erit).

For this reason, the judge allowed her husband to deduct from the entire amount of the dowry some expenses incurred during the marriage. These costs had to be justified and were then freely assessed by the judge. The case law simplified the task of the judge by elaborating a reference case law, to which he could adhere, for example provided for the retention: expenses for the maintenance and education of children (propter liberos) in the case of marriage dissolved on the initiative of the pater familias of the wife or by divorce attributable to the wife. This complex system of retentiones was eliminated by Justinian.

The a. rei uxoriae, in the event of the death of his wife, could be experienced by his paterfamilias and was not transmissible to heirs, in the case of dos profecticia. When her father died, the dowry remained with her husband. In case of death of the husband or divorce the action was up to the wife, if sui iuris, or his pater, if aliens iuris, with the obligation to exercise it only together with the daughter (adiuncta filiae persona). If the wife had died after the divorce the action could not be experienced by the pater, nor passed to the heirs of the uxor. This shows that the right to restitution was considered a personal right of women.

The actio rei uxoriae was in any case limited by the beneficium competentiae, because of which the husband could not be sentenced to give what he could not pay. For this very reason a paradox could occur, consisting in the fact that the woman would have obtained maximum protection against her shrewd husband, who had managed his dowry and his estate well, while she remained unprotected against her husbands, who had squandered their property and endowment. Thus there was a gap in this legislation and the need for a more incisive form of protection of the wife's expectations; Augusto provided it with the lex Iulia de fundo dotali of 18 a. C. (perhaps a chapter of the lex Iulia de adulteriis). With this provision was introduced the prohibition for the husband to alienate funds, without the consent of his wife. The arrangement referred to the endowment fund (dotale praedium) and it was discussed whether it concerned all the funds or only the Italian funds. Justinian eliminated all doubt and made the ban general and mandatory, going so far as never to allow the alienation of funds; not even with the consent of his wife.

But already the disposition wanted by Augustus (to protect marriages) had been shocking, as it reversed the relations between the spouses, making sure that the husband, who previously had been the absolute arbiter of the fate of the wife, now depended on his wife and that at the first opportunity of a more conspicuous dowry he decided to divorce. Moreover, the women, formerly passive, now confident that they could rely on their dowry, began increasingly to take the initiative of divorce themselves, frustrating the Emperor's intention, who had intended to safeguard the talents to make marriages more stable, in order to ensure procreation.

The events of the dowry in Roman law are an example of the research and solutions projected toward the social insertion of man in the community of belonging; which ends up being humanity, with its levels of organization (family, Republic) according to an unavailable order of human life and society.

The history of dowry has been varied.

In the face of societies that already in ancient times provided for an inverse discipline, warning that it was up to the husband and his family to pay to get a girl in marriage, use still present in some societies, in contexts influenced by Roman law the custom of equipping brides has long been preserved and the dowry was present in almost all contemporary codes; especially those derived (directly or indirectly) from the Code Napoleon and in the Islamic world, where, however, it was conferred by her husband. Today it has disappeared or in phase extinction: for example, in 1975 the Italian Civil Code introduced the prohibition of the constitution of dowry, in any form; art. 166a:

> *È nulla ogni convenzione che comunque tenda alla costituzione di beni in dote.*[36]

In contrast, women and their families are still required to donate their dowry to the Indian continent (mainly India, Pakistan, Bangladesh) and to Iran. It is so strong that it constitutes one of the most frequent cases of feminicide, tolerated even by the courts, which often detract from the killing (e.g., of a daughter-in-law who did not give her mother-in-law the refrigerator, the television or the sewing machine promised) domestic accident. The British Empire had already tried to oppose such crimes, but in vain, because yesterday as today they are among the greatest cases of violence against women.

Looking back at the so-called West, we can say that the disappearance of the dowry is the result of the increasing autonomy of women and their consequent insertion in today's societies, with the possibility of autonomous development.

---

36 Every convention is null that however tends to the constitution of assets in dowry.

This has led to the need to provide skills for women who are now able to provide for themselves and their families.

At times, however, the result would be a loss-making view of the family and of sonship, acute at times, not infrequent of serious economic crisis and lack of work; aggravated by the almost exponential centralization of wealth in the hands of more and more few.

Today, it seems to me, there is no longer any concern to put people in a position to marry and we are witnessing the collapse of births and the progressive aging of populations. It promotes the insertion in the world of work (which, for the most part, is the source of sustenance) but there is no direct policy specifically to make available to nubendi what is necessary for marriage and to encourage procreation: with some exceptions, such as that of Poland.

Moreover, it will be necessary to deal with the intrusive, but also irrepressible, advancement of AI (Artificial Intelligence), which, make "people" useless and the institution of the Family obsolete.

12. The ceremony

Finally, it is time to have a look at the ceremonies linked to the wedding rites.

The close link on one hand with the sacred and on the other with the social attitudes, made the wedding ceremonies, inseparable in the archaic age, always assume great importance: "The wedding ceremony was not necessary for the establishment of the legal bond between the spouses; but the tradition and the sacred character that was attached to it made it the most important event of family life." This did not take away the fact that, even today, the marriage could be concluded (on the other hand) with the simple agreement between the nubendi, without any externalization or ceremony. This is demonstrated by the exemplary case of Cato Uticense and Marcia. The friend Hortense (the famous orator often opposed by Cicero), in order to have children to give to the Civitas, asked Cato to give him his daughter Portia, who was already married. Cato, not believing he was breaking his daughter's marriage, instead offered him his wife Marcia. Then, when Hortense died, Marcia asked her husband to return to him: Cato, a good stoic, consented and took her back into the house, thus constituting with the simple agreement, a new marriage. Therefore no ceremony; no presence of others (witnesses or relatives) besides the spouses alone.

Having said that, it must be said that this concerned the legal significance of marriage. In the experience, however, the custom was different and went well beyond the legal configuration and committed families and in particular the patres to strict respect.

This was underlined, at the conclusion of Roman jurisprudence, also by Modestino, who dedicated a special work to the rite:

D. 50. 17. 197, *Modestinus, libro singulari de ritu nuptiarum: Semper in coniunctionibus non solum quid liceat considerandum est, sed et quid honestum sit.*[37]

How was the wedding ceremony?

The news that has reached us are many and refer to the preparatory phase to the conclusion and entry of the woman in the house of her husband (deductio in domu mariti) until the first night, in which the husband untied the double knot, the cingulum herculeum of the wool belt, which tightened the woman's robe, under a saffron-colored cloak or ball.

The woman arrived dressed in white with a long dress that covered her from head to toe and had the caught veiled, a veil flammeum, which, as the name indicates, must have been "flaming," that is red-orange and probably originated from the flaminian Dialis, the wife of Flamen Dialis, priest of Jupiter; who, in fact, wore a dress and a veil of flame color with which, during the sacrifices, the head was veiled.

The reference to the circumstance that the woman should be "veiled" had great importance both in the Roman experience and in the contemporary one: in fact, the term nupta (i.e., "veiled," from the verb nubere, which means, in fact, "veiled") originated from it, indicating the married woman, and nuptiae, synonymous with marriage, transmigrated in our "wedding."

The "ceremony" started from a religious moment: the sacrifice of an animal from the bowels of which the priest (in the case auspex, untranslatable term) desumumeva the "auspicia" and only if he found them favorable he proceeded; otherwise "marriage, disapproved of by the gods, would not be valid."

Established the divine approval followed, as a rule, the signing of the tabulae nuptiales, the marriage contract, in the presence of 10 witnesses. The bride and groom went before the pronuba (a woman, who was to be univirous; that is, who had only one husband) and the groom lifted the veil of the bride; then the pronuba took the right of the spouses, placing them one in the other. This was the dextrarum iunctio, the most solemn moment of the ceremony: tacit exchange of commitment of fidelity among the young spouses, mutual promise of wanting to live together. The woman proclaimed the constitutive formula of the bond: Ubi tu Gaius ego Gaia. Numerous sarcophagi represent the scene; and the symbolic

37 (Tr.: Nei matrimonî occorre sempre tener conto non solo di ciò che è lecito ma anche di ciò che ad essi si addice").

act, which the Church has maintained in the wedding rite, also has meaning and value today.

There are three aspects to this.

The substantial perpetuation of Roman marriage in the marriage rite of Christianity. Carcopino cites Monsignor Duchesne's statement "… all the Roman nuptials have been preserved in Christian usage…"

The formula *Ubi tu Gaius ego Gaia* has been revisited often seeing the expression of an almost romantic declaration of fusion of their lives. In fact, we must be warned that the meaning was quite different. Not "a form in which they seem to confuse their—that is, of both spouses—existence, like their wills," but the proclamation that from now on the woman will live in function and in accordance with the will and life of her husband. In this sense, in fact, the definition (which currently I have often heard, as an example of an equal community created by marriage) of Modestino, who proclaimed marriage as a "common life" with even sharing of the same religion: Mod. D. 23. 2. 1, l. primo regularum: *Nuptiae sunt coniunctio maris et feminae et consortium omnis vitae, divini et humani iuris communicatio*. This definition is also very suggestive, since it means marriage as a sharing of every aspect of life, in the Roman experience was to indicate that the woman from the moment of marriage divided every aspect and moment of her husband's life and made hers the gods venerated by him and the gods of the dead (Lari and Penati) of his family.

The officiant was not male, but female. The union of the hands that yesterday as today concluded the marriage happened in front of the *pronuba*, that was a woman who had not more than one husband; which (perhaps projection of the *pronuba Juno—Iuna pronuba*—Goddess protector of marriage and fertility) sealed the union with the overlap of his hand.

After the rite began the banquet. But before there was a sort of symbolic kidnapping, consisting in a staging of a rat carried out by the groom, who pretended to tear the bride from her mother's arms; probably vestiges of the historical "Rape of the Sabines," the origins of Rome.

The bride was accompanied by a procession, corresponding to the one staged at the Liberalia for males on the occasion of the presentation and entry into the populus. He advanced carrying the spindle and the conocchia, symbols of his new activity as mother of a family preceded by three children's homelands and stepmothers: "two he held hands, a third preceded them by waving a torch of hawthorn (spina alba) lit in the hearth of the bride's house. The sunken leftovers were distributed among the participants, because, so it was believed, they were good luck. (We do the same with orange blossoms)." To this launch could be accompanied that of the nuts: in fact, since the woman had to abandon the toys of her childhood, before leaving home, the use of throwing in the air and to the newlyweds and guests the nuts with which she had dabbled as a girl, whose sound on the pavement now joyfully foreshadowed the fruitful happiness that the future would have reserved for her. Which matches our rice toss.

Upon arrival the woman was raised in her arms and taken to the house. This act, which some sometimes also associate with the Sabine rat, in reality was a precaution aimed at preventing the woman, passing on the doorstep, from slipping, since the brides used to anoint the thresholds of the future house with pig fat (considered a harbinger of well-being); therefore wives were usually called unxores—uxores.

How much this custom has remained up to our days is under the eyes of all.

I would like to suggest a very bold approach. Christian marriage involves the sharing of Holy Communion: you can see a late subliminal heritage and idealized by Christian thought of sharing a muffin of spelt in one with the invocation of the protection of God (Iuppiter farreus) by the spouses, at the time of the monarchy? Of course, however, it appears that the confarreatio (the most ancient marriage rite) whose institution was traced back to Romulus, confirms the religious matrix (in the sacred) of marriage.

At this point I would like to recall another aspect that seems to last, from antiquity to today: that of marriage rings.

Regarding the use of the ring we have the testimony of Aulus Gellius, who linked it to the experience of the Egyptians, whom he himself considered to be masters of science and intelligence. The Carcopino speaks of it: "Whether it was made of an iron circle covered in gold, or of a gold circle similar to our rings, the girlfriend took care to insert it, immediately, to the finger in which still today is usually worn the faith, that is 'in the finger near the little finger of the left hand'".. Precisely for this reason we, with a name derived from the low Latinity (anularius), call it "annular,—without for another reason reminding us of the reason why the Romans had chosen it. Aulus Gellius explains it with a long round of words: "When you open the human body, as the Egyptians do, and you operate the dissections, anatomy to speak like the Greeks, you find a very thin nerve, which starts from the ring finger and reaches the heart. It is considered appropriate to give the honor to bring the ring to this finger rather than to others, for the close connection, for that certain bond that unites it to the main organ"

The circle, without beginning and without end, was considered by the Egyptians the perfect figure of which the ring constituted the aspiration and no matter if the ring was crocodile skin or bone, the only important thing was the circular shape symbol of commonality and prosperity.From the Egyptians the use of the wedding rings passed to the Greeks and, as Aulus Gellius recalled, to the

Romans, who also used to affix a seal, with which the wife would have to mark the property of the house, to prevent its abuse or theft by the slaves. Clement of Alexandria, in the Pedagogue, spoke of this practice, recalling, for this purpose, that it was customary to give the ring to the woman so that she could stamp the household goods. It was typical to seal drawers, utensils and preserves of the pantry, in order to protect them from any theft of slaves. Among the different attitudes to be held, Clement advised against using the rings for mere ornament, recommending, instead, to use them to seal the husband's goods, in accordance with the care of the household; considering this necessary because the lack of education often contributed to the dishonesty of those who lived or attended the house.

So for the Romans there was the use of the ring given by the groom to the bride and, as we said, ringed to the fourth finger of the hand, because of the nerve that went from there to the heart, motor of life and fidelity (fides). The meaning then of this faith is, as has been said, that of expressing the fidelity, due by the wife to her husband; therefore, it was not by chance that we spoke of "faith" and not, for example, of "love"!

It should be added here that the use of the ring had roots also consolidated in ancient China. But with different meanings and values, linked to the conceptions of life and men in the family context. Specifically, each finger represented a pillar of life. The thumb was connected to the parents. The forefinger represented the brothers. The middle finger represented themselves. The ring finger, the finger of the rings, represented the couple and the little finger the children.

As for today's use, it must be traced back to the Church, which opposed, as pagan symbols, the rings sealed and only after 860 d. C. admitted the use for marriage, leaving for them the term "faith" but with a higher sense: as a sign of love and fidelity elevated to the reciprocity of the spouses, which is nourished in love in God, so that the "faith" is no longer referring to the wife who received the ring, but of those who give it, that is, of both spouses.

Bibliography

Albertario, E., "Promessa generica e legato generico di dote," in *Mélanges de droit romain*, Milano 1925.

Amarelli, F., De giovanni, L., Garbarino, P., Marotta, V., Schiavone, A., and Vincenti, U., *Storia del diritto romano e linee di diritto privato*, Torino 2000.

Astolfi, R., *Il fidanzamento nel diritto romano*[3], Padova 1994.

Astolfi, R., *La lex Iulia et Papia*[4], Padova 1996.

Astolfi, R., *La lex Julia et Papia*, Padova 1996.

Astolfi, R., *Il matrimonio nel diritto romano preclassico*, Padova 2000.

Astolfi, R, *Il matrimonio nel diritto romano classico*, 2ª ed., Padova 2014.

Baccari, M. P., *Concepito: l'antico diritto per il nuovo millennio*, Torino 2004.

Baccari, M. P., "Il concetto di civitas augescens: origine e continuità," *SDHI* LXI (1995).

Baccari, M. P., *Matrimonio e donna*, Torino 2013.

Baccari, M. P., "Persone e famiglia: concetti e principi giuridici contra le astrazioni e l'individualismo," *Revista Brasileira de direito comparado* 27 (2005).

Bachofen, J., *Das Mutterrecht. Eine Untersuchung über die Gynaikokratie der alten Welt nach ihrer religiösen und rechtlichen Natur; Urreligion und antike Symbole* (3 Bde., 1926) e *Mutterrecht und Urreligion* (1927).

Bartocci, U., *Le species nuptiarum nell'esperienza romana arcaica. Relazioni matrimoniali e sistemi di potere nella testimonianza delle fonti*, Roma 1999.

Biondetti, L., *Dizionario di mitologia classica*, Milano 1997.

Biondi, B., *Istituzioni di diritto romano*, Milano 1972.

Bonfante, P., *Corso di diritto romano*, cit., 405ff.

Bretone, M., "Pomponio lettore di Cicerone," *Labeo* 16 (1970).

Bretone, M., *Tecniche e ideologie dei giuristi romani*, Napoli 1971.

Bretone, M., *Storia del diritto romano*, Bari 1987.

Calderai, V., and Favilli, C., *Genere, riproduzione, filiazione*, Napoli 2011.

Cantarella, E., *L'amore è un Dio*, Milano 2007.

Carcopino, J., *La vita quotidiana a Roma all'apogeo dell'Impero*, trans. E. Omodeo Zona[12], Bari 2005.

Cardilli, R., *Fondamento romano dei diritti odierni*, Torino 2021.

Casola, M., "Interesse *rei publicae* alla salvezza della dote," in *Ionicae Disputationes—Umo e ambiente. II incontro ionico-polacco*, Taranto, 17–20 settembre 2007, Taranto, 2008.

Casola, M., "Man, Family and Society: From the Experience of Ancient Roma up to Nowadays," in *Quaderni del dipartimento jonico—Pace e sviluppo nell'epoca moderna. Il modello costaricense*, 12, 2019, p. 173ff. Al *sito* http://edizionidjsge.uniba.it/i-quaderni.

Casola, M., "Sponsalia nelle differentiae di Modestino," in *Annali della Facoltà di Giurisprudenza di Taranto*, Anno III, Bari 2010.

Castelli, G., "Intorno all'origine dell'obbligo di dotare in diritto romano," *BIDR* 26 (1913).

Castello, C., "La definizione di matrimonio secondo Modestino," in *Apollinaris* 51.

Catalano, P., *Cittadini popoli e comunione nella legislazione dei secoli IV–VI*, Torino 1996.

Catalano, P., *Diritto e persone—studi su origine e attualità del sistema romano* I, Torino 1990.

Ceci, L., *Le etimologie dei giuristi romani*, Roma 1966.

Champeaux, J., *La religione dei romani* [cur. N. Salomon Traduzione G. Zattoni Nesi], Bologna 2002.

Cristaldi, S. A., "Confarreatio e svolgimento delle nozze," in *Religione e Diritto Romano. La cogenza del rito* [cur. S. Randazzo], Tricase 2015.

De Martino, F., *Storia della costituzione romana.* I, Napoli 1958.

De Robertis, F. M., *La responsabilità contrattuale nel sistema della grande compilazione* I, Bari 1981.

Devoto, G., *Dizionario etimologico. Avviamento alla etimologia italiana*, rist. Firenze 1968.

Devoto, G., *Storia della lingua di Roma*, Bologna 1940.

Dini, *Il potere delle antiche madri*, Firenze 1995.

Dupont, F., *La vita quotidiana nella Roma repubblicana*, Bari 1989.

Engels, F., *L'origine della* famiglia, *della proprietà privata e dello Stato. In rapporto alle indagini di Lewis H. Morgan*, Roma 1955.

Fascione, L., *Storia del diritto privato romano*, Torino 2006.

Fayer, C., *La familia romana: aspetti giuridici ed antiquari*, I, Roma 2005.

Fayer, C., *La familia romana. Aspetti giuridici ed antiquari. Sponsalia matrimonio dote* 2, Roma 2005.

Filoramo, S., *Storia delle religioni. 1. Le religioni antiche*, Bari 1994.

Fiorentini, M., *Ricerche sui culti gentilizi*, Roma 1988.

Flaceliere, R., *Daily Life in Greece*, New York 1974.

Franciosi, G., *Preesistenza della "gens" e "nomen gentilicium,"* in *Ricerche sull'organizzazione gentilizia romana*, cur. G. Franciosi, 1, ed. A. A. Vari, Napoli 1984.

Franciosi, G., *Ricerche sull'organizzazione gentilizia* romana², Napoli 1988.

Franciosi, G., *Clan gentilizio e strutture monogamiche. Contributo alla storia della famiglia* romana⁴, Napoli 1989.

Franciosi, G., *Famiglia e persone in Roma Antica Dall'età arcaica al Principato*, Torino 1989.

Garcia Garrido, M. J., *Diritto privato romano*, ed. it a cura di M. Balzarini, Padova 1992.

Giannini, F., and Baratta, I., "La donna etrusca: indipendente, libera, moderna e bellissima, scritto il 09/06/2018," in Finestre sull'Arte—Arte antica e contemporanea. Al sito: https://www.finestresullarte.info/opere-e-artisti/donna-etrusca-libera-bellissima-moderna.

Gioffredi, C., "Per la storia del matrimonio romano," *Nuovi studi di diritto greco e romano, Roma* 113–144 (1980).

Heyse, G., Mulier non debet abire nuda. *Das Erbrecht und die Versorgung der Witwe in Rom [Europäische Hochschulschriften, Reihe II, Rechtswissenschaft,* Bd. 1541], Frankfurt 1994.

Impellizzeri, S., *La letteratura bizantina da Costantino agli iconoclasti*, Bari 1965.

Ions, V., *Egyptian Mythology*, Hamburg 1973.

Kaplan, J., *Le persone non servono. Lavoro e ricchezza nell'epoca dell'intelligenza artificiale*, trad. I. V. Tomasello, Roma 2016.

Kaser, M., *Das römisches Zivilprozessrecht*, München 1996.

Kaufmann, H., *Die altrömische Miete. Ihre Zusammenhänge mit Gesellschaft, Wirtschaft und staatlicher* Vermögensverwaltung [Forschungen zum römischen Recht, Abh. 18], Köln-Graz 1964.

Kerber, W., *Die quasi-Institute als Methode der Römischen Rechtsfindung*, Münich 1970.

Kuper, A., *Enciclopedia delle scienze sociali*, Treccani, 1998.

Lévi-Strauss, C., *Lo sguardo da lontano*, tr. It. Di P. Levi, Torino 1984.

Lobrano, G., *Uxor quodammodo domina*, Sassari 1989.

Lombardi, G., "*Su alcuni concetti del diritto pubblico romano: 'civitas', 'populus', 'res publica', 'status rei publicae',*" *Archivio Giuridico* 126 (1941).

Lombardi, G., "Libertà di caccia e proprietà privata in diritto romano," *BIDR* 53–54 (1948).

Marotta, V., "Cittadinanza e condizione giuridica delle donne in Roma repubblicana e imperiale (A proposito di Leo Peppe, Civis Romana)," *Diritto@Storia*, riv. *Online*, Tradizione romana 15 (2017).

Marrone, M., *Istituzioni di diritto romano*[3], Palermo 2006.

Mazzarino, S., *L'Impero romano*, 1, Roma-Bari 1984.

Morgan, L., *La società antica. Le linee del progresso umano dallo stato selvaggio alla civiltà*, trans. Casiccia e Trevisan, Milano 1974.

Moriaud, P., "Du consentement du père de famille au mariage en droit classique," in *Mélanges Girard*, Paris 1912.

Onida, P. P., *Studi sulla condizione degli animali non umani nel sistema giuridico romano*, Torino 2002.

Paoli, U. E., *Vita romana*, Firenze 1963.

Peppe, L., *Civis Romana. Forme giuridiche e modelli sociali dell'appartenenza e dell'identità femminili in Roma antica*, Lecce 2016.

Pischedda, E., *I Greci, i Romani e ... le donne*, Roma 2022.

Platner, S. B., *A topogr. Diction. Of ancient Rome*, Oxford 1929.

Pohlenz, M., *Antikes Führertum. Cicero de officiis und das Lebensideal des Panaitios*, Leipzig-Berlin 1934, p. 37 (= *L'ideale della vita attiva secondo Panezio nel de officiis di Cicerone*, Brescia 1970, p. 66).

Pugliese, G., "Precedenti romani della moderna legislazione sui minori," in *Atti dei Convegni Lincei* 59 (1983); *Colloquio italo-polacco: La legislazione sui minori* (Roma, 22–23 novembre 1979).

Pugliese, G., "Appunti sugli impuberi e i minori in diritto romano," *St. Biscardi* IV (1983).

Pugliese, G., "Il ciclo della vita individuale nell'esperienza giuridica romana," *Atti dei Convegni Lincei* 61 (1984); Colloquio: *Il diritto e la vita materiale* (Roma, 22–23 novembre 1982).

Quadrato, R., *Le Institutiones nell'insegnamento di Gaio*, Napoli, 1979.

Quadrato, R., *Sulle tracce dell'annullabilità.* Quasi nullus *nella giurisprudenza romana*, Napoli 1983.

Rangoni, L., *La grande madre. Il culto del femminile nella storia*, Milano 2005.

Rizzelli, G., *Lex Iulia de adulteriis. Studi sulla disciplina di adulterium, lenocinium, stuprum*, Lecce 1997.

Robleda, O., *El matrimonio en derecho romano*, Roma 1970.

Robleda, O., "Il consenso matrimoniale presso i Romani," *Gregorianum* 60/2 (1979), p. 250.

Romanazzi, A., *Guida alla Dea Madre in Italia. Itinerari fra culti e tradizioni popolari*, Roma 2005.

Rothschild, N. H., *Emperor Wu Zhao and Her Pantheon of Devis, Divinities, and Dynastic Mothers*, 16, Giugno 2015.

Saller, R. P., *"Familia," "domus" and the Roman Conception of the Family*, Phenix 38, Phoenix 1984.

Sanfilippo, C., *Corso di diritto romano—La dote*, Catania 1959.

Schiavone, A., *Storia del diritto romano e linee di diritto privato*, Torino 2005.

Serrao, F., *Diritto privato economia e società nella storia di Roma—Prima parte*, Napoli 1984.

Seth Mira, *Women and Development. The Indian Experience*, New Delhi-London 2009.

Shehu, N., “Il diritto romano in Albania: insegnamento e strumenti,” *Diritto@ Storia* 3 (2004).

Sitek, B., “La conception du mariage dans le droit classique romain et la culture juridique en Europe. Quelques reflexions sur le mariage selon le texte de Modestin,” *Czasopismo Prawno Hystoryczne* 50/11–29 (1998).

Steinwenter, A., “Prolegomena zu eine Geschichte der Analogie. II. Das Recht der kaiserlichen Konstitutionen,” in *Studi Arangio-Ruiz* 2, Napoli 1953.

Stella Maranca, F., “Dos necessaria, II,” in *AUBA*, 1929.

Stepkine, A., “Aspetti dell'affectio maritalis nelle dinamiche del matrimonio romano,” in *fhi* (*forum historiae iuris*) 2020, al sito https://forhistiur.net/2020-08-a-stepkine/?l=it.

Strobel, A., “Der Begriff des Hauses im griechischen und römischen Privatrecht,” in *ZSS* 56 (1965), pp. 91–99 [Zeitschr. Neutest. Wissensch. 56, 91–99 (1965)].

Tafaro, S., *Regula e ius antiquum in D. 50.17.23. ricerche sulla responsabilità contrattuale*, Bari 1984.

Tafaro, S., *Pubes e viripotens nella esperienza giuridica romana*, Bari 1988.

Tafaro, S., “Famiglia e matrimonio: le radici romanistiche,” in *Rodizna i spoleczenstwo wczoraj i dzis. Atti del Convegno svoltosi a Bialystok nel novembre del 2004 sulla Famiglia*, Temida 2 (Poland), ed. F. Lempa and S. Tafaro, Bialystok 2006.

Tafaro, S., “La responsabilité de l'enfant dans le droit romain,” in *Enfant et romanité. Analyse comparée de la condition de l'enfant*, Paris 2007.

Tafaro, S., “Riflessioni su familia e societas humana,” in *Filia. Scritti per Gennaro Franciosi* IV, ed. F. M. D'Ippolito, Napoli 2007, p. 2537.

Tafaro, S., *Ius hominum causa constitutum—Un diritto a misura d'uomo*, Napoli 2009.

Tafaro, S., “Persona e familia,” in *Diffusione e sviluppo del sistema del Diritto romano e il Diritto Cinese*, traduzione di Lou Aihua, China, 2015, pp. 218–240.

Talamanca, M., “Lo schema 'genus-species' nelle sistematiche dei giuristi romani,” in *Colloquio Italo-Francese La filosofia greca e il diritto romano (Roma, 14–17 aprile 1973)*, t. II, *Quaderno dell'Accademia nazionale dei Lincei* N. 221, 1977.

Talamanca, M., *Istituzioni di diritto romano*, Milano 1990.

Vaihinger, H., *La filosofia del “come se,”* tr. It., Roma 1967.

Vari, A. A., *Storia delle donne. L'Antichità*, P. Shmitt Pantel, Bari 1990.

Vari, A. A., *Dizionario giuridico romano*[3] [*Introduzione*. A. Guarino; *Presentazione* S. Di Salvo], Napoli 2003.

Veyne, P., *La società romana*, Bari 1990.

Volterra, E., *Lezioni di diritto romano. Il matrimonio romano*. Anno accademico 1960–1961, Roma 1961.

Wesener, G., "Zur Denkform der 'quasi' in der römischen Jurisprudenz," in *Studi Donatuti*, 3, Milano 1973.

Wesener, G., "v. Pubertas," *PWRE* Suppl. XIV (1974), p. I.

Wissowa, G., in Roscher, *Lexicon der griech. Und röm. Mythologie*, II, col. 2462 segg.; id., *Religion und Kultus der Römer*, 2ª ed., Monaco 1912.

Zizza, A., "La moglie 'in prestito': il caso di Marzia e Catone Uticense," in *MediterraneoAntico*, Rivista online al sito https://mediterraneoantico.it/articoli/la-moglie-in-prestito-il-caso-di-marzia-e-catone-uticense/.

Anna Karabowicz

The Roman-Christian roots of the modern institution of marriage: Historical evolution in Europe

Abstract: Marriage law has undergone significant evolution since the time of classical Roman law. In European legal culture, the Roman principle on which the construction and validity of the institution of marriage were based, namely the permanent consent of both spouses to enter into and continue the relationship, the so-called *affectio maritalis*, has acquired a timeless character. In postclassical law and the Church's teaching, the other legal maxim was used: *consensus facit nuptias*. The theory of prior constitutive consent, developed by postclassical Roman jurists and later by Fathers and Doctors, theologians and canonists of the Church, led to the regulation of the institution of marriage in modern Western European civil codes as a civil contract, the conclusion of which is conditional on the existence of the mutual consent of both spouses. Contemporary European civil codifications draw from centuries-old Roman-Christian tradition when regulating matrimonial consent.

Keywords: *affectio maritalis*, civil marriage, consent, contract of marriage, marriage, Austrian civil law, canon law, French civil law, German civil law, Italian civil law, Roman law, Spanish civil law, Portuguese civil law, Swiss civil law

One might think that the modern institution of marriage, which is regulated down to the last detail in the numerous provisions of today's European civil codes, has nothing in common with the marriage provided for in ancient Rome. However, nothing could be further from the truth. There is an undeniable continuity in the interpretation of validly contracted marriage from the time of archaic Roman law through to the current regulations of marriage law. The common link consists of the principle of the spouses' consent to conclude and continue the relationship. This principle was subject to change as early as Roman times. Subsequently, the Fathers and Doctors of the Church, together with modern theologians, shaped their own theory of marriage consent. Accordingly, the current codical provisions on the institution of marriage and its validity are the fruit of more than two thousand years of evolution of this most crucial element of the lawful relationship between two individuals.

Despite the evolution of the character of marriage from a purely *de facto* institution in ancient Rome as a consequence of its religionization in Christian times following its submission to the legislative and jurisdictional monopoly of the Church, and finally through its secularization as a result of exhaustive state regulation during the era of the great codifications, the fundamental and invariable condition for the validity of marriage in the European legal tradition was and still is the consent of the spouses to its conclusion.

The sources of Roman law offer two definitions of marriage in the Corpus Iuris Civilis. The first is by Modestinus, according to which "*nuptiae sunt coniunctio maris et feminae et consortium omnis vitae, divini et humani iuris communicatio*," D. 23, 2, 1 (Mod. 1, Reg.). According to the Justinian Institutes: "*Matrimonium est viri et mulieris coniunctio, individuam consuetudinem vitae continens*" (Inst. 1, 9, 1).

In Roman law, the key term for a valid marriage was *affectio maritalis*, the definition of which varies from author to author. M. Kaser submits that it signified both spouses' awareness that their relationship had the character of a marriage, manifested by the spouses' specific conduct toward each other and toward third parties.[1] Other Romanists assert that it should be understood as the intention to enter into and continue in marriage[2] or simply a will to be husband and wife.[3] According to Marcellus (D. 48, 20, 5, 1) *affectio maritalis* exists when "*nihil prohibet et virum mariti affectionem et mulierem uxoris animum retinere*."[4] In the works of Roman jurists, the notion of *affectio maritalis* was used interchangeably with the term *consensus*: [...] "*nuptias non concubitus sed consensus facit,*" D. 35, 1, 15 (Ulp. 35, ad Sab.) and [...] "*quasi duraverint nuptias: non enim coitus matrimonium facit, sed maritalis affectio*," D. 24, 1, 32, 13 (Ulp. 33, ad Sab.). The difference between the meanings of the

1 M. Kaser, *Derecho Romano Privado*, trans. J. Santa Cruz Teijeiro, Madrid 1982, pp. 256–257.

2 J. Arias Ramos and J. A. Arias Bonet, *Derecho romano*, vol. II: *Obligaciones. Familia Sucesiones*, Madrid 1991, p. 752.

3 R. Domingo, *Roman Law. An Introduction*, London-New York 2018, p. 138; J. Iglesias, *Derecho Romano. Instituciones de derecho privado*, Barcelona 1987, pp. 566–567; É. Stocquart, "Marriage in Roman Law," *Yale Law Journal* XVI/5 (1907), p. 304; A. Borkowski and J. du Plesis Paul, *Borkowski's Textbook on Roman Law*, Oxford 2020, pp. 122–123.

4 R. Astolfi, *Il matrimonio nel diritto romano classico*, Padova 2014, pp. 114–115.

two terms is very subtle.[5] For the purposes of this article, *affectio maritalis* may be identified with the spouses' consent.[6]

The existence of *affectio maritalis* on the part of the spouses was a necessary condition for the legal validity of the marriage. However, the legality of marriage in Rome did not depend in any way on its conclusion or any religious or secular ceremony, the cohabitation of the spouses, the act of betrothal or the establishment of property relations between the parties.[7] It is worth quoting here a passage from Julian's Digest, which, when comparing betrothal and marriage, indicates that the consent of the parties was required for the conclusion of both: "*Sponsalia, sicut nuptiae, consensu contrahentium fiunt* [...]," D. 23, 1, 11 (Iul. Dig. XVI). Indeed, the consensus of the spouses was one of the few conditions for the validity of Roman marriage besides the *connubium*, the appropriate age and the consent of the *paterfamilias* in the case of a union of persons *alieni iuris*: "*Iustum matrimonium est, si inter eos, qui nuptias contrahunt, conubium sit, et tam masculus pubes quam femina potens sit, et utrique consentiant, si sui iuris sunt, aut etiam parentes eorum, si in potestate sunt*" (Ulp. 5, 2).[8]

Affectio maritalis between the spouses must be demonstrated in some manner. Hence, certain archaic traditions and ceremonies developed in Roman law which were regarded as elements *ad probationem* of a validly concluded and continuing marriage, such as *confarreatio*, *coemptio* as *gestum per aes et libram*, cohabitation, *deductio in domum*, *honor matrimonii*, witnesses (*testationes*) and the issue of

---

5 M. I. Núñez Paz, *Consentimiento matrimonial y divorcio en Roma*, Salamanca 1988, pp. 55–56, argues that *consensus* refers to the legal nature of the relationship, while *affectio maritalis* has a more personal or ethical meaning and emphasizes the permanence of the relationship.

6 This view is also shared by some researchers (see J. Zabłocki, "Zgoda małżeńska w prawie rzymskim [Marital Consent in Roman Law]," in *Honeste vivere... Księga pamiątkowa ku czci Profesora Władysława Bojarskiego* [Honeste vivere... Memorial Book in Honour of Professor Władysław Bojarski], ed. A. Sokala and E. Gajda, Toruń 2001, p. 303, which on pp. 307–308 compares the theories of Romanists as to the conditions determining the validity of a Roman marriage.

7 É. Stocquart, *op. cit.*, 303.

8 J. Arias Ramos and J. A. Arias Bonet, *op. cit.*, 753–755; J. Iglesias, *op. cit.*, 568–570. In addition to these conditions, there were, of course, impediments such as kinship, affinity or existing marriage.

marriage documents (*tabulae dotales, nuptiales, instrumentum*).[9] However, none of them determined the union's existence and its legality.

The principle of consent of the spouses has its origins in archaic law in relation to the oldest form of marriage in Rome, namely the institution of *confarreatio*, whereby the bride and groom expressed their will to marry. Throughout Roman times, consent to marriage was manifested in two forms: prior constitutive consent expressed by the spouses at the time of entering into the union and creating a valid relationship; and continuous consent, the existence of which was required throughout the duration of the marriage. Scholars of Roman marriage law point out that during the *ius sacrum* period, the validity of a marriage was determined by the initial will of the spouses. The progressive secularization of Roman law led to the recognition in the classical period that the existence of a permanent intention on both sides to remain in the union was legally relevant for the formation and continuation of a legal marriage. The situation changed again in postclassical law when the original rule was reverted to, namely, when assessing the validity of a marriage the existence of prior consent of the spouses to its conclusion was taken into account.[10] Since the 4th century AD, the rule of *consensus facit nuptias* has been a fundamental principle to determine the legality of a relationship.[11] This undoubtedly reflects the influence of Christian thought, which emphasized the importance of the initial consent, combined with the formalism of the marriage ceremony bearing the symbolism of the pre-Christian era.[12]

Irrespective of the formula in force at the time, the principle of consent of the spouses gave rise to the idea among Roman jurists of the classical period that marriage is a kind of contract between the spouses, who must necessarily express their will to conclude it, and also—throughout its duration—constantly express

9 R. Astolfi, *Il matrimonio, op. cit.*, pp. 92–108. On the form of Christian marriage in the first centuries after Christ, cf. R. Astolfi, *Studi sul matrimonio nel diritto romano postclassico e giustinianeo*, Napoli 2012, pp. 42–45.

10 R. Astolfi argues that during the classical period prior consent was also necessary in addition to continuing consensus, which seems logical because there can be no question of intention to remain in a marriage without the will to enter into it, cf. R. Astolfi, *Il matrimonio, op. cit.*, pp. 82–85; M. Kaser, *Das Römische Privatrecht. Erster Abschnitt. Das altrömische, das vorklassische und klassische Recht*, München 1971, pp. 321–322; M. I. Núñez Paz, *op. cit.*, pp. 56–57.

11 Which found its expression in the imperial constitutions (e.g., Nov. 22, 3: AD 535) and in some (probably interpellated) passages of the Digests, cf. M. I. Núñez Paz, *op. cit.*, p. 57.

12 J. Arias Ramos and J. A. Arias Bonet, *op. cit.*, p. 753.

their consent to its continuation. Hence the formal and *de facto* ease of divorce so characteristic of the late Republic and Empire, when *sine manu* marriage was practically the only type of union. Since the necessary condition for forming and continuing a valid marriage was the consensus of both parties, the logical consequence of the lack of will to continue the marriage was its dissolution.[13] No other additional formality was necessary. The legal construction of marriage was linked with civil law contracts, more specifically the consensual contract of partnership or *societas* already established in contractual theory. This was based on the analogy between marriage and partnership, since the existence and continuity of both requires a subjective element or *animus* called *affectio*. There is also a similarity between the regulation of the institution of marriage in the Digests and the Justinian Codex, where the drafters used the model of civil contracts.[14]

The first Fathers and Doctors of the Church alluded to these elements of Roman marriage, namely the principle of the consent of the spouses in the form of an initial consensus as expressed at the time of the marriage conclusion, as well as to the idea of the analogy of marriage and contract.[15]

Christianity brought about a socio-cultural, ideological and legal revolution. While drawing abundantly from the achievements of Roman law and ancient tradition and philosophy in general, it led to a slow but highly permanent change in the character of many legal institutions. In some cases, the theories of Christian thinkers embodied in the norms of canon law led to the gradual assumption of the legislative competence and subsequently the jurisdiction of lay authorities by the authorities and courts of the Church. This process lasted throughout the Middle Ages, starting at different times in different parts of Europe and with certain local variations. Turning points in this respect were, of course, the moment when the Christian world first split as a consequence of the Great Schism of 1054 into the Western and Eastern Churches, and then after 1517, when the Protestant Church broke away from the Western Church.

Concerning the institution of marriage, the abovementioned tendency of the ecclesiastical authorities to assume a monopoly over its legislation and judicial regulation intensified due to the recognition by Christian theologians of marriage as an institution sanctified by Christ and endowed with special grace by Him,[16] which eventually led to the acknowledgment of marriage as one of the

13 Ibid.; R. Astolfi, *Il matrimonio, op. cit.*, pp. 112–113.

14 M. I. Núñez Paz, *op. cit.*, pp. 55, 77; cf. R. Astolfi, *Il matrimonio, op. cit.*, pp. 110–111.

15 T. Rincón, *El matrimonio, misterio y signo. Siglos IX–XIII*, Pamplona 1971, pp. 16–22.

16 Cf. Letter Conturbatio to Probus, year 417?: A. Sarmiento, J. Escrivá-Ivars, *Enchiridion Familiae. Textos del Magisterio Pontificio y Conciliar sobre el Matrimonio y la Familia*

seven sacraments instituted by the Saviour. This did not occur until the 13th century[17] and was the result of scholastic theology based on the ideas of St. Augustine, who saw in marriage a holy symbol of the union of Christ with the Church, and was completed by the theory of St. Thomas Aquinas.[18]

In the first millennium, the issue of marriage consent began to appear in Church texts. Pope Nicholas I (858–867)[19] explicitly pointed to the principle of consensus as a necessary condition for a valid marriage. According to his words: "*Ubi non est consensus utriusque, ibi non est coniugium*"[20] and "*Sufficiat secundum leges solus eorum consensus, de quorum coniunctionibus agitur. Qui consensus si solus in nuptiis forte defuerit, cetera omnia etiam cum ipso coitu celebrata frustrantur, Iohanne Chrysostomo magno doctore testante, qui ait: 'Matrimonium non facit coitus, sed voluntas.*'"[21]

The abovementioned dilemma of whether a valid marriage was created solely by the spouses' consent or whether sexual intercourse was necessary was raised by scholars in the 1st century of the second millennium.[22] Under the influence of the Roman Digests that had recently been rediscovered, which offered a ready

(Siglos I a XX), vol. I, Pamplona 2003, p. 23; Letter Τοῦ σωτῆρος of Cyril of Alexandria to Nestorius, November 430, read at the Ecumenical Council of Ephesus (Asia Minor), 22.06.431: "*Propter hanc etenim causam dicimus eum dispensatorie et ipsis benedixisse tunc nuntiis, cum in Canan Galilaeae cum sanctis vocatus apostolis adesse dignatus est*," Ibid.

17 Although the term "*Christi et Ecclesiae sacramentum*" appeared earlier in reference to the *societas nuptiarum*, the conjugal community, cf. Leo the Great from his *Epistolas fraternitatis* to Rusticus, Bishop of Narbonne (France), year 458 or 459, resp. IV. Ibid., p. 29. To explain the symbolism of marriage contained in the Gospel, St. Augustine used the term *bonum sacramenti*, and therefore the sacred sign, cf. P. Adnés, *El matrimonio*, Barcelona 1969, p. 98; T. Rincón, *op. cit.*, pp. 25–27; E. Schillebeeckx, *El matrimonio, realidad terrena y misterio de salvación*, vol. I, Salamanca 1968, pp. 247–255.

18 For a description of the development of scholastic doctrine on the sacramental nature of marriage, cf. P. Adnés, *op. cit.*, pp. 112–114, p. 129; A. Sarmiento, *El matrimonio cristiano*, Pamplona 2007, pp. 124–127; E. Schillebeeckx, *op. cit.*, pp. 252–302; scholastic doctrine description, cf. T. Rincón, *op. cit.*, pp. 255–369, with St. Thomas' ideas about marriage as a sacrament, ibid., pp. 347–349.

19 Ibid., pp. 65–67.

20 Decrees or Rescripts of Pope Nicholas I, c. 858, n. III, A. Sarmiento and J. Escrivá-Ivars, *Enchiridion Familiae, op. cit.*, p. 82.

21 Reply to the Bulgarians *Ad consulta vestra*, 13.11.866, chap. III. Ibid., p. 84.

22 The carnal act theory appeared before, in the 9th century, cf. Rincón T., *op. cit.*, pp. 67–85.

answer to this question in excerpts from Ulpian's works D. 35, 1, 15 (Ulp. 35, ad Sab.) and D. 24, 1, 32, 13 (Ulp. 33, ad Sab.), two schools appeared in the 12th century. The first, the Bolognese, whose leading representative was the canonist Gratian, held that marriage was formed by consent but could be dissolved if the spouses did not cohabit.[23] The second, the Parisian, headed by the theologian Peter Lombard, advocated the indissolubility of marriage regardless of the consummation of the union, since only consent was necessary to create the sacrament.[24] Finally, popes Alexander III (1159–1181), Innocent III (1198–1216) and Gregory IX (1227–1241) worked out an indirect solution by concluding that a valid marriage is formed as a sacrament by mutual consent of the spouses but it is possible to dissolve the marriage up until the carnal act has been completed. A compromise between the two positions was the provision that a marriage contracted but not consummated could only be dissolved by a dispensation issued by the ecclesiastical authorities.[25]

From the very beginning, both theological and canonical church doctrine on the institution of marriage has referred to the postclassical formula of the constitutive consent of the spouses as a condition for the validity of the union. This was also a logical consequence of the Catholic theory of the indissolubility of marriage. Since a valid marriage could not be dissolved other than by the death of one of the spouses, the continuing consent of the parties to the marriage was legally irrelevant.[26] As mentioned, the opposite situation existed in classical Roman marriage, the dissolution of which took place automatically without the need for any formal acts with the cessation of *affectio maritalis*, that is, the will to continue living in the union. The postclassical and canonical principle of prior consent expressed at the time of marriage conclusion, which creates a valid marriage due to its status as the only subjective element relevant to its validity, has many severe legal consequences. The most important of these is that in order to affect the validity of the marriage—and thus to be a ground for its annulment—any defects in the marriage consent must necessarily exist at the time of the expression of consent at the conclusion of the marriage.

According to the Code of Canon Law of 1983, "The consent of the parties, legitimately manifested between persons qualified by law, makes marriage [...]"

23 Ibid., pp. 214–243.

24 Ibid., pp. 176–191.

25 Cf. Adnés P., *op. cit.*, pp. 103–105; Rincón T., *op. cit.*, pp. 243–251, 375–385; A. Sarmiento, *op. cit.*, pp. 177–180.

26 Ibid., pp. 173–174.

(Can. 1057 §1). Paragraph 2 of the same provision expressly refers to the legal nature of marital consent as an act of will of the parties expressed once and "by which a man and a woman mutually give and accept each other through an irrevocable covenant in order to establish marriage." According to Canons 1095–1099, 1101–1103, the defects of marriage consent include lack of use of reason, lack of judgment as to the rights and duties of marriage, inability to assume essential marital duties for reasons of a mental nature, minimal knowledge of the nature of marriage, certain types of error, deceit or coercion.[27]

As with the institution of marriage consent, the issue of marriage as a contract arose among theologians and canonists of the University of Bologna. While St. Thomas Aquinas was skeptical, it was the Franciscan doctrine which took up the subject of the contractual nature of marriage. Its representative, Duns Scot, claimed that marriage was a contract.[28] The vast majority of theologians see in matrimonial consent the so-called matter and form of the sacrament. This theory of complete identification between the marriage contract and the sacrament was advocated by St. Thomas Aquinas, Martín de Azpilcueta, Francisco Suárez, Benedict XV and St. John Paul II. Melchior Cano (1509–1561) pointed out that consent is only a matter, while the form of the sacrament is a priestly blessing.[29] Meanwhile, in the 17th century the so-called Regalists who sought to limit the powers of the Church in favor of the monarch considered the matter of the sacrament to be a civil contract. This was the first step toward recognizing the distinction between the marriage contract and the sacrament.[30]

Throughout the Middle Ages, the Church and canon law tolerated marriages according to local, often pagan, customs. However, although the Church considered them valid, over time these clandestine marriages were subject to punishment. At the end of the first millennium, the recommended but non-obligatory form of marriage was a church ceremony where the priest blessed the newlyweds, which in time was combined with the Holy Mass.[31] It was not until the Council of Trent that a compulsory form of marriage was introduced, with failure to

27 *Code of Canon Law* of 1983, text in English: https://www.vatican.va/archive/cod-iuris-canonici/eng/documents/cic_lib4-cann998-1165_en.html#TITLE_VII [accessed: 30.06.2023].

28 J. F. Muñoz García, *El matrimonio, misterio y signo. Siglos XVII y XVIII*, Pamplona 1982, pp. 105–107, 118–120, 294, 341–344, 351–354.

29 Ibid., pp. 88, 285–286, 288, 375–397, 425–475.

30 P. Adnés, *op. cit.*, pp. 129–131; J. F. Muñoz García, *op. cit.*, pp. 397–424, 476–478, 522, 526; A. Sarmiento, *op. cit.*, pp. 185–187.

31 A. Sarmiento, *op. cit.*, pp. 192–193; E. Schillebeeckx, *op. cit.*, pp. 228–237.

comply resulting in the nullity of the marriage.[32] From that time on, a marriage could only be validly contracted following the spouses' declaration of will before the competent parish priest of the place of residence of one of the spouses (or his representative) in the presence of at least two witnesses. In addition, there was an order to read the banns three times before the wedding to reveal any possible impediments to the marriage. Marriages also had to be entered in the register kept by the parish priests.[33]

Roman-canonical solutions—developed during the Middle Ages and the Renaissance by Christian theologians based on Roman postclassical concepts—concerning the form of marriage, prior consent as a condition of validity and the contractual nature of the institution of marriage were referred to by enlightened civilists and codifiers of civil law in the 18th, 19th and 20th centuries. What is particularly interesting is that the achievements of the canonists served as a model not only for the legislators of traditionally Catholic countries but also Protestant countries and even those in which there was an open policy of separation of church and state, as in the case of France.

Not all the state legislators of the era of the great codifications decided to include a definition of marriage in the relevant provisions of the civil codes when regulating the institution of marriage, or to explicitly define its contractual nature and the principle of consent as fundamental elements of the institution of marriage. Among the more enlightened European civil codifications, mention should first be made of the pioneering terms included in legal instruments at the turn of the 18th and 19th centuries. Their authors included relevant provisions on the nature and definition of marriage as an element of protest against the monopoly of the Catholic Church in this sphere. This resulted from the aforementioned Regalist doctrine, a variation of which in France was called Gallicanism. As is well known, it was also referred to by the Austrian monarchs, especially Maria Theresa and her son Joseph II of Habsburg. The Austrian variant of Gallicanism is referred to as Josephinism.[34] It is not surprising, then, that the most

32 The *Tametsi* Decree of 1563 regulating the canonical form of marriage was to apply only in those ecclesiastical provinces where it was officially promulgated, cf. *Tametsi* Decree, Session XXIV, 11.11.1563, chap. 1, 1–4. A. Sarmiento and J. Escrivá-Ivars, *Enchiridion Familiae, op. cit.*, pp. 147–149. It was only by virtue of the *Ne Temere* Decree of 1907 that marriage was universally introduced as a compulsory canonical form for all Catholics, even for mixed marriages. Ibid., pp. 615–617.

33 A. Sarmiento, *op. cit.*, pp. 192–193.

34 Josephinism was a specific religious policy initiated by Maria Theresa of Austria and continued by her son, Joseph II Habsburg, the Holy Roman Emperor. The Austrian

radical regulations, which attempted to break with the ecclesiastical understanding of marriage as an institution subject solely to the legislation and jurisdiction of the Church, are contained in laws promulgated in Austria and France, despite being traditionally Catholic countries.[35]

The Austrian Emperor Joseph II was the first secular legislator to break the Church's legislative and jurisdictional monopoly on matrimonial matters. The marriage patent ("*Ehepatent*") enacted in 1783 regulated issues relating to the form of marriage, the admissibility of divorces and the jurisdiction of courts in matrimonial matters, and it remained in force in the Habsburg Monarchy for over a hundred years.[36] Its § 1 reads: "Marriage in itself, regarded as a civil

---

legislature, based on that doctrine and heralded by the monarch's enactment of the *Toleranzpatent* in 1781, regulated the legal position of three religions alongside Catholicism: Calvinism, Lutheranism and Orthodoxy. A year later a similar act was issued in relation to the Jewish confession. It was not until 1912 that the Muslim faith was recognized. This doctrine led to profound interference by the state and its administration in the internal affairs of religious unions. For more cf. A. Dziadzio, "Osbowe prawo małżeńskie w Austrii na tle stosunków państwo-Kościół katolicki (XVIII–XIX wiek) [Personal Marriage Law in Austria in the Context of State-Catholic Church Relations (18th–19th centuries)]," in *Krakowskie studia z historii państwa i prawa* [Cracow Studies of Constitutional and Legal History], Kraków 2004, pp. 137–146; A. Borowski, "U źródła poglądów liberalnych na małżeństwo [At the Source of Liberal Views on Marriage]," *Przegląd Katolicki* [*Catholic Review*] 70/25 (1932), pp. 390–392; 70/26, pp. 406–408, 70/27, pp. 422–425.

35 In Protestant countries, civil marriages were introduced earlier. Civil marriages existed primarily in the Netherlands, where they were introduced as an optional form of marriage on April 1, 1580. In England, compulsory civil marriages were introduced in 1653, but from 1683 they were an optional form of marriage. W. Abraham, *Forma zawarcia zaręczyn i małżeństwa w najnowszem ustawodawstwie kościelnem* [Form of Betrothal and Marriage in the Latest Ecclesiastical Legislation], Lwów 1909, pp. 148–151.

36 The *Ehepatent* advocated the so-called mixed regulation of matrimonial law. It consisted of a kind of incorporation into state law of the rules already existing in the respective religious unions (in the case of Austria, the marriage law of the Catholic Church, the Orthodox Church, the Lutheran Church, the Calvinist Church and the Mosaic Marriage Law) and recognition by the state of the validity of religious marriages, but all disputes arising from marriage law were subject to state jurisdiction. Initially, Austrian law did not recognize the possibility of marriage before a civil official. Civil unions were introduced on an exceptional basis, such as the so-called *Nothzivilehe* and for non-denominationals only during the constitutional period, namely by the Acts of 1868 and 1870, cf. A. Karabowicz, "Małżeństwo cywilne z konieczności (Notzivilehe) w Galicji w latach 1868–1918 [Civil Marriage of Necessity (Notzivilehe) in Galicia in the Years 1868–1918]," in *Prawo blisko człowieka. Z dziejów prawa rodzinnego i spadkowego*

contract, as well as any rights and obligations arising from this contract, are civil […]."[37] This may be compared with the beginning of § 44 of the Austrian Civil Code (ABGB): "The family relations are established by the marriage contract. In the marriage contract, two persons of different gender legally declare their intent to live in a joint community, to procreate, to raise children and to support each other."[38]

A further step was taken by revolutionary and Napoleonic legislation in France. This broke entirely with the denominationalism of marriage and the only form of marriage recognized as valid by the state was secular marriage. The French Constitution of 1791 established compulsory civil marriage for all regardless of their religion, combined with the general acceptance of divorce and the state's assumption of jurisdiction in matrimonial matters. Its Article 7 contained in Title II: "Of the division of the Kingdom and of the status of citizens," states as follows: "The law considers marriage only as a civil contract."[39] The Napoleonic Civil Code of 1804 was interestingly the only one of the codifications discussed here which in its original wording clearly referred to the Roman-Christian tradition of marriage consent, stating in Article 146: "There can be no marriage where consent is wanting."[40] It is an almost literal translation of the texts of Roman jurists and ecclesiastical theologians and canonists. A practically identical provision was introduced recently in the amended version of Article 45 of the Spanish Civil Code of 1889 as a result of the reform of marriage law in Spain, which took

---

[Law Close to Man. From the History of Family and Inheritance Law], ed. M. Mikuła, Kraków 2008, pp. 59–70. Finally, civil marriages were made compulsory as the only form recognized by the Austrian state in 1938. A. Dziadzio, *op. cit.*, p. 141.

37 Author's trans, *Ehepatent* of 16.01.1783, *Justizgesetzsammlung* 117 (1783), p. 192, https://alex.onb.ac.at/cgi-content/alex?aid=jgs&datum=1001&page=214&size=45 [accessed: 30.06.2023].

38 Author's trans., "*Allgemeines bürgerliches Gesetzbuch für die gesammten deutschen Erbländer der Oesterreichischen Monarchie* [ABGB] of 1.06.1811," *Justizgesetzsammlung* 946 (1811), p. 282, https://alex.onb.ac.at/cgi-content/alex?aid=jgs&datum=1012&page=472&size=45 [accessed: 30.06.2023].

39 French Constitution of 3.09.1791, text in French: https://www.conseil-constitutionnel.fr/les-constitutions-dans-l-histoire/constitution-de-1791 [accessed: 30.06.2023], text in English: https://web.archive.org/web/20111217062556/http://sourcebook.fsc.edu/history/constitutionof1791.html [accessed: 30.06.2023].

40 *Code civil des Français* of 21.03.1804, text in French: https://www.legifrance.gouv.fr/codes/texte_lc/LEGITEXT000006070721/1804-03-29/ [accessed: 30.06.2023], text in English: *The Code Napoleon; or the French Civil Code. Literally Translated from the Original and Official Edition, Published at Paris, in 1804*, London 1827, p. 43.

place in 1981 after the change of political regime and the adoption of the democratic Constitution of 1978: "There is no marriage without marital consent."[41]

The codifications of the second half of the 19th and 20th centuries no longer included such firm expositions of the definition and nature of marriage in their regulations on matrimonial law since, at that time, the secular nature of marriage and the competence of the state to adjudicate matrimonial matters were no longer, in principle, the subject of legal debate in Europe. For example, the Italian Civil Code of 1865,[42] the Spanish Civil Code of 1889,[43] the German BGB of 1896[44] and the Swiss ZGB of 1907[45] no longer contained such definitions and determinations of the nature of marriage. Despite the continued resistance of the hierarchy of the Catholic Church, the process of secularization of the institution of marriage was already unstoppable. In some countries traditionally closely linked to the Catholic Church (Portugal and Spain[46]), it is interesting to

---

41 Author's trans., Ley 30/1981, of 7.07.1981, "Boletín Oficial de Estado," No. 172, of 20.07.1981, pp. 16457–16462, https://www.boe.es/buscar/doc.php?id=BOE-A-1981-16216 [accessed: 30.06.2023].

42 *Codice Civile del Regno d'Italia*, Torino 1865.

43 *Código Civil* of 25.07.1889, "Gaceta de Madrid," No. 206 of 25.07.1889, https://www.boe.es/buscar/act.php?id=BOE-A-1889-4763&tn=1&p=18890725 [accessed: 30.06.2023].

44 *Bürgerliches Gesetzbuch* (BGB) of 18.08.1896, "Reichs-Gesetzblatt," No. 21 of 24.08.1896, pp. 195–603, https://www.reichsgesetzblatt.de/D/RGBl-D/1896/index.htm [accessed: 30.06.2023]; the law of 1875 which introduced the obligatory civil form of marriage in its § 41 stated as follows: "Within the territory of the German Reich, a marriage can only be validly concluded before the registrar" [Author's trans.], *Gesetz über die Beurkundung des Personenstandes und die Eheschließung*, 06.02.1875, "Reichsgesetzblatt," No. 4 of 9.02.1875, p. 31, https://opacplus.bsb-muenchen.de/Vta2/bsb11309201/bsb:10569916?page=3 [accessed: 30.06.2023].

45 *Schweizerisches Zivilgesetzbuch* (ZGB) of 10.12.1907, "Schweizerisches Bundesblatt," No. 54 of 21.12.1907, https://www.fedlex.admin.ch/eli/fga/1907/6_589_429_/de [accessed: 30.06.2023]; text in English: *The Swiss Civil Code of December 10, 1907 (Effective January 1, 1912)*, trans. R. P. Schick, Boston 1915.

46 The first civil codification of the Kingdom of Italy in 1865 provided for a civil form of marriage to be compulsory and only recognized by the state, cf.: Article 93 in: *Codice Civile*, *op. cit.*, p. 25. However, Articles 82 and 83 of the new Civil Code enacted in 1942 and still in force today provide for the possibility, but not the obligation, of marriage before a Catholic priest in accordance with the provisions of the Concordat (added to the Lateran Treaty of 1929) and other special acts or before a minister of other denominations recognized by the state, cf. *Codice civile* of 16.03.1942-XX, No. 262, "Gazzetta Ufficiale," No. 79 of 4.04.1942, https://www.gazzettaufficiale.it/atto/serie_generale/cari

note the dual nature of codical regulations. On the one hand, they introduced the principle of civil marriage; on the other, they regulated so-called Catholic marriages as being compulsory for Catholics. This was an apparent concession to the traditional prerogatives of the Church in matrimonial matters, since the state authorities renounced the role of legislator in Catholic marriages (for their regulation the codifiers referred to the formulations of canon law[47]), as well as their jurisdictional functions by placing matrimonial matters between Catholics in the hands of the ecclesiastical courts.[48]

In this extensive European legal patchwork on the legislation of matrimonial matters, one codification should be singled out which has taken a very original approach to regulation of marriage. Nineteenth-century Portuguese legislators decided not to include the institution of marriage either in the codical book on the law of persons according to the traditional tripartite civil law structure derived from the Roman jurist Gaius (*personae-res-actiones*) or in the book of family law according to the Pandectists' systematization of civil law introduced by German scholars. Instead, marriage law was included in the Portuguese Civil Code of 1867 in Book II: "Rights which are acquired by own act and will, along with act and will of another" under Title II: "Of contracts in particular." Marriage was regulated as the first of the civil contracts.[49] Its Article 1056 stated: "Marriage

caDettaglioAtto/originario?atto.dataPubblicazioneGazzetta=1942-04-04&atto.codiceRedazionale=042U0262 [accessed: 30.06.2023].

47 This was provided for in Article 75 of the Spanish Civil Code of 1889, which was in force until 8.08.1981, *Código civil* of 25.07.1889…, *op. cit.*, and in Articles 1069 to 1070 of the Portuguese Civil Code of 1867, *Codigo civil portuguez. Approvado por Carta de Lei de 1 de julho de 1867*, Lisboa 1868, p. 189, text in English: *Portuguese Civil Code, 1867. Official Translation with Notes*, Panaji (Goa) 2018, p. 239, https://www.indiacode.nic.in/bitstream/123456789/8312/1/ocrportuguesecivilcode.pdf [accessed: 30.06.2023].

48 Article 80 of the Spanish Civil Code of 1889, which was in force until 8.08.1981, *Código civil* of 25.07.1889…, *op. cit.*, and Articles 1086 to 1088 of the Portuguese Civil Code of 1867; *Codigo civil portuguez…*, *op. cit.*, p. 193, *Portuguese Civil Code, 1867…*, *op. cit.*, p. 244, and Articles 1625 to 1626 of the Portuguese Civil Code of 1966, *Código Civil* of 25.11.1966, No. 47344/66, "Diário do Governo" of 25.11.1966, No. 274, https://files.dre.pt/1s/1966/11/27400/18832086.pdf [accessed: 30.06.2023].

49 It is worth noting that the second contract governed by the Portuguese Code of 1867 was the contract of partnership (*Codigo civil portuguez…*, *op. cit.*, pp. 217 et seq., *Portuguese Civil Code, 1867…*, *op. cit.*, p. 274 et. seq.), a fact which evokes associations with the analogy between marriage and partnership highlighted in Roman sources, *vide* fn. 14.

is a perpetual contract made between two persons of different sex with the purpose of legitimately constituting a family."[50]

As a consequence of the transfer of legislative and jurisdictional competence from ecclesiastical hands to lay institutions, together with the introduction of the civil form of marriage, whether on a broader or narrower scale, there was recognition—at least among non-Catholics—of the possibility of civil divorces, and therefore of a formal decision on the dissolution of marriage issued by the state courts based on a hearing, albeit complicated. This break from the principle of the indissolubility of marriage existing in canon law led to the need to introduce changes in the regulation of defects of marital consent. Drawing on the general theory of defects in the declaration of wills and defects in marriage *consensus* developed by the canonists, lay codifiers working on the newly enacted civil codes enumerated in the relevant regulation of marriage law a list of circumstances which—if they existed at the time of its declaration, and therefore at the time of marriage conclusion—gave rise to the annulment of the marriage effective *ex tunc*. A novelty introduced by the 19th-century codifications of civil law relating to the already existing canonical concept of defects in marital consent resulting from the introduction of civil divorces was the inclusion of time limits to petition for annulment of marriage on the grounds of defects in marriage consent. Parties entitled to initiate proceedings in a state court for annulment of a marriage based on defective constitutive consent to the marriage must do so within an appropriate prescription period from the moment they become aware of the given circumstance or the cessation of the situation that led to the defective marital consent. In addition, an absolute deadline was set, after which it was impossible to bring an action for the annulment of the union. Introduction of this prescription period on the right to apply to the court for marriage annulment due to defects of consent was the logical consequence of introducing the possibility of the dissolution of marriage, that is, civil divorce. Secular legislators considered that the existence of a right to apply for the annulment of a union that is unlimited in time creates an undesirable state of legal uncertainty. When the right to apply for annulment of civil marriage has prescribed, the parties always have the right to file for divorce.

This brief overview of the evolution of the principle of marital consent in Europe from Roman law through to practically contemporary civil codifications is a reminder of the historical continuity of legal institutions, the regulation of which today is by no means the invention of any particular codifier or legislator but the

---

50 Portuguese Civil Code, 1867…, *op. cit.*, p. 236.

fruit of the theories of many jurists, thinkers and philosophers, and whose origin and development have been significantly influenced by centuries of social, cultural and intellectual change. Proof of this is the fact that the free consent of both spouses, a condition *sine qua non* for relationships entered into at the dawn of Roman law, continues to be a fundamental requirement for the validity of different- and same-sex relationships in the laws of the 21st century.

Bibliography

Abraham, W., *Forma zawarcia zaręczyn i małżeństwa w najnowszem ustawodawstwie kościelnem* [Form of Betrothal and Marriage in the Latest Ecclesiastical Legislation], Lwów 1909.

Adnés, P., *El matrimonio*, Barcelona 1969.

Arias Ramos, J., Arias Bonet, J. A., *Derecho romano*, vol. II: *Obligaciones. Familia Sucesiones*, Madrid 1991.

Astolfi, R., *Il matrimonio nel diritto romano classico*, Padova 2014.

Astolfi, R., *Studi sul matrimonio nel diritto romano postclassico e giustinianeo*, Napoli 2012.

Borkowski, A., and du Plesis Paul, J., *Borkowski's Textbook on Roman Law*, Oxford 2020.

Borowski, A., "U źródła poglądów liberalnych na małżeństwo [At the Source of Liberal Views on Marriage]," *Przegląd Katolicki* [*Catholic Review*] 70/25 (1932), pp. 390–392, 70/26, pp. 406–408, 70/27, pp. 422–425.

Domingo, R., *Roman Law. An Introduction*, London-New York 2018.

Dziadzio, A., *Osbowe prawo małżeńskie w Austrii na tle stosunków państwo Kościół katolicki (XVIII–XIX wiek)* [Personal Marriage Law in Austria in the Context of State-Catholic Church Relations (18th–19th centuries)], *Krakowskie studia z historii państwa i prawa* [Cracow Studies of Constitutional and Legal History], Kraków 2004, pp. 137–146.

Iglesias, J., *Derecho Romano. Instituciones de derecho privado*, Barcelona 1987.

Karabowicz, A., "Małżeństwo cywilne z konieczności (Notzivilehe) w Galicji w latach 1868–1918 [Civil Marriage of Necessity (Notzivilehe) in Galicia in the Years 1868–1918]," *Prawo blisko człowieka. Z dziejów prawa rodzinnego i spadkowego* [Law Close to Man. From the History of Family and Inheritance Law], ed. M. Mikuła, Kraków 2008, pp. 59–70.

Kaser, M., *Das Römische Privatrecht. Erster Abschnitt. Das altrömische, das vorklassische und klassische Recht*, München 1971.

M. Kaser, *Derecho Romano Privado*, trans. J. Santa Cruz Teijeiro, Madrid 1982.

Muñoz García, J. F., *El matrimonio, misterio y signo. Siglos XVII y XVIII*, Pamplona 1982.

Núñez Paz, M. I., *Consentimiento matrimonial y divorcio en Roma*, Salamanca 1988.

Rincón, T., *El matrimonio, misterio y signo. Siglos IX–XIII*, Pamplona 1971.

Sarmiento, A., *El matrimonio cristiano*, Pamplona 2007.

Sarmiento, A., and Escrivá-Ivars, J., *Enchiridion Familiae. Textos del Magisterio Pontificio y Conciliar sobre el Matrimonio y la Familia (Siglos I a XX)*, vol. I, Pamplona 2003.

Schillebeeckx, E., *El matrimonio, realidad terrena y misterio de salvación*, vol. I, Salamanca 1968.

Stocquart, É., "Marriage in Roman Law," *Yale Law Journal* XVI/5 (1907), pp. 303–327.

Zabłocki, J., "Zgoda małżeńska w prawie rzymskim [Marital Consent in Roman Law]," in *Honeste vivere … Księga pamiątkowa ku czci Profesora Władysława Bojarskiego* [*Honeste vivere … Memorial Book in Honour of Professor Władysław Bojarski*], ed. A. Sokala and E. Gajda, Toruń 2001, pp. 303–312.

Legal acts

Allgemeines bürgerliches Gesetzbuch für die gesammten deutschen Erbländer der Oesterreichischen Monarchie (ABGB) of 01.06.1811, Justizgesetzsammlung, No. 946/1811, p. 282, https://alex.onb.ac.at/cgi-content/alex?aid=jgs&datum=1012&page=472&size=45 [accessed: 30.06.2023].

Bürgerliches Gesetzbuch (BGB) of 18.08.1896, "Reichs-Gesetzblatt," No. 21 of 24.08.1896, pp. 195–603, https://www.reichsgesetzblatt.de/D/RGBl-D/1896/index.htm [accessed: 30.06.2023].

Code civil des Français of 21.03.1804, text in French: https://www.legifrance.gouv.fr/codes/texte_lc/LEGITEXT000006070721/1804-03-29/ [accessed: 30.06.2023], text in English: *The Code Napoleon; or the French Civil Code. Literally Translated from the Original and Official Edition, Published at Paris, in 1804*, London 1827.

Code of Canon Law of 1983, text in English: https://www.vatican.va/archive/cod-iuris-canonici/eng/documents/cic_lib4-cann998-1165_en.html#TITLE_VII [accessed: 30.06.2023].

Codice Civile del Regno d'Italia, Torino 1865.

Codice civile of 16.03.1942-XX, No. 262, "Gazzetta Ufficiale," No. 79 of 4.04.1942, https://www.gazzettaufficiale.it/atto/serie_generale/caricaDettaglioAtto/ori

ginario?atto.dataPubblicazioneGazzetta=1942-04-04&atto.codiceRedazionale=042U0262 [accessed: 30.06.2023].

Codigo civil portuguez. Approvado por Carta de Lei de 1 de julho de 1867, Lisboa 1868, pp. 189, text in English: *Portuguese Civil Code, 1867. Official Translation with Notes*, Panaji (Goa) 2018, https://www.indiacode.nic.in/bitstream/123456789/8312/1/ocrportuguesecivilcode.pdf [accessed: 30.06.2023].

Código Civil of 25.07.1889, "Gaceta de Madrid," No. 206 of 25.07.1889, https://www.boe.es/buscar/act.php?id=BOE-A-1889-4763&tn=1&p=18890725 [accessed: 30.06.2023].

Código Civil of 25.11.1966, No. 47344/66, "Diário do Governo" of 25.11.1966, No. 274, https://files.dre.pt/1s/1966/11/27400/18832086.pdf [accessed: 30.06.2023].

Constitution of 3.09.1791, text in French: https://www.conseil-constitutionnel.fr/les-constitutions-dans-l-histoire/constitution-de-1791 [accessed: 30.06.2023], text in English: https://web.archive.org/web/20111217062556/http://sourcebook.fsc.edu/history/constitutionof1791.html [accessed: 30.06.2023].

Ehepatent of 16.01.1783, *Justizgesetzsammlung* 117 (1783), p. 192, https://alex.onb.ac.at/cgi-content/alex?aid=jgs&datum=1001&page=214&size=45 [accessed: 30.06.2023].

Gesetz über die Beurkundung des Personenstandes und die Eheschließung of 6.02.1875, "Reichs-Gesetzblatt," No 4 of 9.02.1875, pp. 23–40, https://opacplus.bsb-muenchen.de/Vta2/bsb11309201/bsb:10569916?page=3 [accessed: 30.06.2023].

Ley 30/1981, of July, 7, "Boletín Oficial de Estado," No. 172 of 20.07.1981, pp. 16457–16462, https://www.boe.es/buscar/doc.php?id=BOE-A-1981-16216 [accessed: 30.06.2023].

Schweizerisches Zivilgesetzbuch (ZGB) of 10.12.1907, "Schweizerisches Bundesblatt," No. 54 of 21.12.1907, https://www.fedlex.admin.ch/eli/fga/1907/6_589_429_/de [accessed: 30.06.2023]; text in English: *The Swiss Civil Code of December 10, 1907 (Effective January 1, 1912)*, trans. R. P. Schick, Boston 1915.

Chapter II. The family as the foundation of society

Jaime Bonet Navarro

The secularization of marriage in Europe

Abstract: The Protestant Reformation caused, among other consequences, the decline of the marriage system existing in Europe until that moment: the obligatory religious marriage system, which meant that the only marriage admitted was the canonical one. In subsequent centuries, the gradual decline of the influence of the Catholic Church in matrimonial matters caused the consolidation of an unstoppable process of secularization of marriage in Europe; process that gained further momentum after the French Revolution and the Napoleonic Civil Code. From that moment, the establishment of a parallel civil marriage regulation in front of the canonical marriage and its expansion throughout the different European countries determined that in each of these countries, a particular marriage system was established. The secularization process finished, in my opinion, already at the end of the 20th century, with the equalization of marriage and de facto unions. The work starts, as a premise, from the concept of marriage system, to go on to detail of the existing compulsory canonical marriage system in Europe at the time of the Protestant Reformation: the basic characteristics of canonical marriage and, especially, its configuration as a formal contract during the Counter-Reformation, through the Tametsi Decree of the Council of Trento. Next, the numerous attempts to secularize marriage that occurred prior to the French Revolution in various European countries are studied. After, the expansion of the secularization of marriage through the Napoleonic Code is addressed, which, paradoxically, to say the least, it was notably inspired by the formal model of canonical marriage, and which is reflected in the current civil marriage regulation of most countries in Europe. Finally, the work addresses the incidence of de facto unions as the culmination of the process of secularization of marriage. This study has been carried out within the MULTIHURI research project "Diversity and coexistence: human rights as a guide for action," DER 2015–65840-R, MINECO-FEDER.

Keywords: Secularization, marriage, de facto unions, Protestant reform, French revolution, Napoleonic code

1. Introduction: Marriage system and secularization

The relationship between religious marriage and civil marriage is the result of how the process of secularization of marriage has evolved in each country. That process began with the Protestant Reformation and was accentuated after the French Revolution and the French Civil Code, also known as Napoleonic Code, and which, in our opinion, has culminated in the recognition of *de facto* unions in Europe.

Prior to the Protestant Reformation, the only recognized marriage in Europe was canonical one, which was (and it is nowadays) regulated as established by the Catholic Church. Throughout the secularization process, there came a time when, along with canonical marriage, a marriage regulated by civil authorities was created. Since the moment that together with the canonical marriage, of a religious nature, there begins to be a civil regulation of it, it is when we can properly speak of the existence of a marriage system, understood as "the criterion with which each State regulations harmonizes existing legislation regarding the celebration of marriage, both in substantive and procedural law, as well as its civil recognition, respecting the religious convictions of its citizens."[1]

The historical changes derived from the Protestant Reformation determined the confrontation between the powers that were considered competent to regulate marriage: on the one hand, the Catholic Church, which had always possessed it, and, on the other hand, the various States, which had become aware of such competition. In this way, as a consequence of State intervention in matrimonial matters, the coexistence of a civil marriage together with a Catholic religious marriage occurs, and it is at that moment when the concept of "marriage system" appears in the history of legal institutions. From then on, each State will establish the type of marriage system that will be applied within its territory, which will depend on the type of relationship it has with the religious factor, and the vision toward it, specifically if it is a confessional or non-denominational State, and within the latter if it is a secular one, with a hostile attitude toward religion and with an absolute separation between the Church and the State, or if it is a State with a mitigated separation, which has a positive vision toward religion, which is recognized as a social factor, and therefore, it is protected and guaranteed.

This will determine, on the one hand, that secular States establish a marriage system of obligatory civil marriage, in which canonical marriage (or any other religious marriage) lacks recognition and, on the other hand, that in non-denominational countries with a healthy secularism, religious marriage is recognized together with civil one or that Catholic States maintain the exclusive recognition of canonical marriage. This last marriage system is known as compulsory religious marriage, and it was the existing marriage system before the beginning of the secularization process, in which only canonical marriage existed. This marriage system was the logical consequence of the relationship between political and religious powers in Europe during the Middle Ages: a time

1 R. Navarro Valls, "El matrimonio," in *Derecho Eclesiástico del Estado español*, Pamplona, 1980, p. 409.

known as hierocratism, in which the predominance of the Catholic Church and the Pope or Roman Pontiff, which led to the imposition of many canonical rules not only in the spiritual sphere, but also in the civil or political one exerting. In the matrimonial field, the Church had outlined a solid institution which was, one and the same, a contract and a sacrament.

Starting with the Protestant Reformation, the cause of matrimonial secularization, the influence of the Catholic Church and Canon Law declined in all European countries, especially in those where the Reformation was successful, but not only in them, and, in each one, the secularization process followed its own rhythm, according to its particular circumstances. In Spain, for example, the issue was not raised until the Law of 1870 which establish the civil marriage.

In order to adequately understand the secularization of marriage in Europe, it is necessary to start from the existing marriage regulations at the time the process began, characterized by the compulsory religious marriage. Now it will be exposed the basic characteristics of canonical marriage, focusing on its configuration as a contract and sacrament, as well as its formal character.

2. Marriage in Europe until the 16th century

2.1. Basic characteristics of canonical marriage

Following the tradition of Roman Law, Canon Law considers marriage as a contract, and specifically, as a consensual one.[2] Therefore, it is a legal institution prior to Christianity. However, considering that Christ raised the marriage institution to the category of sacrament, the sacramentality of the valid canonical marriage supposes a differentiating element that constitutes it as an important element of a religious nature, as well as a legal and social one. It should not be forgotten that marriage is the only sacrament that, as a social and legal institution, already existed before Christianity.

A sacrament is, for the Catholic Church, an instrument of salvation, which frames it within the same purpose of the Church, which is the salvation of souls or *salus animarum*. Although a contract can be made by anyone, but if both contracting parties are baptized the Church considers that that contract is also

2 About canonical marriage, among others: A. Bernárdez Cantón, *Curso de Derecho matrimonial canónico*, 4ª ed., Madrid 1981; A. Molina Meliá, and M. E. Olmos Ortega, *Derecho matrimonial canónico sustantivo y procesal*, 5 ed., Valencia 1992; J. Fornés, *Derecho matrimonial canónico*, 4ª ed., Madrid 2000; M. López Alarcón, and R. Navarro Valls, *Curso de Derecho matrimonial canónico y concordado*, 7 ed., Madrid 2010.

a sacrament. In the event that, before marriage, both spouses (not just one of them), have received baptism, the marriage contract is also a sacrament is the first sacrament that implies entry into the People of God, into the Church as a lay faithful, and therefore, its consideration as a Christian, and so, the marriage is an instrument of salvation of the spouses themselves. Conversely, if none or only one of the contracting parties is not baptized, the contract will not be sacramental, therefore, the identity between the contract and the sacrament will not occur, at least at the moment of the celebration, since it could become a sacrament later if the unbaptized party were baptized, or both, if neither of them had been baptized before.

The identity between the contract and the sacrament when both spouses are baptized, was decisive for the legal solution that the Roman Pontiff established in the medieval doctrinal discussion between the canonist schools of Bologna and Paris on the legal nature of the marriage contract. The discussion concerned whether the marriage was a consensual contract that, therefore, it would be perfected with the provision of consent by the contracting parties (a position defended by the Paris school, in line with Roman Law), or if it would be a real contract, which require the delivery of the thing or *traditio rei* for its perfection, position defended by the Bologna school. The *traditio rei*, in matrimonial matters, is the sexual union between a man and a woman. Indeed, Pope Innocent III, in the 11th century, established that the marriage bond would arise only by providing consent, although he maintained some relevance to the sexual union in the sense that if the marriage was not consummated through sexual intercourse, could be dissolved. In this way, only the marriage that, after the exchange of consent, is added its consummation will be indissoluble. On the contrary, the marriage ratified (or *rato*, in latín), that means celebrated through the manifestation of consent, but not consummated could be dissolved by the pontifical authority. Canon law has also regulated the requirements for conjugal intercourse to effectively consummate the marriage.

The sexual union between two baptized spouses is the visible fact of the sacrament of marriage, which in its invisible or supernatural reality, from the canonical perspective, it supposes the union of Christ, founder of the Church. So, each marriage constitutes the refounding of the Church. In this way, the identity between contract and sacrament determines that marriage, each marriage, is a constitutive element of the Church itself, therefore it justifies the competence of the Church to regulate the marriage.

On the other hand, the consent of the contracting parties, which is the only thing that is necessary for arising the marriage bond, logically must be provided by people with sufficient capacity. The Church, throughout the centuries, has been developing with canonical norms, and through jurisprudence, a detailed list of different causes of nullity of marriage related to consent (such as fear, malicious error, simulation, or disabilities for psychological reasons) as well as other causes of nullity referring to the ability of the parties as personal situations in which there is a prohibition to contract, known as matrimonial impediments, such as age, impotence or certain degrees of consanguinity, among others.

If any of the causes of nullity is proven in a judicial process, the ecclesiastical judge will rule declaring the nullity of the same, which means that the marriage link did not arise at the moment *in fieri*, which is the moment of consent. However, if the unconsummation of the marriage is proven, we are not dealing with a cause of nullity, but of dissolution, which means that the marriage bond, validly arisen at the time of the Exchange of consent, is nevertheless broken by the decision, in this case, of the Roman Pontiff, who is the only one who has the power to dissolve these valid marriages.

2.2. Canonical marriage as a formal contract

As we have previously indicated, only the consent of the contracting parties is sufficient and essential to originate the marriage bond. Initially, an exchange of matrimonial consent carried out privately between two contracting parties, without publicity, had the same constitutive force of the marriage as if it were done in a public way, for which reason clandestine marriages were as valid as those carried out with publicity, as long as they were carried out by capable and skillful people. Therefore, there was no legal obligation to provide consent observing a certain form of celebration. However, by custom, consent was manifested in front of the priest, who limited himself to giving his blessing. The clandestine marriage was a marriage valid as a contract and it was also at the same time a sacrament if both parties were baptized.

But clandestine marriages left open the possibility of abuse, since there was no publicity, the proof of its celebration was reduced to the word of the contracting parties, and in the event of a contradiction between them, it could not be known who was telling the truth. Such abuses were a particular or private problem for the contracting parties due to the legal uncertainty in which they could be found, and they also represented a problem for the Catholic Church itself because it could not be sure of the existence of a sacrament.

This was the legal-canonical situation of marriage at the time of the Protestant Reformation. During the Counter-Reformation, the Tametsi Decree of the Council of Trent established the obligatory nature of the determined form for the provision of matrimonial consent, which if it was not fulfilled would mean the annulment of the marriage. In this way, the baptized (Catholics) had to express their matrimonial consent in the presence of a priest and two witnesses. The contracting parties are those who carry out the contract and the sacrament before the witnesses, among whom the priest, normally the parish priest, would be a witness qualified by the fact that he is invested with his ecclesial office. The priest receives the consent expressed by the contracting parties on behalf of the Church, so he does not marry them, but the contracting parties are the ones who make the contract (hence the term "contractors") and they are also the ministers of the sacrament that the contract implies.

The described passive presence of the priest during the celebration of the canonical marriage had to be modified because it gave rise to the so-called surprise marriages, which met the indicated formal requirements, but since the intention to celebrate the marriage was not known in advance they were null in many cases, since they could have been carried out between incapable or unskilled people. On the other hand, the nullity of such marriages could only be declared by judicial ruling after the corresponding nullity process, since it is presumed that any marriage celebrated is valid; presumption that can only be broken if the contrary is proven in an annulment process.

It will be necessary to wait for the Ne temere Decree of the Sacred Congregation of the Council of Trent, of August 2, 1907, for the establishment of the passive position of the sacred minister assisting the marriage. So, that Decree established that the consent was expressed at the request of the assistant minister. Thus ended the marriages by surprise, since the active position of the sacred minister supposes the prior communication by the future contracting parties of their intention to contract, which made it possible to inquire about their capacity and ability for the marriage before its celebration. So, it also reduced the possibility that the marriage was null because many possible causes of nullity could be detected before the celebration.

3. The process of secularization of marriage

3.1. The influence of the Protestant Reformation

Among the dogmatic postulates of Protestantism, in matrimonial matters, the denial of its sacramental character stands out. So, marriage is a simple contract originated in the exchange of consent of the parties and that only originates a private or civil bond between them, and marriage has no theological or religious purpose as an instrument for the salvation of the souls of the contracting parties, because marriage is not considered as a sacrament. The solely contractual nature of the marriage, together with the attribution of legislative competence in religious matters to civil authorities, as a consequence of the application of the principle "*cuius regio eius est religió*" reached in the Peace of Westphalia, which ended to the period of the wars of religion in Europe, were the first steps in the process of matrimonial secularization, which has been studied, among other authors, by Bettetini.[3] This process was not limited to the European countries in which Protestantism triumphed, but also extended, to a different extent, to the countries that remained faithful to Catholicism due to the influence of existing jurisdictional doctrines in the various countries with a Catholic majority—as in the case of regalism in Spain, Gallicanism in France, Febronianism in Germany, or Josephinism in Austria. which advocated the separation of marriage as a contract and marriage as a sacrament. These doctrines advocated the competence of the State to regulate the contractual content of marriage, leaving the regulation of its purely religious or sacramental aspect to the Catholic Church.

As indicated, in the Middle Ages, the religious dimension reached its full expression, since it was when the Catholic Church came to have exclusive jurisdiction in matrimonial matters. The Protestant Reformation questioned this exclusive competence due to its particular conception of the Church as a charismatic and non-legal entity. This consideration of the Church itself as an institution implied the denial, on the one hand, of the authority of the Roman Pontiff, and on the other hand, of the legality of canon law and, consequently, of the canonical marriage regulation, promulgated by the Pope. From his point of view, only the political power of the State could be the source of law on marriage, just as it happened in other ecclesiastical matters. In this sense, the process of secularization of marriage is a reflection of the confrontation between the ecclesial and state powers that affirmed their respective competencies in the regulation of marriage.

Therefore, after the Peace of Westphalia there was an evident and increasing state intervention in the regulation of marriage in the different European countries. In some cases, this intervention was a consequence of the fact that the corresponding Reformed Church had been subjected to political power. In other cases, the state competence derived, as has been indicated, from the fact that the Protestant postulates themselves left this issue to the political power.

The fact that States began to intervene in the regulation of marriage did not initially imply a proper secularization of it, since the separation between the civil

---

3 A. Bettetini, *La secularizzazione del matrimonio nell'esperienza giuridica contemporanea*, Padova 1996.

and religious spheres was not yet clearly defined.[4] However, without such state intervention, the secularization of marriage would probably not have happened.

Another factor that influenced the beginning of the process of secularization of marriage was the relative influence of canonical legal doctrine that distinguished between contract and sacrament in the same canonical marriage. According to the defenders of this doctrine, everything related to the contract would be a competence of the State, and the Catholic Church would be only competent in religious aspects, that is, on marriage as a sacrament. However, against this doctrine, the most among canonists advocated the inseparability between contract and sacrament in marriage.

If the bases for the secularization of marriage were laid with Protestantism and jurisdictional doctrines, its definitive embodiment occurred some time later, after the French Revolution, imbued with a secularist conception of religion in general and of the relationship of the State with the Church, characterized by the radical separation between both powers, since both the Church and religion were identified with the Old Regime. However, before the French Revolution there were already some attempts at secularization, as we are going to analyze below.

3.2. Marriage secularization until the French Revolution

The attempts to secularize marriage that occurred between the Protestant Reformation and the French Revolution were a consequence of the solutions that were imposed at the time to the matrimonial problems derived from the religious antagonisms that arose after the Protestant Reformation. This was the case, as Gaudemet points out, in the Netherlands and England.[5]

Thus, in the Netherlands, the Sacred Congregation of the Council, through a Decree of the year 1602, admitted the validity of the marriage celebrated by Catholics before a civil authority in some areas of that country such as Holland, Zealand and Friesland, given the need to arbitrate a system for Catholics to contract a civil marriage before a municipal authority, which could be followed by a religious ceremony.

For his part, in England, Cromwell replaced religious marriage with civil marriage in 1653, with the arguments, on the one hand, of fighting against marriage

---

4 Ibid.

5 J. Gaudemet, *El matrimonio en Occidente*, Madrid 1993, pp. 425–434 and M. T. Regueiro García, "La secularización del matrimonio: Siglos XVI a XVIII," in *Seguridad, extranjería y otros estudios histórico-jurídicos*, ed. A. R. Martín Minguijón and R. Morán Martín, Madrid 2016, p. 659.

clandestinity and, on the other hand, to combat reformist proposals. However, this substitution of religious marriage for civil marriage was short-lived, since it was repealed shortly after, in 1660, by King Charles II of England.

Although to a lesser extent, the fact that, in Bavaria, the 1756 Codex Maximilianus considered the betrothal contract as a civil contract, could also be considered a timid secularizing attempt, although not marriage which continued to be clothed with a religious character.

In the second half of the 18th century, after the triumph of Enlightenment and rationalist ideas, secularization attempts spread to various European countries, with the logical opposition of the papacy. Indeed, the enlightened legislators of some countries were inspired by the French philosophers and jurists who defended Gallicanism, a doctrinal system started in France whose main postulates were the reduction of the power of the Pope in favor of the lower levels of the ecclesiastical hierarchy, as well as the subordination of the Church to the State.

This is what happened, for example, in Protestant Sweden in 1734, where the General Code of Sweden removed the investigation of divorce proceedings from ecclesiastical jurisdictions.

For its part, in Austria, in 1783, at a time when the State had already reserved everything related to the regulation of marriage as a civil contract, a later norm of José II (from whom the Austrian current similar to Gallicanism is named, the so-called Josephinism), in 1786, established that marriages between Catholics should be celebrated before a Catholic priest but if it was a mixed marriage, between a Catholic and a Protestant one, the intervention of the Protestant pastor was recognized. The ecclesiastical courts, in Austria, had recognized competence to judge on the validity of the marriage, although the civil courts were competent in the marriage as a contract. These Josephinist provisions were repealed by King Leopold II in 1791, who established that mixed marriages should be celebrated in the presence of a Catholic priest. Likewise, this king returned to the ecclesiastical courts the exclusive competence for matrimonial causes.

3.3. The French secularizing impulse

The first French rule on civil marriage dates back to the Edict of Nantes of 1598, which established, on the one hand, that Protestants could get married either before the pastor of their confession, or without an official ceremony and, on the other hand, was recognized the civil jurisdiction about the constitution of the matrimonial bond and divorce. Later, the Edict of Fontainebleau, promulgated by Louis XIV in October 1685, which revoked that of Nantes, did not regulate the form of marriage for Protestants, because it falsely assumed that there were no Protestants in France. This legislation meant that Protestants had to submit to the canonical form of marriage celebration, so they could only celebrate their marriage before a Catholic priest, a marriage rite that they rejected. The logical consequence of this situation was that the French authors began to demand their own marriage for Protestants, which led to the establishment of a civil registry for non-Catholics by means of a subsequent edict of 1787. This registry, although it was initially intended for Protestants, was also applied to Jews.

The secularization of marriage was not really a strictly revolutionary measure, but the consequence of the various triggering factors already mentioned: the contractual nature of marriage recognized by philosophers, defended by many jurists and recognized or pointed out by some canonists; the regalist and jurisdictional theses that affirmed the right of civil sovereigns to legislate and judge in matrimonial matters; the secularization attempts that some countries made before the French Revolution, and, finally, the solution that had been adopted in France itself for the marriage of Protestants. The culmination of this process in which the mentioned factors are intermingled, again following Gaudemet, ended, paradoxically, in the establishment of a secular form of marriage celebration that was nothing more than the transposition of the Tridentine form of canonical marriage.[6]

Subsequently, it was the Civil Code of France, or Napoleon's Code, approved by the Law of March 21, 1804, which definitively established the secularization of marriage by establishing the compulsory civil marriage system in France and in the territories subject to sovereignty of France such as the Netherlands, Belgium, Luxembourg, or the German territories west of the Rhine, all of which still maintain this marriage system today. In addition, the Napoleonic Code also established divorce as a procedure for breaking the marriage contract.

This Code considers marriage to be a completely secular act, although in regulating the form of its celebration it was clearly inspired by the form of celebration of canonical marriage, except for some small differences. An example is its article 165, which establishes that the marriage "is celebrated publicly before the civil officer of the domicile of one of the two contracting parties," or article 194, according to which the sole proof of the celebration of the marriage is "the act of celebration registered in the civil status registers." In this way, the French Civil Code assimilated the requirement of publicity of the marriage established by the

6 J. Gaudemet, *El matrimonio en Occidente*, cit., pp. 425–434.

Catholic Church in the Tametsi Decree of the Council of Trent,[7] as well as, evidently, the form of canonical celebration transferred to the civil sphere.

In this sense, in the same way that for the canonical marriage the banns are previously published at the same Sunday mass, article 63 of the Napoleonic Code established the requirement of making two publications made with an interval of eight days before the celebration of the marriage. Civil marriage, according to this same article, had to take place with some curious conditions of place and time: "at the door of the town hall… on Sunday." Likewise, article 213 and following of the Napoleon's Code reminded the woman that she owed obedience to her husband, as well as various obligations and incapacities of the married woman. This civil regulation, as Gaudemet reminds,[8] supposed the transposition to the secular or lay sphere of the Epistle to the Ephesians (5, 22–24) that the priest read at Mass on Sundays: "Wives are subject to their own husbands as to the Lord. For the husband is the head of the wife, just as Christ is the head of the Church; and he is the savior of the body. So, just as the Church is subject to Christ, so also are married women to their husbands in everything."[9]

Also, the presence of two witnesses, established in article 75 of the Napoleonic Code, coincided with the provisions of the Tametsi Decree of the Council of Trent for the canonical form, although it differed, and it is an essential difference, in which the civil marriage bond was not formed until the formula of the union had been pronounced by the civil authority: "I declare you united by marriage," while in the canonical marriage the contracting parties are united and the marriage bond arises by exchange of consent. In other words, in canonical marriage, since the contracting parties are the ministers of the sacrament that involves the same contract, the intervention of the priest is to be a qualified witness of the celebration by the contracting parties through reciprocal exchange of their respective consents, which is what gives rise to the marriage bond. However, in civil marriage regulated by the Napoleonic Code it is the civil authority that receives the consent of the contracting parties and is the one that originates the matrimonial bond, since said authority, normally the mayor, pronounces the declaration of the contracting parties as united by marriage. Therefore, in civil marriage, the declaration of consent by the contracting parties is not enough, rather it is required the aforementioned declaration of the civil authority that receives the consent of the parties and declares them married.

---

7 S. Acuña Guirola, *La forma del matrimonio*, cit., p. 137.
8 J. Gaudemet, *El matrimonio en Occidente*, cit., p. 451.
9 Epistle to the Ephesians 5, 22–24.

So, civil marriage in the Napoleonic Code is more rigorous, since the action of the civil authority is not limited to publicity, to serve as proof of the celebration as a qualified witness, as occurs in canonical marriage; rather, his intervention is decisive, since it constitutes the marriage bond. In this difference lies, in my opinion, the most important distinction between canonical religious marriage and its secularization in civil marriage: in canonical marriage, the spouses "get married," while in civil marriage "they are married." In other words, the Catholic Church does not marry the contracting parties, unlike the civil authority.

This decisive difference regarding the authentic origin of the marriage bond, which in the case of civil marriage is in the hands of the civil authority, entails the consequence that the same civil authority may, where appropriate, also decide on the dissolution through divorce. But in canonical matrimonial law, the ecclesiastical authority cannot dissolve the marriage bond through divorce, precisely because the minister of that marriage was not the priest, and he was neither the one who married the spouses, but that it was the contracting parties who got married among themselves, when expressing their matrimonial consent at the *in fieri* moment of the marriage. Therefore, a possible cause for matrimonial annulment could only be given at *in fieri* moment, the moment of consent, and it would not be possible to allege a hypothetical cause of nullity or dissolution of the bond at a time after the emergence of the bond, at the so-called *in facto esse* moment, during the married life, as it occurs in divorce.

The concept of marriage in the Napoleonic Code spread throughout many European countries, especially in those that, such as the Netherlands, Belgium, Luxembourg and part of present-day Germany, came to be effectively applied due to having been integrated into the first French Empire. In these countries, the French marriage system with a compulsory civil marriage is still applied today. However, not all the countries that were subjected to the French yoke for some time adopted this marriage system immediately, as is the case of Spain, to which we dedicate a specific treatment below.

3.4. The secularization of marriage in Spain

The first milestone in the secularization of marriage in Spain did not happen during the French invasion, but several decades later: it was found in the Provisional Law on Civil Marriage of 1870. Said Law established civil marriage and the French marriage system, with a compulsory civil marriage as in France. Also, it was rejected the state recognition of the marriage that was carried out through a canonical religious form, before the parish priest and two witnesses; marriage celebration that until that year had always been the only one marriage system admitted in Spain.

However, a few years later, in 1875, as a consequence of a political change and the fact that citizens ignored the new civil regulation and continued to marry in canonical form despite the compulsory nature of the civil form, the Ministry of Regency issued several provisions that introduced the Spanish marriage system that lasted until the current Spanish Constitution of 1978, with the exception of the years of the Second Spanish Republic: the marriage system known as subsidiary civil marriage. These are the decrees of January 22 and February 9, 1875, as well as a Royal Order of February 27 of that year. According to this marriage system, Catholics always had to get married in canonical form, while non-Catholics could get married civilly. According to this marriage system, civil marriage is only applicable in the case of spouses not bound by canonical form, that is, who were not baptized or had carried out a formal act of apostasy from the Catholic faith.

4. The secularization of marriage in Europe today: A final reflection

Since the last decades of the 20th century, the perception that marriage is a mere formality, a simple bureaucratic "paperwork" has been consolidated, because in the same way that the judge has been able to marry, he can also "unmarry." If this popular perception, were maintained today only about civil marriage it could be understandable; however, it has also been extended to canonical marriage, as its true significance is unknown. The culmination of this situation, in my opinion, is found in current *de facto* unions, a widespread social phenomenon throughout Europe that dispenses with what is considered useless bureaucracy: any marriage. The recognition of *de facto* unions and their equalization to marriage, supposes the culmination of the process of secularization of marriage.

From a legal-canonical perspective, the civil marriage carried out by a baptized Catholic person, which is bound to the canonical form of celebration, had the qualification of public and notorious concubinage. From the concept of concubinage, the concept of irregular marriage has been developed, which includes unions or life situations established by two people not united in marriage. Traditionally, those two people have been a man and a woman; Currently, many countries have presented *de facto* unions—as well as civil marriages—constituted by people of the same sex: two men or two women.[10]

---

10 M. O. Sánchez Martínez, "Constitución y parejas de hecho. El matrimonio y la

According to canonical doctrine, these unions or life situations have a certain resemblance to the married life, but in them the parties have a concubinage intent, not a marital spirit. Catholic doctrine understands that any illicit sexual relationship must be qualified as fornication or concubinage. Specifically, concubinage would be continued fornication with a certain person, so that it supposes a perseverance in the sexual relationship.[11] These coexistence situations, outside the canonical scope, receive various names: irregular family, extramarital cohabitation, irregular union, common-law couple, or *de facto* unions,[12] that would be included in the set that supposes the "plurality of family structures."[13] Such coexistence situations suppose a way of life that in the various societies has gone through three phases until its social and, later, legal acceptance: at first, it is considered as a deviant social phenomenon, frowned upon and combated by society; in a second phase, most of society accepts or tolerates it, and finally, it comes to be considered a social institution such as marriage.[14] This last situation is only reached when the solution to the problems derived from such factual coexistence is reflected in legislation, and not only at the jurisprudential level.[15]

Europe is currently in the third of the aforementioned phases. At the end of the 20th century, it was still in the transition from the second to the third phase, since then, the majority of European countries had promulgated regulations regarding *de facto* unions. At that time, only Sweden had specific legislation on *de facto* unions, although most European civil marriage laws recognized legal effects, applying the jurisprudential way, not properly legislative one. At the end of the 20th century, at a time when the recognition of same-sex marriage had not yet begun, only Denmark had a regulation aimed at this: the Coexistence Law of

---

pluralidad de estructuras familiares," *Revista Española de Derecho Constitucional* 58 (2000), pp. 45–69.

11 F. Aznar Gil, *Uniones matrimoniales irregulares. Doctrina y pastoral de la Iglesia*, Salamanca 1993, pp. 20–22; L. Bender, "Concubinatus in iure canonico," *Monitor Ecclesiasticus* 87 (1962), p. 541, and J. M. Díaz Moreno, "La Iglesia ante las familias 'de hecho' y monoparentales," in *Familia en un mundo cambiante*, Salamanca 1994, p. 271.

12 A. Bettetini, *La secularizzazione del matrimonio*, *op. cit.*, p. 115, and IDEM, "La disciplina delle unioni di fatto: appunti per un ripensamento critico," in *Il ruolo del matrimonio nel ordinamento giuridico attuale*, ed. F. Finocchiaro, Padova 1990, p. 25.

13 M. O. Sánchez Martínez, *Constitución y parejas de hecho*, cit., p. 45.

14 V. Franceschelli, "La famiglia di fatto da 'deviant phenomenon' a istituzione sociale," in *Diritto di famiglia e delle persone* (1980), p. 1260.

15 M. Martín Casals, "Informe de Derecho comparado sobre la regulación de la pareja de hecho," *Revista de Derecho Privado* (1996), p. 1709.

June 7, 1989, which admitted that homosexual couples could register officially to be able to opt for the same rights as heterosexual couples. At that time, *de facto* couples in European countries were recognized certain rights and, in practice, if they were heterosexual couples, they were equated to marriage.[16]

The main reason for the aforementioned equalization of rights of *de facto* unions to marriages is to consider that what matters is the protection of the family, regardless of its origin, be it a marriage or a *de facto* union. Another reason for such equalization involves considering that the moral qualification of human relations is private issues, without incidence in social life, which also means giving more preponderance to people than to institutions, as well as the application of the principle of equality, that is incompatible with any discrimination, and the protection of the fundamental rights of the person regardless of the situation in which they find themselves.[17]

On this point, it can be affirmed that the centuries-old dispute on jurisdiction over matrimonial matters between the State and the Catholic Church concluded at the beginning of the 19th century, at the Napoleonic Code times, with a victory for the State over the Church, since the latter imposed, not only the existence of a civil marriage together with the canonical one, but in many cases, the compulsory nature of civil marriage and the consequent legal irrelevance of religious marriage. And this, despite the fact that, as has been shown, the regulation of the form of celebration of civil marriage is undeniably inspired by the canonica form established in the Council of Trent. However, in line with the above considerations, I believe it is interesting to reflect on the future of the marriage system, or if preferred, the secularization process, which, in my opinion, in the long term, points to the possible disappearance of civil marriage, due that it is considered a mere formality. Therefore, if the *de facto* unions are formalized by means of a civil contract, this supposes the equating to the matrimonial consent of a non-marital consent, since in the *de facto* unions a mere will to coexistence is expressed. Faced with such a situation, the logical question that inevitably arises is about the difference that may exist between the civil marriage bureaucracy and the bureaucracy of *de facto* unions. In other words, the real question lies in what purpose the civil marriage will serve. Despite the fact that, as Viladrich affirms, marriage cannot be reduced to a conventional legal and social formality

16 F. Aznar Gil, "Las uniones de hecho ante el ordenamiento canónico," *Revista Española de Derecho Canónico* 48 (1991), p. 49.

17 F. Aznar Gil, *Uniones matrimoniales irregulares*, cit., p. 37.

by forgetting its natural reality, which is its primary reality and prior to the legal one,[18] the truth is that this is what it seems to be currently happening.

Finally, from my point of view, the social phenomenon of *de facto* unions, understood as the culmination of the process of secularization of marriage, can only be faced by the Catholic Church, and by Canon Law, as a pastoral issue. The patrimonial and economic aspects derived from the quasi-marital relationship, as occurs with those of the marriage relationship, are and must be regulated by civil law: only this branch of State Law must face the regulation of non-marital cohabitation and provide a solution to the problems that may arise from them.

Bibliography

Acuña Guirola, S., "La forma del matrimonio hasta el Decreto Ne Temere," *Ius Canonicum* 13 (1973), pp. 137–192.

Aznar Gil, F., "Las uniones de hecho ante el ordenamiento canónico," *Revista Española de Derecho Canónico* 48 (1991), pp. 49–80.

Aznar Gil, F., *Uniones matrimoniales irregulares. Doctrina y pastoral de la Iglesia*, Salamanca 1993.

Bender, L., "Concubinatus in iure canonico," *Monitor Ecclesiasticus* 87 (1962), pp. 541–555.

Bernárdez Cantón, A., *Curso de Derecho matrimonial canónico*, 4ª ed., Madrid 1981.

Bettetini, A., "La disciplina delle unioni di fatto: appunti per un ripensamento critico," in *Il ruolo del matrimonio nel ordinamento giuridico attuale*, ed. F. Finocchiaro, Padova 1990, pp. 25–62.

Bettetini, A., *La secularizzazione del matrimonio nell'esperienza giuridica contemporanea*, Padova 1996.

Díaz Moreno, J. M., "La Iglesia ante las familias 'de hecho' y monoparentales," in *Familia en un mundo cambiante*, Salamanca 1994, pp. 271–193.

Diz Franco, A. M., "Del divorcio romano a la sacramentalidad tridentina. Estudio histórico-jurídico." Doctoral thesis defended in UNED, Madrid 2023 (pendiente de publicación).

Escrivá Ivars, J., "El sistema matrimonial español. Eficacia de los matrimonios confesionales," in *Manual de Derecho Eclesiástico del Estado*, ed. D. García Hervás, Madrid 1997, pp. 327–360.

Fornés, J., *Derecho matrimonial canónico*, 4ª ed., Madrid 2000.

18 P. J. Viladrich, *Agonía del matrimonio legal*, Pamplona 1984, pp. 124–125.

Franceschelli, V., "La famiglia di fatto da 'deviant phenomenon' a istituzione sociale," *Diritto di famiglia e delle persone* (1980), pp. 1257–1299.

Gaudemet, J., *El matrimonio en Occidente*, Madrid 1993.

López Alarcón, M., and Navarro Valls, R., *Curso de Derecho matrimonial canónico y concordado*, 7 ed., Madrid 2010.

Martín Casals, M., "Informe de Derecho comparado sobre la regulación de la pareja de hecho," *Revista de Derecho Privado* (1996), pp. 1709–1898.

Martínez Blanco, A., "La familia de hecho ante el Derecho canónico y el Derecho eclesiástico," *Anales de Derecho* (1991), pp. 71–116.

Molina Meliá, A., and Olmos Ortega, M. E., *Derecho matrimonial canónico sustantivo y procesal*, 5 ed., Valencia, 1992.

Navarro Valls, R., "El matrimonio," in *Derecho Eclesiástico del Estado español*, Pamplona 1980, pp. 409–489.

Navarro Valls, R., "El matrimonio religioso," in *Derecho Eclesiástico del Estado Español*, ed. J. Ferrer Ortiz, Pamplona 2012, pp. 293–325.

Prader, G., *Il matrimonio nel mondo*, Padova 1986.

Prader, G., *Il matrimonio in Oriente e Occidente*, Roma 1992.

Reina Bernáldez, V., *Lecciones de Derecho Matrimonial*, Barcelona 1983.

Regueiro García, M. T., "La secularización del matrimonio: Siglos XVI a XVIII," in *Seguridad, extranjería y otros estudios histórico-jurídicos*, ed. A. R. Martín Minguijón and R. Morán Martín, Madrid 2016, pp. 659–670.

Sánchez Martínez, M. O., "Constitución y parejas de hecho. El matrimonio y la pluralidad de estructuras familiares," *Revista Española de Derecho Constitucional* 58 (2000), pp. 45–69.

Viladrich, P. J., *Agonía del matrimonio legal*, Pamplona 1984.

Wójcik, A., "La unión de hecho y el matrimonio, diferencia antropológico-jurídica," *Cuadernos doctorales: derecho canónico, derecho eclesiástico del Estado* 19 (2002), pp. 313–372.

Anna Siemińska

The family as the basis of the richness of civil society: That is, the need to (change) the method of interpreting civil law in Poland

Abstract: The family as the basis of the richness of society—that is, the need to (change) the method of interpreting civil law in Poland. The article covers theoretical and legal considerations explaining the role of the family in society and the economy, in a Western European system of the capitalist type and in a socialist system. It shows how different the roles of the family are in the both systems and the different importance attributed to it for the creation of society and its wealth. The approach to the family from the perspective of material interests and their protection by civil law in this article aims to illustrate how, at different stages in the development of law and society, the family has been the foundation of the richness of Western European capitalist society, from its origins in the Roman Empire to contemporary Western European society, in which the method of civil law interpretation plays a central role. This method makes it possible to create and interpret civil law with a view to the concrete (and not abstract) protection of property interests, which enables a real assessment of legislative solutions, leading inevitably to the conclusion of the need to (change) the method of interpretation of civil law used in Poland today, as inadequate to economic and social needs.

Keywords: theory of civil law, method of civil law interpretation, civil society, family, economic and social development

1. Presentation of the issue

The article covers theoretical and legal considerations, explaining the role of the family in society and the economy, in a Western European system of the capitalist type and in a system of the socialist type. It points out how different roles the family plays in the two indicated systems, as well as—how different importance is attributed to it to create society and its richness. Thus, assuming that in a capitalist economy, the free market is the place where various interests confront each other for the purpose of making profit and accumulating capital, the law (civil law in particular) should ensure the protection of interests that are of particular importance to society and its enrichment.[1] Such interests, as presented

---

1 In recent years, scholars have increasingly recognized the role of law and legal

in the article, are held by the family, whose legal protection is the basis of the richness of Western European capitalist societies, from the Roman Empire to the present day. Thus, the proposed approach to the family is different from the one traditionally considered in Polish civil law dogmatics, explaining the family, as a rule, in social or sociological terms, failing to understand the role of the family in free-market society and the capitalist economy. Such an understanding of the family is, in a way, a legacy of the adoption of Soviet doctrine in the post-war period, combating capitalism and essentially depriving society of the opportunity to become rich, and this through the political ideology adopted, expressed in the method of creating and interpreting civil law.

The approach of the family from the perspective of property interests and their protection by civil law in the article aims to illustrate how, at different stages of the development of law and society, the family has been the foundation of the wealth of Western European capitalist society, from its origins in the Roman Empire to modern Western European society, in which the method of interpretation of civil law plays a central role. This method makes it possible to create and read civil law with a view to the concrete (and not abstract) protection of property interests, which makes it possible to realistically evaluate legislative solutions, leading inevitably to the statement of the need for (change) the method of interpretation of civil law used in Poland today, as inadequate to economic and social needs.

Based on the fundamental assumption that the family in the capitalist economy and its relevant law includes the most important property interests in society and the economy, because the capital accumulated within it affects the richness of society, the following theses are taken up in the article:

1. Civil law should include the protection of the property interests of the family and its economic needs, with the goal of enabling the richness of society.
2. The method of interpretation of civil law should refer to the economy—to consider the economic and social needs of citizens, and in a capitalist

---

institutions in the Roman economy, i.e., in the organization of economic activity and the distribution of richness in society, such as: M. W. Gleason, *Making Men. Sophists and Self-Presentation in Ancient Rome*, Princeton 1995; H. I. Flower, *Ancestor Masks and Aristocratic Power in Roman Culture*, New York 1996; L. Foxhall, *When Men Were Men: Masculinity, Power, and Identity in Classical Antiquity*, London 1998; E. Gunderson, *Staging Masculinity: The Rhetoric of Performance in the Roman World*, Ann Arbor 2000.

economy—to enable the settlement of conflicts of material interests in the free market.

3. The method of legal interpretation, which includes the linguistic examination of legal provisions, does not allow for a proper assessment of conflicting property interests occurring in society, because the purpose of its introduction was different, hence it does not allow for the assessment of existing legal constructions and the creation of new ones, in accordance with the development of the free market and its needs, in particular, the family.

In terms of methodology, the article subscribes to the legal-comparative and historical-descriptive studies of legal theory, making civil law theory, which includes the method of interpretation of civil law, the object of study, within the limits set by the problems developed and the historical context.

2. Ancient Rome: Society, law, and the family

2.1. Roman society as a legal category and the basis of the economy

From the time of its founding, Rome was a city-state (*civitas*, *polis*), which in classical terms is explained as a community of free people living in a small territory and ready to defend it against external interference and participating in decisions aimed at its common good.[2] In the Roman state, which united various peoples, the community of Roman citizens, as the hosts of their state, with the apparatus of power in their hands, decided the most important matters for themselves: they created for centuries the mechanisms and legal constructions that, in the commodity-money economy that gave rise to capitalism,[3] served to protect

2 W. Bojarski, *Prawo rzymskie* [*Roman Law*], Toruń 1994, p. 17. Compare that according to Aristotle, all social development was aimed at the creation of the state: "every community comes into being for the attainment of some good (for all in every action are actuated by what appears to them to be a good), it is clear that, although all [communities] aim at some good, this is done above all by the foremost of all, which has the most important task of all and includes all others. This is the so-called state and the state community": Arystoteles, *Polityka* [*Politics*], trans. Ludwik Piotrowicz, Warszawa 2006, p. 25.

3 "Ancient Rome managed to achieve this high standard of living through the combined operation of moderately stable political conditions and markets for goods, labor and capital, which allowed specialization and efficiency": Peter Temin, "The Economy of the Early Roman Empire," *Journal of Economic Perspectives* 1 (2006), p. 134.

the material interests of Roman citizens and their families, as the richest part of this community.[4]

Roman society was highly differentiated in terms of social and property structure,[5] with the existing legal divisions of society being the result of economic needs and serving their realization.[6] It should be noted that the economy of the Empire was based largely on the labor of slaves, who constituted the primary workforce and a massive social category.[7] Indeed, throughout its history, the Roman state was a state of slave formation, and for this reason, the primary internal task of its ruling class was to maintain authority over slaves and create the conditions for their exploitation.[8] The Roman Empire was a state of slave formation. Freedom was therefore a condition for membership in the community, determining one's status as a subject (free people) or as an object of economic circulation (slaves). The category of free people was subject to a further division at the same time, and that was into Roman citizens (*cives Romani*), Latins and foreigners.[9] This division, too, was economically significant, for only Roman citizens were allowed to participate in economic transactions (e.g., *ius commercii*—the right to enter legal acts recognized by the *ius civile*, or *legis actio*—the right

4 "The Roman State was a family and the gods of the state were the gods of a family (…)": W. K. Lacey, "Patria potestas," in *The Family in Ancient Rome. New Perspectives*, ed. B. Rawson, London 1986, pp. 123 and 125f.

5 Further: W. Eck, "Aristokraten und Plebs: Die geographische, soziale und kulturelle Herkunft der Angehörigen des römischen Heeres in der Hohen Kaiserzeit [Aristocrats and Plebs: The Geographical, Social, and Cultural Origins of Members of the Roman Army in the High Imperial Period," in *Gesellschaft und Administration im Römischen Reich*, ed. A. Kolb, Berlin-Boston 2022, p. 99.

6 About relationship between legal and economic development see: L. de Ligt, "Roman Law and the Roman Economy: Three Case Studies," *Latomus* 66/1 (2007), p. 10 f.

7 R. Schultz, "Die gesellschaftlichen Grundlagen [The Social Foundations]," in *Die römische Republik: Kompaktwissen Geschichte*, ed. G. Henke-Bockschatz, Stuttgart 2014, pp. 36–41: "Over time, slaves became an economically important part of Roman society. (…) Nevertheless, there was no question of them becoming free Roman citizens because they were denied civitas Romana, Roman citizenship."

8 K. Kolańczyk, *Prawo rzymskie* [*Roman Law*], Warszawa 2021, p. 207.

9 about the meaning and the function of the three broad categories (the so-called status: *familia*, *civitas*, *libertas*), which were built in the Roman antiquity and were utilized to include and exclude human beings, defining the person's legal condition and what the subjects could do, what they could own, see: F. Lucrezi, "Citizenship and Religion: Inclusions and Exclusions in the Ancient World," in *Paradoxes of Conflicts*, ed. G. Scarafile and L. G. Gold, Cham 2016, pp. 41–46.

to appear in court to assert their claims under civil law). Consequently, "all the dependent societies of Rome were increasingly relegated to the position of serfs in the vast provinces of the Roman State"[10] for the purpose of profiteering.

The economic needs and property interests of Roman citizens meant that Roman society was not homogeneous, and above all, it was not equal before the law. In fact, the free citizens of the Roman state differed from each other due to their legal, or property-legal position, based on their membership in certain communities.[11] The largest of these was the Roman commune, and the narrowest was the family, within which an individual's legal and property position depended on belonging under the authority of a particular family father, regulating family life in a sovereign manner.[12] This caused that these communities, from the perspective of modern civil law theory, can be considered as peculiar groups of interests,[13] occurring in Roman business and the civil law created on its basis.[14]

---

10 W. Osuchowski, *Prawo rzymskie prywatne. Zarys wykładu* [*Roman Private Law. Lecture Overview*], Warszawa 1988, p. 175.

11 Lacey, "Patria potestas" (cit. n. 4), p. 133f.

12 H. Hausmaninger, *Römisches Privatrecht* [*Roman Private Law*], Wien 2001, p. 280f; H.-R. Wicker, "Matri-, Patrilinearität und die soziale Evolution [Matri-, patrilinearity and the Social Evolution]," in *Leitfaden für die Einführungsvorlesung in Sozialanthropologie, 1995–2012*, Bern, 2012, pp. 27–32. About "patriarchal control" compare also: L. Pensieroso and A. Sommacal, "Economic Development and Family Structure: From pater familias to the Nuclear Family," *European Economic Review* 71 (2014), p. 80f.

13 Comp.: "The civil law of Romans (…) was constructed, so far as the law of persons and property was concerned, with reference primarily to the interests of a close- knit and exclusive groups of persons, the familia, and its property": J. F. Gardner, *Family and Familia in Roman Law and Life*, Oxford 1998 (reprint 2004), p. 16f. See also B. Sitek, "Koncepcja małżeństwa z perspektywy prawa rzymskiego i kanonicznego. Niemodna instytucja? [The Concept of Marriage from the Perspective of Roman and Canon Law. An Unfashionable Institution?]," in *Rodzina w prawie. Księga pamiątkowa dedykowana ks. Prof. Dr. Hab. Ryszardowi Sztychmilerowi z okazji 65. Rocznicy urodzin i 30- lecia pracy naukowej*, ed. M. Różański and J. Krzywkowska, Olsztyn, 2013, p. 297: "Marriage was part of the great Roman family and its interests."

14 "In the suitability and obedience to the pater familias lies the characteristic foundation of the greatness of ancient Rome": R. P. Saller, "Pater familias, mater familias, and the gendered semantics of the roman household," *Classical Philology* 94 (1999), p. 182. See also: W. K. Lacey, which considers the private (family) and public (state) spheres in interaction, with the Roman family, in which the *pater familias* was the sub-primary institution, being the foundation of the state. W. K. Lacey, "Patria potestas," (cit. n. 4), p. 121.

2.2. Law as protection of the property interests of Roman citizens

The civil law of ancient Rome, was a law made by Roman citizens (*civis*) for themselves—"this law, which the people have made for themselves, is their own law and is called *ius civile* (G. 1,1)."[15] The purpose of this law was to protect the material interests of Roman citizens in economic transactions, which explains why the rest of the Roman Empire was not bound by this law, even though they were formally free and part of Roman society. This was due to the principle in force at the time, according to which every citizen was governed by the right of that municipality or civitas to which he belonged, while the right of a particular *civitas* was available only to its citizens.[16] This caused only a member of a Roman civic municipality to participate in the affairs of Roman citizens in the so-called *ius Quiritium*, *ius civilie*.[17] Thus, exclusively within the Roman commune one became a citizen, possession became property and contracts became obligations.[18]

Civil law in classical approach started from "person"—*persona*, as a concept translated by modern scholars regarding the legal situation of individual members of society.[19] At the same time, the division of persons was made according to various criteria, and only some of them were explained in more detail in the sources, nevertheless—its clearer picture can be obtained by referring to modern concepts, in particular, legal capacity. Although this concept was not formulated in Roman law, it was deduced from it, to denote the ability to be the subject of rights and obligations[20] (e.g., to own property, receivables, debts, participate in legal actions, etc.).[21] Legal capacity, at the same time, was not granted to all

15 Bojarski, "Prawo rzymskie" (cit. n. 2), p. 32.

16 H. Hausmaninger and W. Selb, *Römisches Privatrecht* [*Roman Private Law*], Wien 1981, p. 29f.

17 J. A. Crook, "The Law of Statues," in *Law and Life of Rome 90 B.C.–A.D. 2012. Aspects of Greek and Roman Life*, Ithaca 1967, p. 38.

18 Por. O. Behrends and W. Sellert, "Der Kodifikationsgedanke und das Modell des Bürgerlichen Gesetzbuches (BGB). 9. Symposium der Kommission 'Die Funktion des Gesetzes in Geschichte und Gegenwart' [The Codification Idea and the Model of the Civil Code (BGB). 9th Symposium of the Commission 'The Function of the Law in History and Present']," in *Abhandlungen der Akademie der Wissenschaften in Göttingen. Nr 236* Göttingen 2000, p. 13.

19 T. S. Taylor, "Social Status, Legal Status and Legal Privilege," in *The Oxford Handbook of Roman Law and Society*, ed. P. J. du Plessis, C. Ando, and K. Tuori, Oxford 2016, p. 349f.

20 Kolańczyk, "Prawo rzymskie" (cit. n. 8), p. 204.

21 Osuchowski, "Prawo rzymskie" (cit. n. 10), p. 158.

members of society, but only to free people who were Roman citizens, belonging to a certain family.[22] Thus, legal capacity was a prerequisite and important condition for participation in legal life and, thus, in economic life. Its restrictions on non-citizens of Rome thus had a clear social and even political cutting edge, closing off access to Roman private law to slaves, foreigners, or free persons *alieni iuris* (under the authority of *patria potestas*).

Thus, a Roman citizen in the sphere of private law had, among other things, the right to participate in legal transactions, to use the institutions of the law of succession, and to protect his rights through litigation.[23] However, the most important effect of acquiring full legal capacity was the ability to own property and inherit, and thus—to be the subject of obligations under civil law. This meant full participation in economic life and profiting from it in this prototype of the capitalist economy, which was possible only for a narrow group of Roman citizens, resulting in a large disparity of wealth in relation to the rest of society (among others, the plebs). Therefore, the concept of legal capacity manifests to the maximum extent the nature of Roman civil law[24]—the special protection of the interests of the richest part of society.[25]

2.3. The family as a patrician material community protected by the *ius civile*

The Roman family—*familia* was different from the natural family in today's sense, for its characteristic feature (*familia proprio iure*) was the subjection of all members to the same authority (*manus potestas*) of the superior (*pater familias*). This authority, in a broad sense, included both a set of persons and property values belonging to the same house (*domus*),[26] sometimes tightening to the

---

22 K.-J. Hölkeskamp, "Under Roman Roofs: Family, House, and Household," in *The Cambridge Companion to the Roman Republic*, ed. H. I. Flower, Cambridge 2014, p. 101.

23 W. Rozwadowski, *Prawo rzymskie. Zarys wykładu wraz z wyborem źródeł* [*Roman Law. Lecture Outline with a Selection of Sources*], Warszawa 1991, p. 91.

24 H. Hausmaninger and W. Selb, *Römisches Privatrecht* (cit. n. 16), p. 29. See also: J. Pölönen, "Framing 'Law and Society' in the Roman World," in *The Oxford Handbook of Roman Law and Society*, ed. P. J. du Plessis, C. Ando, and K. Tuori, Oxford 2016, p. 16f.

25 Rozwadowski, "Prawo rzymskie" (cit. n. 23), 85.

26 W. Litewski, *Rzymskie prawo prywatne* [*Roman Private Law*], Warszawa 2003, p. 139: "The term *familia* in the latter sense could include either all of that property including slaves (alongside the name *familia pecuniaque* or *pecunia*), or only slave household members (*famuli*)." On the distinction between Familia and domus cf.: R.

property itself, or even to parts of it, such as slaves, belonging to the same owner. In classical law, however, the most proper meaning encompassed the union of free persons: narrower, as a union including the superior and those subordinate to his authority, or broader, all agnates (D. 50, 16, 195, 1–2).[27] Agnation, as a legal bond rather than a blood bond joining relatives in the male line under the authority of the same *pater familas*, at the same time shaped the legal and property position of the members of a given family, for the rules of *ius civile*, concerning statutory succession and guardianship, were based on the principles derived from agnation.[28] At the same time, the family, viewed in this way, was reserved for the wealthy patricians (plebeians remained effectively outside of it, and it was not possible to marry between patricians and plebeians until 445 BC and the lex Canuleia). Thus, the Roman family formed a legal community, and above all—a material community of the richest Roman citizens, regulated and protected by civil law.

At the head of the Roman family was the superior (*pater familias*), who had property capability (*filius nihil suum habere potest*), as a special kind of legal capability,[29] entitling him to own property. As the administrator and sole disposer of the family property, he was also the sole representative of the family externally in legal and property transactions, while all the children's acquisitions fell to him.[30] This caused the family's entrants to share their father's social and

---

P. Saller, "'Familia, Domus', and the Roman Conception of the Family," *Phoenix* 38/4 (1984), p. 337. See also: R. Saller, *Patria potestas and the Stereotype of the Roman Family*, Cambridge 2008, p. 7; K. R. Bradley, *Discovering the Roman Family: Studies in Roman Social History*, New York 1991, p. 653f.: The Ancient Roman family was a complex social structure based mainly on the nuclear family, but could also include various combinations of other members, such as extended family members, household slaves, and freed slaves. Ancient Romans had different names to describe their concept of family, including 'familia' to describe the nuclear family and 'domus' which would have included all the inhabitants of the household."

27 See also: H. Honsell, *Römisches Recht* [*Roman Law*], Zürich 2010, pp. 23–24, 183.

28 "In Latin the term Familia could mean the agnatic lineage (…)." S. Dixon, *The Roman Mother*, Kent 1988, p. 14f.

29 Osuchowski, "Prawo rzymskie prywatne" (cit. n. 10), p. 161. "The most common meaning of *pater familias* is 'estate owner' without reference to familial relations." R. P. Saller, "Pater familias" (cit. n. 14), p. 182.

30 J. A. Crook, *Law and life of Rome*, Ithaca 2006, p. 109; A. Gestrich, *Neuzeit* [*Modern Times*], in *Geschichte der Familie*, ed. A. Gestrich, J.-U. Krause, and M. Mitterauer, Stuttgart 2003, p. 367; B. Linke, *Von der Verwandtschaft zum Staat: die Entstehung politischer Organisationsformen in der frührömischen Geschichte* [*From Kinship to the State: The*

economic position, and, as a rule, inherit his property after his death.[31] The family's property was not a property of the father, but a property of the father. This explained the important social, but above all—economic role of the family,[32] determining the legal and property situation of the members.

The Roman family, understood as a material community of Roman citizens,[33] and in fact reserved only for patricians as the richest part of society, had a special place in civil law, and above all—its protection. In fact, the family was primarily addressed by the provisions of family law, regulating the personal legal relations of family members, found in the sections of matrimonial, paternal and guardianship law. Moreover, because of the family's influence on the legal and property situation of its members, the position an individual occupied within the Roman family determined the extent of his legal and property capacity.[34] For this reason, Book One of the *ius quod ad personas pertinet*—"law that pertains to persons" was also important in determining the legal and property situation. This is because it was not until the pandect system that this matter was separated into personal law more strictly defined, which was included in the general part (section: subjects of the law), and family (familial) law, which was one of the five specific parts of German BGB (along with property, bond and inheritance law). However, this was only an editorial effort to organize the statutory matter,[35] since it is the two parts read together that give a comprehensive picture of the

---

Emergence of Political Forms of Organization in Early Roman History], Stuttgart 1995, pp. 82–83; A. Dębiński, *Rzymskie prawo prywatne. Kompendium* [*Roman Private Law. Compendium*], Warszawa 2011, p. 183.

31 K. Milnor, "Women in Roman Historiography," in *The Cambridge Companion to the Roman Historians*, ed. A. Feldherr, Cambridge 2009, pp. 276–287; D. Herlihy, *Medieval Households*, Cambridge 1985, pp. 2–3.

32 R. P. Saller, "Pater Familias" (cit. n. 14), p. 182; L. Allason-Jones, "The Family in Roman Britain," in *A Companion to Roman Britain*, ed. M. Todd, Malden 2004, p. 282.

33 Based on "financial arrangements" and "political goals," see: P. D. Bardis, Main Features of the Ancient Roman Family," *Social Science* 38/4 (1963), p. 225. See also: R. P. Saller, *Patriarchy, Property and Death in the Roman Family*, Cambridge Studies in Population, Economy and Society in Past Time, Cambridge 1997, p. 226f.

34 Kolańczyk, "Prawo rzymskie" (cit. n. 8), p. 224.

35 Por. S. F. Fortunato, "Vom römisch-gemeinen Recht zum Bürgerlichen Gesetzbuch [From Roman Common Law to the Civil Code]," *Zeitschrift für das Juristische Studium* 4 (2009), p. 334.

protection of the property interests of the wealthiest part of society, on which Rome built its centuries-old tradition.[36]

3. Capitalist law and societies in Western Europe

3.1. Civil society and the material interests of citizens

The modern development of the free market increasingly determined the need to change the understanding of law and society.[37] A change that was aimed at making the property needs of the population visible and enabling them to become rich. The demand for universal freedom and equality before the law, in fact, had (also, or especially) an economic dimension—enabling the mobilization of land and the influx of manpower provided the foundations for the development of the free market. Therefore, freedom and equality, understood in terms of the foundations of the free-market economy, came to be understood as "the one, primary, right ascribed to every human being on the basis of his humanity," from which all other natural rights derive.[38] Consequently, the concepts of the rule of law were based on the emergence of a "'civil society universally governed by law'. (…) The rule of law is a state limited in its scope of action to a law (…) equal for all and an order based on respect for the freedom of citizens."[39] Such a conception of the freedom and equality underlying the law necessitated profound legal transformations, particularly concerning the understanding of

---

36 "Patria potestas was the fundamental institution underlying Roman institutions, and that in consequence, public life followed the assumptions of private life, and not vice versa (…)." W. K. Lacey, "Patria potestas" (cit. n. 4), p. 123.

37 Comp. B. Schäfers, "Vom Dritten Stand zum Bürgertum und zur bürgerlichen Gesellschaft [From the Third Estate to the Bourgeoisie and Civil Society]," in *Die bürgerliche Gesellschaft. Vom revolutionären bürgerlichen Subjekt zur Bürgergesellschaft*, Karlsruhe 2017, p. 1f.

38 H. Coing, *Grundzüge der Rechtsphilosophie*, Berlin-New York 1993, p. 36, referring to: I. Kant, *Metaphysik der Sitten. Einleitung III und Einleitung in die Rechtslehre §3 (Inselausgabe IV)*, Leipzig 1797, pp. 322–323, 337, 345.

39 Comp. A. Sylwestrzak, *Historia doktryn politycznych i prawnych* [*History of Political and Legal Doctrines*], Warszawa 2015, p. 217: "Law is the result of the autonomous conduct of the collective as bearer of the idea of society itself. The basic relationship (…) between the freedom of the individual and the freedom of the other members of the community."

society as a theoretical and legal category for economic development[40] and thus for the enrichment of society within the framework of the developing capitalist free market economy.

Thus, at the basis of the theoretical assumptions of civil (civic) society (*bürgerliche Gesellschaft*) was the economic development of Western Europe, based on which legal concepts were created. This caused civil society to be considered sometimes as a capitalist society, since the development of society was conditioned by this mode of economy. Thus, already according to the philosophy of G. W. F. Hegel (the first theorist of civil society[41]), civil society—understood as a community of citizens—respects the sphere of autonomy of the individual, whose detailed interest is realized within the abstract law and society.[42] At the same time, society is a kind of "ground of intermediation"[43] between the individual and the state, which is carried out through the so-called "system of needs" as a system of free-market economy.[44] The subject of society is the citizen from the point of view of needs, while the satisfaction of needs is achieved through the work of all, constituting a common richness. Consequently, this society is the sphere of private interests and economic needs of citizens and their satisfaction through the production of goods, and therefore—a non-political, civil, private sphere.[45]

The conception of society as economic needs meant that the citizen, as a legal category, was no longer considered by belonging to a community, and began to be recognized as an individual to whom the law confers rights and duties.

---

40 "The citizen no longer wanted to be subject, wanted to enjoy his freedom without the tutelage of the authorities." See f. i.: E. Bloch, *Das Prinzip Hoffnung* [*The Principle of Hope*], Frankfurt am Main 1967, p. 603.

41 M. Riedel, *Bürgerliche Gesellschaft und Staat* [*Civil Society and State*], Neuwied 1970, p. 67.

42 See also: G. W. F. Hegel, *Zasady filozofii prawa* [*Principles of the Philosophy of Law*], trans. A. Landman, Warszawa 1969, § 260, 245–246.

43 G. W. F. Hegel, *Vorlesungen über Rechtsphilosophie* [*Lectures on Philosophy of Law*], Bd. 3, ed. K.-H. von Ilting, Stuttgart-Bad Cannstatt 1974, p. 567.

44 J. Bung, *Die bürgerliche Gesellschaft und das globale subjektive Recht* [*Civil Society and Global Subjective Law*]," in *Die Idee subjektiver Rechte*, ed. E. Hilgendorf and B. Zabel, Berlin-Boston 2021, p. 90f.

45 Comp. P. Załęski, "Etymologia społeczeństwa obywatelskiego: o problemie tłumaczenia nowoczesnej koncepcji bürgerliche Gesellschaft [The Etymology of Civil Society: On the Problem of Translating the Modern Concept of bürgerliche Gesellschaft]," *Acta Philologica* 34 (2008), p. 50, pointing out that its modern equivalent is a free market society.

This individual, therefore, is not free because of the legal community to which he belongs, but because freedom has become a universal right of the citizen. Each citizen, becoming an element of the free market, pursuing his individual economic needs, had to be a subject of the rights and obligations of civil law, regulating this market. This reduced the importance of the legal community, protecting its members (paternal control) until then, who gained independent protection before the law and the ability to be the subject of civil law rights and obligations. Thus, the needs arising from the conditions of the free market consequently led to the development by representatives of the science of law—a new way of "binding" the law to the subject and object of the law. The legal protection of civil law was no longer entitled on the basis of membership in a particular social class or category of persons, but equally extended to all citizens (lat. *civis* = German: *der Bürger*), as members of the political and legal community, creating BGB (German Civil Code) and civil life.[46]

3.2. Civil law as the resolution of conflicts of interest of citizens

A consequence of considering society as the economic needs and material interests of citizens is the concept of civil law, according to which—citizens (*Bürgern*) in the free market enter into various relationships with each other in order to realize their material interests and economic needs.[47] This often results in conflicts, which civil law must resolve, protecting specific property interests of citizens in specific cases.[48] The norms of civil law therefore include the settlement of conflicts of interests of citizens and their groups, with the aim of further and

46 As for the term *bürgerlich* in German BGB: K. Adomeit, *Das bürgerliche Recht, das Bürgerliche Gesetzbuch und die bürgerliche Gesellschaft. Würzburger Vortäge zur Rechtsphilosophie, Rechtstheorie und Rechtssoziologie* [*Civil Law, the Civil Code and Civil Society. Würzburg Lectures on Philosophy of Law, Legal Theory and Sociology of Law*], ed. H. Hofmann, E. M. Wenz, and D. Willoweits, Baden-Baden, pp. 7–15.

47 "The BGB promotes the desire for self-direction, independence and autonomy norm by norm. The goals of the BGB citizen, which this code imposes upon him, are: to engage in business, to acquire a fortune, to found a family—if not a clan, so that in the end as much as possible is to be inherited by as many as possible." K. Adomeit, *Das bürgerliche Recht* (cit. n. 46), p. 8.

48 Comp. m. in. R. Zippelius, *Rechtsphilosophie. Ein Studienbuch* [*Philosophy of Law. A Study Book*], München 2011, p. 211; P. Heck, *Begriffsbildung und Interessenjurisprudenz* [*Terminology and Jurisprudence of Interests*], Berlin-Zürich 1968, p. 72; P. Heck, "Gesetzesauslegung und Interessenjurisprudenz [Interpretation of the Law and Jurisprudence of Interests]," *Archiv für die civilistische Praxis* 112 (1914), p. 60.

continuous economic development. The norms of civil law therefore regulate the private sphere of citizens, hence civil law is the private law of civil (*civic*) society, that is, the law that this society is governed by in the free market, regulating the economic needs and material interests of citizens vis-à-vis each other.

The concept of civil law, as the regulation of economic interests in the free market, determines the specificity of the method of interpreting civil law, as a method of reading the law and its further development, separate from administrative or criminal law. This is because civil law as private law regulates economic relations between citizens, hence the absence or maximum limitation of the state's sovereign interference, is dictated by the absence of state interests found in administrative and criminal law. In contrast, in civil law, as the private law of citizens, there are rifts of conflicts of interest of citizens toward each other, or toward the community, which is the essential criterion for the division of civil law, that is, on the basis of the similarity of the problems of conflicts of interest. For example, in contract law, the interests of members of the community against each other, that is, citizens entering into a certain contract,[49] are regulated for resolving conflicts of interest, based on equal terms for the parties,[50] which the parties can modify based on their own economic needs. In property law, on the other hand, in addition, there are also—interests of the public (*Interessen der Allgemeinheit*),[51] understood as the interests of civil society, resulting, among other things, from the certainty of trading as the basis of the free market. Therefore, the property law contains several resolutions of conflicts of interest of the owner against the interests of the society, considering the interests of society rather than the interests of the individual.[52]

---

49 Comp about obligation as conflict of interests: P. Heck, *Grundriß des Schuldrechts* [*Outline of the Law of Obligations*], Tübingen 1929, pp. 2, 6.

50 See: J. Busche, "Die Begründung von Schuldverhältnissen [The Creation of Debt Relationships]," in *J. von Staudingers Kommentar zum Bürgerlichen Gesetzbuch mit Einführungsgesetz und Nebengesetzen, Eckpfeiler des Zivilrechts*, ed. M. Martinek, Berlin 2008, p. 187; K. Larenz, C.-W. Canaris, *Lehrbuch des Schuldrechts*, 2. Bd, Besonderer Teil, Zweiter Halbband [*Textbook of the Law of Obligations*, Vol. 2, Special Part, Second Half-Volume], München 1994, p. 129.

51 In this meaning compare also: P. Heck, *Grundriss des Sachenrechts* [*Outline of the Property Law*], Tübingen 1930, p. 8.

52 Interest of the public comes from the neighborhood regulations and other civil or public law regulations under the German *Grundgesetz* vom 24.05.1949, land-use planning law, construction law and others.

3.3. Family as property interests of citizens in the free market

The specifics of the free-market economy that determine the understanding of society and on the creation and interpretation of civil law, also affect the concept of family. This is because family, in the economic perspective of civil law theory, refers to the material interests and economic needs of a group of citizens in the free market. The material interests of the family are not economically different from the material interests of other citizens and their groups, for they are united by the economic goal of capital accumulation. As a result, the economically determined material interests of the family can be compared to the interests of the company—for its purpose is also the accumulation of capital, seen as the achievement of a common economic goal. However, while the source of the company's material interests is the contract of the parties,[53] obliging the partners to pursue an economic goal, the source of the family's material interests is the legal bond, uniting citizens in accordance with the principles derived from family and guardianship law. Likewise, the material interests of the family are of particular importance to society, as they affect the accumulation of capital, leading to the enrichment of society.[54] In this ability to accumulate and make society rich lies the special feature of the family's material interests in a free-market economy.

The material interests of the family are subject to legal protection, relying on the accepted method of interpreting civil law. This protection, based on the reading of legal norms as settlements of material conflicts of interest, consists in giving priority in specific cases to the material interests of the family over the interests of other citizens (employers, developers, banks, vendors, etc.). Thus, the protection of the material interests of the family is not absolute but is the result of considering each case from the point of view of economic development. This consideration of interests, makes it possible to create family property in the long term based on the economic needs of citizens, providing a theoretical and legal foundation for the family, which is considered when creating civil laws.

The material interests of the family are the foundation of the wealth and economic success of capitalist societies, based economically on family businesses. This long tradition dates back as far as ancient Rome, where the material interests of the patrician family formed the basis of the economy and its wealth.

53 Comp. f. i. Art. 860 § 1 polish Civil Code: "By the partnership agreement the partners agree to pursue a common economic goal (…)," Dz. U. 2022 pos. 1360.

54 About Minimal Formula of Capitalism as a demand for unlimited capital accumulation through the use of formally peaceful means as central: L. Boltanski, È. Chiapello, *Der neue Geist der Kapitalismus* [*The New Spirit of Capitalism*], Köln 2018, p. 39 a.f.

Today, too, the material interests of the family are of particular importance in the Western European economy, forming its core.[55]

4. Poland-society, law, and family

4.1. Society as political interests and lack of connection with the economy

The end of World War II meant for Poland the political and economic domination of the USSR and the adoption of a new socialist system. At its core was first and foremost the fight against capitalism, as the economic system of Western Europe, serving the enrichment of the bourgeoisie, that is, citizens acting with each other in a free market, protected by law. This free market, as well as the resulting economic needs of citizens, based on private property and economic freedom, were replaced by a centrally controlled market, that is, the state (or more precisely, by a political party, in accordance with the constitutional principle of the unity of state power, amounting to the sole rule of a political party).[56] This resulted in the subordination of the economy to politics, serving to monopolize and control all areas of citizen activity by the political party, while excluding their influence on the state authorities.[57] The economy of the country was also subordinated to the state.

The centrally controlled economy resulted in the political determination of its development, that is, based on political guidelines and the current demand of the ruling party.[58] In this way, the economic needs of society and the economic

---

55 The largest family-owned companies in Germany are: Volkswagen AG, BMW AG, Metro AG, Aldii, Otto Group, Henkel, Rossmann, Deichmann, in Spain: Mercadona, Inditex, El Corte Ingles, or in Italy: Holding Edizione (f.i. Benetton), holding Exor (f. i. Fiat-concern), or Ferrero International. In Germany family business are considered an important economic factor—90% of Germany's four million companies are run by families or owners (according to the Federation of German Industries), providing 58% of all jobs in Germany (according to the Institute for Research on Small and Medium-Sized Enterprises).

56 PRL Constitution dated 1952, Dz. U. 1952 no. 33 pos. 232.

57 W. Bokajło, "Społeczeństwo obywatelskie: sfera publiczna jako problem teorii demokracji [Civil Society: The Public Sphere as a Problem of Democratic Theory]," in *Społeczeństwo obywatelskie*, ed. W. Bokajło and K. Dziubka, Wrocław 2001, p. 33; M. Buchowski, "Communist Governmentality and Civil Society," in *Civil Society: Challenging Western Models*, ed. E. Dunn and C. Hann, London-New York 1996, p. 87ff.

58 See also: D. Lane, *The Capitalist Transformation of State Socialism. The Making and Breaking of State Socialist Society and What Followed*, New York 2014, pp. 6, 23f.

interests of citizens were determined, which, due to the replacement of the free market with a politically regulated market, were of little importance. Their replacement by political (party) interests, however, led to the identification of the civil sphere (economic interests) with the political sphere[59] (political interests). As a result, political interests determined the economic needs and property interests of citizens, while socialist society itself thus constituted an expression of the politicization of the economic sphere[60] that determined the needs of citizens of the totalitarian state.[61]

In opposition to the politically controlled socialist society, was formed after the period of systemic transformation—the modern view of society, that is, as a part of social life, not subject to state control. Indeed, the need for freedom and democracy, expressed in the struggle against authoritarian and totalitarian socialist rule, led to social self-organization,[62] independent of the state and aimed at rebuilding an autonomous social space,[63] as the foundation of the civil society being created. However, this led to the framing of society as an autonomous sector separate from the state and the economy, creating: a public sector (the state), a private sector (the economy) and a nonprofit, or simply a third sector (civil society). The civil society sector thus constitutes an area in which citizens voluntarily and autonomously form associations, foundations, movements, unions, oriented toward the expression, defense or realization of their needs and aspirations.[64] However, in such a view, the needs and aspirations of

59 Załęski, "Etymologia" (cit. n. 45), p. 50.

60 Comp. J. Staniszkis, "On Some Contradictions of Socialist Society: The Case of Poland," *Soviet Studies* 31/2 (1979), p. 167f.

61 About the role of ideology see also: R. Taras, *Ideology in a Socialist State. Poland 1956–1983*, Cambridge 1984, p. 1.

62 E. Górski, "Idea społeczeństwa obywatelskiego w Polsce i Europie Środkowowschodniej [The Idea of Civil Society in Poland and Central and Eastern Europe]," in *Rozważania o społeczeństwie obywatelskim i inne studia z historii ideii*, Warszawa 2003, p. 58; J. Frentzel-Zagorska, "Civil Society in Poland and Hungary," *Soviet Studies* 42/4 (1990), p. 759f.

63 Bp E. Frankowski, "Od społeczeństwa totalitarnego do obywatelskiego [From Totalitarian to Civil Society]," in *Społeczeństwo obywatelskie. Modele teoretyczne i praktyka społeczna*, ed. E. Balawajder Lublin 2007, p. 259.

64 Comp. P. Gliński, "Przemiany sektora obywatelskiego po roku 2000—analiza porównawcza wybranych wyników badań empirycznych [The Transformation of the Civic Sector after 2000—a Comparative Analysis of Selected Empirical Findings]," in *Samoorganizacja społeczeństwa polskiego: III Sektor i wspólnoty lokalne w jednoczacej się Europie*, ed. P. Gliński, B. Lewenstein, and A. Siciński, Warszawa 2004, pp. 59–65;

citizens cannot relate to their economic interests, as these are autonomous areas (!).[65] Consequently, contemporary Polish civil society has little in common with the concepts of classical Western European theorists[66] and the economic needs of citizens.[67]

1.2. Law as an expression of political interests

Law during the communist period, like society (as a legal category), was created and read under the domination of the USSR, encompassing both legal regulations and legal dogma. Thus, the creation and reading of the law (the method of interpreting the law) was carried out based on communist ideology,[68] being an expression of partisan and current political interests, replacing the real economic interests and needs of citizens with the interests of the political party. This resulted in the need to remove the study of interests from the interpretation of the law, in order to make it impossible to evaluate legislative solutions in terms of their usefulness for economic life, replaced by propaganda.

Therefore, it is not surprising to adopt (still during the period of socialism)—legal positivism, which, rejecting philosophical assumptions (in particular, political philosophy, or the philosophy of economics), fully corresponded to political demand, fitting into the ideology of political subordination of society and law-state. This explains, the commonly accepted notion of law, as a set of norms, coming from the state and secured by coercion, making it impossible to consider the norm of law, as a resolution of the conflict of interests and economic needs of citizens. On the other hand, the scientific rhetoric of socialism was ideally

---

M. Magner, "Civil Society in Poland after 1989: A Legacy of Socialism?," *Revue Canadienne des Slavistes* 47/1–2 (2005), p. 50f.: "The communist era, in short, was decisive in shaping contemporary CSOs. Associational life after 1989 displays considerable inertia and while it is difficult to determine whether it retards the process of systemic change, it surely is not the sphere of social life that can currently accelerate it."

65 A. Łoś-Tomiak, "Społeczeństwo obywatelskie—kryzys idei, czy recepta na kryzys? [Civil Society—a Crisis of Ideas or a Recipe for Crisis]," *Zeszyty Naukowe Polskiego Towarzystwa Ekonomicznego w Zielonej Górze* 2 (2015), p. 97.

66 A. Smolar, "Przygody społeczeństwa obywatelskiego [Adventures of Civil Society]," in *Tabu i niewinność*, Kraków 2010, p. 99.

67 Bp Frankowski, "Od społeczeństwa" (cit. n. 63), p. 259.

68 Comp. f. i. Art. 1 Ustawy z dnia 18. lipca 1959 r. Przepisy ogólne prawa cywilnego [Law of 18. July 1959 General Provisions of Civil Law] (Dz. U. Nr 34): "Civil laws are to be interpreted and applied in accordance with the principles of the system and objectives of the People's State."

matched by the analytical methods of reading the law (linguistic and logical)[69] that were proper to positivism, and thus—the linguistic analysis of legal provisions,[70] which is the basic method of interpreting the law even today. This is because both the clarification and derivation[71] methods of interpreting the law are based on the linguistic study of law and language,[72] taking the law as a linguistic message,[73] "as a way of understanding the linguistic message, as linguists do."[74] Such a method of studying the law makes it impossible to evaluate legislative solutions for economic life, because by not studying economic interests (occurring in the free market), it does not allow for an evaluation of the statutory resolution of conflicts of interest and their impact on the lives of citizens. A linguistic examination of the law, on the other hand, allows the law to maintain its autonomy from the economic needs of citizens.

The consequence of the accepted-language way of reading the law (interpretation of the law) is that the method of interpreting the law has no influence on the further development of the law, responding to the needs of the economy. This is

69 See: L. Morawski, *Filozofia prawa* [*Philosophy of Law*], Toruń 2014, p. 31; J. Stelmach, *Ryszard Sarkowicz, Filozofia prawa XIX i XX wieku* [*Philosophy of Law of the 19th and 20th Centuries*], Kraków 1998, p. 23f.

70 M. Zieliński, *Wykładnia prawa—zasady—reguły—wskazówki* [*Interpretation of law—principles—rules—guidelines*], Warszawa 2017, p. 47.

71 M. Zieliński, "Derywacyjna koncepcja wykładni jako koncepcja zintegrowana [The Derivational Concept of Interpretation as an Integrated Concept]," *Ruch Prawniczy, Ekonomiczny I Socjologiczny* 3 (2006), p. 94.

72 F. i. L. Morawski, *Wykładnia w orzecznictwie sądów. Komentarz* [*Interpretation in the Jurisprudence of the Courts. Commentary*], Toruń 2002, p. 27f.; K. Płeszka, "Językowe znaczenie tekstu prawnego jako granica wykładni [The Linguistic Meaning of a Legal Text as a Limit to Interpretation]," in *Filozoficzno- teoretyczne problemy sądowego stosowania prawa*, ed. M. Zirk-Sadowski, Łódź 1997, pp. 69–77; M. Zieliński, O. Bogucki, A. Choduń, S. Czepita, B. Kanarek, and A. Municzewski, "Zintegrowanie polskich koncepcji wykładni prawa [Integrating Polish Concepts of Legal Interpretation]," *Ruch Prawniczy, Ekonomiczny i Socjologiczny* 4 (2009), p. 25f.

73 Comp. M. Romanowicz, "Teoria klaryfikacyjna wykładni prawa jako teoria uzasadnienia. Perspektywa psycholingwistyczna a pozytywistyczna koncepcja wykładni prawa [The Clarification Theory of Legal Interpretation as a Theory of Justification. A Psycholinguistic Perspective Versus a Positivist Conception of Legal Interpretation]," *Archiwum Filozofii Prawa i Filozofii Społecznej* 1 (2011), p. 57; J. Wróblewski, *Rozumienie prawa i jego wykładnia* [*Understanding the Law and Interpreting It*], Wrocław-Warszawa-Kraków-Gdańsk-Łódź 1990, p. 52.

74 Zieliński, "Wykładnia" (cit. n. 70), p. 47.

because political interests, determining the creation and reading of the law, cause the law to be an expression of the political vision of the political party that won a given parliamentary election. This vision determines the values that legitimize the law and how they are understood. The direction of the development of the law changes on the basis of a change in political vision, that is, both as a result of an intra-state change in the political party winning the election, and also, as a result of a change in the international political situation. This causes instability and unpredictability not only in the direction of the development of the law but also in the outcome of the interpretation of existing laws, affecting the instability of the economy and, consequently, the difficulty of accumulating capital.

4.3. The family, as an instrument of the state's political influence on citizens

The post-war domination of the USSR and the suppression of capitalism, as an economic system serving the wealth of the Western European bourgeoisie, were also evident in the family. The Sovietization of law (and the system), which began in 1948, was associated with the view that civil law should be the foundation for building a communist system. In this system, the law was to play a completely different role than in the system of capitalist states, including family law.[75] A great popularization of Soviet family law[76] began, assuming that family relations were based on family ties, rather than on property ties (as in capitalism). In doing so, it was emphasized that in the embattled capitalism, the family, was created because of the "property order" of bourgeois society, based on private property, which caused (in the terms of socialist propaganda) the weakening of family ties.[77] Therefore, in the socialist state, the family in the capitalist view became a completely superfluous institution,[78] whose place was taken by a completely new

75 Comp. M. Molyneux, "Family Reform in Socialist States: The Hidden Agenda," *Feminist Review* 21/1 (1985), p. 47f.

76 P. Fiedorczyk, "Prawo rodzinne Polski Ludowej jako przedmiot badań historyczno-prawnych (1944–1964) [Family Law of the People's Republic of Poland as a Subject of Historical and Legal Research (1944–1964)]," *Czasopismo Prawno—Historyczne* LV/2 (2003), pp. 147–148.

77 Comp. G. M. Swierodłow, *Małżeństwo i rodzina w państwie radzieckim* [*Marriage and Family in the Soviet State*], Warszawa 1949, pp. 8–9.

78 T. Guz, "Koncepcje małżeństwa i rodziny w nowożytnej filozofii [Concepts of Marriage and Family in Modern Philosophy]," in *Prawo rodzinne w dobie przemian*, ed. P. Kasprzyk and P. Wiśniewski, Lublin 2009, p. 15.

understanding of the family—one that was not based on and did not refer to its material interests and their protection.

The family in the socialist system was based on family ties, as personal and biological ties of its members. The material interests of the family, on the other hand, as its capitalist and weakening foundation, were not considered to such an extent that, to supposedly strengthen it, Soviet law (and after it—Polish law) included the family in a separate code.[79] However, this was not merely a systematizing procedure, but in a way a political one—for with the abovementioned break with the capitalist order in mind, the regulation of family law in a separate code may have been intended to break with the recognition of the family, property, and contract as the foundations of the capitalist order, in which property interests are protected. Hence, family law, as a part of civil law, contains statutory settlements of conflicts of property interests, constituting the entire regulation of the economic needs of citizens, to which the same (i.e., based on the examination of such interests) method of civil law interpretation is applied. Meanwhile, the regulation of family law on the Soviet model meant that the property interests of the family were of no practical importance, while the family itself became an instrument of state influence over citizens building a new regime.

The removal of the study of material interests from the interpretation of civil law and the creation of the family on the Soviet model, as based on personal rather than property ties, has resulted in a failure to recognize the property potential of the family as the foundation of society's richness in the capitalist system that was adopted in Poland in 1989.[80] This is reflected in an economy in which family businesses do not have a strong market position, while the largest companies are state-owned enterprises. It is only recently that representatives of the Polish doctrine of civil and family law have been pointing out the importance of the so-called family property, while emphasizing that it is an issue that has been

---

79 S. Szer, *Prawo rodzinne* [*Family Law*], Warszawa 1954, pp. 15–16; P. Fiedorczyk, "Z dziejów polskiego prawa rodzinnego w XX wieku [From the History of Polish Family Law in the 20th Century]," in *Rodzina i społeczeństwo. Wczoraj i dziś*, ed. F. Lempa and S. Tafaro, Białystok 2006, p. 243.

80 See: C. Creighton, "Family, Property and Relations of Production in Western Europe," *Economy and Society* 9/2 (1980), p. 129f., where the Author develops the contention that family structures and their transformation can be understood only in relation to property rights and to the social relations of production.

neglected in the science of law,[81] undoubtedly representing a legacy of the previous regime and its associated treatment of law, society and the family.

5. Conclusion

The family is a legal category, the importance of which is determined by the economic (and political) system as well as the underlying philosophical or ideological assumptions and theoretical and legal concepts. Therefore, the consideration of civil law theory, considering the historical development and comparative legal context of the family, shows that its role is extremely momentous in building and strengthening each economic system. Indeed, in Western Europe, which was built on capitalism, from the time of the Roman Empire, the wealth of society was based on the wealth of the families of Roman citizens (patricians). The family, as a reference of the provisions of the (entire!) *ius civile*, not only regulated the legal and property status of its members at that time, but above all, it enabled the richest part of society to participate in commercial transactions, providing them with the protection of the *ius civile*. The concept of modern society and the family in the capitalist system is also embedded on this economic plane. Also in this regime, the family is understood by the material interests of the citizens, which are the foundation of the free market, and the protection of these interests by civil law regulates the rules of this market, in a way that allows society to become richer, by making families richer. Civil law is therefore created in a way that protects the material interests of the family in the free market, allowing to build capital, both of the family itself and of family businesses, which constitute the success of Western European economies.

From the perspective of the theory of civil law, the issue of the family as the basis of the wealth of society is considered based on the accepted concept of law, and first of all—the method of interpretation of civil law appropriate to it. This method is conditioned by the close connection of law with the economy, allowing lawyers (practitioners and legal theorists) to read the norms of civil law as specific needs and property interests of citizens, as well as conflicts of these interests in the free market. This way of reading legal norms makes it possible to evaluate legal regulations in terms of their usefulness for solving economic problems,

81 Comp. P. Telusiewicz, "The Concept of the Existence and Functioning of the Family Property. A New Approach," in *Rodzina w prawie. Księga pamiątkowa dedykowana ks. Prof. Dr. Hab. Ryszardowi Sztychmilerowi z okazji 65. Rocznicy urodzin i 30- lecia pracy naukowej*, ed. M. Różański and J. Krzywkowska, Olsztyn 2013, p. 346.

showing which interests of citizens the legislature protects and why. Thus, the scientific discussion is based on legal and economic arguments, explaining the strengths and weaknesses of the legislator's intentions. On the contrary, the removal in the socialist science of law and the method of interpreting the law—an examination of the property interests underlying civil law—causes, on the one hand, the impossibility of evaluating legislative solutions in terms of their usefulness for the economy and, on the other hand, the use of propaganda or political arguments in legal discussion.

At the same time, the method of interpreting civil law in capitalist regimes is common to all parts of civil law, including, among others, property law, contract law, as well as family law, forming a coherent whole of statutory settlements of citizens' property interests, contained in civil law. For this reason, the family, like property or contract, are important economic foundations of the capitalist system, which system determines the legal significance of these basic dogmatic constructs. In doing so, the economic importance of the family helps to explain the family's property potential, exploited for the enrichment of Western European societies. However, this economic significance of the family remains underestimated in Polish theory and civil law dogma, which is largely a legacy of socialist legal science and the adopted method of civil law interpretation. Because of these, the family ceased to be treated in terms of property, and became, as a rule, an issue for socio-legal discussion (leaving aside the narrow area of alimony, or spousal property community). This situation is reflected in the economy, constantly raising new questions about the role of legal theory in Poland, its relationship to the economy, and in particular, contributing to the discussion of the need to change the method of interpreting civil law in Poland.

Monika Nowikowska

Protecting children online

Abstract: The aim of this article is to review main issues connected with the protection of a child in the cyberspace. It indicates the issue of the scientific discourse within the key terms: cyberspace and security of an underage in the online and offline environment. The rapid developments in Information and Communication Technologies have increased the opportunities children have access to online, as well as the risks they presented with. On the Internet, we can find information about almost anything. However, when it comes to our children's online activities, we need to make sure they're protected against contact with undesirable people, inappropriate or harmful content and malicious software or attacks. Internet is also a space where children are more easily exposed to violence, abuse or exploitation and therefore at risk of having their rights violated, in particular their right to be protected and to live in a safe environment, in accordance with their best interests. To develop effective measures on child online protection, children need to be involved in the development and implementation of relevant frameworks—and therefore need to be equipped with the digital skills and the necessary knowledge to become digitally literate and resilient for themselves and for others.

Keywords: harmful content, children, digital environment, Internet, protection, cyberbullying

1. Introduction

Child protection in cyberspace, understood in the informative context, is a complex subject of consideration of almost all fields and many scientific disciplines.[1] Today's children have entirely integrated the Internet in their interaction with others. They have adopted specific communication habits which have significant influence on their role in society and the way in which they can exercise their rights. The Internet provides many opportunities for children to spend their leisure time, to learn, to express themselves and to influence decision-making.[2] On the other hand, it is also a space where children are more easily exposed to violence, abuse or exploitation and therefore at risk of having their rights violated,

1 K. Landgren, "The Protective Environment: Development Support for Child Protection," *Human Rights Quarterly* 27/1 (2005), p. 214.

2 S. Hick, and E. Halpin, "Children's Rights and the Internet," *The Annals of the American Academy of Political and Social Science* 575 (2001), p. 56.

in particular their right to be protected and to live in a safe environment, in accordance with their best interests.[3] The Internet is having profound impact on children's rights around the world. Its impact is both negative, such us with the proliferation of child pornography, and positive, in providing child advocates with the new tools to promote and protect the rights of children.[4]

The definition of "child" is set out in Article 1 of the Convention on the Rights of the Child of November 11, 1989.[5] According to this article, for the purposes of the present Convention, a child means every human being below the age of 18 years unless under the law applicable to the child, majority is attained earlier. Article 2 indicates that States Parties shall respect and ensure the rights set forth in the present Convention to each child within their jurisdiction without discrimination of any kind, irrespective of the child's or his or her parent's or legal guardian's race, color, sex, language, religion, political or other opinion, national, ethnic or social origin, property, disability, birth or other status. States Parties shall take all appropriate measures to ensure that the child is protected against all forms of discrimination or punishment on the basis of the status, activities, expressed opinions, or beliefs of the child's parents, legal guardians, or family members.

In the aspect of this article, another important concept is cyberspace. Cyberspace has become a domain which pertains to many areas of human life.[6] Although still considered a "novum," the term was first used in the 1980s by W. Gibson, who described it as follows: A consensual hallucination experienced daily by billions of legitimate operators, in every nation, by children being taught mathematical concepts. A graphical representation of data abstracted from the banks of every computer in the human system. Unthinkable complexity (…). Lines of light ranged in the non-space of the mind, clusters and constellations of

---

3 https://www.coe.int/en/web/portal/children-and-the-internet (accessed: 04.06.2023).

4 S. Hick, and E. Halpin, *op. cit*, p. 56.

5 Convention on the Rights of the Child Adopted and opened for signature, ratification and accession by General Assembly resolution 44/25 of November 20, 1989 entry into force September 2, 1990, in accordance with article 49.

6 See more: A. Mukerji, "The Need for an International Convention on Cyberspace," *Horizons: Journal of International Relations and Sustainable Development* 16 (2020), pp. 198–209; D. R. Johnson, and D. Post, "Law and Borders: The Rise of law in Cyberspace," *Stanford Law Review* 48/5 (1996), pp. 1367–1402; G. Brown, and K. Poellet, "The Customary International Law of Cyberspace," *Strategic Studies Quarterly* 6/3 (2012), pp. 126–145; M. Karpiuk, "Cybersecurity as an Element in the Planning Activities of Public Administration," *Cybersecurity and Law* 5/1 (2021), pp. 45–52.

data.[7] Gibson pointed out some characteristic features of the environment: unlimited time and space, virtuality, complexity, and the collation of all resources in one huge database.[8]

D. E. Denning defines cyberspace (its technical aspect) as the space of information created by all computer networks put together.[9] A similar definition is formulated by G. T. Rattray. "A physical domain which is the result of the creation of information systems and networks which enable mutual interactions through electronic communication."[10] K. Chałubińska-Jentkiewicz indicates, that one of the defining features of cyberspace is its network character. It is very often associated with the information revolution, and is undoubtedly connected with the rapid growth of telecommunications and the popularization of the Internet.[11]

The above definition refers merely to the technological dimension of cyberspace. It does not make any references to the social sphere, to mankind, the user of cyberspace. In addition, the definition firmly ascribes the hardware aspect of infrastructure with the leading role of the Internet.[12] The development of new communication technologies and the evolution of the Internet have led to a vacuum in appropriate measures to protect children against content carrying a risk of harm. While the protection against content in the offline world is, in most cases, much easier to guarantee, it has become significantly more difficult to do so in the online world, especially considering that every action to restrict access to content is potentially in conflict with the right to freedom of expression and information as enshrined in Article 10 of the European Convention on Human Rights.[13] At the same time states also have a legitimate right,

7 W. Gibson, *Neuromancer*, Katowice 2009, p. 59.

8 E. Szczepaniuk, *Bezpieczeństwo struktur administracyjnych w warunkach zagrożeń cyberprzestrzeni państwa*, Warszawa 2016, p. 69.

9 D. E. Denning, *Wojna informacyjna i bezpieczeństwo informacji*, Warszawa 2002, p. 24.

10 G. T. Rattray, *Wojna strategiczna w cyberprzestrzeni*, Warszawa 2004, p. 30.

11 K. Chałubińska-Jentkiewicz, "Cyberspace as an Area of Legal Regulation," in *Cybersecurity in Poland. Legal aspects*, ed. K. Chałubińska-Jentkiewicz, F. Radoniewicz, and T. Zieliński, Cham 2021, p. 28.

12 C. Chang, "Internet Safety Survey: Who Will Protect the Children," Berkeley Technology Law Journal 25/1 (2010), pp. 501–527; R. Kuś, in *Ustawa o krajowym systemie cyberbezpieczeństwa. Komentarz*, ed. K. Chałubińska-Jentkiwiecz, M. Karpiuk, J. Kostrubiec, Warszawa 2022, p. 35.

13 K. Chałubińska-Jentkiewicz, "Freedom of Speech in International Regulations in the Face of Digital Media Development," *Cybersecurity and Law* 1/9 (2023), p. 11.

and even an obligation, to protect children from content which is unsuitable or inappropriate.[14]

2. Selected methods of child protection in cyberspace

The purpose of protecting a child in cyberspace is, on the one hand, to ensure the child's safety and, on the other, to ensure proper conditions of the child's development. Referring to the aspect of counteracting children's threats on the Internet, a very important document is Council of Europe Convention on the Protection of Children against Sexual Exploitation and Sexual Abuse (25.10.2007).[15] Contains provisions criminalizing the use of new technologies—the Internet in particular—to sexually harm or abuse children. It is open to any country in the world. Available data suggest that about one in five children in Europe are victims of some form of sexual violence. Convention on the Protection of Children against Sexual Exploitation and Sexual Abuse is the international treaty to make sexual abuse a criminal offense, with criminal penalties for (1) those who recruit children into prostitution[16]; (2) the production, supply, distribution and possession of child pornography and online access to it (3) soliciting children on chat rooms or online game sites for sexual purposes.[17]

As a preventive measure, the convention recommends that primary and secondary school children be informed of the risks of Internet use. In accordance with Art. 6 "Each Party shall take the necessary legislative or other measures to ensure that children, during primary and secondary education, receive information on the risks of sexual exploitation and sexual abuse, as well as on the means to protect themselves, adapted to their evolving capacity. This information,

14 Recommendation CM/Rec(2009)5 of the Committee of Ministers to member states on measures to protect children against harmful content and behavior and to promote their active participation in the new information and communications environment (Adopted by the Committee of Ministers on July 8, 2009 at the 1063rd meeting of the Ministers' Deputies).

15 Council of Europe Treaty Series—No. 201 Council of Europe Convention on the Protection of Children against Sexual Exploitation and Sexual Abuse, Lanzarote, 25.10.2007.

16 F. R. Barri, "The Sex Trade Industry's Worldwide Exploitation of Children," *The Annals of the American Academy of Political and Social Science* 575 (2001), p. 147, http://www.jstor.org/stable/1049185.

17 D. Thornburgh, and H. Lin, "Youth, Pornography, and the Internet," *Issues in Science and Technology* 20/2 (2004), pp. 43–48.

provided in collaboration with parents, where appropriate, shall be given within a more general context of information on sexuality and shall pay special attention to situations of risk, especially those involving the use of new information and communication technologies."

Another tool developed by the Council of Europe is transversal program "Building a Europe for and with children." The program "Building a Europe for and with children," launched in 2006, aims to ensure an integrated approach to promoting children's rights in the Council of Europe's policies and help decision-makers to develop national strategies. Its objectives are to promote children's rights, and to eliminate all forms of violence against children. As part of these activities in 2007, the Council of Europe designed an online game "Through the Wild Web Woods" to help children learn basic Internet safety rules. The game used familiar fairy tales to guide children through a maze of potential dangers on the way to the fabulous e-city Komet, while teaching them: (1) how to protect identity and personal data; (2) how to participate safely in chat rooms; (3) how to recognize sites and online games containing harmful content; (4) how to develop a critical approach toward information found on the Internet; (5) how to protect their computers against spam and viruses; (6) how to promote such key concepts and values underlying the work of the Council of Europe as democracy, respect for others and children's rights.

There is a need to provide children with the knowledge, skills, understanding, attitudes, human rights values and behavior necessary to participate actively in social and public life, and to act responsibly while respecting the rights of others.

Noteworthy are also Recommendations of the Committee of Ministers on:

(1) Measures to protect children against harmful content and behavior and to promote their active participation in the new information and communications environment (2009);
(2) Measures to promote the respect of freedom of expression and information with regard to Internet filters (2008), with specific provisions on children[18];
(3) Declaration of the Committee of Ministers on protecting the dignity, security and privacy of children on the Internet (2008).

---

18 See more: M. M. McCartby, "Filtering the Internet: The Children's Internet Protection Act," *Education Horizons: "No Child Left Behind: Failed Schools-Or Failed Law?"* 82/2 (2004), pp. 108–113.

Ad 1. In Recommendation of the Committee of Ministers to member states on measures to protect children against harmful content and behavior and to promote their active participation in the new information and communications environment (2009)[19] highlighted, that protecting freedom of expression and human dignity in the information and communications environment by ensuring a coherent level of protection for minors against harmful content and developing children's media literacy skills is a priority for the Council of Europe. The risk of harm may arise from content and behavior, such as online pornography, the degrading and stereotyped portrayal of women, the portrayal and glorification of violence and self-harm, demeaning, discriminatory or racist expressions or apologia for such conduct, solicitation (grooming), the recruitment of child victims of trafficking in human beings, bullying, stalking and other forms of harassment, which are capable of adversely affecting the physical, emotional and psychological well-being of children.

There is a need to provide children with the knowledge, skills, understanding, attitudes, human rights values and behavior necessary to participate actively in social and public life, and to act responsibly while respecting the rights of others.

There is also the need to encourage trust and promote confidence on the Internet, in particular by neutral labeling of content to enable both children and adults to make their own value judgments regarding Internet content. The Committee of Ministers recommends that member states, in cooperation with private sector actors and civil society, develop and promote coherent strategies to protect children against content and behavior carrying a risk of harm while advocating their active participation in and best possible use of the new information and communications environment, in particular by: (1) encouraging the development and use of safe spaces (walled gardens), as well as other tools facilitating access to websites and Internet content appropriate for children; (2) promoting the further development and voluntary use of labels and trustmarks allowing parents and children to easily distinguish non-harmful content from content carrying a risk of harm; (3) promoting the development of skills among children, parents and educators to understand better and deal with content and behavior

---

19 Recommendation CM/Rec(2009)5 of the Committee of Ministers to member states on measures to protect children against harmful content and *behavior and to promote their active participation in the new information and communications environment (Adopted by the Committee of Ministers on 8.07.2009 at the 1063rd meeting of the Ministers' Deputies).*

that carries a risk of harm; (4) bringing this recommendation and its appended guidelines to the attention of all relevant private and public sector stakeholders.

Ad 2. There is an increasing demand for systems which help to protect children from content carrying a risk of harm. The development of Internet content filters has provided one form of protection which subsequently led to the adoption of Recommendation CM/Rec(2008)6 of the Committee of Ministers on measures to promote the respect for freedom of expression and information with regard to Internet filters.[20] The Internet has significantly increased the number and diversity of ideas, information and opinions which people may receive and impart in the fulfillment of their right to freedom of expression and information without interference by public authorities and regardless of frontiers. At the same time, it has increased the amount of readily available content carrying a risk of harm, particularly for children and young people.[21]

To satisfy the legitimate desire and duty of member states to protect children and young people from content carrying a risk of harm, the proportionate use of filters can constitute an appropriate means of encouraging access to and confident use of the Internet and be a complement to other strategies on how to tackle harmful content, such as the development and provision of information literacy.

In this context, member states should:

(a) facilitate the development of strategies to identify content carrying a risk of harm for children and young people, taking into account the diversity of cultures, values and opinions;

(b) cooperate with the private sector and civil society to avoid over-protection of children and young people by, inter alia, supporting research and development for the production of "intelligent" filters that take more account of the context in which the information is provided (for example by differentiating between harmful content itself and unproblematic references to it, such as may be found on scientific websites)[22];

20 Recommendation CM/Rec(2008)6 of the Committee of Ministers to member states on measures to promote the respect for freedom of expression and information with regard to Internet filters.

21 K. Chałubińska-Jentkiewicz, and M. Nowikowska, *Prawo mediów*, Warszawa 2021, p. 36.

22 M. M. McCartby, *op. cit.*, p. 109.

(c) facilitate and promote initiatives that assist parents and educators in the selection and use of developmental-age-appropriate filters for children and young people;
(d) inform children and young people about the benefits and dangers of Internet content and its filtering as part of media education strategies in formal and non-formal education.

3. Children and the Internet: the phenomenon of cyberbullying

Every child must be protected from violence, exploitation and abuse on the internet.[23] The problem of children on the Internet is also pointed out by UNICEF.[24] Children are spending more time online than ever before. And they're getting there sooner. Around the world, a child goes online for the first time every half second. Growing up online offers limitless opportunities. Through computers, smartphones, gaming consoles, and televisions, children learn, imagine and develop their social networks.[25] When used in the right way—and accessible to all—the internet has the potential to broaden horizons and ignite creativity the world over.[26]

But with these opportunities come serious risks. Cyberbullying and other forms of peer-to-peer violence can affect young people each time they log in to social media or instant messaging platforms. When browsing the internet, children may be exposed to hate speech and violent content—including messages

---

23 E. Landstedt, and S. Persson, "Bullying, Cyberbullying, and Mental Health in Young People," *Scandinavian Journal of Public Health* 42/4 (2014), p. 393.

24 UNICEF is the successor of the United Nations International Children's Emergency Fund, created on December 11, 1946, in New York. Now officially United Nations Children's Fund, is an agency of the United Nations responsible for providing humanitarian and developmental aid to children worldwide. The agency is among the most widespread and recognizable social welfare organizations in the world, with a presence in 192 countries and territories. UNICEF's activities include providing immunizations and disease prevention, administering treatment for children and mothers with HI, enhancing childhood and maternal nutrition, improving sanitation, promoting education, and providing emergency relief in response to disasters.

25 A. M. Dodge, N. Husain, and N. K. Duke, "Connected Kids? K-2 Children's Use and Understanding of the Internet," *Language Arts* 89/2 (2011), p. 86.

26 https://www.unicef.org/protection/violence-against-children-online (accessed: 04.06.2023).

that incite self-harm and even suicide.[27] Children can also be put at risk when tech companies breach their privacy to collect data for marketing purposes. Child-targeted marketing through apps—and the excessive screen time it often results in—can compromise a child's healthy development. More than a third of young people in 30 countries report being cyberbullied, with 1 in 5 skipping school because of it.

UNICEF draws attention to a new phenomenon: cyberbullying. What is cyberbullying?

Cyberbullying is bullying with the use of digital technologies. It can take place on social media, messaging platforms, gaming platforms and mobile phones. It is repeated behavior, aimed at scaring, angering or shaming those who are targeted. Examples include: (1) spreading lies about or posting embarrassing photos or videos of someone on social media, (2) sending hurtful, abusive or threatening messages, images or videos via messaging platforms, (3) impersonating someone and sending mean messages to others on their behalf or through fake accounts. Face-to-face bullying and cyberbullying can often happen alongside each other. But cyberbullying leaves a digital footprint—a record that can prove useful and provide evidence to help stop the abuse.[28]

What are the effects of cyberbullying? When bullying happens online it can feel as if you're being attacked everywhere, even inside your own home. It can seem like there's no escape. The effects can last a long time and affect a person in many ways: (1) mentally—feeling upset, embarrassed, stupid, even afraid or angry, (2) emotionally—feeling ashamed or losing interest in the things you love, (3) physically—tired (loss of sleep), or experiencing symptoms like stomach aches and headaches. The feeling of being laughed at or harassed by others, can prevent people from speaking up or trying to deal with the problem. In extreme cases, cyberbullying can even lead to people taking their own lives. Cyberbullying can affect us in many ways. But these can be overcome and people can regain their confidence and health.

---

27 G. Angrove, "'She's Such a Slut!': The Sexualized Cyberbullying of Teen Girls and the Education Law Response," in *eGirls, eCitizens: Putting Technology, Theory and Policy into Dialogue with Girls' and Young Women's Voices*, ed. J. Bailey and V. Steeves, Ottawa 2015, p. 307.

28 https://www.unicef.org/end-violence/how-to-stop-cyberbullying (accessed: 04.06.2023).

To meet the problems of the dangers posed by cyberspace, it is worth taking preventive measures to make children, adolescents and adults aware that the development and use of modern technology pose dangers that can affect everyone. It should be said that cyberspace as a source of dehumanization particularly jeopardizes human health, and has quite an impact on the manifestation of the loss of a sense of reality.[29]

Most alarming is the threat of online sexual exploitation and abuse. It has never been easier for child sex offenders to contact their potential victims, share imagery and encourage others to commit offenses. Children may be victimized through the production, distribution and consumption of sexual abuse material, or they may be groomed for sexual exploitation, with abusers attempting to meet them in person or exhort them for explicit content.

In the digital world, any person from any location can create and store sexually exploitative content. Child sex offenders may even livestream sexual abuse from the confines of their homes, directing on-demand abuse of children far away. Some 80% of children in 25 countries report feeling in danger of sexual abuse or exploitation online.[30]

As children embrace more digital platforms, they too may self-generate sexually explicit imagery. And though these images might be intended for an age-appropriate relationship, they can end up widely shared without consent. Sometimes, trusted adults solicit children to share imagery. For a child victim, this may result in social isolation, mental health issues, substance abuse, self-harm or suicide, as well as an increased likelihood of exhibiting abusive behaviors themselves in adulthood.

4. Summary

Ensuring digital safety in the online environment, especially for children, requires a global approach based on internationally recognized standards and recommendations. Collaboration at national, regional and international level through the development of harmonized frameworks, integrated approaches are necessary. Integrated approaches include legal and regulatory frameworks,

---

29 A. Pieczywok, "Cyberspace as a Source of Dehumanization of the Human Being," *Cybersecurity and Law* 1/19 (2023), p. 46.

30 J. D. Osofsky, "The Impact of Violence on Children," *The Future of Children* 9/3 (1999), p. 33.

technical and procedural measures, organizational structures, capacity building, and international cooperation, are necessary.

In the literature on the subject K. Badźmirowska-Masłowska indicates that research should be focused on creating a national strategy for the protection of a minor. When considering the issues of child protection in cyberspace, conclusions should be presented regarding initiatives and actions that should be raised to increase its effectiveness. The first issue is conducting extensive research in the field of (1) terminological arrangements as to the concept of (a) cyberspace—as an environment for the functioning of a minor; (b) the status of the child in the context of being recognized as an object of protection for its proper development; (c) security—as an aspect of research on these issues.[31]

Globally, there is a lack of official tools, resources, and educational programs on child online protection developed in coordination with relevant national and international stakeholders. However, to effectively protect and empower children online, all relevant stakeholders need to have the awareness, knowledge, and skills to play their part. These stakeholders include children, parents, carers and educators, the ICT industry and policymakers. To develop effective measures on child online protection, children need to be involved in the development and implementation of relevant frameworks—and therefore need to be equipped with the digital skills and the necessary knowledge to become digitally literate and resilient for themselves and for others. The development of child online protection strategies, including policies, legislation, and regulations based on internationally recognized recommendations is therefore necessary in order to achieve change in protecting children's rights in the digital environment.[32]

Bibliography

Angrove, G., "'She's Such a Slut!': The Sexualized Cyberbullying of Teen Girls and the Education Law Response," in *eGirls, eCitizens: Putting Technology, Theory and Policy into Dialogue with Girls' and Young Women's Voices*, ed. J. Bailey and V. Steeves, Ottawa 2015.

31 K. Badźmirowska-Masłowska, "Child Protection in Cyberspace," *Cybersecurity and Law* 1 (2019), p. 221; K. Badźmirowska-Masłowska, and J. Rosa, "Wybrane aspekty prawne przeciwdziałania przestępczości seksualnej," *Przegląd Policyjny* 143 (2021), pp. 203–233.

32 K. C. Montgomery, "Protecting Children's Privacy Online: The Battle Continues," *Human Rights* 39/3 (2013), p. 6.

Badźmirowska-Masłowska, K., "Child Protection in Cyberspace," *Cybersecurity and Law* 1 (2019).

Badźmirowska-Masłowska, K., and Rosa, J., "Wybrane aspekty prawne przeciwdziałania przestępczości seksualnej," *Przegląd Policyjny* 143 (2021).

Barri, F. R., "The Sex Trade Industry's Worldwide Exploitation of Children," *The Annals of the American Academy of Political and Social Science* 575 (2001).

Brown, G., and Poellet, K., "The Customary International Law of Cyberspace," *Strategic Studies Quarterly* 6/3 (2012).

Chałubińska-Jentkiewicz, K., "Cyberspace as an Area of Legal Regulation," in *Cybersecurity in Poland. Legal aspects*, ed. K. Chałubińska-Jentkiewicz, F. Radoniewicz, and T. Zieliński, Cham 2021.

Chałubińska-Jentkiewicz, K., "Freedom of Speech in International Regulations in the Face of Digital Media Development," *Cybersecurity and Law* 1/9 (2023).

Chałubińska-Jentkiewicz, K., and Nowikowska, M., *Prawo mediów*, Warszawa 2021.

Chang, C., "Internet Safety Survey: Who Will Protect the Children," *Berkeley Technology Law Journal* 25/1 (2010).

Denning, D. E., *Wojna informacyjna i bezpieczeństwo informacji*, Warszawa 2002.

Dodge, A. M., Husain, N., and Duke, N. K., "Connected Kids? K-2 Children's Use and Understanding of the Internet," *Language Arts* 89/2 (2011).

Gibson, W., *Neuromancer*, Katowice 2009.

Hick, S., and Halpin, E., "Children's Rights and the Internet," *The Annals of the American Academy of Political and Social Science* 575 (2001).

Johnson, D. R., and Post, D., "Law and Bodrers: The Rise of law in Cyberspace," *Stanford Law Review* 48/5 (1996).

Karpiuk, M., "Cybersecurity as an Element in the Planning Activities of Public Administration," *Cybersecurity and Law* 5/1 (2021).

Kuś, R., in *Ustawa o krajowym systemie cyberbezpieczeństwa. Komentarz*, ed. K. Chałubińska-Jentkiwiecz, M. Karpiuk, and J. Kostrubiec, Warszawa 2022.

Landgren, K., "The Protective Environment: Development Support for Child Protection," *Human Rights Quarterly* 27/1 (2005).

Landstedt, E., and Persson, S., "Bullying, Cyberbullying, and Mental Health in Young People," *Scandinavian Journal of Public Health* 42/4 (2014).

McCartby, M. M., "Filtering the Internet: The Children's Internet Protection Act," *Education Horizons: "No Child Left Behind: Failed Schools-Or Failed Law?"* 82/2 (2004).

Montgomery, K. C., "Protecting Children's Privacy Online: The Battle Continues," *Human Rights* 39/3 (2013).

Mukerji, A., "The Need for an International Convention on Cyberspace," *Horizons: Journal of International Relations and Sustainable Development* 16 (2020).

Osofsky, J. D., "The Impact of Violence on Children," *The Future of Children* 9/3 (1999).

Pieczywok, A., "Cyberspace as a Source of Dehumanization of the Human Being," *Cyberesurity and Law* 1/19 (2023).

Rattray, G. T., *Wojna strategiczna w cyberprzestrzeni*, Warszawa 2004.

Szczepaniuk, E., *Bezpieczeństwo struktur administracyjnych w warunkach zagrożeń cyberprzestrzeni państwa*, Warszawa 2016.

Thornburgh, D., and Lin, H., "Youth, Pornography, and the Internet," *Issues in Science and Technology* 20/2 (2004).

List of legal acts

Convention on the Rights of the Child Adopted and opened for signature, ratification and accession by General Assembly resolution 44/25 of November 20, 1989 entry into force September 2, 1990.

Council of Europe Convention on the Protection of Children against Sexual Exploitation and Sexual Abuse, Lanzarote, 25.10.2007.

Recommendation CM/Rec(2009)5 of the Committee of Ministers to member states on measures to protect children against harmful content and behaviour and to promote their active participation in the new information and communications environment (Adopted by the Committee of Ministers on July 8, 2009 at the 1063rd meeting of the Ministers' Deputies).

Recommendation CM/Rec(2009)5 of the Committee of Ministers to member states on measures to protect children against harmful content and behaviour and to promote their active participation in the new information and communications environment (Adopted by the Committee of Ministers on 8.07.2009 at the 1063rd meeting of the Ministers' Deputies).

Recommendation CM/Rec(2008)6 of the Committee of Ministers to member states on measures to promote the respect for freedom of expression and information with regard to Internet filters.

Internet sources

https://www.unicef.org/protection/violence-against-children-online.
https://www.unicef.org/end-violence/how-to-stop-cyberbullying.
https://www.coe.int/en/web/portal/children-and-the-internet.

Rosa Indellicato

Social transformations: The family as the fundamental nucleus for education in values

Abstract: In this contribution we aim to highlight, in the light of the new social transformations that have taken place in recent years, the role of today's family in the upbringing of children and consequently in the formation of the future citizen. The first and complex hermeneutic question concerns family identity. The transformations taking place today in the structure of the family make it uncertain and difficult to define its physiognomy, which is increasingly heterogeneous in its composition, type, relational bonds, and ways of bringing up children. In considering the changes that have taken place in the family in recent decades, the need to develop training projects for parenting, as a resource and understanding of the emotional and relational problems that are created in the family, is emphasized. This is why we believe that family pedagogy can help us and represent a good opportunity to respond to the new challenges of parenthood.

Keywords: family, bringing up children, identity, family pedagogy

1. Identity and pedagogy of the family in a complex society

The specificity of pedagogy aimed at the study of the family highlights the problematic nature and plurality of the relationships[1] that characterize families today and that require targeted educational and training interventions for a conscious and rational management.

The first complex hermeneutic question concerns family identity. The transformations taking place today in the structure of the family make the definition of its physiognomy uncertain and difficult, since "we are faced not with the family, but with a constellation of families"[2] increasingly heterogeneous in composition, typology, relational bonds, and ways of educating.

It is clear that the face of the modern family has changed very rapidly, the types of nucleus and relationship, parental roles, and intergenerational relations are undergoing important metamorphoses that have been the subject of much

1 Cf. P. Donati (ed.), *Identità e varietà dell'essere famiglia. Il fenomeno della "pluralizzazione,"* Milano 2001.

2 N. Galli, *Educazione familiare e società complessa*, Milano 1991, p. 351.

research and debate[3] in recent years. Rather, the current reality shows a dilation of the concept of family and the difficulty of providing an unambiguous definition.

It is undeniable that despite everything the family remains the central fulcrum in the subject's education, the value of family education, understood as a relational process, is a decisive element for the harmonious growth of individual personalities, for the formation of the citizen and the advent of a society on a human scale, indispensable "both for the democratic qualification of the State and for the determination of family policy in the perspective of education."[4]

The affective relationships[5] and identity constructions that develop in the family sphere have made this, the family, the subject of educational reflection and socio-cultural research, also as a consequence of the radical transformations that the family nucleus has undergone during the 20th century and that have structured it in ways that are completely different from the past; an articulated and plural identity linked to the many types of family that characterize the contemporary way of life and that activate a bundle of roles and internal dynamics that are increasingly complex and difficult for the members themselves to understand.

The patriarchal family of the past, as well as the more recent bourgeois family, founded on the hierarchical fixity of roles, on paternal authority and on the transmission of social norms, has dissolved since 1968, which questioned its values, the presumed naturalness of women's role as mothers and housewives, the centrality of the father, the pyramidal and substantially repressive structure.

Beyond the different representations, what is certain is that the family is not a natural entity as some consider it but a historical-cultural institution that evolves in forms and functions in relation to economic (work), social (demographic decline) and cultural (spread of education media culture), assuming, as in recent decades, a plural, single-parent, separate, extended, hetero—or homosexual physiognomy, and an unstable structure, open and permeable on the outside, with fluid, horizontal, more intimate and personal ties on the inside.[6] It has to be said, however, that in the plurality of its forms, it remains an "ecosystem of education" open to dynamic interaction with the context and its constituent elements.[7]

---

3 Ibid.
4 N. Galli, *Educazione dei coniugi alla famiglia*, Milano 1992, p. 19.
5 Cf. T. Parsons and R. Bales, *Famiglia e socializzazione*, Segrate 1974.
6 Cf. A. Gigli, *Famiglie mutanti. Pedagogia e famiglie nella società globalizzata*, Pisa 2007.
7 Cf. R. Viganò, *Ricerca educativa e pedagogia della famiglia*, Brescia 1997.

Today's family is not only radically changed but also profoundly differentiated internally, where the dynamics between parents and children revolve around the dimension of affection, friendship and brotherhood.

In the "liquid family" all too often there is no definition of roles, there are adult children, children who are the "object" of contention between parents in conflict, the mother friend and the father older brother, and in this sense the authoritativeness of parents who should assume the responsibility of educating is lost, turning into a group of friends who, horizontally, live everything and everything together, forgetting that minors are not emotionally and biologically ready to live this climate that takes on negative connotations from the educational[8] point of view. The call, therefore, is for respect for roles, for the verticality of the adult-minor relationship, meaning a two-way respect not only from the children toward the parents, but also in the opposite direction.

Considering the changes that have taken place in the family in recent decades, the need to develop parenting[9] training projects is emphasized, as a resource and understanding of the emotional and relational problems that are created in the family.

The pedagogy of the family[10] is a concrete expression of the school-family educational co-responsibility pact, an example of the possibility of living in a participatory and responsible manner the path of the child's harmonious development toward conscious autonomy and the acquisition of fundamental values.[11]

It is a winning model of a pedagogy that recognizes a central role for parents in their child's education and also in the network of co-responsibility that involves both school and family.

The family pedagogy[12] was born precisely as an enhancement of the family's parental skills and knowledge. The starting point is the consideration of the family in its value as an essential and irreplaceable component of education[13]: parents

8 Cf. R. Indellicato, *La dispersione scolastica nel terzo millennio. Analisi e prospettive pedagogiche tra vecchi bisogni e nuove sfide*, Lecce 2020, p. 73.

9 Cf. A. D'Antone, *Il sostegno educativo alla famiglia e alla genitorialità. Contenuti, strumenti e strategie per la formazione delle figure professionali a valenza pedagogica*, Milano 2020.

10 Cf. L. Pati, *Scuola e famiglia. Relazione e corresponsabilità educativa*, Brescia 2019.

11 Cf. M. Corsi and M. Stramaglia, *Dentro la famiglia. Pedagogia delle relazioni educative familiari*, Roma 2009.

12 Cf. L. Pati (ed.), *Pedagogia della famiglia*, Brescia 2014.

13 Cf. A. Bellingreri, *La famiglia come esistenziale. Saggio di antropologia pedagogica*, Brescia 2014.

know their children better than anyone else, and their point of view is an indispensable element of the educational process.

This is why we believe that the pedagogy of the family is a good opportunity to transmit firm values[14] while respecting the differences in educational styles, representing at the same time, a space for sharing, listening and confrontation, an example of the good family that is born from the positive and proactive relationship with families.

2. The family: A privileged place for shaping the future citizen

The family, therefore, the foothold and refuge of everyone, especially the child. Parents and educators in general not only condition the educandi, through the basic anthropological choice made for the educational pathway to be implemented,[15] but with behavior, attitudes, ways of doing and being, they suggest to the minors what will be both the life choices and the educational choices of their children when they grow up and become parents in turn.

The first form of acceptance between people occurs precisely in the family unit. Spouses, united with each other and with their children, are sharers in an original story of love and hope, and so they make up a group, which, while it structures itself in solidarity, produces it. The propitious ages for arousing similar attitudes in them are pre-adolescence and adolescence, when boys and girls become capable of understanding the reasons for domestic community, of appreciating it, of participating in it. Adolescents begin to manifest feelings of esteem and gratitude to their parents, which will then increase and specify themselves in traits of particular sensitivity in the later stages of their lives.

The family remains the most valid "school of humanity," in which generations learn to accept and understand each other, to prevent and ease the tensions caused by their relationships, and to grasp the value of an ordered and peaceful coexistence. A policy for the family[16] today finds consensus on the following three guiding criteria: economic and social autonomy, which means guaranteeing all families a minimum level of dignity, outside the logic of welfare;

---

14 Cf. J. Juul, *La famiglia che vogliamo. Nuovi valori guida nell'educazione dei figli e nei rapporti di coppia*, Milano 2012.

15 Cf. S. Grilli, *Antropologia delle famiglie contemporanee*, Roma 2019.

16 Cf. G. Elia and A. Rubini (eds.), "Famiglie politiche sociali e prospettive pedagogiche," in *Pedagogia della cura—Famiglie, comunità, legami sociali*, Lecce 2022.

the principle of freedom in the choice of services available to families, that is, arranging the choice of schools, health and social facilities; the third criterion concerns the solidaristic treatment of families, they must be guaranteed essential services and, if necessary, supported with support measures.

In this context, attention to the reality of families, rightly considered as a "resource" but to which specific support measures must be reserved, is therefore central. The family, as both subject and privileged object of social policies, is the foundation and primary resource of society. It must be helped to recognize and identify these resources within it and to make the most of them. It is only by bringing to light all the wealth it possesses that a real promotion of its well-being and a renewed way of conceiving and fostering the relationship between families and services can arise. The family, as a fundamental place in the development of the human person, is decisive in the formation of the child and also plays an important role in education in adulthood.[17] It constitutes a very significant environment for the development of children and young people, in particular for the relationships that are created there and that profoundly influence the process of identity construction.

Family education activities, in fact, contribute to promoting people's psychological well-being, putting them in a position to better manage their relationships with their children and with people in general; in this way they also show their "civil" connotation, aimed at improving the "quality of life" of citizens.

Family didactics and methodology, therefore, being foundational elements in the conquest of the skill of credibility itself, represent the fulcrum of family life within which everyone learns the possibility of being credible and happy or not. This as an essential and indispensable value for the collective balance of today's society that is too focused on productivity and economic aspects instead of on the well-being of its members. A family, which intends to foster harmony, joy, serenity and happiness, must build an adequate educational relationship between its members; it must contradict the pursuit of solitude, isolation or a lack of interpersonal and inter-human communication; it must reset the intergenerational relationship through the participation, sharing and commitment of each person to family life.[18] All this regardless of the age of each family member.

---

17 Cf. D. Bacchini (ed.), *Il ruolo educativo della famiglia. Essere genitori nella società contemporanea*, Trento 2013.

18 Cf. L. Fruggeri, *Famiglie d'oggi. Quotidianità, dinamiche e processi psicosociali*, Roma 2018.

A lack of relationship and intra-family dialogue between the components present in the family nucleus, on the other hand, produces a distortion of interpersonal communication with consequent fractures in the relationship and dialogical[19] exchange between the parties involved. So that the family is no longer a harmonious entity in which to find refuge in times of need, but rather a place in which individuals share only a physical space.

The studies conducted outline a society full of family instability[20] and intergenerational fractures, resulting in a worsening of everyone's civic commitment and, hence, of the social climate. the responsibility is attributed to the general lack of trust of man toward other man toward other man and institutions.

This being so, the parental and adult commitment in the education of offspring takes on a very fundamental and unique value in order to re-organize and re-educate societies to a sense of the human that has almost completely disappeared. In our time, therefore, the family needs to regain its role of responsibility to respond to the educational needs of children precisely through that patient exercise of love[21] that alone can sustain an educational practice that cares for the child and arouses his trust, and this must be done not only by parents, but also by teachers because only in this way will the learner be captured by the interest in knowledge and become an active subject in search of what he lacks. The irreplaceable role of the family in the education of children is the guiding idea on which the reflections conducted thus far are based. The family is a fundamental element of the educational experience, just as the educational dimension is a fundamental peculiarity of it, too important for it not to be developed, albeit through a new conceptual effort (thinking philosophically about the family) and under conditions of new contextual difficulties. An organic and scientifically founded philosophy of the family[22] and for the family must therefore be pursued, both so as not to be left without educational answers in the face of its new dimensions, and as a condition for designing and evaluating social services in a promotional perspective. However, even today, despite some significant exceptions, there is still no widespread awareness of the importance of philosophical reflection on the family and of the appropriate instruments for its promotion.

---

19 Cf. P. Milani, *Educazione e famiglie. Ricerca e nuove pratiche per la genitorialità*, Roma 2018.

20 Cf. J. Horvat and D. Platt (eds.), *The Child's World. The Essential Guide to Assessing Vulnerable Children, Young People, and their Families*, London 2019.

21 Cf. G. Simmel, *Filosofia dell'amore*, Roma 2001.

22 Cf. G. Riconda, *Filosofia della famiglia*, Brescia 2014.

On the other hand, the renewed interest in family pedagogy cannot be separated from the contribution of theoretical elaboration, research and operational intervention offered by the philosophical knowledge system. The areas of family pedagogy, aimed at guiding and supporting reciprocity in the couple's journey, educational commitment and care for their children, are situated in the more general context of adult education. The family today is "orphaned" of models in a longitudinal sense and poor in comparisons in a transversal sense. Everyday life, the expression of complex and articulated organization and planning strategies, of solidarity pacts, of solutions for everyday life, tests the possibility of building a stable path.

It is therefore necessary to activate resources capable of supporting the family in its educational projects[23] and tasks, in relation to the demands of everyday life. In this respect, the promotion of education and the need to feel invested with responsibility is indispensable, even when the relationship breaks down, parents remain parents for life. The attitude that must be present in the family is solidarity,[24] which must take concrete form in a set of measures aimed at humanizing the person, with the intention of promoting man according to the law of love. The unknowns present in our reality must become resources from which to propose constructive paths. Beyond the existing family models, parents must be trained to assume the awareness of educating in a complex society like ours.

Bibliography

Bacchini, D. (ed.), *Il ruolo educativo della famiglia. Essere genitori nella società contemporanea*, Trento 2013.

Bellingreri, A., *La famiglia come esistenziale. Saggio di antropologia pedagogica*, Brescia 2014.

Corsi, M., and Stramaglia, M., *Dentro la famiglia. Pedagogia delle relazioni educative familiari*, Roma 2009.

D'Antone, A., *Il sostegno educativo alla famiglia e alla genitorialità. Contenuti, strumenti e strategie per laformazione delle figure professionali a valenza pedagogica*, Milano 2020.

Donati, P. (ed.), *Identità e varietà dell'essere famiglia. Il fenomeno della "pluralizzazione,"* Milano 2001.

23 Cf. J. P. McHale, *La sfida della genitorialità*, Milano 2010.

24 Cf. P. Gambini, *Psicologia della famiglia. La prospettiva sistemico-relazionale*, Milano 2016.

Elia, G., and Rubini, A. (eds.), "Famiglie politiche sociali e prospettive pedagogiche," in *Pedagogia della cura—Famiglie, comunità, legami sociali*, Lecce 2022.

Fruggeri, L., *Famiglie d'oggi. Quotidianità, dinamiche e processi psicosociali*, Roma 2018.

Galli, N., *Educazione familiare e società complessa*, Milano 1991, p. 351.

Galli, N., *Educazione dei coniugi alla famiglia*, Milano 1992, p. 19.

Gambini, P., *Psicologia della famiglia. La prospettiva sistemico-relazionale*, Milano 2016.

Gigli, A., *Famiglie mutanti. Pedagogia e famiglie nella società globalizzata*, Pisa 2007.

Grilli, S., *Antropologia delle famiglie contemporanee*, Roma 2019.

Horvat, J., and Platt, D. (eds.), *The Child's World. The Essential Guide to Assessing Vulnerable Children, Young People, and their Families*, London 2019.

Indellicato, R., *La dispersione scolastica nel terzo millennio. Analisi e prospettive pedagogiche tra vecchi bisogni e nuove sfide*, Lecce 2020, p. 73.

Juul, J., *La famiglia che vogliamo. Nuovi valori guida nell'educazione dei figli e nei rapporti di coppia*, Milano 2012.

McHale J. P., *La sfida della genitorialità*, Milano 2010.

Milani, P., *Educazione e famiglie. Ricerca e nuove pratiche per la genitorialità*, Roma 2018.

Parsons, T., and Bales, R., *Famiglia e socializzazione*, Segrate 1974.

Pati, L. (ed.), *Pedagogia della famiglia*, Brescia 2014.

Pati, L., *Scuola e famiglia. Relazione e corresponsabilità educativa*, Brescia 2019.

Riconda, G., *Filosofia della famiglia*, Brescia 2014.

Simmel, G., *Filosofia dell'amore, Donzelli*, Roma 2001.

Viganò, R., *Ricerca educativa e pedagogia della famiglia*, Brescia 1997.

Chapter III. Family, constitution and fundamental rights

Marta Cantín Larumbe

The paradigm of the family in the Spanish Constitution of 1931[1]

Abstract: The family is commonly identified as the cell of humanity, with inherent natural rights over and above the State. As the fundamental nucleus of society, it cannot be reduced solely to the private sphere, as it constitutes a plural and dynamic reality in constant evolution, generating changes as well because of them.

However, in the 20th century, the Constitution made provisions for marriage and the family in its articles. The Mexican Constitution of 1917, in article 130, affirms the contractual nature of marriage, being the exclusive competence of civil servants and authorities.

Likewise, the Weimar Constitution of 1919, in Articles 119–122, regulates marriage and the family more precisely. Firstly, it states that marriage, the foundation of family life and the preservation and growth of the nation, is under the special protection of the Constitution. It proclaims the legal equality of the sexes and provides for the protection and assistance of motherhood. Finally, it entrusted parents with the education of their offspring and placed illegitimate children on the same legal footing as legitimate children.

The 1931 Constitution will regulate marriage and the family similarly. There are many reasons for the constitutional regulation of marriage and the family: the social transformation after the proclamation of the republic, the feminist movement, the rise of socio-Marxist ideologies, and the secularization of the state.

However, does the family paradigm embodied in the Constitution correspond to social reality, or was it merely an attempt by the Second Republic to transform the foundations of society, such as the family and marriage?

Keywords: Family law, Constitution, the secularization of marriage

---

1 Communication given in the 13th Annual Spanish-Polish Conference in Barcelona (April 21, 2023).

1. Introduction

Until the Republican Constitution, family law remained outside public law.[2] The Civil Code regulated the relations, duties, and rights between spouses and children born in wedlock.

The classic constitutions of the 19th century were limited to regulating in their organic part the body of the powers of the State, and in the dogmatic position, to recognizing the rights of man and the citizen and the fundamental political liberties.

The Constitutions of the 20th century institutionalized the protection of the family, inscribed in them as a political program pleasing to political parties of all tendencies. It seems that a Constitution of the end of the 19th century in Costa Rica initiated this process of constitutionalizing the family.

Several original ideological and political factors led to the constitutional protection of marriage and the family:

(a) The effort of the constitutions of the time to enshrine social rights.
(b) The attempt of the constitutions to declare the fundamental factors of power constitutionalized.
(c) The political consensus tacitly agreed upon between the bourgeoisie, addicted to conservative family values.

2. The legal background to the 1931 Constitution

Until the compulsory civil marriage law of 1870, a valid marriage was celebrated according to canon law.[3] The Royal Decree of 1564 by Philip II incorporated into national legislation the provisions of the Council of Trent on matrimonial matters, introducing compulsory canonical marriage for the baptized.

The explanatory memorandum of this law recognizes marriage as the basis of all human institutions—including the family—the generative element of society itself. It states that without marriage, there is no family; without it, there is no society.[4]

2 Except for the Penal Code, which regulated both the crime of adultery and the crime of adultery, crimes intimately related to marriage and family.
3 However, the existence of clandestine marriages—sham marriages—valid but subject to sanctions is worth mentioning.
4 *Journal of Sessions*, December 17, 1869, Appendix 3, p. 1.

However, enacting this law meant a change in the marriage paradigm, as it established compulsory civil marriage, with canonical marriage having no effect, despite recognizing marriage as a religious institution.[5]

The 1869 Constitution, of a liberal democratic nature, is characterized by its extensive declaration of rights in Title I, including freedom of conscience and worship (Art. 21). this freedom of religion and conscience underlies the establishment of compulsory civil marriage. Thus, Mr. Eugenio Montero Ríos, in a session of the Cortes, stated:

> Civil marriage is a necessary consequence of religious freedom. Marriage is one of life's most essential, transcendental acts; marriage is the basis of the family, just as the family is the basis of the State: the family is where the whole of society is reflected, and the ends of humanity are realized. For if there is religious freedom, if there is even tolerance of worship, even if the Church is not completely separated from the State, the State must see not the faithful, but citizens, in contracting this act; the ideas of the faithful and citizens must be separated; the civil contract and the sacrament must also be separated; this civil contract must be organized according to the sound principles of natural law, according to the eternal principles of justice.[6]

The enactment of this law is a consequence of the liberalism characteristic of the 19th century, which affirms that state-legal regulations cannot take the Church or ecclesiastics into account but must be produced solely to protect legal situations that are based on the development of powers and rights deriving from the State itself.[7] Pi y Margall expressed himself in these terms:

> It is necessary, gentlemen, to know well what the Church is: we must know well what the enemy before us is: we must understand perfectly well what the great difficulty is for the freedom of thought to be complete. The real problem is the Church (...). So, if we wish to have freedom of thought and total freedom in religious matters, we must always try to separate the Church from the State: for in this way, the Church cannot count on the protection of the State to make its anathemas and prohibitions real.[8]

The then Minister of Grace and Justice, Luis Zorrilla, when presenting the draft law to the Cortes[9] -as we have announced above-recognized the dual nature of

5 *Journal of Sessions*, December 17, 1869, Appendix 3, p. 1.

6 *Journal of Sessions*, March 15, 1869, p. 510.

7 Grahit Ferrer, E., "El matrimonio civil obligatorio: Ley española de 1870. The promoters of civil marriage in defence of indissolubility," *Cuadernos doctorales, Derecho canónico, derecho eclesiástico del Estado* 10 (1992), p. 506.

8 *Journal of Sessions*, March 24, 1869, p. 705.

9 *Journal of Sessions*, December 17, 1869, Appendix 3.

marriage. For this reason, he justified the concurrence of both powers in matrimonial matters. Religion legislated on marriage insofar as it is an institution transcendental to man's spiritual and moral life. The State should also legislate on it because it constitutes an essential element of existence. He differentiates civil marriage from the sacrament depending on who legislates on the institution. If it is the State, we speak of civil marriage; if it is the Church, marriage is a sacrament. That is why he justifies that civil marriage was confused with the sacrament when there was legislative unification until the enactment of this law.

2.1. Indissolubility of marriage

As for the indissolubility of marriage, far from considering it as a religious or sacramental characteristic, it affirms that it manifests the principles of justice and equity proper to natural law. The legislator recognizes that marriage is a natural complement to the human personality, which does not only have as its purpose the perpetuation of the species but also responds to the fulfillment of social needs, such as the education of children or support between spouses:

> In marriage, the spouses unite to realize the rational ends of life; not only procreation but also the education of offspring and the cooperation of the spouses in fulfilling their respective and natural destinies. If perpetuity is destroyed, realizing the ends above will be hindered or rendered impossible.[10]

Therefore, if marriage is stripped of its perpetual and indissoluble character, the social aims it pursues can hardly be realized.

2.2. Divorce

The indissolubility of marriage determines the nature of divorce. Divorce would not dissolve the conjugal bond; it would only be exempt from the obligation to live together. The explanatory memorandum clarifies that the commitment to live together does not correspond exclusively to private law since "its main basis is morality and public order, so that the spouses may not divorce or separate of their own free will as long as there is no enforceable judgment." As divorce affects society and public order, provides exhaustively, in Article 87, those causes that would give rise to divorce.

This law already announces, albeit timidly, the public nature of marriage, which should be kept from the will of the spouses.

10 *Journal of Sessions*, December 17, 1869, Appendix 3, p. 3.

Finally, the 1870 law would be the first to secularize marriage based on the freedom of worship and conscience enshrined in the 1869 Constitution. However, part of the doctrine considered that enacting this law meant a mismatch between legal regulations and social reality. Spanish society was not very favorable to the secularization of Marriage.[11] Even though this Law would not recognize civil effects to canonical marriage, an Order of June 20, 1874 prevented civil marriage when a non-dissolved canonical marriage bound the contracting parties.

This law would lose its validity after promulgating the Decree of February 9, 1875, which would recognize the civil effects of marriages contracted according to the sacred canons.

2.3. Promulgation of the Civil Code

The debate on the validity of the different forms of marriage was familiar to the parliamentary debate during the drafting of the Civil Code.[12] Article 42 of the original draft of the Civil Code of 1889 established two forms of marriage: the canonical marriage, compulsory for all those professing the Catholic religion,[13] and the civil union, to be celebrated in a manner determined by the Code.

This article results from the Government's negotiations with the Holy See, conducted by Alejandro Groizard. It is interesting to note the three points that the Holy See sought to clarify during the talks: firstly, that the civil effects of canonical marriage should be recognized; secondly, that the presence of a State representative at the celebration of a canonical marriage should be for the sole

---

11 Manuel Marañón y Gómez-Acebo, "Examen del decreto de 9 de febrero de 1875 reformando la ley de matrimonio civil." *Revista General de Jurisprudencia y legislación* 15 (1877), p. 5: "(…) the legislator forgetting that the first condition for the law to be fulfilled is not its absolute divorce with the customs and tendencies of those who must observe it, as happened with the law on civil marriage, dictated more than anything else by the impulse of a political requirement." Iván C. Iban also gathers some of the opinions of the doctrine in his work "Matrimonio civil y matrimonio canónico en la legislación española (1870–1978)," *Anuario de Derecho Civil ADC* XXXII/1 (1979), p. 94: It "marred the pages of our patriotic matrimonial law," "caused many and very deep disturbances in families and public morality," "clashed with patriotic traditions and with the social environment," etc.

12 v. Fosar Benlloch, E. *Estudios de derecho de familia*, vol. III, Madrid 1982, pp. 520ff.

13 The term *profess*, as its scope was not precisely defined, led to doctrinal interpretations. *v* Iban, I. C., "Matrimonio civil y matrimonio canónico," pp. 111ff.

purpose of immediate registration in the civil registry; and, finally, that the State should limit itself to establishing prohibitive impediments.[14]

The Civil Code of 1889 also recognized the competence of the ecclesiastical courts to hear claims for marriages celebrated according to canon law.

3. The family in the 1931 Constitution

The proclamation of the Second Republic—following the victory of the Republican parties in the central provinces—brought with it the promulgation of a Constitution. The Republican Constitution, like the Constitution of 1812, aroused their interest in trying to break with the past and find a new Spanish state.

Before explaining the family regulation in the 1931 Constitution, we must dwell on the Preliminary Draft of Ángel Ossorio y Gallardo, which was not submitted to the Cortes for debate but outlined the bases of the 1931 Fundamental Law.

3.1. Preliminary constitutional draft

Before the elections to the Constituent Courts were called, the preliminary draft was entrusted to a Legal Advisory Commission, which depended on the Ministry of Justice. Subsequently, this commission delegated responsibility to a Subcommission headed by Ángel Ossorio y Gallardo, comprised of 12 members.

His proposal was a moderate constitution inspired by Spain's constitutional tradition (Constitutions of 1812, 1837, and 1869) and the Weimar Constitution.[15] It consisted of 104 articles divided into nine titles.

---

14 Fuenmayor de, A., "El matrimonio en el Código civil," *Ius canonicium* 59 (1990), p. 225.

15 The similarity with the Weimar constitutional text is palpable in the regulation of the family. Article 119 of the Weimar Constitution stated that "marriage, the foundation of family life and the preservation and increase of the nation, is under the special protection of the Constitution. It is based on the legal equality of the two sexes. It is incumbent upon the State and the municipalities to ensure the family's purity, health, and improvement. Large families are entitled to compensatory protection measures. Motherhood is entitled to the protection and assistance of the state."
On the other hand, as discussed below, Article 27 of the preliminary draft provided that "marriage, the basis of the family, is under the special protection of the State. It is based on equal rights for both sexes. Parents shall be obliged to feed their children, keep them in their company, educate them, and instruct them. The state shall ensure the fulfillment of these duties. Civil laws shall regulate the rights of children born out of wedlock and the investigation of paternity in their defence."

The explanatory memorandum accompanying the draft bill unpacks some of the reasons or ideas underlying the text, such as the separation of church and state:

> The religious issue, of primary interest everywhere and of special concern among Spaniards, has been dealt with as it is already in all peoples, even in those with the strongest Catholic sentiment, namely, separating the Church from the State and respecting without hesitation the freedom of conscience and freedom of worship, proclaimed in more than one passage of the text.
>
> No one can see a persecutory spirit or destructive sectarianism in these declarations. Even if some members of the Commission had wished to see a Christian orientation in the moral activities of the State expressly safeguarded, it seemed preferable not to make a declaration on the matter and to leave the two powers independent, albeit in agreement, as is generally the case today.[16]

Despite establishing a non-denominational state, it recognized a special status for the Church by considering it an "institution of public law" and guaranteeing religious education. It also recognized the Church's social strength and historical significance. Thus, Article 8 read as follows:

> There is no state religion. The Catholic Church shall be considered a Corporation under public law. Other religious denominations may have the same status when they so request and, by their constitution and the number of their members, offer guarantees of subsistence.

According to the Explanatory Memorandum and the recognition of political and civil rights,[17] social and economic rights, characteristic of contemporary Constitutions, were included to regulate issues of high social interest. Hence, the Chapter entitled "Family, economy and Culture" was incorporated.

---

16 The Preliminary Draft is available at https://www.cervantesvirtual.com/obra-visor/anteproyecto-de-constitucion-de-la-republica-espanola-de-1931/html/.

17 Among others, unlawful arrests and the responsibility of the agents and officials who enforce them (Art. 14); the affirmation of trade union freedom to consider trade unions as bodies under public law so that they may intervene in the social and economic policy of the State (Art. 23); the principle of equality of the sexes in working life (Art. 24); and the acceptance of civil servants' associations, provided they do not interfere in the public service entrusted to them (Art. 25). 23); the principle of equality of the sexes in working life (Art. 24); and the acceptance of Associations of civil servants, provided that they do not interfere with the public service entrusted to them, as well as the recognition of the right of such Associations to appeal to the Courts in defense of their members (Art. 25).

Firstly, Article 27 proclaims marriage as the basis of the family and places it under the special protection of the State, based on equal rights for both sexes.[18] It also provides for the duties of parental authority, the rights of children born out of wedlock, and the investigation of paternity.

Unlike Article 43 of the 1943 constitution -which would establish divorce as a constitutional issue—this draft omitted any reference to divorce.

Numerous individual opinions accompanied this preliminary draft. None referred to the family question, although many referred to the religious question.[19]

The dissenting vote on Article 8 by Ángel Ossorio, Manuel Pérez Rodríguez, and José Manuel Puebla is noteworthy, as they considered that "if the constitution] is to teach the children of their country if it is to legislate on the family if it is to watch over ethics in contracts if it is to watch over customs, it will be difficult for them to fulfill such arduous duties without having a firm idea of the spiritual foundations of life, which can only be found in religious belief." For this reason, they proposed that Article 8 should be worded as follows: "There is no official religion of the State, which shall protect freedom of worship, but shall base its actions and legislation on the norms of Christian morality."

Although the intention was for this preliminary draft to become a project, given the Government's disagreements, the Cortes, once constituted, appointed a special Commission to be in charge of drawing up a project.

3.2. Draft constitution and debate in the constitutional courts

On July 28, 1931, the 21 members of the Constitutional Commission that would draw up the draft constitution, chaired by Luis Jiménez de Asúa, were elected.

On August 27, with a speech by the President of the Commission, the debate in the constituent courts began. In this speech, Jiménez de Asúa justified the

---

18 The Weimar Constitution influences the family question, Article 119 states: "Marriage, the foundation of family life and the preservation and increase of the nation, is under the special protection of the Constitution. It is based on the legal equality of the two sexes."

19 Fernández Clérigo, in his dissenting opinion, proposed the establishment of a secular State: "The State does not profess any religion. The Catholic Church and other religious confessions will only be considered as associations. They will be obliged to comply with the precepts established in the special law regulating them." In similar terms, E. Ramos put the wording of Article 8 in similar terms: "There is no state religion. Freedom of worship is guaranteed. Churches shall be considered worship establishments and regulated by a special law."

inclusion of the rights of collective entities such as trade unions or the family, a trend already adopted in the Mexican Constitution of 1917, the Russian Constitution of 1918, and the Weimar Constitution of 1919.

Some issues were hotly debated, notably the religious question, the definition of the family, and the establishment of divorce.

3.2.1 The religious question concerning the family

The religious question provoked a clear division not only among parliamentarians but also among the Spanish population.[20] Article 3 of the Constitution established a secular state. Secularism permeated the entire constitutional text, as Deputy Molina Nieto pointed out:

> This atheism is also exacerbated in Article 41 of the same draft Constitution, in which an attack is made, a brutal blow to the family; in which, not only is it stripped of all religious principles, but which, if approved as it is in the first paragraph of the article above, would truly constitute a principle and a focus of social dissolution.[21]

In the same sense, Deputy Álvarez Rodríguez understood that the Constitution attacked the Catholic population, the school, and the family head-on; not only that, but he also reproached the Commission for attributing the misfortunes and crimes of the monarchy to the Catholic religion.[22]

The Deputy for the Union of the Right party, Santiago Guallar, presented in the Cortes the Catholic doctrine on marriage, alleging that the marriage contract is utterly inseparable from the sacrament, in such a way that marriage being a sacred thing, its ordination and jurisdiction belong entirely and exclusively to the Church. Finally, he affirms that any interference of the civil power in this matter is a sacrilegious usurpation, an outrage to the rights of the Church, and an attack on the Catholic conscience and freedom of conscience.[23]

The words of the Radical-Socialist Member of Parliament, Gordón Ordás, are essential to understand the relationship between secularization and the regulation of the family in the Constitution: "The Free State cannot exist until the other state that governs and directs it is removed from it, and this state is the Church;

---

20 Manuel Azaña, in his speech to the Cortes on October 14, 1931, stated, "Spain had ceased to be Catholic." However, this statement does not seem to correspond to social reality.

21 *Journal of Sessions*, August 27, 1931, p. 649.

22 *Journal of Sessions*, August 28, 1931, p. 667.

23 *Journal of Sessions*, June 17, 1932, p. 6287.

the Church as the fundamental basis of power, of the family, of property and education."[24]

3.2.2. *The social function of the Family*

All that has been said so far does not imply that the sole motivation of the constituent legislator in regulating the family was the separation of Church and State. The legislator recognizes the social function and importance of the family:

> The family factor has a great importance in our social life, a transcendence of such a nature that, not only in the atmosphere of the Chamber but also the corridors and cafés and in all the homes of Spain, discussions are being held about the possibilities, the concept and the results that the decisions of the Chamber can bring to this institution.[25]

The State should protect the family in marriage because, in addition to being a natural organism, "it is also a political, legal and moral organism, constituting a nucleus of the family, a point where future citizens germinate."[26] Ricardo Semper, a member of the Constitutional Project Commission, asserts:

> These principles of divorce, of equal rights between husband and wife within marriage, of the investigation of paternity and, finally, of the equal duties of the father towards legitimate and natural children, are so important and, in a certain way, so incorporated in the political programs that have constituted the essence of this national movement, that they must be enshrined in the Constitution.[27]

Another MP, speaking on the dissolution of marriage, states that marriage "is not merely a thing of two persons, that it does not belong only to the conjugal partnership, but that the partnership has or should have a social action when it is in the public interest to dissolve the marriage."[28]

However, despite the social function played by the family, we can deduct from the debates in the Cortes that there was no unanimity among the deputies

---

24 *Journal of Sessions*, September 1, 1931, p. 705.

25 *Journal of Sessions*, September 29, 1931, p. 1536.

26 Review of the Courts and Universal Legislation 67 (1933), pp. 313–171.

27 *Journal of Sessions*, October 15, 1931, p. 1755.

28 *Journal of Sessions*, February 5, 1932, p. 3643. Ricardo Samper expressed himself in similar terms: "The dissolution of marriage, which is the legal fact, is harmful to the social interest, as all disturbances of the legal order are harmful; but the principle of dissolubility, which is the remedy that the law applies to avoid great evils that occur within marriage and which determine the effective or legal fact of its dissolution, far from being evil, is a good thing, because, to use a simile, the amputation of a limb of an individual is evil for him and society" (*Journal of Sessions*, October 15, 1931, p. 1755).

when it came to constitutionalizing family law. Thus, Deputy Castrillo wondered whether life issues such as family, religion, or property should be included in the Constitution, as it is part of civil life that divides the parties and mankind into two camps.[29]

And if it was to be regulated, in what terms? Unlike the preliminary draft of the Constitution, which placed marriage as the basis of the family, the republican constitution bases it on consanguinity. Moreover, Clara Campoamor, in one of her speeches in Congress, stated that "not all the family is marriage; that there is a natural and spiritual family" and that "there is also a multitude of families that do not have their origin in paternity or maternity."[30]

3.2.3. *Divorce*

The debate intensified even more on whether or not to regulate divorce as a constitutional issue. Some MEPs—including Óscar Casanova—considered that establishing divorce as a constitutional issue responded only to partisan interests. He compared the case of divorce to the peaceful turn of the parties during the 19th century:

> (…) Did Cánovas come to power? Would the conservatives fall and the liberals rise? All those who had been appointed before suffered the same fate. Well, something similar happens when they insist on giving laws retroactive effect. For example, in the current case: What does the left command? To divorce even D. Ángel's cat, even if the marriage was contracted based on indissolubility. What does the right-wing command one day? Nobody gets divorced, even if the marriage was entered on the condition that it could be dissolved if it went badly for the contracting parties. You must realize, Members of Parliament, that this would be an upheaval for everyone, and you must realize that those of you who are on top now may at some point fall underneath.[31]

Ossorio y Gallardo, despite defending the conception of marriage as a contract, considers:

> Is required of marriage what is not required of any contract, which is the possibility of withdrawal, because in all contracts there is an element of individual interest, almost always patrimonial, but also a concept of social interest. We ask one extraordinary thing of marriage: that it can be undone as soon as someone does not agree with having entered into it. So, it is no longer a contract; according to this thesis, it is the last, most

29 *Journal of Sessions*, October 15, 1931, p. 1753.
30 *Journal of Sessions*, October 15, 1931, p. 1749.
31 *Journal of Sessions*, February 5, 1932, p. 3640.

> despicable, and smallest of contracts. What no one would dare to break in a sale, in a loan, is intended to be broken by dissolving the bond in a marriage.[32]

And, in any case, he considers that "the declaration and regulation of divorce is a matter for civil law, not for a Constitution. And I say in this what I have had to say on other issues: let us not bring into the Constitution legal matters that may need to be amended tomorrow, and if they are not amended, they may constitute social damage."[33]

The Minister of Finance replied in the following terms: "We have a fundamental reason for bringing it into the Constitution, and that is that until this civil law is passed, the previous code, which refers the hearing of divorce cases to the ecclesiastical courts, will remain in force."[34]

4. Recap

The constitutionalization of the family resulted from the Republic's desire to transform society, and this transformation implied the secularization of marriage and the family.

Until then, the Church had been responsible for safeguarding morals, customs, and, of course, the family.[35] Therefore, by establishing a secular state, the Church was to be stripped of its power in favor of state power. Thus, whereas previously the family, specifically marriage, was regulated by canonical provisions, it is now the State that must take on this task because of the social function of the family.

And, as deputy López Varela of the radical Republican party said:

> A society is revolutionized and transformed when it transforms its institutions since society is a harmony of the most important institutions such as the family, the state, property, and religion. A revolution that produced a social upheaval but left these institutions intact would not have revolutionized anything.

---

32 *Journal of Sessions*, October 15, 1931, p. 1746.

33 *Journal of Sessions*, October 15, 1931, no. 57, p. 1747.

34 *Journal of Sessions*, October 15, 1931, no. 57, p. 1748. The Civil Code of 1888/1889 established that the ecclesiastical courts would hear cases of separation and divorce from marriages celebrated according to canonical provisions.

35 It is enough to look at Article 11 of the 1876 Constitution: "The Roman Catholic, Apostolic and Roman religion is the religion of the State," obliging the Nation to maintain the cult and its ministers. Thus, it is clear that no one shall be disturbed in Spanish territory for their religious opinions, nor for the exercise of their respective worship, *except for the respect due to Christian morality*."

The Republic, in the Constitution and then in the development of the laws that came to complete it, has made this great transformation of Spanish society: from the theological family perpetually bound by divine bonds, to a human family, based on conjugal love and filial piety.

Bibliography

Legal acts

Act of March 11, 1932 on Divorce.

Act of June 18, 1870 on Civil Marriage.

Civil Code of 1888.

Constitution of 1931.

Literature

Battle Y Vázquez, M., *Repercusiones de la Constitución en el Derecho Privado*, Madrid 1933.

Corcuera Atienza, J., "La constitución española de 1931 en la historia constitucional comparada," *Fundamentos: Cuadernos monográficos de teoría del estado, derecho público e historia constitucional* 2 (2000), pp. 629–695.

Díez-Picazo, L., *Familia y Derecho*, Civitas 1984.

Falcón y Tella, F., "La familia, el Estado, la Iglesia: pasado y nuevos horizontes," *Anuario de Derechos Humanos*, Nueva Época 5 (2004), p. 191.

Fosar Benlloch, E., *Estudios de derecho de familia*, vol. III, Madrid 1982, pp. 520ff.

Fuenmayor de, A., "El matrimonio en el Código civil," *Ius canonicum* 59 (1990), pp. 223–241.

Gomá, I., *La familia según el Derecho Natural y cristiano*, Barcelona 1931.

Grahit Ferrer, E., "El matrimonio civil obligatorio: Ley española de 1870. Los promotores del matrimonio civil en defensa de la indisolubilidad," *Cuadernos doctorales. Derecho canónico, Derecho eclesiástico del Estado* 10 (1992), pp. 501–560.

Iván, C., "Matrimonio civil y matrimonio canónico en la legislación española (1870–1978)," *Anuario de Derecho Civil ADC* XXXII/1 (1979), pp. 83–175.

Jiménez de Asúa, L., *La constitución de la República*, Madrid 1932.

Manuel Marañón y Gómez-Acebo, "Examen del decreto de 9 de febrero de 1875 reformando la ley de matrimonio civil," *Revista General de Jurisprudencia y legislación* 15 (1877), pp. 257–276.

Marzal Rodríguez, P., *El derecho de familia entre la II república y el primer franquismo*, Aranzadi 2022.

Oliver Araujo, J., and Ruiz Robledo, A. (dirs.), *Comentarios a la constitución española de 1931 en su 90 aniversario*, Madrid 2021.

Pérez Serrano, N., *La Constitución española de 1931*, Madrid 1932.

Pidal Rodrigalvares, L., *La revolución y el derecho privado* (ensayo crítico), Madrid 1934.

Quintana Reynés, L., *Derecho matrimonial y familiar del Estado Español 1936–1942*, Barcelona 1943.

Valpuesta Fernández, R., *La disciplina constitucional de la familia en la experiencia europea*, Valencia 2022.

Vázquez, de Prada, M., "Para una historia de la familia española en el siglo XX," *Memoria y Civilización* (M&C) 8 (2005), pp. 115–170.

Iwona Florek

Changes in Polish labor law to support parents on the labor market

Abstract: Recent changes to the Polish Labor Code (amendment of the act in March 2023) implementing Directive 2019/1158 are aimed at supporting families, especially parents in the labor market.

However, these changes were not only a response to the dramatic demographic situation in Europe and equal opportunities for women on the labor market, but also to the entire changing labor market. A new generation, the so-called Generation Z has different life priorities, and thus perceives professional commitments differently.

The article presents changes on the Polish labor market against the background of Europe, taking into account not only the legal obligation to implement the directive, but also social conditions.

Keywords: Labor law, labor market, work-life balance, generation Z

1. Introduction

In March 2023, new labor law provisions were introduced into the Polish legal system to facilitate the professional functioning of parents and persons caring for family members.

The changes were dictated by the obligation to implement the Work-Life Balance Directive,[1] but the author suggests that it is based not only on the legal obligation, but also on social changes taking place both in Polish and European societies.

Directive 2019/1158 establishes minimum requirements to achieve equality between women and men in terms of labor market opportunities and treatment at work by making it easier for employees who are parents or carers to reconcile work and family life. Mainly the law focus on inclusion women at labor market. As it is stated in the justification for the Labor Law "a significant factor contributing to the underrepresentation of women in the labor market is the difficulty in reconciling professional and family responsibilities. Women who have children tend to spend fewer hours working and more time fulfilling unpaid caring responsibilities. The fact of having a sick or dependent relative also turns out to

---

1 Directive (EU) 2019/1158 of the European Parliament and of the Council of June 20, 2019 on work-life balance for parents and carers and repealing Council Directive 2010/18/EU.

have a negative impact on women's employment and causes some of them to completely withdraw from the labor market."

The current European legal framework offers few incentives for men to share caring duties equally. This inequality between women and men in work-life balance policies exacerbates gender gaps in work and care. Fathers' use of work-life balance arrangements, such as leave or flexible working arrangements, will have a positive effect in reducing the amount of unpaid family work carried out by women and leave them more time for paid work.

The Work-life Balance Directive introduces a set of legislative actions designed to modernize the existing EU legal and policy frameworks, with the aims of better supporting a work-life balance for parents and carers, encouraging a more equal sharing of parental leave between men and women, and addressing women's underrepresentation in the labor market.

Changes in Polish labor law were forced by policy and regulations in this area at the EU level. But what are the reasons for this new approach to the regulation of employment relations? The author of the study argues that this is caused by generational and demographic changes in Europe.

The main three reasons for implementation changes in labor law:

1. the labor market has switched from an "employer's market" to an "employee's market"
2. demographic situation
3. gender differences in the labor market.

2. The entrance of Z Generation to the labor market

Generation Z, or the digital generation, includes people born between 1997 and 2012. This group is very heterogeneous, but there are some general trends regarding their values and perception of work. It is very important to emphasize the attitude of this group to diversity. Generation Z often places a high value on equality and respects diversity in society, including different ethnicities, sexual orientations and gender identities. Generation Z is often more open to different views and cultures than previous generations. They may be more willing to accept other perspectives and lifestyles. Perhaps this is due to the times in which they grew up being connected with the whole world thanks to information technologies.[2]

---

2 Scholz, C., "The Generations Z in Europe—An Introduction," in *Generations Z in Europe (The Changing Context of Managing People)*, ed. C. Scholz and A. Rennig, Bingley 2019, pp. 3–31, https://doi.org/10.1108/978-1-78973-491-120191001.

People of this generation are often more concerned about the environment and sustainability. Many of them are actively involved in environmental protection activities. Many members of Generation Z focus on a sustainable lifestyle, which includes taking care of mental and physical health, care for the natural environment and social relations.

People from Generation Z treat work as an expression of identity. For many Gen Z people, work plays an important role in expressing their identity and passion. They often try to find a job that is in line with their values and allows them to develop their interests.

People from this generation are often looking for a job that gives them the opportunity to develop and self-fulfillment. They may prefer flexibility and the ability to take on a variety of tasks, as well as innovative and creative work environments. Generation Z recognizes the importance of maintaining a work-life balance. They prefer flexible work schedules and the possibility of working remotely to better reconcile their private and professional lives.[3]

The value for generation Z is personal development, acquiring new skills and continuous learning. Many of them strive to obtain a high education and undertake various forms of learning, both formal and informal. Therefore, at work, they care about development opportunities. Pay is not the most important motivator.

Generation Z shows interest in social impact and willingly engages in social activities. They may prefer work that has a positive impact on society and the opportunity to make a difference. This is consistent with the growing trend to introduce CRS values in organizations.[4]

Many researchers made studies on this specific group. Here are some results of the research.

---

3 Musinszki, Z., Vallasek, M., Mélypataki, G., Csolák, E. H., and Lipták, K., Workaholism and a New Generation—Labour Market Survey among Hungarian and Romanian Youth," *Amfiteatru Economic* 22/14 (2020), pp. 1227–1242.

4 Thomas, S., Bhatt, V., and Patel, R., "Impact of Skepticism on CRM Luxury Campaign Participation Intention of Generation Z," *International Journal of Emerging Markets* (ahead-of-print, 2022), https://doi.org/10.1108/IJOEM-10-2021-1568; Anisiewicz, U., Wołowiec, T., Społeczna odpowiedzialność biznesu a integracyjna wizja społeczeństwa—uwarunkowania ekonomiczne i społeczne," *Journal of Modern Science* 48/1 (2022), pp. 207–230, https://doi.org/10.13166/jms/150756.

"Z" generation in the labor market	
Muster, R.[5]	Generation Z is dynamic, demanding, shows no loyalty and attachment to the company
Schroth, H.[6]	Gen Z employees often have an idealistic picture that the work will be interesting and meaningful, that their managers will want to hear and implement their ideas, that they will have flexibility in the schedule, and that they will enjoy everyone they work with. (…) Autonomy can be fostered by managers showing trust and support for new employees to make decisions, allowing them to take eventual ownership over projects and have greater control over their time management and how they complete tasks
Leslie B. et al.[7]	Results indicated three distinct subgroups within generation Z: Social Investors, Chill Worker Bees, and Go Getters Social Investors valued a work-life balance, Chill Worker Bees desired a comfortable workplace environment, and Go Getters prioritized advancing their career. All three groups reported prioritizing companies with high moral and ethical standards
Kirchmayer, Z., Fratričová, J.[8]	Motivating factors at work: enthusiasm, co-workers (atmosphere), financial reward, achievement, career advancement, personal development, recognition, workplace

As it can be seen, the new generation has different requirements than its predecessors. Work is a value for them, but not the most important, it does not define their

5 M. Rafał, "Pokolenie 'Z' na współczesnym rynku pracy w opiniach pracodawców," *Humanizacja pracy* 1 (2020), pp. 131–146.

6 Schroth, H., "Are You Ready for Gen Z in the Workplace?," *California Management Review* (2019), 000812561984100, https://doi.org/10.1177/0008125619841006.

7 Leslie, B., Anderson, C., Bickham, C., et al., "Generation Z Perceptions of a Positive Workplace Environment," Employee Responsibilities and Rights Journal 33 (2021), pp. 171–187, https://doi.org/10.1007/s10672-021-09366-2.

8 Kirchmayer, Z., and Fratričová, J., "What Motivates Generation Z at Work? Insights into Motivation Drivers of Business Students in Slovakia," *Proceedings of the Innovation Management and Education Excellence through Vision*, 6019, 6030 (2020).

lifestyle. The job can be changed if necessary, if it does not give satisfaction not only financially, but also in terms of pursuing passion, self-development.

3. Labor market on the verge of a demographic crisis in Poland

The current demographic situation in Poland affects the labor market in various aspects. The key factors here are the aging of the population and changes in the age structure. Poland is a country where the aging process of the society is observed. An increasing number of people are retiring, leading to labor shortages in some sectors. In addition, many people of the young generation leave Poland in order to look for better earning opportunities abroad. This phenomenon, known as economic migration, leads to the draining of the workforce, especially highly skilled ones. The lack of younger workers may be driving up labor costs and shortages in some industries, such as healthcare and elderly care. Young people who enter the labor market have a greater choice of jobs and may place higher demands on employers.

Poland is also experiencing changes in the age structure of the population. The proportion of working age people is decreasing while the proportion of younger people is increasing. This can lead to more competition in the labor market among younger people and affect their employment opportunities.[9]

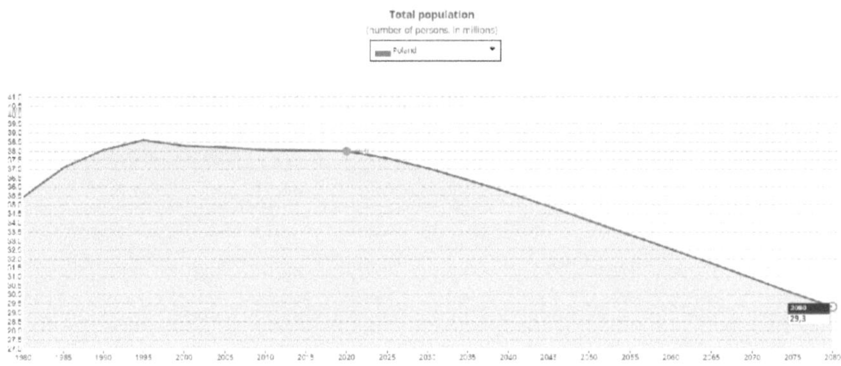

9 Drela, K., "Zmiany demograficzne a rynek pracy w Polsce," *Prace Naukowe Uniwersytetu Ekonomicznego we Wrocławiu* 489 (2017), pp. 78–89.

Source: Eurostat [accessed: 13.04.2023]

To sum up, the demographic situation in Poland, including the aging of the population and economic migration, has an impact on the labor market. This requires adjustments by government, businesses and others to manage the labor shortage, adjust pension and social policies, and develop strategies to attract and retain young talent. Also, legal changes in the field of greater protection of employees are forced, among others, by demographic changes in the labor market.

The total number of population will be decreasing in the next decades, with the estimated drop up to 29.3 million people in 2080, according to the estimations of European Statistical Office.

4. Gender pay gap in EU

The gender pay gap is a significant problem that many countries, including European countries, still struggle with. Despite advances in gender equality, there is statistical evidence of a gender pay gap. Statistics show that in Europe, on average, women earn less than men. According to Eurostat data, in 2021 the gender pay gap rate was almost 13% in the European Union Member States. However, these differences may vary from country to country and in some cases may even be more than 20%.

The gender pay gap is due to a variety of factors. Factors often cited include occupational segregation, with women concentrated in lower-paying sectors and occupations, inequalities in access to career advancement, limited access to management positions, underutilization of women's professional skills, and inequalities in internal pay in some companies.

The gender pay gap has negative consequences for both women and society as a whole. For women, this means lower incomes, greater economic dependence, and hindered professional development and promotion. In addition, wage inequality contributes to maintaining stereotypes and social inequalities, limiting social and economic potential.

Equal pay between the sexes is a desirable goal, both from the perspective of social justice and from the point of view of socio-economic development. At the European level, it takes action to reduce the pay gap through the introduction of legislation, the promotion of equality and awareness, the close monitoring of pay inequalities and initiatives to increase the participation of women in leadership and management.

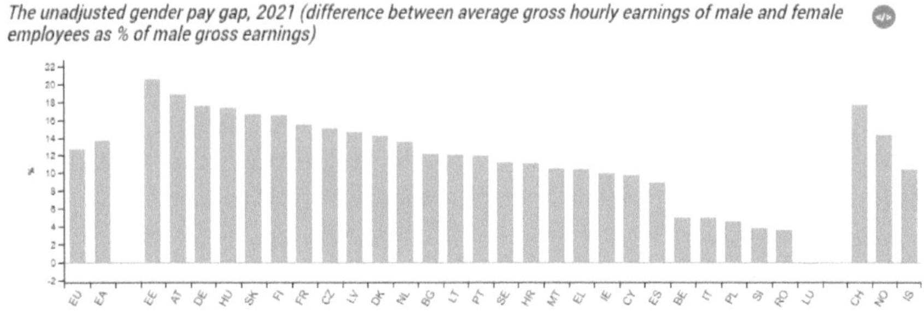

Source: Eurostat [accessed: 12.04.2023]

In 2021, women's gross hourly earnings were on average 12.7% below those of men in the EU.

In Poland, differences in remuneration of women are significant in the private sector—in companies and enterprises managed by private persons. Standards of equal pay between the sexes are maintained in the public sector.

As it can be seen, the situation in Poland is better than in many other European countries, but it is not perfect yet. The role of the legislator is to create such a law that will protect weaker individuals on the labor market, in this case women.

5. Changes in Labor Law[10] in favor of parents

The latest amendments in Polish labor law introduces many changes, not only addressed to working parents, but also regarding remote work or transparent working conditions, which also partially improve the working conditions of parents.

10 Act of June 26, 1974. Labor Code (Journal of Laws 1974 No. 24 item 141 with amendments).

The unadjusted gender pay gap by economic control (%), 2021

	Public	Private
Belgium	1.1	8.1
Bulgaria	11.0	13.6
Czechia(²)	12.2	19.5
Denmark	10.8	13.7
Germany	9.2	22.1
Spain	8.4	13.4
Croatia	10.7	13.9
Italy	5.5	15.5
Cyprus	-0.2	19.3
Latvia	15.6	15.5
Lithuania	9.7	14.3
Hungary	17.2	16.9
Netherlands	11.1	19.2
Poland	-0.6	13.0
Portugal	15.0	13.4
Romania(¹)	1.7	10.2
Slovenia	5.1	10.8
Slovakia	12.3	18.4
Finland	17.1	16.4
Sweden	7.8	10.1
Iceland	10.3	13.9
Norway	6.8	18.0
Switzerland	15.5	18.5

Note: For all the countries except Czechia: data for enterprises employing 10 or more employees, NACE Rev. 2 B to S (-O); for Czechia: enterprises employing 1 or more employees, NACE Rev. 2 B to S;
Data not available for EE, IE, EL, FR, LU, MT, AT
Gender pay gap data for 2021 are provisional until benchmark figures, taken from the Structure of Earnings survey, become available in December 2024

(¹) Estimated data.
(²) Definition differs (see metadata)
Source: Eurostat (online data code: earn_gr_gpgr2ct)

eurostat

The most important facilitations addressed mainly to parents include: additional days off for childcare, force majeure, paternity leave.

1. Prohibition of refusal to work remotely. The employer will not be able to refuse to work remotely (remote work can be total, hybrid or occasional) a pregnant employee, an employee raising a child until the child is 4 years old, an employee taking care of another member of the immediate family or another person remaining in the same household, holding a certificate of disability or a certificate of severe disability. However, it should be remembered that remote work is not possible for all professions and workplaces. In any case, the employer may refuse it if it is not possible due to the organization of work or the type of work performed by the employee.
2. Obligatory leave for fathers. Each parent will have 9 weeks of non-transferable leave (at the moment, Polish fathers can use a two-week paternity leave).
3. Parental leave, after the implementation of the work-life balance directive, will be 41 weeks, and in the case of multiple pregnancies—43 weeks (currently 32 and 34 weeks, respectively). As part of parental leave, each parent will receive 9 weeks of leave for exclusive use. This means that one of the parents can take parental leave for a maximum of 32 weeks or 34 weeks (in the case of multiple pregnancies). The remaining 9 weeks are left to be used by the other parent, usually the child's father. For the 9-week parental leave, the employee-father will receive a maternity allowance in the amount of 70% of the basis of remuneration. Adoptive parents will be entitled to the same amount of leave as biological parents.
   Ex.: 20 weeks of maternity leave, 32 weeks parental leave for the mother, 9 weeks parental week for the father.
4. According to the provisions of the directive, every worker in the EU is entitled to have 5 days off a year. Carer's leave is to be used to care for or support a relative or a person living with an employee in the same household who requires significant care or significant support for serious medical reasons—and such provisions will be included in Polish legislation. In Poland, carer's leave will cover children, parents and spouse. Carer's leave will not be included in the holiday leave pool, but it will be unpaid leave.
5. Additional time off will be due, among others, to: due to "force majeure," there will be 2 additional days off or 16 hours per calendar year. It will have to relate to the worker's family life and covers events such as accident or illness. Time off due to "force majeure" will be granted on different terms than leave on demand. First of all, these are additional days off—they are not included in the general pool of holiday leave—using this time off, we do not reduce the amount of leave to which we are entitled in a given year. In addition, for the period of taking time off due to "force majeure," you are entitled to 50%. remuneration calculated as remuneration for the period of holiday leave.

To encourage parents to take up work, policymakers can consider various support tools.

Providing flexible working hours or remote work options can be very appealing to parents. It will allow them to adjust their work to their schedules related to childcare, such as picking up from school or attending important school events. As Such-Pyrgiel points out, the family's financial situation is one of the determinants of its quality of life (objective dimension), next to attitude toward people, values (psychological dimension) and views (cultural dimension).[11]

Additional benefits such as paid parental leave, extra days off to care for a child in case of illness, or childcare subsidies can be a powerful incentive for parents to take up work. The provision of paid parental leave is an important factor in encouraging parents to take up work. It allows them to spend time with the child in key stages of development and provides financial support during this period. Providing extra days off to care for a sick child will help parents organize work and child care more effectively. Moreover, in Poland there is a financial benefit for parents of all children up to the age of 18. The introduction of subsidies to the cost of childcare eases the financial burden of childcare for parents.

Introducing employment stability, as well as clear career paths for employees, can help parents feel more secure and encourage them to take up work.

Ensuring greater employment stability is crucial for parents. This may include long-term contracts, a certain level of working hours, or long-term projects that give parents a sense of financial security and stability.

6. Conclusions

It is important that policymakers consider the diverse needs and challenges that parents face. By adopting a flexible and supportive approach, they can create a working environment that encourages parents to take up employment while allowing them to effectively combine work and family life. Providing fringe benefits and reducing job insecurity are long-term investments that can bring many benefits. By attracting and retaining parents in the labor market, organizations can benefit from the experience, knowledge, and skills of these employees, which can have a positive impact on productivity and workplace atmosphere. Taking care of work-life balance is beneficial for the employee, but also for the

11 Such-Pyrgiel, M., "Rodzina i jakość jej życia we współczesnym społeczeństwie polskim. Zarys problematyki," in *Bezpieczeństwo i jakość życia we współczesnym społeczeństwie polskim. Studium interdyscyplinarne*, Józefów 2015, pp. 13–34.

employer, who will have among his resources a more efficient, effective and satisfied employee.[12]

Changes addressed mainly to parents dictated by the changing workforce on the labor market will be used by the next generations, which are more demanding.

In the light of this changing labor market and the growing flexibility and turbulence of careers, European national labor policies should continue to consider the balance between flexibility and security (***flexicurity***). The guarantee of security through transitions into (long-term) open-ended employment is becoming increasingly weaker. However, one should be careful not to label all non-standard forms of employment as precarious work. Some transitions in a turbulent labor market are inclusive (at least in hindsight). The institutional framework could play an important role in providing security and guaranteeing certain rights (including for those who are in non-standard forms of employment). This gives rise to several policy options. On the one hand, security could be made inherent to the non-standard employment status by lowering the risks of unemployment and income reduction weighing on non-standard workers.[13]

Bibliography

Legal acts

Act of June 26, 1974. Labor Code (Journal of Laws 1974 No. 24 item 141 with ammendments).

Directive (EU) 2019/1158 of the European Parliament and of the Council of June 20, 2019 on work-life balance for parents and carers and repealing Council Directive 2010/18/EU.

Literature

Anisiewicz, U., and Wołowiec, T., "Społeczna odpowiedzialność biznesu a integracyjna wizja społeczeństwa—uwarunkowania ekonomiczne i społeczne," *Journal of Modern Science* 48.1 (2022), pp. 207–230, https://doi.org/10.13166/jms/150756.

12 Szejniuk, A., "Równowaga praca—życie osobiste," *Journal of Modern Science* 21/2 (2014), pp. 313–326.

13 S. Bekker and I. Deurzen, "Photographs of Young Generations on the Dutch Labour Market," *International Labour Review* (2019), https://doi.org/10.1111/ilr.12139.

Bekker, S., and Deurzen, I., "Photographs of Young Generations on the Dutch Labour Market." *International Labour Review* (2019), https://doi.org/10.1111/ilr.12139.

Drela, K., "Zmiany demograficzne a rynek pracy w Polsce," *Prace Naukowe Uniwersytetu Ekonomicznego we Wrocławiu* 489 (2017), pp. 78–89.

Kirchmayer, Z., and Fratričová, J., "What Motivates Generation Z at Work? Insights into Motivation Drivers of Business Students in Slovakia," *Proceedings of the Innovation Management and Education Excellence through Vision* 6019, 6030 (2020).

Leslie, B., Anderson, C., Bickham, C., et al., "Generation Z Perceptions of a Positive Workplace Environment," Employee Responsibilities and Rights Journal 33 (2021), pp. 171–187, https://doi.org/10.1007/s10672-021-09366-2.

Musinszki, Z., Vallasek, M., Mélypataki, G., Csolák, E. H., and Lipták, K., "Workaholism and a New Generation—Labour Market Survey among Hungarian and Romanian Youth," *Amfiteatru Economic* 22/14 (2020), pp. 1227–1242.

Rafał, M., "Pokolenie 'Z' na współczesnym rynku pracy w opiniach pracodawców," *Humanizacja pracy* 1 (2020), pp. 131–146.

Scholz, C., "The Generations Z in Europe—an Introduction," in *Generations Z in Europe (The Changing Context of Managing People)*, ed. C. Scholz and A. Rennig, Bingley 2019, pp. 3–31, https://doi.org/10.1108/978-1-78973-491-120191001.

Schroth, H., "Are You Ready for Gen Z in the Workplace?," *California Management Review* (2019), 000812561984100, https://doi.org/10.1177/0008125619841006.

Such-Pyrgiel, M., "Rodzina i jakość jej życia we współczesnym społeczeństwie polskim. Zarys problematyki," in *Bezpieczeństwo i jakość życia we współczesnym społeczeństwie polskim. Studium interdyscyplinarne*, Józefów 2015, pp. 13–34. WSGE.

Szejniuk, A., "Równowaga praca—życie osobiste," *Journal of Modern Science* 21/2 (2014), pp. 313–326.

Thomas, S., Bhatt, V., and Patel, R., "Impact of Skepticism on CRM Luxury Campaign Participation Intention of Generation Z," *International Journal of Emerging Markets* (ahead-of-print, 2022), https://doi.org/10.1108/IJOEM-10-2021-1568.

Kinga Flaga-Gieruszyńska & Aleksandra Klich

The community interview in Polish civil proceedings: Selected issues

Abstract: The community interview is used in the Code of Civil Procedure in those cases where the court should, for the accuracy of its decision, have full knowledge of the living conditions of the persons who are to be affected by the decision. This instrument for obtaining information is of an optional nature, and it is applied only in cases strictly specified in the procedural act. The purpose of this paper is to present and resolve interpretative problems relating to the community interview as a source of information for the authority issuing a decision in a matrimonial, family or guardianship case and, at the same time, a document with certain characteristics, as well as its status within the framework of the evidence procedure. The question of the correct execution of the community interview in order to optimize its substantive value for the shaping of the framework of an effective evidentiary procedure is also not without significance.

Keywords: community interview, civil procedure, probation officer

1. Introduction

In Polish civil proceedings, the principle of truth is of fundamental importance, which however suffers from limitations resulting from the passivity of the parties (participants) to the proceedings who fail to present their claims and evidence in support thereof. However, the situation is slightly different in relation to proceedings relating to broadly understood family, guardianship and matrimonial matters in which the court ex officio has to take care of the welfare of children or persons subject to guardianship or guardianship or other persons with special needs who are not able to take care of their own interests. In such a situation, the legislator places more emphasis on the necessity for the court to act ex officio in order to establish information that is relevant for making a decision securing the interests of these persons, in particular by establishing their living conditions, the extent to which their material and non-material needs are met, the provision of an adequate basis for development and a dignified life. For example, it appears that an interview is a good means of substantiation to assist the court in granting safeguards in both custody and contact cases, as well as maintenance.[1]

1 M. Cieśliński, "Komentarz do art. 434 KPC," in *Kodeks postępowania cywilnego.*

Consequently, it should be assumed that the community interview is applicable in the Code of Civil Procedure[2] in those cases where the court should, for the accuracy of its decision, have full knowledge of the living conditions of the persons who are to be affected by the decision. This instrument of obtaining information is of an optional nature,[3] and it is applied only in cases strictly specified in the procedural act. The legitimacy of its application depends on the specific case and on the disclosed circumstances to be established in the course of the evidentiary proceedings. However, W. Stojanowska emphasizes the need to introduce the obligatory nature of conducting a community interview.[4] It should be acknowledged that such a solution may be too far-reaching, taking into account the fact that the court may obtain the necessary information in a specific proceeding already at the stage of exchange of first pleadings between the parties (participants) to the proceedings or from the content of the submitted preparatory pleadings.

The aim of this study is to present and resolve interpretative problems relating to the community interview as a source of information for the authority issuing a decision in a matrimonial, family or guardianship case, and at the same time a document with certain characteristics, as well as its status within the framework of evidentiary proceedings. The main thesis of the thesis is to show that the community interview is not a means of evidence, but a source of information constituting the basis for evidence proceedings. The question of the correct conduct of the community interview in order to optimize its substantive value for shaping the framework of an effective evidentiary procedure is also not without significance. In this respect, a number of specific issues arise, primarily concerning the potential infringement of the privacy rights of third parties not involved in the proceedings, as well as the objectivity of the person conducting the community interview, who may reflect his or her subjective beliefs in the information provided to the court, indirectly influencing further proceedings and the final decision.

Komentarz, ed. P. Rylski, Warszawa 2022, Legalis.

2 Act of 17.11.1964—Code of Civil Procedure—Journal of Laws 2021, item 1805, hereinafter referred to as the CCP.

3 Judgment of the Supreme Court of 10.05.2000, III CKN 881/00, Legalis.

4 M. Cieśliński, Legalis.

2. The procedural nature of the community interview

As already indicated, there is a doctrinal dispute as to the procedural nature of the community interview in civil proceedings. Some scholars consider the community interview as an unnamed means of evidence, due to the fact that it is not defined *expressis verbis* in Part One of Book One, Title VI, Section III of the Code of Civil Procedure devoted to evidence. In such a case, it is indicated that the community interview is similar in nature to the expert opinion and visual inspection.[5] For example, Z. Krzemiński considered that the material collected during a community interview may undoubtedly constitute evidence in a pending divorce case.[6]

According to the researchers representing the view that the community interview is evidence, its status is evident from the content of Article 434 CCP, and this in juxtaposition with Article 441 CCP, as well as from the content of Articles 561^1, 565^1 and 570^1 CCP. They accept that the absence of the inclusion of a community interview in the general rules of evidence cannot mean that such an interview is not evidence. According to this position, the placement of Article 434 CCP in the general rules of evidence in matrimonial proceedings proves that in trial proceedings the community interview is evidence at least in these separate proceedings. On the other hand, the regulations contained in Articles 561^1, 565^1 and 570^1 CCP—according to this position—allow the inference that in non-trial proceedings the community interview is evidence in certain family law, guardianship and custody cases.[7] Consistently assuming that a community interview is evidence, it would have to be considered that the order for a community interview to be conducted by a designated person takes the form of an order issued by the court. This order should be made in closed session (Article 148 § 3 CCP). Going further, if the community interview is to be treated as evidence, the parties (participants) to the proceedings should be given the opportunity to challenge it. In such a situation, it would be appropriate to allow the application

5 W. Stojanowska, *Rozwód a dobro dziecka*, Warszawa 1979, p. 125; Z. Krzemiński, *Rozwód. Komentarz do przepisów. Orzecznictwo. Piśmiennictwo. Wzory pism*, Warszawa 2004, p. 209.

6 Z. Krzemiński, *op. cit.*, p. 214.

7 H. Haak and A. Haak-Trzuskawska, "Komentarz do art. 434 KC," in *Małżeństwo (zawarcie małżeństwa, prawa i obowiązki małżonków). Komentarz do art. 1–30 KRO i powiązanych przepisów KPC (art. 7, 15, 17, 41, 47, 57, 66, 98, 100–102, 117, 177, 187, 189, 193, 203, 204, 2054, 316, 367, 400, 425–435, 447–451, 561–565(1))*, Warszawa 2020, Legalis.

by analogy of Article 286 CCP, allowing the interviewer to request an oral or written explanation of the content of the document submitted.

However, in putting forward such a thesis about the nature of the community interview, it is first necessary to consider the way in which the information contained in it is obtained and its value. Seemingly, the community interview can be considered as indirect evidence. However, indirect evidence occurs when the fact in evidence is established on the basis of other facts, such as the observation of a witness or expert. As noted in the literature, the strength of the evidence depends on the number of intermediate members separating the judge from the fact in evidence.[8] Based on this criterion, W. Siedlecki introduces first-degree indirect evidence (e.g., testimony of a witness about what he heard or saw), and second-degree indirect evidence (e.g., testimony of a witness about what he heard from someone else).[9] This classification can be applied to the community interview, the manner in which it is conducted and the evidentiary value of the information thus established. In this respect, one has to agree with F. Zedler that the poor evidentiary value and the difficult to verify indirect message often contained in the community interview put into question the advisability of considering it as evidence, which, in view of the need to preserve the constitutional principle of a fair trial in every civil case, can never be disregarded.[10] Not only does the community interview contain the observations of the person conducting it, which may be evaluative and subjective in nature, but it may also contain highly subjective accounts provided by third parties (neighbors, teachers, fact-finders), which lengthens the number of links between the facts and the court and consequently makes it problematic to consider the information contained in the community interview or the evidentiary interview itself as evidence.

In contrast, another position, which in our view is accurate, considers that a community interview is not evidence, as it has a different purpose and is not provided for in the system of evidence proceedings.[11] The community interview cannot replace the evidentiary procedure. Its task is to prepare it properly,[12] and

8 Z. Resich and T. Misiuk-Jodłowska, in *Postępowanie cywilne*, ed. J. Jodłowski, Z. Resich, J. Lapierre, T. Misiuk-Jodłowska, and K. Weitz, Warszawa 2014, p. 392.

9 W. Siedlecki, in *Postępowanie cywilne. Zarys wykładu*, ed. W. Siedlecki and Z. Świeboda, Warszawa 2003, p. 227.

10 F. Zedler, "Dowód nienazwany w postępowaniu cywilnym," *Polski Proces Cywilny* 4 (2018), p. 477.

11 T. Żyznowski, "Komentarz do art. 434," in *Kodeks postępowania cywilnego. Komentarz*, t. II, ed. A. Marciniak, Warszawa 2020, Legalis.

12 J. Sztombka, "Wywiad środowiskowy w sprawach rozwodowych," *Nowe Prawo* 5 (1978), p. 737.

above all to provide the starting material for assessing whether and what evidence still needs to be carried out in a given case.[13] In this case, an evidentiary proceeding is understood as the totality of procedural acts carried out by both the parties and the procedural authorities in order to prove the truth of the facts alleged by the parties in support of their claims and allegations.[14] In practice, the determination that a community interview is not evidence is very important, because, for example, in the case where, in a divorce or separation case, spouses with a minor child agree on the resolution of all the issues covered by Article 58 CCP, the court may not be content with limiting the evidentiary proceedings to hearing the parties and conducting a community interview (Article 441 CCP).[15] As a consequence, the interview may also be an impetus, for example, for the admission of evidence ex officio (Article 232 sentence 2 CCP).[16] Certainly, such evidence can be evidence from the testimony of a witness, which will be, for example, the person drawing up the interview, especially if it is requested by a party (participant) challenging the veracity of the interview. This remark also applies to the problem of third parties who provided the information reflected in the content of the community interview. If one is going to treat the community interview as evidence, it would be necessary to give the parties (participants) to the proceedings the opportunity to ask questions and refer to any statement made by a person who provided even fragmentary information for the purposes of the community interview. In the meantime, it would be far better to establish in this way the facts that need to be verified in the course of the evidentiary proceedings and the evidence to support them, which should be carried out in order to make an accurate decision.

In summary, it should be considered that the latter position, denying the status of evidence to a community interview in civil proceedings, is accurate. As T. Żyznowski rightly points out, such evidence has not been provided for in the system of evidentiary proceedings. According to this author, the search for similarity to expert opinion evidence or visual inspection evidence does not take into account the fundamental premise of evidence proceedings conducted with

13 W. Stojanowska, in *System prawa prywatnego, Prawo rodzinne i opiekuńcze*, ed. T. Smyczyński, t. 11, Warszawa 2014, p. 659.

14 E. Rudkowska-Ząbczyk, "Postępowanie dowodowe," in *Dowody w postępowaniu cywilnym*, ed. Ł. Błaszczak, K. Markiewicz, and E. Rudkowska-Ząbczyk, Warszawa 2010, p. 287.

15 M. Cieśliński, Legalis.

16 A. Horoch, "Próba sformalizowania wywiadu środowiskowego w sprawach rozwodowych," *Nowe Prawo* 6 (1987), p. 82.

the participation of an expert, which is the need to prove a given circumstance. Only circumstances the determination or evaluation of which requires special knowledge are involved (Article 278 CCP). If the expert performs his activities under the conditions indicated in Article 284 CCP, in this situation the examination material viewed by the expert constitutes the factual basis for his opinion. On the other hand, in the case of visual evidence, the court has the opportunity to make direct observations, through the senses of the members of the panel, of the facts that are the subject of the evidence. The source of these observations is the characteristics of the place or objects inspected (Article 292 CCP). Treating the community interview as evidence would impose the need to allow the parties to take part in carrying out and documenting the activities carried out by the person appointed to conduct the community interview,[17] as is the case with other means of evidence. It is not insignificant that the community interview has been structured in the Code of Civil Procedure in a different way from the sources of information considered as means of evidence, including with the omission of terminology and rules concerning these means.

The effect of the community interview is primarily a material substrate in the form of private or official document evidence. In practice, the activities aimed at gathering the relevant information as part of the community interview result in a document of a reporting nature. In practice, the court may limit itself to reading the contents of the document, but may question the probation officer who conducted the community interview as a witness, and the parties to the proceedings then have the right to ask him/her questions. As U. Dąbrowska states, it is necessary to allow the parties to give explanations as to the circumstances stated in the interview conducted during the informational hearing and later during the hearing of the parties.[18]

This is pointed out by F. Zedler, pointing out, in light of the current legislation, a community interview is undoubtedly a document. However, this does not mean that it can still be document evidence in the case in which it was conducted. According to this author, the application of the provision of Article 309 CCP to a community interview would also lead to a circumvention of the rules on evidence and prima facie evidence; the rules on document evidence would be applied to an institution that has not been called statutory evidence. It is difficult to reconcile such an interpretation with the principles of a rational

17 T. Żyznowski, *Komentarz*, Legalis.

18 U. Dąbrowska, "Komentarz do art. 434 KPC," in *Rozwód i separacja*, ed. J. Ignaczewski, Warszawa 2021, Legalis.

legislator. Therefore, a community interview cannot be considered as evidence. As F. Zedler notes, in its essence it is only a form of investigation, and the facts given in a community interview should be considered only as probable circumstances.[19] Consequently, the community interview, both in its functional and structural aspects, cannot be a means of evidence, even if an attempt is made to include it in the open catalog of unnamed evidence within the meaning of the Code of Civil Procedure.

3. Scope of the community interview

As indicated, the legislator precisely defines in the Procedural Act the cases in which the court should consider the use of a community interview as a source of information to effectively shape the evidentiary proceedings with respect to the welfare of the child or the person subject to guardianship or curatorship or other person subject to the community interview.

Pursuant to Article 434 CCP, in separate proceedings in matrimonial cases, the court may order an interview to be conducted by an appointed person in order to ascertain the conditions in which the children of the parties live and grow up. This category of cases includes cases of divorce, separation at the request of one spouse, annulment of marriage and determination of the existence or non-existence of marriage. As emphasized by Z. Krzemiński, conducting a community interview in separation cases is also taken into account when there is a dispute between the parties on the exercise of parental authority.[20] The purpose of the community interview can only be to establish the conditions in which the children of the parties live and grow up. The linguistic interpretation of the provision in question allows for such a conclusion. The subject of the interview cannot therefore be other disputed or necessary circumstances and relations between the spouses, unless they are in relation to the situation of the children as referred to in Article 434 CCP. In practice, this means gathering information about the housing conditions (size and condition of the premises in which the children live, relations between the children and those in the joint household, conditions for studying, etc.), as well as establishing the details of the children's daily life (the way in which parental authority is exercised, fulfillment of compulsory schooling, extracurricular activities, parents' relations with teachers, etc.).

---

19 F. Zedler, *op. cit.*, p. 478.

20 M. Białecki, "Komentarz do art. 434 KPC," in *Separacja. Komentarz. Wzory pism*, ed. M. Białecki, Warszawa 2014, Legalis.

During the community interview, arrangements are sometimes made to establish contact with the children or their parents. The cited provision is functionally linked to the provisions of Article 441 CCP, which stipulates that the evidentiary proceedings are intended, inter alia, to establish the circumstances concerning the children of the parties and their situation. It should be added that in a matrimonial case the court assumes the role of the guardianship court, so it seems necessary for it to establish in the course of the conducted case the necessary data concerning the minor and his/her environment (Article 570[1] CCP). As M. Cieśliński aptly observes, a worrying situation often existing in practice is when the course of a divorce case results in the weakened protection of a child—the district court loses to a large extent its competences (in particular in the area of parental authority and contacts), while the divorce court focuses mainly on the matrimonial dispute and limits its activity to the minimum in the care sphere.[21]

Pursuant to Article 561[1] CCP, in non-trial proceedings for marriage license cases, the court may order a probation officer to conduct a community interview to establish the conditions in which the applicants live. Marriage license cases relate to women under the age of 18, persons suffering from mental illness or cognitive impairment and persons related in direct line. It is designed to gather information on the living conditions of the parties, but also on their relationship with each other or on the opinion of the community in which they live. It is intended to be an important tool in obtaining objective knowledge of the real situation of persons who wish to marry.[22] It is correct that in the case of separate residence of the parties, the interview should be conducted at the home of each of them, and this is the most common judicial practice.[23] As K. Flaga-Gieruszyńska points out, the above solution is always applied when there is a suspicion that the conditions in which the nuptuptial couple live will not be conducive to the permanence and proper functioning of the marriage; thus, the specific object of the curator's findings must be to determine in what conditions the

21 M. Cieśliński, "Commentary on Art. 434 CCP," in *Kodeks postępowania cywilnego. Komentarz*, ed. P. Rylski, Warsaw 2022, Legalis.

22 P. Jastrzemska, "Komentarz do art. 561(1) KPC," in *Kodeks postępowania cywilnego. Komentarz. Art. 506–1217*, ed. T. Szanciło, t. II, Warszawa 2023, Legalis.

23 M. Domański, "Orzekanie o zezwoleniu na zawarcie małżeństwa kobiecie, którzy nie wieku 18 lat," in *Stosowanie prawa, Księga Jubileuszowa z okazji XX-lecia Instytutu Wymiaru Sprawiedliwości*, ed. A. Siemaszko, Warszawa 2011, p. 342 i n.

future spouses will live after the marriage.[24] As emphasized in the literature, the conditions in which the persons seeking permission to marry live will have a significant impact on the life of the future family. Therefore, the court may, or rather should—although the provision does not impose such an obligation—order a community interview to be conducted by the probation officer. If it is clear from the interview that the spouses will have very poor living conditions—the court should dismiss the application, unless, despite this obstacle, exceptional circumstances support its granting.[25] When issuing the permission referred to in the provision contained in Article 561 CCP, the court should be guided primarily by the good of the future marriage, the family to be established and the good of the joint children the spouses may have.

The community interview will also find application in non-proceedings in certain matrimonial matters: (1) to decide on important family matters in the absence of an agreement of the spouses, (2) to authorize an act for which the consent of the other spouse is required or to which the other spouse has objected, (3) to order the court that the remuneration for work or other dues accruing to one spouse be paid in whole or in part to the other spouse; (4) to decide or overturn a decision to exclude the spouse's liability for obligations incurred by the other spouse in matters arising from the satisfaction of ordinary family needs (Article 565^1 CCP). The community interview is aimed at establishing the conditions in which the spouses live, which includes not only their material situation, housing situation or the amount of their income, but also other characterizing circumstances, such as, inter alia, the personal situation of each of them, their education, their employment, as well as their relations with other family members. In this category of cases, it is primarily a matter of verifying the material conditions in which the family concerned lives. Again, the legislature's use of the phrase "the court may" means that the body adjudicating the case has complete discretion to use the community interview as a means of making findings in cases involving significant family issues.

On the other hand, in guardianship cases, the guardianship court may order the court superintendent to conduct a community interview in order to collect information concerning the minor and his/her environment, in particular his/

24 K. Flaga-Gieruszyńska, "Komentarz do art. 561(1) Kodeksu postępowania cywilnego," in *Kodeks postępowania cywilnego. Komentarz*, ed. K. Flaga-Gieruszyńska and A. Zieliński, Warszawa 2022, Legalis.

25 N. Krej, "Komentarz do art. 561 § 1 k.p.k.," in *Kodeks postępowania cywilnego. Komentarz*, ed. E. Marszałkowska-Krześ and I. Gil, Warszawa 2023, Legalis.

her behavior, upbringing and living conditions, including the living situation of the family, the course of the minor's education and the way he/she spends his/her free time, his/her community contacts, the attitude of his/her parents or guardians toward him/her, upbringing interventions undertaken, the minor's health condition and addictions known in the environment. This solution also applies when the guardianship court becomes aware of an event justifying the initiation of proceedings ex officio and in the course of enforcement proceedings (Article 570^1 CCP). The expression "in particular" used in the wording of the provision indicates an exemplary, rather than enumerative, listing of the information to be collected. The court has broad powers to establish data on the minor and his/her environment, so it may order the guardian to collect also other data on the minor than those listed, if it is justified by the type and nature of the case. Consequently, the guardianship court may order the probation officer to interview information beyond those indicated in Article 570^1 § 1 of the Code of Civil Procedure.[26] Therefore, the court should provide the necessary data in sufficient detail so that the guardian, given the nature of the case, can collect as much information as possible to establish the facts in accordance with the reality.[27] This regulation is a guarantee that the guardianship court will rule on the case with a real understanding of the case. A realistic opportunity to know the living situation and the environmental assessment of the person or persons concerned is essential for the guardianship court to make a correct judgment.

It is worth noting that the Supreme Court pointed out that also in this provision, although the legislator used the phrase "the guardianship court may," there is no doubt that whenever there is such a need, it is the duty of the guardianship court to use the means provided for in Article 570^1 of the Code of Civil Procedure to obtain knowledge of the situation of the minor. It should be noted that the cited ruling was issued against the background of disciplinary proceedings conducted against a judge for, inter alia, the fact that the accused allegedly failed to establish the real situation of children residing in a foster family.[28]

In addition, the guardianship court may order a community interview to be conducted by the probation officer in the course of the proceedings conducted in cases concerning the establishment of guardianship or custody and the enforcement proceedings conducted in these cases in order to determine the

26 Judgment of the Supreme Court of 13.12.2013, SNO 35/13, Legalis.

27 A. Góra-Błaszczykowska, "Komentarz do art. 570(1) KPC," in *Kodeks postępowania cywilnego. Komentarz. Tom III. Art. 506–729*, ed. T. Wiśniewski, Warszawa 2021, Lex.

28 Judgment of the Supreme Court of 13.12.2013, SNO 35/13, Legalis.

possibility or manner in which the guardianship or custody is to be exercised and the living conditions of the person concerned (Article 570[1a] CCP). However, unlike the community interview concerning a minor, in this provision the law defines a clearly narrower scope of the interview. This provision is located in the general provisions concerning the procedure for other family cases and guardianship cases, which are heard by non-trial procedure (Articles 506–525 CCP). This allows for the use of the community interview in all the abovementioned cases (other family and guardianship cases), that is, parent-child relationship cases (Articles 579–584 CCP), adoption (Articles 585–589 CCP), guardianship (Articles 590–598 CCP), removal of a person subject to parental authority or guardianship (Articles 598[1]–598[14] CCP), child contact enforcement (Articles 598[15]–598[22] CCP), guardianship (Articles 599–605 CCP).

The community interview is also used in relation to foster care cases for minors. Before placing a child with a candidate qualified to act as a foster family, a candidate qualified to run a family-type children's home, a foster family or a family-type children's home, the court, as well as in the event that the court needs to obtain information about a candidate qualified to act as a foster family candidate qualified to run a family foster home, foster family or family foster home other than that contained in the register, the court may order a probation officer to carry out a community interview in the place of residence of the candidate to act as a foster family or to run a family foster home, in particular with regard to: (1) personal data; (2) degree of relationship with the child; (3) criminal record and proceedings pending with him/her concerning parental authority; (4) state of health; (5) professional status; (6) addictions; (7) living and family situation; (8) attitude toward the child; (9) presented educational model; (10) manner of functioning in the environment.

The considerations relating to the scope of application of the community interview would be incomplete if the most relevant regulations relating to this issue located outside the Code of Civil Procedure were omitted.

The court may order the probation officer to conduct a community interview in order to establish the circumstances indicating alcohol abuse by the person subject to the proceedings and his/her disturbance of the peace or public order, as well as his/her relations within the family, behavior toward minors and attitude toward work, pursuant to the provision of Article 30a of the Act on Upbringing in Sobriety and Counteracting Alcoholism.[29] The information obtained by conducting an interview is intended to assist the court in making its decision.

29 Journal of Laws 2023, item 165.

On the basis of the interview, certain facts are established, which are then subject to the court's free assessment. In making its decision, the court must take into account the totality of the circumstances of the case. However, in the circumstances of a particular case, the court may therefore not take into account all the circumstances indicated in the interview—arguing this on the basis of other circumstances present in the case.[30]

The court may also order the probation officer to conduct a community interview in order to establish the living conditions of the person affected by the proceedings initiated under the Mental Health Act of 19.8.1994.[31] This applies in particular to proceedings for admission to a therapeutic hospital, admission to a social welfare home and the functioning of the person concerned in the community, in accordance with the provision contained in Article 42a of this Act.

The essence of the latter two regulations is the collection, in the course of a community interview, by a probation officer of information that may prove helpful in the court's assessment of the possible existence of non-medical premises referred to in Article 24 of the Act on Upbringing in Sobriety and Counteracting Alcoholism (i.e., causing the disintegration of family life, demoralizing minors, evading work or systematically disturbing the peace or public order), as well as in determining the facts necessary for a decision on the obligation to undertake rehab treatment, and a decision on its termination or a change of the type of rehab treatment facility. On the other hand, on the basis of the Mental Health Act, this information is necessary to establish the prerequisites indicated in Article 29(1)(2) of this Act (inability to meet the needs of life on their own) in the case of a potential placement in a psychiatric hospital without consent, as well as Article 38 of the Act (possibility of receiving care from other persons) in the case of a possible referral to a social welfare home without consent.

The most recent solution relating to the community interview was introduced in the field of family matters by an amendment contained in the Act of 26.01.2023 amending the Act—Code of Civil Procedure and some other acts.[32] Thus, Section IIDA was introduced into the Code of Civil Procedure, regulating the issue of certificates concerning judgments in matrimonial cases and in cases of parental responsibility. The abovementioned regulation refers to the issuance in individual European Union Member States of certificates to the judgments

30 G. Krawiec, "Komentarz do art. 30a ustawy," in *Ustawa o wychowaniu w trzeźwości i przeciwdziałaniu alkoholizmowi. Komentarz*, ed. G. Krawiec, Warszawa 2021, Legalis.

31 Journal of Laws 2022, item 2123.

32 Journal of Laws 2023, item 403.

of their courts in matters falling within the scope of Regulation No 2019/1111, with a view to their automatic recognition or enforcement in another European Union Member State. The competent court to issue the certificate is the court which issued the judgment. The issue of an appeal against the order on the certificate has also been regulated, bearing in mind that under the Regulation no remedy is provided against the issuance of a certificate. The current Article 795^{11a} § 2 CCP introduces the possibility of appealing only against the refusal to issue the certificate, as its absence would impede the recognition or enforcement of the judgment in another EU Member State (Article 31 of Regulation No 2019/1111 introduces the possibility of submitting an equivalent document and adds the possibility of exemption from submitting the certificate, so the failure to issue the certificate does not foreclose a party from recognizing and enforcing in another EU Member State the judgment of a Polish court). The envisaged complaint against the court's decision on the certificate will be subject to recognition by a higher court (as a decision ending the proceedings—Article 394 § 1 CCP), which is in line with the hitherto existing model of proceedings in cases concerning appeals against decisions on certificates issued on the basis of other EU regulations, which are included in Part Three and Title I of the Code of Civil Procedure.[33]

In summary, the community interview is a source of information, devoid of the status of evidence, which, in the categories of cases indicated, fundamentally shapes the course and scope of the evidence procedure and is important for establishing the factual basis for the decision, to the extent relevant for the protection of values such as the welfare of the child, the welfare of the person subject to guardianship or custody or the welfare of the family.

4. Selected problems of conducting a community interview

Regardless of the proceedings in which the need for a community interview is actualized, the entity that decides whether to conduct one is the court. This is confirmed by the wording of Article 434 CCP, Article 561^1 CCP, Article 565^1 CCP and Article 570^1 CCP. The form in which the court decides on the necessity of conducting a community interview is an order. According to Article 47 § 3^1 CCP, the order is issued by the chairman. This terminology is relevant for cases decided in multi-member panels. When the court decides a case in a

33 Explanatory Memorandum to the Bill, Parliamentary Paper No 2860, Sejm of IX tenure, p. 7.

single-member composition, the judge has the rights and duties of the chairman. In the above-quoted regulations of the Code of Civil Procedure, the court explicitly defines the individual responsible for conducting the community interview. As indicated, this person in a determining number of cases is the superintendent, who conducts the interview through legal aid. Given the important role played by the community interview, the person appointed by the court to conduct the community interview should have the appropriate qualifications. This is justified primarily by the fact that conducting a community interview is one of the most responsible tasks of family probation officers. On the basis of the facts established therein, the diagnosis of the case and the conclusions developed, the court decides, among other things, on the form and manner of providing legal protection to the child.[34] That is why, in practice, courts commission probation officers or social probation officers to conduct a community interview (Articles 11(2) and 91(1)(2) of the Laws on probation officers).[35] Of particular importance are undoubtedly family probation officers involved in virtually all phases of court proceedings. This includes both exploratory and executive proceedings.[36] The curator acts on the basis of the Act of 27.07.2001 on court curators[37] and the Regulation of the Minister of Justice of 12.06.2003 on the detailed exercise of powers and duties of court curators.[38] The indicated Ordinance concerns the exercise of powers and duties by probation officers in family and juvenile matters.

The legislature specifies in Article 2 of the UKS that probation officers are professional probation officers and community probation officers. Probation officers who execute judgments in criminal cases are adult probation officers, and those who execute judgments in family and juvenile cases are family probation officers. The difference between the designated probation officers is that a probation officer is appointed, transferred to another court or probation team, or suspended from duty by the president of the district court, either ex officio or at the request of the district probation officer, subject to the powers of the Minister of Justice

34 D. Wybrańczyk, "3. Wywiad środowiskowy," in *Sytuacja prawna małoletniego dziecka rozwodzącego się z rodzicem*, Warszawa 2022; T. Jedynak and K. Stasiak, in *Zarys metodyki pracy kuratora sądowego*, ed. K. Stasiak, Warszawa 2018, p. 689.

35 So also J. Bodio, in *Kodeks postępowania cywilnego*, t. 1, Komentarz do art. 1–729, ed. A. Jakubecki, Warszawa 2017, p. 706, Nb 1; Act of July 27, 2001 on court superintendents (unified text Journal of Laws of 2023, item 1095).

36 G. Ott, in *Prawo o ustroju sądów powszechnych. Komentarz*, ed. A. Górski, Warszawa, p. 616, nb 15.

37 i.e., OJ 2023, item 1095, hereinafter: UKS.

38 i.e., OJ 2014, item 989, hereinafter: RKS.

set forth in the law. Pursuant to Article 9 of the SCS, in carrying out his official duties, the probation officer has the right to visit from 7 a.m. to 10 p.m. the persons under investigation at their place of residence or stay, as well as in closed institutions. He has the ability to demand that the person under investigation show a document that allows him to establish his identity, as well as to demand the necessary explanations and information from the wards under supervision, surveillance or any other form of control ordered by the court. At the same time, the probation officer is entitled to review Court records and make copies from them in connection with his official activities, as well as to access records concerning the ward and other persons under investigation. He may also request assistance from the Police and other state bodies or institutions, local government bodies, associations and social organizations within the scope of their activities, as well as from individuals in the performance of official activities. The social probation officer, in turn, is appointed, suspended and dismissed by the district court president at the request of the head of the probation team. He performs his function socially in one team. The teams in question are formed in the district court. They carry out decisions in criminal cases and in family and juvenile cases. The social superintendent is entered in the list of superintendents at the president of the district court.

According to Section 6 of the RKS, the family probation officer, when conducting a community interview, has the duty to establish the circumstances specified by the court or judge. At the same time, his activity may involve controlling the manner in which the judgment is implemented by authorized entities. The provisions of §1 (1) and (2), §2, §3, §4 and §7 of the Ordinance of the Minister of Justice of 11.06.2003 on the rules of activity for conducting a community interview and the model questionnaire for this interview[39] apply accordingly to the family superintendent's interview. After conducting the interview, the family superintendent is obliged to prepare a written report on the interview. It should include the name of the person conducting the interview, a description of the activities performed and the circumstances found, resulting from the interview order, the date of the interview and the signature of the person conducting the interview. The superintendent is required to submit the interview report within 14 days of receiving the interview order. However, a different deadline for submitting the report may be indicated in the order. In such a situation, the deadline indicated in the order is binding. If the court determines that the interview needs to be supplemented, the superintendent is obliged to supplement it upon

39 OJ No. 108, item 1018.

the express order of the court (§ 7 RKS). The cited regulations, however, do not apply in the case of a community interview prepared under the Juvenile Justice Act. Importantly, in the case of conducting a community interview in cases of marriage annulment, determination of the existence or non-existence of marriage, divorce, separation, the community superintendent is entitled to a lump sum (Article 91(1)(2) of the RKS).

In attempting to analyze selected problems relating to conducting an environmental interview, it is worth noting that in addition to the regulations contained in the Code of Civil Procedure, the legislature regulates in detail the conduct of community interviews in specific categories of cases. Such practice confirms the importance of the community interview as an informational instrument to support ongoing proceedings, not only civil but also criminal or administrative (e.g., for obtaining support and social assistance). As indicated, it is optional in nature. Observation of practice indicates that it is possible to note peculiar regionalisms, since in some courts this possibility is used relatively often, while in others the courts practically do not use this institution.[40] Given the limited framework of this paper, it is only worth noting that on November 15, 2021, the Decree of the Minister of Family and Social Policy of April 8, 2021 on the family environmental interview came into force.[41] This interview is conducted with individuals and families receiving or applying for social assistance benefits in order to determine their personal, family, income and property situation. Also, in cases where a minor shows signs of demoralization or has committed a criminal act, a community interview is conducted based on the provisions of the Ordinance of the Minister of Justice of October 12, 2022 on conducting community interviews about minors.[42] The doctrine perceives the view that the probation officer should not make an appointment to conduct the interview, which, as a rule, should be conducted at the place of residence of the parties or the party.[43] In practice, it is also indicated that in most cases, community interviews are conducted only at the place of permanent residence of that parent with whom the child permanently resides. Most often this is the mother. As a rule, courts do not order community interviews at the place of permanent residence of the other parent.[44]

40 M. Cieśliński, *op. cit.*, Legalis.
41 Journal of Laws 2021, item 893.
42 OJ 2022, item 2143.
43 For more on the powers and duties of probation officers, see T. Jedynak and K. Stasiak, p. 96 i n.
44 M. Domański, "Powierzenie wykonywania władzy rodzicielskiej jednemu z rodziców w wyroku rozwodowym," *Prawo w Działaniu* 21 (2015), p. 76.

It is also correct that in the case of separate residence of the parties, the interview should be conducted at each of them, and this is the most common judicial practice.[45] It also seems reasonable that the probation officer should not make an appointment in advance to conduct a community interview. Such a practice will minimize the risk of adequate preparation of the persons interviewed. This, in turn, will have a positive effect on the determination of the real and not a created state of facts relevant to the court issuing the substantive decision.

5. Conclusions

The community interview is an extremely important tool that is used in civil cases, especially in cases involving child custody, child support, adoption, separation, divorce and other family-legal issues. It is—as indicated—conducted to gather information about the environment in which the people involved in the case live (i.e., family, children, guardians or relatives). Among the reasons justifying its conduct, the first is the need to verify the living conditions of those whose rights and obligations will be affected by the settlement. Its scope includes, depending on the category of the case, an analysis of housing conditions, accessibility to education and the manner of fulfillment of related obligations, but also health, care, or possible risks that may affect the situation of children or other family members. In addition, the interview sometimes also aims to determine family relations as well. Conducting it also makes it possible to determine whether there is domestic violence, conflicts or other unfavorable situations in the investigated environment that may affect the judgment of the court. Direct contact with the family also makes it possible to analyze parental capacity. Although this is a difficult process, it helps to estimate what capacity parents have to care for and raise their children. It is then necessary to take into account what the parents' skills are, their abilities, but also the resources they have and the support they have from other family members and social support. Finally, the community interview allows an analysis of the social environment, as well as serves to assess the safety of the child or the person who is a party or participant in the proceedings.

There is no doubt that the person conducting the community interview has a duty to act in a maximally objectified manner. The conclusions she formulates should not depend on any subjective impulses. The person conducting the community interview should be focused on gathering reliable information,

45 M. Domański, *Orzekanie*, pp. 342–345.

unencumbered by flaws in the form of conjecture or doubt. This is an extremely difficult task. But gathering reliable information serves to support the court in making substantive decisions.

It should also be emphasized that a community interview can be used as a source of information in a civil case. It is not considered evidence in civil proceedings. In litigation, it has the role of providing data on the basis of which the parties and participants in the proceedings can formulate their positions, as well as take evidence. This tool is auxiliary and subsidiary in the determination of living conditions, family relations, parental capacity or other aspects relevant to the substantive decision of the court. As indicated, the conduct of a community interview is subject to certain standards and procedures designed to guarantee fairness and objectivity.

Bibliography

Białecki, M., "Komentarz do art. 434 KPC," in *Separacja. Komentarz. Wzory pism*, Warszawa 2014.

Bodio, J., *Kodeks postępowania cywilnego*, t. 1, Komentarz do art. 1–729, ed. A. Jakubecki, Warszawa 2017.

Cieśliński, M., "Komentarz do art. 434 KPC," in *Kodeks postępowania cywilnego. Komentarz*, ed. P. Rylski, Warszawa 2022.

Dąbrowska, U., "Komentarz do art. 434 KPC," in *Rozwód i separacja*, ed. J. Ignaczewski, Warszawa 2021.

Domański, M., "Orzekanie o zezwoleniu na zawarcie małżeństwa z kobietą, która nie ukończyła 18 lat," in *Stosowanie prawa, Księga Jubileuszowa z okazji 20-lecia Instytutu Wymiaru Sprawiedliwości*, ed. A. Siemaszko, Warszawa 2011.

Domański, M., "Powierzenie wykonywania władzy rodzicielskiej jednemu z rodziców w wyroku rozwodowym," *Prawo w Działaniu* 21 (2015).

Flaga-Gieruszyńska, K., "Komentarz do art. 561(1) Kodeksu postępowania cywilnego," in *Kodeks postępowania cywilnego. Komentarz*, ed. K. Flaga-Gieruszyńska and A. Zieliński, Warszawa 2022.

Góra-Błaszczykowska, A., "Komentarz do art. 570(1) KPC," in *Kodeks postępowania cywilnego. Komentarz. Tom III. Art. 506–729*, ed. T. Wiśniewski, Warszawa 2021.

Haak, H., and Haak-Trzuskawska, A., "Komentarz do art. 434 KC," in *Małżeństwo (zawarcie małżeństwa, prawa i obowiązki małżonków). Komentarz do art. 1–30 KRO i powiązanych przepisów KPC (art. 7, 15, 17, 41, 47, 57, 66, 98, 100–102, 117, 177, 187, 189, 193, 203, 204, 2054, 316, 367, 400, 425–435, 447–451, 561–565(1))*, Warszawa 2020.

Horoch, A., "Próba sformalizowania wywiadu środowiskowego w sprawach rozwodowych," *Nowe Prawo* 6 (1987).

Jastrzemska, P., "Komentarz do art. 561(1) KPC," in *Kodeks postępowania cywilnego. Komentarz. Art. 506–1217*, ed. T. Szanciło, t. II, Warszawa 2023.

Jedynak, T., and Stasiak, K., *Zarys metodyki pracy kuratora sądowego*, ed. K. Stasiak, Warszawa 2018.

Krawiec, G., "Komentarz do art. 30a ustawy," in *Ustawa o wychowaniu w trzeźwości i przeciwdziałaniu alkoholizmowi. Komentarz*, ed. G. Krawiec, Warszawa 2021.

Krej, N., "Komentarz do art. 561 § 1 k.p.k.," in *Kodeks postępowania cywilnego. Komentarz*, ed. E. Marszałkowska-Krześ and I. Gil, Warszawa 2023.

Krzemiński, Z., *Rozwód. Komentarz do przepisów. Orzecznictwo. Piśmiennictwo. Wzory pism*, Warszawa 2004.

Ott, G., *Prawo o ustroju sądów powszechnych. Komentarz*, ed. A. Górski, Warszawa 2013.

Resich, Z., Misiuk-Jodłowska, T., in *Postępowanie cywilne*, ed. J. Jodłowski, Z. Resich, J. Lapierre, T. Misiuk-Jodłowska, and K. Weitz, Warszawa 2014.

Rudkowska-Ząbczyk, E., "Postępowanie dowodowe," in *Dowody w postępowaniu cywilnym*, ed. Ł. Błaszczak, K. Markiewicz, and E. Rudkowska-Ząbczyk, Warszawa 2010.

Siedlecki, W., in *Postępowanie cywilne. Zarys wykładu*, ed. W. Siedlecki and Z. Świeboda, Warszawa 2003.

Stojanowska, W., *Rozwód a dobro dziecka*, Warszawa 1979.

Stojanowska, W., in *System prawa prywatnego, Prawo rodzinne i opiekuńcze*, ed. T. Smyczyński, t. 11, Warszawa 2014.

Sztombka, J., "Wywiad środowiskowy w sprawach rozwodowych," *Nowe Prawo* 5 (1978).

Wybrańczyk, D., "Wywiad środowiskowy," in *Sytuacja prawna małoletniego dziecka rozwodzącego się z rodzicem*, Warszawa 2022.

Wyrok SN z 10.05.2000, III CKN 881/00, Legalis.

Wyrok SN z Court of 13.12.2013, SNO 35/13, Legalis.

Zedler, F., "Dowód nienazwany w postępowaniu cywilnym," *Polski Proces Cywilny* 4 (2018).

Żyznowski, T., "Komentarz do art. 434," in *Kodeks postępowania cywilnego. Komentarz*, t. II, ed. A. Marciniak, Warszawa 2020.

Beata Stępień-Załucka

The lengthiness of court proceedings in Poland as more than a systemic problem

Abstract: The right to a court is a fundamental human right. It is protected under a number of regulations of international, EU but also domestic law. It also finds a special place in the Constitution of the Republic of Poland, which in Article 45(1) indicates: "Everyone has the right to a fair and public hearing without undue delay by a competent, independent, impartial and independent court."

According to the wording of this provision, an inseparable part of the right to a court is "to have a case heard without undue delay." Unfortunately, the practice of court proceedings shows that the understanding of this term does not always remain uniform. The term is seen differently by the parties, differently by the attorneys, and still differently by the court. Hence, for each of these entities, the time for timely consideration of a case is understood differently. This is important insofar as it forces a discussion of when a given proceeding becomes protracted. Therefore, the purpose of this study is to show when we have to deal with the so-called protraction of proceedings, as well as to identify the causes of this phenomenon. Such a delimited research area forces us to put forward several theses. First, it is not always the nature of a long-running proceeding to be protracted. Secondly, the protractedness of proceedings consists not only of systemic but also extra-systemic reasons. The dogmatic-legal and theoretical-legal method was used.

Keywords: right to a court, judicial decisions, the slowness of judicial procedures

1. Theoretical and practical text

The right to a court is a fundamental human right.[1] It is protected by a number of regulations under international, EU but also national law. One of the most important is the Universal Declaration of Human Rights of December 10, 1948, Article 10 of which states that "everyone is entitled, under conditions of full equality, to a fair and public hearing by an independent and impartial tribunal

1 More about that I wrote in: *Sprawowanie wymiaru sprawiedliwości przez Sad Najwyższy w Polsce*, Warsaw 2016, p. 32.

to decide on his rights and obligations or on the merits of any criminal charge against him."[2]

Internationally, this regulation has become the starting point for further ones. These are manifested, inter alia, in Article 6 of the Convention for the Protection of Human Rights and Fundamental Freedoms, which states that "everyone is entitled to a fair and public hearing within a reasonable time by an independent and impartial tribunal established by law, to decide on his civil rights and obligations or on the merits of any criminal charge brought against him,"[3] and Article 14 of the 1966 International Covenant on Civil and Political Rights, recognizing that "everyone is entitled to a fair and public hearing by a competent, independent and impartial tribunal established by law, to decide on the merits of any criminal charge against him or his rights and obligations in civil matters."[4] The importance and significance of this right has led the EU legislature to also bow to it by indicating in Article 47 of the Charter of Fundamental Rights of the European Union that "everyone is entitled to a fair and public hearing within a reasonable time by an independent and impartial tribunal previously established by law."[5]

The right to a court also finds a special place in the Constitution of the Republic of Poland, which in Article 45(1) indicates: "Everyone has the right to a fair and public hearing without undue delay by a competent, independent, impartial and independent court."[6]

According to the wording of this provision, an integral part of the right to a court is "to have a case heard without undue delay." Unfortunately, the practice of court proceedings shows that the understanding of this term does not always remain uniform. The term is seen differently by the parties, differently by the

---

2 United Nations General Assembly Resolution 217 A (III) of 10.12.1948, data after website: http://www.un.org/Overview/rights.html. Data as of 11.01.2011. Hereinafter as PDPC.

3 Convention for the Protection of Human Rights and Fundamental Freedoms, Rome, 4.11.1950, as amended by Protocols 3, 5, 8, and supplemented by Protocol No. 2 (*Journal of Laws* 1993, no. 61, item 284, as amended).

4 International Covenant on Civil and Political Rights, opened for signature in New York on 19.12.1966 (OJ 1977, no. 38, item 167), Annex.

5 Charter of Fundamental Rights of the European Union (2000/C364/01), data behind website: http://www.europarl.europa.eu/charter/pdf/text_en.pdf, Polish version: http://www.ms.gov.pl/ue/translation/32000X1218(01).doc. Data as at 11.01.2011.

6 Constitution of the Republic of Poland of April 2, 1997, *Journal of Laws* 1997, no. 78, item 483.

attorneys and still differently by the court. Hence, for each of these entities the time limit for timely consideration of the case is understood differently. This is important insofar as it forces a discussion on when a given proceeding becomes protracted. Therefore, the aim of this study is to show when we are dealing with the so-called protraction of proceedings, as well as to indicate the causes of this phenomenon. The research area so delineated forces us to put forward several theses. Firstly, it is not always the case that long proceedings are protracted. Secondly, the lengthiness of proceedings consists not only of systemic, but also of non-systemic reasons. The dogmatic-legal and theoretical-legal method has been used to achieve the presented research goal and to verify the abovementioned theses.

In order to present the essence of the problem we are facing, it is necessary to refer directly to statistics. Basically, after 2015 until 2020, the average duration of trials before district courts deciding cases at first instance has not changed and is around 8 months. In contrast, there has been a change in the case of district courts, an increase from 4 to more than 5 months can be noted here.

In district courts, labor law cases took the longest time to resolve, taking between 9.9 months and 14 months between 2011 and 2018. Criminal cases were the second longest, ranging from 7.6 months to 10.3 months. Civil cases, on the other hand, took the shortest time—from 6.8 months to 7.8 months.[7]

In district courts, on the other hand, insurance cases took the longest time between 2011 and 2018—from 7.1 to 10.9 months. Another category was labor law cases—from 6.3 to 9.5 months. On the other hand, criminal cases took the shortest time—from 3.3 to 3.6 months. However, it must be borne in mind that the values presented are averages.[8]

2. Complaint for protraction vs. protraction of proceedings

The lengthiness of proceedings in Poland is verified by means of the specially enacted Act of June 17, 2004, on a complaint for violation of a party's right to have a case heard in court proceedings without undue delay.[9] Its adoption was

---

7 Przewlekłość postępowań sądowych w Raporcie HFPC. Ministerstwo Sprawiedliwości nie udostępnia danych, https://monitorkonstytucyjny.eu/archiwa/17237.

8 Ibid.

9 Act of 17.6.2004. *Journal of Laws* Dz. U. 2004, no. 179, item 1843 Ustawa of June 17, 2004 on a Complaint for Infringement of a Party's Right to Investigate a Case in Pre-trial Proceedings Conducted or Supervised by a Public Prosecutor and in Court Proceedings Without Undue Delay (*Journal of Laws*, no. 179, item 1843). Hereinafter

the result of legislative actions aimed at implementing the judgment of the European Court of Human Rights (ECtHR), in the case of Kudła v. Poland. These actions were aimed at enacting a direct institution, a means of asserting the rights of an individual to a court in relation to the claims for damages provided for in the Civil Code.[10]

It should be recalled that the essence of the said judgment was that the European Court stated the existence of an obligation on the part of the States Parties to the Convention, based on Article 6(1) of the Convention ("Everyone is entitled to a fair and public hearing within a reasonable time by an independent and impartial tribunal established by law, to decide on his civil rights and obligations or on the merits of any criminal charge brought against him (….)" in conjunction with Article 13 of the ECHR, which states that "everyone whose rights and freedoms have been violated should have an effective remedy before a competent State authority, including where the violation has been committed by persons acting in an official capacity," the provision of legal remedies at national level to review judicial decisions, including allowing for the possibility of a claim for damages. These remedies, in turn, are used, inter alia, in situations of protraction of judicial proceedings as an integral part of the right to a court.[11]

This line of jurisprudence of the ECtHR is consistent with domestic case law, where the Constitutional Court in its judgments emphasize the importance of the timeliness of proceedings for the realization of the right to a court.

Among others, the judgment of July 28, 2004, is worth mentioning in this respect,[12] in which the Constitutional Court held that the right to a court includes, in addition to access to a court, the right to a court verdict, the right to an appropriate form of court procedure in accordance with the requirements of fairness and publicity and within a reasonable time.[13] On the other hand, in another

as the Act on Complaint (Ustawa z 17.6.2004 r. Dz. U. 2004 Nr 179 poz. 1843 U S T AWA z dnia 17 czerwca 2004 r. o skardze na naruszenie prawa strony do rozpoznania sprawy w postępowaniu przygotowawczym prowadzonym lub nadzorowanym przez prokuratora i postępowaniu sądowym bez nieuzasadnionej zwłoki (Dz. U. Nr 179, poz. 1843)).

10 P. Ostaszewski and E. Melaniuk, *Kwerenda spraw ze skargi na przewlekłość postępowania sądowego. Analizy wymiaru sprawiedliwości*, Warszawa 2019, p. 7.

11 Judgment. ECHR of 26.10. in Kudła v. Poland, Application no. 30210/96.

12 Judgment of the Constitutional Tribunal of 28.07.2004, P 2/04, OTK ZU 2004, No. 7/ A, item 72.

13 See judgments of the Constitutional Court of: 16.3.1999, SK 19/98, OTK ZU 1999, No 3, item 36 and 13.5.2002, SK 32/01, OTK ZU 2002, No. 3/A, item 31.

judgment, that is, in the order of October 30, 2006. The Court emphasized that the right to have a case decided by a court without undue delay is an essential element of the constitutional right to a court. At the same time, the Court has repeatedly drawn attention to the necessity to maintain a specific balance between rendering justice and timely disposal of a case, such position was taken, inter alia, in the judgment of July 9, 2002, P 4/01, recognizing that the requirements of fairness of proceedings allow for such a balancing of decisions taken in the sphere of human rights that they take into account the maintenance of a specific optimum between the requirements of justice and efficiency of proceedings.[14]

The key prerequisite for bringing an action is to establish when one is dealing with the so-called protraction of proceedings.

Article 2, paragraph 1. of the Act on Complaints, which reads: "A party may file a complaint that in the proceedings to which the complaint relates, his or her right to have a case heard without undue delay has been violated, if the proceedings aimed at issuing a decision ending the proceedings in the case last longer than it is necessary to clarify the relevant factual and legal circumstances or longer than it is necessary to settle an enforcement or other case concerning the enforcement of a court decision (protraction of proceedings)." is relevant here.[15] In addition, paragraph 2 of the aforementioned provision specifies the aforementioned conditions by stating that in determining whether there is a protraction of proceedings in a given case, the timeliness and correctness of actions taken by the court "for the purpose of issuing a final decision in the case, or actions taken by a prosecutor conducting or supervising pre-trial proceedings for the purpose of completing pre-trial proceedings, or actions taken by a court or bailiff for the purpose of conducting and completing an enforcement case or another case concerning the enforcement of a court decision should be assessed in the first instance." The assessment of such timeliness and regularity shall take into account the entire cumulative duration of the proceedings from the moment of their commencement to the moment of the examination of the complaint, irrespective of the stage at which the complaint was lodged, the nature of the case, the degree of its factual and legal complexity, the importance of the case for the party who lodged the complaint, the issues resolved therein and the

14 Judgment of the Constitutional Court of 9.7.2002, P 4/01, OTK-A 2002, No. 4, item 52; cf. also P. Wiliński, *Rzetelny proces karny w orzecznictwie sądów polskich i międzynarodowych*, Warsaw 2009, pp. 306–322.

15 P. Górecki, S. Stachowiak, and P. Wiliński, *Skarga na przewlekłość postępowania sądowego. Komentarz*, Warsaw 2007, p. 28 and n.

conduct of the parties and, above all, the party who alleged that the proceedings were protracted.

At the same time, although the Polish legal system is not a system of precedent only, the case law of the Supreme Court has an important guideline for the lower courts. The latter has repeatedly expressed its opinion on the issue of when lengthiness of proceedings occurs. Thus, in the decision of the Supreme Court—Chamber of Labour, Social Insurance and Public Affairs of May 12, 2005 (III SPP 96/2005, OSNP 2005, No. 23, item 384), the Supreme Court held that a 12-month-long inactivity of the second instance court, consisting in failure to schedule the appeal hearing, justifies a complaint for protraction of proceedings. Another circumstance justifying such a complaint and supporting the increase of the appropriate sum of money awarded to a party by the State Treasury is the forwarding, with a significant delay, of a complaint for protraction of proceedings to the court having jurisdiction to examine it (Judgment of the Supreme Court—Labour, Social Insurance and Public Affairs Chamber of November 13, 2007, III SPP 44/2007, LexPolonica no 1965208, OSNP 2008, No. 23–24, item 368.). What is more, the Supreme Court has also formulated the obligation of the state to organize conditions for the proper exercise of jurisdiction, including ensuring optimal staffing of appellate courts, in order to prevent the lengthiness of proceedings (Decision of the Supreme Court—Labour, Social Insurance and Public Affairs Chamber of March 8, 2005, III SPP 34/2005, LexPolonica no. 388832, OSNP 2005, No. 20, item 327). Thus, he stated that the influx of a number of cases from a certain category to the court, which results in the impossibility of their examination within a "reasonable time" in a specifically indicated court, does not justify the state authorities, unless it is of a sudden, unforeseeable and temporary character and no legislative, organizational and financial measures have been taken, which would allow examination of specific cases without undue delay.[16] On the other hand, the assessment as to whether a case has been protracted does not relate to its earlier stages, which have already been completed. It refers only to the stage of the proceedings in progress, whereby it is possible to take into account the progress of the case to date.[17]

16 Order of the Supreme Court—Chamber of Labour, Social Insurance and Public Affairs of 6.1.2006, II SPP 154/2005, LexPolonica no. 418954, OSNP 2006, No. 21–22, item 342.

17 Order of the Supreme Court—Labour, Social Security and Public Affairs Chamber of 18.2.2005, II SPP 19/2005, LexPolonica no. 384764, OSNP 2005, No. 17, item 277.

In yet another reasoning of the order of June 22, 2016 (III CSP 1/16, LEX no. 2099033), the Supreme Court held that the provisions of the Act on Complaint for Lengthy Proceedings do not specify what period of waiting for the cognizance of a case is to be regarded as unjustified delay. However, it should be inferred from the wording of these provisions that unjustified delay leading to protraction of proceedings is when the court, by making decisions with delay or with defects, has not made a decision on the merits of the case in due time. He also pointed out that the condition for the validity of a complaint for lengthiness of proceedings is an unjustified delay in the merits of the case and not the failure of the court to take any procedural action.

In the context of referring to a specific time limit that would indicate a failure to act without undue delay, Supreme Court in case referred to Article 14 of the Act. According to which, a renewed action for protraction of proceedings in the same case may be brought after the lapse of 12 months from the date of the court's decision resolving the previous action. Thus, the legislator considered that the protraction of proceedings may be referred to—if the prerequisites indicated in the Act are met—with regard to proceedings that last longer than 12 months. In the jurisprudence of the Supreme Court to date, it has been assumed that the protraction of appeal proceedings can be referred to in the case of a court's inaction lasting for at least 12 months.[18]

3. Grounds for bringing a complaint for protraction of proceedings

According to Article 3 of the Act, the persons entitled to lodge a complaint are as follows:

- in proceedings for fiscal offenses and fiscal offenses—a party,
- in proceedings for misdemeanors—a party,
- in proceedings for liability of collective entities for acts prohibited under penalty—a party or an applicant,
- in criminal proceedings—a party and a victim, even if not a party,
- in civil proceedings—a party, an ancillary intervener and a party to the proceedings,

18 *Przewlekłość postępowania cywilnego w świetle orzecznictwa Sądu Najwyższego*, https://www.temidium.pl/artykul/przewleklosc_postepowania_cywilnego_w_swietle_orzecznictwa_sadu_najwyzszego-3264.html.

- in enforcement proceedings and in other proceedings concerning the enforcement of a judicial decision—a party and another person exercising his or her rights in those proceedings.

In principle, it should be assumed that a complaint is filed with the court before which the proceedings are pending (Article 4 of the Act).

If the complaint concerns the lengthiness of proceedings before the district court and the circuit court—the court of appeal is competent to hear the complaint in its entirety.

If, on the other hand, the complaint concerns the lengthiness of proceedings before the circuit court and the court of appeal—the court of appeal has jurisdiction to hear the complaint in its entirety.

On the other hand, if the complaint concerns the lengthiness of proceedings before a court of appeal or the Supreme Court—the Supreme Court shall have jurisdiction to hear the complaint.

The court with jurisdiction to hear a complaint concerning the lengthiness of enforcement proceedings or other proceedings concerning the enforcement of a judicial decision shall be the district court in whose district the enforcement is conducted or other actions are performed, and when enforcement or other proceedings concerning the enforcement of a judicial decision are conducted in two or more districts, the court in whose district the first action was performed.

If, on the other hand, the complaint concerns the lengthiness of pre-trial proceedings, the court superior to the court that would have had substantive jurisdiction to hear the case shall have jurisdiction to hear it.

The court hearing the case in a three-judge panel (Article 8(1) of the Act) is obliged to give its decision within two months, counting from the date on which the complaint was filed (Article 11 of the Act).

The decision in the case amounts to either upholding the complaint or dismissing it. If the complaint is upheld, the court shall declare that the proceedings to which the complaint relates have been protracted. In addition, at the request of the applicant or ex officio, the court shall recommend that the court with jurisdiction over the merits of the case take appropriate action within a specified period of time, unless making such recommendations is manifestly unnecessary. The recommendations may not interfere with the factual and legal assessment of the case. At the same time, if the complaint is upheld, the court, at the request of the complainant, awards a sum of money[19] from the State Treasury in

19 Cz. P. Kłak, "Skarga na przewlekłość postępowania a rozwiązania przyjęte w wybranych krajach europejskich jako 'środki odwoławcze' na nadmierną długość

the amount of PLN 2,000 to PLN 20,000. In turn, in the case of an unfounded complaint, the court dismisses the complaint (Article 12 of the Act). The provisions of the Act assume a single-instance procedure for the examination of such a complaint, and do not grant the party the right to appeal.[20]

4. Procedural rules in the fight against protraction of proceedings

The basic provision in civil proceedings that forces the courts not to delay cases is Article 6, which states that "the court should counteract the protraction of proceedings and should aim to reach a decision at the first hearing if this is possible without prejudice to the clarification of the case" of the Act of November 17, 1964—Code of Civil Procedure. According to the wording of this provision, the court has a duty to prevent protraction of the proceedings and to gather all the procedural material so that a decision is reached at the first hearing, with the proviso that this must not be done at the expense of clarifying the case. The necessity to decide the case quickly and in accordance with the applicable legal provisions may not induce the court to apply simplifications which may have an adverse effect on the settlement of the case contrary to the truth.[21] At the same time, the rationality of the court's behavior is assessed above all in the light of the disposition of Article 6(1) of Kodeks Postępowania Cywilnego (the Code of Civil Procedure), which by its actions should make the trial last as short as possible, and additionally be the least burdensome for the parties and the cheapest. Therefore, the evidence proceedings should be purposeful and efficiently conducted. The court, in turn, should act in such a way as to exercise its powers and fulfill its duties in an appropriate manner. Indeed, prolonging the proceedings poses a threat to the correctness of the decision, as after a longer period of time, it becomes more difficult to clarify essential factual elements, as some evidence may no longer be available and the value of others decreases.[22]

---

postępowania – podobieństwa i różnice (cz. 2)," *Palestra* 5–6 (2012), p. 91.

20 K. Sobczak, *Można dochodzić odszkodowania za przewlekłość* postępowania, https://www.prawo.pl/prawnicy-sady/odszkodowanie-za-przewleklosc-postepowania,184448.html.

21 Judgment of the Supreme Court of 19.5.1976, IV PRN 9/76, NP 1977, No. 9, p. 1299.

22 Ł. Kozłowski, *Rozprawa doktorska, Korzystanie w procesie cywilnym z dowodów uzyskanych sprzecznie z prawem*, https://repozytorium.amu.edu.pl/bitstream/10593/26474/1/Doktorat%20_%C5%81ukasz%20Koz%C5%82owski_.pdf, p. 81.

In the case of criminal proceedings, the principle of procedural speed is shaped by Article 2 § 1 item 4 of the Act of June 6, 1997—Code of Criminal Procedure, which indicates that the provisions of the Code are intended to shape criminal proceedings in such a way that, inter alia, the case is resolved within a reasonable time. This principle is expressed here in the directive to eliminate all unnecessary delays and delays from the criminal process and to conduct the proceedings quickly and efficiently. However, the speed of the proceedings must not be achieved to the detriment of the objectives of the criminal trial and the statutorily guaranteed interests of the parties.[23]

Another principle that is important from the point of view under examination is the principle of the adversarial system, which makes the course of the evidence proceedings dependent on the will of the parties, and where the parties fail to make further requests for evidence, the court closes the trial and passes judgment. In practice, however, the operation of this principle remains limited, as 747 pieces of evidence were taken in the 204 cases examined, of which 219 (29.3%) were still ex officio. Another regulation that affects the course of the trial is the 7-day short deadline for completing formal deficiencies in the proceedings. On the other hand, the institutions regulated in Article 136–139 of the Code of Civil Procedure on the one hand allow for the delivery of pleadings in the place where the addressee can be found, but they also oblige the party to notify the court about the change of his/her place of residence. On the other hand, a hearing may be postponed at the unanimous request of the parties, but only for an important reason. These reasons include, inter alia: the parties' consent to conclude an agreement, evidence preclusion, according to which evidence which is significant for the determination of the case is to be taken (Article 227 of the Code of Civil Procedure), judgment by default (Article 339 et seq.), and special procedures: simplified, order and writ of payment proceedings.[24]

Nevertheless, despite the clear guidelines of the legislator, there is still a problem with the efficiency of the proceedings in the Polish legal system, which is reflected in the numbers.

---

23 More about that, J. Kluza, "Wpływ ostatnich nowelizacji Kodeksu postępowania karnego na szybkość i rzetelność procesu karnego. Studium przypadku," *Studenckie Zeszyty Naukowe* XX/32 (2017), 51 and n.

24 A. Kucharska, *Przyczyny przewlekłości postępowań cywilnych w sądach rejonowych*, https://iws.gov.pl/wp-content/uploads/2018/09/Anna-Kucharska-Przyczyny-przewlek%C5%82o%C5%9Bci-post%C4%99powa%C5%84-cywilnych-w-s%C4%85dach-rejonowych-109.pdf, p. 111.

5. Causes of the lengthiness of court proceedings in Poland

Essentially, I will posit at the outset that these causes are not uniform, although those relating to the system obviously predominate.

One of the causes of the lengthiness of proceedings should be identified as issues of organization in the courts, or rather sometimes the lack thereof. In other words, when a judge is planning a hearing, he or she is first and foremost mindful of the time he or she has to devote to writing justifications and taking specific action in the case. Consequently, he does so primarily on the basis of his time. It should be the case that this time should be divided between the judge and his assistant, but this is not always the case. This, in turn, is primarily due to staff shortages in the courts. This problem, in turn, is deeper, as the shortage of assistants is due to low salaries and a heavy workload for assistants.[25]

The delays in the work of the judges themselves are also due to various problems. The primary one in this respect is the changing law. The speed of the changing law, as well as the short periods of vocatio legis,[26] mean that judges have to assimilate new developments in a very short period of time, which "puts them off" adjudicating. An example of this is the criminal procedure, where it happens that in one day judges take five different criminal codes for five hearings, depending on when the criminal act was committed. In turn, this state of affairs translates into a lack of stability of jurisprudence, which is a fundamental flaw in judicial procedure in a democratic state under the rule of law. Indeed, the law is often changed not because a change in social relations requires it, but because of social expectations or political marketing.

In addition, the problem of expert witnesses in courts, that is, specialists writing expert opinions in court cases, is also a key problem.[27] On the one hand,

---

25 P. Szymaniak, "Nikt się nie garnie do pracy w sądzie: Brakuje asystentów s*ędziów, protokolantów i sekretarzy*," *Dziennik Gazeta Prawna*, December 5, 2018, https://prawo.gazetaprawna.pl/artykuly/1378812,braki-kadrowe-w-sadach-pracownicy-sadow-domagaja-sie-podwyzek.html.

26 The Covid Laws are an example in this respect.

27 A. Jędrzejczyk, *Zbyt mało biegłych sądowych w sprawach cywilnych. To poważny problem, któremu przygląda się Rzecznik*, https://bip.brpo.gov.pl/pl/content/zbyt-ma%C5%82o-bieg%C5%82ych-s%C4%85dowych-w-sprawach-cywilnych-powa%C5%BCny-problem-kt%C3%B3remu-przygl%C4%85da-si%C4%99-rzecznik. "An expert witness is an auxiliary body of the court, appointed to prepare a written opinion containing answers to questions asked by the court, which will enable an unequivocal answer to be obtained to clarify the circumstances of the case. Being a person of public trust, he or she must demonstrate knowledge and impartiality as well as conscientiousness in

it is all too often the case that the court waits too long for expert opinions, sometimes being urged to do so. There are various reasons for the lengthiness of expert witnesses' work, sometimes as a result of the difficulty and complexity of the case, sometimes due to the lack of knowledge of the experts and the need to train them, and sometimes due to the fact that they are overloaded with the number of opinions commissioned by the court. On the other hand, this overburdening of experts is due to the fact that there is a shortage of experts in a particular narrow field, which causes them to be overburdened and unable to produce opinions in a timely manner. On the other hand, it should be noted that it is not easy to change the status quo, as more experts are needed to save the situation, but the problem is that they cannot be found just like that. As they are specialists in a given field, they work for many years to build up their knowledge, and this in turn makes becoming a given specialist—an expert in a given field—a lengthy process. What is more, having a given expertise means that expert witnesses, given the choice between the public sector and the court-ordered work of drawing up an opinion and the private sector—which is much better paid—choose, as it were, the latter.

The length of proceedings is also still a social problem.

It stems from the fact that there is still a problem of litigation, that is, filing lawsuits and appeals to the court "on principle," that is, a party knows that he or she is wrong but continues to defend his or her position on principle, which, I am sorry to say, is fostered by the situation of exemption from court costs for a party who is unable to cover his or her own and his or her family's living expenses.[28] However, the elimination of this instrument would not be appropriate because it would limit access to court for the poorest. Obviously, the solution is to grant exemption only when a party actually meets the criteria, but it is one thing to have a difficult situation and its assessment and another to decide on the legitimacy of a lawsuit or an appeal. The legislator is taking remedies in the form of alternative dispute resolution methods like the promotion of mediation, but it is insufficient in the domestic system as of today.

---

giving an opinion. He or she is obliged to read the case file very carefully and, where possible and necessary, to contact the parties to the proceedings. The expert's opinion must be clearly and completely formulated for the court and each party." https://www.infodent24.pl/lexdentpost/dlaczego-jest-tak-malo-bieglych-sadowych,116549.html.

28 L. Jamróz, *Prawo do sądu a zjawisko pieniactwa sądowego*, Prawo do sądu a zjawisko pieniactwa sądowego (uni.wroc.pl), cf. Article 102(1) of the Act of July 28, 2005 on court costs in civil cases, Journal of Laws 2022, 1125.

Another problem with this is that the number of attorneys offering their services on the market affects the fight for clients, which in turn also leads to a situation in which attorneys are not always ethical in their actions and drag out trials artificially, for example, by citing new evidence, which also affects the proceedings.[29]

6. Summary

The lengthiness of proceedings is a problem that occurs in every procedure. And with a certain degree of conviction it must be said that it cannot be completely eliminated, but certainly also every effort must be made to marginalize the problem. For this to happen, however, the legislator has an absolute obligation to respond to all signals concerning the lengthiness of proceedings. Ignoring them will lead to a growing problem, piling up of complaints about lengthy proceedings, but will also lead to a loss of trust in the judiciary, which is by all means undesirable. In Poland, the problem of lengthiness of proceedings, although to a large extent has a systemic background, which is influenced mainly by the issue of organization of work in courts, too few assistants or experts, it is also a social problem, resulting from "getting used to judging." Getting used to the judicial method of settling disputes. Thus, these reasons lead to the academic postulation of an increase in the amounts of decoding for protracted proceedings. On the other hand, it seems that it will be much more effective not to pay higher damages but to eliminate the causes of protraction.

Bibliography

Górecki, P., Stachowiak, S., and Wiliński, P., *Skarga na przewlekłość postępowania sądowego. Komentarz*, Warsaw 2007.

Jędrzejczyk, A., *Zbyt mało biegłych sądowych w sprawach cywilnych. To poważny problem, któremu przygląda się Rzecznik*, https://bip.brpo.gov.pl/pl/content/zbyt-ma%C5%82o-bieg%C5%82ych-s%C4%85dowych-w-sprawach-cywilnych-powa%C5%BCny-problem-kt%C3%B3remu-przygl%C4%85da-si%C4%99-rzecznik.

Kluza, J., "Wpływ ostatnich nowelizacji Kodeksu postępowania karnego na szybkość i rzetelność procesu karnego. Studium przypadku," *Studenckie Zeszyty Naukowe* XX/32 (2017).

29 Cf. Article 183 Act of November 17, 1964—Code of Civil Procedure Dz.U.2021.0.1805, 23a—Act of June 6, 1997—Code of Criminal Procedure Dz.U.2022.0.1375.

Kłak, Cz. P., "Skarga na przewlekłość postępowania a rozwiązania przyjęte w wybranych krajach europejskich jako 'środki odwoławcze' na nadmierną długość postępowania—podobieństwa i różnice (cz. 2)," *Palestra* 5–6 (2012).

Kozłowski, Ł., *Rozprawa doktorska, Korzystanie w procesie cywilnym z dowodów uzyskanych sprzecznie z prawem*, https://repozytorium.amu.edu.pl/bitstream/10593/26474/1/Doktorat%20_%C5%81ukasz%20Koz%C5%82owski_.pdf.

Kucharska, A., *Przyczyny przewlekłości postępowań cywilnych w sądach rejonowych*, https://iws.gov.pl/wp-content/uploads/2018/09/Anna-Kucharska-Przyczyny-przewlek%C5%82o%C5%9Bci-post%C4%99powa%C5%84-cywilnych-w-s%C4%85dach-rejonowych-109.pdf.

Ostaszewski, P., and Melaniuk, E., *Kwerenda spraw ze skargi na przewlekłość postępowania sądowego. Analizy wymiaru sprawiedliwości*, Warszawa 2019.

Przewlekłość postępowania cywilnego w świetle orzecznictwa Sądu Najwyższego, https://www.temidium.pl/artykul/przewleklosc_postepowania_cywilnego_w_swietle_orzecznictwa_sadu_najwyzszego-3264.html.

Sobczak, K., *Można dochodzić odszkodowania za przewlekłość postępowania*, https://www.prawo.pl/prawnicy-sady/odszkodowanie-za-przewleklosc-postepowania,184448.html.

Stępień-Załucka, B., *Sprawowanie wymiaru sprawiedliwości przez Sad Najwyższy w Polsce*, Warszawa 2016, p. 32.

Szymaniak, P., "Nikt się nie garnie do pracy w sądzie: Brakuje asystentów sędziów, protokolantów i sekretarzy," *Dziennik Gazeta Prawna*, 5 december 2018, https://prawo.gazetaprawna.pl/artykuly/1378812,braki-kadrowe-w-sadach-pracownicy-sadow-domagaja-sie-podwyzek.html.

Wiliński, P., *Rzetelny proces karny w orzecznictwie sądów polskich i międzynarodowych*, Warsaw 2009.

Patricia Panero Oria

The existence of filiation between a woman and a child born of another pregnant woman from the Roman juridical experience

Abstract: In order to face the question of whether or not it is convenient to reform the cases of filiation included in our legislation, it may be of interest to observe the cases of cession of wives that the Roman sources provide us with. The constant refusals of the Spanish courts to consider the filiation between a woman and a child born of another woman by virtue of the possession of state, raised from the Roman Law can be resolved in a contrary way. This makes this work a review of the subject from the Roman Law, analyzing, on the one hand, the types of women who are resorted to as expectant mothers, and on the other hand, examining the existing forms of filiation

Keywords: roman law, filiation, possession of state, surrogacy, surrogate motherhood

1. Introduction

I am aware that nowadays it is not easy to present a paper on surrogacy, not only because of all that has been written about it, but also because of the debate it raises in different ethical, legal, psychological, social, economic, religious, and scientific aspects. In a legal sphere, and in spite of the clarity of Spanish regulations prohibiting this type of reproduction technique,[1] there are numerous cases of children entering Spain without issues and eventually not only becoming part of a specific family nucleus, but also being registered in the Civil Registry if certain requirements are met.

The continued use of this practice in particular, and in general the irruption of new assisted reproduction techniques and new means to form a family, has meant that the cases of filiation provided for in article 108 of the Civil Code (filiation by nature—matrimonial[2] or non-matrimonial—and filiation by adoption),

1 The Law on Assisted Human Reproduction Techniques (Law 14/2006, of May 26, on assisted human reproduction techniques) in its art. 10 expressly declares the nullity of the surrogacy contract.

2 Matrimonial (art. 115 Cc) or non-matrimonial (art. 120 Cc). In the latter, birth is the biological fact that legally determines maternal filiation (arts. 120.5 Cc and 44.4 pf. 2.°

have become obsolete[3] and do not conform to the social reality, in which every day there are more cases of children conceived through surrogacy, crossing our borders and becoming part of a family nucleus. Faced with these cases, the courts have no choice but to legislate, and thus other forms of filiation are appearing in our legal system which, although they are not *ex lege*, *de facto* solve the problems that arise for cases of children born abroad through this praxis, in which the following are present: (1) the volitional or intentional element of wanting to be a father or a mother; (2) the suitability to be one; (3) the best interests of the child; and (4) possession of status, ascertained by the existence of a *de facto* paternal-filial relationship.[4]

A few considerations on the concept and function of possession of status before continuing:

> It is a factual situation which, according to doctrine[5] and jurisprudence, is characterised by three elements: the *nomen*, the *tractatus* and reputation (*reputatio*).

The first—*nomen*—refers to the customary use of the parent's surname by the minor; *tractatus* is the treatment that the father or the mother give to another person as a son or daughter, which is manifested not only in the assumption of economic obligations, but mainly in the affective relationship, in the ordinary and habitual activities they share, in acts and attitudes typical of a parent; and *reputatio* implies that these acts have transcendence in the public or social

---

LRC 2011), and the recognition of the child as one's own, whether or not it is biologically, paternal filiation (art. 120.1.°, 2.° and 3.° Cc and 7 LTRHA).

3 This has been recognized by the Supreme Court itself in STS no. 45/2022, of January 27: *Pending* a necessary revision of the whole system of filiation (… that adequately accommodates that derived from the use of assisted reproduction techniques, both in terms of extrajudicial determination and judicial actions for claiming and challenging …), to resolve the appeal we must look at the deficient regulation in force and the court's jurisprudence adapted to the circumstances of the present case.

4 Possession of status is understood as the existence of a paternal-filial relationship in cases where there is no biological bond between the parties. Thais means without there being a biological paternity, the roles of father and son are recognized as such in society.

5 Cf., for example, M. Navarro-Michel, "La filiación derivada de gestación por sustitución: posesión de estado e interés del menor, orden público y derechos fundamentales," *Rev. Bioética y Derecho* [online] 56 (2022) [cited July 5, 2023], pp. 4–28, 10–11. Available at: http://scielo.isciii.es/scielo.php?script=sci_arttext&pid=S1886588720 22000300004&lng=es&nrm=iso. Epub June 26, 2023. https://dx.doi.org/10.1344/rbd2 022.56.40741.

sphere, acts that according to jurisprudence-must be continuous and repeated.[6] It is, ultimately the appearance of a "constant" and public family relationship,[7] or in other words *de facto* family life.

The Spanish Civil Code regulates actions to claim filiation, whether maternal or paternal, and the first paragraph of article 131 Cc, states that "any person with a legitimate interest has an action to have filiation declared by the constant possession of status," its main function being, probative. This is why this article is included in the chapter dedicated to judicial actions of filiation. With that being said, the possession of status is considered more as a means of proving filiation than determining it. Since it is not included in the provisions that determine filiation, it does not, by itself, allow for the formal establishment of filiation.[8]

In light of this, it is logical that the Supreme Court had not previously ruled on filiation claims regarding non-biological children—born through surrogacy—based on possession of status,[9] as we have just seen, that possession of status is an indirect means of proving filiation, which serves to demonstrate that a person

---

6 The *tractatus* is the internal manifestation of the filiation relationship, and the *reputatio,* the external one: Thus, as M. Navarro-Michel, "La filiación derivada de gestación por sustitución: posesión de estado e interés del menor, orden público y derechos fundamentales," cit, pp. 10 and 11, treating a person as a child is not confined to the internal domestic sphere, but this treatment is externalized, both because third parties see and perceive this mother-child treatment, and because of the way of relating to third parties, so that everyone comes to believe that they are, in fact, mother and child. Friends, neighbors, the school, the primary care center identify the behavior as a filial relationship. Doesn't it remind you of the elements of marriage? *Affectio maritalis* and *honor matrimonii*?

7 M. Navarro-Michel, "La filiación derivada de gestación por sustitución: posesión de estado e interés del menor, orden público y derechos fundamentales," cit., p. 11.

8 Civil law doctrine differentiates between means of determining filiation and means of accrediting filiation. The former makes it possible to legally establish the legal bond of filiation, while the latter give legal standing to act in legal transactions. Cf. M. Navarro-Michel, "La filiación derivada de gestación por sustitución: posesión de estado e interés del menor, orden público y derechos fundamentales," cit. 11ff.

9 The Provincial Courts of Madrid and Navarre have done so in ST of December 1, 2020 and March 25, 2022, respectively. The former has been the subject of cassation by the Public Prosecutor's Office, mainly alleging that "*the substantive rule infringed is art. 131 in fine of the Civil Code in relation to art. 10 of the LAHRT*." Further examples can be found in the SAP Barcelona, ST of April 6, 2021, or in the SAP Balearic Islands ST April 27, 2021. However, not all the courts agree on this issue, with some judgments denying the claim of the plaintiffs to determine the filiation of children born through surrogacy on the sole basis of possession of status.

behaves as a father or mother because they are in fact, genetically connected to the child being claimed for filiation.

However, it did so, just over a year ago, resolving a filiation action brought by a single woman based on possession of status over a child conceived through surrogacy with whom she has no biological connection.[10] At the time being, the Court has not addressed the issue again.

2. The Supreme Court ruling of March 31, 2022: Is there a filiation bond between a woman and a child born from another pregnant woman, without the first providing any genetic material?

An intended grandfather brought an action for filiation to declare the existence of that bond between his daughter (the commissioning mother) and a child born in Mexico through a surrogacy contract. Although child's filiation is not recognized in Spain, the Spanish authorities allowed the woman and the child to enter our country, where they have been living together ever since. The Provincial Court of Madrid, in the second instance, established the maternal filiation based on possession of status, valuing the best interest of the child who is already integrated into the family. However, the Public Prosecutor's Office appealed the Court's decision in cassation, and the Supreme Court overturned the Provincial Court's ruling.

The aim is to determine the child's filiation under Spanish law, specifically art. 131 Cc, as we have seen regarding possession of status. The commissioning mother can demonstrate that she has been taking care of the child born through surrogacy, although she has no genetic connection to the child.

However, the High Court has once again, pronounced against surrogacy, not only deeming it null but warning that it violates public order, fundamental rights recognized in the Constitution, and international conventions on human rights.[11]

---

10 STS 277/2022 of March 31, 2022. See the criticisms of this judgment in Álvarez González, S., "Gestación por sustitución y Tribunal Supremo español: Nota breve a la STS de 31 de marzo de 2022," *Diario La Ley*, n. 10.069, Sección Tribuna, May 16, 2022.

11 There is not much case law on the matter, although the High Court has already declared in its ruling 835/2013 of February 6, 2014, that surrogacy contracts violate the fundamental rights of both the pregnant woman and the child and are therefore manifestly contrary to our public order. On that occasion, the registration in the Civil Registry was rejected by means of the validation of what had been agreed in the California Registry.

Many questions arise from this ruling,[12] but they are beyond the scope of my work. Therefore, I will focus solely on two: (1) On one hand, it urges the commissioning parents to consider adoption, providing some legal certainty given the existing discrepancy among certain courts that were denying access to adoption in some surrogacy cases, establishing a precedent to adopt the same criteria for all future cases. (2) It brings back to the forefront a complex issue of whether or not there is a filiation bond between a woman and a child born from another pregnant woman, without the first providing any genetic material. The aim is to determine the child's possession based on art. 131 of the Civil Code.

1. Regarding the first point, as the judgment itself states, under our legal system, children born abroad through surrogacy are considered the children of the woman who gave birth, even if she is willing to carry the pregnancy for others, (art. 10.2 LTRHA). Only if the commissioning father is the biological father who provided his gametes, he could pursue an action to claim paternity in accordance with art. 10.3 LTRHA.[13]
   However, when the commissioning mother is the one seeking the recognition of the filial relationship, the pathway which filiation must be determined is adoption. This is also the route to which Spanish courts refer when dismissing the claim, and it is recommended by the ECHR Advisory Opinion of April 10, 2019.[14]
   Thus, our legal system already provides a pathway to claim maternity in cases such as the one described: a single woman who wishes to have a child

---

12 As stated by Mª Dolores Muelas, member of AEFA, in *La sentencia del Supremo sobre gestación subrogada refuerza el acceso a la adopción por parte de los comitentes* (n.f.). AEFA, https://www.aeafa.es/noticias-ampliadas/2429/2/la-sentencia-del-supremo-sobre-gestacin-subrogada-refuerza-el-acceso-a-la-adopcin-por-parte-de-los-comitentes/.

13 However, I agree with Álvarez González, "Gestación por sustitución y Tribunal Supremo español: Nota breve a la STS de 31 de marzo de 2022," cit., the man who provides his genetic material is a father by that fact alone and there is no reason why his filiation with respect to the child should not be accredited by any other means: registration in the civil registry, fulfilling the requirements of the applicable law, voluntary acknowledgment of paternity, etc.

14 Accepted as one of the mechanisms to satisfy the child´s best interests in such cases "adoption by the commissioning mother […] to the extent that the procedure established by national law ensures they can be implemented promptly and effectively, in accordance with the child's best interests."

through surrogacy abroad without providing genetic material, will do so through adoption.

2. Regarding the second, point, the existence or not of a filiation bond between a woman and a child born from another pregnant woman, or as Álvarez González[15] states, the relevance of such a bond exists based on possession of status, as declared in the judgment of the Courts of Appeals of Madrid, and then contested in the recent Supreme Court ruling, demonstrates for the time being, that the maternal filiation of a child born through surrogacy will be determined by the birth, following the traditional principle of Roman Law, *mater semper certa est.*

Despite this, we are all aware this issue will continue to be raised in the near future. Therefore, when considering whether or not it is advisable to reform the conditions of filiation provided in our legislation, it may be of interest to once again look back at Roman Law and observe cases of—*uxoris cessio*—(wives' cessions) found in Roman sources. Through these examples, I will try to demonstrate it becomes evident that the mother is considered to be the woman who marries the father, regardless of whether or not she is the biological mother of the child, even against the well-known Paulus principle.

This prompts a re-examination of the topic of surrogacy in this paper, exploring it from the perspective of Roman Law. Analyzing cases collected in historical sources sheds light on the conditions necessary to discuss this issue. This includes considering; (a) The type of women who serve as surrogate mothers, (b) The nature of their relationship with the future father, as significant differences arise among children born depending on the mother's situation and the type of relationship, and (c) The existing forms of filiation, taking into account the Roman concept *procreatio filiorum* as the purpose of marriage.

Additionally, it's important to consider that during that era, marriage was a powerful tool for strengthening alliances among prominent Roman families, ensuring their presence in the ruling elite.[16] As a result, having offspring became a social and political necessity, leading many Romans to resort to any means to secure an heir.

This analysis seeks to understand why in Roman Law, the mother is considered the woman who marries the father, rather than the biological mother of the

---

15 S. Álvarez González, "Gestación por sustitución y Tribunal Supremo español: Nota breve a la STS de 31 de marzo de 2022," cit.

16 S. Castán, "El matrimonio como estrategia en la carrera política durante el último tramo de la república," *RIDROM* 7 (2015), pp. 1–59.

child. This approach reinforces the principle: *pater is est quem nuptiae demonstrant*, while weakening its predecessor: *mater semper certa est*. These principles have been questioned with the appearance of new assisted reproduction techniques, and I dare to venture, in some cases, a new applicable one: *mater ea est quam nuptiae demonstrant.*

3. The *uxoris cessio*: cases

The starting point of this work is the concept of *uxoris cessio* (wives cession); In Roman legal experience, once again ahead of its time, we find texts where a husband would cede his still fertile wife, even if pregnant, to another man with the purpose of having children, akin to a more traditional version of surrogacy. Not only that, but she could later return to her original husband, leaving those children in the care of a new wife who, if she married the father, would become the mother of those children, perhaps through a form of possession of status as discussed earlier.

Much has been said about the cession of Roman women from various perspectives.[17] Many literary texts refer to cases of marriages being dissolved so that the husband can have offspring with another woman. These cases commonly share two characteristics: (a) The involvement of illustrious, well-known, and high-class individuals; and (b) The timeframe, which is limited to the late Roman Republic and early Principate.

---

17 Cfr. On the subject, Núñez Paz, I., "La *voluntas* de las madres comitentes *versus* el *uterus* de las madres gestantes," pp. 23–52, in *Mujer sujeto u objeto de derechos reproductivos*, ed. L. Suárez Llanos, Valencia, 2019; which approaches the topic from the female´s will and consent point of view both the gestational mother and the commissioning mother, although I do not agree with the author's assertions that only midwives have the possibility of choosing. Recent bibliography, the same author "On *cessio ventris* in ancient Rome. Transcendencia socio-jurídica del principio *mater semper certa est*," *e-Legal History Review* (2018), pp. 49–66, p. 9; P. Panero Oria, "Surrogacy; A Regression to a Patriarchal Society Free of Social Policies?," *Journal of Modern Science* 40/1 (2019), pp. 115–124, and "Precedentes de la gestación por sustitución," *A locatio conductio. Influência nois direitos actuáis*, Oporto 2018, pp. 787–795; M. De Simone, "Sulle tracce di un'antica prassi: la c.d. cessione della moglie," *Annali del seminario giuridico dell'Università degli studi di Palermo* AUPA 44 (2010–2011), pp. 9–54; M. E. Fernández Baquero, "La cesión de la mujer con fines de procreación según la concepción de la familia romana arcaica y preclásica," *Revista de la facultad de Derecho de la Universidad de Granada* 4/201 (2001), pp. 273–298.

There are several examples provided by the sources, although the best known and most outstanding case is that of Marcia, Cato and Hortensius, a case referred to by some authors as the "strange triangle,"[18] and reported by Plutarch[19] and Lucan.[20]

The story takes place in 56 BC at the end of the Republican era, which is significant for two reasons (1) The prevailing conceptions of marriage and divorce at the time, and (2) The political and social panorama of that period.

Hortensius, a close friend of Cato's, desires to connect himself to Cato's family, and asks for his daughter Porcia's hand in marriage. Porcia is already married to Marcus Calpurnius Bibulus, who served as consul in 59 BC, and they had two children together. Hortensius's sole intention is to have Porcia bear him a child, and once that goal is achieved, he plans to return her to her husband.

When Cato refuses Hortensius request, Hortensius proposes an alternative: that Cato should cede his wife Marcia, to him. Hortensius points out that Marcia is still young enough to bear him children, since Cato's succession is already assured with two children.[21]

After consulting with his father-in-law, Lucius Marcius Philippus, Marcia's father, Cato, agrees to the arrangement. Thus, in the year 56 BC, Marcia becomes Hortensius' wife and bears him two sons. Six years later, after Hortensius' death, Cato then remarries Marcia[22] and as highlighted by CANTARELLA,[23] he had lent her to Hortensius, still young and now a wealthy widow.

Another example of *uxoris cessio* is that of Livia Drusilla, the wife of Tiberius Claudius Nero and already mother of the future emperor Tiberius. While pregnant with her second child, Drusus, (the future father of Emperor Claudius), she

---

18 E. Cantarella, *Pasado Próximo. Roman women from Tacitus to Sulpicia*, cit., p. 141. following H. L. Gordon, "The Eternal Triangle. First Century B.C.," *Clasical Journal* 28 (1933), pp. 574 ff. The characters are indeed three: Cato of Utica (the husband); Marcia (his wife) and Quintus Hortensius Hortalus (the third), although as will be seen Cato's daughter—Porcia—also plays a prominent role in the case.

19 Plutarch, *Cato Minor*, p. 25.

20 Lucan, *Pharsalia*, II, 331; *Comenta Lucani*, II, 33; and *Adnotationes Lucani*, II, 339.

21 Lucan, *Pharsalia*, II, 331 speaks of Cato's three sons, but it seems that the third, although fathered by Cato, was born after Marcia's marriage to Hortensius, and was therefore considered to be the son of Hortensius. This reinforces the idea that it is the father who proves the marriage.

22 Apianus, *Bellis civilibus*, II, 14.9.

23 *The Near Past. Roman Women from Tacitus to Sulpicia*, Madrid 1997, p. 146.

was ceded to Octavian the future Augustus,[24] in the year 38 BC. becoming his third wife.[25] Even with her visible pregnancy, Livia divorced Tiberius Claudius Nero and married Augustus. Three months after the marriage, Drusus was born. Apparently, the future Emperor sought permission from the Pontifical College for the wedding ritual, and Tiberius Claudius Nero actively took part in the celebration of the new marriage, which lasted for over 50 years, despite not having more children.[26]

Other cases include Livia Orestilla[27] who was ceded to Caligula and Poppea Sabina,[28] who was ceded to Otto. In my opinion, these are not examples of *cessio ventris,* but I consider it important to mention because they serve as examples for some of the assertions we will be making throughout this work. Let's take a close look at them:

Caligula, the guest of honour attended the betrothal ceremony of Livia Orestilla and Gaius Calpurnius Pison, who belonged to one of the important families at the time. After the banquet Caligula took the bride to his home and married her. However, the marriage ended a few days later.

Poppea Sabina married the young senator Marcus Salvius Otho (who later became emperor in the year 69). Otho openly praised his young wife in front of Nero, that the emperor fell in love with her. To make her his mistress, Nero did not hesitate to send his friend as governor to Lusitania. Nero divorced his first wife, Octavia and 12 days later, he married Poppea. In the year 63, Poppea gave birth to a daughter named Claudia, who died shortly after birth.

24 Very controversial case because it seems that Augustus stole it. It can be read in Tacitus *Annales*, I.10.5 and 12.6.

25 The sources consulted on Livia are: Dion Cassius, *Roman History*, 48.15.3–4, 34.3, 44; 49.38.1; 53.33.4; 54.19.3–4; 55.2.5–6, 10, 14, 32,1; 56.30.5–32.1–2, 46.1–3, 47.1; 57.3, 5–6 and 60.5.2. 57.12; 58.2.1–6; 59.2.3; Suetonius, *Divus Augustus,* 62.2; 63.1; 84.2 and 101.2, and *Tiberius,* 4.3; 6.1–3; 10.2; 12.1; 13.2; 50.2–3; and 51; *Caligula* 10.1; *Claudius,* 1.1; 4; 11.2; *Galba*, 5.2; 16.3 and 23.2. Tacitus, *Annales,* 1.3–7, 8, 10, 13–14, 33; 2.14, 34, 43, 77, 82; 3.15, 17, 34, 64, 71; 4.8, 12, 16, 21–22, 57, 71; 5.13; 6.5, 26, 29; y 12.69.

26 In addition to achieving reconciliation between the gens Claudia and the Julii.

27 Although Cassius Dion, 59.8.7, calls her Cornelia Orestilla. Suetonius, *Caligula*, 25.1, who says that he abducted her "after the manner of Romulus and Augustus," in reference to the latter's marriage to Livia.

28 The sources consulted on Poppea Sabina are: Dion Cassius, *Roman History*, 62.11.2–3, 12.1, 13.1–2, 28.1–2; and 63.26.4, Plutarch, *Galba*, 19.2–5. Suetonius, *Nero* 35.1–3 and *Otho* 3.1–2. Tacitus, *Annales,* 13.45–46; 14.1–2, 59–65; 15.23; 16.6–7, and *History*, 1.13, 22 and 78.

There are more cases involving well-known characters, although they might not be precisely about cessions of wives, but rather daughters. One example is that of Sulla, who arranged for his daughter Emilia (daughter of his fourth wife, Metella with her first husband, Q. Aemilius Scaurus), to divorce her first husband, Manius Acilius Glabrio, with whom she was expecting a child, in order to marry, Pompey (81 BC).[29] However, it seems that this decision was more to do with political ambitions than a desire to continue the family linage.[30] The marriage was short-lived, as Aemilia died during childbirth, giving birth to a daughter who also died shortly afterward.

All these examples show how both the cession of wives and daughters were a widespread practice among the upper classes. It was not uncommon for a husband or father once having enough children, to cede his own wife or daughter to another man with the purpose of having children in another family, in order to strengthen social and political alliances. This was not merely for personal or family interests, but rather to serve the interests of the city-state, fulfilling their duty to the State.[31] As Núñez Paz points out, it may have been justified under the sacred *officium amicitiae*,[32] whereby one could request the cession of their fertile wife from a close friend to fulfill the desire for offspring.[33]

29 Plutarch, *Sulla* 33. Who in turn repudiated his first wife to marry her, and according to Plutarch, in a cruel and ignominious manner, Plutarch, *Parallel Lives, Pompey*, p. 10.

30 C. García Fernández, "Edad, salud y capacidad adquisitiva en la formación de los diferentes tipos de familia. La cesión del *venter*," in *Mujer sujeto u objeto de derechos reproductivos. Derecho de los menores y maternidad por sustitución*, Valencia 2019, p. 70.

31 It should be noted that the public duties of the Roman matron are not limited to her own family but transcend the public interest. I., Núñez Paz, "Progresivo y limitado reconocimiento de la figura materna en el Derecho Romano. De la cesión del vientre al ejercicio de la tutela," in *Madres y maternidades. Construcciones culturales en la civilización clásica*, Oviedo 2009, pp. 255–291, p. 266.

32 Seneca, *De Beneficiis*, 1.9.3, in speaking of the services that friends render to each other, mentions the loan of wives.

33 *Amicitia*, explains S. Castán, "El papel de la mujer romana en la política del s. I. a. C. ¿influencia política, participación indirecta o influencia social?," *RIDROM* 24 (2020), pp. 540–601, p. 560, was for the Romans a special status linked to the virtue to which all good people should aspire in their personal lives and which attained a formal and objective value and treatment.

Many Roman scholars, including myself, view in this practice a precedent of today's surrogacy, albeit in a more traditional version: with one's own genetic material and without financial compensation.[34]

4. The *uxoris cessio*: Requirements

For this *cessio ventris* to happen, in my opinion, the following requirements must be met[35]:

1. The woman being ceded (or acting as a surrogate) must be married and already have had children. 2. The future father (intended father or commissioning father) must be married. 3. Both men, the current husband of the surrogate woman and the intended father, must agree. 4. The parties involved must divorce their respective spouses. 5. The cession must take place within the context of marriage. 6. The ceded women must be pregnant.

1. Certainly, if we are talking about the cession of a wife, it is logical to consider that the surrogate woman should already be married to another man, and not only that, but she must have already given birth. This is evident in all the cases presented. In the first case, despite Hortensius' proposal to marry Porcia (Cato's daughter) did not succeed, she was married to Marcus Calpurnius Bibulus, with whom she already had two children.[36]

---

34 Classification on types of surrogacy: (a) according to whether or not there is financial consideration, and (b) according to whether or not the mother has a genetic relationship with the child born. (a) In the first case, surrogacy can be carried out in an "altruistic" manner, without any consideration in return, or under the modality known as "commercial surrogacy" in which the surrogate mother will carry out the pregnancy in exchange for a price. (b) The second classification raises two more variants; the so-called "gestational" in which the surrogate mother will only carry out the pregnancy and won't have any genetic relationship with the baby, or the "traditional" in which the gestational carrier will provide her womb and her own ova which will be fertilised. Cf. P. Panero Oria, "'Precedentes de la Gestación por—sustitución,' Fundamentos romanísticos del Derecho Contemporáneo," *BOE* VII (2021), pp. 2045–2054, and *A locatio conductio. Influência nois direitos actuáis*, Oporto 2018, pp. 787–795.

35 M. De Simone, "Una congettura sull'arcaico filiam abducere," *Annali del seminario giuridico dell'università degli studi di Palermo (AUPA)* 55 (2012), pp. 321–384, p. 26. Although the author refers to a hypothetical reconstruction of this figure in archaic times, I consider that they are more in line with the period to which I am referring, that is, late pre-classical and early classical times.

36 Cato's daughter marries Marcus Junius Brutus, son of Caesar, on the death of her first husband.

Marcia was Cato's wife with whom she had two children; Livia Orestilla was married to Gaius Calpurnius Pison, an excellent orator of the time, and Poppaea Sabina was married to the young senator Marcus Salvius Otho.[37] In the case of Livia and Aemilia, both were also married. Livia to Tiberius Claudius Nero with whom she had a son -Tiberius- and Emilia to Manius Acilius Glabrion, with whom she was pregnant.

In all the abovementioned it appears that the marriages were *cum manu,* in which the husband held the marital power, known as -*manus*[38]—and the wife came under the authority of the husband if he was a *paterfamilias* or under the authority of her father-in-law if her husband was under his own father's authority meaning he was. *alieni iuris.* Thus, the wife was separated from her family of origin, her cognates or blood relatives, to become part of her husband's family as a daughter or granddaughter, depending on whether the *manus* was exercised by her husband or her husband's father.[39] This makes her a legitimate heir alongside her children, or if her husband was under his own *paterfamilias*, being *alieni iuris,* she acquires the *status* of her husband's sister.[40]

On the other hand, in the case of daughters, the fact that they were married confirms the existence of a common practice, at least until the 2nd century, the so-called *abductio filiae*,[41] a power held in the *patria potestas*, which allow the *paterfamilias* to interrupt the marriages of his daughters and sons whenever he wished. For this very reason, if the parties were *alieni iuris*, the consent of the *paterfamilias* was an essential requirement in order to marry.[42]

---

37 She was previously married to Crispino, with whom she had a son, Rufrio Crispino.

38 Included in the ancient trichotomy enjoyed by the *paterfamilias*: *potestas*, *manus* and *mancipium*. The first exercised over the children, the second over the wife, and the third over slaves and free persons acquired by the *pater in causa mancipii.*

39 Alongside this type of marriage, there were others, the *sine manu,* which began to be progressively introduced, whereby the woman did not submit to her husband's family: she remained under the parental authority of her own *paterfamilias* (if she had one), without breaking with her family of origin, which revalued cognatic ties to the detriment of agnatic ones and favored the natural family over the legal family. All this will lead to a new situation for married women.

40 C. Fayer, *La famiglia romana. Parte terza: Concubinato, divorzio e adulterio*, Roma 2015, p. 118.

41 On this figure see, for example, M. De Simone, "Una congettura sull'arcaico filiam abducere," cit., pp. 321–384.

42 E. Cantarella, *Pasado Próximo. Roman women from Tacitus to Sulpicia*, cit., p. 113. D. 23.2.2 (*Paul. 25 ad Ed*). The consent of the natural father is also required when he is not her *paterfamilias*.

This happened with Emilia, Sulla's daughter, whom her father forced her to divorce. Or like Porcia, Cato's own daughter, whom was Hortensius' first choice.

The singularity of what we have observed, displays an ideology and family customs of the ancient Roman society different from ours. However, the tone in which these events are reported in historical sources is normal, without scandals or condemnations, despite dealing with events that were widely known in antiquity, mainly due to the notoriety of the individuals involved—let us remember that Cato became Praetor of Rome, Hortensius was a prestigious orator, and of course, Augustus, Sulla, and Caligula were prominent characters.

The requirement for the women who were ceded, in other words, our surrogate mothers, was to have already given birth. This serves a dual purpose: on one hand, they had fulfilled their duty toward their husbands and Rome, and on the other hand, it guarantees that they are fertile and capable of procreation, this aspect is closely connected to:

– *The liberorum quaerendorum (procreandorum)* purpose of the Roman marriage[43] foundations

It is *communis opinio* among Roman scholars that the main purpose of the marital union was indeed *procreatio filiorum*,[44] even though it is not explicitly stated in classical Roman legal sources.[45] As highlighted in rare occasions, children guarantee the continuity of the family lineage,[46] and provide new citizens for the Republic. Men who were unable to have biological offspring resorted to various methods to secure an heir, such as (a) Marrying fertile or younger women, preferably married ones, (b) Turning to adoption,[47] or (c) Even resorting to practices

43 See the expressions liberorum quaerendorum causa uxorem duxerit in the Tituli ex corpore Ulpiani, III.3 and liberorum procreandorum causa in C. 5.4.9.

44 O. Robleda, *El matrimonio en Derecho Romano. Esencia, requisitos de validez, efectos, disolubilidad*, Roma 1970, p. 62 and G. Franciosi, *Famiglia e persone in Roma antica. Dall'etá arcaica al principato*, Torino 1992, p. 34 and p. 13.

45 However, this is clear from the texts of Modestinus, D. 23.2.1 (1 *Regul.*) and Justinian (I. 1.9.1) who, in defining marriage, refer to its natural basis, which is also applicable to other stable unions such as concubinage or the union between slaves.

46 Cicero, *De Officiis*, 1.4.1; *De Finibus*, 3.19.64. Suetonius, *Iulius*, 52. Quintilian, *Declamationes*, 147 and D. 1.1.1.3 (*Ulp. 1 Inst.*).

47 S. Castán, "El papel de la mujer romana en la política del s. I. a. C. ¿influencia política, participación indirecta o influencia social?," p. 557.

like the one we are witnessing with the cession of daughters or wives, which bear similarities to modern surrogacy.

The requirement for the woman being ceded to be married and having already borne children served as a guarantee of her fertility, ensuring the future husband's ability to produce offspring, being the main purpose. During the late Roman Republic, upper-class families formed powerful alliances through strategic marriages to consolidate their social, economic, or political positions. Marriages became tools at the disposal of the *paterfamilias* to strengthen and enhance the family's status within society.[48] Consequently, in addition to the practices mentioned, marriages were often arranged through betrothal,[49] guaranteeing the growth of the community with new citizens and securing the family's continuity and influence.

In this context, there is no doubt that the primary role of Roman women was as wives and equally important, as mothers. Their life's purpose evolved around marriage, ensuring the procreation of offspring for their husbands, and thereby legitimizing their children. It was crucial to have children within marriage as it was the most common way for the father to acquire *patria potestas*, the legal authority over his children. Legitimate (*iusti or legitimi*) children inherited the status of the father at birth while illegitimate (*non-iusti*) children inherit the status of the mother at birth.

This relates to the second necessary requirement for the cession of the wife:

2. The intended or commissioning father must be married.

Although this condition is not explicitly mentioned in the sources, it can be presumed from the lives of the characters involved. For instance, in the case of Marcia and Hortensius, he was married to Lucia, Catulus' daughter, with whom he apparently had no offspring.[50] Augustus had been married twice before

---

48 S. Castán, "El matrimonio como estrategia en la carrera política durante el último tramo de la república," *RIDROM* 7 (2011), pp. 367–423, cit., p. 371, this same author recounts in his work the political-familial alliances entered into by key figures of this period such as Caesar, Pompey, Cicero and Mark Antony.

49 In order to secure these future alliances, there are cases of girls who entrust themselves to the family of their future husbands before they have reached the age of 12 (the age established for marriage) and live in the house of their future in-laws until the time of the celebration of the marriage, D. 23.2.4 (*Pomp. 3 ad Sab.*), D. 23.1.9 (*Ulp. 35 ad Ed.*), D. 48.5.14 (13).8 (*Ulp. 2 de Adult.*).

50 Apianus, *Bellis civilibus*, II 99, 413; but according to F. Münzer, *Römische Adelsparteien und Adelsfamilien*, Stutgart 1963, pp. 342 ff. 286 and 343 he had a son with her, Q.

marrying Livia; first to Claudia, with whom he did not consummate the marriage,[51] and then to Scribonia, with whom he had a daughter, Julia the Elder, who interestingly was born on the day Augustus was celebrating his betrothal with Livia.[52] Nero was married to Octavia, whom he repudiated to marry Livia Orestilla. The same happened in the case of Pompey, who, as described by Suetonius, repudiated his first wife, Antistia, in a dishonorable and cruel manner.[53] Despite this, there is no reason to believe that a married man could not cede his wife to someone else who was unmarried, but it is surprising that the texts do not clearly mention it.[54] This could be related to the need for the cession to take place if the intended or commissioning father was not only married but also married to an infertile woman?

This argument finds its justification in the very foundation of marriage. If, as previously mentioned, the importance laid in having offspring (either for the desire to have children *liberorum quaerendorum causa*,[55] or to strengthen political alliances) and if the woman did not fulfill this purpose, the man could divorce her and look for another wife.

Fertility was of vital importance in Roman society, to the extent that it determined women[56] health, and since the regal laws, also was grounds for divorce.

Leaving descendants was crucial to such a point that a woman's sterility became a reason for divorce, as happened with Spurius Carvilius Ruga (around 230 BC),[57] who repudiated his deeply loved wife because she could not have children.[58] There is no certainty if this was the first divorce in Rome, but there is

---

Hortensius, which others attribute to Marcia herself, *cit.* F., De Simone, "Una congettura sull'arcaico filiam abducere," cit., p. 27, n. 62.

51 Suetonius, *Augustus*, 62. 1; Dion Cassius, *Roman History*, 48. 5. 3.

52 Suetonius, *Augustus*, 62.1–2; but it seems that they divorced because of the disarrangement of the Emperor's customs, *Augustus*, 69.1.

53 Suetonius, *Parallel Lives*, *Pompey*, 9.

54 The exception is Caligula, who was not married when he stole Livia Orestilla.

55 This has been pointed out by F., De Simone, "Una congettura sull'arcaico filiam abducere," cit., p. 27, who argues that one of the prerequisites for cession in archaic times was the need for the man claiming it to be married to an infertile woman.

56 Thus *ad exemplum*, D. 21.1.7 and 14 (*Ulp. 1 ad Ed. Aed. Curul.*); or 15 (*Paul. 11 ad Sab.*), which consider a barren woman to be in poor health.

57 Among other sources, Dionysius Halicarnassus, *Antiguitatum Rom.*, II.25.7; Valerius Maximus, *Facta et dictia memorabilia*, II.9.2; Plutarch, *Questiones Romanae*, 14 and 25.

58 *Cfr.* on the subject I. Núñez Paz, *Matrimonio y divorcio en Roma*, Salamanca 1988, pp. 89 et seq.

no doubt it was the first one carried out due to infertility.[59] This wasn't a socially accepted reason,[60] and that is why it was severely censured. However, his name has undoubtedly gone down in history for opening the way to many others who, since then, and for the same reason, preferred to try to provide themselves with an heir through a new marriage rather than keep their wife.[61]

The purpose of marriage, *liberorum quaerendorum (procreandorum causa)*, affects both spouses, but the consequences are much worse for women than for men, by facing criminal charges.

Indeed, during the Roman Republic, specifically after the Punic Wars, there was a moral relaxation, and divorce became more frequent, particularly among the higher social strata[62] due to various reasons. However, the sources do not refer to divorces of women from lower class, likely because they were not of any political or social interest. It is then that the cases of wife cession analyzed are mentioned, but the sources do not explicitly indicate the need for the intended or commissioning father to be married or for his wives to be infertile. For instance, it is not clear whether Hortensius already had a child; Augustus was not a father when the cession of Livia, but he had a daughter on the day of their marriage, and Pompey repudiated his wife Antistia to marry Emilia.[63] Caligula and Nero had not yet had descendants, which suggests that they may have been seeking an heir at any cost.

What is beyond doubt is that the man who intended to marry the ceded woman had to be married himself. As for the fertility of the woman, it fits perfectly with the prevailing mentality of the time and the purpose of marriage, which was "*procreatio filiorum*" If the woman was fertile, it aligned with the traditional understanding of marriage, while if she was infertile, the cession could be motivated by State affairs, family alliances, or even the interests of the Republic. This period marked a time of change for Rome, where both forms of understanding

---

59 Mª E., Fernández Baquero, *Repudium-Divortium (Origen y configuración jurídica hasta la legislación matrimonial de Augusto)*, Granada 1987, pp. 312 ff. In this case it was motivated by the censorial oath that Carvilio Ruga had to take, as a candidate for censorship, to have a child, which, as his wife was sterile, was not possible.

60 Since Romulus, the husband has had the power to repudiate his wife, but only in certain cases, among which sterility is not contemplated: attempted poisoning, supposition of children, falsification of keys and poisoning. Plutarch, *Questiones Romanae*, p. 22.

61 S. Castán, "El matrimonio como estrategia," cit., p. 379.

62 Women follow the social status of their fathers or husbands, procuring their own honor through marriage—honor *matrimonii.*

63 Suetonius, *Parallel Lives, Pompey*, 4, 9 and 10.

marriage might have coexisted[64]; marriage *cum manu* or *sine manu* much like other matters such as guardianship, and agnatic and cognatic ties.

3. The third requirement concerns the consent of the men involved. The sources do not mention the need for the woman's consent; rather, they emphasize the need for the men to give their consent. Both the husband of the surrogate woman (the ceding party) and the intended father must agree to the *uxoris cessio,* or in modern terms, to the surrogacy. In the cases described, we see that Cato not only has to consent to ceding his daughter and then his wife but also consults with his father-in-law, Lucius Marcius Philippus, who insists on the need for his agreement but also his presence. Philippus declares that if Cato does not agree, he will not hand over Marcia to Hortensius.[65] The same applies to Tiberius, who not only cedes his wife Livia to Octavius but also plays an active role in the celebration of the new marriage.[66] In Nero's case, Odo agreed to the cession of his wife, Poppaea Sabina, for personal interests.[67] Similarly, in Emilia's case, her husband Glabrio was forced to divorce her at Sulla's request, who was fully in favor of the cession.

---

64 Thus De Simone, "Sulle tracce di una antica prassi," cit., pp. 31–34, reconstructs the cession of women in the archaic period and its development at the end of the Republic. The author tries to show that the most ancient cession is *liberorum quaerendorum causa*, thus consecrating the purpose of marriage, while at the end of the Republic and during the Principate, it pursues a more political purpose: to weave a network of personal and family relationships.

65 According to E. Cantarella, *Matrimonio e sessualità nella Roma repubblicana: una storia romana di amore coniugale*, Firenze 2005, pp. 123 ff, the fact that Cato had to consult his father-in-law shows that it was a marriage *sine manu*, so that Philip would be the holder of parental authority. If so, he would be the only one who could authorize the divorce of the daughter, which would be an *abductio filiae, so it* would not be a case of cession of the wife. I do not share this opinion, and I believe, along the lines of De Simone, "Sulle tracce di una antica prassi," cit, *Il matrimonio nel diritto romano preclassico*, Milano 2001, pp. 9–54, p. 188, among others, that the consultation of Marcia's father is more a social than a legal question: if it is true that in this period most marriages were already *sine manu, with* the woman enjoying greater autonomy and greater protection by the praetorium, it is no less true that in practice personal relations were regulated more by custom than by the legal system.

66 Dion Cassius, *Roman History.* 48.44, and Vell. Pat. *Hist.* 2.79.2; 2.94 and 2.95.1. This is a controversial issue because it has been claimed that Augustus married Livia against the will of her husband, Tiberius Claudius.

67 However, in the case of Caligula, it seems that he stole it from her husband, as we have said, on the day of the betrothal.

Regarding the consent of women, whether those who agree to have others conceive due to their infertility or those who agree to become surrogates, it is essential to consider the specific period of time in question, between the late Roman Republic and the early Principate, known as the "golden age" of female emancipation.[68] In early and even later times, their consent was not taken into account when it came to being ceded for procreation. In archaic law, girls were given away at very young ages even before reaching puberty to preserve their virginity. During this time, it does not seem likely that wife cessions were carried out, despite Plutarch, mentioning a *lex regia* attributed to Numa[69] according to which a man who had a sufficient number of children could give his wife to another man who had no offspring, so that he fulfilled his civic duty.[70]

During the period where our cases appear, as previously cited, marriage and divorce were entirely free, representing the peak of women's autonomy in giving their consent to marry or divorce. It is crucial to underline the necessity for their consent, both for women who accept being ceded to other men and those who agree to let their husbands have children with another woman, even if it resulted in divorce. For example, Marcia's case exemplifies the acceptance of her role as a dutiful citizen when she agrees to marry Hortensius, even though no one asks for her consent. Furthermore, after Hortensius's death, she remarries Cato, seemingly without holding any resentments.[71] Livia's loyalty to Augustus is beyond doubt, as they were married for over 40 years, and Poppea Sabina's interest in being close to Nero is evident. As for Emilia, little can be said since she died during childbirth shortly after marrying Pompey.

4. The fourth requirement refers to the need for the parties to divorce before the cession takes place.

From the woman's perspective on being ceded, the legal framework in which it was done could be by two means: (1) Without divorcing, thus remaining married

68 Núñez Paz, "Sobre la cessio ventris en la antigua Roma. Transcendencia socio jurídica del principio "mater sempre certa est," cit., p. 17.

69 *Ligurco-Numae*. 3.1.2 y 4.1.2.

70 *Cf.* on the assignment of the wife in earlier times, De Simone, "Sulle tracce di una antica prassi," cit., pp. 9–54.

71 Marcia had inherited a fortune from her second husband, Hortensius, and according to Caesar this was the reason why Cato took her back in marriage. Plutarch, *Cato Minor* 52.6. *Although it* has been argued that it was because of the political enmity between the two. Cf. E. Cantarella, *Pasado Próximo. Roman women from Tacitus to Sulpicia*, cit., p. 147.

to the husband ceding her to another man, without losing the "*manus*" or authority over her,[72] and once the purpose is achieved, she may or may not be recovered by her original husband, or (2) Divorcing him, as in the cases we have reviewed.

(1) Regarding the first aspect, Plutarch text, *Comp. Lyc et Numae*, 3.1.2, refers to the regal law attributed to Numa, where a husband who already had children was granted the ability to either permanently leave his wife in the hands of a new husband or reclaim her. A very ancient practice that likely did not persist.

A passage in the Digest also mentions that if the woman returns to the same husband, the marriage remains intact (D. 23.2.33; *Marc., 3 ad leg. Iul. et Pap.*). However, it notes that not much time should have passed, and neither party should have married someone else afterward. In my opinion, this may not align perfectly with the cases of wife cession we are analyzing, but it does show it was a common practice.

As we previously underlined, in the case of daughters, the *paterfamilias* could interrupt their marriage (*abducere filiam*), and the possibility that the woman may not divorce and later be reclaimed, proves that these are marriages *cum manu*[73] where the husband's power extends beyond the divorce itself.[74]

(2) Perhaps in a remote time, these practices were allowed, mainly during the archaic era when divorce was infrequent and contrary to social morality. However, in the pre-classical period, as social morality relaxed, and divorce became more frequent, particularly among the upper classes, the general

---

72 This is a similar case to when children were ceded as labor force *in mancipium* to another family, as stated in the Law of the XII Tables. M. De Simone, "Sulle tracce di una antica prassi," cit., p. 27, hypothesizes that the way of carrying out the cession for earlier times would be by means of a *mancipatio fidi fiduciae causa*: the divorce takes place and the woman contracts a new marriage with the aim of procuring offspring for the new husband. Once this objective has been achieved, the new husband can remarry her and divorce her according to the fiduciary agreements reached during the marriage.

73 This is a controversial issue among Romanists: they consider that it is a question of marriages *sine manu*, J. Gaudemet, "Observations sur la manus," in *Etudes de Droit Romain,* Napoli 1979, pp. 338, 345; PIRO, *Usu in manu convenire*, Napoli 1994, p. 93 et seq. 345; M. Against De Simone, "Sulle tracce di una antica prassi," cit., p. 27.

74 C. Fayer, *La familia romana, Parte terza: Concubinato, Divorzio e Adulterio*, Roma 2005, p. 82.

trend was for the woman who was ceded to divorce her husband but always after the future husband, or intended father, requested the cession. Therefore, it is not a spontaneous act by the husband but rather the result of a proposal from a third party (in the case of Marcia, proposed by Hortensius, in the case of Livia, Livia Orestilla, and Poppea Sabina, at the request of Augustus, Caligula, and Nero, respectively. About Emilia, we do not know anything, although it could be assumed that it was the same). This proposal was made through reflection and considering the benefits this cession would bring, either to fulfill the desire to become a father or, as more commonly in the late Republic and early Principate, to fulfill the State's duty resulting from the institution of marriage.

Hence, from the woman's perspective, she usually divorced her husband, and from the future husband's perspective (intended or commissioning father), as noted in the mentioned cases, a divorce from their first wife also took place, although the sources are not explicit on this matter.

In the case of Marcia and Cato, there were two divorces (Hortensius-Lucia and Cato-Marcia) and two marriages (Marcia-Hortensius and later Marcia-Cato); in the case of Livia and Augustus, two divorces too (Livia-Tiberius Claudius and Augustus-Escribonia)[75] and one marriage (Augustus-Livia[76]). In Emilia's case, two divorces (hers with Glabrion and Pompey-Antisia) and one marriage (Emilia-Pompey). In the case of Otho and Poppea, Poppea technically did not divorce Nero,[77] but a sort of marriage was celebrated with Otho. As for Caligula, there was a divorce (Pisone-Livia Orestilla) and a marriage (Caligula-Livia Orestilla).

5. It is important to emphasize the need for a woman's cession to take place within marriage. In fact, Roman women were obliged to have sexual relations only with their husbands, and they could be accused of adultery if they were married, or of *stuprum* if they were not.[78] From Augustus' legislation onwards, the number of women with whom one could marry is notably

75 It should not be forgotten that Augustus had been married to Claudia before.

76 Coincidentally, the marriage of Augustus and Livia is celebrated onthe same day as the birth of Julia Major, the daughter of Augustus and his former wife.

77 In Nero's case there is a divorce (Nero-Octavia) and a marriage (Poppea-Crispino) and a marriage (Nero-Poppea).

78 This is understood as the sexual intercourse of a virgin or widow. D. 50.16.101pr. (*Mod. l. 9 Diff.*) Cf. On the subject P. Panero Oria, *Ius occidendi et Ius Accusandi en la Lex Iulia de Adulteriis coercendis*, Valencia 2001, p. 53.

> restricted: certain unions were prohibited—*Lex Iulia et Papia Poppaea*—and not only were certain extramarital relations declared illicit—*Lex Iulia de adulteriis*—with certain types of women, but a category was established within them, with whom *stuprum* could not be committed and therefore, with whom thus, a *iustum matrimonium* could not be entered.

For a legitimate marriage (*iustum*) to take place, specific requirements must be fulfilled[79]: the existence of *conubium* between the man and the woman[80] their natural capacity to contract[81] and, the consent,[82] of the parties involved, as well as their *patresfamiliae* permission if necessary. When all of these conditions are met, we can speak of a *iustum matrimonium.* A direct consequence is the legitimation of the children, who, being procreated within these marriages, follow the status of the father from the moment of conception.[83] This leads to the well-known principle of Paulus *pater vero is est quem nuptiae demonstrant,* also cited by Celsus in D. 1.5.19 (*29 ad Ed.*).[84]

In contrast, the illegitimate children follow the mother's status from birth. In some cases, they may not even be considered as children; for example, if they are the result of a concubinage relationship they were called *spurii,* but if they were born to a single mother, they were referred to as *vulgo concepti.*[85] These children have no kinship ties with anyone and are *sui iuris* from birth, as the mother

79 Collected in the *Tituli ex Corpore Ulpiani* 5.2.

80 Let the woman be *viri potens* and the man pubescent.

81 The consent of the man and the woman is embodied in the intention to contract—*affectio maritalis,* which is indispensable for the existence of marriage.

82 It should be noted that in Rome, for legal purposes, the most relevant moment is the moment of conception, not the moment of birth.

83 *Quum legitimae nuptiae factae sint, patrem liberi sequuntur.*

84 The names given to these children willchange throughout the ages, and they are generally considered illegitimate in the *ius commune.* As A. Torrent, *Diccionario de Derecho Romano,* voz *filius,* Madrid 2005, cit., p. 367, makes clear, in Rome the modern distinction between legitimate and illegitimate filiation, or matrimonial or non-matrimonial, cannot be applied *strictu sensu,* but in any case, the Roman jurists noted different categories of children, with different attributions of rights to each of the categories, being able to equate the iusti with the legitimate ones.

85 For these *filii to become iusti* it is decisive that the mother marries, and only in the case of concubinage can the children *subsequens matrimonium* be legitimized, C.Th. 4.6.2–3.

cannot hold *potestas,* nor do they have agnatic ties. From Constantine onwards, this type of filiation began to be taken into account for inheritance purposes.[86]

Returning to legitimate children, law and society had a very dignified role for women with offspring, but always within marriage. This translates into a series of social and legal prerogatives. However, unmarried women of a certain age or married women with no children are given almost no social consideration, since they are seen as not having contributed to the common interest.[87]

Indeed, just as women's sterility and that of men, was punished,[88] motherhood—and fatherhood—was rewarded,[89] especially in the time of Augustus, who, through a very strict marriage policy[90] sought to encourage marriages and the procreation of Roman citizens born of legitimate marriages, in order to restore ancient Roman values.[91]

In this context the concept of *uxoris cessio* is understood as the cession of a wife by her husband. If the Roman husband, had a sufficient number of children and another man desired to have offspring, the husband would separate from his wife and cede her to the other man so that they could marry and have children together.

---

86 Cf. on the scarce social visibility of unmarried women, in Mª C. Lázaro Guillamón, "Redescubriendo a las mujeres de la antigua Roma: los derechos sucesorios de la mujer soltera en el derecho romano arcaico y preclásico," *RIDROM* 23 (2019), pp. 228–272, p. 229.

87 Thus the *caelibes*—unmarried—were punished, first by the censors, and then by the laws of Augustus, which provided that they were incapable of acquiring inheritances or legacies deferred in their favor. *Gaius*, I., 2.286.

88 Those who had three children in Rome, four in Italy and five in the provinces were exempted from certain burdens. Males were granted access to public office before the age of majority, and women were *granted ius liberorum*, which freed them from male guardianship and allowed them access to the property of which they were heirs or legatees only if they had three or four children.

89 It consists of three well-known laws: the *Lex Iulia de maritandis ordinibus* (18 BC), the *Lex Iulia et Papia Poppaea nuptalis* (9 BC), and the *Lex Iulia de Adulteris Coercendis*, possibly published between the two previous ones.

90 P. Panero Oria, *Ius Occidendi et Ius Accusandi in the Lex Iulia de adulteris coercendis*, cit.

91 E. Cantarella, *Pasado Próximo. Roman women from Tacitus to Sulpicia*, cit., pp. 157ff., refers to these women as *ventres,* extending by metonymy the term assigned to the continent, to the content. In fact, *venter* is first of all the foetus in the womb, and the Italian author extends it to the pregnant woman.

6. The last and arguably most important requirement for *uxoris cessio* to occur is that the women being ceded (our surrogate mothers-to-be), must already be pregnant.[92]

This happened with all the women mentioned. They were pregnant before being ceded: Marcia was pregnant when she was given to Hortensius, resulting in one of the children from that marriage being Cato's. Livia was pregnant with her second child, Drusus, when she was given to Augustus, and Emilia married Pompey while pregnant. As for Poppea Sabina and Livia Orestilla, the sources are not exact, but there is no indication that they were pregnant, which leads to doubts about whether they were actually part of the practice of ceding wives. Nevertheless, Caligula, desperate for an heir after divorcing Livia Orestilla, married Milonia Cesoria, a very prolific commoner who had three children and was pregnant. It is said that on the very day of the wedding, she gave birth to a girl, Julia Drusilla, which further supports the Roman custom of marrying pregnant women.

It seems Romans not only ceded their wives but also did when they were already pregnant. However, there seems to be no doubt regarding the child's paternity who were mostly considered to be the legitimate children of the intended fathers.

Traditionally, paternity has always been surrounded by doubts and uncertainties, which are resolved in the second part of the well-known text by Paulus: *Pater vero is est quem nuptiae demonstrant* (D. 2.4.5; *Paul. 4 ad Ed.*), meaning that marriage grants the husband the status of father.[93] Indeed, children born within marriage, in addition to inheriting the status of the father from the moment of conception, are considered legitimate (*iusti*),[94] therefore, marriage is the most common form of filiation, resulting in the direct subjection of the children (*filii*) to the *patria potestas* of the father. In the ancient times, children conceived

92 As T. Duplá, "El presente del pasado: el principio mater semper certa est y su reflejo en la actual legislación sobre reproducción humana asistida," *RIDROM* 1/22 (2019), pp. 289–325, pp. 292 and 293, states, it is only true, in principle, in the case of marriage; and this idea, which seems to extend and consolidate in the mind of Roman jurisprudence, is taken up by the Justinian compilers. Gaius states, *qui nascuntur, patris, non matris familiam sequuntur*, and Ulpianus, in D. 50.16.196.1 (*16 ad Ed. Prov.*) in speaking of the *status libertatis*, notes, *conubio interueniente liberi semper patrem sequuntur.*

93 Ulpian in D. 1.1.6 (*9 Sab.*).

94 The concept of family *proprio iure* should be taken into account, which designates a group of persons who are subject—*quae sunt*—to the same power. D. 50.16.195.2 (*Ulp. 46 ad Ed.*).

within marriage became part of the father's family, as agnatic kinship was based on the authority of the *paterfamilias* and was transmitted solely through the male line. When this type of kinship gives way to consanguineous kinship, women, who until now were not considered family to their own children[95] or to their ancestors or collateral relatives, were also legally considered family. However, they still could not exercise *patria potestas* over their descendants,[96] and could only opt for a kind of *moral auctoritas* over them, a merely fictitious tie without any legal content, which continued to be held by the husband.[97]

Despite the fact that *auctoritas* was recognized in Rome for respectable and dignified people, such as senators or jurists, the sources show numerous testimonies of women with *auctoritas* carrying out functions related to education and moral values[98] all of them from the upper social class, such as matrons or vestals. This reveals that only certain women endowed with that *auctoritas* could be ceded for such purposes. They were women of a certain social status, capable of bearing children, but always within marriage,[99]

Children born out of wedlock followed the status of the mother, being considered *spurii or vulgo concepti*, depending on whether they were the result of a stable union such as concubinage or if the father was uncertain. In some cases, as Ulpianus states, they do not even deserve the name of *filius*[100] (son). The reference point for their status is the moment of birth, and they follow the condition of the mother, making them *sui iuris* and taking the mother's *nomen*.

95 Neither tobe guardians of their own children, nor to adopt, as they are the beginning and end of their own family.

96 Mothers are limited to fulfilling their reproductive and educating mission for their children: they must look after them and feed them, and transmit patriarchal values to them and continue to exercise their *munium matris*, I. Núñez Paz, "Auctoritas y mujeres romanas ¿ejercicio o sumisión?," *Arenal, Revista de Historia de las mujeres* 22/2 (2015), pp. 352–356.

97 D. 43.30.3 (*Ulp. 71 ad Ed.*), when speaking of mothers, it is understood that they are women of recognized authority.

98 In relation to Roman matrons, the term has been identified with that of *materfamilias, a* term which, as I have already pointed out in another work, Roman doctrine has not gone into much depth in this area. P., Panero Oria, *Ius Occidendi*, cit.: (1) woman subject to the family or authority of the husband; (2) woman *sui iuris*, (3) woman who lives *non inhonestate*, according to the *boni mores*. It is in the latter meaning that our matrons are to be found, or, as is clear from the sources, who lives according to the customs appropriate to the position of the matron. Cf., D. 50. 16.46.1 (*Ulp. 59 ad Ed*).

99 *Ep. Ulp*. V. 7 and 8.

100 D.38.16.3.11 and 12 (*Ulp. 10 ad Sab.*).

Therefore, the presumptions *iuris tantum* of paternity in favor of the husband, becomes decisive, taking as starting point the nine months that a pregnancy usually lasts. According to these presumptions, children born after 182 days following the celebration of marriage are considered to be fathered by the husband, as well as those born before 300 days following the dissolution of the marriage.[101]

The fact that the legitimacy of offspring depends on whether the mother is married or not determines the *tempus lugendi* that the widow must respect first and the divorced woman later in order to avoid *turbatio sanguinis* and to eliminate any doubt about the father's identity for filiation purposes, by controlling the time that must elapse between marriages with different men.

Returning to the cases we have been analyzing, none of the sources refer to the need to respect this *tempus lugendi*. In my opinion, the reason is clear: since the women who are ceded are already pregnant[102] there is no need to avoid *turbatio sanguinis* because it is perfectly known who the legitimate father of those children is or will be.

All of this takes us to affirm that these new husbands, to whom the women are ceded, are not biological fathers but rather intended or commissioning fathers. However, this does not prevent the legitimacy of these children: they are accepted as if they were their own, exercising paternal authority over them, and thus becoming *filii* through the acceptance by the father, the last requirement for legitimization by birth. Regarding acceptance, let us recall the ancient *tollere liberos* ceremony, consisting of showing the newborn child to the *pater* so that he would lift the baby, taking it into his arms and thus demonstrating his recognition as *filiusfamilias*.[103] If it was a girl, it was necessary to order that she was nourished—*iubere alere*—to be recognized.

Otherwise, the father could exercise the *ius exponendi*. Constantine (in 331) banned this power and penalized those fathers who abandoned their children by revoking their parental authority. Subsequent emperors criminally punished the abandonment of children, who, if not taken in by someone else, could easily die of starvation.[104]

---

101 Whether of the first husbands, or of the new husbands, as has been hypothesized, for example, in the case of Augustus.

102 It is a figure found in literary sources, which is not very clear and which has given rise to doctrinal controversy, cf., for example, A. Torrent, *Diccionario*, cit., voz *tollere liberos*, p. 1392.

103 C. Th.9.5.1 and C. 8.5.1.2.

104 *Laudatio Turiae* I, 37–39, FIRA, III (*negotia*), Florence, 1953. Cf. R. Mentxaca, "Turia. Un ejemplo de mulier fortis romana," in *Mujeres en tiempos de Augusto. Realidad social*

In my opinion, these non-biological fathers legitimize their children through what is now called "possession of status" by meeting the required criteria: *nomen*, *tractatus*, and *reputatio* -through the *tollere liberos*—ceremony. However, if we consider the presumptions of paternity, they likely do not meet the required 180 days for birth. Nevertheless, for filiation to occur, marriage must take place because otherwise, the children would follow the mother's condition.

Certainly, the father will be the man who marries the ceded mother. For example, in the case of Marcia, her third child, despite being conceived by Cato, was born after her marriage to Hortensius and was considered his legitimate child. Another example is Emilia's daughter, who lived and died in Pompey's house. In Augustus case, the two children brought to the marriage by Livia were conceived by Tiberius Claudius, her first husband, although Drusus was born in Augustus's house, it was believed he was Augustus's child, the result of a previous adulterous relationship with Livia.

5. *Mater semper certa est versus mater ea est quam nuptiae demonstrant*

Concluding this work, a final consideration should be taken into account: the fact that these ceded women (pregnant mothers) could, once the purpose was achieved, either stay with the new husband, as in the case of Livia, or go, leaving their biological children under the paternal authority, since it is the husband who determines filiation. In the event they left, they could make way for a new wife (commissioning mother) who, through marriage, would become the mother of those children. Thus, the new wife will exercise *auctoritas* over the children.

An example can be found in Turia, a sterile woman who was willing to accept as her own the children conceived by another woman with her husband. The case is known from the famous *laudatio* delivered by her husband to Quintus Lucretius Vespilon on the occasion of his death in the year IV, during the Augustan era. He praised her as a chaste and respectful woman, she was unable to give her husband a child, and her nobility was such, that she even proposed he divorce her, offering to leave the home to the fertility of another woman and to accept the children he had as her own, a proposal that her husband rejected.[105]

---

e imposición legal, ed. R. Rodríguez López and M. J. Y Bravo Bosch, Valencia 2016, pp. 90–120.

105 In the words of E. Cantarella, *Pasado Próximo. Roman women from Tacitus to Sulpicia*, cit., pp. 151 and 152.

The behavior of Turia's husband is contrasted with that of Cato's, although both cases, in my opinion, follow the same pattern: fixed-term marriages destined to be dissolved once the wife fulfilled her duty, that is, a reproductive strategy of the Roman aristocracy.[106]

The parties in both cases, had surpassed youthful romanticism and held a moderate view of marriage in accordance with the times. Indeed, for Cato, marriage was merely a mean to ensure offspring,[107] and fulfill his duty with the State. Since Marcia had already borne him several children, he considered the social benefit in addition to his affection toward Hortensius and accepted his friend's request ceding his fertile wife[108] and divorcing her.

In the case of Turia, we find ourselves before a matron of high social standing, known for her great generosity, who considers giving up her husband in favor of having offspring. By Roman matron, we refer to those women who possess certain virtues such as generosity and *pudicitia*,[109] as well as a sense of duty toward her family and Rome. These women are ideal candidates to carrying out the cession of the wife for reproductive purposes. On the other hand, women who lacked modesty, single mothers or those who belonged to lower social class were not suitable for this purpose, due to their low social status. In fact, the sources do not mention cases related to these women. However, this does not mean that they could not occur, but we must not forget that these cessions during the era in which we are analyzing were driven by the desire to procreate and seek family alliances.

If Turia's proposal had been carried out, we do not know if it would have been a formal -*uxoris cessio*.[110] Still, it fits perfectly with the thesis that Roman Law had something similar to surrogacy. In modern terms Turia would be the commissioning mother, and the woman who would conceive her husband's children would be the surrogate mother. Turia would have accepted the children her husband had with the surrogate mother (after they divorced and only if Turia

106 Lucan 2, 387 ff.

107 Plutarch, *Cato Minor*, 25.1.

108 *Pudicitia* understood as modesty, honesty, chastity, i.e., the modesty that is preached by women. There are a series of offenses against them that have already been sanctioned by the curule aediles.

109 Since this was not done, it can only be hypothesized whether the woman who would have given birth to her husband's children was married or not, or whether she was even already pregnant, which I consider necessary for the *uxoris cessio to* take place.

110 Although hedoes not give them the *nomen,* he would give them the *tractatus and* the *reputatio.*

remarried him), becoming the mother of her husband's children, as the father determines filiation.

Turia would have become the intended or commissioning mother, and her husband the biological father. She would have been the mother through marriage, or even, as we said at the beginning through the so-called possession of status,[111] proving that the mother is the one who is married to the father, although she does not exercise parental authority.

Taking it a step further, based on the examples provided by the sources, and if Turia's husband had married a woman who was already pregnant, becoming a commissioning father through marriage, once he remarried Turia, she would become the intended or commissioning mother.

When the commissioning mother accepts the children, they cease to belong to the biological mother's and become the children of the receiving mother, but only if she is married to the father (biological or not) of the children.

Nowadays, many authors,[112] uphold that surrogacy challenges the traditional principles of Roman Law such as *mater semper certa est* and *pater vero is est quem nuptiae demostrant.*[113] While both principles have taken different paths throughout history, the fact that cases of surrogacy were already documented in Roman experience implies: (a) The certainty of the mother may be called into question, suggesting that is not an entirely new concept in our positive law and (b) The notion that the father is the one proven by marriage may be further affirmed.

---

111 Cf. on the subject M. T. Duplá Marín, "El principio Mater semper certa est, ¿a Debate? La nueva legislación sobre reproducción asistida y sus consecuencias," in *FUNDAMENTA IURIS. Terminologia, principios e interpretatio*, Almería 2012, pp. 309–320.

112 D. 2.4.5 (*Paul. lib. IV ad Ed.*) since (a) it allows the separation of the fact of having children from the complementarity between the man and the woman necessary to conceive, (b) it contemplates the possibility of being able to procreate without the biological-genetic participation of the couple and/or without their knowledge, and (c) it raises problems of filiation since there can be cases of double or even triple filiation, as in the case of one woman commissioning the baby, another carrying it, and a third woman donating her gametes.

113 D. 2.4.5 (*Paul. lib. IV ad Ed*), (a) allows for the separation of the act of having children from the complementarity between a man and a woman necessary for conception; (b) contemplates the possibility of procreation without the biological-genetic involvement of the couple and/or without their knowledge; and (c) raises issues of filiation, as it can lead to cases of double or even triple filiation. An example of this would be a situation where one woman commissions the baby, another woman carries the pregnancy, and a third woman donates her gametes.

It has been said time and again that while maternity is certain, paternity is uncertain. However, throughout this journey, we have analyzed situations that demonstrate precisely the opposite, allowing us to conclude that in certain cases, based on the examples we have seen, *mater ea est quam nuptiae demonstrant* applies, not only to the one who gives birth.

And so we see that the same question that was mentioned in the beginning of this paper, and which the Spanish Supreme Court has currently settled, namely, whether or not there is a filiation bond between a woman and a child born to another woman, raised from Roman Law, can be resolved differently, that is, affirming that such bond can indeed exist between a woman and a child born to another woman, since the mother is the one who marries the father.

Perhaps this relationship -which in Rome, let us not forget, is merely factual- was based on something similar to the possession of state: those mothers who were comitents, after all, took care of the care of those children, of their feeding and education, establishing between them a true paternal-filial relationship, which although originated as a consequence of marriage, since as we have seen Roman Law does not accept any other type of filiation, creates between them a true de facto filiation by *possession.*[114]

Bibliography

Literature

Álvarez González, S., "Gestación por sustitución y Tribunal Supremo español: Nota breve a la STS de 31 de marzo de 2022", *Diario La Ley*, n. 10.069, Sección Tribuna, 16 May 2022.

Cantarella, E., *Pasado Próximo. Roman women from Tacitus to Sulpicia.* Colección Feminismos, 1996.

Cantarella, E., Matrimonio e sessualità nella Roma repubblicana: una storia romana di amore coniugale, Firenze 2005.

Castán, S., "El matrimonio como estrategia en la carrera política durante el último tramo de la república", *RIDROM,* 7 (2015), pp. 1-59.

114 Certainly, if we allow the comparison and playing with the analogy of possession, while recognizing the differences, the three required elements for possession would be present: the *corpus* (the child), the *animus* (or intention to recognize it as one's own), and the *Iusta Causa* (marriage).

Castán, S., "El papel de la mujer romana en la política del s. I. a. C. ¿influencia política, participación indirecta o influencia social?," RIDROM 24 (2020), pp. 540–601.

De Simone, M., "Sulle tracce di un'antica prassi: la c.d. cessione della moglie" *Annali del seminario giuridico dell'Università degli studi di Palermo* AUPA, vol. 44 (2010-2011), pp. 9-54.

De Simone, M., "Una congettura sull'arcaico filiam abducere," Annali del seminario giuridico dell'università degli studi di Palermo (AUPA) 55 (2012), pp. 321–384.

Duplá Marín, M.T, "El principio Mater semper certa est, ¿a Debate? La nueva legislación sobre reproducción asistida y sus consecuencias," in FUNDAMENTA IURIS. Terminologia, principios e interpretatio, Almería 2012, pp. 309–320.

Duplá Marín, M.T., "El presente del pasado: el principio mater semper certa est y su reflejo en la actual legislación sobre reproducción humana asistida," RIDROM 1/22 (2019), pp. 289–325.

Fayer, C., La famiglia romana. Parte terza: Concubinato, Divorzio e adulterio, Roma 2015.

Franciosi, G., *Famiglia e persone in Roma antica. Dall'etá arcaica al principato,* Torino, 1992.

Fernández Baquero, Mª E., Repudium-Divortium (Origen y configuración jurídica hasta la legislación matrimonial de Augusto), Granada 1987.

Fernández Baquero, M.E., "La cesión de la mujer con fines de procreación según la concepción de la familia romana arcaica y preclásica", *Revista de la facultad de Derecho de la Universidad de Granada,* 4, 201, (2001), pp. 273-298.

García Fernández, C., "Edad, salud y capacidad adquisitiva en la formación de los diferentes tipos de familia. La cesión del *venter*" in *Mujer sujeto u objeto de derechos reproductivos. Derecho de los menores y maternidad por sustitución,* Valencia, 2019.

Gaudemet, J., "Observations sur la manus" in *Etudes de Droit Romain,* Napoli, 1979.

Lázaro Guillamón, M.C., "Redescubriendo a las mujeres de la antigua Roma: los derechos sucesorios de la mujer soltera en el derecho romano arcaico y preclásico," RIDROM 23 (2019), pp. 228–272

Muelas, Mª D., *La sentencia del Supremo sobre gestación subrogada refuerza el acceso a la adopción por parte de los comitentes.* (s. f.). AEFA, https://www.aeafa.es/noticias-ampliadas/2429/2/la-sentencia-del-supremo-sobre-gestacin-subrogada-refuerza-el-acceso-a-la-adopcin-por-parte-de-los-comitentes/.

Navarro Michel, M., “La filiación derivada de gestación por sustitución: posesión de estado e interés del menor, orden público y derechos fundamentales”, *Rev. Bioética y Derecho* [online]. 2022, n. 56.pp. 4-28.

<http://scielo.isciii.es/scielo.php?script=sci_arttext&pid=S188658872022000300004&lng=es&nrm=iso>. Epub 26-Jun-2023. https://dx.doi.org/10.1344/rbd2022.56.40741.

Robleda, O., *El matrimonio en Derecho Romano. Esencia, requisitos de validez, efectos, disolubilidad,* Roma, 1970,

Núñez Paz, I., Matrimonio y divorcio en Roma, Salamanca 1988.

Nuñez Paz, I., “Progresivo y limitado reconocimiento de la figura materna en el Derecho Romano. De la cesión del vientre al ejercicio de la tutela” in *Madres y maternidades. Construcciones culturales en la civilización clásica,* Oviedo, 2009, pp. 255-291.

Núñez Paz, I., “Auctoritas y mujeres romanas ¿ejercicio o sumisión?,” Arenal, Revista de Historia de las mujeres 22/2 (2015), pp. 352–356.

Nuñez Paz, I., “On *cessio ventris* in ancient Rome. Transcendencia socio-jurídica del principio *mater semper certa est”, e-Legal History Review* (2018), pp. 49-66.

Nuñez Paz, I., “La *voluntas* de las madres comitentes *versus* el *uterus* de las madres gestantes”, pp 23-52, in *Mujer sujeto u objeto de derechos reproductivos,* ed. L. SUÁREZ LLANOS, L., Valencia, 2019.

Panero Oria, P., Ius occidendi et Ius Accusandi en la Lex Iulia de Adulteriis coercendis, Valencia 2001.

Panero Oria, P., “Surrogacy; A regression to a patriarchal society free of social policies?”, *Journal of Modern Science,* (2019), 40, 1, pp. 115-124.

P Panero Oria, “‘Precedentes de la Gestación por sustitución,’ Fundamentos romanísticos del Derecho Contemporáneo,” BOE VII (2021), pp. 2045–2054, A locatio conductio. Influência nois direitos actuáis, Oporto 2018, pp. 787–795.

Piro, D., *Usu in manu convenire*, Napoli, 1994.

Torrent, A., Diccionario de Derecho Romano, Madrid 2005.

Mentxaca, R., “Turia. Un ejemplo de mulier fortis romana,” in Mujeres en tiempos de Augusto. Realidad social e imposición legal, ed. R. Rodríguez López and M. J. Bravo Bosch, Valencia 2016.

Law 14/2006, of 26 May, on assisted human reproduction techniques (LRTHA)

Case of Law

Spanish Suprem Court, STS 835/2013 6 February 2014.

Spanish Suprem Court, STS no. 45/2022 January 27.
Spanish Suprem Court, STS 277/2022, 31 March 2022.
Audiencia Provincial de Madrid, ST de 1 Decembre 2020.
Audiencia Provincial de Barcelona, ST 06 April 2021.
Audiencia Provincial de Navarre, ST de 25 March 2022
Audiencia Provincial Balearic Islands, ST 27 April 2021.

Act of Law

Spanish Civil Code
Law 14/2006, of May 26, on assisted human reproduction techniques

Małgorzata Eysymontt

Application for the Court's authorisation to perform, on behalf of a minor, an act exceeding the scope of ordinary administration of the child's property in the light of Polish law: Practical remarks

Abstract: The scope of parental authority is defined broadly—it includes the duty and right of the parents to exercise custody over the child's person and property and to bring up the child, respecting the child's dignity and rights, as well as the child's representation. The administration of the child's property refers to the total assets and liabilities belonging to the child but does not include the child's non-property matters and person. Parents are obliged to manage the property of a child under their parental authority with due diligence. In certain cases, the administration of the child's property suffers significant restrictions. Pursuant to art. 101 § 3 of the Polish Family and Guardianship Code, parents may not, without the authorization of the guardianship court, perform acts exceeding the scope of ordinary administration or consent to the child performing such acts. Actions exceeding the scope of ordinary administration have not been defined or typified. They are measured by the gravity of the activity, its effects on the minor's property, the value of the subject of the activity and the broadly understood welfare of the child and the protection of his or her life interests. They include, *inter alia*, rejection of an inheritance, withdrawal of a considerable amount of money by a parent from the child's bank account, conclusion of an agreement or waiver of a claim. The performance of such acts by a parent requires the prior consent of the guardianship court, under pain of nullity. An application for the court's authorisation to perform such an act may be submitted by one or both parents, must meet the formal requirements set out by law and must be consistent with the minor's welfare. It is ruled on in non-contentious (non-procedural proceeedings).

Keywords: parental authority, court authorization, administration of the child's property, acts beyond the ordinary administration of the child's property

1. Introduction

The purpose of this article is to characterize the institution of court authorization of an act by the parents which exceeds the ordinary administration of the child's property, from the perspective of the child's welfare and respect for the child's legal subjectivity. As a research hypothesis, it was stated that in proceedings concerning the court's authorisation for parents to carry out on behalf of a minor an act that exceeds the scope of ordinary administration of the child's property, special consideration is required for the minor's welfare, which should consequently have the effect of increasing his or her participation in such proceedings, for example, by changing his or her status from that of a third party to that of a participant. In order to verify such a hypothesis, the article poses the following research questions:

1. Should the role of the court be reduced to the minimum necessary in carrying out *ex ante* control of the acts performed by parents on behalf of their minor children? Should there be more decision-making autonomy for parents in this regard?
2. Should the catalogue of acts considered by the law to be outside the scope of ordinary administration of the child's property be clarified so as to indicate examples of them, if only by using the wording "in particular"?
3. What is the participation of a minor in proceedings for court authorisation to carry out an act on behalf of a minor which exceeds the scope of ordinary administration of the child's property? Should evidence of a hearing of the minor be mandatory in such proceedings?
4. In the event of the death of one of the parents, should the participation of a court guardian in proceedings for court authorization to carry out an act on behalf of a minor which exceeds the scope of ordinary administration of the child's property be mandatory or is it unnecessary?

The legal analysis covers the legal provisions of the laws in force in Poland, that is, the Family and Guardianship Code, the Civil Code and the Code of Civil Procedure, as well as numerous views of the doctrine (commentaries to selected provisions and monographs) and the judicature. The study used a number of research methods, in particular the descriptive method, the theoretical-legal method and the dogmatic-legal method, which served to characterize and analyze the legal provisions concerning the issue in question, based on the available views of doctrine and jurisprudence.

2. Attributes of parental authority

The legislator has devoted the issue of parental authority to the provisions of Articles 92–112 of the Polish Family and Guardianship Code[1] (hereinafter

1 Act of February 25, 1964 Family and Guardianship Code (consolidated text: Dz. U. (*Journal of Laws*) of 2020, item 1359, as amended: https://isap.sejm.gov.pl/isap.nsf/

also: "FGC"). This notion does not have a legal definition, but instead finds clarification in the judicature and doctrine. The Supreme Court emphasizes that it follows from the entirety of the provisions of the Family and Guardianship Code that parental authority "constitutes a set of duties and rights in relation to the child aimed at ensuring his/her due care and guarding his/her interests."[2] The doctrine also points out that parental authority, constitutes "one of the most important legal institutions, regulated in the Family and Guardianship Code," which "plays a key role in determining the rights and obligations between parents and children," and its content "is determined by the supreme principle of family law, which is the principle of the welfare of the child."[3]

The concept of parental authority refers to the relationship of parents toward children. Indeed, according to art. 92 FGC, a child remains under parental authority until the age of majority. At the same time, the jurisprudence indicates: "The age of majority only sets the upper temporal limit of parental authority. In exceptional cases, for reasons dependent on or beyond the control of the parents, this authority may cease before the child reaches the age of majority (for example, as a result of the court withdrawing parental authority, the child being adopted by another person or the death of the minor). With the termination of parental authority, the right and obligation to bring up the child automatically ceases, irrespective of the child's age."[4]

According to art. 10 § 1 of the Civil Code[5] (hereinafter also: "CC"), as a general rule, a person over the age of majority is a person who has attained 18 years of age. However, a minor (only women) also comes of age through marriage, the status of which does not disappear if the marriage is annulled (art. 10 § 2 CC) or terminated for other reasons, such as death of the spouse or divorce.[6] Indeed, the guardianship court may "for important reasons" allow a woman who has reached

---

download.xsp/WDU19640090059/U/D19640059Lj.pdf).

2 Order of the Supreme Court of May 5, 2000, II CKN 761/00, LEX no. 51982.

3 A. Pośpiech, "Commentary to art. 95 FCG," in *Kodeks rodzinny i opiekuńczy. Komentarz*, ed. M. Fras and M. Habdas, Warsaw 2021.

4 Judgment of the Provincial Administrative Court in Warsaw of February 25, 2020, II SA/Wa 2038/19, LEX no. 3015103.

5 Act of April 23, 1964 Civil Code (consolidated text: Dz. U. (*Journal of Laws*) of 2022, item 1360, as amended: https://isap.sejm.gov.pl/isap.nsf/download.xsp/WDU19640160093/U/D19640093Lj.pdf).

6 T. Sokołowski, "Commentary to art. 10 CC," in *Kodeks cywilny. Komentarz. Tom I. Część ogólna*, wyd. II (II ed.), ed. A. Kidyba, Warsaw 2012.

the age of 16 to marry when the circumstances show that the marriage will be compatible with the good of the established family (art. 10 § 1 sent. 2 FGC).

As a general rule, (full) parental authority is vested in both parents (art. 93 § 1 FGC), however, if the child's best interests so require, the court, in its judgment establishing the child's parentage, may rule on the suspension, restriction or termination of parental authority of one or both parents (art. 93 § 2 FGC). This may also occur as a result of divorce (art. 58 § 1-1a and 112 FGC) or separation (art. 61^3 § 1 and 112 FGC), as well as during the marriage and during or when the parents of children from non-formalized unions separate (art. 107 and 110–111 FGC). The above is confirmed by the case law according to which "The content of parental authority is different from its exercise, and the mere possession of parental authority does not imply its exercise. (…) Exercise of parental authority means that the parent is personally involved in the child's affairs. It involves the exercise of all the duties that will ensure that the child is brought up in a way that ensures his or her proper development. Parental authority should be exercised by both parents, but it may happen that, due to various circumstances, the exercise of parental authority is entrusted to one parent without depriving the other parent of parental rights."[7]

The scope of parental authority is broad, encompassing an open catalogue of parental duties and powers, referred to in the literature as attributes of parental authority. Pursuant to art. 95 § 1 FGC, parental authority includes, in particular the duty and right of parents to exercise custody over the child's person and property and to bring up the child, with respect for the child's dignity and rights. On the one hand, a child under parental authority owes obedience to the parents and, in matters in which he or she can make decisions and declarations of intent independently, should listen to the opinions and recommendations of the parents formulated for his or her good (art. 95 § 2 FGC). At the same time, parental authority should be exercised in such a way as the child's best interests and the public interest require (art. 95 § 3 FGC). On the other hand, before making decisions on major matters concerning the child's person or property, the parents should listen to the child, if the child's mental development, state of health and degree of maturity so permit, and take the child's reasonable wishes into account as far as possible (art. 95 § 4 FGC). According to well-established case law, among the parental duties and powers (referred to as "the totality of the child's affairs"), three important groups of them can be distinguished: firstly, the

7 Judgment of the Provincial Administrative Court in Warsaw of November 10, 2005, II SA/Wa 1475/05, LEX no. 192582.

so-called custody of the person of the child, secondly, the administration of the child's property (to which this article is devoted) and thirdly, the representation of the child, whereby it is for the parents, in particular, to give the child's upbringing a fundamental direction.[8]

The first essential element of parental authority is the custody (called custody in the science of psychology) of the child, which is the so-called personal element of parental authority.[9] It is regulated in art. 96 § 1 FGC, according to which the parents not only bring up and direct the child under their parental authority but are also obliged to take care of the physical and spiritual development of the child and prepare him/her duly for work for the good of society in accordance with his/her talents. The case law points out that "Parental authority, by its very nature, exhibits, as a subjective right, special characteristics. Its essential characteristic is that its attributes are both a duty of the parents and its primary purpose is a protective function toward the child. Satisfying the child's natural and fundamental need to be in contact with his or her parents is part of the parents' concern for the child (custody)."[10] The jurisprudence emphasizes that the custody of the person of the child first and foremost includes the upbringing of the child, the management of the child, the provision of suitable living conditions, the care of the child's health and safety, and the upbringing of the child "thus amounts to deciding on all educational matters relating to the person of the child, including, e.g., secular, religious upbringing, along with the choice of religion, the formation of the child's ethics and character, diligence, conscientiousness, etc. (…) It is also necessary to take into account the protection of the child from the bad influences of the environment of both other children and adults, e.g. drug abuse, paedophilia, etc. No less important is the preparation of the child for social life. Parents also have a duty to provide the child with appropriate living conditions and to strive for the child's mental and physical health. (…) The child's duty of upbringing includes caring for the child's physical and spiritual development,

8 Resolution of the SN(CI) of 9.06.1976, III CZP 46/75, OSNC 1976, no. 9, item 184.
9 M. Stępień, "Atrybuty władzy rodzicielskiej," in *Prawo wobec wyzwań współczesności. Wybrane problemy teoretycznoprawne i dogmatycznoprawne*. E-Wydawnictwo. Prawnicza i Ekonomiczna Biblioteka Cyfrowa. Wydział Prawa, Administracji i Ekonomii Uniwersytetu Wrocławskiego, ed. J. Helios, W. Jedlecka, and A. Kwieciński, Wrocław 2019, p. 226 - see https://repozytorium.uni.wroc.pl/Content/95905/PDF/20_M_Stepien_Atrybuty_wladzy_rodzicielskiej.pdf (accessed: 10.06.2023).
10 Resolution of the Supreme Court (7) of March 8, 2006, III CZP 98/05, OSNc 2006, no. 10, item 158.

taking into account the child's talents and interests (…)."[11] In doing so, the doctrine emphasizes that the management of a child includes the performance of both factual and legal acts, including determining the child's whereabouts, taking the child away from an unauthorized person or controlling the child's leisure activities.[12]

The second important element of parental authority is the already mentioned administration of the child's property, which is analyzed in detail in this study later on.

The third element of parental authority is the representation of the child by the parents which includes the child's performance of both legal and procedural acts. According to art. 98 FGC, parents are the legal representatives of the child who remains under their parental authority, and if the child remains under parental authority of both parents, then each of them may act independently as the child's legal representative (§ 1). However, neither of them may represent the child in two cases—in legal acts between children under their parental authority and in legal acts between the child and one of the parents or his or her spouse, unless the legal act consists in a gratuitous adoption in favor of the child or concerns maintenance and upbringing owed to the child by the other parent (§ 2). The representation of the child by the parents, is referred to as an "attribute of representation" and a technical legal instrument, with a servile role vis-à-vis the other attributes of parental authority, which enables the parents to take formalized actions concerning their child.[13]

3. Administration of the child's property by the parents

3.1. Child's property

In this study, the main focus is on the sphere of the administration of the child's property by the parents. In this case, it concerns matters of a property nature, that is, exclusively concerning the property and not the person of the child. Pursuant to art. 101 § 1 of the FGC, parents are obliged to exercise due care in the administration of the property of a child under their parental authority. Parents are thus obliged, and at the same time entitled, to exercise custody and property

---

11 Judgment of the Court of Appeal in Szczecin of June 6, 2019, III AUa 30/19, LEX no. 2692946.

12 E. Trybulska-Skoczelas, "Commentary to art. 95 FGC," in *Kodeks rodzinny i opiekuńczy. Komentarz*, ed. J. Wierciński, Warsaw 2014.

13 M. Stępień, ibid., p. 234.

of the child. The child's property should be understood as all the assets and liabilities belonging to the minor, irrespective of the manner in which they were acquired (e.g., through donation or inheritance). The child's property may include both movables and immovable property, as well as capital, funds received as compensation or damages, alimony (however, according to the well-established doctrine, the child's property does not include the right to alimony[14] or originating from competition or lottery winnings, as well as animals[15]).

As indicated above, the parents of a child under their parental authority are obliged to manage the child's property "with due diligence." According to the views of the doctrine, "The measure of due diligence means that the diligence inherent in typical parents in typical social relations, rather than the highest attainable diligence, is sufficient," as "an excessively high measure of diligence could constitute an impediment to the proper exercise and evaluation of the parents' administration," and in turn, "the consequence of failing to exercise due diligence and causing damage to the child's property may be that the parents are liable for damages to the child itself."[16] It is pointed out that this is a "reasonable" and "not excessive measure of diligence" that "prevents possible, and unjustified, disputes between parents living apart who could too easily claim to entrust sole administration to only one of them, merely proving that only one of them is able to increase the profits made from the child's assets."[17] It is worth noting at this point that, according to § 2 of the art. 101 of the FGC, the administration exercised by the parents does not include the child's earnings or objects given to him or her for their free use. The above means that the administration exercised by the parents over the child's property, as a general rule, covers all of the child's property, apart from the child's earnings and objects put at his or her free use (by the parents or third parties, with the parents' consent) (see art 22 CC). At the same time, pursuant to art. 21 CC, for important reasons, the guardianship court may limit or exclude the disposal of earnings by the child as a person with limited legal capacity.

---

14 J. Gwiazdomorski, "Krewni uprawnieni do żądania i obowiązani do dostarczania środków utrzymania," *PiP* 1 (1954), p. 82.

15 As to the administration of animals—see the comments of P. Wicherek, "Commentary to art. 101 FGC," in *Kodeks rodzinny i opiekuńczy. Komentarz*, ed. M. Fras and M. Habdas, Warsaw 2021.

16 P. Wicherek, ibid.

17 T. Sokołowski, "Commentary to the art. 101 FGC," in *Kodeks rodzinny i opiekuńczy. Komentarz*, wyd. II (II ed.), ed. H. Dolecki, Warsaw 2013.

3.2. Factual, legal and procedural acts

The literature expresses the view that the scope of custody of the child's property is broadly construed as including the following elements: the administration of the child's property; the disposition of the pure income from the property; the accounting for the administration of the property; the control of the child's property situation and the prevention of irregularities in the administration by others.[18] According to the judicature, "The administration of the child's property includes factual, legal and procedural actions (in court and administrative proceedings) concerning the objects of the property, their acquisition, encumbrance and disposal."[19] Among representatives of the doctrine, the predominant view is that "The administration of the child's property is all kinds of dispositions and actions relating to individual assets, just as the administration of an object means all kinds of dispositions and actions relating to that object. (…) the administration of the child's property as an aggregate of assets and liabilities, includes behaviour and legal and factual acts affecting the child's property situation in the broadest sense. These are behaviours aimed at the preservation of this property, actions causing its decrease, through the disposal or encumbrance of its components, as well as actions causing the increase of this property, through the acquisition of new property items or reduction of existing encumbrances (…)."[20] The administration of the child's property thus encompasses a broad and genre-diverse catalogue of acts. Firstly, among the *de facto* acts carried out by the parents, one may distinguish, *inter alia*, carrying out repairs or demolishing a building or repairing equipment belonging to the child, changing the use of property (e.g., converting an outbuilding to residential purposes), carrying out acts related to the running of a farm. Secondly, in the case of legal acts, it is in particular the conclusion of various types of contracts in the name and on behalf of the child, for example, purchase, sale, donation, taking out a loan for the renovation of a building, or mortgaging a property. In the case of a wrongful performance of a factual act by a parent related to the administration of the child's property, a possible liability for damages is triggered, while a defectively performed legal act entails the effect of the nullity of such act. Thirdly, in the case of procedural acts undertaken by the parents in relation to the administration of the child's property, that is, acts before the courts or other state or local authorities, particular

18 *Ibid.*
19 Order of the Supreme Court of January 21, 2022, III CZ 21/22.
20 T. Sokołowski, "Commentary to the art. 101 FGC," *op. cit.*

mention should be made of those that aim to preserve or increase the substance of the child's property.

3.3. Acts of ordinary administration and acts beyond the ordinary administration of the child's property

In addition to the above division of activities, another one is worth noting. As stipulated in art. 101 § 3 FGC, parents may not, without the authorization of the guardianship court, perform actions exceeding the scope of ordinary administration or consent to the child performing such actions. It follows from this provision that actions related to the administration of the child's property are divided into actions of ordinary administration and actions exceeding the scope of ordinary administration. However, there is no legal definition of these two terms. The fundamental difference between them lies in the manner in which they are carried out. Furthermore, the literature emphasizes that in order to distinguish actions exceeding the scope of ordinary administration of children's property, both objective criteria (i.e., a commonly accepted division of actions) and subjective criteria (here attention is paid to the assessment of the financial situation of the minor "holder" of a given property, primarily to the value and nature of the action performed in relation to the value and nature of the entire property, that is, its main components, as well as to the circumstance whether it is a matter of acquiring an object against payment or free of charge, that is, without any encumbrances) are helpful.[21] It should be noted that, in the absence of a statutory definition, in order for an act to be considered an act exceeding the scope of ordinary administration, it should meet the criteria indicated below. In this respect, it is worth referring to the jurisprudence of the Supreme Court which indicates that the objective and verifiable measure of actions exceeding the scope of ordinary administration is the gravity of the action performed, its effects in the sphere of the minor's property, the value of the object of the given dispositive action expressed in the court proceedings and the broadly understood welfare of the child and protection of his/her life interests.[22] The consequence of the lack of authorization from the guardianship court under art. 101 § 3 FGC is the invalidity of the act performed. According to the Supreme Court, "When interpreting the concept of actions exceeding the scope of ordinary administration within the

21 T. Sokołowski, "Commentary to the art. 101 FGC," *op. cit.*

22 Compare: Judgment of the Supreme Court of November 16, 1982, I CR 234/82, LEX no. 8486 and Order of the Supreme Court of October 17, 2000, I CKN 319/00, LEX no. 536776.

meaning of Art. 101 § 3 FGC the objective and verifiable—in the circumstances of the case in question—criteria should be applied, which, *inter alia*, include the gravity and value of the object of the action performed, its consequences in the sphere of the minor's property, the broadly understood good of the child and the protection of the child's life interests."[23]

The doctrine stresses that, according to the general rule for qualifying actions as exceeding the scope of ordinary administration of the child's property, they must, even if only hypothetically, threaten to damage the child's property interests.[24] However, for the correct legal qualification to be made, it is important that the nature of the act in question be considered on a case-by-case basis. The above is confirmed by the jurisprudence of the Supreme Court, which, referring to art. 58 § 1 sent. 2 FGC, pointed out that the scope of one's administration as defined in this provision "is not generally defined and may be assessed differently depending on the circumstances of the particular case, and in particular on the value of the asset to which the action relates, on the relation of this value to the collateral held or the assets to the prompt satisfaction of claims in difficult times"—in this context, the Supreme Court held, "It is not beyond the limits of ordinary administration as well as a violation of the legitimate interests of the employee's children for their mother, as a statutory representative, to enter into such a settlement by virtue of which they obtained compensation commensurate with the damage suffered."[25]

4. Authorization to carry out an act exceeding the scope of ordinary administration of the child's property: Legal characteristics of the institution

Indeed, acts of ordinary administration may be undertaken by the parents—as legal representatives of the children—independently (by one or both parents), without the control of the guardianship court. Such acts include both those which do not concern the child's essential affairs and those related to such affairs. Pursuant to art. 97 FGC, it is stipulated that if parental authority is vested in both parents, in such a situation each parent is both obliged and entitled to exercise it, and furthermore, the essential matters of the child are decided jointly by the parents, in turn, in the absence of an agreement between them, the guardianship

---

23 Order of the Supreme Court of October 17, 2000, I CKN 319/00, LEX no. 536776.

24 P. Wicherek, ibid.

25 Judgment of the Supreme Court of October 22, 1968, II PR 433/68, LEX no. 1672949.

court decides. The acts of ordinary administration of the child's property should be considered to be those which consist in arranging, in the name and on behalf of the child, the day-to-day matters relating to the ordinary use of the things that are part of the child's property. The above is confirmed in the literature, where it is indicated that among the acts of ordinary administration are physical and legal acts related to the ordinary use of the property, which are aimed at preserving its substance in an unchanged and undamaged state, as well as "the exchange of typical components of the property mass without changing its purpose, ordinary day-to-day repairs of the assets, payment of fees, taxes, fixed payments, etc."[26]

On the other hand, acts which exceed the scope of the child's ordinary assets require the prior authorization of the guardianship court, as will be discussed further below. However, acts exceeding the scope of ordinary administration are neither enumeratively nor exemplarily listed in the Act. In this respect, the views developed in the field of property law should be followed. For example, the doctrine indicates that "Undoubtedly, also within the meaning of art. 101 § 3, acts which exceed the scope of ordinary administration should be deemed to be directly dispositive (*in rem*) or obliging to dispose of (obliging), and which concern the disposal of the substance of the property, encumbering it with limited rights in rem or changing its purpose. It is not possible to list all acts that exceed the scope of ordinary administration in a taxative manner, especially as this criterion is not absolute and may be assessed differently—depending on the value of the asset to which the act relates, the value of the child's estate, the mutual relationship between the two values and other circumstances. For example, as acts exceeding ordinary administration, in addition to those cited above, it is possible to mention contracting loans and promissory notes, making donations, renouncing the right to inherit."[27] In addition, the literature gives as examples of actions exceeding the scope of ordinary administration "the acquisition, disposal, relinquishment or substantial encumbrance of real estate and rights of greater value, a change in the administration of an important asset, a change in the use of part of the real estate, a major renovation or reconstruction of a building, the establishment of separate ownership of premises, the division of real estate," while also pointing out that "Subjective criteria require, in particular, that it be determined whether the action in question concerns a value that represents a significant, substantial fraction of the value of the entire estate."[28]

26 T. Sokołowski, "Commentary to the Article 101 of the FGC," *op. cit.*

27 H. Ciepła, "Commentary to the art. 101 FGC," in *Kodeks rodzinny i opiekuńczy. Komentarz,* wyd. V (V ed.), ed. K. Piasecki, Warsaw 2011.

28 T. Sokołowski, "Commentary to the art. 101 FGC," *op. cit.*

At present, despite such postulates, there seems to be no need to specify the catalog of actions exceeding the scope of ordinary administration of the child's property, if only by adding the phrase "in particular" to the wording of art. 101 § 3 FGC, which gives the guardianship court greater freedom in assessing individual actions. Moreover, as the actions exceeding the scope of ordinary administration of the child's property are not specified anywhere (open catalogue), following the views expressed in the doctrine and the judicature, the following actions should be classified as such: a division of the joint property in which the children participate as heirs[29]; renunciation of the succession, rejection of the inheritance (whereby it is irrelevant whether the value of the liabilities exceeds the value of the assets or whether the inheritance consists only of liabilities) or acceptance of the inheritance outright[30]; acts of disposition undertaken in legal proceedings by parents on behalf of a minor child, such as the conclusion of a settlement not of a purely causal nature on a matter going beyond the day-to-day administration of the child's property, *inter alia*, as regards the sharing of the inheritance, the liquidation of a joint property or the compensation due to the child[31]; making a declaration on behalf of a minor in a succession case waiving the inheritance payments due to him or her[32]; the filing by the parent of a minor co-owner of real estate of a statement that a mortgage has been created on the minor's interest in the real estate[33]; conclusion of a civil partnership agreement on behalf of a minor child[34]; liquidating a minor's housing passbook and depriving him or her of the right to a guarantee premium[35]; the withdrawal of a substantial amount from a child's account[36]; conclusion of the lease

29 Compare: Ibid. with reference to the judgment of the Supreme Court of May 19, 2005, V CK 648/04, Rzeczpospolita 2005, no. 122, p. 7, LEX no. 380939.

30 Compare: Resolution of the Supreme Court of May 22, 2018, III CZP 102/17, LEX no. 2488790; Order of the Supreme Court of July 15, 2005, IV CK 20/05, OSNC 2006, no. 6; Order of the Supreme Court of November 13, 1998, II CKU 64/98, LEX no. 1215083 and Order of the Supreme Court of May 27, 1998, I CKU 181/97, not published.

31 Compare: Order of the Supreme Court of September 9, 1997, I CKU 13/97, LEX no. 32373; G. Jędrejek, "Commentary to the art. 101 FGC," in *Kodeks rodzinny i opiekuńczy. Komentarz aktualizowany*, Warsaw 2019 and P. Wicherek, Ibid.

32 Order of the Supreme Court of July 23, 1998, III CKU 34/98, LEX no. 1232690.

33 Order of the Supreme Court of December 12, 1997, III CKU 92/97, LEX no. 1226976.

34 Judgment of the NSA OZ in Poznań of April 8, 1997, II SA/Po 1438/96, Pr. Gosp. 1998, no. 1, p. 31.

35 Judgment of the Supreme Court of November 23, 1995, I C 172/94, Pr. Bank. 1997, no. 4, p. 83.

36 Judgment of the Supreme Court of November 16, 1982, I CR 234/82, LEX no. 8486.

agreement[37]; transfer of agricultural parcels for free use[38]; the waiver of a claim for damages on behalf of minor children against a person obliged to compensate for the damage is among the acts which exceed the ordinary administration of the child's property[39]; the withdrawal of a claim brought by a minor in order to establish his/her state rights in a manner consistent with reality[40]; the acquisition by parents for a child under their parental authority of immovable property on the basis of a contract of sale, even if the money for the purchase comes from an intentional donation made by them[41]; as well as—depending on the circumstances—the parents' consent to the insurance company's proposed shortening of the insurance period under the children's supply contract and acceptance of the benefit without the reservation of valorization provided for in art. 358^1 § 3 CC may be regarded as acts exceeding the scope of ordinary administration within the meaning of art. 101 § 3 FGC.[42]

Pursuant to the wording of art. 101 § 3 of the FGC, parents may only carry out acts exceeding the scope of ordinary administration of the child's property with the prior authorization of the court, apart from the exception provided for in art. 104 § 2 of the FGC, according to which "The guardianship court may, in justified cases, determine the value of dispositions concerning movable property, money and securities which the child or the parents may make each year without the authorisation of the guardianship court, subject to art. 103." Certain exceptions to the rule provided for in art. 101 § 3 FGC also result from case law. For example, the Supreme Court indicated: "Parents may, without the authorisation of the guardianship court provided for in art. 101 § 3 of the Family and Guardianship Code, acquire real estate for a minor child under a donation agreement in a state free from obligations to the donor or third parties."[43]

---

37 Judgment of the Supreme Court of April 3, 2007, II UK 178/06, OSNP 2008, no. 9–10, item 141.

38 Judgment of the Supreme Administrative Court of March 13, 2014, II GSK 2102/12, LEX no. 1447211.

39 Judgment (Orzeczenie) of the Supreme Court of March 5, 1962, 4 CR 578/61, OSNC 1963, no. 6, item 127.

40 Judgment of the Supreme Court of August 1, 1966, II CR 279/66, OSNPG 1966, no. 11–12, item 58.

41 Resolution of the Supreme Court of February 15, 2019, III CZP 85/18, OSNC 2020, no. 2, item 14.

42 Resolution of the Supreme Court of February 4, 1997, III CZP 127/96, OSNC 1997, no. 5, item 50.

43 Resolution of the Supreme Court of April 30, 1977, III CZP 73/76, OSNC 1978, no. 2, item 19.

It should be emphasized that the provision of art. 101 § 3 FGC refers to the fact that the court grants authourisation, not consent. This means that if the parents perform an act that exceeds the scope of ordinary administration of the child's property, the consequence is that such an act is treated as absolutely null and void, and thus, it is not subject to convalidation.

The purpose of the parents' administration of the child's property is primarily to preserve that property for the future, that is, for the time when the child reaches the age of majority, and to pass it on to the child as an adult in an undisturbed state. While parents are not obliged to increase the child's assets, they should nevertheless exercise due diligence in caring for them so that these assets are not depleted, unless this is justified by the child's welfare and the natural wear and tear of the assets.

As already indicated above, the exercise of parental authority insofar as it concerns the administration of the child's assets is subject to supervision (control) by the guardianship court *ex lege*. This is the so-called *ex ante* control. It is emphasized in the judicature that "pursuant to art. 101 § 3 of the of FGC, parents may not, without the authorisation of the guardianship court, perform acts exceeding the scope of ordinary administration or consent to such acts being performed by the child," as "the cited provision refers to the authorisation of a state authority and not to the consent of a third party within the meaning of art. 63 CC."[44] Thus, authorisation to perform a legal act exceeding the scope of ordinary administration of the child's property cannot be granted *ex post*, that is, after the act has been performed. This is because in accordance with the wording of art. 101 § 3 of FGC, if it is necessary to perform an action exceeding the scope of ordinary administration of the child's property, the parents may not act on their own, but are obliged to first apply for the guardianship court's authorisation to perform such an action.

According to the Supreme Court, if a legal action concerning a minor's property has been carried out by the minor's statutory representative without prior authorization from the guardianship authority, it is invalid and cannot be convalidated.[45] As a result, such a substantive legal action is unconditionally invalid as an action contrary to the law, which follows directly from the art. 101 § 3 FGC in conjunction with art. 58 § 1 FGC. Similarly, the Supreme Court takes the position that a bilateral legal action performed by a minor with limited legal capacity (i.e., a child over 13 years of age), without the legally required consent

44 Order of the Supreme Court of May 19, 2005, V CK 669/04, LEX no. 603871.
45 Resolution of the SN(CI) of June 24, 1961, 1 CO 16/61, OSNC 1963, no. 9, item 187.

of his/her statutory representative, may be convalidated in the indicated cases by the statutory representative either with the prior consent of the guardianship authority for such convalidation, or by the minor himself/herself after he/she has acquired full capacity to perform legal actions.[46] On the one hand, this may seem to constitute a significant interference by the court in the sphere of their parental powers, especially their decision-making autonomy. On the other hand, however, particularly in situations where the parents live apart or are highly conflicted, it must be examined in each case whether the action taken by one of the parents, is compatible with the child's welfare and takes into account the child's interests. Therefore, in these cases, an enhanced role for the court in this respect seems justified.

6. The course of the proceedings and its procedural consequences

Pursuant to art. 583 sent. 1 of the Code of Civil Procedure[47] (hereinafter: "CCP"), the guardianship court grants authorisation for the parents to perform an act exceeding the scope of ordinary administration of the child's property or for the parents to consent to the child performing such an act at the request of one of the parents after hearing the other parent. In view of the content of the above provision, it should be pointed out that the procedure for granting authorisation for the parents to carry out an act exceeding the scope of ordinary administration of the child's property or for the parents to consent to the child carrying out such an act is conducted in non-contentious court proceedings upon application (the court does not act in this respect *ex officio*). At the same time, the mere granting of authorisation by the guardianship court does not imply the necessity of the child's parents to carry out the act in question (they may refrain from doing so) but opens up the possibility for them to do so.

The application must be submitted to the guardianship court, which is the family court (art. 568 CCP). The material competence to rule on this application is the district court (art. 507 CCP). On the other hand, as far as the territorial jurisdiction of the court is concerned, pursuant to art. 569 CCP, only the guardianship court of the place of residence of the person to whom the proceedings

---

46 Ibid.

47 Act of November 17, 1964 Code of Civil Procedure (consolidated text: Dz. U. (*Journal of Laws*) of 2021, item 1805, as amended: https://isap.sejm.gov.pl/isap.nsf/download.xsp/WDU19640430296/U/D19640296Lj.pdf).

relate is competent, and if there is no place of residence—the guardianship court of the place of his/her residence. If both of these grounds are lacking, the district court for the capital city of Warsaw has jurisdiction (§ 1); however, in urgent cases, the guardianship court issues all necessary orders *ex officio* even with regard to persons who do not fall under its local jurisdiction, notifying the guardianship court with local jurisdiction (§ 2). In this situation, the person whose domicile or place of residence determines the local jurisdiction of the guardianship court is the child, whereby—according to the rules arising from art. 26 CC—however, the place of residence of a minor is the place of residence of his/her legal guardian (art. 26 CC). It should be emphasized at this point, however, that a child, although his/her property is involved in the proceedings, is not a participant in the proceedings, even if he/she is at least 13 years old (age of limited legal capacity), as the case concerns his/her property and not his/her person. This may raise concerns relating to the child's lack of active participation in the proceedings and raise doubts as to the respect of his/her legal subjectivity, since he/she appears as a third party and not as an active participant in the proceedings. Nevertheless, it finds its justification. Article 573 § 1 CCP provides that a person under parental authority, custody or guardianship has the capacity to take action in proceedings concerning his or her person, unless he or she has no legal capacity. Moreover, according to a well-established view of the case law, "Neither the content of art. 101 FGC nor the content of art. 583 CCP implies that a child has the right to be a participant in the proceedings for the authorisation of an action by the parents which exceeds the scope of ordinary administration of their property. This means that hearing the case only with the participation of the parents is procedurally correct."[48] In order to ensure that the child has an opportunity to be heard in a matter concerning an action that goes beyond the ordinary administration of his or her property, it would be advisable to consider hearing the child in every such matter whenever possible—this should become the standard. In particular, that according to the wording of art. 576 § 2 sent. 1 FGC, "The court in matters concerning the person or property of the child shall hear the child, if his/her mental development, state of health and degree of maturity so permit, taking into account his/her reasonable wishes as far as possible." Moreover, in certain cases, the guardianship court, pursuant to art. 570[1] § 1 CCP, may order that a court guardian conduct a community interview in order to collect information concerning the minor and his or her environment, which may

48 Order of the Supreme Court of February 11, 1997, II CKN 90/96, LEX no. 1228425.

prove helpful in assessing the legitimacy of a certain action taken by the parents with effect on the minor.

Insofar as the parents have parental authority over the child, pursuant to art. 583 CCP, they should appear in the case—either unanimously as applicants, or—in the case of a divergence of their positions as to the necessity of carrying out a given action exceeding the scope of ordinary administration of the child's property—one as an applicant and the other as a participant. Where both parents are involved in the case, particularly where one of them has the status of applicant, it is necessary to hear the other parent, which may make it necessary for the court to set a hearing (although this is not obligatory). On the other hand, in the event of the death of one of the parents, it must be presumed that the parent in charge of the child's estate with parental responsibility acts as applicant. There is then no obligation to name a participant or to appoint a court guardian on their side. In addition, interested parties (see art. 510 CCP) and the public prosecutor (see art. 60 CCP) may also be participants in the proceedings.

A request for authorisation for the parents to perform an act exceeding the scope of ordinary administration of the child's property or for the parents to consent to the child performing such an act should correspond to the general conditions provided for pleadings, taking into account the specificity of non-litigation proceedings (see art. 511 § 1 CCP in conjunction with art. 126 and 187 CCP, however—pursuant to art. 128 CCP—in the absence of other, except for the applicant, participants of the proceedings, enclosing copies is unnecessary. At the same time, the application in question should precisely specify the most important elements of the legal act the guardianship court is to authorize. The above is reflected in the established position of the judicature and doctrine. Indeed, as the Supreme Court indicates, "When granting an application under art. 583 CCP, the guardianship court should precisely specify the specific content of the action exceeding ordinary administration for which it gives its authorisation."[49] It is stated in the literature that, as a general rule, the authorization referred to in art. 101 § 3 of the FGC may be of a general nature if this is necessary for the proper running of the farm or business, but it cannot generally cover all unspecified actions, but should at least specify such elements as the category of the action, the conditions for its execution (e.g., the object and the price), as well as set a deadline for submitting to the court an account of the transaction concluded.[50] Furthermore, "the guardianship court, when granting authorisation in

49 Ibid.
50 H. Ciepła, Ibid.

the above-mentioned cases, cannot limit itself to a formal control of the legality of the parents' activities, but should examine each case also in terms of economic expediency and the benefit achieved for the child's welfare. The authorisation should include in its content all the essential elements of the act in question (*essentialia negotii*). If ancillary clauses are included, they are absolutely binding and their violation may render the entire act invalid (…)."[51] The so-called *in abstracto* authorisation is therefore inadmissible. An application for a authorisation for the parents to perform an act which exceeds the scope of ordinary administration of the child's property or for the parents to consent to the child performing such an act is subject to a fixed court fee of PLN 100.[52]

It should also be pointed out that if any proceedings are pending, whether in a contentious or non-contentious procedure, in the course of which a settlement is to be concluded that will affect the child's property, then it constitutes a legal act exceeding the scope of ordinary administration. In such a situation, it is required that the court before which the proceedings are pending suspends the proceedings and sends the file to the guardianship court to authorize the settlement or, if the case is pending in the same court of fact and jurisdiction, withholds court approval of the settlement until the guardianship court has ruled on the authorization.[53]

According to a well-established jurisprudential view, "the guardianship court shall assess the intended act in terms of exceeding ordinary administration according to the state of affairs on the date of the decision."[54] The literature indicates that "the jurisdiction of the court includes an assessment of whether the intended action is taken in the interests of the child, as well as an assessment of the advisability of the action and of the economic benefits that the action entails."[55] Moreover, pursuant to the second sent. of art. 583 CCP, a decision of the guardianship court on this subject becomes effective only when it becomes final and cannot be modified or revoked if legal effects toward third parties have been produced on the basis of the authorisation. The abovementioned regulation

51 Ibid.

52 Article 23 point 1 of the Act of July 28, 2005 on court costs in civil cases (consolidated text: Dz. U. (*Journal of Laws*) of 2023, item 1144, as amended: https://isap.sejm.gov.pl/isap.nsf/download.xsp/WDU20051671398/U/D20051398Lj.pdf).

53 See: Articles 570 and 572 CCP.

54 Resolution of the Supreme Court of February 15, 2019, III CZP 85/18, OSNC 2020, no. 2, item 14.

55 P. Pruś, "Commentary to the art. 583 CCP," in *Kodeks postępowania cywilnego. Komentarz aktualizowany. Tom II. Art. 478–1217*, ed. M. Manowska, Warsaw 2022.

is an exception to the general rule applicable to non-contentious proceedings expressed in art. 577 CCP ("The guardianship court may change its decision, even a final one, if the welfare of the person concerned so requires.").

It is also worth mentioning that if the administration of the child's property is carried out in an irregular or even defective manner, then there are grounds for limiting parental authority, in particular, if the child's welfare is at risk. In such a situation, on the basis of art. 109 § 1 and 2 FGC, the guardianship court will issue appropriate orders (e.g., specifying what actions cannot be performed by the parents without the court's permission or subjecting the parents to such restrictions as the guardian is subject to, including, for example, obliging them to draw up an inventory of the child's property (see art. 104 § 1 FGC), to report annually on their administration or to establish security for the transactions they intend to perform by insuring them or establishing a bank guarantee), and pursuant to § 3 of the provision, it may also entrust the administration of the minor's property to a guardian appointed for that purpose.

7. Conclusions

The best interests of the minor should be specifically protected in law. It is worth considering the possibility of changing his or her status in proceedings for court authorisation to carry out an act on behalf of a minor which exceeds the scope of ordinary administration of the child's property from that of a third party (who is not its subject) to that of a participant actively involved in the proceedings (whose position should be duly taken into account) or at least by introducing a mandatory hearing of the minor in such cases. However, the current legislation does not provide for a possibility of such a change and according to the well-established position of the jurisprudence, the mechanisms available make it possible to ensure that the child's welfare and interests are properly taken care of.

Bibliography

Literature

Ciepła, H., "Commentary to the Article 101 of the FGC," in *Kodeks rodzinny i opiekuńczy. Komentarz*, wyd. V (V ed.), ed. K. Piasecki, Warsaw 2011.

Gwiazdomorski, J., "Krewni uprawnieni do żądania i obowiązani do dostarczania środków utrzymania," *PiP* 1 (1954).

Jędrejek, G., "Commentary to the Article 101 of the FGC," in *Kodeks rodzinny i opiekuńczy. Komentarz aktualizowany*, Warsaw 2019.

Pośpiech, A., "Commentary to art. 95 FCG," in *Kodeks rodzinny i opiekuńczy. Komentarz*, ed. M. Fras and M. Habdas, Warsaw 2021.

Pruś, P., "Commentary to the art. 583 CCP," in *Kodeks postępowania cywilnego. Komentarz aktualizowany. Tom II. Art. 478–1217*, ed. M. Manowska, Warsaw 2022.

Sokołowski, T., "Commentary to art. 10 CC," in *Kodeks cywilny. Komentarz. Tom I. Część ogólna*, wyd. II (II ed.), ed. A. Kidyba, Warsaw 2012.

Sokołowski, T., "Commentary to the art. 101 FGC," in *Kodeks rodzinny i opiekuńczy. Komentarz*, wyd. II (II ed.), ed. H. Dolecki, Warsaw 2013.

Stępień, M., "Atrybuty władzy rodzicielskiej," in *Prawo wobec wyzwań współczesności. Wybrane problemy teoretycznoprawne i dogmatycznoprawne*, E-Wydawnictwo. Prawnicza i Ekonomiczna Biblioteka Cyfrowa. Wydział Prawa, Administracji i Ekonomii Uniwersytetu Wrocławskiego, ed. J. Helios, W. Jedlecka, and A. Kwieciński, Wrocław 2019 - see https://repozytorium.uni.wroc.pl/Content/95905/PDF/20_M_Stepien_Atrybuty_wladzy_rodzicielskiej.pdf (accessed: 10.06.2023).

Trybulska-Skoczelas, E., "Commentary to art. 95 FGC," in *Kodeks rodzinny i opiekuńczy. Komentarz*, ed. J. Wierciński, Warsaw 2014.

Wicherek, P., "Commentary to art. 101 FGC," in *Kodeks rodzinny i opiekuńczy. Komentarz*, ed. M. Fras and M. Habdas, Warsaw 2021.

Acts of law

Act of February 25, 1964, Family and Guardianship Code (consolidated text: Dz. U. (*Journal of Laws*) of 2020, item 1359, as amended: https://isap.sejm.gov.pl/isap.nsf/download.xsp/WDU19640090059/U/D19640059Lj.pdf).

Act of April 23, 1964, Civil Code (consolidated text: Dz. U. (*Journal of Laws*) of 2022, item 1360, as amended: https://isap.sejm.gov.pl/isap.nsf/download.xsp/WDU19640160093/U/D19640093Lj.pdf).

Act of November 17, 1964, Code of Civil Procedure (consolidated text: Dz. U. (*Journal of Laws*) of 2021, item 1805, as amended: https://isap.sejm.gov.pl/isap.nsf/download.xsp/WDU19640430296/U/D19640296Lj.pdf).

Act of July 28, 2005, on court costs in civil cases (consolidated text: Dz. U. (*Journal of Laws*) of 2023, item 1144, as amended: https://isap.sejm.gov.pl/isap.nsf/download.xsp/WDU20051671398/U/D20051398Lj.pdf).

Case law

Judgment (Orzeczenie) of the Supreme Court of March 5, 1962, 4 CR 578/61, OSNC 1963, no. 6, item 127.

Judgment of the Court of Appeal in Szczecin of June 6, 2019, III AUa 30/19, LEX no. 2692946.

Judgment of the NSA OZ in Poznań of April 8, 1997, II SA/Po 1438/96, Pr. Gosp. 1998, no. 1, p. 31.

Judgment of the Provincial Administrative Court in Warsaw of November 10, 2005, II SA/Wa 1475/05, LEX no. 192582.

Judgment of the Provincial Administrative Court in Warsaw of February 25, 2020, II SA/Wa 2038/19, LEX no. 3015103.

Judgment of the Supreme Administrative Court of March 13, 2014, II GSK 2102/12, LEX no. 1447211.

Judgment of the Supreme Court of August 1, 1966, II CR 279/66, OSNPG 1966, no. 11–12, item 58.

Judgment of the Supreme Court of November 16, 1982, I CR 234/82, LEX no. 8486.

Judgment of the Supreme Court of May 19, 2005, V CK 648/04, Rzeczpospolita 2005, no. 122, p. 7, LEX no. 380939.

Judgment of the Supreme Court of October 22, 1968, II PR 433/68, LEX no. 1672949.

Judgment of the Supreme Court of November 23, 1995, I C 172/94, Pr. Bank. 1997, no. 4, p. 83.

Judgment of the Supreme Court of April 3, 2007, II UK 178/06, OSNP 2008, no. 9–10, item 141.

Order of the Supreme Court of February 11, 1997, II CKN 90/96, LEX no. 1228425.

Order of the Supreme Court of December 12, 1997, III CKU 92/97, LEX no. 1226976.

Order of the Supreme Court of November 13, 1998, II CKU 64/98, LEX no. 1215083.

Order of the Supreme Court of July 15, 2005, IV CK 20/05, OSNC 2006, no. 6.

Order of the Supreme Court of October 17, 2000, I CKN 319/00, LEX no. 536776.

Order of the Supreme Court of May 19, 2005, V CK 669/04, LEX no. 603871.

Order of the Supreme Court of January 21, 2022, III CZ 21/22.

Order of the Supreme Court of July 23, 1998, III CKU 34/98, LEX no. 1232690.

Order of the Supreme Court of May 27, 1998, I CKU 181/97, not published.

Order of the Supreme Court of May 5, 2000, II CKN 761/00, LEX no. 51982.

Order of the Supreme Court of September 9, 1997, I CKU 13/97, LEX no. 32373.

Resolution of the SN (CI) of June 24, 1961, 1 CO 16/61, OSNC 1963, no. 9, item 187.

Resolution of the SN (CI) of 9.06.1976, III CZP 46/75, OSNC 1976, no. 9, item 184.

Resolution of the Supreme Court (7) of March 8, 2006, III CZP 98/05, OSNC 2006, no. 10, item 158.

Resolution of the Supreme Court of February 15, 2019, III CZP 85/18, OSNC 2020, no. 2, item 14.

Resolution of the Supreme Court of February 15, 2019, III CZP 85/18, OSNC 2020, no. 2, item 14.

Resolution of the Supreme Court of May 22, 2018, III CZP 102/17, LEX no. 2488790.

Resolution of the Supreme Court of April 30, 1977, III CZP 73/76, OSNC 1978, no. 2, item 19.

Resolution of the Supreme Court of February 4, 1997, III CZP 127/96, OSNC 1997, no. 5, item 50.

Chapter IV. The family in an inclusive and global society: Changes in the family structures

Teresa Duplá Marín

The intestate succession of "half-brothers" in the current family structure: A proposal for a return to the original Roman regulation

Abstract: In the context of today's globalized society, but, above all, inclusive and protective of fundamental rights, the maintenance of the expression "half-brothers," present, among others, in our State Civil Code, specifically in arts. 949 to 951, is curious and, to say the least, questionable. If, in addition, it can bring, as a legal consequence, a possible discrimination in the distribution of a family inheritance, contrary to the essence, principles and configuration of legal succession, it seems reasonable to spend time analyzing its origin, historical evolution and subsequent reinterpretation. and, of course, the causes that may justify the elimination not only of said expression, but also of the current content of this standard in full s. XXI. All of this is the subject of this study, in which, based on the essential principles of intestate succession in Roman Law and the call for collateral in it, it goes on to explain its reception by the Spanish Civil Code of 1889 in the that has not suffered, since its publication more than a century ago, unlike what happened in some regional rights, any type of modification.

Keywords: intestate succession, half-brothers, discrimination, family

Summary: 1. Introduction: *status quaestionis*, objectives of the study and the factual situation. 2. Analysis of the origin of the intestate appeal to uterine and consanguineous siblings in Roman Law and its subsequent legal evolution. 3. Some brief considerations on the current Spanish regulation: articles 949–951 of the Spanish Civil Code versus article 442–10 of Book 4 of the Catalan Civil Code and some special rules. 4. By way of conclusions and a proposal *de lege ferenda*: the elimination of the exception and the return to the archaic Roman origin of intestate succession.

1. Introduction: *status quaestionis*, objectives of the study and the factual situation

In the context of today's globalized society, but, above all, inclusive and protective of fundamental rights, the maintenance of the expression "half-siblings," present, among others, in our Spanish State Civil Code (hereinafter C.C.), specifically in Articles 949 to 951 in the area of intestate succession, is, in my opinion, curious and, to say the least, questionable. If, as we shall see in the following pages, it can also lead, as a legal consequence, to possible discrimination in the distribution of a family inheritance, contrary to the essence, principles and configuration of legal succession, it seems reasonable to devote some time to analyzing its origin, historical evolution and subsequent reinterpretation. As well as, of course, trying to identify the causes, if there are any, that could justify the elimination not only of this expression, but also of the current content of this rule and its effects in the middle of the 21st century.

All of this is the subject of the present study, in which, starting from the essential principles of intestate succession in Roman Law, and the call to collaterals in the intestate succession of Justinian Law, specifically Novel 118.2, the unquestionable precedent of the current Spanish regulation, I will stop briefly to show the reinterpretation that was made of it in Las Partidas (13th century), specifically Partida 6ª ley 13, to then go on to explain its reception by the Spanish Civil Code of 1889. And all this because, although it has not undergone, since its publication more than a century ago, any kind of modification, as Pacheco[1] pointed out at the time, *"the discipline of intestate succession before the Code was the result of the contribution of the Visigoth tradition that had passed into the Royal Charter, of the Justinian contribution through the Partidas and of the modifications made by the legislation in modern and contemporary times."* Finally, I will refer, by way of example, to the possible beginning of the change manifested, in origin, in the adaptation that the Catalan legislator made with the publication of Law 10/2008, of 10 July of Book 4 of the Catalan Civil Code, and some other law that, outside the field of succession, curiously enough, deals with this subject.

But before doing so, and in order to situate us in the underlying problems, I will begin by configuring and describing the factual assumption that I will analyze in the following pages and which, being timeless, as you will see, can be useful, not only today, but throughout legal history.

We are dealing with an intestate succession. Our deceased, Claudia, the *de cuius*, dies without having made a will. Her family situation is as follows: she has no descendants, no ascendants, no spouse (or stable partner, as the case may be). When her succession is open, in this case, the law, from Rome to the present day, calls upon the collaterals, first and foremost, the siblings. Claudia has four siblings, two from the same father and mother, and two from another couple that her mother married after her father's divorce. Claudia has always had a very good relationship with all of them, as she has lived with them all her life, like a

1 F. C. Pachecho Caballero, "Derecho histórico y Codificación. El derecho sucesorio," *AHDE* LXXXII (2012), p. 138.

normal family. But she dies without having made a will and a dispute arises over the distribution of her inheritance between the two brothers with whom she shares father and mother, that is, the so-called double brothers, and the other two from her mother's second marriage, that is, the single brothers. The legal basis for this dispute lies in the fact that the former (double-bonded siblings), in accordance with the provisions of our state legal system today, claim double shares in the distribution of Claudia's inheritance. Specifically, Art. 949 of the C.C. provides as follows:

> If siblings of father and mother concur with half-siblings, the former shall take double the share of the latter in the inheritance.

That is to say, the aforementioned article, without making any different treatment with regard to the offer—*ius delationis*—to the siblings, does establish an exception to the rule of distribution established in intestate succession law of the division by heads in the cases of equal degree of call. In short, therefore, although no discrimination can be seen as far as the offer of inheritance is concerned, there is inequality of treatment in the distribution between siblings, depending on the origin or birth of the siblings. We will return to this issue later on.

Continuing with the inheritance and family problems raised, let us now assume another slightly different scenario, but also present and possible throughout history and in our current society. It turns out that Claudia does not have siblings, but only two "half-siblings," one on her mother's side from that second marriage, and the other on her father's side, that is, from her father's second marriage. He has always had a wonderful relationship with them as a normal family. In this specific case, it should be borne in mind that, if her intestate succession is open, the provisions of Art. 950 of the C.C. could be invoked:

> In the event that there are only half siblings, some on the father's side and others on the mother's side, they will all inherit in equal shares, without any distinction of assets.

This is, in this case, similar to the previous one as far as the family model is concerned,[2] but different only as far as the number of children is concerned.

---

2 In both cases we would be dealing with what has come to be known as a reconstituted, recomposed or step-family. In this respect, see M. T. Duplá Marín, "Potestad parental catalana y autoridad familiar aragonesa: breve análisis comparativo de las facultades otorgadas a los padrastros respecto de los hijos menores del cónyuge o conviviente," in *El nuevo derecho de la persona y de la familia: (libro segundo del Código Civil de Cataluña), Reyes Barrada Orellana (aut.), Martín Garrido Melero (aut.), Sergio Nasarre Aznar (aut.)*, ed. Bosch, Barcelona 2011, pp. 735–746.

And the difference is that surely here there will no longer be a dispute between them over the distribution because the rule, expressly and clearly appealing to the difference in treatment in the previous case "without any distinction of assets," indicates for this one equal treatment in the distribution and, consequently, non-discriminatory, since all Claudia's siblings will inherit in equal shares.

Given these two factual scenarios, which are perfectly identifiable in Rome and today, the question that arises is the following: is it really justified to maintain the different treatment established by the rule today? The answer to this question, in my opinion, must be in the negative. If we take into account the preferential and protective place attributed in our current society to fundamental rights, the non-discrimination of children on the basis of their birth, which has been established in our legal system for decades, and the consequent equal treatment in the intestate succession of parents, it is appropriate, in my opinion, to take a closer look at this case, in order to analyze whether it is possible to maintain it in the case of intestate inheritance between siblings. I will deal with this in the following sections.

2. Analysis of the origin of the intestate appeal to uterine and consanguineous siblings in Roman Law and its subsequent legal evolution

In order to understand the justification for this current regulation, in my opinion, it is necessary to take as a starting point the origin and context in which it was born, and its evolution up to the present day. This means going back to its origin, that is, archaic Roman law and its consolidation in Justinian law. We will briefly analyze its subsequent reception in the Partidas in order to focus our attention on the regulation of the Spanish State Civil Code, making a brief allusion to the reform of the regulation of Catalan civil law in 2008, in order to support a *lege ferenda* proposal for reinterpretation that I mention in the title of this study.

I begin, then, with the regulation in its Roman origins. And I do so on the understanding that it is not the aim of this work to carry out a new analysis of intestate succession in Roman law, but to focus my attention on the Roman regulation of the intestate succession of siblings, a question which is certainly complex and which, as we shall see below, has been scarcely dealt with by the doctrine.

The first thing to note is that the regulation of intestate succession between brothers and sisters began in the archaic period when, according to what has come down to us from the XII Tables, in the absence of *sui heredes*, the *agnati* were called upon, that is, as Herrero[3] points out, the closest collateral relatives in the male line, that is, brothers and sisters.

The brothers, in turn, are distinguished into *consanguinei* and *agnati,* the former being called, as Voci[4] rightly points out, the brothers and sisters who have the same father, even if born of a different mother.[5] And this is what Gaius states in his Institutions:

> Vocantur autem adgnati, qui legitima cognatione iuncti sunt. Legitima autem cognatio est ea, quae per virilis sexus personas coniungitur. Itaque eodem patre nati fatres agnati sibi sunt, qui etiam consanguinei vocantur, nec requiritur, an etiam matrem eandem habuerint. (Gai III, 10)

In this sense, *agnati* are the rest of the collaterals in the male line, from the third degree of kinship onwards and, as Finazzi[6] points out, it seems that with a limit in the sixth degree of kinship.[7]

Moreover, as pointed out by *Gaius*, only in the sphere of *consanguinei* do men and women inherit:

> ...Itaque soror fratri sororiue legitima heres est, amita vero et fratris filia legitima heres esse non potest. (Gai. III,14)[8]

3 On the doctrinal debate on the distinction between *sui heredes* and *proximi agnati*, see, for example, the synthesis of Herrero Medina, M., *Génesis del sistema sucesorio romano*, ed. Comares, Colección Derecho Romano y Ciencia Jurídica Europea, Granada, 2020, p. 186, n. 2.

4 Voci, P., *Diritto ereditario romano*, vol. secondo, parte especiale, 2ª ed., Milano 1963, p. 7.

5 Cf. D. 38, 16, 2, 1 (Ulp. Lib. XIII ad Sab.): "Agnati autem sunt cognati virilis sexus ab eodem orti; nam post suos et consanguineos statim mihi proximus est consanguinei mei filius, et ego ei; patris quoque frater, qui patruus appellatur; deincepsque ceteri, si qui sunt, hinc orti in infinitum." In the same sense I. 3.2.1.

6 "La succesione ab intestato," in *XII Tabulae. Testo e commento. Tomo I*, ed. M. F. Cursi, Napoli 2018, pp. 231–296, p. 245.

7 Thus, in the absence of siblings, the uncles and aunts of the deceased would be called, then the uncles and aunts of his father, until reaching the children of the male siblings of the *de cuius*. See, in this respect, S. Castán, "Reflexiones sobre el origen de las sucesiones en Roma. El '*testamentum calatis comitis*' y su relación con la sucesión intestada," *RIDROM* 11 (2013), pp. 238–239.

8 Cf. I. 3.2.3.

To which it should be added that, excluding the right of representation (*successio in locum*) in this appeal,[9] even a brother of the father alone could have preference over the children of a brother, of both father and mother, who had died beforehand.[10]

In short, and for all that has been described above, it can be concluded that in the first regulation of Roman intestate succession contained in the Law of the XII Tables, that is, in civil law intestate succession, in the absence of *sui heredes* (who are mainly descendants), siblings[11] in the father's line and without distinction of sex are called in the first place and preferentially. Romanist doctrine has understood that it is in these cases that we can really speak of hereditary successors, rather than "continuators of the family" as occurs in the case of *sui heredes.*[12]

And what is even more important, for the purposes of the problem we are analyzing here, without any distinction of quotas between the so-called "half-siblings." And even, in some cases, with preference for the latter over the children of pre-dead double-bonded siblings.

We continue with the system of praetorian law, that is, the *bonorum possessio sine tabulis testamenti*, indicating that it presents some changes which, in my opinion, are relevant in the appeal we are analyzing: (a) it refers to the rules of ius civile with regard to the appeal to the *legitimi*[13]; (b) brothers are also contemplated in the following appeal to the *cognati,* taking into account, in the latter, that successive delation (*successio ordinum et graduum*)[14] is admitted; (c) finally, and as Voci[15] points out, uterines are included here, that is, brothers on the mother's side who can succeed each other.

The regime of intestate succession between brothers improved from Constantine until Justinian, and was articulated through a series of novelties contained

---

9 In the same sense it is maintained later in the late classical period, as is recorded in C. 6.58.3 (*Imp. Dcius A. Asc.*).

10 Cf. I. 3.2.4. In any case, always siblings born of *iustae nuptiae*, since it should be remembered that, at that time, purely natural filiation did not confer inheritance rights, except in cases of adoption.

11 Who are related in the second-degree crosswise, as indicated in I.3.6.2.

12 Vid. for all, M. Herrero, *Génesis del sistema sucesorio romano*, *op. cit.*, pp. 191 n. 20 y 192–194.

13 With the exception of the controversy raised by *Gaius* in his Institutions regarding the maintenance, or not, of the *successio in gradum*. Cf. in this respect, *Gai* III, 28.

14 Cf. In this sense, D. 38, 9 *De Successorio Edicto*.

15 *Dir. er.*, cit., p. 38.

in different imperial Constitutions which, on the whole, established a somewhat confused regime, namely:

(a) In a Constitution of Anastasius (before 498),[16] the emancipated brother has access to the succession of his brothers, albeit at a lower rate than the rest of the non-emancipated brothers, if he competes with them. It is evident that emancipation, and consequent independent patrimony, must have justified the inequality of quota in this case, an inequality which, as we shall see, came to an end in the Justinian period:

> Quum igitur praetorem filium emancipatum, licet subtili iure capite fuerat deminutus, attamen in patris successionem sine ulla deminutione vocare manifestum est, non eodem autem iure etiam ad fratrum suorum successiones ab eo vocabatur, sed nec filii eius iure legitimo suis patruis succedebant, necessarium duximus hoc primum corrigere, et legem Anastasianam iusto incremento perfectam ostendere, ut emancipatus filius et filia non solum in paternis bonis ad suorum similitudinem succedant, sed etiam in fratrum vel soronum suarum successione, sive omnes sui, sive omnes emancipati sunt, sive permixti, aequo iure invicem sibi succedant, et non secundum legem Anastasianam parte aliqua deminuta. Et haec quidem de filiis emancipatis sancire bellissimum nobis visum est. (C. 6.58.15.1 Ioanni P.P)

(b) Another later Constitution (502) establishes the reciprocity of this right, that is, the possibility for the brothers of the emancipated person to have access to his inheritance:

> Si ab eo, qui ex sacro rescripto secundum nostram constitutionem fieri postulaverit emancipationem liberorum, petitum sit, quatenus ei, qui emancipandus emnacipandave est, minime legitima iura per emancipationem exstinguatur, eadem iura tam emancipatio vel emancipatae contra personas alias hoc modo sibi coniunctas, quam aliis itidem contra eum vel eam in hereditatibus, vel successionibus, et tutelis, nec non ceteris serventur intacta.... (C. 6.58.11 Imp. Anast. A. Const. P.P.)

(c) Justinian, in a Constitution of 534 (C. 6.58.15.1 and 2 Imp. Iust. A. Ioanni P.P.), equalizes the dues of brothers regardless of whether they are emancipated or not:

> ...ut emancipatus filius et filia non solum in paternis bonis ad suorum similitudinem succedant, sed etiam in fratrum vel sororum suarum successione, sive omnes sui, sive omnes emancipati sunt, sive permixti, aequo iure invicem sibi succedant, et non secundum legem Anastasianam parte aliqua deminuta...

16 Which has not reached us. Cf. I. 3.5.1.

(d) And, furthermore, it equals in degree (second, *agnati*) blood brothers and uterine brothers (C. 6.58.15.2 *Imp. Iust. A. Ioanni P.P.*)[17]:

> Sed nec fratrem vel sororem uterinos concedimus in cognationis loco relinqui. Quum enim tam próximo gradu sunt, merito eos sine ulla diferentia, tanquam si consanguinei fuerant, cum legitimis fratribus et sororibus vocandos esse sancimus, ut secundo gradu constituti, et legitima sucessione digni reperti, aliis omnibus, qui sunt ulterioris gradus, licet legitimi sint, praecellant. El haec quidem de secundi gradus successione satis abundeque a nobis cum suma utilitate disposita sunt.

(e) In another Constitution of the same year (C. 6.58.13 *Imp. Iust. A. Ioanni P.P.*), he calls in the same order the brothers and sisters together with the surviving father, granting the usufruct to the father and the bare ownership to the brothers and sisters:

> … Huiusmodi dubitationem compendioso responso duximus esse finiendam, ideoque sancimus, ad similitudinem maternarum rerum aliarumque, de quibus iam a nobis lex posita est, et huiusmodi hereditatem iure quidem dominii ad fratres vel sorores in totum pervenire, usumfructum autem eius patri totum, sive priorem torum servaverit, sive ad secundas migraverit nuptias, acquiri, sive per sacrum oraculum emancipatio procedat, sive alio legitimo modo a sacris paternis fuerint absoluti. Quum enim et pater utitur usufructu, et votum eius est, ad alios filios suas res pervenire, quapropter quum ex lege Anastasiana in alium articulum fratribus prospectum est, nunc a nobis in hac specie plenius eius subvenitur, ut pater inabeat usumfructum, fratres autem vel sórores dominium rerum relictarum …

Nevertheless, it is common knowledge that Justinian's reforms in Novels 118 (543) and 127 (548) brought the evolution of intestate succession to a close, and the cognatic kinship was definitively imposed over the agnatic one, merging the civil and praetorian systems. As Fadda[18] rightly points out, recalling the words of Marchi, just as it would be excessive to affirm that Christianity had not influenced the Justinian reforms of intestate succession law, so it would be the same to pretend to exclude it completely from the reforms. It is a system, as Fadda continues, that is articulated around nature and that is what makes the cognates

---

17 And, consequently, in the third degree to the children of blood and uterine siblings. Cf. C.6.58.15.3.

18 G. Fadda, *Concetti fondamentali del Diritto ereditario romano*, vol. I, Milano 1949, p. 333, 335 and 337.

enter into the orbit of the *legitimi*, with the civil parentage coinciding with the natural one.[19]

Thus, as far as we are concerned, in the first place the children and descendants of the deceased are called, regardless of parental authority, sex[20] or degree of kinship; in the second place the paternal and maternal ascendants of the deceased, together with the Germanic siblings (father and mother) and the children of the pre-deceased Germanic siblings by right of representation (novel 118, ch. 3). If ascendants and Germanic siblings concur, the inheritance is divided by heads and the right of representation is only admitted from novel 127 onwards; and in 3rd place, and therefore only in the absence of the above, to the siblings of simple bond, whether on the father's side (*consanguinei*) or on the mother's side (*uterini*), and also to the children of the pre-deceased siblings. We do not refer to the rest of the appeals because they are beyond the scope of this work.

With regard to the case we are analyzing, that is, the call to the intestate succession of siblings, the following should be noted:

1. That it is the first time that the distinction between cognates in general and siblings appears expressly, giving priority to the latter over the rest of the collaterals.
2. That it is also the first time that a distinction is made, for the purposes of intestate succession, between Germanic siblings (with a double bond) and uterine or consanguineous siblings, with a single bond.[21]
3. Furthermore, siblings of double bond are placed in a preferential order, since they are called together with the ascendants and, in second place, only in the absence of descendants. This is clearly provided for in Nov. 118 ch. 2 and Nov. 127 ch. 1,[22] the children of pre-deceased Germanic brothers being preferred to brothers of simple bond:

> Cessante successione lineae descendentis et eius, quae sola sit adscendentis, vocantur primo fratres fratrisque praemortui filii in stirpes. Dico autem de fratre eiusque fratris filiis, qui ex utroque parente contingunt eum, de cuius hereditate nunc agitur. Quae

19 Vid. in the same sense, a recent interesting and profound study by B. García Fueyo, "Hijas e hijos legítimos en la sucesión intestada de su progenitor: de Roma a los códigos civiles (Igualdad y género)," *RIDROM* 28 (2022), p. 86.

20 The general principle of equalization was consolidated at this time.

21 However, as A. D'Ors, in *Derecho Privado Romano*, 8ª ed. rev., Pamplona 1991, pp. 321–325, pointed out, in the Theodosian Code the term "*germani*" refers to the brothers of the father, as opposed to the *uterini*, of the mother.

22 C.6.58.3. Cf. In the same sense Nov. 84 cap. 1 (C.6.59.11 Imp. Iust. A. Demos.).

personae veniunt et sine defunctae nunc personae parentibus, et cum proximis gradu adscendentibus. Et quidem praedicti fratris filius, etsi tertio gradu sit, praefertur fratribus defuncti, qui ex uno tantum parente cognati sunt. In hac successione omnis differentia sexus et emancipationis cessat.

4. And, in short, that the Justinian law makes a call in different degree according to the "type" of brother that is, being preferential the brother of double bond that not only concurs with the ascendants, but, in addition, excludes, the call to the brothers of simple bond, if there are any, since they pass to occupy the third order of calls, as it is provided in Nov. 118 cap. 3:

Post fratres autem ex utroque parente et eorum filios admittuntur ex uno latere fratres sororesve, cum quibus et filii eorum, si qui ex eis iam decesserint. Hi autem fratrum filii, quum pares sint defuncti fratribus, praeferuntur procul dubio eiusdem defuncti patruis et aliis similibus. Et in his successionibus omnino cessat sexus et agnationis ratio.

That is to say, in the Roman Justinian period, in the hypothesis posed at the beginning of Claudia's intestate succession, the brothers with a double bond would inherit, and those with a single bond would not.

We continue with a brief analysis of the content of PART 6, Title XIII, which regulates intestate succession and which, as we all know, has its source in Roman Justinian law.[23] Specifically, Laws 4, 5 and 6 provide us with information on how succession should work in these cases, both in terms of calling and distribution.

In them, the reinterpretation of the Justinian rule of succession is as follows:

1. Law 4, in the absence of descendants, the Roman Justinian call to the ascendants together with the brothers of father and mother (double bond), and to the children of pre-deceased Germanic brothers, is taken up.
2. Law 5 also includes the incompatibility of the calls with siblings with a simple link, who only inherit in the absence of the previous ones.
3. Law 6 establishes, as a novelty, a special distribution in the case of siblings with a simple link, indicating that they can only inherit the assets that come from their mother or father. And those that come directly from the earnings of the deceased sibling, will be divided in equal parts. This is, as Pérez Martín[24] points out, a gradual linear or parental linkage system.

23 See, for example, the interesting synthesis of A. Pérez Martín, "Fuentes romanas en las Partidas," *GLOSSAE. REVISTA DE HISTORIA DEL DERECHO EUROPEO* 4 (1992), pp. 215–246.

24 Fuentes romanas en las Partidas, *op. cit.*, p. 243.

4. And Law 12 establishes a singular rule with regard to the intestate succession of a natural sibling, that is, one who is not born of legitimate marriage.

In short, the reinterpretation of the regulation we are analyzing, the intestate succession of siblings, in the Partidas, introduces the principle of truncation in the distribution of the assets of half-siblings, as a clear manifestation of the Visigothic influence, as well as a special regulation of the case of natural children, which I will not go into as it exceeds the objectives of this work.

In any case, we can conclude from the above:

1. On the one hand, that, according to the doctrine, the joint call with the ascendants seems to be justified by the fact that they had to be taken into consideration in the calls, but taking into account that in many cases they were no longer alive when the succession was opened.
2. And on the other hand, that the distinction and preference of appeals between siblings of double and single bond, had much to do with the conception and patrimonial organization of the families, and the maintenance of the goods within the family *"strictu sensu,"* a fact that is reaffirmed with the reinterpretation made in Las Partidas regarding the specific trunk division of the goods in the case of the siblings of single bond. Once again, this is a clear manifestation of the direct connection between intestate succession and the protection of the nuclear family which, as we shall see, also exists today, but adapted to the new social reality.

3. Some brief considerations on the current Spanish regulation: articles 949–951 of the Spanish Civil Code versus article 442–10 of Book 4 of the Catalan Civil Code and some specialrules.

I shall continue by returning to the beginning of the paper, that is, to the case of Claudia's succession and to current law. As I have indicated, our State Civil Code includes in arts. 949 to 951 the appeal to siblings in intestate succession which, as we have seen and as the doctrine points out, undoubtedly represents a reinterpretation of the Roman rule contained in the Partidas, noting the following relevant changes, for the purposes of the matter we are analyzing:

1. Siblings are no longer called together with ascendants, but in the absence of ascendants and spouse (the latter is included in this position after the modification by Law 11/1981).[25]

---

25 Ley 11/1981, de 13 de mayo, de modificación del Código Civil en materia de filiación,

2. Furthermore, siblings are placed on the same level regardless of their filiation, that is, siblings with double and single filiation are called together, which is undoubtedly a step forward, but, having said that, it is a step forward.
3. Once the siblings are placed on an equal footing in the same order, a rule of distribution is established which, ignoring the truncation of Las Partidas (which is already fulfilled with the figure of the reserves) leads to a division of the relict patrimony which is not equal, and clearly to the detriment or discrimination of the inheritance rights of the siblings with a simple link.

And it is this rule of distribution that, in my opinion, makes no sense in the current family context, as it can lead to results that are certainly discriminatory, as was the case at the beginning of Claudia's succession. Above all, if we take into account the reality in which we find ourselves and which we cannot forget: we are in intestate succession, that is, subsidiary and in the absence of a will. In other words, the future testatrix, in our case Claudia, if she has no relationship with any of her siblings, either single or double, she can always choose to make a will and distribute her estate as she wishes, excluding, in this case, the sibling of her choice.

In addition, it is worth recalling the judicial doctrine on the application of the principle of equality and non-discrimination of art. 14 of the Spanish Constitution. To which we must add, among others, art. 39.1 which states "that the public authorities shall ensure the social, economic and legal protection of the family." In view of this, I pose the following question: when considering all the siblings called in the same order, is the sibling with the simple link really less of a sibling when it comes to the distribution of the estate of another deceased intestate sibling? This is really the fundamental question.

And the doctrine on this point is divided.[26] In my opinion, the answer, as I pointed out at the beginning, must be negative, and I corroborate this with the evolution that has begun in this sense in our country, in the first place, with the modification, if you like reinterpretation, that the Catalan legislator made when publishing Book 4 of the Civil Code (hereinafter, Cccat.), dedicated to successions. Thus, according to the provisions of art. 442–10.1 Cccat:

---

patria potestad y régimen económico del matrimonio.

26 Vid. for all, analysis of M. Nuñez Nuñez, Reglas del Código civil y legislaciones forales sobre la sucesión intestada de los parientes colaterales," in *La sucesión intestada de los parientes colaterales*, Madrid 2008, pp. 257–266.

> Siblings, in their own right, and the children of siblings, by right of representation, succeed to the succession of the deceased in preference to other collaterals, without distinction between siblings of double or single bond.

As the doctrine points out, the distinction is dispensed with in view of social changes and the increasingly frequent reality of reconstituted families, families, let's not forget, such as Claudia's.

And finally, it is curious that the Supreme Court itself has recognized and admitted, by way of example, when specifying the scope of civil liability ex delicto, the possibility of compensating the victims' siblings, without distinguishing between siblings with a double or single relationship, even when there is no proof of an effective relationship of cohabitation, and also concurring with other closer relatives.

Thus, by way of example, in STS 879/2005, of July 4, the following is said: "siblings belong to the family, who as such, even if there is no reference in the judgment to a relationship of cohabitation or of particular affection, are legitimised to receive iure propio the compensation for non-pecuniary damage when there are no other closer relatives … since siblings are part of a natural order of affection, paladinly recognised by certain penal precepts (concealment, excuse for acquittal, etc.) and in civil institutions in matters of intestate succession, guardianship and alimony debt."

And it is also appropriate to recall that this equalization has been included in other areas, for example, as recalled in the STSJ Castilla-La Mancha 16/2019, of June 13, 2019 (pp. 70–71), in Law 35/2015, of September 22, on the reform of the system for the assessment of damages and losses caused to persons in traffic accidents, which adapts the Spanish system of scales to the set of reforms generated at the Community level in relation to automobile insurance, and which tend to increase the protection of victims by guaranteeing sufficient compensation. Thus, in the field of basic personal injury due to death, the status of injured parties is recognized for siblings, specifically and in what is of interest here, it expressly equates in Art. 66 siblings with a double link with those with a single link.

> (1) Each brother receives a fixed amount which varies according to his age, depending on whether he is up to 30 or over 30 years of age. (2) For these purposes, a single-bonded sibling shall be treated in the same way as a dual-bonded sibling.

4. Byway of conclusions and a proposal *de lege ferenda*: the elimination of the exception and the return to the archaic Roman origin of intestate succession.

In short, the extension of the classic concept of family is a reality in the current European and global context and includes a variety of family models. And this indisputable reality, in my opinion, should also encourage an adaptation of this Roman rule contained in the Partidas, so as not to have to resort, in cases such as those of the succession of Claudia's brothers, to an interpretation of the rule which, going beyond its words, should consider in its practical application, what art. 3.1 of the CC provides, that is: *"the context, the historical and legislative background, and the social reality of the time in which they are to be applied, fundamentally taking into account the spirit and purpose of the rule."*

By way of conclusion. This being the current situation, given that the legal and family consequences derived from their application could generate situations of discrimination or difference of treatment between siblings, in the succession of a sibling, the proposal *de lege ferenda* set out here should involve: (a) on the one hand, the elimination of the use of the term "half-siblings" which, today, can certainly be contrary to the defense of fundamental rights; (b) on the other, a return to the original regulation of intestate succession contained in the XII Tables, in which, as we have seen, no such distinction was made; and (c) finally, the same would entail the elimination of the exception, in my opinion unjustified, to the essential principle of distribution *in capita* in the case of delation and concurrence of relatives of the same degree in intestate succession.

Bibliography

Castán, S., "Reflexiones sobre el origen de las sucesiones en Roma. El '*testamentum calatis comitis*' y su relación con la sucesión intestada," *RIDROM* 11 (2013), pp. 238–239.

D'Ors, A., *Derecho Privado Romano*, 8ª ed. rev., Pamplona 1991.

Duplá Marín, M. T., "Potestad parental catalana y autoridad familiar aragonesa: breve análisis comparativo de las facultades otorgadas a los padrastros respecto de los hijos menores del cónyuge o conviviente," in *El nuevo derecho de la persona y de la familia (libro segundo del Código Civil de Cataluña), Reyes Barrada Orellana (aut.), Martín Garrido Melero (aut.), Sergio Nasarre Aznar (aut.)*, ed. Bosch, Barcelona 2011.

Fadda, G., *Concetti fondamentali del Diritto ereditario romano*, vol. I, Milano 1949.

Finazzi, G., "La successione ab intestato," in *XII Tabulae. Testo e commento*. Tomo I, ed. M. F. Cursi, Napoli 2018, pp. 231–296.

García Fueyo, B., "Hijas e hijos legítimos en la sucesión intestada de su progenitor: de Roma a los códigos civiles (Igualdad y género)," *RIDROM* 28 (2022), pp. 60–184.

Herrero Medina, M., *Génesis del sistema sucesorio romano*, ed. Comares, Colección Derecho Romano y Ciencia Jurídica Europea, Granada 2020.

Nuñez Nuñez, M., "Reglas del Código civil y legislaciones forales sobre la sucesión intestada de los parientes colaterales," in *La sucesión intestada de los parientes colaterales*, Madrid 2008, pp. 257–266.

Pachecho Caballero, F. C., "Derecho histórico y Codificación. El derecho sucesorio," *AHDE* LXXXII (2012), pp. 113–147.

Pérez Martín, A., "Fuentes romanas en las Partidas," *GLOSSAE. REVISTA DE HISTORIA DEL DERECHO EUROPEO* 4 (1992), pp. 215–246.

Pulitanò, F., *Richerce sulla Bonorum Possessio ab intestato nell'età tardo-romana*, Torino 1999.

Voci, P., *Diritto ereditario romano, vol. secondo, parte especiale*, 2ª ed., Milano 1963.

Ewa Dawidziuk

Prisoners' contact with their families: Current problems based on the 2022 amendment of the Executive Penal Code and penitentiary practice in Poland

Abstract: The right to contact with family and outside world is very important for convicts and pre-trial detainees. Keeping in touch with families is an influential factor for people deprived of liberty. The major amendment to the Executive Penal Code in August 2022 introduced a number of changes in Poland regarding this issue, limiting both telephone and correspondence contacts. In the text I am discussing these changes, showing the practice of implementation of the new legislation. I am also presenting information on the possibility of using Internet to maintain contact with families and regulations regarding standard visits.

Keywords: prisoner, contact with the outside world, right to family life, phone calls, internet connections, visits, correspondence

1. Introduction

The issue of contact between convicts and their families is systematically discussed in the literature and plays a crucial role in the readaptation process. Reporting on the results of her research, Niełaczna indicates that prisoners ranked contact with the family fourth among the measures that help to achieve the goals of prison sentence. Prison officers, on the other hand, indicated that the family builds motivation and provides perspective, which is important for the successful implementation of the sentence.[1]

However, the amendment of the Executive Penal Code (later on: Code) of August 5, 2022[2] introduced a number of restrictions on this contact and as a result it was broadly discussed in Poland. It introduced fundamental changes with regard to the possibility for convicted persons and pre-trial detainees to have contact

1 M. Niełaczna, *Mechanizm nie-doskonały? Dobra administracja więzienna—ustalenia i konkluzje badawcze*, Warszawa 2017, p. 108.

2 *Journal of Law* 2022, item 1855, https://isap.sejm.gov.pl/isap.nsf/DocDetails.xsp?id=WDU20220001855 (accessed: 12.07.2023).

with their family members while keeping in touch with the outside world is an influential factor for all inmates. It has limited both telephone and correspondence contacts.

This is a major amendment to this Code,[3] which also introduced a limited period of seven days to file a complaint to the enforcement authorities, a fee for the use of electrical facilities in the cell, made it more difficult to contact a lawyer, and made it obligatory in principle to pay for all correspondence sent by convicts.[4]

I agree with Kwieciński that the role of the legislator is to create an appropriate legal framework allowing family ties to be maintained, so that, while meeting the needs of the detainee's minor family members, contribute at the same time to the success of his social readaptation.[5] Hence, the text analyses the current legal regulations in that context, comparing them with the previously applicable ones.

2. Means of contact between prisoners and their families

Article 102 of the Code contains a catalog of the rights of convicted persons. It places the right to maintain contacts with family and other relatives in the second position. Furthermore, Article 67 of the Code specifies the objectives of a custodial sentence. It is to arouse in a prisoner the will to cooperate in the formation of his socially desirable attitudes, in particular, a sense of responsibility and the need to respect legal order and thus to refrain from returning to crime. In the pursuit of these objectives, a very important role is played by maintaining contacts with the family and the outside world. The influence on the convicted persons shall also take into account work, education, cultural, educational and sporting activities as well as therapeutic measures.

3 The previous major revision took place in 2015. However, the changes implemented in 2022 tighten the regime of imprisonment or the execution of pre-trial detention, hence they draw particular attention. The content of the critical opinions submitted at the public consultation stage is available on the website of the Government Legislation Centre: https://legislacja.gov.pl/projekt/12353001/katalog/12826466#12826466, number of the project: UD282.

4 Extensive opinions at the drafting stage of the legal act were provided *inter alia* by the Ombudsman, HFHR, Prisoners' Families, https://legislacja.gov.pl/projekt/12353001/katalog/12826466#12826466 (accessed: 2.07.2023).

5 Kwieciński, A., "Skazani rodzice. Sytuacja prawna osadzonych sprawujących opiekę nad dziećmi," *Nowa Kodyfikacja Prawa Karnego* XXVIII (2012), p. 188.

The prisoner shall be enabled to maintain links primarily with his family and other relatives by such means as: visits, correspondence, telephone calls, parcels and in justified cases, with the approval of the director of the prison, also by other means of communication which in practice means the use of Skype. As Przesławski and Rokosz underline, the decision of the director regarding the other means of communication belongs to the group of decisions but is bound by legal norms defining: the entity entitled to issue the decision, the prerequisites and the procedure for issuing the decision, as well as the limits of the discretion, which must take into account the constitutional principle of social justice.[6] Nevertheless, in practice, it would be difficult to successfully challenge a negative decision of the director if other forms of contact with the family are provided. Besides, it is still not a right of the convicted person to communicate by electronic means with family members.

The censorship of correspondence, the supervision of visits, the control of conversations during visits, telephone conversations and conversations carried out by other means of communication, depends basically on the type of prison.

3. Phone calls

In the past, prisoners relied heavily on phone calls as the most convenient means of staying in touch with their families, with the ability to make daily calls for up to 5 minutes. However, following the amendment of the Code in 2022, the regulations changed to require contact "at least once a week," for approximately 10 minutes. Unfortunately, such vague regulations often result in a decrease in the frequency of communication and limiting it to only once per week.

We have previously witnessed a similar situation in the past concerning a regulation that mandated prisoners to shower "at least once a week." This requirement had been narrowly interpreted for many years, resulting in prisoners being allowed to shower only once a week.[7] The interpretation of this provision regarding the frequency of showers changed after the Constitutional Tribunal[8] took up the case. Although the Tribunal did not declare this type of legal norm

6 T. Przesławski and M. Rokosz, in *Kodeks karny wykonawczy. Komentarz*, ed. W. Sych, Warszawa 2023, art. 105.

7 The Ombudsman's application to the Constitutional Court dated July 3, 2014, case number KMP.571.26.2014.MMa/ST, https://bip.brpo.gov.pl/pl/content/trybunal-ws-kapieli-wiezniow (accessed: 20.06.2023).

8 Judgment of the Constitutional Court of March 31, 2015, Ref. U 6/14, https://trybunal.gov.pl/s/u-614 (accessed: 1.07.2023).

unconstitutional, it prompted the Prison Service to increase the bathing frequency from once to twice per week. However, based on past experience, there are concerns that the provision "at least" one telephone call per week may also be narrowly interpreted.

Practice in the application of this provision has demonstrated the validity of these concerns. In a significant number of units, a policy of using the phone to the family only once a week has been introduced. Within this limit, making phone calls to government offices were also possible.[9]

This is a drastic reduction in the frequency of telephone calls, which before the amendment were possible for about 5 minutes but every day (the length of the conversation is always regulated within internal order). Little is changed by the provision, which adds that in justified cases, the director of the prison may grant permission to use a telephone at the expense of the penitentiary. In particularly justified cases, especially when direct contact is impossible or particularly difficult or when it results from an urgent life situation, the director of the prison may grant permission to use a telephone to contact family and other close persons outside the time limits established in the internal order. However, the construction of this provision and the invocation of "justified cases" means that it will be difficult for convicts to obtain permission for an additional phone call, beyond the limit. Practice has shown that even a request for an additional call on a child's birthday, or the illness of a family member, was not sufficient justification and directors did not agree to an additional phone call.[10] This problem was presented by the Supreme Bar Council[11] as well as the Ombudsman.[12] The Director General of the Prison Service, replying to the Ombudsman, pointed out that the legislator had left the organization of the use of telephone sets to the directors of prisons, who take into account, inter alia, the organizational possibilities of the

---

9 Article 8(4) of the Code sets an additional time limit only for phone calls to defense counsel, an attorney who is a lawyer and a representative who is not an advocate or a legal adviser, which has been approved by the President of the Chamber of the European Court of Human Rights to represent the sentenced person before that Court.

10 Detailed description of sch situations can be found in the visit reposts conducted after 22 amendment, www.rpo.gov.pl.

11 Letter of 30.11.2022 of the President of the Supreme Bar Council to the Director General of the Prison Service, https://www.adwokatura.pl/admin/wgrane_pliki/file-20221130-pismo-do-czsw-36046.pdf.

12 The Ombudsman described in details the analysis of internal orders and the findings of the visits to penitentiary units. See more in general letter: https://bip.brpo.gov.pl/sites/default/files/2023-03/do_DGSW_telefon_kontakt_zewnetrzny_28.02.23.pdf.

unit, the number of telephones, as well as the necessity of realizing all statutory tasks of the Prison Service. Hence, in closed-type establishments, they may also indicate the day or days for making calls.[13]

Postulski stresses that access to the telephone must be made real by providing an adequate number of telephones.[14] In practice, however, this is not a problem as a larger number of telephones were installed in units during COVID-19. The essence of the problem lies in the restriction to only one call to the family. The telephones therefore remain unusable most of the time.

The implementation of the restrictions mainly refers to a closed-type facility. In the case of semi-open and open custodial establishments, it is in practice possible to call several times a week or even every day. Therefore, convicts serving sentences in closed prisons and their families have submitted several hundred complaints to the Polish Ombudsman since the amendment to the Code entered into force. The complaints point to the right of every child to have contact with each parent, even these deprived of liberty.[15] The detainees indicate that the sudden cessation of daily telephone contact negatively affects their families, especially the children, who cannot understand why father/mother used to call more often taking an interest in the children's daily problems, but now this is not possible. Considering the previous discontinued contacts during the pandemic, in view of the failure to organize visits, it is important to see the negative consequences for the children of parents deprived of their liberty.[16]

In the case of pre-trial detainees, the Code contains separate regulations for contact with the family. Article 217c § 1c states that a pre-trial detainee, in particularly justified cases, especially when direct contact is impossible or particularly difficult, or when it is due to an urgent life situation, may use, at times established in the internal order in force in the pre-trial detention center, a self-dialing telephone to contact a person other than a lawyer. The carrying out of the conversation requires each time the consent of the authority at whose disposal the pre-trial detainee remains. The authority at whose disposal the provisionally

---

13 See the whole answer: https://bip.brpo.gov.pl/sites/default/files/2023-04/Odpowiedz_DGSW_telefon_kontakt_03.04.2023.pdf.

14 See more: Postulski… p. 512.

15 In the letters the authors of complaints underlined that this right is regulated in Article 9(3) of the Convention on the Rights of the Child, https://www.ohchr.org/en/instruments-mechanisms/instruments/convention-rights-child.

16 S. Minson and C. Flynn, "Symbiotic Harms of Imprisonment and the Effect on Children's Right to Family Life," *The International Journal of Children's Rights* 29/2 (2021) pp. 308–309.

detained person remains shall issue an order authorizing the use of a self-dialing telephone unless there is a reasonable fear that it will be used: (1) to unlawfully obstruct criminal proceedings; (2) to commit an offense, in particular incitement to commit an offense.

In practice, this kind of statutory provision means that the disposing authority will only give its consent to a person in pre-trial detention in special circumstances when family members do not have permission to see the detainee. Complaints about the lack of consent to telephone contact with a pre-trial detainee often reach the Ombudsman. Since the disposing authorities do not trust telephone calls to lawyers and it happens more and more often that they do not consent to such telephone contact, it is even more so that they refuse telephone contact with family members. They argue this on the grounds of the stage of the criminal proceedings, the fear of obstruction, the uncertainty of who will be on the other end of the phone. During the COVID-19 pandemic, when visits were not implemented so pre-trial detainees were in a particularly difficult situation. Usually they were not given permission to make contact with their families via the telephone, which, in the absence of visits, meant that they could only send letters and thus maintain contact with the outside world.

Prior to the 2022 amendments to the Code, the disposing authority did not consent to telephone contact when there was a reasonable fear that it would be used: (1) to unlawfully obstruct criminal proceedings; (2) to commit an offense, in particular, incitement to commit an offense. In contrast, the legislation did not specify that telephone calls to the family could only be authorized in particularly justified cases. The amendment has significantly altered the situation, resulting in fewer instances where permission is granted to contact the family by telephone. Instead, there is now a preference for visits within the custodial area. Online meetings with the family are not allowed for pre-trial detainees, as described below.

The topic was noticed within the Global Prison Trends 2023 from the financial point of view. It illustrates that globally families face multiple costs in maintaining contact with persons in prison through paying to receive phone calls or loading money on phone accounts. However, communication services in prisons tend to be monopolized by a few companies that charge unaffordable rates.[17]

17 Penal Reform International, Global Prison Trends 2023, p. 137.

4. Visits

Associated costs with visiting someone in prison remain unaffordable for large segments of people affected.[18] This s a global trend which is noticed also in Poland. Particularly after COVID-19 and in view of placing prisoners far from their families' home, the frequency of visits within the prisons is not high.

The visit lasts 60 minutes and the convicted person has the right to see a family member or other close person. Other persons may be allowed to visit after receiving permission from the director of the prison and being put on the list of visitors. The frequency of visits depends on the type of prison. In a closed-type unit it is two visits per month, in a semi-open unit with three and in an open unit with an unlimited number of visits.

A pre-trial detainee may be granted visitation after a consent order has been issued by the authority at whose disposal he remains and he is entitled to at least one visit per month with a person close to him. Consent to visitation may only be refused if there is a well-founded fear that the visitation will be used: (1) to unlawfully obstruct criminal proceedings; (2) to commit an offense, in particular incitement to commit an offense. This means that pre-trial detainees are not always allowed to see family members or other relatives. However, in the ECtHR's view, restrictions on a pre-trial detainee, including restrictions on visits with family, do not in principle constitute a violation of Article 8 of the European Convention of Human Rights. The key point, however, is that these restrictions must be justified and proportionate.[19] For example in the new judgment of the ECtHR against Lithuania, the detainee's inability to see his wife and daughter for as long as nine months was judged by the Court to be "not necessary in a democratic society" and therefore in breach of Article 8 ECHR.[20]

Dawidziuk and Kotowska also point to the aspect of visits by two persons who are deprived of their liberty, in particular when they are spouses which, without the support of the prison administration, is not really possible. There are also

18 Ibid., p. 37.

19 See the ECtHR judgment of 11.10.2005 in the case of Bagiński v. Poland, application no. 37444/97.

20 European Court of Human Rights, Case of Deltuva v. Lithuania, Application no. 38144/20, March 21, 2023, point 44–49.

aspects of so-called "intimate visits" or visits with children in institutions.[21] In this context, however, the amendment in 2022 did not introduce anything new.[22]

5. Online visits with the family via Skype

Online visits play an important role for prisoners who are serving the sentence. It's hard to explain why within the Polish penitentiary institutions it's allowed to use only Skype while at the same time Zoom, Teams, Google Meets or other forms of instant communication are forbidden. However, it must be underlined that only people who are serving the sentence can meet online with their families. Pre-trial detainees cannot use this form of communication as Article 217c of the Code states that a pre-trial detainee may not use means of communication other than a telephone.[23]

In practice during the COVID-19 pandemic regular visits were not organized within Polish penitentiary units[24] at all for many months[25] so as a result Internet communicator Skype was used instead. However, this trend was characteristic not only for Poland, but for many other countries in the world.[26] It

21 E. Dawidziuk and K. Kotowska, "Nowe technologie w komunikacji skazanych i tymczasowo aresztowanych ze światem zewnętrznym," *Archiwum Kryminologii, PAN* 43/2 (2021), pp. 11–12.

22 Intimate visitation is a form of reward referred to in the Code as "visitation in a separate room without a supervisor" (Article 138 § 1, point 3), and visitation with children in a foster care facility can in principle only take place by way of a pass granted on a discretionary basis by the director of the prison on the basis of Article 141a of the Code.

23 Till 1.07.2015 the use of phone by the pre-trial detainees was forbidden. The law changed on the base of the judgment of the Constitutional Court of November 25, 2014. K 54/13 states that the provision of Article 217c, in so far as it absolutely prohibited the use of a telephone by a pre-trial detainee to communicate with his lawyer, is incompatible with Article 42(2) in conjunction with Article 31(3) of the Constitution of the Republic of Poland.

24 During COVID-19 all prohibitions were based on Article 247 of the Code which states that in cases justified by special sanitary or health reasons or by a serious threat to security, the director of a penal institution may, for a limited period of time, inter allies withhold or restrict the granting of visits and walks, the carrying out of collective activities, worship and religious services, shopping, receiving parcels, and the use of telephones, or even order the closure of cells.

25 The decision to stop visitation was taken by the Prison Service in March 2020. Only solicitors and barristers, as well as chaplains who were employees of the units, were allowed on the premises of prisons and detention centers.

26 Penal Reform International, Global Prison Trends 2021, p. 33.

was comfortable way to see online with the members of inmates' families and, at the same time, a form of protection for prisoners from contracting coronavirus, which in places of isolation could potentially lead to large outbreaks of infection.[27] After coronavirus period of time, the use of Skype was limited to one or two conversations per month for about 20 minutes.[28] However, nowadays families do not come to prisons in order to take part in visitations as often as it was in the past because of the distance from their homes or costs connected with that.

The prisoner shall submit a request to the director of a prison for permission to visit online. In the request he shall specify the data and degree of relationship of the person with whom he wishes to carry out the visit. This information is checked in the Central Database of Persons Deprived of Liberty. The date of the interview is established earlier and indicated in the request to the director of the unit for permission for online visitation or only after the positive consideration of the request of the convicted person. The convict himself notifies the family of the date of the meeting.[29]

Still the communication through Internet is not described within the Code as the right of a prisoner. It's regulated only within internal regulations and it differs in each penitentiary unit.

In my view, it is reasonable to create a *de lege ferenda* postulate to regulate in the Code both the right of convicted persons to visit via Internet links and the right of pre-trial detainees to such visits, provided that there are no grounds for refusing to allow a detained person to see a particular family member. Skype visits are controlled, a prison officer has control over who the prisoner is talking to. Therefore, it appears that this form of visitation can be safe for the prison and is a convenient form of contact for prisoners as well as their families.

---

27 WHO has developed a set of publications on preparedness, prevention and control of COVID-19 in prisons, https://www.who.int/europe/emergencies/situations/covid-19/prisons-and-covid-19 (accessed: 2.07.2023).

28 A content analysis of the internal orders in force at the end of December 2022 makes it possible to indicate just such an acceptable frequency even though more computers were bought during pandemic.

29 See more: E. Dawidziuk and K. Kotowska, "Nowe technologie w komunikacji skazanych i tymczasowo aresztowanych ze światem zewnętrznym," *Archiwum Kryminologii, PAN* 43/2 (2021), pp. 176–178.

6. Correspondence between prisoners and family

According to new law, the convict shall bear the costs of all correspondence, including those to families or official correspondence (even to a lawyer, Ombudsman). In particularly justified cases, a prisoner who does not have cash may receive postage stamps for correspondence from the prison administration (Article 105 par. 6a of the Code). It refers also to pre-trial detainees. Postulski underlies that this is a true limitation of the right to correspondence and discrimination of prisoners. However, the detainee has the right to file the complaint to the penitentiary court in case of any decision of the director that limits the contact with the outside world.[30]

The Prison Service indicates that previously the possibility to receive two stamps per month, and in the case of complaints or requests for further funding, was abused. The expenses of penitentiary units, indicated in the justification to the draft amendment, reached sometimes as much as PLN 23,000 (€4,800) per year per inmate. This created a sense of social injustice by providing funding to persons deprived of liberty, from which persons outside the prison couldn't benefit.[31] It is worth noting that complaints from prisoners about this legislative change do not reach the Office of the Ombudsman in Poland.[32] It is therefore not the kind of amendment that would be perceptible or make contact with the family so difficult that it becomes the subject of numerous complaints, which was the case in the context of limiting the frequency of telephone calls.

A convicted person's correspondence with his or her family is subject to censorship and supervision, unless the Code states otherwise (Article 8a of the Code). It is described more precisely in provisions relating to the different types of prison. In a closed establishment, correspondence is subject to censorship (Article 90 point 8 of the Code), while in a semi-open and open establishment it may be subject to censorship (Article 91 point 10 and Article 92 point 13). Prior to the 2022 amendment, correspondence was not censored in an open penitentiary units. The amendment also introduced in open prisons the possibility to control conversations during visits and telephone or Skype conversations of prisoners.

30 J. Postulski, "Komentarz do art. 105 k.k.w.," in *Kodeks karny wykonawczy. Komentarz*, 5 wydanie, ed. J. Lachowski, Warszawa 2023, p. 509.

31 Explanatory Memorandum to the Draft Law on Amendments to the Act—Executive Penal Code and Certain Other Laws of 21.06.2022, 9th term, Sejm. print no. 2376, https://sejm.gov.pl/Sejm9.nsf/druk.xsp?nr=2376 (accessed: 10.07.2023).

32 As Director of the Team in the Ombudsman's Office that receives prisoners' complaints, I observe a certain trend in the topics that convicted and pre-trial detainees.

Conducting these checks in an open-type unit is always optional and the rationale is the security of the prison and the protection of society from crime.[33] It can therefore be expected that such forms of control in open prisons will take place in exceptional situations.

Pre-trial detainee's correspondence with members of family may be kept, censored or supervised by the authority at whose disposal he remains, unless that authority orders otherwise. In the absence of such action by the disposing authority, the decision to keep, censor or supervise may be taken by the director of the pre-trial detention center, who shall notify the detainee, the penitentiary judge and the authority at whose disposal the detainee remains of the reasons for such action (Article 217a of the Code).

7. Conclusions

Contacts with the outside world constitute implementation of the integration rule,[34] especially contact with family is crucial for a person who is deprived liberty. At the level of *soft law*, international organizations stress the need to ensure such contact regardless of whether we are dealing with a convicted person (including extremely long sentences) or a person in pre-trial detention.[35] The use of information and communication technology such as video-conferencing, telephone systems or internet shall be facilitated between face-to-face visits and should not involve excessive costs. Besides rules for making and receiving telephone calls and other forms of communication with children shall be applied flexibly to maximize communication between imprisoned parents and their

---

33 T. Przesławski and M. Rokosz, in *Kodeks karny wykonawczy. Komentarz*, ed. W. Sych, Warszawa 2023, art. 92.

34 M. Niełaczna and W. Klaus, "Wykonywanie przez polskie władze zalecenia Europejskiego Komitetu do Spraw Zapobiegania Torturom oraz Nieludzkiemu lub Poniżającemu Traktowaniu lub Karaniu (CPT). Raport z badan," in *Przestrzeganie praw osób pozbawionych wolności. O monitorowaniu jednostek penitencjarnych*, ed. W. Klaus and M. Niełaczna, Warsaw 2008, p. 156.

35 Nelson Mandela Rules reg. 58—Resolution adopted by the General Assembly on December 17, 2015, A/RES/70/175. United Nations Standard Minimum Rules for the Treatment of Prisoners (the Nelson Mandela Rules); European Prison Rules, reg. 24—Recommendation Rec (2006)2-version of the Committee of Ministers to member states of the Council of Europe on the European Prison Rules, adopted by the Committee of Ministers on January 11, 2006 at the 952 meeting of the ministers' deputies, revised and supplemented by the Committee of Ministers on July 1, 2020, at the 1380th meeting of the Ministers' Deputies (2006).

children.[36] The CPT goes even farther and presents its recommendations that remand prisoners should be allowed to communicate with their family and other persons in the same way as sentenced prisoners. Besides all inmates should have visits at least one hour every week and possibility to call at least once a week.[37]

We are far from the solutions presented in the abovementioned international recommendations in Poland, and the just introduced amendments to the provisions of the Code make contact with the family even more difficult. Hence, it is important to emphasized that close family ties provide protection against feelings of alienation, strengthening mental resilience and can be a source of support in critical situations, including times of radical change such as the incarceration of a family member. At the same time they are one of the basic variables for the success of the rehabilitation process of prisoners.[38] Emotional ties with the family of persons deprived of their liberty have a positive effect on reducing the emotional tensions experienced by prisoners, give them a sense of belonging to a family and thus motivate them to participate in the rehabilitation process.[39]

The implemented provisions of the Code limiting the frequency of telephone contacts, an obligation in principle to pay for all correspondence, the low frequency of Skype visits and the costs that the family has to incur for coming to the prison to participate in the visit, make the negative changes for all inmates. At the same time, a lot depends on the prison officers themselves, who may interpret the provision stipulating "at least one conversation per week" in favor of the convicted persons. This should be encouraged, taking into account how important a role the convicted person's family plays in the readaptation process.

Last but not least, in the context of the issues presented, it is worth recalling once again what the Strasbourg Court has raised on several occasions. Namely, with incarceration in a penitentiary institution a person loses the right

---

36 Recommendation CM/Rec(2018)5 of the Committee of Ministers to member States concerning children with imprisoned parents, adopted by the Committee of Ministers on April 4, 2018 at the 1312th meeting of the Ministers' Deputies, point 25 and 26.

37 The 26th General Report of the European Committee for the Prevention of Torture and Inhuman or Degrading Treatment or Punishment (CPT), published in 2017 (CPT/Inf(2017)5), point 59.

38 S. Bębas, "Skutki uwięzienia członka rodziny i znaczenie rodziny dla więziennego funkcjonowania osadzonych oraz ich resocjalizacji i readaptacji," *Ruch Pedagogiczny* 4 (2017), p. 121.

39 More in A. Rzepliński, *Rodziny więźniów długoterminowych*, Wrocław 1981; T. Sakowicz, *Wybrane aspekty środowiska rodzinnego w percepcji i ocenie osób osadzonych w polskich zakładach karnych*, Kraków 2009.

to personal liberty, but enjoys all the other fundamental rights regulated by the European Convention on Human Rights. This includes the right to respect for family law. Any limitation of this right must be justified on an individual basis.[40]

Bibliography

Bębas, S., "Skutki uwięzienia członka rodziny i znaczenie rodziny dla więziennego funkcjonowania osadzonych oraz ich resocjalizacji i readaptacji," *Ruch Pedagogiczny* 4 (2017).

Dawidziuk, E., and Kotowska, K., "Nowe technologie w komunikacji skazanych i tymczasowo aresztowanych ze światem zewnętrznym," *Archiwum Kryminologii, PAN* 43/2 (2021).

European Court of Human Rights, Case of Deltuva v. Lithuania, Application no. 38144/20, March 21, 2023.

European Court of Human Rights, Case of Bagiński v. Poland, Application no. 37444/97, October 11, 2005.

European Court of Human Rights, Case of Mirgadirov. v. Azerbaijan and Turkey, Application no. 62775/14, September 17, 2020.

European Court of Human Rights, Case of Andrey Smirnov v. Russia, Application no. 43149/10, February 13, 2018.

General letter of the Polish Ombudsman of 28.02.2023 to General Director of the Prison Service, https://bip.brpo.gov.pl/sites/default/files/2023-03/do_DGSW_telefon_kontakt_zewnetrzny_28.02.23.pdf.

Klaus, W., and Niełaczna, M. (eds.), *Przestrzeganie praw osób pozbawionych wolności. O monitorowaniu jednostek penitencjarnych*, Warszawa 2008.

Kwieciński, A., "Skazani rodzice. Sytuacja prawna osadzonych sprawujących opiekę nad dziećmi," *Nowa Kodyfikacja Prawa Karnego* XXVIII (2012).

Lachowski, J. (ed.), *Kodeks karny wykonawczy. Komentarz*, 5 wydanie, Warszawa 2023.

Letter of the President of the Supreme Bar Council of 30.11.2022 to the Director General of the Prison Service, https://www.adwokatura.pl/admin/wgrane_pliki/file-20221130-pismo-do-czsw-36046.pdf.

Machel, H., "Rodzina skazanego jako współuczestnik jego resocjalizacji penitencjarnej, readaptacji i reintegracji społecznej," *Resocjalizacja Polska* 7 (2014).

40 Judgment of the ECHR in case Mirgadirov. v. Azerbaijan and Turkey, case no. 62775/14; Andrey Smirnov v. Russia, no. 43149/10.

Minson, S., and Flynn, C., "Symbiotic Harms of Imprisonment and the Effect on Children's Right to Family Life," *The International Journal of Children's Rights* 29/2 (2021).

Niełaczna, M., *Mechanizm nie-doskonały? Dobra administracja więzienna—ustalenia i konkluzje badawcze*, Warszawa 2017.

Przesławski, T., and Rokosz, M., "Komentarz do art. 105," in *Kodeks karny wykonawczy. Komentarz*, ed. W. Sych, Warszawa 2023.

Penal Reform International, Global Prison Trends, 2021.

Penal Reform International, Global Prison Trends, 2023.

Resolution adopted by the General Assembly on December 17, 2015, A/RES/70/175. United Nations Standard Minimum Rules for the Treatment of Prisoners (the Nelson Mandela Rules).

Recommendation Rec (2006)2-version of the Committee of Ministers to member states of the Council of Europe on the European Prison Rules, adopted by the Committee of Ministers on January 11, 2006, at the 952 meeting of the ministers' deputies, revised and supplemented by the Committee of Ministers on July 1, 2020, at the 1380th meeting of the Ministers' Deputies (2006).

Recommendation CM/Rec(2018)5 of the Committee of Ministers to member States concerning children with imprisoned parents, adopted by the Committee of Ministers on April 4, 2018, at the 1312th meeting of the Ministers' Deputies, points 25 and 26.

Rzepliński, A., *Rodziny więźniów długoterminowych*, Wrocław 1981.

Sakowicz, T., *Wybrane aspekty środowiska rodzinnego w percepcji i ocenie osób osadzonych w polskich zakładach karnych*, Kraków 2009.

Siemaszko, A., *Granice tolerancji*, Warszawa 1993.

Szymanowska, A., *Więzienie i co dalej*, Warszawa 2003.

The 26th General Report of the European Committee for the Prevention of Torture and Inhuman or Degrading Treatment or Punishment (CPT), published in 2017 (CPT/Inf(2017)5).

World Health Organization, Preparedness, prevention and control of COVID-19 in prisons and other places of detention, Copenhagen: WHO Regional Office for Europe, 2021. License: CC BY-NC-SA 3.0 IGO.

Anna Wilk

New problem in family law: "Animal family members" after divorce—Reflections in the context of Polish and Spanish law

Abstract: The article will refer to the legal consequences of a new trend in modern families: treating animals as family members. More and more people treat animals not only as creatures useful in the farm or accompanying people, but as full members of the family, sometimes even "substituting" their own offspring. In case of a divorce of the spouses, there is the problem—who should stay with the animal and what the possible contacts of the other spouse with this animal should look like. This issue may lead to conflicts between former spouses, resulting even in the attempts to kidnap the animals by one of the spouses. The article will take into account the recent changes in Spanish law, aimed at regulating the situation of animals after divorce, as well as the position of Polish doctrine and jurisprudence. In Spanish law, the judicial authority must entrust the care of the companion animals to one or both spouses, and determine the way of contacts with the animal, as well as the distribution of the charges associated with the care of the animal, all taking into account the interest of the family members and the well-being of the animal. The way of treating animals can also influence the decision of custody over children, because the court shall not grant the custody to a parent guilty of mistreating animals. The Author will also present *de lege ferenda* conclusions, regarding the possibility of regulating these issues in Polish law, because Polish law, in contrast to Spanish law, does not include any provisions regarding the fate of animals in case of divorce. In the Author's opinion, if Poland decides to regulate animals' situation after the divorce, Spanish experiences should set an example. Obviously, not everyone may accept the trend of treating animals as family members, but this trend is real, and the law should address the needs of the society.

Keywords: animals, family, divorce, spouses

1. Introduction

There is no doubt that currently, mainly in Western countries, the issue of broadly understood animal welfare plays an increasingly important role. This is due, firstly, to the growing power of the ecological movement and the development of philosophical concepts of animal rights,[1] and secondly to the growing

---

1 See T. Pietrzykowski, "Problem podmiotowości prawnej zwierząt z perspektywy filozofii prawa," *Przegląd Filozoficzny—Nowa Seria* 94 (2015), p. 247.

importance of animals in society and the change in attitudes toward them. More and more people treat animals not only as creatures useful in the farm or accompanying people, but as full members of the family, sometimes even "substituting" offspring.[2] In the case of family breakdown and divorce of spouses, there arises the problem of determining which of the divorced spouses should take care of the animal and what the other spouse's possible contacts with this animal should look like.

As T. Pietrzykowski rightly notes, "the fact that some animals have an experiential (sensitive) awareness and the perception of its moral significance has resulted in the so-called dereification of animals in many legal systems. It means the formal exclusion of animals from the legal category of 'things' (…) However, this is not accompanied by their personification, and therefore animals are not at the same time included in the category of 'persons'. Although they are not things, they do not become subjects of law. Their handling is subjected to legal restrictions, but they themselves remain more subject of man's duties, rather than subject to any rights ascribed to them."[3] Thus, Polish civil law, and also family law, is adapted to treat animals as objects forming part of the joint property of the spouses, rather than as beings whose welfare should be taken into account in the proceedings for the division of property.

2. Situation of animals after divorce in Polish law

Pursuant to the Polish Act of August 21, 1997, on the Protection of Animals,[4] an animal, as a living being capable of suffering, is not a thing, and a human owes it respect, protection and care. However, the same act provides that in matters not regulated therein, the provisions concerning things shall apply accordingly to animals. Therefore, in proceedings for the division of joint property between former spouses, the animal simply has the status of joint property that must be divided. Of course, due to the fact that physical division will be impossible in this case, it will be necessary to make a decision to grant the sole ownership

---

2 See A. Dawidczyk, *Zwierzęta zamiast dzieci? Coraz więcej par podejmuje taką decyzję*, http://www.kobieta.pl, 18.9.2019 [accessed: 5.5.2023]; A. Wilk, "Problem uznania więzi emocjonalnej ze zwierzęciem za dobro osobiste w orzecznictwie sądów polskich," *Monitor Prawniczy* 22 (2022), p. 1115; Wilk A., "Zwierzę jako podmiot prawa spadkowego? Uwagi de lege lata i de lege ferenda," *Edukacja Prawnicza* 2 (2022/2023), p. 50.

3 See T. Pietrzykowski, "Problem podmiotowości," p. 247. See also A. Wilk, "Problem uznania," p. 1115; A. Wilk, "Zwierzę jako podmiot," p. 50.

4 Consolidated text *Journal of Laws* 2022, item 572, 2375 as amended.

of an animal to one of the spouses. The Polish Civil Code[5] only provides that an indivisible thing may be awarded to one of the co-owners, according to the circumstances, with the obligation to repay the remaining owners (Article 212 § 2 of the Civil Code). It does not, however, specify any important circumstances to be taken into account when disposing of the co-ownership of an animal. Also, the Polish Family Code[6] does not refer to the issue of animals at all, regulating in the event of divorce only the manner of adjudication of parental authority, contacts with children and the possible division of joint property.[7] Therefore, neither the issues of circumstances affecting the decision to grant an animal to a specific person, nor the problem of contacts of former spouses with an animal after divorce, are regulated in Polish law. The lack of regulations causes disputes that often deepen the conflict between former spouses—there have already been cases such as the husband kidnapping a dog, which was taken by the wife after the divorce.[8]

T. Justyński has a negative opinion on the possibility of applying by analogy the provisions on parent-child contact, approving the thesis that the structure and justification of contact with children are not transferable to the "master-dog" relationship, pointing out that even a more "veiled" approach, referring to the need to take into account the specificity of the subject of division, that is, the special status of animals, is also unacceptable.[9] The aforementioned Author points at previous German and French judicature, where the courts emphasized the need to take into account the special status of animals in the proceedings for the division of joint property, but considered it unacceptable to regulate contacts with them—the special status of an animal should therefore only affect the decision to grant it to a specific person, but it cannot be the basis for creating a right to contact with animals.[10]

---

5 Act of April 23, 1964—Civil Code, consolidated text *Journal of Laws* 2023, item 326 as amended.

6 Act of February 25, 1964, Family and Guardianship Code, consolidated text *Journal of Laws* 2022, item 2140 as amended.

7 See K. Flaga-Gieruszyńska and A. Zieliński, *Rozwód. Materialnoprawne podstawy rozwodu oraz postępowanie odrębne w sprawie o rozwód. Komentarz praktyczny z orzecznictwem. Wzory pism procesowych*, Warszawa 2021, p. 100.

8 https://www.rp.pl/prawo-rodzinne/art19277411-rozwod-z-domowym-czworonogiem, 12.1.2022 [accessed: 5.5.2023].

9 T. Justyński, "Znak czasu. Porozwodowe 'prawo do kontaktów' z domowymi czworonogami?," *Rodzina i Prawo* 14–15 (2010), p. 101.

10 Ibid., pp. 99–100.

However, in Polish literature and judicature, there were also attempts to improve the animals' situation in civil law in general, by using the construction of personal rights. The emotional bond with an animal is not listed in the catalog of personal rights indicated in art. 23 of the Civil Code, however, this catalog is open, which makes it possible to seek legal protection also for personal rights not listed in it. The content of this catalog is affected by the revaluation taking place in the social consciousness, related to the progress of civilization and changes in culture and customs.[11] Therefore, in jurisprudence, values not explicitly mentioned in the jurisprudence were also considered as such goods—particularly the values concerning the emotional relations of a person, such as, for example, a bond with a family member[12] or the cult of a deceased loved one.[13] On the other hand, attempts to recognize human-animal bonds as personal goods have already been the subject of legal analyses, but they met with various assessments, both positive and negative.[14]

Some Polish courts stated in favor considering an emotional bond with animals as a personal right. However, these cases did not concern the divorce, but mainly the compensation liability for an animal's death as a result of a bite, an accident or an unsuccessful veterinary surgery.

For example, in the judgment of the District Court in Kraków of 7.9.2017 II Ca 1111/17,[15] it was stated that "the tragic consequences of biting the plaintiff's dog led to a violation of the plaintiff's personal good in the form of a special and

11 J. Panowicz-Lipska, in *Kodeks cywilny. Komentarz. Tom I. Komentarz do art. 1–352*, ed. M. Gutowski, 3rd ed., Warszawa 2021, Legalis, art. 23, Nb 5.

12 See judgment of Polish Supreme Court of 27.3.2018, III CZP 60/17, Legalis; A. Wilk, "Zadośćuczynienie za krzywdę osobom najbliższym poszkodowanego—glosa do uchwały SN z dnia 27.3.2018r., III CZP 60/17," *Monitor Prawniczy* 15 (2018), pp. 830–835. However, considering family bond as a personal right was also criticized—see J. Sadomski, in *Kodeks cywilny. Komentarz. Część ogólna. Przepisy wprowadzające Kodeks cywilny. Prawo o notariacie (art. 79–95 i 96–99)*, ed. Osajda K., 30th ed., Warszawa 2022, Legalis, art. 23, Nb 14; T. Grzeszak, "Dobro osobiste jako dobro zindywidualizowane," *Przegląd Sądowy* 4 (2018), p. 37.

13 See judgments of Polish Supreme Court of 31.3.1980r, II CR 88/80, Legalis and 23.9.2009r., I CSK 346/08, Legalis; Ł. Cudny and K. Kryla, "Kult pamięci osoby zmarłej jako dobro osobiste," *Monitor Prawniczy* 16 (2011), p. 897.

14 K. Panfil, "Więź emocjonalna ze zwierzęciem a dobra osobiste," *Radca Prawny. Zeszyty Naukowe* 3 (2021), p. 149; A. Wilk, "Problem uznania," pp. 1115–1121.

15 http://orzeczenia.krakow.so.gov.pl/content/$N/152010000001003_II_Ca_001111_2017_Uz_2017-09-07_002 [accessed: 5.5.2023]. See also A. Wilk, "Problem uznania," pp. 1115–1121.

authentic bond that he had with this animal. This event and its consequences also had an impact on the functioning of the plaintiff's family, affected by the effects of the event itself, which had a drastic course, the suffering of the dog and finally its death. In this context, the infringement of the plaintiff's personal good should be seen." The court emphasized that if the defendant had properly secured her animal, the plaintiff's dog would not have been bitten to death, which resulted in a number of consequences and adversely affected the mental sphere of the plaintiff and his family. In the opinion of the Court, if it had not been for this event, the plaintiff and his family would have functioned in the same way, and the plaintiff would not have to face not only his own sadness and mental suffering resulting from the loss of the dog to which he was attached, but also to see how members of his immediate family, especially children, are experiencing sadness and grief. Considering the above, the Court recognized the rightness of the demand to award compensation for the loss of the dog and indicated that this amount should compensate the plaintiff for the harm suffered by him, resulting from the violation of personal rights, which was a special and authentic bond with the dog that occupied a special place in the plaintiff's home—the dog was a family companion, a favorite and a source of joy. This ruling correctly captures the basic aspect of the discussed issue, which is the mental suffering of the animal's guardian as a result of its death.

Similar argumentation was presented in the judgment of the District Court in Bełchatów of 16.10.2017, I C 74/16,[16] in which it was indicated that a dog or a cat is a creature with the ability to feel joy and attachment, and an emotional bond between a human and an animal may be formed. The breaking of this bond often results in a long-lasting feeling of sadness. The reparation in this case was intended to fulfill the role of satisfaction and thus is aimed at alleviating suffering.

In turn, the District Court in Kraków, in its judgment of 22.11.2016, II Ca 1883/16,[17] also pointed out that "there is no doubt that in culture, and not only Polish, dogs are favored in many respects. Dogs not only accompany in everyday life, but also perform their traditional duties, warning against the intrusion of an intruder and defending against direct attack. It is clear from the established facts

16 http://orzeczenia.belchatow.sr.gov.pl/content/$N/152515050000503_I_C_000074_2016_Uz_2017-10-16_001 [accessed: 5.5.2023]. See also A. Wilk, "Problem uznania …," pp. 1115–1121.

17 http://orzeczenia.krakow.so.gov.pl/content/$N/152010000001003_II_Ca_001883_2016_Uz_2016-11-22_002 [accessed: 5.5.2023]. See also A. Wilk, "Problem uznania," pp. 1115–1121.

that the plaintiff's dog served as a family and companion dog. In the common perception, a dog is a symbol of faithfulness and selfless friendship, and the loyalty and devotion it shows are part of its natural instinct, closely related to the human sense of love and friendship. Thanks to this, many dog owners treat them as full members of the family. As a side note, it is worth mentioning that the dog is the most popular pet in Poland. Due to its features, it is an animal with which man has deep, multidimensional relationships. Not only is it called man's best friend, but it is also the most predestined to establish a strong bond with man. Losing it is an irreparable loss, resulting in suffering, grief and tears."

If, according to some Polish courts, an emotional bond with animals can be recognized as a personal right, it should have an impact on the decision who should stay with the animal after the divorce. However, cases concerning compensation for breakup of emotional bond with animals are still rather rare and some of the courts remain skeptical toward the idea of considering an emotional bond with an animal as a personal right.[18] Therefore, also the fate of animals after the divorce is very rarely the subject of Polish courts' deliberation. Due to the lack of legal regulations, the disputes between former spouses concerning the animals are rather solved in a conciliatory way than in courts. The deeper conflicts, concerning a "kidnapping" of an animal by one of the spouses are sometimes reported to the Police, but if an animal belongs to both spouses, there is no theft. In a rare example of a judgment referring to the animal's fate after separation of the partners—the judgment of the District Court for Warszawa-Wola in Warsaw of 24.11.2020, I C1855/19,[19] the Court awarded custody of the dog to a partner who was neither listed in the dog's health book as a guardian nor paid for the dog from his account. However, in the opinion of the Court, in accordance with the principles of social coexistence, it was reasonable to leave the dog with him. The judge indicated that the dog, as a sentient being, needs a certain stability in life and changing the pet's home would be associated with unnecessary stress. According to the Court, dog is not something that can be freely moved and expected to adapt to the plans and changes in the life of its owner. The Court stated that the removal of the dog from the environment in which it lives can have a negative impact on it, because it would be deprived of

18 For examples of such critical judgments see A. Wilk, "Problem uznania," pp. 1115–1121.

19 Unpublished—cited after B. Michalski, "Spór o wydanie psa. Sąd: zwierzę nie jest rzeczą, którą można dowolnie przestawiać," *Gazeta Prawna* 18.2.2021, https://serwisy.gazetaprawna.pl/orzeczenia/artykuly/8098085,spor-o-wydanie-psa-zasady-wspolzycia-spolecznego-zwierze-sad.html [accessed: 5.5.2023].

the apartment and the company of other dogs. The judgment also indicates that, as a being capable of feeling, the dog feels longing and stress. Thus, a change of residence after such a period of time would have a very negative effect on the behavior of this animal. As an additional argument, the Court also pointed out that the principles of life experience show that when couples decide to take care of an animal, they make such a decision together. It is natural that the animal is treated almost like a family member and is not the sole property of one of the people in the relationship.

3. Situation of animals after divorce in Spanish law

Spanish doctrine elaborated the special legal term—*semoviente*—to classify animals as exceptional movables, "living things" capable of reproduction and movement.[20] Before 2021, *semovientes* were not a third category of things, different from movables and immovables, as Spanish law stood by the classic, Roman dichotomy between objects and subjects of law.[21] This division was comprehensive, because Spanish civil law indicated an enumerative list of assets classified as immovables, and remaining assets should be classified as movable goods.[22] However, this dichotomy was criticized in case of animals—for example, M. Gimenez-Candela notes that "the key terms 'sentience' or 'sentient beings' (…) have still not been integrated in our technical legal language when speaking about animals. For animal welfare science—the place from where the term is derived—the term 'sentience', as in the term 'sentient beings', refers to the capacity of animals to feel not only pain, but also suffering and positive emotions."[23]

However, in 2017, one of parliamentary groups proposed an amendment to the Civil Code, Mortgages Act and Civil Procedure Code regarding the legal status of animals—the proposition of revision urged the Government to promote the legal reforms necessary for creating a special category in the Civil Code[24] referring to animals; as well as plan the necessary legal reforms to ensure that

20 E. Kudasik-Gil, "Spanish Animal Protection Law—an Overwiev of Civil, Criminal and Administrative Provisions Concerning Animal Welfare," in *Legal Protection of Animals*, ed. E. Kruk, G. Lubeńczuk, and H. Spasowska-Czarny, Lublin 2020, p. 345.

21 Ibid.

22 E. Kudasik-Gil, "Spanish Animal Protection Law," p. 344.

23 M. Gimenez-Candela, "The De-Objectification of Animals in the Spanish Civil Code," *Derecho Animal (Forum of Animal Law Studies)* 9/3 (2018), p. 30.

24 The Royal Decree of July 24, 1889—Spanish Civil Code, http://mjusticia.gob.es [accessed: 5.5.2023].

companion animals cannot be considered as seizable objects in any legal procedure.[25] That was an introduction to revolutionary changes in Spanish law, that affected a lot of provisions of the Civil Code, such as animals' status during and after the divorce or obligations of the owner in relation to animals, because all these legal reforms were planned to ensure that companion animals cannot be considered as seizable objects in any legal procedure.[26] The proposal approved in Parliament referred to the creation of a special category in the Civil Code for animals, where they are defined as living beings endowed with sensibility.[27]

Regardless of the parliamentary works, the change of attitude toward animals, not only in the society in general, but also among the lawyers, was visible. For example, on May 27, 2019, a Spanish court in Valladolid granted shared custody of dog Cachas, ordering that he should spend six months with each spouse, allowing visitations on weekends.[28] Therefore, the consideration of some animals as family members has pushed judges to apply family law to animals, acknowledging that their legal status as property is unsuitable for solving these types of cases.[29] M. Montes-Franceschini notes that not only were family law courts recognizing companion animals as family members—for instance, Argentinian criminal judge Gustavo Daniel Castro recognized dog Tita, who was shot dead by a policeman, as a "nonhuman daughter" and recognized the plaintiff as Tita's "father," as well as recognizing Tita a subject of rights and nonhuman person.[30]

The Law 17/2021 of December 15, 2021,[31] which amended the Spanish Civil Code, regulated companion animals' shared custody and visitation in divorce and separation cases, ordering judges to consider the animal's welfare when deciding these cases.[32] The Law 17/2021 has amended several articles of the Spanish Civil Code and Law of Civil Procedure to pay regard to the welfare requirements of animals. The actual version of the Civil Code takes into account that animals are

---

25 M. Gimenez-Candela, "The De-Objectification," p. 29.

26 Ibid.

27 M. Gimenez-Candela, "The De-Objectification," *op. cit.*, p. 29.

28 M. Montes-Franceschini, "Traditional Conceptions of the Legal Person and Nonhuman Animals," *Animals* 12 (2022), p. 3.

29 Ibid.

30 M. Montes-Franceschini, "Traditional Conceptions," p. 4.

31 The Law 17/2021 of December 15, 2021, Amending the Civil Code, the Mortgage Law and the Law of Civil Procedure, on the Legal Regime of Animals. Boletín Oficial del Estado [BOE], no. 30, https://www.boe.es/diario_boe/txt.php?id=BOE-A-2021-20727 [accessed: 5.5.2023].

32 A. Abraizar, *Pets on Family Law in Spain*, https://arbaizarabogados.com/en/pets-on-family-law-in-spain [accessed: 05.05.2023].

sentient beings and have a special relationship with man.[33] According to the new article 333 bis of the Civil Code,[34] animals are living beings endowed with sensitivity. The legal regime of goods and things will only be applicable to them to the extent that it is compatible with their nature or with the provisions intended for their protection. The owner, possessor or holder of any other right over an animal must exercise their rights over it and their duties of care respecting its quality of being sentient, ensuring its well-being according to the characteristics of each species and respecting the limitations established in legal regulations. Expenses for the treatment and care of an injured or abandoned animal are recoverable by whoever has paid for them through the exercise of recourse action against the owner of the animal. In the event that the pet's injury has caused its death or serious impairment to its physical or mental health, both its owner and those who live with the animal are entitled to compensation that includes compensation for non-material damage caused. Pets also cannot be seized in enforcement proceedings.

The new provisions affects also the Spanish family Law. According to art. 90 of the Civil Code, in case of divorce or separation the fate of the companion animals, if they exist, must be decided taking into account the interest of the family members and the welfare of the animal. The same refers to the distribution of the times of coexistence and care, as well as the charges associated with the care of the animal. Art. 94 bis of the Civil Code states that the judicial authority will entrust the care of the companion animals to one or both spouses, and will determine, where appropriate, the way in which the spouse to whom they have not been entrusted may have them in their company. The judge should also order the distribution of the charges associated with the care of the animal, all taking into account the interest of the family members and the well-being of the animal, regardless of its proprietary ownership and who has been entrusted with its care. This circumstance will be recorded in the corresponding animal identification record. Pursuant to art. 92 of the Civil Code, joint custody of children in case of divorce or separation will not proceed when either of the parents is involved in a criminal proceeding initiated for attempting to threaten the life, physical integrity, freedom, moral integrity or freedom and sexual indemnity of the other spouse or of the children who live with both (the court will base on the allegations of the parties and the well-founded evidence of domestic or gender violence). For these purposes, the existence of mistreatment of animals, or the threat of causing them, as a mean to control or victimize any of these people will

33 Ibid.

34 The provisions of the Spanish Civil Code were translated by the Author by the text provided on http://mjusticia.gob.es [accessed: 5.5.2023].

also be treated as domestic violence. This means that the way of treating animals can also influence the decision of custody over children, because the court shall not grant the custody to a parent guilty of mistreating animals.

4. Conclusions

If Poland decides to regulate animals' situation after the divorce, Spanish experiences should set an example. Obviously, not everyone may accept the trend of treating animals as family members, but this trend is real, and the law should address the needs of the society. It is not fair that in Polish Civil Code there are instructions on how to divide a farm, regarding a special social significance of the agriculture (which is beyond discussion), but the law remains completely silent when it comes to make decisions about the fate of living and sentient beings. It also seems that in the context of the issue of the situation of animals after divorce in Polish jurisprudence, one more important issue is overlooked by focusing on the contact of former spouses with animals, namely the contact of children of the spouses with these animals. In a situation where a child is strongly associated with an animal, it should be granted to the spouse with whom the child will live after the divorce, and if for some reason this proves impossible, the child should have the right to have contact with the animal.

Bibliography

Literature

Abraizar, A., *Pets on Family Law in Spain*, https://arbaizarabogados.com/en/pets-on-family-law-in-spain [accessed: 5.5.2023].

Cudny, Ł., and Kryla, K., "Kult pamięci osoby zmarłej jako dobro osobiste," *Monitor Prawniczy* 16 (2011).

Dawidczyk, A., *Zwierzęta zamiast dzieci? Coraz więcej par podejmuje taką decyzję*, http://www.kobieta.pl, 18.9.2019 [accessed: 5.5.2023].

Flaga-Gieruszyńska, K., and Zieliński, A., *Rozwód. Materialnoprawne podstawy rozwodu oraz postępowanie odrębne w sprawie o rozwód. Komentarz praktyczny z orzecznictwem. Wzory pism procesowych*, Warszawa 2021.

Gimenez-Candela, M., "The De-Objectification of Animals in the Spanish Civil Code," *Derecho Animal (Forum of Animal Law Studies)* 9/3 (2018).

Grzeszak, T., "Dobro osobiste jako dobro zindywidualizowane," *Przegląd Sądowy* 4 (2018).

Gutowski, M. (ed.), *Kodeks cywilny. Komentarz. Tom I. Komentarz do art. 1–352*, 3rd ed., Warszawa 2021, Legalis.

https://www.rp.pl/prawo-rodzinne/art19277411-rozwod-z-domowym-czworonogiem, 12.1.2022 [accessed: 05.05.2023].

Justyński, T., "Znak czasu. Porozwodowe 'prawo do kontaktów' z domowymi czworonogami?," *Rodzina i Prawo* 14–15 (2010).

Kudasik-Gil, E., "Spanish Animal Protection Law—an Overview of Civil, Criminal and Administrative Provisions Concerning Animal Welfare," in *Legal Protection of Animals*, ed. E. Kruk, G. Lubeńczuk, and H. Spasowska-Czarny, Lublin 2020.

Michalski, B., *Spór o wydanie psa. Sąd: zwierzę nie jest rzeczą, którą można dowolnie przestawiać*, Gazeta Prawna 18.2.2021, https://serwisy.gazetaprawna.pl/orzeczenia/artykuly/8098085,spor-o-wydanie-psa-zasady-wspolzycia-spolecznego-zwierze-sad.html [accessed: 5.5.2023].

Montes-Franceschini, M., "Traditional Conceptions of the Legal Person and Nonhuman Animals," *Animals* 12 (2022).

Osajda, K. (ed.), *Kodeks cywilny. Komentarz. Część ogólna. Przepisy wprowadzające Kodeks cywilny. Prawo o notariacie (art. 79–95 i 96–99)*, 30th ed., Warszawa 2022, Legalis.

Panfil, K., "Więź emocjonalna ze zwierzęciem a dobra osobiste," *Radca Prawny. Zeszyty Naukowe* 3 (2021).

Pietrzykowski, T., "Problem podmiotowości prawnej zwierząt z perspektywy filozofii prawa," *Przegląd Filozoficzny—Nowa Seria* 2/94 (2015).

Wilk, A., "Problem uznania więzi emocjonalnej ze zwierzęciem za dobro osobiste w orzecznictwie sądów polskich," *Monitor Prawniczy* 22 (2022).

Wilk, A., "Zadośćuczynienie za krzywdę osobom najbliższym poszkodowanego—glosa do uchwały SN z dnia 27.3.2018r., III CZP 60/17," *Monitor Prawniczy* 15 (2018).

Wilk, A., "Zwierzę jako podmiot prawa spadkowego? Uwagi de lege lata i de lege ferenda," *Edukacja Prawnicza* 2 (2022/2023).

Legal acts

The Royal Decree of July 24, 1889, Spanish Civil Code, http://mjusticia.gob.es [accessed: 5.5.2023].

Act of February 25, 1964, Family and Guardianship Code, consolidated text Journal of Laws 2022, item 2140 as amended.

Act of April 23, 1964, Civil Code, consolidated text Journal of Laws 2023, item 326 as amended.

Act of August 21, 1997, on the Protection of Animals, consolidated text Journal of Laws 2022, item 572, 2375 as amended.

The Law 17/2021 of December 15, 2021, Amending the Civil Code, the Mortgage Law and the Law of Civil Procedure, on the Legal Regime of Animals. Boletín Oficial del Estado [BOE], No. 30, https://www.boe.es/diario_boe/txt.php?id=BOE-A-2021-20727 [accessed: 5.5.2023].

Case law

Judgment of Polish Supreme Court of 31.3.1980r, II CR 88/80, Legalis.

Judgment of Polish Supreme Court of 23.9.2009r., I CSK 346/08, Legalis.

Judgment of the District Court in Kraków of 22.11.2016, II Ca 1883/16, http://orzeczenia.krakow.so.gov.pl/content/$N/152010000001003_II_Ca_001883_2016_Uz_2016-11-22_002 [accessed: 5.5.2023].

Judgment of the District Court in Kraków of 7.9.2017, II Ca 1111/171, http://orzeczenia.krakow.so.gov.pl/content/$N/152010000001003_II_Ca_001111_2017_Uz_2017-09-07_002 [accessed: 5.5.2023].

Judgment of the District Court in Bełchatów of 16.10.2017, I C 74/16, http://orzeczenia.belchatow.sr.gov.pl/content/$N/152515050000503_I_C_000074_2016_Uz_2017-10-16_001 [accessed: 5.5.2023].

Judgment of Polish Supreme Court of 27.3.2018, III CZP 60/17, Legalis.

Judgment of the District Court for Warszawa-Wola in Warsaw of 24.11.2020, I C 1855/19, unpublished—cited after *B. Michalski*, Spór o wydanie psa. Sąd: zwierzę nie jest rzeczą, którą można dowolnie przestawiać, Gazeta Prawna 18.2.2021, https://serwisy.gazetaprawna.pl/orzeczenia/artykuly/8098085,spor-o-wydanie-psa-zasady-wspolzycia-spolecznego-zwierze-sad.html [accessed: 5.5.2023].

Joanna Bocianowska

Psychoanalysis in the field of law: The analysis of the notion of ownership and its limits

Abstract: First of all, what is worth noticing, when we talk about different scholar disciplines, at first sight is seems quite strange to combine psychoanalysis and law. There is no doubt that it is more natural to speak in this field of psychology, economics or sociology, but the idea of using psychoanalytical concepts in law is a novelty. However, is this really the case.

It must be recognized that the modern psychoanalyst—Jacques Lacan used the concept of "jouissance" in the Freudian sense to explain legal phenomena. In particular, he explained to some extent the problem of abuse, crossing property lines and wastage due to ego.

Although at first glance these concepts seem quite ridiculous, with a deeper analysis they become very rational. Jacques Lacan, in his seminar which was given in 1972 at the Sorbonne at the faculty of law, used two metaphors. First of them was in the form of a symbol—the conjugal bed—to describe limits of possibility of satisfying our right, in particular when this enjoyment takes into account the need to obtain the consent of the other person or when it is a question of joint possession. Lacan described it with the example of a marriage bed which really shows only a small individual context where abuse is possible and where "jouissance" can be pushed beyond the threshold of pain.

Another metaphor that was used by Lacan was one that comes from an anecdote about Picasso and his parrot. Briefly, the anecdote talks about a situation where the parrot falls in love with Picasso's shirt. The animal does not know that it is not possible for the shirt (and more particularly its collar) to return the feeling. The other aspect of this situation is Picasso's attitude. He was not interested in the courtship of the parrot. But, at the same time, he did not decide to change the shirt… maybe for something without a collar… In the end the question that arises is—was he actually responsible—by the choice of his clothes—for the reaction of the animal?

Now, one may ask where in these digressions is the space for the theory of law, and in particular the theory of ownership. The analysis given in this article tries to answer this question in a most thoughtful manner. It also sheds light to a modern, psychanalytical approach toward the notion of ownership and in particular the responsibility that comes with it.

Keywords: ownership, wastage, responsibility, zero waste, psychoanalysis, abuse

1. Introduction

The notion of ownership is a very multidimensional one and in order to fully understand its function and importance for overall human existence one needs to search in different disciplines, not only in the field of law. Yet this reflection does not really seem very revealing since the multidisciplinary discussion about the institution of ownership has existed since the beginning of early social structures. Throughout the years it evolved and changed its status many times. It was considered as "an idea, a right, a value, a myth, a rule, a foundation, a goal but it has also been 'a theft' or 'misfortune.'"[1] However, it needs to be noticed that even though in the discussion about the complexity of ownership it is natural to include such disciplines as psychology, economics or sociology, the idea of using psychoanalytical concepts in law seems to be quite a novelty. What is more, the fact that psychoanalysis was outwardly introduced and used in particular during the 20th century, does not negate its influence nowadays. The reason for this is that psychoanalysis seems to be an extremely valuable, yet a bit underestimated field which helps in explanation of many complex notions. This article focuses on the psychoanalytical approach introduced by Jacques Lacan, in particular the prominent notion of "*jouissance*" that he coined, which shall be explained in the further analysis.

As an explanatory remark, it needs to be pointed out that the subject of this article was also included in Hélène Thomas's piece: "Le regard politique et psychanalytique. Un lit, un oiseau, une table et un sentier. Variations sur le concept de propriété,"[2] yet in a different perspective. In this publication the attention is drawn mainly to the importance of utilization of psychoanalysis in order to discover more profound sense of ownership, its functions and its limitations.

2. Lacanian concepts: General remarks

It must be recognized that the modern psychoanalyst—Jacques Lacan used the notion of "*jouissance*" in the Freudian sense to explain legal phenomena. In particular, he explained to some extent the problem of abuse, crossing property lines

1 J. Jabłońska-Bonca, "Własność—w labiryncie interdyscyplinarnych problemów, Kilka uwag wstępnych" in *Krytyka prawa. Niezależne studia nad prawem. Vol. 1: Własność*, ed. J. Jabłońska-Bonca, Warsaw 2009, p. 11.

2 H. Thomas, "Le regard politique et psychanalytique. Un lit, un oiseau, une table et un sentier. Variations sur le concept de propriété," in *Les propriétés*, ed. G. Lardeux, Aix-en-Provence 2022, pp. 53–79.

and wastage due to ego. Although at first glance these concepts seem too far-fetched, with a deeper analysis they become quite rational.

The term "*jouissance*" which could be translated as "enjoyment," in Latin as *usus*, *ususfruct*,[3] that has a strong sexual context, in professional literature is rather left in the original form as it better depicts its particularity. The general concept in the Lacanian model revolves around the phenomenon in which crossing the point of desire—*jouissance* instead of being a source of pleasure—turns into pain. In broader sense it focuses on the moment when exercising the privilege leads to abuse which may result in damage inflicted not only on a user or an owner but also on an object itself.

To explain this quite disturbing concept, Jacques Lacan, in his seminar "*Encore*"[4] which was given in 1972 at the Sorbonne in the faculty of law, used two metaphors. First of them was the conjugal bed—used as a symbol to describe limits of possibility of satisfying our right, in particular when this enjoyment takes into account the need to obtain the consent of the other person (a spouse) or when it is a question of joint possession—that is, the marriage bed, which, by definition has to be shared. Lacan's in this very particular example, seemingly shows only a small individual context where abuse is possible and where *jouissance* can be pushed beyond the threshold of pain. However, it can be easily expanded toward the phenomena far more universal—such as responsibility for shared natural sources or crossing somebody's limits in different relationships that one enters into on a daily basis where question of mutual consent arises quite often.

Another metaphor that was used by Lacan was one that comes from an anecdote about Picasso and his parrot. Briefly, the anecdote depicts a situation where the parrot falls in love with Picasso's shirt. The animal does not know that it is not possible for the shirt (and more particularly its collar) to return the feeling. The other aspect of this situation is Picasso's attitude. He was not interested in the courtship of the parrot. But, at the same time, he did not decide to change his shirt. In the end, the question that arises is—was Picasso actually responsible—by the choice of his clothes—for the reaction of the animal? Now, one may ask where in these digressions is the space for the theory of law, and in particular the theory of ownership. This shall be presented in the following part of the article.

3 H. Thomas, "Le regard politique et psychanalytique. Un lit, un oiseau, une table et un sentier. Variations sur le concept de propriété," in *Les propriétés*, ed. G. Lardeux, Aix-en-Provence 2022, p. 61.

4 J. Lacan, *Le séminaire, Livre XX 1972–1973: Encore, Seuil*, Paris 1975.

3. Lacanian concepts in the domain of law

The problems that the said anecdote sheds light on are actually very universal ones. Firstly, we may contemplate the already mentioned borders of jouissance, with regard to not only the relations between living beings but also the objects. In this manner, the "moral" of the anecdote is that *jouissance* must be based on mutual relation. In the juridical meaning we may extract from this narration the reflections onto the problems of (1) responsibility of the owners for their resources, (2) from "the parrot's perspective"—the necessity to see the other person as a partner, which leads us to the principle of reciprocity—the will to establish a relation and finally, a very deep concept of (3) responsibility for what we surround ourselves with and what we declare through it toward other participants of different relations that we enter in our everyday life, and most importantly, how it influences the environment.

In the Lacanian concept the connecting point of two disciplines—psychoanalysis and law—seems to be the moment when the pain arises, the pressure—*l'entreinte*.[5] The reason for that is crossing the border of pleasure leads toward a rather painful exploitation. In juridical sense, but also in moral and ethical one, this conclusion leads us to the problem of the attitude of an owner toward a thing which is being divided, occupied, cultivated. It draws our attention to the issue of how not to cross the border of the proper exploitation of a thing in our possession. In particular, this case is visible in the exploitation of crucial sources for all mankind as fresh water or energy. The described concepts lead us to a question of awareness of the fact that the exploitation of possessions which is not useful or necessary should be carefully considered, limited and redistributed.[6]

What is more, the psychoanalytic concept coined in the form of the notion of "*jouissance*" leads us to the problem of wasting resources. According to the Freudian model, presented in the seminar "*Encore*," what pushes us toward it is our *ego*. All the excess that goes beyond our balanced, natural needs, that serves gaining superfluous power, instead of leading a well-adjusted life, where the need of possession is harmonized with the environment and our whole surrounding, is caused by *ego*.

---

5 H. Thomas, "Le regard politique et psychanalytique. Un lit, un oiseau, une table et un sentier. Variations sur le concept de propriété," in *Les propriétés*, ed. G. Lardeux, Aix-en-Provence 2022, p. 58.

6 H. Thomas, "Le regard politique," p. 65.

The balance point in law that might be derived from the concepts of Lacan revolves around the idea that having a right does not mean a coercion but something we can actually decide to use or not.[7] The fact that we are given a possibility to possess certain goods or exploit resources under our control does not mean we are obliged to use this power to its full extent. What is more, we need to be aware that the power endowed on us with the status of being owners is solely an option. We obviously use it in certain limits given by regulations but the other limits—moral and ethical ones should be within us.

In this field we may seek solution via psychoanalysis. Since this is the method that enables us to pose questions and search in our inner selves for profound answers that might explain actions we take as well as understand our actual motivation for undertaking them.

In today's world, where religion was substituted, to a great extent, by other systems and explanations of the world, including psychoanalysis, it is necessary to recognize this shift and adjust it properly also to the theory of law—in this case—the theory regarding ownership.

It goes without saying that the method of forced limitation and control of our assets (*la règlementation*) which was characteristic for socialist regimes, today is known to be the source of rather pathological abuse by some at the expense of others, instead of being a credible source of well-balanced distribution of goods. With that experience hopefully behind us, nowadays we need to focus on a more profound understanding and sensitivity toward our needs in a more holistic aspect. It seems that a solution for this might be introduced by the Lacanian concepts, especially in the context of psychoanalysis as described above.

One needs to notice also that the problem of exceeding the norms in using the law is directly combined with its abuse—*l'abus*. This juridical issue could be also widely explored in connection to the domain of psychoanalysis. Yet the issue of abuse of law deserves a wider contemplation in a separate article, so here the matter is only promptly signalized.[8]

---

7 See: H. Thomas, "Le regard politique," p. 63.

8 For more on this matter see: V. Bolgár, "Abuse of Rights in France, Germany, and Switzerland: A Survey of a Recent Chapter in Legal Doctrine," *Louisiana Law Review*, Special Issue 35/5 (1975), https://digitalcommons.law.lsu.edu/cgi/viewcontent.cgi?article=4114&context=lalrev (accessed: May 30, 2023).

4. Psychoanalysis as an indication for legal regulations

The question that needs to be asked is how could psychoanalysis actually function in the field of law. Obviously, regulations are needed since we cannot rely solely on moral and ethical guidance. Yet the process of formulating the regulations that are aimed at the responsible ownership and well-balanced possessions should be harmonized with the said holistic approach, which derives in particular from the process of self-awareness and true responsibility that derives from this attitude. It is obvious that this remark may not be particularly revealing since the creation of law has always included different disciplines as economy or sociology, unless we add the said psychoanalytical approach which might be, in fact, a novelty.

On the one hand, we need to remember that: "Generally, it is acknowledged in the democratic systems that property right is one of the basic human rights and it provides the individual with two main psychological effects: the feeling of security in a social group in which he/she operates and the effect of 'complementing I'. Lack of property means exclusion and deprivation of the possibility to 'complement personality.'"[9] The importance of this institution, as it was already said, is not only because it is crucial for our being but also because it is very complex and multidimensional. From the many dimensions it comes with, we need to strongly underline the ethical and moral dimensions that come with possessions but this time not so much as from the traditional outside (e.g., religious) perspective that is imposed, but from our own inner contemplation which stems from our more profound awareness and understanding of the unity of the world and our place in it. The egoistic drive, that actually echoes the concept of "the holy ownership" coined by the French Revolution and established by Napoleon,[10] has been already questioned many times as rather a myth than an actual phenomenon.[11]

Since no one lives in a vacuum, each decision that we make and action that we undertake influences the outside world—both animate and inanimate. Lacan in his seminar underlined the importance of the inanimate world too. In the above-described anecdote of Picasso and his parrot, the concept of how we use our possessions echoes quite strongly. We may transfer this example onto matters of

---

9 J. Jabłońska-Bonca, "Własność—w labiryncie interdyscyplinarnych problemów," p. 11.

10 K. Sójka-Zielńska, *Kodeks Napoleona. Historia i współczesność*, Warsaw 2008, p. 101.

11 See, for example: J. Comby, "Un droit inviolable et sacré," *ADEF* (1990), https://www.agter.asso.fr/IMG/pdf/Comby_impossible_propriete_absolue.pdf (accessed: May 30, 2023).

more importance, such as responsibility for plastic production or fast-fashion, but also to the liability of how and for what reasons natural sources are overexploited. It seems that in this matter psychoanalysis might be helpful as it may lead to the greater motivation to act in a conscious balanced way. What is more, on the basis of this deeper understanding human nature, with a right amount of focus and contemplation, the true regulations may also be introduced. With this attitude, there may be created a set of rules that reflect holistically the nature of things and the genuine reasons for such institutions as ownership.

5. Summary

In conclusion, the analysis given in this article tries to answer the question where in the theory of law, and in particular the theory of ownership is the space for the psychanalytical concepts. It also sheds light to a modern, psychanalytical approach toward the notion of ownership and in particular the responsibility that comes with it.

It is common knowledge that the direction of the progress has always been set by the developed countries of the world. In modern history one of these countries was France which actually introduced the notion of holy/absolute ownership which nowadays goes through a deep crisis. It is therefore not surprising, that from the same country came another theory—which is in the opposition to the classical one. And, with a proper interpretation, we may say that one of its authors is a French psychanalysist—Jacques Lacan. It is also in France where modern commentators such as Hélène Thomas from the University of Marseilles makes analysis and promotes these concepts onto the domain of ownership. Moreover, the reflections given in this piece aim to find the answers to a question of how to adjust the institution of ownership to modern reality, where humanity needs to be more sensible than ever. The field in which this awareness and wise regulations are in particular needed is our approach to our material needs and their excessive production in times of deep ecological crisis. Hopefully, the concepts such as described in this article may, in time, lead us to a more meaningful and balanced consumption and holistic regulations in this matter.

Bibliography

Bolgár, V., "Abuse of Rights in France, Germany, and Switzerland: A Survey of a Recent Chapter in Legal Doctrine," *Louisiana Law Review*, Special Issue 35/5 (1975), https://digitalcommons.law.lsu.edu/cgi/viewcontent.cgi?article=4114&context=lalrev (accessed: May 30, 2023).

Boudot, M., and Veillon, D. (eds.), *Les propriétés*, Potiers, 2016.

Comby, J., "Un droit inviolable et sacré," *ADEF* (1990), https://www.agter.asso.fr/IMG/pdf/Comby_impossible_propriete_absolue.pdf (accessed: May 30, 2023).

Jabłońska-Bonca, J. (ed.), *Krytyka prawa. Niezależne studia nad prawem. Vol. 1: Własność*, Warsaw 2009.

Lacan, J., *Le séminaire, Livre XX 1972–1973: Encore, Seuil*, Paris 1975.

Lardeux, G. (ed.), *Les propriétés*, Aix-en-Provence 2022.

Malabat, V., and Zabalza, A., *La propriété au 21e siecle*, Paris 2021.

Renaut, M.-H., *Histoire du droit de la propriété*, Paris 2004.

Sójka-Zielńska, K., *Kodeks Napoleona. Historia i współczesność*, Warsaw 2008.

Sergio Barbaro

Datafication, family and the protection of children's privacy

Abstract: The term datafication is used to describe the technological process involving the transformation of every aspect of a person's individual or social life into data that can also have a significant economic value. In particular, through access to social media, habits, preferences, tastes and even friendships are transformed into bytes that circulate freely through the network. It is clear that this phenomenon entails several risks, firstly, concerning the misuse of data by the very platforms that provide access to online services and social media, but also by the network users themselves.

The purpose of this paper is to look specifically at the risks arising from the circulation of children's data on the Internet, both in the case where it is the children themselves who post information online, and in the increasingly frequent case where it is their parents who voluntarily post videos and images of their children on social media.

In particular, this paper aims to take into consideration the widespread habit of parents to publish photos of their children on social networks when they are still very young. This phenomenon is defined as "shareting," a fusion of the words "parenting," parental role and "share," sharing.

Alongside shareting, another phenomenon that compares the media exposure of minors is that of baby influencers, represented by the habit of parents posting videos of the everyday lives of children and adolescents on the web, often for the purpose of promoting commercial goods, products, and services for children.

Both phenomena do not currently find legal regulation in most national legal systems. The only exception is France, which has created a legal framework to protect minors in relation to potential abuse resulting from excessive media overexposure.

Keywords: Datafication, minors, consent, protection, shareting, baby influencer, regulatory gaps

1. Introduction: Data circulation on the web and protection of minors

The English term datafication is intended to describe the technological process that involves the transformation of every aspect of a person's individual or social life into data that can also have a significant economic value.[1] In particular,

1 On this point with particular reference to minors, see: E. Battelli, "Il trattamento dei dati nel prisma della tutela della persona minore di età," *Diritto dell'Informazione e*

through access to social media, habits, preferences, tastes and even friendships are transformed into bytes that circulate freely through the network. It is clear that this phenomenon entails several risks, firstly, concerning the misuse of data by the very platforms that provide access services to online services and social media, but also by the network users themselves.

The purpose of this paper is to look specifically at the risks arising from the circulation of children's data on the Internet, both in the case where it is the children themselves who post information online, and in the increasingly frequent case where it is their parents who voluntarily post videos and images of their children on social media.

The interests at stake are different. On the one hand, children and adolescents cannot be denied access to the Internet and to communication and information platforms, which constitutes a right instrumental to the development of the child's personal identity and his or her socialization.[2] Equally undeniable is the need to protect minors from abuse arising from the misuse of data entered the network.

The question to start from in addressing the issue is what is in the best interest of the child in this case: free and unlimited access to online platforms for socializing and entertainment or the adoption of incisive measures to protect and control the behavior of minors in the digital environment. It is clear that a balance must be struck between the right of access to the web, which can now be considered a constitutional right to the exercise of which the state must not put obstacles[3] and the equally important need to protect minors from the traps and pitfalls of the web.

2. EU Regulation 2016/679 and the consent of the child

Several scholars believe that the existing data protection measures for minors based on the acquisition of informed consent from parents or from the child

---

dell'Informatica (Il), fasc. 2 1 (2022), p. 267. For an in-depth look at the phenomenon of datafication in general see: J. Sadowski, "When Data Is Capital: Datafication, Accumulation, and Extraction," *Big Data & Society* (2019), 1–12.

2 E. Frosini, "Il Costituzionalismo nella società tecnologica," *Diritto dell'Informazione e dell'Informatica*, f. 3 (2020), pp. 465ff.

3 Ibid.

himself who has passed a certain, conventionally agreed age, are insufficient to adequately protect them.[4]

To delve into this debate, it is necessary to start from the relevant European legal framework: Regulation (EU) 2016/679, better known by the acronym GDPR (*General Data Protection Regulation*), implemented in Italy by Legislative Decree No. 101 of August 10, 2018, that provides for specific regulations on the consent of the child in relation to information society services.[5]

Article 8 GDPR deals with the "Conditions applicable to the consent of minors in connection with information society services" and states that the processing of data is lawful if the subject is at least sixteen years old, unless a national minimum age threshold, between thirteen and sixteen, applies.

In cases where the child has not yet reached that age, the processing of the data is lawful if "consent is given or authorised by the holder of parental responsibility."

In Italy, Legislative Decree No. 196/2003, as amended following Legislative Decree No. 101/2018, has identified, in the text of Article *2-quinquies*, the limit

---

4 E. Battelli, "Il trattamento dei dati nel prisma," cit., p. 301; "Minori e social network: cyberbullismo e limiti della parental responsibility," *Il Corriere giuridico*, f. 9 (2021), pp. 1269–1277.

5 For an in-depth study on the EU Regulation 2016/679 see without claiming to be exhaustive: R. D'Orazio, G. Finocchiaro, O. Pollicino, and G. Resta (eds.), *Codice della Privacy e Data Protection*, Milan 2021; V. Cuffaro, R. D'Orazio, and V. Ricciuto (eds.), *I dati personali nel diritto europeo*, Torino 2020; A. Iunker, "The New Requirements of The EU General Data Protection Regulation 2016/679 GDPR," *Conferința Internațională de Drept, Studii Europene și Relații Internaționale* VII (2019), pp. 106–113; M. Krzysztofek, *GDPR: General Data Protection Regulation (EU) 2016/679: Post-Reform Personal Data Protection in the European Union*, Alphen aan den Rijn 2019; E. Lucchini Guastalla, "Il nuovo regolamento europeo sul trattamento dei dati personali: i principi ispiratori," in *Contratto e impresa* (2018), pp. 106ff.; V. Cuffaro, "Il regolamento generale sulla protezione dei dati," in *Trattamento dei dati personali e Regolamento UE n. 2016/679, Speciali digitali del Corriere giuridico*, 2018, pp. 2ff.; A. Mantelero and D. Poletti (eds.), *Regolare la tecnologia: il Reg. UE 2016/679 e la protezione dei dati personali. Un dialogo tra Italia e Spagna*, Pisa 2018; S. Bhaimia, "The General Data Protection Regulation: The Next Generation of EU Data Protection," *Legal Information Management* 18/1 (2018), pp. 21–28, https://doi.org/10.1017/S1472669618000051; G. Finocchiaro (ed.), *Il nuovo Regolamento europeo sulla privacy e sulla protezione dei dati personali*, Bologna 2017; P. Voigt and A. von dem Bussche, *The EU General Data Protection Regulation (GDPR), A Practical Guide*, Berlino 2017; E. Pelino, *Il Regolamento Privacy europeo. Commentario alla nuova disciplina sulla protezione dei dati personali*, Milano 2016.

in fourteen years for the lawfulness of the processing of a minor's personal data after acquiring the minor's consent. In the case of a younger age, the consent of the person exercising parental responsibility or guardian is required.

Article 8 of the GDPR thus provides for a "special capacity to act" by fixing it at the age of sixteen, which is therefore a prerequisite for access to the various social platforms.

The consideration for access to social platforms, although the basic service is often advertised as free of charge, is the transfer of user data. Every person who wishes to access the services provided by social networks "pays" for them by registering with their personal data. Access to social networks is therefore based on a contract of exchange between personal information on the part of the user and services on the part of the social platform.[6]

Minors are often unaware that access to social networks involves the processing and circulation of their data, including special data, and the use of such data for targeted marketing and profiling purposes.[7]

A prerequisite of the privacy framework is that consent is formed in a free, knowing, and informed manner.

Certainly, these conditions are difficult to fulfill in the case of minors in the presence of unclear or cryptic and hidden information, and the circumstance that failure to provide consent results in the *de facto* non-provision of the service.[8]

Moreover, as noted by the scholars, there is no obligation on the part of providers to actually verify the real age of minors accessing social networks or prior parental consent, which can easily be falsified by the users themselves.[9]

---

6 See: M. Ciancimino, "La libertà di espressione nel mondo digitale: alcune coordinate civilistiche in tema di contenuti controversi sui social network," *Diritto di Famiglia e delle Persone (Il)*, fasc. 1 (2022), p. 360; E. Battelli, "Il trattamento dei dati nel prisma," cit., pp. 299ff.

7 E. Battelli, "Il trattamento dei dati nel prisma," cit., pp. 299ff.; A. Batuecas Caletrío, "Nuove tecnologie e protezione del minore nel diritto privato spagnolo," *Europa e Diritto Privato*, f. 4 (2020), p. 1214; M. Diffenderfer, "The Rights of Privacy and Plublicity for Minor Online: Protecting the Privilege of Dissafirmance in the Digital," *U. Louisville L. Rev.* 54 (2016), p. 131.

8 E. Battelli, "Il trattamento dei dati nel prisma," cit., pp. 271 ff.

9 E. Battelli, "Il trattamento dei dati nel prisma," cit., pp. 271 ff.; A. Astone, "L'accesso dei minori d'età ai servizi della c.d. Società dell'informazione: l'art. 8 del Reg. (UE) 2016/679 e i suoi riflessi sul Codice per la protezione dei dati personali," *Contratto e Impresa* (2019), pp. 633–634; C. Perlingeri, "La tutela dei minori di età nei social networks," *Rassegna di diritto civile*, f. 4 (2016), pp. 1324–1340.

Acquiring the child's informed consent, therefore, is not necessarily to be considered an expression of autonomy nor does it ensure real protection of the child's fundamental rights. Similarly, parental consent may, as we shall see in the course of this work, not represent the best interest of the child, or be aligned with the real will of the children.[10]

The consent of the child or parents therefore ends up becoming a mere formalism, insufficient to guarantee effective protection of the same.[11]

It is not surprising, therefore, that part of the scholars proposes the adoption of different and more effective tools than mere consent, such as, for instance, prior and subsequent public control of the algorithms used by the various platforms by authorized third parties.[12]

Another proposed instrument is the recognition of exponential bodies representing the interests of individuals with a right-duty to intervene, with powers of representation, including procedural powers.[13]

It cannot be overlooked here how the European Union legislator has shown, even in some recent regulatory interventions on the digital world, particular attention to the protection of minors in the online environment.

The Digital Service act[14] contains specific provisions on the protection of minors, which is one of the main aims of the European regulation under consideration.[15]

---

10 On this point, see the Report of J. A. Cannataci, "Rapporteur of the United Nations General Assembly: Artificial Intelligence and Privacy, and Children's Privacy," Report of the Special Rapporteur on the right to privacy, January 25, 2021, p. 19.

11 Some scholars speak of consent as a mere simulacrum of self-determination and an inadequate instrument of protection: A. Astone, "L'accesso dei minori d'età ai servizi della c.d. Società dell'informazione: l'art. 8 del Reg. (UE) 2016/679 e i suoi riflessi sul Codice per la protezione dei dati personali," *Contratto e Impresa* (2019), pp. 633–634; C. Perlingeri, "La tutela dei minori di età nei social networks," *Rassegna di diritto civile*, f. 4 (2016), pp. 1324–1340; L. Bozzi, "I dati del minore tra protezione e circolazione: per una lettura non retorica del fenomeno," *Europa e Diritto Privato, Milano*, f. 1 (2020), pp. 251–275.

12 A. Mantelero, "Rilevanza e tutela della dimensione collettiva della protezione dei dati personali," *Contratto e impresa. Europa* (2015), p. 155; E. Batelli, "Il trattamento dei dati nel prisma," cit., p. 301.

13 A. Mantelero, "Rilevanza e tutela della dimensione collettiva," cit., p. 155; E. Batelli, "Il trattamento dei dati nel prisma," cit., p. 301.

14 Regulation (EU) 2022/2065 of the European Parliament and of the Council of October 19, 2022 on a single market for digital services and amending Directive 2000/31/EC (Digital Services Regulation) (Text with EEA relevance).

15 See in particular recitals 71 and 81 of the Regulation.

The text of the law under consideration states that providers of online platforms used by minors should, already at the design stage, take appropriate and proportionate measures to protect minors by designing online interfaces or parts thereof in such a way as to ensure the highest level of privacy, security, and protection for minors.[16]

In addition, Article 28 regulation provides for an express prohibition on the use of targeting or profiling techniques that target the personal data of minors or vulnerable persons for the purpose of displaying advertising, a prohibition already established by EU Directive 2018/1808 on audio-visual services.

Finally, Article 34 of the Digital Service Act obliges digital platforms to carry out systemic risk impact assessments concerning possible negative effects on the exercise of the fundamental rights to respect for private and family life and to freedom of expression and information, the right to non-discrimination and the rights of the child.

In conclusion, it should be emphasized in this part of this paper that, irrespective of the existing legal safeguards on the subject, a fundamental role in protecting minors lies in the vigilance of parents, who cannot relinquish control even when the existing legal framework allows minors to exercise autonomous consent.[17]

Not least, it is important that families and parents are themselves aware of and trained in what the use of apps, social networks, and electronic devices in general entails for data processing.

But what happens when it is the parents themselves who publish pictures and data of under-14-year-old children on the web?

---

16 Recital 71.

17 C. Sartoris, "Minors' Data Protection between e-Learning and Social Network Platforms," *European Journal of Privacy Law & Technologies* 2 (2020), p. 147. See also: D. Krivokapic and J. Adamovic, "Impact of General Data Protection Regulation on Children's Rights in Digital Environment," *Anali Pravnog fakulteta u Beogradu* 64/3 (2016), p. 220; P. Ni, "Research on Legal Protection of Minors' Data in Digital Age," *International Journal of Education and Humanities* 8/3 (2023), pp. 53–56.

3. Shareting and baby influencers: which instruments of protection?

It is increasingly common for parents to post photos of their children on social networking sites while they are still very young. This phenomenon is called *shareting*, a fusion of the words "parenting," parental role, and "share," sharing.[18]

Alongside *shareting*, another phenomenon that compares the media exposure of minors is that of baby influencers, represented by the habit of parents posting videos of the everyday lives of children and adolescents on the web, often for the purpose of promoting commercial goods, products, and services for children.[19]

Such behavior entails numerous risks for children and adolescents.

Firstly, there is the danger of violation of the privacy and confidentiality of children's personal data due to misuse by third parties. Secondly, the dissemination of images on the Internet and social networks may involve the risk of loss of control of information and content concerning minors, with potential negative consequences on the digital identity of the child and psychological repercussions on the well-being of children, in particular, when the child starts surfing the net independently after having been exposed to the judgment of others for years.

---

18 For a more detailed discussion on the subject see: K. Haley, "Shareting and the (Potential) Right to Be Forgotten," Ind. L. J. 95 (2020), pp. 1005–1020; T. Leaver, "Balancing Privacy. Shareting, Intimate Surveillance and the Right to Be Forgotten," in *The Routledge Companion to Digital Media and Children*, Chapter 22, L. Green et al., New York 2020, pp. 235–244; A. Brosch, "Sharenting, Why Do Parents Violate Their Children's Privacy?," *The New Educational Review* 54 (2018), pp. 75–85; D. Cino and S. Demozzi, "Figli 'in vetrina'. Il fenomeno dello sharenting in un'indagine esplorativa," *Riv. it. edu. fam.* 2 (2017), pp. 153–184; S. Steinberg, "Sharenting: Children's Privacy in The Age of Social Media," *Emory Law Journal* 66 (2017), pp. 839–1007.

19 On the baby influencer phenomenon see: E. E. O'Neill, "Influencing the Future: Compensating Children in the Age of Social-Media Influencer Marketing," *Stan. L. Rev. Online* 72 (2019–2020), p. 42; H. Bosher, "Influencer Marketing and Law," in *Influencer Marketing Building Brand Communities and Engagement*, ed. S. Yesiloglu and J. Costello, London 2020, pp. 235–249; M. M. Masterson, "When Play Becomes Work: Child Labor Laws in the Era of "Kidfluencers,"" *U. Pa. L. Rev.* 169 (2020–2021), pp. 577–607; E., Madyson, *Children Are Making It Big (For Everyone Else): The Need for Child Labor Laws Protecting Child Influencers* (February 8, 2023). Texas Tech University, School of Law, Available at SSRN: https://ssrn.com/abstract=4351827 or http://dx.doi.org/10.2139/ssrn.4351827.

Clearly, this can create tensions and conflicts in the family that can turn into legal disputes in which parents are held accountable for forcing their children into excessive media exposure at an early age.

Images of children and adolescents can easily be manipulated and become child pornography. "Innocent but intimate photos or videos can be shared by anyone; screenshots of screens are possible; they can be downloaded and placed in other online environments by anyone for other purposes. [...] In addition, with the help of simple photo editing programmes accessible to anyone, images can be 'manipulated', turning them into child pornography."[20]

The dissemination online of information on children's lives, passions, habits, and acquaintances can facilitate approach and grooming by malicious persons. Finally, there is a clear risk of exploitation of the child's image by parents or third parties for commercial and profit-making purposes.[21]

The phenomenon of baby influencers, like *shareting*, is a harbinger of potential negative consequences for the psycho-physical development of children and adolescents. Firstly, there is a clear danger that the child involved in what he or she considers a game and entertainment, which takes place exclusively behind a camera or online, loses the dimension of reality and control over reality.

The use of children and adolescents as influencers also entails the danger of child exploitation for commercial purposes.

Finally, the dissemination among young people of videos and images containing dangerous behavior can lead to an emulation effect by other users of such images and content. Indeed, there have been several cases of so-called "challenges" on social platforms such as TikTok in which minors "challenged" other minors to engage in self-harming, dangerous or illegal behavior, and these challenges have sometimes led to tragic consequences such as serious self-mutilation or even the death of the minors involved.[22]

---

20 Save the children, *Shareting: Cosa significa e quali sono i rischi per i bambini?*, 14.09.2021, available online at https://www.savethechildren.it/blog-notizie/sharenting-cosa-significa-e-quali-sono-i-rischi-i-bambini.

21 Ibid.

22 On this point, see: A. Johannes, F. Nilsson, and N. Sandström, *It's time to TikTok: Exploring Generation Z's motivations to participate in #Challenge*, Digitala Vetenskapliga Arkivet, 2023, available online at https://www.diva-portal.org/smash/get/diva2:1434091/FULLTEXT01.pdf; A. Lavorgna, M. Tartari, and P. Ugwudike, "Criminogenic and Harm-Enabling Features of Social Media Platforms: The Case of Sharenting Practices," *European Journal of Criminology* (2022), https://doi.org/10.1177/14773708221131659; A. Elkhazeen, C. Poulos, X. Zhang, J. Cavanaugh, and M. A.

The problem therefore arises of identifying potential remedies to such behavior. Several scholars emphasize the need to increase parental vigilance by raising parents' awareness of these phenomena and of existing control mechanisms and safeguards.[23] A key role is played by the moderation mechanisms to be implemented by social media aimed at removing contents that are dangerous or harmful to the dignity of minors online.

It is common ground that these remedies cannot suffice and that specific regulatory interventions to regulate these phenomena are also necessary.

4. The absence of a regulatory framework on the subject and potential remedies

EU Regulation 2016/679 makes no reference to such cases, and in Italy and most EU countries, there is no specific legislation on the subject.[24]

With reference to the Italian legal system, there are only sporadic interventions by the ordinary judiciary on the use of the image of minors. The Court of Mantua by order of 19.09.2017[25] and the Court of Rieti by decisions of 07.03.2019[26] and 15.10.22[27] have established that the publication of photos of children under 14 on social networks requires the consent of both parents.

Regarding the exercise of parental responsibility and baby influencers, two recent important decisions by the Court of Milan and the Court of Appeal of Milan can be mentioned. The judgments in question deal specifically with the validity of baby influencer sponsorship contracts signed by one parent without the other's knowledge.

Cain, "TikTok™ 'Benadryl Challenge' Death—A Case Report and Review of the Literature," *Journal of Forensic Science* 68 (2023), pp. 339–342. https://doi.org/10.1111/1556-4029.15149.

23 Subjecting educators and parents to digital civics courses, for example. See on this point: C. Cernicchiano, *La sicurezza on-line dei minori in rapporto all'età del consenso digitale*, Altalex, 18.12.2020; I. A., Caggiano, "Protecting Minors as Technologically Vulnerable Persons through Data Protection: An Analysis on the Effectiveness of Law," EJPLT 1 (2022), pp. 27–44, specif. 44. https://doi.org/10.57230/EJPLT221IAC.

24 Some scholars consider the lack of tools to protect children under the age of 13 against the publication of videos and other materials by their parents to be one of the main shortcomings of the GDPR. On this point: S. Donovan, "'Sharenting": The Forgotten Children of the GDPR," *Peace Human Rights Governance* 4/1 (2020), pp. 35–59.

25 Court of Mantua Order of 19.09.2017, in jusdicere.it.

26 Court of Rieti order of 7.03.19, in dejure.it.

27 Court of Rieti Order of 15.10.22, in dejure.it.

The Court of Milan, in Judgment 4379 of July 16, 2020, ruled that in the case of joint exercise of parental responsibility, both parents must sign the sponsorship contracts with the brand since they affect the image of the minor child and therefore the very personal rights of the same.[28]

The same principle was established by the Court of Appeal of Milan's judgment no. 3647/22,[29] which upheld the request of the father of a little influencer to delete the photos and videos posted by his mother, his ex-wife, on social networks, but did not decide to award damages to the plaintiff.

On *shareting*, there are only a few guidelines from the Italian Data Protection Authority entitled, translated from Italian: "Sharenting—Tips for parents to limit the online dissemination of content about their children."[30]

The text under review advises parents against publishing pictures of their own online and suggests, in case they do, certain precautions that parents should follow such as:

- make the child's face unrecognizable (e.g., by using graphics programs to "pixelate" faces, also available free online);
- simply cover faces with an emoticon "smiley face";
- Restrict the visibility settings of images on social networks to only people you know or trust and do not share them without permission when sending them on an instant messaging program;
- avoid the creation of a social account dedicated to the child;
- read and understand the privacy policies of the social networks on which we upload photographs.

The text under review also tries to inform and raise awareness among parents about the risks of publishing their children's images and videos online. Firstly, the Italian Data Protection Authority's document suggests that parents should reflect on the fact that posting pictures and videos of different moments in their children's lives, perhaps accompanied by information including their name or age or the place where they were filmed, helps to define their online image and reputation. Secondly, the office of the Italian Privacy Guarantor dwells on the

28 Court of Milan judgment of 16.07.2020 no. 4379, in dejure.it.

29 Court of Appeal of Milan judgment no. 3647/22, in dejure.it.

30 Garante per la protezione dei dati, Sharenting—Suggerimenti ai genitori *per limitare la diffusione online di contenuti che riguardano i propri figli*, 2021, Doc-web 9862214, available online at https://www.garanteprivacy.it/web/guest/home/docweb/-/docweb-display/docweb/9862214.

risk of misuse of minors' data, reminding parents that what is published online or shared in messaging chats is no longer in our control, and this is even more true in the case of minors. When something appears on a screen, not only can it be captured and reused without our knowledge by anyone for improper purposes or illegal activities, but it contains more information than we think, such as geolocation data. Furthermore, the text under review suggests that parents should always ask themselves whether their children in the future will be happy to find images of themselves available for all to see or disagree with the self-image their parents are constructing.

The Italian Data Protection Supervisor particularly emphasizes the importance for "grown-ups" to increase their awareness of the prejudices to which they subject minors by exposing their children's photos on the web, also in terms of the use of the images for child pornographic, retaliatory, or otherwise improper purposes by third parties. In conclusion, the "*Garante*" points out that parents must be aware that providing details of their children's lives from an early age may influence their personality and relational dimension in the future.

5. Loi n° 2020–1266 du 19 octobre 2020 visant à encadrer l'exploitation commerciale de l'image d'enfants de moins de seize ans sur les plateformes en ligne and the French legal framework

Internationally, the only country that has tried to establish regulatory principles on this issue is France. With the Loi n° 2020–1266 du 19 octobre 2020 visant à encadrer l'exploitation commerciale de l'image d'enfants de moins de seize ans sur les plateformes en ligne, the French legislator has regulated the phenomenon of baby influencers, through an amendment to the labor code and assimilating this case to child labor in the presence of certain factors established by the legislation.[31] Producing and filming videos of minors and disseminating them online constitutes child labor in the presence of three requirements:

31 On the debate in France, see: A. Bousmanne, *L'exploitation commerciale de l'image des enfants sur les plateformes en ligne: quelle protection pour les enfants influenceurs?*, Ottignies-Louvain-la-Neuve 2021; P. L. Duverney, "Quelles mesures pour la protection et la mise en oeuvre des droits des enfants exposé-e-s sur les réseaux sociaux à des fins lucratives?" *Présenté au Centre interfacultaire en droits de l'enfant (CIDE) de l'Université de Genève en vue de l'obtention de la Maîtrise universitaire interdisciplinaire en droits de l'enfant*, 2022; M. Saulier, "Utiles précisions sur la protection du droit à l'image du mineur," *Actualité juridique Famille* 04 (2022), p. 231; A. Edney, "'I Don't

(a) the existence of directives on the part of the person creating, producing, or distributing the content;
(b) the use of the child's image for commercial purposes;
(c) the existence of remuneration exceeding a certain threshold fixed by decree of the Council of State;
(d) the duration and continuity of the service, also taking into account the child's school obligations.

In these cases, the law stipulates that a child under the age of 16 cannot work continuously as an influencer without prior authorization from the administrative authority, which assesses the "best interest of the child."

In addition, all direct and indirect proceeds of this activity must be deposited in an escrow account in favor of the child with the *Caisse des dépôts et consignations* and managed by this fund until the child reaches the age of majority or, if appropriate, until the date of his or her emancipation.

The legislation places an obligation on platforms to make parents and minors themselves aware of the consequences of disseminating images of their children on a video-sharing platform in terms of psychological and legal risks and the means available to protect their rights, dignity, and moral and physical integrity.

Finally, Article 6 of the law provides for the child's power to exercise his or her right to be forgotten by asking the data controller to delete all data concerning him or her even against and irrespective of the wishes of the parents.

Following the introduction of this legislation in France, there are, however, gray areas that are not covered by the law examined and that fall within the phenomenon of *shareting*.

To cover these regulatory gaps in France, a new bill was proposed and approved by Parliament on March 6, "Proposition de loi, adoptée, par l'Assemblée nationale visant à garantir le respect du droit à l'image des enfants, n° 396."

The bill signed by parliamentarian Bruno Studer provides for the French Civil Code (Articles 371, 373, 377) to be amended by introducing the following provisions:

(a) the duty of parents to protect the image and private life of children as a specific and imperative duty (Art. 1 of the bill);
(b) the provision of the need for the joint authorization of both parents for the publication of the image of minors (Art. 3 of the bill);

Work for Free': The Unpaid Labor of Child Social Media Stars," *U. Fla. J. L. & Pub. Pol'y* 32 (2021–2022), p. 547.

(c) in the event of disagreements or violations of the child's dignity and moral integrity, the judge may appoint a guardian for the child to exercise the child's right to the child's image, after hearing his or her express opinion (Art. 4 of the bill).

The text of the law therefore affirms the principle that it is the specific and mandatory duty of parents to protect the image and private life of children. The most significant provision of the proposed law is undoubtedly the provision that in the event of disagreements or violations of the child's dignity and moral integrity, parents may forfeit all rights to the image of their children and that the judge may appoint a guardian of the child to exercise the right to the child's image in place of the parents.

The legislative tightening underway in the French legal system to protect minors and new technologies could be completed with the adoption of a bill currently being debated in the transalpine parliament, the "*Proposition de loi relative à la prévention de l'exposition excessive des enfants aux écrans*" of March 8, which aims to encourage parental education on the dangers of a high level of use of electronic devices by children and adolescents and which prescribes that the packaging of televisions computers, tablets and mobile phones must contain a warning about the risks to the psycho-physical and cognitive development of minors arising from the excessive use of such devices.

6. Conclusions: A legislative gap that needs to be filled

It is clear that in Italy, too, it would be appropriate for the legislature to take steps to introduce a regulatory framework comparable to that in force beyond the Alps.

The Italian legal system, as well as other legal systems cannot remain passive in the face of a regulatory vacuum that must be immediately filled.[32]

It comes as no surprise to the writer, therefore, that even in the United States, a country notoriously reluctant to place limits on freedom of expression, the need for legislation to combat the exploitation of baby influencers and the practice of shareting[33] is being discussed.

---

32 R. Fishbain, "Growing up Viral: 'Kidfluencers' as the New Face of Child Labor and the Need for Protective Legislation in the United Kingdom," *Geo. Wash. Int'l L. Rev.* 54 (2022), p. 127.

33 A. Zaragoza, "The Kids Are Alright? The Need for Kidfluencer Protections," *Am. U. J. Gender Soc. Pol'y & L.* 28 (2019–2020), p. 575; J. Reardon, "New Kidfluencers on the Block: The Need to Update California's Coogan Law to Ensure Adequate Protection

The overriding interest of the child cannot remain a mere formal statement devoid of a concrete declination, particularly within a sector such as that of new technologies where there is great superficiality on the part of parents, who are incapable of performing their parental function in the face of risks and dangers that can often irreversibly affect the psycho-physical development and personal identity of children and adolescents.

It is therefore necessary, in addition to the development of such regulatory instruments, to make parents responsible, who, first and foremost do not understand or underestimate the consequences resulting from the dissemination of their children's images and data.

Therefore, in addition to the implementation of a regulatory framework on the subject, there is also an urgent need to raise awareness among parents and minors, which could be implemented through the organization of training courses by local authorities on the risks of datafication and data circulation.

Bibliography

Astone, A., "L'accesso dei minori d'età ai servizi della c.d. Società dell'informazione: l'art. 8 del Reg. (UE) 2016/679 e i suoi riflessi sul Codice per la protezione dei dati personali," *Contratto e Impresa* (2019), pp. 633–634.

Battelli, E., "Minori e social network: cyberbullismo e limiti della parental responsibility," *Il Corriere giuridico*, f. 9 (2021), pp. 1269–1277.

Battelli, E., "Il trattamento dei dati nel prisma della tutela della persona minore di età," *Diritto dell'Informazione e dell'Informatica (Il)*, fasc.2 1 (2022), pp. 267–301.

Batuecas Caletrío, A., "Nuove tecnologie e protezione del minore nel diritto privato spagnolo," *Europa e Diritto Privato*, f. 4 (2020), pp. 1213–1257.

Bhaimia, S., "The General Data Protection Regulation: The Next Generation of EU Data Protection," *Legal Information Management* 18/1 (2018), pp. 21–28.

---

for Child Influencers," *Case Western. Rsrv. L. Rev.* 73 (2022), p. 165; J. Patch-Friedman, "The Monetization of Childhood: How Child Social Media Stars Are Unprotected from Exploitation in the United States," *Cardozo J. Equal Rts. & Soc. Just.* 28 (2021–2022), p. 361; N. McGinnis, ""They're Just Playing": Why Child Social Media Stars Need Enhanced Coogan Protections to Save Them from Their Parents," *Missouri. L. Rev.* 87 (2022), p. 247.

Bosher, H., "Influencer Marketing and Law," in *Influencer Marketing Building Brand Communities and Engagement*, ed. S. Yesiloglu and J. Costello, London 2020, pp. 235–249.

Bousmanne, A., *L'exploitation commerciale de l'image des enfants sur les plateformes en ligne: quelle protection pour les enfants influenceurs?*, Ottignies-Louvain-la-Neuve 2021.

Bozzi, L., "I dati del minore tra protezione e circolazione: per una lettura non retorica del fenomeno," *Europa e Diritto Privato*, f. 1 (2020), pp. 251–275.

Brosch, A., "Sharenting, Why Do Parents Violate Their Children's Privacy?," *The New Educational Review* 54 (2018), pp. 75–85.

Caggiano, I.-A., "Protecting Minors as Technologically Vulnerable Persons through Data Protection: An Analysis on the Effectiveness of Law," *EJPLT* 1 (2022), pp. 27–44.

Cannataci, J. A., "Rapporteur of United Nations General Assembly: Artificial Intelligence and Privacy, and Children's Privacy," Report of the Special Rapporteur on the right to privacy, January 25, 2021.

Cernicchiano, C., *La sicurezza on-line dei minori in rapporto all'età del consenso digitale*, Altalex, 18.12.2020, https://www.altalex.com/documents/news/2020/12/18/sicurezza-on-line-minori-rapporto-eta-consenso-digitale.

Ciancimino, C., "La libertà di espressione nel mondo digitale: alcune coordinate civilistiche in tema di contenuti controversi sui social network," *Diritto di Famiglia e delle Persone (Il)*, f. 1 (2022), pp. 360–389.

Cino, D., and Demozzi, S., "Figli 'in vetrina'. Il fenomeno dello sharenting in un'indagine esplorativa," *Riv. it. edu. fam.* 2 (2017), pp. 153–184.

Cuffaro, V., "Il regolamento generale sulla protezione dei dati," in *Trattamento dei dati personali e Regolamento UE n. 2016/679*, Speciali digitali del Corriere giuridico, 2018.

Cuffaro, V., in *I dati personali nel diritto europeo*, ed. R. D'Orazio and V. Ricciuto, Turin 2020.

Diffenderfer, M., "The Rights of Privacy and Publicity for Minor Online: Protecting the Privilege of Dissafirmance in the Digital," *U. Louisville L. Rev.* 54 (2016), p. 131.

Donovan, S., "'Sharenting': The Forgotten Children of the GDPR," *Peace Human Rights Governance* 4/1 (2020), pp. 35–59.

D'Orazio, R., Finocchiaro, G., Pollicino, O., and Resta, G. (eds.), *Codice della Privacy e Data Protection*, Milan 2021.

Duverney, P. L., "Quelles mesures pour la protection et la mise en oeuvre des droits des enfants exposé·e·s sur les réseaux sociaux à des fins lucratives?,"

Présenté au Centre interfacultaire en droits de l'enfant (CIDE) de l'Université de Genève en vue de l'obtention de la Maîtrise universitaire interdisciplinaire en droits de l'enfant, 2022.

Edney, A., "'I Don't Work for Free': The Unpaid Labor of Child Social Media Stars," *U. Fla. J. L. & Pub. Pol'y* 32 (2021–2022), p. 547.

Elkhazeen, A., Poulos, C., Zhang, X., Cavanaugh, J., and Cain, M. A., "TikTok™ 'Benadryl Challenge' Death—A Case Report and Review of the Literature," *Journal of Forensic Science* 68 (2023), pp. 339–342.

Finocchiaro, G. (ed.), *Il nuovo Regolamento europeo sulla privacy e sulla protezione dei dati personali*, Bologna 2017.

Fishbain, R., "Growing up Viral: 'Kidfluencers' as the New Face of Child Labor and the Need for Protective Legislation in the United Kingdom," *Geo. Wash. Int'l L. Rev.* 54 (2022), p. 127.

Frosini, E., "Il Costituzionalismo nella società tecnologica," *Diritto dell'Informazione e dell'Informatica*, f. 3 (2020), pp. 465–484.

Garante per la protezione dei dati, Sharenting—*Suggerimenti ai genitori per limitare la diffusione online di contenuti che riguardano i propri figli*, 2021, Docweb 9862214, disponibile in rete a https://www.garanteprivacy.it/web/guest/home/docweb/-/docweb-display/docweb/9862214.

Haley, K., "Shareting and the (Potential) Right to Be Forgotten," *Ind. L. J.* 95 (2020), pp. 1005–1020.

Iunker, A., "The New Requirements of The EU General Data Protection Regulation 2016/679 GDPR," *Conferința Internațională de Drept, Studii Europene și Relații Internaționale* VII, (2019), pp. 106–113.

Johannes, F., Nilsson, N., and Sandström, N., *It's time to TikTok : Exploring Generation Z's motivations to participate in #Challenge*, Digitala Vetenskapliga Arkivet, 2023, disponibile in rete a https://www.diva-portal.org/smash/get/diva2:1434091/FULLTEXT01.pdf.

Lavorgna, A., Tartari, M., and Ugwudike, P., "Criminogenic and Harm-Enabling Features of Social Media Platforms: The Case of Sharenting Practices," *European Journal of Criminology* (2022), https://doi.org/10.1177/14773708221131659.

Leaver, L., "Balancing privacy. Shareting, Intimate Surveillance and the Right to Be Forgotten," in *The Routledge Companion to Digital Media and Children*, Chapter 22, ed. L. Green et al., New York 2020, pp. 235–244.

Lucchini Guastalla, E., "Il nuovo regolamento europeo sul trattamento dei dati personali: i principi ispiratori," *Contratto. e impresa*. (2018), pp. 106–126.

Madyson, E., *Children Are Making It Big (For Everyone Else): The Need For Child Labor Laws Protecting Child Influencers* (February 8, 2023). Texas Tech

University, School of Law, Available at SSRN: https://ssrn.com/abstract=4351827 or http://dx.doi.org/10.2139/ssrn.4351827.

Mantelero, A., "Responsabilità e rischio nel Reg. UE 679/2016," *Nuove leggi civ. comm.* (2017), pp. 144–164.

Mantelero, A., "Rilevanza e tutela della dimensione collettiva della protezione dei dati personali," *Contratto e impresa. Europa* (2015), pp. 137–158.

Mantelero, A., and Poletti, D. (eds.), *Regolare la tecnologia: il Reg. UE 2016/679 e la protezione dei dati personali. Un dialogo tra Italia e Spagna*, Pisa 2018.

Masterson, M. M., "When Play Becomes Work: Child Labor Laws in the Era of 'Kidfluencers,'" *U. Pa. L. Rev.* 169/577 (2020–2021), pp. 577–607.

McGinnis N., "'They're Just Playing': Why Child Social Media Stars Need Enhanced Coogan Protections to Save Them from Their Parents," *Missouri. L. Rev.* 87 (2022), pp. 247–267.

Ni, P., "Research on Legal Protection of Minors' Data in Digital Age," *International Journal of Education and Humanities* 8/3 (2023), pp. 53–56.

Krzysztofek, M., *GDPR: General Data Protection Regulation (EU) 2016/679: Post-Reform Personal Data Protection in the European Union*, Alphen aan den Rijn 2019.

Krivokapic, D., and Adamovic, J., "Impact of General Data Protection Regulation on Children's Rights in Digital Environment," *Anali Pravnog fakulteta u Beogradu* 64/3 (2016), pp. 205–220.

O'Neill, E. E., "Influencing the Future: Compensating Children in the Age of Social-Media Influencer Marketing," *Stan. L. Rev. Online* 72 (2019–2020), 42–52.

Patch-Friedman, J., "The Monetization of Childhood: How Child Social Media Stars Are Unprotected from Exploitation in the United States," *Cardozo J. Equal Rts. & Soc. Just.* 28 (2021–2022), pp. 361–387.

Pelino, E., *Il Regolamento Privacy europeo. Commentario alla nuova disciplina sulla protezione dei dati personali*, Milan 2016.

Perlingeri, C., "La tutela dei minori di età nei social networks," *Rassegna di diritto civile*, f. 4 (2016), pp. 1324–1340.

Reardon, J., "New Kidfluencers on the Block: The Need to Update California's Coogan Law to Ensure Adequate Protection for Child Influencers," *Case Western. Rsrv. L. Rev.* 73 (2022) 165–189.

Sadowski, J., "When data is capital: Datafication, accumulation, and extraction," *Big Data & Society* (2019), 1–12.

Saragoza, A., "The Kids Are Alright? The Need for Kidfluencer Protections," *Am. U. J. Gender Soc. Pol'y & L.* 28 (2019–2020), pp. 575–602.

Sartoris, C., "Minors' Data Protection between e-Learning and Social Network Platforms," *European Journal of Privacy Law & Technologies* 2 (2020), pp. 138–147.

Saulier, M., "Utiles précisions sur la protection du droit à l'image du mineur," *Actualité juridique Famille* 04 (2022), pp. 231–238.

Save the children, *Shareting: cosa significa e quali sono i rischi per i bambini?*, 14.09.2021, disponibile in rete a https://www.savethechildren.it/blog-notizie/sharenting-cosa-significa-e-quali-sono-i-rischi-i-bambini.

Steinberg, S., "Sharenting: Children's Privacy in The Age of Social Media," *Emory Law Journal* 66 (2017), pp. 839–1007.

Thiene, A., "L'inconsistente tutela dei minori nel mondo digitale," *Studium iuris* (2012), pp. 528–535.

Voigt, P., and von dem Bussche, A., *The EU General Data Protection Regulation (GDPR), A Practical Guide*, Berlin 2017.

Salvatore Antonello Parente

Toward a new family-friendly tax system: Which tax regime?

Abstract: In the Italian legal system, the tax rules underlying the taxation of family income have undergone profound changes over the years, in line with the reform of family systems, which marked the transition from the patriarchal family, founded on the figure of the *pater familias*, to the nuclear one, made up of partners and children. Originally, the system chosen was that of juridical cumulation, consisting in the attribution to the husband, in his role as head of the family, of the income produced by the members of the family nucleus; following the intervention of the Constitutional Court, we moved from the principle of legal cumulation to that of decumulation, characterized by the individual (or separate) taxation of the income produced by each member of the family nucleus, allowing the single taxpayer to see the income independently taxed product, regardless of any assessment concerning one's family situation. With the evolution of family models, the current legislation has also raised many critical issues. It is therefore necessary to implement a structural reform relating to family taxation, in the context of income taxation, in order to prepare a tax regime that complies with the principles and values expressed by the Constitution and repeatedly reiterated by the judge of laws.

Keywords: family income, tax regime, models and perspectives

Summary: 1. Introduction. 2. The diachrony of family income taxation models: analysis of the problems. 3. The difficulty of valuing the family nucleus as an economic unit of reference for a different and independent ability to pay compared to that of the individual members. The need to give spouses the right to opt for a different tax regime. 4. The "splitting" system. 5. The "family quotient" mechanism. 6. Critical profiles and further solutions: the deductibility of all expenses incurred by taxpayers for family loads; the institution of the "family factor". 7. Conclusions.

1. Introduction

The family, as a socially relevant aggregating model, assumes importance not only in civil law, but also in tax law,[1] as a place of production of

1 Comp. R. Braccini, "Osservazioni sulla rilevanza tributaria dei doveri economici familiari," *Dir. prat. trib.* I (1977), p. 1239ff.; P. Filippi, "voice Famiglia VII) Diritto tributario," in *Enc. giur. Treccani*, vol. XIV, Roma 1989, p. 1ff.; M. Leccisotti and V. Patrizii,

wealth, as well as of affections, and, therefore, an expression of ability to pay.[2]

In the less recent past, some taxes, such as the focatic[3] and the testatic,[4] affected, in a broad sense, the family aggregation.

With the advent of income tax, which has a personal nature, the taxation of income produced by family members has given rise to a series of application problems, given that, in most countries of the Western world, this tax has the characteristics of globality and progressiveness, as the tax base—into which all the income possessed converge—is divided into brackets, each of which corresponds to an increasing rate.

Therefore, it is not irrelevant, for the purposes of the *quantum debeatur* as a tax, to establish whether the income produced within the family unit must be taxed autonomously by the individual beneficiary or, rather, accumulated by a single subject, normally identified in the *pater familias*.

Il trattamento fiscale della famiglia nei paesi industrializzati, Torino 2002; C. Scalinci, "La famiglia 'community care' nell'imposizione sul reddito," *Dir. prat. trib.* II (2004), p. 864ff.; G. Gaffuri and M. V. Cernigliaro Dini, "La tassazione della famiglia (trattamento fiscale della famiglia: favore o disfavore del Legislatore?)," in *Iustitia*, 2005, p. 134ff.; C. Declich and V. Polin, "Individuo e famiglia: quale fisco?," *Riv. dir. fin. sc. fin.* (2007), p. 5ff.; G. Scarlata, "voice Famiglia e impresa familiare," in *Il diritto. Enciclopedia giuridica del Sole 24 Ore*, vol. 6, ed. S. Patti, Milano 2007, pp. 344–345; F. Farri, *Un fisco sostenibile per la famiglia in Italia*, Milano 2018; S. Gianoncelli, "La famiglia inquadrata nella prospettiva dell'ordinamento tributario," *Riv. dir. fin. sc. fin.* 4 (2018), p. 406ff.; A. Contrino, "Sulla riforma della fiscalità della famiglia: una proposta strutturale e articolata, che va oltre il c.d. assegno unico, tra ineludibili moniti del giudice delle leggi ed eliminabili effetti collaterali in punto di disincentivo al lavoro femminile," *Riv. dir. trib.—Suppl. online*, December 31, 2020, p. 1ff.; S. A. Parente, "Family Income Taxation Models in the Italian Legal System: Analysis and Perspectives," *Białostockie Studia Prawnicze* 3 (2022), p. 207ff.

2 Comp. A. Giovannini, "Famiglia E capacità contributiva," *Riv. dir. trib.* I/3 (2013), p. 221ff.

3 Comp. F. Di Renzo, "voice *Focatico*," in *Noviss. dig. it.*, vol. VII, Torino 1961, pp. 418–419.

4 Comp. Q. Mirti Della Valle, "voice *Testatico*," in *Dig. it.*, vol. XXIII, Torino 1925, p. 1023ff.; F. Di Renzo, "voice *Testatico*," in *Noviss. dig. it.*, vol. XIX, Torino 1973, pp. 273–274.

In abstract, depending on the tax policy choices made by the individual domestic system, three different models can be used: individual taxation, taxation by parts or compulsory cumulation.[5]

In a system of individual taxation, each taxpayer declares his income and the tax is calculated on all of it; the presence of a spouse, children or other dependent family members is relevant only for the purposes of tax deductions or allowances. In the case of taxation by parts, the sum of the income of the spouses (and possibly of the dependent minor children) is added together and then divided; in the case of compulsory cumulation, on the other hand, the income of the spouse is added to that of the head of the family.[6]

2. The diachrony of family income taxation models: Analysis of the problems

In the regime of sources of Italian law, the fiscal rules underlying the taxation of family income,[7] over the years, have undergone profound changes, in line with the reform of family systems (Law May 19, 1975, no. 151), conditioned by the economic and social balances that have characterized the structure, marking the transition from the patriarchal family, based on the figure of the *pater familias*, to the nuclear one, made up of partners and children.

Originally, family relationships took on prominence in the context of family tax,[8] introduced in the tax system of local authorities with the Law July 26, 1868, no. 4513.[9] Subsequently, under the force of the progressive supplementary

---

5 Comp. R. Paladini, *Famiglia (tassazione della)*, https://www.treccani.it/Enciclopedia/tassazione-della-famiglia_%28Dizionario-di-Economia-e-Finanza%29/.

6 Comp. C. Sacchetto, "voice *Famiglia (dir. trib.)*," in *Diritto on line* (2015), https://www.treccani.it/enciclopedia/famiglia-dir-trib_(Diritto-on-line)/.

7 Comp. N. D'Amati, "Le basi civilistiche della fattispecie soggettiva dell'imposta di famiglia," *Riv. dir. civ.* II (1971), p. 67ff.; N. D'Amati, *Progettazione giuridica del reddito*, vol. I, *Le ipotesi della riforma tributaria*, Padova 1973, p. 229ff.; V. Capozzi, "La famiglia nella riforma Irpef," *Riv. dir. trib.* I (2005), p. 333ff.

8 Comp. F. Di Renzo, *L'imposta di famiglia nella dottrina e nella pratica tributaria*, Milano 1954; A. Bernardino, "voice *Famiglia (imposta di)*," in *Noviss. dig. it.*, vol. VII, Torino 1961, p. 73ff.; M. Morelli, "voice *Famiglia (imposta di)*," in *Enc. dir.*, vol. XVI, Milano 1967, p. 808ff.; C. Zoppis, *Imposta di famiglia*, Milano 1968; N. D'Amati, "voice *Famiglia (imposta di)*," in *Noviss. dig. it., Appendice*, vol. III, Torino 1982, p. 647ff.

9 Comp. V. Ficari and F. Paparella, "L'imposta sul reddito delle persone fisiche (Irpef)," in *Corso di diritto tributario*, ed. A. Fantozzi, Torino 2004, p. 385.

income tax,[10] the taxation system chosen was that of legal cumulation (article 2, paragraph 2, r.d. December 30, 1923, no. 3062),[11] consisting in the taxation of the husband, in addition to his own income, even those possessed by his wife, being the latter aimed at satisfying family needs.

This tax model was suitable for a patriarchal family, in which the family unit was represented before the tax authorities by the *pater familias*, who was responsible for all the income produced by the spouses and minor children.[12]

The principle was first reaffirmed, albeit in different declinations, by article 131, paragraph 2, d.P.R. January 20, 1958, no. 645 (consolidated text of the laws on direct taxes), and subsequently by article 4, d.P.R. September 29, 1973, no. 597, on the occasion of the seventies tax reform,[13] attributing to the husband, in his role as head of the family, alongside his own income and those of others,

---

10 Comp. A. Boidi, *Commento alla legge sulla imposta complementare progressiva del reddito*, Torino 1956, p. 21ff.; O. Poli, *L'imposta complementare progressiva sul reddito*, Milano 1969, p. 96ff.

11 Comp. G. Marongiu, "Il 'cumulo' al vaglio della Corte Costituzionale," *Dir. prat. trib.* II (1975), p. 177; E. De Mita, "L'illegittimità costituzionale del c.d. cumulo," *Dir. prat. trib.* II (1976), p. 337; A. Fedele, "'Possesso' di redditi, capacità contributiva ed incostituzionalità del 'cumulo,'" *Giur. cost.* I (1976), p. 2159; M.A. Grippa Salvetti, "Cumulo dei redditi e Costituzione," *Foro It.* I (1976), p. 2530; F. Gallo, *Regime fiscale della famiglia e principio di capacità contributiva, Riv. dir. fin. sc. fin.* I (1977), p. 92ff.; A. Fantozzi, "Regime tributario," in *La comunione legale*, vol. II, ed. C. M. Bianca, Milano 1989, p. 1083ff.; F. Moschetti, "voice Capacità contributiva," in *Enc. giur. Treccani*, vol. V, Roma 1988, pp. 11–12; S. Mencarelli, "Art. 4—Coniugi e figli minori," in *Commentario al testo unico delle imposte sui redditi*, ed. G. Tinelli, Padova 2009, p. 46ff.; A. Turchi, *La famiglia nell'ordinamento tributario. Parte prima. I modelli di tassazione dei redditi familiari*, Torino 2012, p. 59ff.; A. Giovannini, "Famiglia e capacità contributiva," cit., p. 228; A. Turchi, *La famiglia nell'ordinamento Tributario. Parte seconda. Tra favore e limiti del sistema*, Torino 2015; C. Sacchetto, "voice Famiglia (dir. trib.)," cit.

12 Comp. G. Nava, "Imposta sul reddito delle persone fisiche e tassazione dei coniugi: prospettive della riforma tributaria e comparazioni nell'ambito della Comunità europea," *Boll. trib.* (1974), p. 1286; V. Capozzi, "Commento all'art. 4, d.P.R. 22 dicembre 1986, n. 917," in *Commentario breve alle leggi tributarie*, tomo III, *Testo unico delle imposte sui redditi e leggi complementari*, ed. G. Falsitta, A. Fantozzi, G. Marongiu, and F. Moschetti, Padova 2010, p. 33; V. Capozzi, "Commento all'art. 4, d.P.R. 22 dicembre 1986, n. 917," in *Codice del notaio annotato con la dottrina e la giurisprudenza. Catasto—Pubblicità immobiliare—Tributi*, ed. A. A. Carrabba and G. Perlingieri, Napoli 2019, p. 1305.

13 Comp. G. Zingali, "La famiglia nella Costituzione e nella riforma tributaria," *Dir. prat. trib.* I (1971), p. 701ff.

freely available or administered without the obligation of reckoning, also the income produced by the members of the family unit (wife and non-emancipated minor children living with the taxpayer).[14]

This resulted in the recognition of the head of household's tax liability also for the income produced by the other members of the family community, without autonomous fiscal subjectivity. From an accounting point of view, the head of the family was obliged to indicate in the tax return, in addition to their own income, also those of the members of the family unit, with the obligation for the latter to indicate to the former the income produced.

In Italy, this criterion, conforming to the patriarchal structure of the family, was declared unconstitutional,[15] by contrast with articles 3, 29, 31 and 53 of the Constitution, since attributing to a single subject the income produced by those who were part of the same family unit entailed an inevitable inequality of treatment, especially after the recognition of legal equality between the spouses operated by the Law May 19, 1975, no. 151 (so-called "reform of family law"), in response to the changes that had occurred at the social level, as well as the infringement of the principle of protection of the family and of the canons of ability to pay and progressiveness of the tax system.[16]

Following the intervention of the Constitutional Court, the matter of the taxation of family income was redesigned by the Law April 13, 1977, no. 114, which marked the transition from the principle of legal cumulation to that of decumulation, later merged into article 4, d.P.R. December 22, 1986, no. 917 (so-called

---

14 Comp. N. D'Amati, *Istituzioni di diritto tributario*, Bari 2006, p. 149.

15 Comp. Corte Cost., 15 luglio 1976, n. 179, in https://www.cortecostituzionale.it/actionPronuncia.do, con note di: A. E. Granelli, "Finalmente abolita la … 'tassa di maritaggio,'" *Boll. trib.* 15–16 (1976), p. 1172ff.; L. Perrone, "Il cumulo dei redditi familiari: costituzionalmente illegittimo o soltanto iniquo?," *Giur. cost.* I/12 (1976), p. 2188ff.; G. Provini, "Il cumulo e la diversificazione dei redditi," *Boll. trib.* 19 (1976), p. 1401ff.; G. Stefani, "Imposta personale, cumulo dei redditi e capacità contributiva," *Boll. trib.* 22 (1976), p. 1637ff.; A. G. Zorzi, "Ma il cumulo dei redditi è davvero illegittimo?," *Giur. cost.* 12 (1976), p. 2207ff.

16 Comp. L. Perrone, "Il cumulo dei redditi, il principio della capacità contributiva e la progressività del sistema tributario," *Riv. dir. fin. sc. fin.* 2 (1977), p. 113ff.; V. Ficari and F. Paparella, "L'imposta sul reddito delle persone fisiche (Irpef)," cit., pp. 385–386; F. Tesauro, *Istituzioni di diritto tributario*, vol. 2, Parte speciale, Torino 2008, p. 28; R. Schiavolin, "L'imposta sul reddito delle persone fisiche," in *Corso istituzionale di diritto tributario*, ed. G. Falsitta, Padova 2014, p. 455.

T.U.I.R.), characterized by individual (or separate) taxation of the income produced by each member of the family unit.[17]

In this way, each taxpayer sees the income produced independently taxed, regardless of any assessment inherent in his own family situation, except in relation to the deductions for dependent family members, with consequent penalization of single-income households compared to those who use the income produced from multiple components.[18]

3. The difficulty of valuing the family nucleus as an economic unit of reference for a different and independent ability to pay compared to that of the individual members. The need to give spouses the right to opt for a different tax regime

The regulatory framework thus outlined has remained substantially unchanged over the years, as the tax system is still today marked by an atomistic vision of interpersonal relationships inspired by an accentuated individualism, which does not give prominence to the family as an autonomous subject of income imputation, if not for the recognition of modest deductions and tax credits.[19]

In this perspective, the family becomes a unitary subject in the expenditure allocation phase, rather than in the wealth production phase.[20]

Therefore, the Italian tax legislator, despite the attention shown toward the institution of the family, by subjecting to taxation the income of which each spouse is the direct recipient, still shows difficulties in valuing the family nucleus as an

17 Comp. V. Ficari and F. Paparella, "L'imposta sul reddito delle persone fisiche (Irpef)," cit., p. 386; N. D'Amati and A. Uricchio, *Corso di diritto tributario*, Padova 2008, p. 122; V. Capozzi, "Commento all'art. 4, d.P.R. 22 dicembre 1986, n. 917," cit., p. 34; V. Capozzi, "Commento all'art. 4, d.P.R. 22 dicembre 1986, n. 917," cit., p. 1306; A. F. Uricchio, *Percorsi di diritto tributario*, Bari 2017, p. 206; A. F. Uricchio, *Manuale di diritto tributario*, Bari 2020, p. 242.; F. Scialpi, "Imputazione del maggior reddito accertato nell'impresa familiare," *Tax news* 1 (2023), p. 69ff.

18 Comp. R. Tallarico, "La tassazione delle famiglie monoreddito tra Corte Costituzionale e prospettive di riforma," in *Tributi*, 1998, p. 965ff.; F. Tesauro, *Istituzioni di Diritto tributario*, vol. 2, Parte speciale, cit., p. 28.

19 Comp. A. Turchi, "voice *Famiglia nel diritto tributario*," in *Dig. disc. priv., sez. comm., Aggiornamento*, vol. 7, Milanofiori Assago 2015, p. 307.

20 Comp. M. V. Cernigliaro Dini, "voice *Famiglia nel diritto tributario*," in *Dig. disc. Priv., sez. comm., Aggiornamento*, vol. 3, Torino 2007, p. 386.

economic unit of reference for an ability to pay different and autonomous from that of the individual members.[21]

In this view, despite the importance assumed on the fiscal level by the family, also in the light of the continuous wishes addressed by the Constitutional Court to the legislator, with which, in a system ordered to the separate taxation of income, the need to confer spouses the right to opt for a different tax regime has been repeatedly expressed, the Italian tax system still today appears to be focused on the individual nature of taxation,[22] as the family is excluded from the list of taxable subjects.[23]

Therefore, with the evolution of family models, the legislation in force has also raised quite a few critical issues, in the absence of an organic tax regime designed for families.[24] In fact, there are still today profiles of inconsistency, inadequacy and criticality that make a structural reform necessary,[25] rather than a mere regulatory restyling, in order to prepare a tax regime that complies with the principles and values expressed by the Constitution and repeatedly reaffirmed by the judge of the laws, intended to facilitate the formation and development of the family, as a unit of consumption and savings, as well as social formation protected on a constitutional level.[26]

The current income tax system is of a personal nature, with certain correctives of a "family" nature aimed at guaranteeing the horizontal fairness of the tax levy,

---

21 Comp. C. Sacchetto, "voice Famiglia (dir. trib.)," cit.; A. Contrino, "Sulla riforma della fiscalità della famiglia: una proposta strutturale e articolata, che va oltre il c.d. assegno unico, tra ineludibili moniti del giudice delle leggi ed eliminabili effetti collaterali in punto di disincentivo al lavoro femminile," cit.

22 Comp. M. Logozzo, "Il trattamento della famiglia nell'ordinamento tributario," in *Temi di diritto tributario*, Pisa 2019, pp. 261–272.

23 On topic, comp. L. Tosi, "Considerazioni sul regime fiscale della famiglia: discriminazioni ai danni delle famiglie monoreddito, prospettive di riforma e problematiche di ordine costituzionale," *Rass. trib.* I (1988), p. 344; P. Filippi, "voice Famiglia VII) Diritto tributario," cit., p. 1; M. A. Grippa Salvetti, "voice Famiglia nel diritto tributario," in *Dig. disc. priv., sez. comm.*, vol. V, Torino 1990, p. 476ff.; A. M. Proto, "Riflessioni in tema di tassazione dei redditi del nucleo familiare," *Riv. dir. trib.* I (1991), p. 795ff.

24 Comp. A. Turchi, *Diritto tributario di famiglia*, Torino 2022, p. 307.

25 Comp. F. Farri, "Punti fermi e profili di irrazionalità nel regime fiscale della famiglia," *Riv. dir. trib.* I (2016), p. 89ff.

26 Comp. Corte Cost., 24 marzo 1983, n. 76, in Giur. it., 1983, I, 1, 1766; M. Logozzo, "Il trattamento della famiglia nell'ordinamento tributario," cit., p. 272. On topic, comp. A. Turchi, "Proposte legislative e spunti per un riordino della tassazione dei redditi familiari," *Riv. dir. trib.—Suppl. online*, June 7, 2022, p. 2.

with a view to individualizing the tax: the application of these correctives is not exempt from criticality, since these are tax measures anchored to the personal situation of the taxpayer and related to the entity of the total income.[27]

From this point of view, the taxation of family income could be rethought from a twofold perspective: on the one hand, through the provision of an alternative system to that of taxation on an individual basis, taking up the mechanisms of splitting (of the German and US systems) and the family quotient (typical of the French system)[28]; on the other hand, by restructuring the deductible charges and tax deductions, tax measures recognized in direct reference to the taxpayer's family situation, so as to commensurate the levy with the income actually possessed, taking into account the assistance and maintenance obligations affecting the spouses and avoiding unequal treatment between subjects burdened with similar burdens.[29]

4. The "splitting" system

The splitting and family quotient systems base the taxation on the total family income or on a portion of it, rather than on the income of each member of the family community: the basis of these taxation criteria lies in the consideration that the ability to pay is influenced not only by the income of the individual taxpayer but also by the resources available to the household to which the same taxpayer belongs and by the number of the same, since the fiscal unit is not the individual, but the family.[30]

The "splitting" system, widespread on an optional basis in the German[31] and US legal systems, makes it possible to determine the total family income,

27 Comp. M. Logozzo, "Il trattamento della famiglia nell'ordinamento tributario," cit., p. 262.

28 Comp. A. Turchi, "voice Famiglia nel diritto tributario," cit., p. 333; T. Yang, "Tassazione della famiglia e riforma fiscale: alcune note in tema di eguaglianza e imposizioni sostitutive," *Riv. dir. trib.—Suppl. online*, February 9, 2022, pp. 3–4.

29 Comp. M. V. Cernigliaro Dini, "voice Famiglia nel diritto tributario," cit., p. 392; A. Turchi, "Proposte legislative e spunti per un riordino della tassazione dei redditi familiari," cit., p. 2; A. Turchi, *Diritto tributario di famiglia*, cit., p. 307.

30 Comp. M. Logozzo, "Il trattamento della famiglia nell'ordinamento tributario," cit., p. 263.

31 Comp. D. Birk, *Diritto tributario tedesco*, trans. and ed. E. De Mita, Milano 2006; P. Kirchhof, "Die Steuern," in *Handbuch des Staatsrechts der Bundesrepublik Deutschland*, ed. J. Isensee and P. Kirchhof, Heidelberg 2007, p. 1037.

through the articulation of two operations: firstly, by adding up the incomes of the family members; secondly, by applying the expected average rate to the resulting amount.[32]

In particular, the total family income, resulting from the sum of the spouses' income, is divided by two and the rate is applied to the part obtained: the tax thus determined is multiplied by two, so as to obtain the tax income of the nucleus, which takes into account the presence of children or other dependent family members through specific deductions from the tax base and tax allowances.[33]

If the spouses decide to take advantage of splitting, they will proceed to pay a single tax and submit a joint return.[34]

The application of splitting produces the same state of affairs that would exist if both spouses have the same income and are taxed individually, as the incomes are calculated together and then the tax is applied on half.[35]

As a result of this system, a reduction of the tax base and the rate is therefore obtained, in the presence of a progressive tax.[36]

Consequently, this method of taxing family income produces the maximum advantage in single-income families or in those in which there is a great disproportion between the incomes of the spouses; when, on the other hand, the spouses have an equivalent income, splitting does not produce any advantage over the individual taxation system.[37]

5. The "family quotient" mechanism

The "family quotient" mechanism, widespread in the French system, as an evolution of splitting, makes it possible to take into account, alongside the income owned by the spouses, also that produced by the other members of the family, to whom a weight is attributed (i.e., a quotient).[38]

---

32 Comp. M. Logozzo, "Il trattamento della famiglia nell'ordinamento tributario," cit., p. 263.

33 Comp. M. V. Cernigliaro Dini, "voice Famiglia nel diritto tributario," cit., p. 391; M. Logozzo, "Il trattamento della famiglia nell'ordinamento tributario," cit., p. 263.

34 Comp. M. Logozzo, "Il trattamento della famiglia nell'ordinamento tributario," cit., p. 263.

35 Comp. M. Logozzo, "Il trattamento della famiglia nell'ordinamento tributario," cit., p. 263.

36 Comp. M. V. Cernigliaro Dini, "voice *Famiglia nel diritto tributario*," cit., p. 391.

37 Comp. M. Logozzo, "Il trattamento della famiglia nell'ordinamento tributario," cit., p. 263.

38 Comp. M. V. Cernigliaro Dini, "voice *Famiglia nel diritto tributario*," cit., p. 391.

Using this taxation method, the rate to be applied and the part of the income on which to pay the tax are determined by dividing the total family income by a quotient obtained by attributing a coefficient to each individual, based on the composition of the household family and the personal condition of each of its members: the total tax due is obtained by multiplying the tax calculated on each part by the aforementioned quotient.[39]

In other words, as a result of this mechanism, the cumulative income of the family is divided by the sum of the shares and, to the result thus obtained, the corresponding average rate is applied, with a consequent reduction in the rates applicable to the entire family income, without excessive inequalities between single-income families and multi-income families.[40]

As anticipated above, the family quotient mechanism differs from the splitting system in that the subdivision operates not only between the spouses, but also between the children, allowing the tax to be divided according to the portion of the income: the result is a global taxation of the family's ability to pay, considered, from an economic point of view, as a tax unit, so as to subject each taxpayer to an income tax on all the incomes possessed by the members of the "fiscal family" (consisting of the taxpayer, spouse, unmarried children under the age of 18 and children living in the same household).[41]

In the French system, due to the application of the family quotient, the number of income recipients does not constitute a significant variable, as the two spouses both weigh one unit, regardless of whether or not they are income recipients; moreover, a particular advantage is attributed to families with at least three children, since the presence of the third child determines the increase of one unit of the quotient, resulting in a more significant reduction in the tax burden compared to that established for the first two children.[42]

Thus emerges a system of favors for the family, with the provision of tax advantages that increase as income and family members grow, so as to eliminate the inequities deriving from the application of the individual taxation system, in

39 Comp. M. Logozzo, "Il trattamento della famiglia nell'ordinamento tributario," cit., p. 264.

40 Comp. M. V. Cernigliaro Dini, "voice *Famiglia nel diritto tributario*," cit., p. 391.

41 Comp. M. Logozzo, "Il trattamento della famiglia nell'ordinamento tributario," cit., p. 264.

42 Comp. M. Logozzo, "Il trattamento della famiglia nell'ordinamento tributario," cit., p. 265.

which, for the same total income, single-income households are disadvantaged compared to multi-income households.[43]

With the application of the "family quotient," on the other hand, the tax burden is mitigated in relation to large families in a more incisive way compared to what happens in a system based only on deductions and allowances; this works to a greater extent the smaller the number of income-producing family members.[44]

6. Critical profiles and further solutions: The deductibility of all expenses incurred by taxpayers for family loads; the institution of the "family factor"

Even in the Italian legal system, the solution of the "family quotient" was proposed with Law December 29, 1990, no. 428, relating to the revision of the tax treatment of family income[45]: the delegation, which remained unimplemented, was intended to introduce a family taxation regime, left to the choice of individual taxpayers, on the basis of principles similar to those of the French system.[46]

Among the directive criteria of the delegation was the faculty to opt for the cumulation of income, together with the possibility of commensurating the tax with the income strength of the family nucleus (based on the number of its members and the income they possess) and the provision of the mechanism of the "family quotient," a preordained tool for the implementation of progressivity.[47]

In reality, the taxation of family income "by parts" presents many critical issues: firstly, on a constitutional level, the possibility of transferring the tax burden to a family member who does not contribute to producing the taxed wealth is doubtful; secondly, a taxation by parts cannot be separated from the

43 Comp. M. Logozzo, "Il trattamento della famiglia nell'ordinamento tributario," cit., p. 265.

44 Comp. M. V. Cernigliaro Dini, "voice *Famiglia nel diritto tributario*," cit., p. 391.

45 Comp. M. A. "Grippa Salvetti, Note in margine alla legge delega sull'introduzione del quoziente familiare," *Riv. dir trib.* I (1991), p. 473ff.; V. Visco, "Razionalità ed effetti dell'introduzione del quoziente familiare," *Riv. dir. trib.* (1991), p. 26ff.

46 Comp. M. Logozzo, "Il trattamento della famiglia nell'ordinamento tributario," cit., p. 269.

47 Comp. M. Logozzo, "Il trattamento della famiglia nell'ordinamento tributario," cit., pp. 269–270.

presentation of a joint declaration, with which to highlight the income from which the family benefits[48]; on an operational level, then, both the splitting and the family quotient would favor families with higher incomes to the detriment of those in which income is equally produced by several components; finally, by reducing the progressiveness of the income tax produced by the husband, these systems could constitute a disincentive to female work.[49]

Not to mention that the mechanism of the "family quotient" benefits more single-income families, which do not always coincide with families with lower incomes, thus generating antinomic effects on the taxation level.[50]

Even in the French legal system,[51] the mechanism of the "family quotient" has raised, not without contrasts,[52] perplexities both on an ethical level and for the deleterious effects produced on the labor market.[53]

To overcome these critical issues and give value to the family in terms of taxation, one could think of building a tax system aimed at recognizing the deductibility and allowance of all expenses incurred by taxpayers for family expenses, also giving value to the contribution that family members without income can provide in terms of assistance and services.[54]

Another solution, partly proposed by the Law April 7, 2003, no. 80 and then remained unimplemented, could reside in the establishment of the "family factor," with the provision of an income base not subject to tax, coinciding with the "minimum subsistence,"[55] that is, a "no tax area" determined for each taxpayer due to his real family burden, which rises to a constitutional right deducible from the principle of ability to pay; his real family burden

---

48 Comp. M. V. Cernigliaro Dini, "voice *Famiglia nel diritto tributario*," cit., p. 391.

49 Comp. A. Turchi, "voice *Famiglia nel diritto tributario*," cit., p. 333.

50 Comp. M. V. Cernigliaro Dini, "voice *Famiglia nel diritto tributario*," cit., p. 391.

51 Comp. J. Grosclaude and P. Marchessou, *Diritto tributario francese. Le imposte—Le procedure*, trans. and ed. E. De Mita, Milano 2006, p. 409; M. Collet, *Droit Fiscal*, Paris 2015, p. 61.

52 Comp. P. Beltrame, "Famille et impôt. La prise en compte des charges de famille en droit fiscal français," in *La tassazione della famiglia: aspetti nazionali e comparati*, ed. C. Sacchetto, Soveria Mannelli 2010, p. 28.

53 Comp. C. Landais, T. Piketty, and E. Saez, *Pour une révolution fiscale. Un impôt sur le revenu pour le XXI siécle*, Condé-sur-Noireau 2011, p. 7ff.; A. Turchi, "voice *Famiglia nel diritto tributario*," cit., p. 334.

54 Comp. A. Turchi, "voice *Famiglia nel diritto tributario*," cit., p. 334.

55 Comp. L. Antonini, "La tutela costituzionale del minimo esente, personale e familiare," *Riv. dir. trib.* I (1999), p. 867ff.

derives from the application of a coefficient parameterized to the number and type of family burdens weighing on the income recipient.[56]

Income exceeding the "no tax area" would discount the ordinary rates, while those below would benefit from a negative taxation, through the provision of a cash allowance equal to the tax benefit not enjoyed.[57] In this way, tax credits would be attributed to taxpayers with insufficient income compared to the deductions for other dependent family members.[58]

7. Conclusions

Although the need for a family tax reform has been felt for several decades, the Italian tax system has remained indifferent and neutral for too long, relying on an episodic, fragmentary and occasional regulation.[59]

There have been no lack of preordained attempts to promote the formation and development of the family on a fiscal level: only during the 18th legislature were various bills presented which proposed the increase in deductions for dependent children (a measure later superseded by the single and universal allowance provided for in the Law April 1, 2021, no. 46[60]), the provision of tax breaks for young couples,[61] including through financial support measures for families with children,[62] the introduction of the "fiscal family," in order to identify the basis of the income tax payable by its members[63] or a possible flat-rate tax regime,[64] the subjection to taxation, according to the criterion of the "family quotient,"[65] of the income owned by the family.[66]

---

56 Comp. A. Turchi, "voice Famiglia nel diritto tributario," cit., p. 334; M. Logozzo, "Il trattamento della famiglia nell'ordinamento tributario," cit., pp. 270–271.

57 Comp. A. Turchi, "voice Famiglia nel diritto tributario," cit., p. 334; M. Logozzo, "Il trattamento della famiglia nell'ordinamento tributario," cit., p. 271.

58 Comp. A. Turchi, "voice *Famiglia nel diritto tributario*," cit., p. 334.

59 Comp. M. V. Cernigliaro Dini, "voice *Famiglia nel diritto tributario*," cit., p. 390.

60 Comp. F. Pepe, "Vantaggi, criticità ed implicazioni sistematiche dell'istituendo 'Assegno Unico e Universale per Figli a carico,'" *Riv. dir. Trib.—Suppl. online*, October 9, 2020, p. 1ff.; M. De Vita, "Solidarietà fiscale e assegno unico universale," *Riv. trim. dir. trib.* 1 (2023), p. 81ff.

61 Comp. Bill S1175 of March 27, 2019.

62 Comp. Bill C2561 of June 25, 2020.

63 Comp. Bill S1435 of July 25, 2019.

64 Comp. Bill S1831 of May 27, 2020.

65 Comp. Bill C706 of June 7, 2018; Bill S547 of June 29, 2018; Bill S1678 of January 22, 2020.

66 Comp. A. Turchi, *Diritto tributario di famiglia*, cit., p. 308–309.

Following the failure to implement these proposals, our tax system in family matters is still anchored to an individual taxation regime, outlined by the tax reform of the seventies, which, although consistent with the reference civil law, is certainly not in able to attribute to the family the role of primary social importance that the Constitution reserves for it.[67]

In our constitutional order, the family constitutes the most appropriate unit for defining the potential for well-being and, therefore, also the ability to pay of the associates.[68]

Nonetheless, the needs for the protection and promotion of the family, as a primary and vital nucleus to be promoted, have almost always been sacrificed for the pursuit of mere purposes of revenue or contrast to elusive or evasive conduct.[69]

It is therefore necessary to adopt suitable measures to place the family at the center of the tax system, in order to outline a model that is not only rational and coherent in its approach, but also designed and applied "on a family scale."[70]

Looking ahead, rather than limiting itself to achieving mere revenue needs, tax legislation should ensure the pursuit of the ends entrusted to the family in compliance with the constitutional principles governing tax matters. These principles must necessarily direct any legislative intervention on family taxation,[71] so as to enhance the solidarity and emotional aspects that constitute the foundation of all family aggregations.[72]

---

67 Comp. A. Turchi, "voice Famiglia nel diritto tributario," cit., p. 334; M. Logozzo, "Il trattamento della famiglia nell'ordinamento tributario," cit., p. 271.

68 Comp. C. Sacchetto, "La tassazione della famiglia: il modello italiano," in *La tassazione della famiglia: aspetti nazionali e comparati*, Soveria Mannelli 2010, p. 91.

69 Comp. A. Turchi, "voice Famiglia nel diritto tributario," cit., p. 334; M. Logozzo, "Il trattamento della famiglia nell'ordinamento tributario," cit., p. 271.

70 Comp. A. Turchi, "voice Famiglia nel diritto tributario," cit., p. 334; M. Logozzo, "Il trattamento della famiglia nell'ordinamento tributario," cit., p. 272; A. Turchi, *Diritto tributario di famiglia*, cit., p. 308.

71 Comp. A. Contrino, "Sulla riforma della fiscalità della famiglia: una proposta strutturale e articolata, che va oltre il c.d. assegno unico, tra ineludibili moniti del giudice delle leggi ed eliminabili effetti collaterali in punto di disincentivo al lavoro femminile," cit.

72 Comp. C. Sacchetto, "voice *Famiglia (dir. trib.)*," cit.

Bibliography

Antonini, L., "La tutela costituzionale del minimo esente, personale e familiare," *Riv. dir. trib.* I (1999), p. 867ff.

Beltrame, P., "Famille et impôt. La prise en compte des charges de famille en droit fiscal français," in *La tassazione della famiglia: aspetti nazionali e comparati*, ed. C. Sacchetto, Soveria Mannelli 2010, p. 28.

Bernardino, A., "voice Famiglia (imposta di)," in *Noviss. dig. it.*, vol. VII, Torino 1961, p. 73ff.

Birk, D., *Diritto tributario tedesco*, trans. and ed. E. De Mita, Milano 2006.

Boidi, A., *Commento alla legge sulla imposta complementare progressiva del reddito*, Torino 1956, p. 21ff.

Braccini, R., "Osservazioni sulla rilevanza tributaria dei doveri economici familiari," *Dir. prat. trib.* I (1977), p. 1239ff.

Capozzi, V., "La famiglia nella riforma Irpef," *Riv. dir. trib.* I (2005), p. 333ff.

Capozzi, V., "Commento all'art. 4, d.P.R. 22 dicembre 1986, n. 917," in *Commentario breve alle leggi tributarie*, tomo III, *Testo unico delle imposte sui redditi e leggi complementari*, ed. G. Falsitta, A. Fantozzi, G. Marongiu, and F. Moschetti, Padova 2010, p. 33.

Capozzi, V., "Commento all'art. 4, d.P.R. 22 dicembre 1986, n. 917," in *Codice del notaio annotato con la dottrina e la giurisprudenza. Catasto—Pubblicità immobiliare—Tributi*, ed. A. A. Carrabba and G. Perlingieri, Napoli 2019, p. 1305.

Cernigliaro Dini, M. V., "voice Famiglia nel diritto tributario," in *Dig. disc. priv., sez. comm., Aggiornamento*, vol. 3, Torino 2007, p. 386.

Collet, M., *Droit Fiscal*, Paris 2015, p. 61.

Contrino, A., "Sulla riforma della fiscalità della famiglia: una proposta strutturale e articolata, che va oltre il c.d. assegno unico, tra ineludibili moniti del giudice delle leggi ed eliminabili effetti collaterali in punto di disincentivo al lavoro femminile," *Riv. dir. trib.—Suppl. online*, December 31, 2020, p. 1ff.

D'Amati, N., "Le basi civilistiche della fattispecie soggettiva dell'imposta di famiglia," *Riv. dir. civ.* II (1971), p. 67ff.

D'amati, N., *Progettazione giuridica del reddito*, vol. I, *Le ipotesi della riforma tributaria*, Padova 1973, p. 229ff.

D'amati, N., "voice Famiglia (imposta di)," in *Noviss. dig. it., Appendice*, vol. III, Torino 1982, p. 647ff.

D'amati, N., *Istituzioni di diritto tributario*, Bari 2006, p. 149.

D'Amati, N., and Uricchio, A., *Corso di diritto tributario*, Padova 2008, p. 122.

Declich, C., and Polin, V., "Individuo e famiglia: quale fisco?," *Riv. dir. fin. sc. fin.* (2007), p. 5ff.

De Mita, E., "L'illegittimità costituzionale del c.d. cumulo," *Dir. prat. trib.* II (1976), p. 337.

De Vita, M., "Solidarietà fiscale e assegno unico universale," *Riv. trim. dir. trib.* 1 (2023), p. 81ff.

Di Renzo, F., "voice Focatico," in *Noviss. dig. it.*, vol. VII, Torino 1961, pp. 418–419.

Di Renzo, F., "voice Testatico," in *Noviss. dig. it.*, vol. XIX, Torino 1973, pp. 273–274.

Di Renzo, F., *L'imposta di famiglia nella dottrina e nella pratica tributaria*, Milano 1954.

Fantozzi, A., "Regime tributario," in *La comunione legale*, vol. II, ed. C. M. Bianca, Milano 1989, p. 1083ff.

Farri, F., "Punti fermi e profili di irrazionalità nel regime fiscale della famiglia," in *Riv. dir. trib.* I (2016), p. 89ff.

Farri, F., *Un fisco sostenibile per la famiglia in Italia*, Milano 2018.

Fedele, A., "'Possesso' di redditi, capacità contributiva ed incostituzionalità del 'cumulo,'" *Giur. cost.* I (1976), p. 2159.

Ficari, V., and Paparella, F., "L'imposta sul reddito delle persone fisiche (Irpef)," in *Corso di diritto tributario*, ed. A. Fantozzi, Torino 2004, p. 385.

Filippi, P., "voice Famiglia VII) Diritto tributario," in *Enc. giur. Treccani*, vol. XIV, Roma 1989, p. 1ff.

Gaffuri, G., and Cernigliaro Dini, M. V., "La tassazione della famiglia (trattamento fiscale della famiglia: favore o disfavore del legislatore?)," in *Iustitia*, 2005, p. 134ff.

Gallo, F., "Regime fiscale della famiglia e principio di capacità contributiva," *Riv. dir. fin. sc. fin.* I (1977), p. 92ff.

Gianoncelli, S., "La famiglia inquadrata nella prospettiva dell'ordinamento tributario," *Riv. dir. fin. sc. fin.* 4 (2018), p. 406ff.

Giovannini, A., "Famiglia e capacità contributiva," *Riv. dir. trib.* I/3 (2013), p. 221ff.

Granelli, A. E., "Finalmente abolita la … 'tassa di maritaggio,'" in *Boll. trib.* 15–16 (1976), p. 1172ff.

Grippa Salvetti, M. A., "Cumulo dei redditi e Costituzione," *Foro it.* I (1976), p. 2530.

Grippa Salvetti, M. A., "voice *Famiglia nel diritto tributario*," in *Dig. disc. priv., sez. comm.*, vol. V, Torino 1990, p. 476ff.

Grippa Salvetti, M. A., "Note in margine alla legge delega sull'introduzione del quoziente familiare," *Riv. dir trib.* I (1991), p. 473ff.

Grosclaude, J., and Marchessou, P., *Diritto tributario francese. Le imposte—Le procedure*, trans. and ed. E. De Mita, Milano 2006, p. 409.

Kirchhof, P., "Die Steuern," in *Handbuch des Staatsrechts der Bundesrepublik Deutschland*, ed. J. Isensee and P. Kirchhof, Heidelberg 2007, p. 1037.

Landais, C., Piketty, T., and Saez, E., *Pour une révolution fiscale. Un impôt sur le revenu pour le XXI siécle*, Condé-sur-Noireau, Seuil, 2011, p. 7ff.

Leccisotti, M., and Patrizii, V., *Il trattamento fiscale della famiglia nei paesi industrializzati*, Torino 2002.

Logozzo, M., "Il trattamento della famiglia nell'ordinamento tributario," in *Temi di diritto tributario*, Pisa 2019, pp. 261–272.

Marongiu, G., "Il 'cumulo' al vaglio della Corte Costituzionale," *Dir. prat. trib.* II (1975), p. 177.

Mencarelli, S., "Art. 4—Coniugi e figli minori," in *Commentario al testo unico delle imposte sui redditi*, ed. G. Tinelli, Padova 2009, p. 46ff.

Mirti Della Valle, Q., "voice Testatico," in *Dig. it.*, vol. XXIII, Torino 1925, p. 1023ff.

Morelli, M., "voice Famiglia (imposta di)," in *Enc. dir.*, vol. XVI, Milano 1967, p. 808ff.

Moschetti, F., "voice Capacità contributiva," in *Enc. giur. Treccani*, vol. V, Roma 1988, pp. 11–12.

Nava, G., "Imposta sul reddito delle persone fisiche e tassazione dei coniugi: prospettive della riforma tributaria e comparazioni nell'ambito della Comunità europea," in *Boll. trib.*, 1974, p. 1286.

Paladini, R., "Famiglia (tassazione della)," https://www.treccani.it/enciclopedia/tassazione-della-famiglia_%28Dizionario-di-Economia-e-Finanza%29/.

Parente, S. A., "Family Income Taxation Models in the Italian Legal System: Analysis and Perspectives," *Białostockie Studia Prawnicze* 3 (2022), p. 207ff.

Pepe, F., "Vantaggi, criticità ed implicazioni sistematiche dell'istituendo 'Assegno Unico e Universale per Figli a carico,'" *Riv. dir. trib.—Suppl. online*, October 9, 2020, p. 1ff.

Perrone, L., "Il cumulo dei redditi familiari: costituzionalmente illegittimo o soltanto iniquo?," *Giur. cost.* I/12 (1976), p. 2188ff.

Perrone, L., "Il cumulo dei redditi, il principio della capacità contributiva e la progressività del sistema tributario," *Riv. dir. fin. sc. fin.* 2 (1977), p. 113ff.

Poli, O., *L'imposta complementare progressiva sul reddito*, Milano 1969, p. 96ff.

Proto, A. M., "Riflessioni in tema di tassazione dei redditi del nucleo familiare," *Riv. dir. trib.* I (1991), p. 795ff.

Provini, G., "Il cumulo e la diversificazione dei redditi," *Boll. trib.* 19 (1976), p. 1401ff.

Sacchetto, C., "voice Famiglia (dir. trib.)," in *Diritto online* (2015), https://www.treccani.it/enciclopedia/famiglia-dir-trib_(Diritto-on-line)/.

Sacchetto, C., "La tassazione della famiglia: il modello italiano," in *La tassazione della famiglia: aspetti nazionali e comparati*, ed. C. Sacchetto, Soveria Mannelli, 2010, p. 91.

Scalinci, C., "La famiglia 'community care' nell'imposizione sul reddito," *Dir. prat. trib.* II (2004), p. 864ff.

Scarlata, G., "voice Famiglia e impresa familiare," in *Il diritto. Enciclopedia giuridica del Sole 24 Ore*, vol. 6, ed. S. Patti, Milano 2007, pp. 344–345.

Schiavolin, R., "L'imposta sul reddito delle persone fisiche," in *Corso istituzionale di diritto tributario*, ed. G. Falsitta, Padova 2014, p. 455.

Scialpi, F., "Imputazione del maggior reddito accertato nell'impresa familiare," *Tax news* 1 (2023), p. 69ff.

Stefani, G., "Imposta personale, cumulo dei redditi e capacità contributiva," *Boll. trib.* 22 (1976), p. 1637ff.

Tallarico, R., "La tassazione delle famiglie monoreddito tra Corte Costituzionale e prospettive di riforma," *Tributi* (1998), p. 965ff.

Tesauro, F., *Istituzioni di diritto tributario*, vol. 2, *Parte speciale*, Torino 2008, p. 28.

Tosi, L., "Considerazioni sul regime fiscale della famiglia: discriminazioni ai danni delle famiglie monoreddito, prospettive di riforma e problematiche di ordine costituzionale," *Rass. trib.* I (1988), p. 344.

Turchi, A., *La famiglia nell'ordinamento tributario. Parte prima. I modelli di tassazione dei redditi familiari*, Torino 2012, p. 59ff.

Turchi, A., *La famiglia nell'ordinamento tributario. Parte seconda. Tra favore e limiti del sistema*, Torino 2015.

Turchi, A., "voice Famiglia nel diritto tributario," in *Dig. disc. priv., sez. comm., Aggiornamento*, vol. 7, Milanofiori Assago 2015, p. 307.

Turchi, A., *Diritto tributario di famiglia*, Torino 2022, p. 307.

Turchi, A., "Proposte legislative e spunti per un riordino della tassazione dei redditi familiari," *Riv. dir. trib.—Suppl. online*, June 7, 2022, p. 2.

Uricchio, A. F., *Percorsi di diritto tributario*, Bari 2017, p. 206.

Uricchio, A. F., *Manuale di diritto tributario*, Bari 2020, p. 242.

Visco, V., "Razionalità ed effetti dell'introduzione del quoziente familiare," *Riv. dir. trib.* (1991), p. 26ff.

Yang, T., "Tassazione della famiglia e riforma fiscale: alcune note in tema di eguaglianza e imposizioni sostitutive," *Riv. dir. trib.—Suppl. online*, February 9, 2022, pp. 3–4.

Zingali, G., "La famiglia nella Costituzione e nella riforma tributaria," *Dir. prat. trib.* I (1971), p. 701ff.

Zoppis, C., *Imposta di famiglia*, Milano 1968.

Zorzi, A. G., "Ma il cumulo dei redditi è davvero illegittimo?," *Giur. cost.* 12 (1976), p. 2207ff.

Chapter V. The family of the 21st century and the crisis of values

Laura Tafaro

Family, new vulnerabilities and metaverse between protection needs and opportunities

Abstract: In the 21st century family, alongside traditional frailties, new vulnerabilities emerge, in connection with technological developments. With specific reference to the metaverse, in this virtual environment both new aggressions arise and, consequently, new protection needs for the members of the family nucleus, as well as unprecedented opportunities for the promotion of the weak person, which the European jurist must know how to grasp and fully exploit.

Keywords: family, metaverse, new protection needs, opportunities

1. Family of the 21st century and solidarity

The family of the 21st century, crossed by multiple changes, continues to be the (first) social formation where the human personality takes place (art. 2 Costituzione italiana)[1] (Rescigno, 1980; Perlingieri, 1979, p. 1253; Id., 1982, p. 8). In it, the realization of the full development of each of the components (art. 3 Cost) (Perlingieri, 2005, p. 370) is made possible by the fulfillment, by others, of the mandatory duties of solidarity, as required by art. 2 of the Italian Constitution. Family solidarity enables the full development of the human person, first of all in the family and constitutes its foundation.

The 21st-century family reflects the profound social changes that have taken place in recent decades and it is now indubitable that, on the one hand, the right to marry is distinct from the right to found a family, as established by art. 12 of

1 Article 2 Constitution: "The Republic recognizes and guarantees the inviolable rights of man, both as an individual and in the social formations where his personality takes place, and requires the fulfillment of the mandatory duties of political, economic and social solidarity."

the ECHR[2] and, on the other, that alongside the family founded on marriage (art. 29 of the Constitution), other family models coexist (Mengoni, 1990, p. 11; Busnelli, 2002, I, p. 509; Uccella, 2005, p. 447; Polidori, 2009. p. 127; Parente, 2014, p. 388; Ruscello, 2015, p. 97).

The model of family based on marriage (art. 29 of the Constitution) has been progressively replaced by more family-type communities: single-parent, single-parent, reconstituted, extended, patchwork, homoparental, rainbow, variable-geometry, liquid families (Mazzoni, 1999, p. 369; Id., 2002; Busnelli, 2002, p. 509; D'Angelo, 2011, 13; Paradiso, 2016, p. 1306; Femia, 2016, 255) and the profound changes that have taken place for parenthood, no longer exclusively due to biology, have affected the very way of conceiving the family and its legal notion; Today's family, as sociological studies show, "is neither more nor less perfect than it once was: it is different, because the circumstances are different" (Durkheim, 1888, p. 37).

What unites all family-type communities is the need for members to take care of each other to allow each one to realize his own life project, especially for the weakest, in the concreteness of the situations and conditions in which they find themselves, through the fulfillment, on the part of others, of the duty of solidarity (Bugetti, 2017, pp. 313–322).

Violation of this duty entails penalties (Spena, 2022. pp. 97–158; Urciuoli, 2010) and, today more than ever, family law seems to be crossed by a "penetrating sanctioning policy especially toward parents who do not comply with their duties toward their children" (Paradiso, 2013, p. 557; conf. Oliviero; 2014, p. 35). Consider, for instance, the regulation of protection orders against family abuse.[3] It is in continuity with the pre-existing one relating to the forfeiture of

---

2 Article 12 of the European Convention on Human Rights states: "Men and women of suitable age shall have the right to marry and to found a family in accordance with national laws governing the exercise of this right."

3 The regulation of protection orders against family abuse is contained in Articles. 342 bis and following of the Italian Civil Code. Article 342 bis states that "when the conduct of the spouse or other cohabitant is a cause of serious damage to the physical or moral integrity or freedom of the other spouse or cohabitant, the judge, at the request of the party, may adopt by decree one or more of the measures referred to in art. 342 ter." Pursuant to art. 342 ter, "with the decree referred to in art. Art. 342 bis, the court orders the spouse or cohabitant who has engaged in the prejudicial conduct to cease the same conduct and orders the removal from the family home of the spouse or cohabitant who has held the prejudicial conduct, also prescribing him, where necessary, not to approach the places usually frequented by the applicant [...] The judge may also order, where necessary, the intervention of the social services of the territory or of a

parental responsibility over the children (art. 330 c.c.)[4] and the consequences of the parent's conduct detrimental to the children (art. 333, comma 1, c.c.)[5] as well as with the punitive purpose of the discipline of compensation for intra-family offense (Paradiso, 2011, p. 14; Camilleri, 2010, p. 148; Patti, 1984, p. 51; Id., 2011; Fraccon, 2002; Facci, 2003; Ead., 2019, p. 421; Virgadamo, 2006, p. 1894; Sesta, 2017, p. 289; Sebastio, 2004; p. 187; Rossi, 2017; Nazzaro, 2016, p. 827), in addition to the sanctions provided for in the event of termination (for forfeiture) of the person entitled to parental responsibility over the children (provided for in Article 448 bis of the Civil Code[6]) relating to two expressions, so to speak, classic of family solidarity: the fulfillment of the obligation to provide maintenance and inheritance rights.

---

family mediation center, as well as associations whose statutory purpose is the support and reception of women and minors or other victims of abuse and mistreatment; periodic payment of an allowance to persons living in partnership who, as a result of the measures referred to in the first subparagraph, are deprived of adequate means, laying down the terms and periods for payment and prescribing, where appropriate, that the sum be paid directly to the person entitled by the employer of the obligor, deducting it from the remuneration due to him."

4 Article 330 of the Italian Civil Code: "The court may pronounce the forfeiture of parental responsibility when the parent violates or neglects the duties inherent to it [147; 30 Cost.; 570 c.p.] or abuses the relative powers [320, 323, 324; 571ff. c.p.] with serious prejudice to the child.
In such a case, for serious reasons, the court may order the removal of the child from the family residence [333] or the removal of the parent or cohabitant who abuses or abuses the child."

5 Article 330, paragraph one, of the Italian Civil Code: "When the conduct of one or both parents is not such as to give rise to the revocation order provided for in Article 330, but still appears detrimental to the child, the judge, depending on the circumstances, may take appropriate measures and may also order the removal of him from the family residence or the removal of the parent or cohabitant who mistreats or abuses the child."

6 Pursuant to art. 448 bis of the Civil Code, "the child, including an adopted child, and, in his absence, the next of kin descendants are not required to fulfill the obligation to provide maintenance to the parent against whom the forfeiture of parental responsibility has been pronounced and, for facts that do not integrate the cases of unworthiness referred to in Article 463, may exclude him from succession."

2. The paradigm of the obligation to eat between solidarity and personalism

Specifically the maintenance obligation, it constitutes a provision of material assistance to family members who are in need and are unable to provide their own maintenance (Article 438 of the Civil Code),[7] in order to meet the essential needs of life. The obligor is obliged to it by reason of family ties (article 433 of the Civil Code)[8] (Auletta, 1984; Id., 2011; Dogliotti, 1994) as well as for bonds of gratitude (the donor, by reason of the donation received, is held with precedence over any other obliged to provide maintenance to the donor[9]) (Maiorca, 1940. p. 760; Sala, 1997, p. 527; Cian, 1977, p. 815).

The systematic placement of the discipline of food—provided for in Articles. 433 ss. c.c.—in a special title (XIII) of the first book, at the end of the provisions on family law, it is significant of the intent to create a link between the maintenance obligation (of legal source) and the family: the obligation to provide maintenance is an expression of (family) solidarity deriving from belonging to the same family group, characterized by ties that translate into mutual duties of moral and material assistance of the components, with a quantitative and qualitative graduation in relation to the legal relationship between the obligor and the

7 Art. 438 c.c. states: "Maintenance can only be requested by those who are in need and are unable to provide for their maintenance.
They must be assigned in proportion to the needs of those who request them and the economic conditions of those who must administer them. They must not, however, exceed what is necessary for the life of the food, but having regard to his social position. The donor shall not be held beyond the value of the donation which still exists in his assets."

8 Art. Article 433 of the Italian Civil Code provides that "The obligation to provide maintenance is required, in the following order:
1) the spouse;
2) children [legitimate or legitimized or natural or adopted] also adopted, and, in their absence, the next of kin[, including natural];
3) the parents and, in their absence, the next of kin; adopters;
4) sons-in-law and daughters-in-law;
5) father-in-law and mother-in-law;
6) German or unilateral brothers and sisters, with Germans taking precedence over unilaterals."

9 Article 437 of the Italian Civil Code provides: "The donor is required, with precedence over any other obligor, to provide maintenance to the donor, unless it is a donation made in respect of a marriage or a remunerative donation."

person entitled and according to concrete circumstances (Palazzolo, 2008, p. 31) and whose violation, as mentioned, determines sanctions.

In particular, the sanction provided for a parent who has forfeited parental responsibility, the aforementioned Article 448 bis of the Civil Code, requires the parent to comply with the law. Article 448 bis of the Civil Code provides for the loss of the right to maintenance and inheritance rights. In this provision, in fact, as has been pointed out, there is a lack of bilaterality (Paradiso, 2013, p. 557; Laghi, 2016, pp. 73–100; Gigliotti, 2014, pp. 1096–1119) because there is an imbalance of mutual parent-child rights and duties: the sanction of the loss of maintenance and succession rights is provided only for parents who have lost responsibility and not for children who may have been guilty of similar violations of the duty of family solidarity toward their parents (e.g., a child who does not take care of the elderly parent).

This asymmetry in the relationship between parents and children constitutes "a concrete expression of that tendency toward the accentuation of parental obligations, without paying the slightest attention to the concrete behaviour of children toward their ascendants" (Laghi, 2016, p. 73). Family solidarity, however, cannot be unidirectional; it consists in an interweaving of reciprocal rights and obligations between the members of the family, which leads to a "reciprocal responsibility between them, thus the violation of the duties imposed on each of the members of the family [… gives rise] to the use of sanctioning instruments […] having bilateral operation" (Laghi, 2016, pp. 73–100).

The obligation to provide alimony—an expression of the mandatory duty of solidarity toward those in a state of need and unable to provide for their own maintenance (Article 438 of the Civil Code)—is provided for, in the order peremptorily determined by the legislator, toward the family member who has the economic possibility of fulfilling it, who must take charge of what is necessary for life.

It is true that the Constitution, in Articles 2 and 38, paragraphs 1 and 2, Const.,[10] requires to provide for the satisfaction of the needs of citizens in need, but the duty of social solidarity takes on peculiar connotations as a result of belonging to a family group.

---

10 Article 38 of the Italian Constitution prescribes: "Every citizen unable to work and lacking the necessary means to live has the right to maintenance and social assistance. Workers have the right to be provided for and insured with means appropriate to their living needs in the event of accident, illness, invalidity and old age, involuntary unemployment."

Ultimately, belonging to a family community determines the emergence of rights, but also of (related) obligations and duties. Think, for example, of the obligations of parents and children to contribute to the needs of the family (art. 143, paragraph 3,[11] e 315 bis, paragraph 4,[12] of the Civil Code) or the obligations of parents to support their children (art. 147,[13] 148,[14] 316 bis, paragraph 1,[15] of the Civil Code).

Constitutional solidarity, pursuant to art. 2 Cost., is intertwined with personalism (Perlingieri, 1972, 161; Id., 2006, 433; Lipari, 2017, p. 261) and leads, even in the family, to the overcoming of any "merely selfish and individualistic attitude to make room for sharing the needs and requirements of others" (Ferrando, 2000, pp. 52). Family solidarity is certainly the basis, as spouses or children, of demands on the other members of the family, but it is also a source of responsibility toward them (Maisto, 2010, p. 41).

The obligation to provide maintenance—an expression of the duty of solidarity understood as responsibility—derives from belonging to the same family group and increasingly follows not only from blood ties, but also from voluntary choices of the person, involving an assumption of responsibility. Think, for example, of the choice of the cd. Social parenting (Saitta, 2006, p. 19; Stanzione, 2010; *Ead.*, 2012; Recinto, 2016; Cinque, 2017, pp. 1475–1502; Ead., 2019, p. 58): The obligation of maintenance belongs to the social parent, if the biological

---

11 Article 143(3) of the Civil Code requires that "[b]oth spouses are required, each in relation to their own substance and their capacity for professional or household work, to contribute to the needs of the family."

12 According to art. 315 bis, paragraph 4, of the Civil Code, "The child must respect his parents and must contribute, in relation to his abilities, his assets and his income, to the maintenance of the family as long as he lives with it."

13 Art. 147 of the Civil Code states: "Marriage imposes on both spouses the obligation to maintain, instruct, educate and morally assist their children, with respect for their abilities, natural inclinations and aspirations, in accordance with the provisions of Article 315-bis."

14 According to art. 148 of the Civil Code, "The spouses must fulfill the obligation referred to in Article 147, in accordance with the provisions of Article 316-bis."

15 Article 316 bis of the Civil Code requires that "[p]arents must fulfil their obligations towards their children in proportion to their respective substances and according to their capacity for professional or household work. When the parents do not have sufficient means, the other relatives in the ascending line, in order of proximity, are obliged to provide the parents with the necessary means to enable them to fulfil their duties towards their children."

parent does not provide it, even after the interruption of the cohabitation (Veronesi, 2015, p. 1549; Collura, 2018, p. 37).

3. Sanctions for violation of family solidarity

In the current legal system, the violation of the duty of family solidarity determines sanctioning consequences. For example, Article 448 bis provides, as mentioned, for the child, first of all to cease to be obliged to provide maintenance to the parent who has engaged in conduct such serious as to result in the forfeiture of parental responsibility.

Indeed, in the obligation to provide maintenance, the legal duty coincides with the moral duty. Already in the first half of the 20th century it was noted that "the duty to help those in need is imposed by a moral precept of human solidarity, especially on those who are closest to him by virtue of specific family ties [...] Moral duty is then transformed into a juridical obligation" (Provera, 1987, pp. 260–261). The moral duty (left to the free adhesion of the obligators), burdened primarily on the persons closest to the subject by virtue of family ties, is transformed into a legal duty (actionable in court).

The concept is well known: the wealthier family member is obliged, even morally, to make the relative who is in need share the advantages of the patrimony which, in a certain sense, belongs to all the members of the family (Ricci, 1884). It finds its foundation in the publicistic and hierarchical conception of the family, understood as the center of superior interests, in which the members are not bearers of their own interests, but must pursue the higher end of the family's interest. In this view, the maintenance obligation, although arising from a commonality of life, affections and interests, is functional to ensure not so much an advantage of the nourishing, as an interest of a higher order, the superior family interest (Cicu, 1910, p. 145). The food service is therefore aimed at achieving social goals (Tamburrino, 1976, p. 376) and is based on "the same principle of social solidarity that is in the regulation of public assistance" (Maiorca, 1940. p. 760): The private maintenance obligation and that of social security in favor of those who do not have the necessary means to live are considered, in that view, to be competitors for the "attainment of the same end" (Provera, 1972).

In the current legal system, the basis of the maintenance obligation is quite different: although it has a patrimonial content, it does not have a patrimonial nature: its object is patrimonial, since the maintenance service is susceptible to economic evaluation (Auletta, 1984, p. 28), but it has a personal nature. This obligation is in fact preordained to ensure the right to a dignified life of those in need and is directed to the care of the person through the satisfaction of his essential needs (Perlingieri, 2006, p. 553).

Since "in satisfying the fundamental needs of life of those in need, food ultimately safeguards life itself and the dignity of the person" (Auletta, 1984), the right to food is closely inherent in the person, it is a very personal and fundamental right of the person and is one of the "fundamental rights of solidarity that are realized through the cooperation of others" (Galletta, 2007, p. 927; Sala, 2007, p. 601).

The obligation to provide maintenance must therefore be compared to the axiology of the order and to the consequent change in the conception of the family, no longer an institution, but a *community* (Perlingieri, 2006, 919; Paradiso, 1984; Scalisi, 2013, pp. 1043 e 1287), whose interests are not placed on a superordinate level, but are identified with those of solidarity with their own components (Perlingieri, 1982, p. 8).

Ultimately, the justification for the obligation to provide maintenance to the family member in need, giving him what he needs for the necessities of life, goes straight to the heart of the way of conceiving the family in a given society and to the functions entrusted to it.

Since "the sustenance of the foodman is a fundamental condition for the exercise of any right" (Ferrando, 2000, p. 51), the fulfillment of the mandatory duties of solidarity, in the current legal system, requires above all to provide for the satisfaction of primary needs and the protection of human beings in a state of need (Sesta, 2017, p. 567; Tondi della Mura, 2005, p. 340), first of all on the part of family members: the protection of human beings in need is entrusted above all to family solidarity through the obligation to provide maintenance, the loss of which constitutes a sanction under civil law, with general preventive effects and "mainly punitive intent" (Palazzolo, 2014).

4. Family and new vulnerabilities: The metaverse

Family solidarity is therefore entrusted with the care of the weakest members, not only in the hypothesis of the family member in need (art. 438 c.c.) but, more generally, toward the members of the family group in conditions of vulnerability. Consider, in particular, the vulnerability linked to new technologies and, specifically of digital environments, to the Metaverse.

In the Metaverse, indeed, one accesses and interacts through Avatar (Lamberti, 2023, p. 209; Cheong, 2022, pp. 1–28; Gibbons, 2009, p. 899). Each member of the family, therefore, can participate in business meetings, sell and buy (using cryptocurrencies) services and goods such as, for example, limited edition bags or digital art objects in a unique copy (Rubino De Ritis, 2021, p. 3), organize or attend fashion shows or concerts through Avatar (Lamberti, 2023, p. 205; Lazzari, 2021; Celotto, 2022).

The Avatar is something more than a longa manus of the real person, it is a symbol of it, it represents it (Nava G. and Tomazzoli, 2023, pp. 135–172) and must at this point remember that the term person, according to thc most accredited opinion, derives from the Greek Prósôpon. It was used to indicate the "mask"—depicting the image of the character represented—with which, in the Greek theater, the actor covered the face (Cotta, 1983, p. 159).

While philosophers emphasize that the term person does not designate man (*ánthropos*), but the character (who acts, moves in the scene, plays a part) (Viola, 1999, pp. 621–641; Berti, 1992, p. 43) and point out that "while, therefore, man is real, the person [...] it is fictitious and playful appearance" (Cotta, 1983, p. 159), for legal science, according to a first conception, the concept of person indicates "*qui in utero est*" (Albanese, 1983, p. 170) while, in a second and prevalent conception, *homo naturae, persona iuris civilis vocabulum* (Albanese, 1983, p. 170). This concept will be at the foundation of the juridical categories of "subject of law" and "legal capacity" and the person thus becomes an abstract category, unlike man, a real being (Viola, 1999, pp. 621–641).

With regard to this—formal and abstract—category of natural person in Book I of the Civil Code, some Italian civilists of the 21st century (Oppo, 2002, p. 829; Rodotà, 2007) have referred to the need to move from this notion to that of "human reality that pre-exists, even legally, positive law" (Oppo, 2002, pp. 829–836), human person (Busnelli, 2004, p. 540) considered, in an axiological conception of law, as a normative value (set out in Articles 2 and 3 of the Republican Constitution) at the top of the hierarchy of values of the legal system (Perlingieri P., 1972, pp. 12, 175 e 189; Id., 2005, p. 13; Id., 2006, 720) and, in the opposite nihilist conception, a word among those densely emotional words (Irti, 2003, p. 97; Id., 1995, pp. 289–345), which "grip us in our deepest choices; they demand from each of us a stance" (Irti, 2003, p. 97).

In the Metaverse, with the Avatar, we return to the origins: real is man, while the "metaverse person" is appearance. The real person in the Metaverse is represented by a mask, a character, the Avatar. The "mask-avatar" covers what "lies behind," that is, the real person, the concrete man, with the peculiarities of the existential conditions in which he lives in the real world.

The Avatar is not only an expression of personal identity in the Metaverse (Nazzaro, 2023, p. 59; De Vivo, 2009, pp. 191–225; Bavetta, p. 174): the Avatar is what "appears" and is shown, compared to the real person behind and before.

However, the peculiarity of the Metaverse (the circumstance that it is accessed and interacted with through Avatars), could make this digital environment a place where the human person not only needs to be protected (De Vivo, 2009, pp. 191–225; Di Porto, 2022; Garon, 2022; Barker, 2016, pp. 62–70), but can also be promoted, thereby contributing to the removal of obstacles to the realization of substantive equality (art. 3 Cost.).

In the metaverse, indeed, there are instances of protection and promotion with respect to old fragilities (Bernardini, 2020, p. 5) arising from age (for minors and the elderly) or from health conditions (for mental and physical infirmity) and new ones, linked to the peculiarities of the metaverse context.

In such a digital environment, different vulnerability conditions (so-called intersectional or multiple vulnerabilities) can be added (Pastore, 2022, p. 3; Id, 2021, p. 77; Pastore, 2020, p. 8; Id., 2018, pp. 127–131; Furia, Zullo, 2020; Zanetti, 2019; Fusaro, 2019, pp. 39–63; Bernardini, 2017, pp. 365–384; Chenal, 2018, pp. 35–56; Casadei, 2012; Luciani, 2022, p. 3; Diciotti, 2018, pp. 13–34; Callegari, 2018, p. 1; Gentili, 2019, pp. 41–64); to the original condition of fragility is added a further condition of weakness due to the specificities of the meta-versal context, as in the case of minors, for whom the so-called technological vulnerability (Mollo, 2021, p. 201; Gatt, Gaeta, Aulino, Grimaldi, 2020, pp. 7–11) is added to the vulnerability determined by age.

5. Family, metaverse and minor

With reference to the protection needs of minors in the Metaverse (Caggiano, 2021, pp. 189–214; Caggiano, 2018; Naddeo, 2018, pp. 27–64), it must first be pointed out that with reference, more generally, to the digital environment, Article 8 of the GDPR and Article 2-quinquies Privacy Code (as amended by Legislative Decree 2018 No. 101), regulate the consent of minors to the processing of personal data and set at 14 years the age threshold for access to the information society and digital services (Astone, 2019, pp. 614–648; Bozzi, 2020, pp. 251–275; Garaci, 2019, pp. 59–86; Maestri, 2019, pp. 5–36).

Digital platforms, however, although they provide such an age limit for accessing them, in fact, do not carry out any verification, relying on the user's self-declaration and, as a result, allow minors under the age of 14 to access them.

The Italian Childhood and Adolescence Authority, in order to combat this phenomenon, has recently proposed, in addition to raising the age limit to 16 years with the provision of sanctions for platforms that do not ascertain the accuracy of the declared personal age (which could contribute to their accountability and force them to carry out verifications), the adoption of a sort of Spid, that is, a system for age verification based on identity certification by third parties (AgID Determination no. 51 of March 3, 2022—Adoption and application of the "Operational guidelines for the use of SPID services by minors").

For minors, as mentioned, in the Metaverse, age-dependent vulnerability is compounded by so-called technological vulnerability. With respect to the latter, the need for protection against profiling activities is particularly important (Garaci, 2022, pp. 1–15).

It should be noted that Regulation (EU) 2016/679 (GDPR) does not provide for an absolute ban on the profiling of children for commercial purposes. In fact, although recitals 38 and 71 of the GDPR indicate an intention to exclude minors from profiling, Article 22, in allowing automated decisions and profiling in certain exceptional cases, does not distinguish between adults and minors.

It follows that once the child has legitimately given consent to access digital services, his or her personal data can also be used for commercial purposes and automated decisions and profiling concerning him or her are lawful.

The need for the protection of minors and, more generally, of vulnerable persons and their freedom of self-determination with respect to profiling activities is pursued by regulatory interventions subsequent to the GDPR.

For example, EU Directive EU/2018/1808, transposed into Italian law by Legislative Decree No. 208 of November 8, 2021, expressly prohibits digital media providers in on-demand and video-sharing platforms from processing "the personal data of minors collected or otherwise generated by media service providers" for commercial purposes, such as "direct marketing, profiling and targeted advertising."

A similar prohibition on the use of "targeting or amplification techniques that process, reveal or infer the personal data of minors or vulnerable persons for the purpose of displaying advertising" also is contained in Article 24 of the Digital Services Act of 2022, and the European Parliament, in approving it, specified that even in the digital environment, the "Best interest of the child" must be realized (Garaci, 2021, pp. 800–826).

Similarly, Article 5 of the proposed Artificial Intelligence Act of 2021 (Artificial Intelligence Act) prohibits the use of AI systems that exploit the "vulnerability of a specific group of people, due to age or physical or mental disability."

Finally, with reference to so-called technological vulnerability, it must be considered that for minors, in the Metaverse, the need for protection against Internet addiction, now scientifically recognized as a psychiatric pathology, arises more strongly (Golberg, 1995, pp. 6–7; Kimberly, 1998, pp. 237–244; Ferraro, Caci, D'amico, Di Blasi, 2007, pp. 170–175). This addiction leads, with reference to all ages, to loneliness, isolation and forms of rejection of the real life of those who are hyper-connected (the so-called mass hermits) (Spitzer, 2016, p. 15); for the underage child, however, the Hikikomori phenomenon is of greater concern and raises the need for its adequate protection (Porcelli, 2020, pp. 229–261; Ricci, 2017; Parsi, Campanella, 2017).

6. Family and metaverse between the needs of protection and promotion: the elderly and the mentally and physically infirm

The Metaverse undoubtedly represents a context in which new needs for the protection of the person emerge but, at the same time, due to its peculiarity represented by the fact that in this digital environment it is accessed and interacted through Avatar, it can prove to be a place of promotion of the human person.

One thinks, in particular, of the elderly person. With reference to the weakness resulting from the elderly age, protection needs also arise in the Metaverse, which are destined to grow in proportion to the increase in the number of the elderly who increasingly access and will access the new technologies, in view not only of the aging of the population but also the growth of the digital literacy of the elderly, which has undergone a strong impetus and acceleration due to the social isolation imposed by the measures to contain the COVID-19 pandemic, due to the need to resort to such technologies to communicate with the outside world, first and foremost with loved ones.

Alongside these needs for the protection of the elderly in the Metaverse, to be evaluated concretely—given that age does not automatically produce the same effects for everyone and, in order to assess the incidence of age on capacity, it is necessary to look not merely at the fact of (elderly) age, but at the subject's overall personal condition (Perlingieri, 1990, p. 91; Stanzione, 1989, p. 447; Lisella, 1989, p. 800)—the Metaverse can also be a place of promotion and inclusion, instrumental in removing obstacles to effective equality.

Think of the elderly man who, no longer able to do so in real life due to physical weakening, in the Metaverse, with his Avatar, plays football with his "metaversal friends" or participates in competitive sports competitions or, simply, when his health condition or loneliness—due to the distance of his children (few, given our country's high denatality rate) and the disappearance of lifelong friends—prevents him from having a minimum of social life in real life, he interacts in the Metaverse by going to the barber's shop, chatting about current affairs, perhaps without having to worry about being slower, with less memory, and, ultimately, less efficient and performing than he used to be.

The same opportunities for the promotion of the person in the Metaverse can be found in reference to the weakness caused by mental illness, especially in view of the fact that the expectations of social inclusion and integration aroused, in Italy, by the Basaglia law (l. 180/78), have largely gone unfulfilled.

For the same reasons, also for persons with physical impairments, the Metaverse can prove to be a place of inclusion, suitable for the removal of an obstacle to the full development of persons with severe physical disabilities, implementing the fundamental principles and rights recognized and protected in international law—in particular, the United Nations Convention on the Rights of Persons with Disabilities (UNCRPD) of 2006, ratified in Italy by Law no. 18 of March 3, 2009, which commits the signatory states to promote and protect persons with disabilities also through "alternative and augmentative modes, means and formats of communication, including accessible communication and information technologies" (Art. 2), as well as to promote "the availability and use of new technologies" (Art. 4)—and constitutional legality (pursuant to Articles 2 and 3 of the Constitution and the framework law on assistance, social integration and the rights of disabled persons, Law No 104 of February 5, 1992) and European law, considering that Article 10 of the TFEU prohibits discrimination on grounds of disability and the Nice Charter, in addition to prohibiting, in Article 21, "any form of discrimination based, in particular, […] [on] disability," requires, in Article 26, the promotion of the autonomy, social and occupational integration and participation of persons with physical disabilities. Moreover, more recently, the protection and promotion of persons with physical disabilities is pursued, specifically in the digital environment, by the European Commission's 2021–2030 Strategy for the Rights of Persons with Disabilities, by Dir. 2016/2102/EU (the so-called Web Accessibility Directive) and by the so-called European Accessibility Act, partly merged into EU Dir. 2019/882).

With reference to physical infirmity, the Metaverse can be an opportunity, in particular, for patients with amyotrophic lateral sclerosis (ALS), a neuromuscular disease resulting in the progressive loss of the voluntary use of muscles (and, with it, as the disease progresses, of the ability to interact with the outside world). In fact, today, new technologies, in association with neuroscientific techniques and applications, allow people with severe, purely physical disabilities who retain intact cognitive and volitional capacities, to interact with the external environment through the use of residual muscular movements or even only through neuronal brain activity (Pizzetti, 2010, p. 3; Tafaro, 2021, pp. 307–324). 3; Tafaro, 2021, pp. 307–324), thereby realizing even direct communication (i.e., without the use of nerves or muscles) between a human brain and an external peripheral (an electronic brain) through the combination of brain imaging techniques (morphological and functional neuroimaging) and the Brain-Computer Interface (Pizzetti, 2020, p. 291; Pizzetti, 2011, p. 34; Tafaro, 2021, 2021, pp. 471–495).

In the Metaverse, the person with an impaired or non-existent capacity for muscular movement, capable of communicating with the external environment by means of such technologies, can take full advantage of this sole remaining avenue of communication, accessing and interacting with an albeit minimal motor act (think of the blinking of eyelashes or the eye or cheek muscle used by astrophysicist Hawking) or even without any muscular movement, with purely neuronal (brain) activity, simply by imagining performing a certain action (Pizzetti, 2010, p. 3).

The Avatars of such persons are in no way different from the Avatars of persons without physical disabilities, and it is up to the person in question to choose whether or not to show the condition of severe disability "hidden" by the Avatar, that is, to communicate in the virtual world that, behind the Avatar, there is a real person with severe physical disabilities.

All that has been noted so far leads to the conclusion that the family of the twenty-first century has duties of solidarity also with respect to the vulnerabilities linked to new digital environments such as the Metaverse, since what happens in this digital place has concrete and real reflections and reverberations on the real life of the members of the family. The family must therefore continue to them the appropriate place to allow the development of the human personality, pursuant to Articles. 2 and 3 Cost. and 2 and 21 T.U.E.

Bibliography

Albanese, B., "Persona (dir. rom.)," in *Enc.dir.* XXXIII, Milano 1983.

Astone, A., "L'accesso dei minori d'età ai servizi della c.d. Società dell'informazione: l'art. 8 del Reg. (UE) 2016/679 e i suoi riflessi sul Codice per la protezione dei dati personali," in *Contr. impr.* (2019), pp. 614–648.

Auletta, T., *Alimenti e solidarietà familiare*, Milano 1984.

Auletta, T., *Diritto di famiglia*, X ed., Torino 2011.

Barker, K., "Virtual spaces and virtual layers–governing the ungovernable?," *Information & Communications Technology Law* 25/1 (2016), pp. 62–70, https://doi.org/10.1080/13600834.2015.1134146.

Bavetta, F., "Metaverso e protezione dei dati personali," in *Metaverso*, ed. G. Cassano and G. Scorsa, Pisa 2023, pp. 173–196.

Bernardini, M. G., "(In)visibili? La vulnerabilità alla violenza di chi non ha l'età," *GenIUS* (2020), p. 5.

Bernardini, M. G., "Il soggetto vulnerabile. Status e prospettive di una categoria (giuridicamente) controversa," in *Rivista di filosofia del diritto, Journal of Legal Philosophy* 2 (2017), pp. 365–384.

Berti, E., "Il concetto di persona nella storia del pensiero filosofico," in *Persona e personalismo*, Padova 1992, p. 43ff.

Bilotta, F., and Raimondi, F. (eds.), *Il Soggetto di diritto. Storia ed evoluzione di un concetto nel diritto privato*, Napoli 2020.

Bozzi, L., "I dati del minore fra protezione e circolazione: per una lettura non retorica del fenomeno," *Europa dir. priv.* (2020), pp. 251–275.

Bugetti, M. N., "La solidarietà tra genitori e figli e tra figli e genitori anziani," *Familia* (2017), pp. 313–322.

Busnelli, F. D., "La famiglia e l'arcipelago familiare," *Riv. dir. civ.* I (2002), p. 509ff.

Busnelli, F. D., "La famiglia e l'arcipelago familiare," *Riv. dir. civ.* I (2002), p. 509ff.

Busnelli, F. D., "L'inizio della vita umana," *Riv. dir. civ.* I (2004), pp. 533–568 (p. 540).

Caggiano, I. A., "'Privacy' e minori nell'era digitale. Il consenso al trattamento dei dati dei minori all'indomani del Regolamento UE 2016/679, tra diritto e tecno-regolazione," in *Familia*, 2018, http://www.ejplt.tatodpr.eu/Article/Archive/index_html?ida=24&idn=2&idi=-1&idu=-1.

Caggiano, I. A., "Minori d'età e GDPR," in *Diritto di Famiglia e nuove tecnologie*, ed. E. De Belvis, Napoli 2021, pp. 189–214.

Callegari, A., *Il paradigma della vulnerabilità: brevi riflessioni per una riconfigurazione del dilemma equality-difference*, www.questionegiustizia.it, 2018, p. 1.

Camilleri, E., "Illeciti endofamiliari e sistema della responsabilità civile nella prospettiva dell'European tort law," *Eur. dir. priv.* (2010), p. 148.

Carpenter, S., "Mark Zuckerberg explains Meta's plans at SXSW," in *Spectrum News* 1, https://spectrumlocalnews.com/tx/south-texas-el-paso/news/2022/03/15/mark-zuckerbergexplains-meta-s-plans-at-sxsw.

Casadei, T., *Diritti umani e soggetti vulnerabili. Violazioni, trasformazioni, aporie*, Torino 2012.

Celotto, A., Audizione Senato della Repubblica—6 luglio 2022 *Tema del metaverso" e delle sue implicazioni per l'ordinamento giuridico.*

Chenal, R., "La definizione della nozione di vulnerabilità e la tutela dei diritti fondamentali," *Ars Interpretandi* 2 (2018), pp. 35–56.

Cheong, B. C., "Avatars in the Metaverse: Potential Legal Issues and Remedies," *International Cybersecurity Law Review* (2022), pp. 1–28.

Cian, G., "Alimenti," in *Comm. Alla riforma del diritto di famiglia*, Padova 1977, p. 815.

Cicu, A., "La natura giuridica dell'obbligo alimentare tra congiunti," *Riv. dir. civ.* (1910), p. 145.

Cinque, M., "Quale statuto per il 'genitore sociale'?," *Riv. dir. civ.* 63/6 (2017), pp. 1475–1502.

Cinque, M., La famiglia si allarga ai "nonni sociali," *Dir. succ. fam.* 1 (2019), p. 58.

Collura, G., "'Le famiglie degli affetti' e le nuove genitorialità," *Rass. dir. civ.* 1 (2018), p. 37ff.

Cotta, S., "Persona (Filosofia del diritto)," *Enc. dir.*, XXXIII, Milano 1983, p. 159.

D'angelo, A., "La famiglia nel XX secolo: il fenomeno delle famiglie ricomposte," *Riv. dir. civ.* (2011), p. 13ff.

De Vivo, M. C., "Viaggio nei metaversi alla ricerca del diritto perduto," *Informatica e diritto* 1 (2009), pp. 191–225.

Di Porto, F., "Metaversi e aspirazioni di intervento regolatorio: quali prospettive?," Audizione informale presso la I Commissione Affari costituzionali del Senato della Repubblica, 14 luglio 2022, p. 5ff.

Diciotti, E., "La vulnerabilità nelle sentenze della Corte europea dei diritti dell'uomo," *Ars interpretandi* 2 (2018), pp. 13–34.

Dogliotti, M., "Doveri familiari e obbligazione alimentare," in *Tratt. Cicu-Messineo*, Milano 1994.

Durkheim, É., *Introduction à la sociologie de la famille*, Roma 1888.

Facci, G., *I nuovi danni della famiglia che cambia*, Milano 2004.

Facci, G., "Gli illeciti endofamiliari tra risarcimento e sanzione," *Responsabilità civile e previdenza* 2 (2019), p. 421.

Femia, P., "Dichiarazioni d'amore. Fattispecie e convivenza tra matrimonio e unioni civili," in *La famiglia all'imperfetto?*, ed. A. Busacca, Napoli 2016, p. 255ff.

Ferrando, G., "Alimenti," in *Dig. disc. priv., sez. civ., Agg.*, Torino 2000, pp. 51–52.

Ferraro, G., Caci, B., D'Amico, A., and Di Blasi, M., "Internet Addiction Disorder: An Italian Study," *CyberPsychology & Behavior* 10/2 (2007), pp. 170–175.

Fraccon, A., *Relazioni familiari e responsabilità civile*, Milano 2003.

Furia, A., and Zullo, S. (eds.), *La vulnerabilità come metodo*, Roma 2020.

Fusaro, A., "Il negozio della persona vulnerabile e il linguaggio delle invalidità," *Ars Interpretandi* (2019), pp. 39–63.

Galletta, F., "Gli alimenti," in *Trattato Ferrando*, II, Bologna 2007, p. 927.

Garaci, I., "La 'capacità digitale' del minore nella società dell'informazione. Riflessioni sul corretto esercizio della responsabilità genitoriale fra esigenze di autonomia e di protezione," *Nuovo diritto civile* (2019), pp. 59–86.

Garaci, I., "Il 'superiore interesse del minore' nel quadro di uno sviluppo sostenibile dell'ambiente digitale," in *Nuove leggi civili commentate* (2021), pp. 800–826.

Garaci, I., "Minori e pubblicità mirata," *Diritto mercato tecnologia* (14 gennaio 2022), pp. 1–15.

Garon, J. M., *Legal Implications of a Ubiquitous Metaverse and a Web3 Future* (January 3, 2022), http://dx.doi.org/10.2139/ssrn.4002551.

Gatt, L., Gaeta, M. C., Aulino, L., and Grimaldi, P. (2020). "The Vulnerability of the Human Being in a Technological Environment: The Need for Protective Regulation," in *Social Networks and Multimedia Habits*, ed. L. Gatt, Napoli, 2020, pp. 7–11.

Gentili, A., "La vulnerabilità sociale. Un modello teorico per il trattamento legale," in *Riv. crit. dir. priv.* (2019), pp. 41–64 (p. 42).

Gibbons, L. J., "Law and the emotive avatar," in *Vanderbilt Journal of Entertainment and Technology Law* 11 (2009), p. 899, https://scholarship.law.vanderbilt.edu/jetlaw/vol11/iss4/6.

Gigliotti, F., "L'esclusione della successione nell'art 448 bis cod civ. Luci (poche) ed ombre (molte) di una disposizione scarsamente meditata," *Rass. dir. civ.* (2014), pp. 1096–1119.

Goldberg, I., "IAD," in *Internet Addiction Disorder un fenomeno sociale in espansione*, ed. M. E. Cinti, 1995, pp. 6–7, http://www.iucf.indiana.edu/brown/hyplan/addict.html.

https://www.youtube.com/watch?v=pjNI9K1D_xo.

Irti, N., "Persona e mercato," in *L'ordine giuridico del mercato*, Roma-Bari 2003, p. 97, già in *Riv. dir. civ.* I (1995), pp. 289–345.

Kimberly Young, S., "Internet Addiction: The Emergence of a New Clinical Disorder," *CyberPsychology & Behavior* 1/3 (1998), pp. 237–244, https://doi.org/10.1089/cpb.1998.1.237.

Laghi, P., "Note critiche sull'art. 448 bis c.c.," in *Dir. success. fam.* 2016, pp. 73–100.

Lamberti, F., "Il metaverso: profili giuslavoristici tra rischi nuovi e tutele tradizionali," *Federalismi* 4 (2023), pp. 205–238 (p. 207).

Lazzari, S., "Il Metaverso. Immaginario, promessa, applicazione," *Filodoritto.com* (2021).

Lipari, N., "Personalità e dignità nella giurisprudenza costituzionale," in *Principi, regole, interpretazione. Contratti e obbligazioni, famiglie e successioni. Scritti in onore di Giovanni Furgiuele*, I, ed. G. Conte and S. Landini, Mantova 2017, p. 261ff.

Lisella, G., "Rilevanza della 'condizione di anziano' nell'ordinamento giuridico," *Rass. dir. civ.* (1989), p. 800.

Luciani, M., *Le persone vulnerabili e la Costituzione, Intervento di discussione della Lectio magistralis del Presidente della Corte europea dei diritti dell'uomo, Prof. Robert Spano, Diritti umani e persone vulnerabili*, Roma 22 aprile 2022, spec. 3ff., www.cortecostituzionale.it.

Maestri, E., "L'identità perduta. Internet of things, smart devices e privacy dei minori sul web," in *Minori e privacy. La tutela dei dati personali dei bambini e degli adolescenti alla luce del Regolamento (UE) 2016/679*, ed. A. Annoni and A. Thiene, Napoli 2019, pp. 5–36.

Maiorca, C., "Gli alimenti," in *Commentario cod. civ.*, I, ed. D'Amelio, Firenze 1940, p. 760.

Maisto, F., *Personalismo e Solidarismo familiare nel diritto internazionale privato. Il ruolo del principio di sussidarietà nell'impiego delle norme civilistiche straniere*, Napoli 2010, p. 41.

Mazzoni, S., *Nuove costellazioni familiari: le famiglie ricomposte*, Milano 2002.

Mazzoni, S., "Le famiglie ricomposte: dall'arrivo dei nuovi partners alla costellazione familiare ricomposta," *Dir. famiglia* (1999), p. 369.

Mengoni, L., "La famiglia in una società complessa," *Iustitia* (1990), p. 11ff.

Mollo, A. A., "La vulnerabilità tecnologica. Neurorights ed esigenze di tutela: profili etici e giuridici," *European Journal of Privacy Law & Technologies* 1 (2021), p. 201.

Monti, A., "Metaverso e convergenza tecnologica: aspetti (geo) politici, giuridici e regolamentari," in *Metaverso. Diritti degli utenti, piattaforme digitali, privacy, diritto d'autore, profili penali, blockchain e NFT*, ed. G. Cassano and G. Scorza, Pisa 2023, https://doi.org/10.13140/RG.2.2.18181.22247.

Naddeo, F., "Il consenso al trattamento dei dati personali del minore," *Dir. dell'inf.* (2018), pp. 27–64.

Nazzaro, A. C., "La natura giuridica del Metaverso tra Stato, Essential facility e giardino privato," in *Metaverso*, ed. G. Cassano and G. Scorsa, Pisa 2023, pp. 55–64.

Nazzaro, A. C., "Danno endofamiliare e danni nei rapporti tra 'familiari,'" *Giustizia civile* (2016), fasc. 4, p. 827.

Núñez, R. M., *Le avventure del soggetto. Contributo teorico-comparativo sulle nuove forme di soggettività giuridica*, Milano-Udine 2018.

Núñez, R. M., "Soggettività giuridica e natura. Spunti per una riflessione civilistica," www.dirittoequestionipubbliche.org, 2020, p. 29ff.

Oliviero, F., "Decadenza dalla responsabilità genitoriale e diritti successori," *Riv. dir. civ.* (2014), p. 35ff.

Oppo, G., "Declino del soggetto e ascesa della persona," *Riv. dir. civ.* I (2002), pp. 829–836.

Palazzolo, G., *Alimenti dovuti e mantenimento negoziato*, Napoli 2008, p. 31ff.

Palazzolo, G., "Alimenti e indegnità a succedere nel nuovo art. 448 bis c.c.,", www.personae-danno.it, 2014.

Paradiso, M., *La comunità familiare*, Milano 1984.

Paradiso, M., "Famiglia e responsabilità civile endofamiliare," *Fam. pers. succ.* (2011), p. 14ff.

Paradiso, M., "Decadenza dalla potestà, alimenti e diseredazione nella riforma della filiazione," *Nuove leggi civili commentate* (2013), p. 557ff.

Paradiso, M., "Navigando nell'arcipelago familiare. Itaca non c'è," *Riv. dir. civ.* 62/5 (2016), p. 1306ff.

Parente, F., "L'evoluzione dei modelli familiari: dal principio di autorità alla tutela delle libertà personali," *Rass. dir. civ.* (2014), p. 388.

Parsi, M. R., and Campanella, M., *Generazione, H. Comprendere e riconnettersi con gli adolescenti sperduti nel web tra Blue whale, Hikikomori e sexting*, Torino 2017.

Pastore, B., "Soggettività giuridica e vulnerabilità," in *Vulnerabilità. Analisi, Vulnerabilità. Analisi multidisciplinare di un concetto*, ed. O. Giolo and B. Pastore, Roma 2018, pp. 127–131.

Pastore, B., "Introduzione a di B. Pastore (ed. by), Capacità di agire e vulnerabilità. Una prospettiva interdisciplinare," in *Diritto e questioni pubbliche*, Palermo 2020, p. 8.

Pastore, B., *Semantica della vulnerabilità, soggetto, cultura giuridica*, Torino 2021, p. 77.

Pastore, B., "Vulnerabilità, diritto, ragionamento giuridico," www.teoriaestoriadeldirittoprivato.com, 2022, p. 3.

Patti, S., *Famiglia e responsabilità civile*, Milano 1984, p. 51.

Patti, S., "Famiglia e responsabilità civile, un lungo itinerario," in *La responsabilità nelle relazioni familiari*, ed. M. Sesta, Torino 2011.

Perlingieri, C. "Diritto privato delle nuove tecnologie: contenuti e competenze," *Tecnologie e diritto* 2 (2021), pp. 70–88.

Perlingieri, P., "Diritti della persona anziana, diritto civile e stato sociale," *Rass. dir. civ.* (1990), p. 91.

Perlingieri, P., *La personalità umana nell'ordinamento giuridico*, Napoli 1972, p. 161ff.

Perlingieri, P., "Sui rapporti personali nella famiglia," in *Diritto di famiglia e delle persone*, Napoli 1979, pp. 1253ff.

Perlingieri, P., "Riflessioni sull' 'unità della famiglia,'" in *Rapporti personali nella famiglia*, ed. P. Perlingieri, Napoli 1982, p. 8ff.

Perlingieri, P., "Famiglia e diritti fondamentali della persona," in *La persona e i suoi diritti. Problemi del diritto civile*, ed. P. Perlingieri, Napoli 2005, p. 370.

Perlingieri, P., *La personalità umana nell'ordinamento giuridico*, Camerino-Napoli 1972, spec. pp. 12, 175 and 189f.

Perlingieri, P., "La personalità umana nell'ordinamento giuridico," in *La persona e i suoi diritti. Problemi del diritto civile*, ed. P. Perlingieri, Napoli 2005, p. 5ff., p. 13.

Perlingieri, P., *Il diritto civile nella legalità costituzionale secondo il sistema italo-comunitario delle fonti*, Napoli 2006, pp. 433ff., 720, 919.

Pizzetti, F. G., "Recenti sviluppi delle neuroscienze e nuove questioni per il diritto: la manifestazione di volontà mediante 'interfaccia cervello–computer' fra promozione e protezione della persona con (gravissima) menomazione," *Astrid Rassegna* 127/22 (December 22, 2010), p. 3, spec. note 8 and 9.

Pizzetti, F. G., "Brain-Computer Interfaces and the Protection of the Fundamental Rights of the Vulnerable Persons," in *Neuroscience and Law. Complicated Crossings and New Perspectives*, ed. A. D'Aloia and M. C. Errigo, Cham 2020, p. 291ff.

Pizzetti, F. G., "Libertà di autodeterminazione e protezione del malato nel 'Brain-Computer interfacing': un nuovo ruolo per l'amministratore di sostegno?," *Riv. crit. dir. priv.* (2011), p. 34.

Polidori, S., "Le famiglie non fondate sul matrimonio: ruolo del diritto e tecniche d'intervento del sistema," in *Rapporti familiari e regolazione: mutamenti e prospettive*, ed. M. Francesca and M. Gorgoni, Napoli 2009, p. 127ff.

Porcelli, G., "Nativi digitali e l'entropia della partecipazione: gli 'hikikomori' in Italia," in *Di fronte al futuro. i giovani e le sfide della partecipazione*, ed. G. Delli Zotti and G. Blasutig, Torino 2020, pp. 229–261.

Provera, G., "Degli alimenti," in *Comm. c.c. Scialoja Branca*, Bologna-Roma, 1972.

Provera, G., "Alimenti," in *Dig. disc. priv., sez. civ.*, I, Torino 1987, pp. 260–261.

Pugliatti, S., "Autoresponsabilità," in *Enciclopedia del diritto*, vol. IV, Milano 1959. p. 452ff.

Recinto, G., *Le genitorialità. Dai genitori ai figli e ritorno*, Napoli 2016.

Rescigno, P., "La comunità familiare come formazione sociale," in *Rapporti personali nella famiglia*, Quaderni del CSM, Roma 1980, p. 366.

Ricci, C., *Hikikomori: adolescenti in volontaria reclusione*, Milano 2017.

Ricci, F., *Corso teorico-pratico di diritto civile*, Torino 1884.

Rodotà, S., *Dal soggetto alla persona*, Napoli 2007.

Rossi, R., *Le regole del risarcimento dei danni endo ed esofamiliari*, Milano 2017.

Rubino De Ritis, M., "L'espansione economica nel Metaverso: I No Fungible Token (NFT)," *Giustiziacivile.com* (2021), p. 3.

Ruscello, F., "La famiglia nella società contemporanea," *Vita not.* (2015), p. 97.

Saitta, P., "La genitorialità 'sociale' e la sua regolazione. Una rassegna europea," in *Quaderni della Sezione Diritto e Comunicazioni Sociali*, 2006, p. 19ff., http://www.cirsdig.it/Pubblicazioni/saittastepparents.pdf.

Sala, M., "Gli alimenti," in *Tratt. Bonilini Cattaneo*, II, Torino 1997, p. 527.

Sala, M., "Gli alimenti," in *Trattato Bonilini-Cattaneo, Il diritto di famiglia*, II, 2°ed., Torino 2007, p. 601.

Scalisi, V., "Le stagioni della famiglia nel diritto dall'unità d'Italia a oggi. Parte prima: Dalla 'famiglia-istituzione' alla 'famiglia-comunità': centralità del 'rapporto' e primato della 'persona,'" *Riv. dir. civ.* (2013), p. 1043ff. and *ivi* parte seconda, 6 (2013), p. 1287ff.

Sebastio, G., "La responsabilità civile endo-familiare," in *I rapporti familiari tra autonomia e responsabilità*, ed. R. Torino, Torino 2004, p. 187.

Sesta, M., "La famiglia tra funzione sociale e tutele individuali," *Riv. trim. dir. proc. civ.* (2017), p. 567ff.

Sesta, M., "Il danno nelle relazioni familiari tra risarcimento e finalità punitiva," *Famiglia e diritto* 3 (2017), p. 289.

Spena, A., "Violazione degli obblighi di solidarietà familiare," in *Reati contro la famiglia*, ed. M. Bertolino, Torino 2022, pp. 97–158.

Spitzer, M., *Solitudine digitale. Disadattati, isolati, capaci solo di una vita virtuale?*, trad. it., Milano 2016, p. 15.

Stanzione, M. G., *Filiazione e "genitorialità." Il problema del terzo genitore*, Torino 2010.

Stanzione, M. G., "Rapporti di filiazione e 'terzo genitore': le esperienze francese e italiana," *Fam. dir.* (2012), part. p. 204ff.

Stanzione, P., "Le età dell'uomo e la tutela della persona: gli anziani," *Riv. dir. civ.* I (1989), p. 447.

Tafaro, L., "Il diritto alla 'comunicazione non verbale' mediante Brain-Computer Interface-Spelling: gli atti neuronali," *Dirittifondamentali.it* 1 (2021), pp. 307–324.

Tafaro, L., "Oltre gli atti muti: gli atti neuronali. I Brain's Acts a contenuto non patrimoniale, l'uomo postumano e la sua custodia," *BioLaw Journal- Rivista di BioDiritto* 2 (2021), pp. 471–495.

Tamburrino, G., *Lineamenti del nuovo diritto di famiglia italiano*, Torino 1976, p. 376.

Tondi della Mura, V., "Famiglia e sussidiarietà, ovvero: dei diritti (sociali) della famiglia," in *Modelli familiari tra diritti e servizi*, ed. M. Gorgoni, Napoli 2005, p. 340.

Uccella, F., "Dalla 'famiglia pluriematica' alla 'famiglia putativa' come soggetto giuridico: prime considerazioni," *Familia* (2005), p. 447ff.

Urciuoli, M. A., *Rapporti familiari tra libertà e strumenti di controllo*, Napoli 2010.

Veronesi, S., "Genitore 'sociale' e relazioni di fatto: riconosciuta la rilevanza dell'interesse del minore a mantenere un rapporto stabile e significativo con il convivente del genitore biologico," *Corr. giur.* 12 (2015), p. 1549ff.

Viola, F., "Lo statuto giuridico della persona in prospettiva storica," in *Studi in memoria di Italo Mancini*, ed. D. Pansini, Napoli 1999, pp. 621–641.

Virgadamo, P., "Rapporti familiari e danno non patrimoniale: la tutela dell'individuo tra diritti personali a inviolabilità strutturale e interessi familiari a inviolabilità dinamica," *Dir. fam. pers.* (2006), p. 1894.

Virgilio, M., "La vulnerabilità nelle fonti normative italiane e dell'Unione Europea: definizioni e contesti," in *Vulnerabilità. Analisi multidisciplinare di un concetto*, ed. O. Giolo and B. Pastore, Roma 2018, pp. 161–170.

Zanetti, G., *Filosofia della vulnerabilità*, Roma 2019.

Mariusz Załucki

The approach of family and succession law to digital assets

Abstract: Digital assets have been an increasingly important component of our wealth for some time. Against the background of a person's presence in the virtual world, many legal questions arise. Some of these concern family law and, consequently, after the death of family members, also inheritance law. The provision of electronic services usually starts with the creation of a virtual account to access them. Facebook, Twitter or regular email are services that are provided in this way. One may be concerned about the status of such an account, especially in the context of its possible affiliation to the property of the spouses, as well as its possible inheritance. Hence, the purpose of the author's contribution is to present the basic dilemmas of this area, possible concepts and some proposals for necessary solutions.

Keywords: digital assets, joint property, virtual account, digital estate, inheritance, succession

1. Introduction

The issue of new technologies, especially those used by the public on a daily basis via the Internet, has already been the subject of various scientific inquiries.[1] From a private law perspective, these considerations have mainly concerned contract law,[2] intellectual property law,[3] the area of personal data protection,[4]

1 Cf., e.g.: T. Kerikmae (ed.), *Regulating eTechnologies in the European Union. Normative Realities and Trends*, Cham-Heidelberg-New York-Dordrecht-London 2014, passim. Research results are part of a research project funded by the National Science Centre (Poland), agreement No. UMO-2018/31/B/HS5/01061.

2 Cf. A. Savelyev, "Contract Law 2.0: 'Smart' Contracts as the Beginning of the End of Classic Contract Law," *Information and Communications Technology Law* 26/2 (2017), pp. 116–134.

3 Cf. C. R. Davies, "An Evolutionary Step in Intellectual Property Rights—Artificial Intelligence and Intellectual Property," *Computer Law and Security Review* 27/6 (2011), p. 601 ff.

4 H. Beverley-Smith, A. Ohly, and A. Lucs-Schloetter, *Privacy, Property and Personality. Civil Law Perspectives on Commercial Appropriation*, Cambridge 2005, p. 1ff.

but also family law and the law of succession.[5] Nevertheless, one gets the impression that the discussion in this area is not yet exhausted. Moreover, it seems that some of the contributions of science even encourage further discourse.[6] This is the case, inter alia, in the area of digital (virtual) goods, where, in the context of their circulation, both *inter vivos* and *mortis causa*, no consensus has yet been reached and the positions of some discussants either overlook certain aspects of virtual goods or are far from debatable.

One of the reasons for this is that many legislators have not decided to change their law in the context of digital (virtual) goods, assuming, inter alia, that the law should be technologically neutral, and that the existing regulations should enable the resolution of potential doubts also in this relatively new area.[7] However, there are also those who have decided on specific changes, introducing specific solutions to regulate the trade in digital (virtual) goods into their legal system.[8] These, too, while resolving some existing doubts, also bring other doubts. This is because they are often *ad hoc* changes made under the influence of specific events occurring in practice. There is usually a lack of comprehensive legal regulation, which is due, for example, to the fact that the authors of most of the basic laws in the area of family law and inheritance law, at least from the perspective of European countries, could not have imagined at the time when these acts were created that certain legal problems in this area would apply not only to the real

---

5 Cf., e.g.: G. W. Beyer, "Estate Planning for Digital Assets," *Estate Planning Studies* 1 (2015), p. 1ff; M. Esperança Ginebra Molins, "Voluntades digitales: disposiciones mortis causa," in *En derecho privado en el nuevo paradigma digital*, vol. X, ed. E. A. Amayuelas and S. C. Lapuente, Madrid-Barceliona-Buenos Aires-Sao Paulo 2017, p. 210ff; A. Gebicka and A. Heinemann, "Social Media & Competition Law," *World Competition* 37/2 (2014), pp. 149–172; E. Harbinja, *Digital Death, Digital Assets and Post-mortem Privacy*, Edinburgh 2023, p. 84ff; A. Kamalnath, "The Law of Cryptoassets Is the Law of the Horse," *Banking & Finance Law Review* 36 (2020), pp. 135–143; B. B. Merhi, *L'émergence de l'identité numérique: l'influence de la révolution numérique sur l'environnement juridique*, Paris 2022, p. 10ff.

6 R. Berti and S. Zanetti, "La trasmissione mortis causa del patrimonio e dell'identità digitale: strumenti giuridici, operativi e prospettive de iure condendo," *Law and Media Working Paper Series* 18 (2016), pp. 1–25; M. Załucki, "Digital Content Left On-line after Death of a User. On the Research that Needs to Be Conducted," *Legal and Administrative Studies* 19/1 (2020), pp. 53–66.

7 Cf., e.g.: A. Janssen, "Das digitale Erbe eines Menschen," *European Review of Private Law* 4 (2017), p. 697 ff.

8 M. Mądel, "Następstwo prawne treści cyfrowych z perspektywy prawa Stanów Zjednoczonych Ameryki," *Prawo Mediów Elektronicznych* 1 (2016), p. 1ff.

world, but also to the virtual one.[9] However, time passes quickly and regulations enacted often in the last century are not necessarily relevant to the needs of practice today. On the other hand, the Internet today is widely used in households and the use of a number of services available through it escapes traditional legal constructions.[10]

In this context, it is important to point out that the provision of electronic services usually starts with the creation of a virtual account that allows access to them. Facebook, Twitter or ordinary email are services that are provided in just such a way.[11] Numerous questions arise against the background of the use of these services, which some legislators, as well as the jurisprudence, have so far tried to deal with, especially, however, in the context of their inheritance legal status (including personal and patrimonial aspects). Few, on the other hand, have recognized the family law problems involved. In the meantime, it is, one might think, above all, the legal-family qualification of certain assets in the digital world that may be of considerable importance for the question of inheritance. If it turns out that an account which is the basis for the provision of electronic services, for example, an account allowing access to Facebook, is a component of family property (above all marital property), then its legal-succession character would also have to be determined by its status (at least in part).

For this reason, it is worth taking a look at this issue and trying to identify the dilemmas whose prior resolution should be relevant to the legal-family and then legal-succession status of digital assets. Hence, the purpose of this contribution is therefore to present the basic dilemmas of this area, possible concepts and some proposals for the necessary solutions.

2. Transformation to the digital world

Analyzing the current legal solutions, one can get the impression that the law has not kept up with the virtual world. Virtual reality is such that part of human life

9 B. Mceniery, "Succession Law Keeping Pace with Changes in Technology and Community Expectations—Informal Wills," *Journal of New Business Ideas & Trends* 12/1 (2014), pp. 1–10.

10 Cf. A. J. Hirsch, "Technology Adrift: In Search of a Role for Electronic Wills," *Boston College Law Review* 61/3 (2020).

11 J. A. T. Fairfield, "Virtual Property," *Boston University Law Review* 85/4 (2005), p. 1047ff.

has moved from the analog world to the digital world.[12] We rarely use traditional cameras, for example, because we usually take photos with our smartphones and at the same time we do not develop them in the traditional way, but save them in the cloud, sometimes creating digital albums.[13] The same is true of music, we buy CDs or DVDs less and less, and we also access music via online services, where we create our virtual collections.[14] We communicate with the world through various types of instant messaging, not to mention the widely and extensively used social networks. We no longer write letters but send e-mails.[15] A large part of our life activity also involves computer games, which we of course also play online. Thus, providers of all kinds of products and services have moved into the world of the Internet, becoming Internet service providers, offering them via the Internet.[16] In order to use most of these services, it is first necessary to register virtually, thus creating an appropriate virtual account. For many online services, universal accounts such as those provided by Google, Microsoft or Meta (formerly Facebook) are sufficient.[17] It is therefore impossible to say that life and the needs associated with it are the same today as they were without the Internet or when it was still in its infancy. Today, therefore, our daily activities leave a "digital footprint."[18] We create, acquire, obtain the right to use or access digital goods or content, use digital services for various purposes, often also pursuing our economic interests in this way.

The legal status of this type of virtual account, as well as its contents, is debatable. There are basically no legal regulations in the various countries that clarify this status. And those that do exist may be questionable to many, if only because

12 Cf. W. Barfield, "Intellectual Property Rights in Virtual Environments: Considering the Rights of Owners, Programmers and Virtual Avatars," *Akron Law Review* 39 (2006), p. 649ff.

13 J. A. T. Fairfield, "Virtual Property," *op. cit.*, p. 1055ff.

14 P. Szulewski, "Śmierć 2.0—problematyka dóbr cyfrowych," in *Non omnis moriar. Osobiste i majątkowe aspekty prawne śmierci człowieka. Zagadnienia wybrane*, ed. J. Gołaczyński, J. Mazurkiewicz, J. Turłukowski, and D. Karkut, Wrocław 2015, pp. 731–749.

15 E. Harbinja, "Legal Nature of e-mails: A Comparative Perspective," *Duke Law & Technology Review* 14/1 (2016), pp. 227–255.

16 A. Savelyev, "Contract Law 2.0: 'Smart' Contracts as the Beginning of the End of Classic Contract Law," *op. cit.*, p. 116ff.

17 See, however: A. Carr, "Facebook Everywhere," *Fastcompany.com* 7/8 (2014), pp. 56–92.

18 S. S. Varnado, "Your Digital Footprint Left behind at Death: An Illustration of Technology Leaving the Law Behind," *Louisiana Law Review* 74/3 (2014), pp. 719–775.

they are national in nature, while the Internet is a space that knows no borders. One of the most important issues in this respect is the status of the digital goods used by the user of online services in the context of his/her virtual account.

It should also be noted that, as of today, what we encounter on the Internet, the trace we leave there, is a phenomenon that has not yet been uniformly defined. If one looks at the various statements made on this subject, one can see a number of divergent and heterogeneous elements, referred to as "digital goods,"[19] "digital content,"[20] "digital assets,"[21] "digital services," "digital products," or whatever.[22] The conceptual scope of all these terms is not precise. In the current normative state of many countries, there is basically no definition of these terms (which, however, is not necessarily flawed), significant divergences in their meaning also occur in practice. The development of different technological instruments, the lack of uniformity of practice or identical legislative solutions in individual countries, dictates that any definition of these phenomena, which collectively for the purposes of this speech may be called "digital goods,"[23] should be approached with caution. Despite the fact that, in recent times, it is possible to speak of an increasing clarification of the meaning of all these concepts, it is nevertheless necessary to make the far-reaching reservation (out of an excess of caution) that all these phenomena—from the perspective of legal science—have not yet been

19 L. Edwards and E. Harbinja, "'What Happens to My Facebook Profile When I Die?' Legal Issues Around Transmission of Digital Assets on Death," *CREATe Working Paper* 5/5 (2013), p. 2.

20 R. Matanovac Vučković and I. Kanceljak, "Does the Right to Use Digital Content Affect Our Digital Inheritance?," *Eu and Member States—Legal and Economic Issues* 3/3 (2019), p. 724ff. It has to be mentioned that *Directive 2011/83/EU of the European Parliament and of the Council of October 25, 2011 (on consumer rights)* uses the term „digital content" (art. 2.11) and provides that it means „data which are produced and supplied in digital form."

21 N. M. Banta, "Minors and Digital Asset Succession," *Iowa Law Review* 104/4 (2019), p. 1699ff. American *Uniform Fiduciary Access to Digital Assets Act* uses the term "digital assets" (Section 2.1) and explains that it means „an electronic record in which an individual has a right or interest."

22 S. Herzog, "Der digitale Nachlass und das Erbrecht," *Anwaltsblatt Online* 6 (2018), pp. 471–481; M. Kubis et al., *Der digitale Nachlass. Eine Untersuchung aus rechtlicher und technischer Sicht*, Bremen-Regensburg 2019, passim; A. Magnani, "L'eredità digitale," *Notariato* 5 (2014), p. 1281ff.; M. Marinioni, *Patrimonio digitale: analisi comparata dei profili successori*, Padova 2016, passim.

23 L. Edwards and E. Harbinja, "'What Happens to My Facebook Profile When I Die?' Legal Issues Around Transmission of Digital Assets on Death," *op. cit.*, p. 2.

properly studied and diagnosed. Moreover, there is, as one might think, a need for a flexible approach in this regard, so that the conceptual scope of the digital footprint of the human being on the Internet is resilient to innovations that may, and certainly will, arise in the future.[24]

These remarks already indicate that we are dealing with specific phenomena which escape the traditional conceptual apparatus, which must give rise to, and usually does give rise to, various doubts. The different conceptual scopes, and thus the different understandings of the various terms, cannot fail to make a difference in the context of trying to agree on whether these phenomena can be governed by rules familiar from family law or succession law.

Several concepts have emerged worldwide as to how the law should treat such digital goods (or to put it another way: virtual objects). The most far-reaching conception advocates the application of property law to these objects (rather, however, by analogy). In this case, the object of ownership would be reduced to the computer code stored on the server of the entity that owns the rights to the online service in question. There are also concepts, which tend to be the majority view, focusing on contract law, indicating that the user of an Internet service is linked to the Internet Service Provider (ISP) by a license agreement, which should set out the terms and conditions for the use of specific virtual objects. There are also ideas proposing the use of a deposit contract structure. The latter assumes that, in addition to the license agreement, the user and the ISP are linked by a deposit agreement, where the user could store the virtual objects "belonging" to him or her. Other positions can of course also be encountered.[25]

The legal nature of the account and the virtual objects (digital goods) accessible through it is therefore not a foregone conclusion. The statements of civil law doctrine and jurisprudence to date are not clear. At the same time, there are those who consider such an account and its associated content to be of a property nature, especially if it serves to realize an individual's property interest.[26] In the case of email, social networking sites or virtual computer games, it seems that such a legal qualification can be discussed, especially since practice shows

---

24 B. B. Merhi, "L'émergence de l'identité numérique: l'influence de la révolution numérique sur l'environnement juridique," *op. cit.*, passim.

25 These concepts are described in more detail in e.g.: M. Esperança Ginebra Molins, "Voluntades digitales: disposiciones mortis causa," *op. cit.*, p. 210ff.

26 Cf. A. Fuchs, "What Happens to Your Social Media Account When You Die? The First German Judgments on Digital Legacy," *ERA Forum* 22 (2021), pp. 1–7.

that some accounts bring their beneficiary significant property benefits.[27] For example, the Facebook account of any celebrity can be pointed out here. It is usually a significant carrier of property values. This in turn must somewhat impinge on the optics with which the legal status of such an account will be viewed. If one assumes, not without some doubt, that a virtual account for the use of online services is of an asset nature, for which there are many reasons, the consequences of such a view may be far-reaching, both from the point of view of family law and inheritance law. It is important to look at the possible dilemmas associated with this.

3. Family law doubts and challenges

In the context of family law, far-reaching doubts arise in relation to determining to which property (whose property) the virtual account in question belongs, if of course we classify it as an asset. Such a legal qualification, if only due to the content of the contracts concluded by the users of Internet services with the ISPs, is debatable.[28] Nevertheless, it is obvious that when the applicable legal provision regulates something differently from the contract, and it is not dispositive in nature, then it is the legal provision and not the contract that will take precedence. Hence, at least initially, the content of ISP contracts does not prevent the qualification of the digital good in question from being different from that which would result from the contract.[29] This problem becomes particularly apparent when dealing with spouses in a matrimonial property regime of joint ownership.[30] Many legal systems provide for such constructions. According to the regulations generally applicable there, the joint property of the spouses includes all property belonging to them which is not excluded from the joint property.[31]

27 M. Załucki, "Digital Inheritance: Key Issues and Doubts. The Challenges of Succession Law in the Face of New Technologies," in *Future Law*, Vol. II, ed. F. da S. Veiga, P. de Brito, and Z. L. Pierdoná, Porto 2021, p. 671ff.

28 R. Polčák, "The Legal Classification of ISPs," *Journal of Intellectual Property, Information Technology and E-Commerce Law* 3/1 (2010), p. 172 ff.

29 See, e.g.: Report on *Digital Assets and Private Law. Public Consultation (Study LXXXII)*, International Institute for the Unification of Private Law (UNIDROIT), Rome 2023, passim.

30 D. Damascelli, "La legge applicabile ai rapporti patrimoniali tra coniugi, uniti civilmente e conviventi di fatto nel diritto internazionale privato italiano ed europeo," *Rivista di Diritto Internazionale* 6 (2017).

31 Cf. L. Ruggeri, I. Kunda, and S. Winkler (eds.), *Family Property and Succession in EU Member States. National Reports on the Collected Data*, Rijeka 2019.

This is, arguably, an important argument in the context of various attempts to qualify the legal status of digital assets. Although ISP contracts sometimes contain restrictions on the use of an online account by other persons,[32] as it seems, these provisions are of particular interest in the context of the existence of precisely this kind of regulation in family law as regards the assets of spouses.

A kind of obstacle to the qualification of a virtual account and related digital assets, at least raised by some, is the nature of this account, which is closely linked to its user.[33] This is supposed to be a prejudicial argument for the exclusion of such assets from the joint property of spouses.[34] This close connection between the account and the person, in many cases, is indeed strong, however, well-known examples from case law, including European case law, concerning admittedly inheritance rather than family matters, have tended to present a view of the property, hereditary nature of the account, which must also imply the possibility of trading it *inter vivos* (which can be contractually excluded to some extent) and rather disqualify the idea of its exclusively personal nature.

The community property regime is often the regime preferred by the legislator and has the character of a universal property regime. In the legal systems that provide for such a regime (e.g., Poland, but also the general law of Spain[35] and the law of some Spanish autonomous communities, such as Aragon or Navarre[36]), it is often argued that it serves to realize the fundamental principles of family law, in particular the principle of equality between men and women and the principle of protection of marriage and the family, contributing to strengthening the position of the economically weaker spouse and to stabilizing the material situation of the family founded by the spouses.[37] It is aimed at enabling the spouses to cooperate as fully as possible in the property sphere. According to the established view in

32 Cf. Report on ISP Interconnection and its Impact on Consumer Internet Performance—A Measurement Lab Consortium Technical Report, Measurement Lab Consortium Technical, Washington, DC 2014, passim.

33 Cf. M. V. Naseh, "Person and Personality in Cyber Space: A Legal Analysis of Virtual Identity," *Masaryk University Journal of Law and Technology* 10/1 (2016), pp. 1–22.

34 Cf. M. Esperança Ginebra Molins, "Voluntades digitales en caso de muerte," *Cuadernos de Derecho Transnacional* 12/1 (2020), p. 911ff.

35 *The concept of sociedad de gananciales*, Art. 1344 et seq. of the Spanish General Civil Code.

36 *The concept of consorcio conyugal*, see e.g.: Art. 210 et seq. of the Regional Legal Code of Aragon (Código de Derecho Foral de Aragón), Art. 87 et seq. of the New Legal Code of Navarre—(Fuero Nuevo de Navarra).

37 Cf. resolution of the Polish Supreme Court of 9.06.1976, III CZP 46/75.

such systems, any doubts concerning the belonging of an object to the joint property or to the personal property of a spouse should be resolved in favor of the former. Only those objects which are expressly mentioned in the provisions of the law may belong to personal property. Other assets are included in the joint property of the spouses. Since there is usually no specific regulation concerning digital goods (as for example in Poland and in principle in the common law in Spain, where reference is made to data protection provisions), the conclusions of such argumentation seem obvious. Potentially, individual digital goods are joint goods of the spouses. This raises important consequences, related to the management of joint property. This is an aspect that needs to be taken into account when designing legislation in this area. On the other hand, however, the view can be defended that the participation of an individual on the Internet is relevant from the point of view precisely of the protection of personal data, which could allow, inter alia, to limit the access of third parties to specific digital goods without the consent of the person concerned. A certain conflict between the proprietary and personal nature of such online presence is apparent here. The lack of a clear regulation means uncertainty and deepening doubts.

4. Inheritance law doubts and challenges

Similar uncertainty exists in inheritance law, especially in those countries where there is no relevant specific legal regulation, as for example in Poland. The well-known judgments of the German courts on the inheritance of a Facebook account[38] have contributed a great deal to the discussion in this regard. It has been ruled there that access to the deceased's user account and the content contained therein is hereditary and does not conflict with postmortem personal rights, telecommunications secrecy, data protection regulations or the general personal rights of the deceased's communication partners.[39] This does not mean, however, that this has ended the discussion, although in countries which have similar

38 Cf. the following judgments: *Landgericht Berlin*, judgment of 17.12.2015, 20 O 172/15; *Kammergericht Berlin*, judgment of 31.05.2017, 21 U 9/16; Bundesgerichtshof, judgment of 12.07.2018, III ZR 183/17; *Landgericht Berlin*, judgment of 13.02.2019, 20 O 172/15; Kammergericht Berlin, judgment of 9.12.2019, 21 W 11/19; Bundesgerichtshof, judgment of 27.08.2020, III ZB 30/20. The cases are presented extensively in M. Załucki, "Contractual Limitations in the Mortis Causa Legal Succession on the Example of the Facebook Contract. The German Facebook Case," *Istorie, Cultura, Cetatenie in Uniunea Europeana* 13/1 (2021).

39 Ibid.

regulations to the one under German law, the hereditary status of virtual goods only appears to be a foregone conclusion. This is because the German court still does not seem to have answered the question of who owns the content of the deceased Facebook user's account, but has only ruled on the question of access to the content (although this can probably also be understood differently).[40] It is also interesting to note that even if one were to assume full heredity of the content stored in this way, what relevance would there be in this context of a different will expressed by the deceased Facebook user,[41] which the deceased Facebook user is entitled to under, inter alia, one of the provisions of the Terms of Service: "Deleting your account when you pass away: You can choose to have your account permanently deleted should you pass away. This means that when someone lets us know that you've passed away, all of your messages, photos, comments, relations and info will be immediately and permanently removed from Facebook."[42] Therefore, is the German case and its emerging developments a well-done lesson for the future?

The US judicature can also serve as an interesting point of reference.[43] In this context, it may be recalled the case, which was widely discussed in the media at the time, concerning access to the email of an American soldier who was killed in Iraq.[44] The father of the deceased sought access to his email account because of his wish to publish a memoir, which was the testator's previously expressed intention. The email provider, "Yahoo," refused this access on the grounds of privacy considerations and the rules of use of the email service, which stipulated that access to the account could not be shared with third parties. In April 2005, however, the succession court ordered that the data from the testator's email account be made available, thus prejudging the possibility of the testator's successors in title entering into his virtual rights and obligations.[45] In turn, the conclusions of this case, as well as those of the German case, can and certainly

---

40 K. Seidler, "Der digitale Nachlass—ein Zwischenstand," *Neue Zeitschrift für Familienrecht* 7/4 (2020), p. 141 ff.

41 N. M. Banta, "Electronic Wills and Digital Assets: Reassessing Formality in the Digital Age," *Baylor Law Review* 71/3 (2020), p. 547ff.

42 Cf. Facebook's Terms of Service.

43 M. D. Walker, "The New Uniform Digital Assets Law: Estate Planning and Administration in the Information Age," *Real Property, Trust and Estate Law Journal* 52 (2017), pp. 51–78.

44 For more on the case and its consequences, see http://www.justinellsworth.net/.

45 D. Horton, "Tomorrow's Inheritance: the Frontiers of Estate Planning Formalism," *Boston College Law Review* 58/2 (2017), p. 543ff.

have already inspired on more than one occasion the addressing of the problems of virtual goods in the legal context of succession.

Therefore, can the spouse of the account holder have any claims regarding access to the account? Are these claims only inter vivos or mortis causa? Also, can other persons, including the heirs of the account holder, have claims in relation to this, or do they inherit the account and its contents? These are fundamental questions that need to be decided in national law. Perhaps a solution would be an appropriate legal regulation in which it would be up to the account holder to decide this, thus protecting his privacy, the privacy of his communication partners or the secrecy of his correspondence. In that case, if the legislator so decided, it could be assumed that these are such assets, the status of which is decided by the person entitled from them. Since it is generally possible to dispose of ownership of an item, it would certainly also be possible to decide that the rights to an account and its contents expire, for example, on the death of the holder. However, as long as there is no such regulation (as in most European countries), the problems of family law and inheritance law indicated here will arise in practice and produce different solutions, depending on the applicable law and jurisdiction, which seems undesirable.

5. The approach of some legislators

The approach of some legislators is interesting against this background. Indeed, there are legal systems in the world which, in connection with digital assets, have decided to introduce specific legal regulations primarily concerning the issue of possible legal succession arising here. Essentially two approaches can be noted here: patrimonial and personal.[16] The former will imply the proprietary nature of digital assets, which will determine their legal-succession status. The latter, on the other hand, is a concept that takes into account the personal link between the digital goods and the user of the virtual accounts, prejudging the need to look at this problem primarily from the perspective of personal data.

This first approach can be seen, for example, in the US Model Law[47] or the Canadian Model Law.[48] It essentially implies the inheritance (legal succession)

46 M. Esperança Ginebra Molins, "Voluntades digitales: disposiciones mortis causa," *op. cit.*, p. 210ff.

47 Uniform Fiduciary Access to Digital Assets Act (2015) [RUFADAA].

48 Uniform Access To Digital Assets By Fiduciaries Act (2016) [UADAFA].

of digital assets. In contrast, the recently enacted Portuguese[49] or universal Spanish[50] laws refer to the European General Data Protection Regulation.[51] They imply, among other things, the possibility for the deceased to decide on the status of digital assets *ante mortem*, and the possible prohibition of access to data "does not affect the rights of the heirs to access the data of the deceased's estate." A slightly different perspective arises, for example, from Italian law, where it is provided that when the data subject has prohibited the exercise of rights, such a prohibition may not have a detrimental effect on the exercise by third parties of economic rights arising from the death of the data subject.[52]

Thus, one can notice a trend toward entrusting the decision on the further fate of digital assets to the right holder *ante mortem*. Such a trend seems to be noticeable not only in European legislation, but also in the terms and conditions of service of individual ISPs, which certainly seems to be an interesting paradigm. While a certain conflict of interest between the patrimonial, proprietary nature of digital assets and the possible decision to extinguish them is already prima facie apparent here, this is, one might think, a kind of compromise between the perceived problems of the personal nature of some content found in the virtual world, or the protection needs of third parties.

Here, too, there is a need for further discussion and agreement on standards, for which the model laws (American or Canadian) are an interesting stimulus, as they recognize the need for a uniform approach in separate regional (state or provincial) systems. Perhaps the divergence in the wording of the various

49 Cf. Portugese law implementing the GDPR: Lei n.° 58/2019 de 8 de Agosto—Assegura a execução, na ordem jurídica nacional, do Regulamento (UE) 2016/679 do Parlamento e do Conselho, de 27 de abril de 2016, relativo à proteção das pessoas singulares no que diz respeito ao tratamento de dados pessoais e à livre circulação desses dados.

50 Cf. Spanish law implementing the GDPR: Ley Orgánica 3/2018, de 5 de diciembre, de Protección de Datos Personales y garantía de los derechos digitales [LOPD].

51 Regulation (EU) 2016/679 of the European Parliament and of the Council of April 27, 2016 on the protection of natural persons with regard to the processing of personal data and on the free movement of such data.

52 Cf. Italian law on GDPR: Disposizioni per l'adeguamento della normativa nazionale alle disposizioni del regolamento (UE) 2016/679 del Parlamento europeo e del Consiglio, del 27 aprile 2016, relativo alla protezione delle persone fisiche con riguardo al trattamento dei dati personali, nonchè alla libera circolazione di tali dati e che abroga la direttiva 95/46/CE (regolamento generale sulla protezione dei dati), Codice in materia di protezione dei dati personali.

European laws will also give further impetus in future to the emergence of a uniform substantive law of succession, at least within the EU countries.

The Catalan law on digital wills, for example, appears to be a pioneer in solving the problem of inheritance of digital assets.[53] This law essentially makes the succession of legal heirs to the deceased's rights in the context of digital assets conditional on the deceased's willingness to do so, while also indicating possible competencies, including requiring the deceased to delete active accounts or transferring outstanding content to specific individuals. This is a very interesting solution that could perhaps form the basis of a general European project in the future. The consequences of this solution are that it shifts the burden of the decision as to the further fate of the digital assets to the rightsholder, who should express the relevant decision ante mortem.[54] This seems an apt solution, especially as it is the rightsholder who will generally be in a position to assess the nature of his or her digital footprint and the possible consequences of making it available to third parties. It is worth looking at the Catalan practice in this regard.

6. Some conclusions

Digital assets, as one may judge, are also problems of family law and inheritance law. Without detailed legal regulation, doubts may arise as to their legal nature and possible belonging to particular estates, both *inter vivos* and *mortis causa*. When considering the introduction of a legal regulation in this area, a number of different aspects need to be taken into account, starting with the question of the legitimacy of the impact of the will expressed by the holder of digital assets ante mortem on their subsequent fate. Regulations according to which the account holder decides whether the account should be terminated, closed or allowed to be used by third parties are possible. However, it is important to bear in mind the current family and inheritance law regulations, which have specific provisions for assets. As of today, there are many questions in this area and they are still unanswered in many jurisdictions. These doubts should be discussed and eventually lead to a situation where a uniform legal regulation is created in this area, at least from the perspective of the European states.

53 La Ley catalana 10/2017, de 27 de junio, de las voluntades digitales y de modificación de los libros segundo y cuarto del Código civil de Cataluña.

54 Cf. M. Esperança Ginebra Molins, "Voluntades digitales en caso de muerte," *op. cit.*, p. 919ff.

Bibliography

Banta, N. M., "Minors and Digital Asset Succession," *Iowa Law Review* 104/4 (2019).

Banta, N. M., "Electronic Wills and Digital Assets: Reassessing Formality in the Digital Age," *Baylor Law Review* 71/3 (2020).

Barfield, W., "Intellectual Property Rights in Virtual Environments: Considering the Rights of Owners, Programmers and Virtual Avatars," *Akron Law Review* 39 (2006).

Berti, R., and Zanetti, S., "La trasmissione mortis causa del patrimonio e dell'identità digitale: strumenti giuridici, operativi e prospettive de iure condendo," *Law and Media Working Paper Series* 18 (2016).

Beverley-Smith, H., Ohly, A., and Lucs-Schloetter, A., *Privacy, Property and Personality. Civil Law Perspectives on Commercial Appropriation*, Cambridge 2005.

Beyer, G. W., "Estate Planning for Digital Assets," *Estate Planning Studies* 1 (2015).

Carr, A., "Facebook Everywhere," *Fastcompany.com* 7/8 (2014).

Damascelli, D., "La legge applicabile ai rapporti patrimoniali tra coniugi, uniti civilmente e conviventi di fatto nel diritto internazionale privato italiano ed europeo," *Rivista di Diritto Internazionale* 6 (2017).

Davies, C. R., "An evolutionary step in intellectual property rights—Artificial intelligence and intellectual property," *Computer Law and Security Review* 27/6 (2011).

Digital Assets and Private Law. Public Consultation (Study LXXXII), International Institute for the Unification of Private Law (UNIDROIT), Rome 2023.

Edwards, L., and Harbinja, E., "'What Happens to My Facebook Profile When I Die?' Legal Issues Around Transmission of Digital Assets on Death," *CREATe Working Paper* 5/5 (2013).

Esperança Ginebra Molins, M., "Voluntades digitales: disposiciones mortis causa," in *En derecho privado en el nuevo paradigma digital*, vol. X, ed. E. A. Amayuelas, S. C. Lapuente, Madrid-Barceliona-Buenos Aires-Sao Paulo 2017.

Esperança Ginebra Molins, M., "Voluntades digitales en caso de muerte," *Cuadernos de Derecho Transnacional* 12/1 (2020).

Fairfield, J. A. T., "Virtual Property," *Boston University Law Review* 85/4 (2005).

Fuchs, A., "What Happens to Your Social Media Account When You Die? The First German Judgments on Digital Legacy," *ERA Forum* 22 (2021).

Gebicka, A., and Heinemann, A., "Social Media & Competition Law," *World Competition* 37/2 (2014).

Harbinja, E., "Legal Nature of e-mails: A Comparative Perspective," *Duke Law & Technology Review* 14/1 (2016).

Harbinja, E., *Digital Death, Digital Assets and Post-mortem Privacy*, Edinburgh 2023.

Herzog, S., "Der digitale Nachlass und das Erbrecht," *Anwaltsblatt Online* 6 (2018).

Hirsch, A. J., "Technology Adrift: In Search of a Role for Electronic Wills," *Boston College Law Review* 61/3 (2020).

Horton, D., "Tomorrow's Inheritance: the Frontiers of Estate Planning Formalism," *Boston College Law Review* 58/2 (2017).

ISP Interconnection and its Impact on Consumer Internet Performance—A Measurement Lab Consortium Technical Report, Measurement Lab Consortium Technical, Washington, DC 2014.

Janssen, A., "Das digitale Erbe eines Menschen," *European Review of Private Law* 4 (2017).

Kamalnath, A., "The Law of Cryptoassets Is the Law of the Horse," *Banking & Finance Law Review* 36 (2020).

Kerikmae, T., *Regulating eTechnologies in the European Union. Normative Realities and Trends*, Cham-Heidelberg-New York-Dordrecht-London 2014.

Kubis, M. et al., *Der digitale Nachlass. Eine Untersuchung aus rechtlicher und technischer Sicht*, Bremen-Regensburg 2019.

Mądel, M., "Następstwo prawne treści cyfrowych z perspektywy prawa Stanów Zjednoczonych Ameryki," *Prawo Mediów Elektronicznych* 1 (2016).

Magnani, A., "L'eredità digitale," *Notariato* 5/5 (2014).

Marinioni, M., *Patrimonio digitale: analisi comparata dei profili successori*, Padova 2016.

Matanovac Vučković, R., and Kanceljak, I., "Does the Right to Use Digital Content Affect Our Digital Inheritance?," *Eu and Member States—Legal and Economic Issues* 3/3 (2019).

Mceniery, B., "Succession Law Keeping Pace with Changes in Technology and Community Expectations—Informal Wills," *Journal of New Business Ideas & Trends* 12/1 (2014).

Merhi, B. B., *L'émergence de l'identité numérique: l'influence de la révolution numérique sur l'environnement juridique*, Paris 2022.

Naseh, M. V., "Person and Personality in Cyber Space: A Legal Analysis of Virtual Identity," *Masaryk University Journal of Law and Technology* 10/1 (2016).

Polčák, R., "The Legal Classification of ISPs," *Journal of Intellectual Property, Information Technology and E-Commerce Law* 3/1 (2010).

Ruggeri, L., Kunda, I., and Winkler, S. (eds.), *Family Property and Succession in EU Member States. National Reports on the Collected Data*, Rijeka 2019.

Savelyev, A., "Contract Law 2.0: 'Smart' Contracts as the Beginning of the End of Classic Contract Law," *Information and Communications Technology Law* 26/2 (2017).

Seidler, K., "Der digitale Nachlass—ein Zwischenstand," *Neue Zeitschrift für Familienrecht* 7/4 (2020).

Szulewski, P., *Śmierć 2.0—problematyka dóbr cyfrowych* [in:] *Non omnis moriar. Osobiste i majątkowe aspekty prawne śmierci człowieka. Zagadnienia wybrane*, ed. J. Gołaczyński, J. Mazurkiewicz, J. Turłukowski, and D. Karkut, Wrocław 2015.

Varnado, S. S., "Your Digital Footprint Left Behind at Death: An Illustration of Technology Leaving the Law Behind," *Louisiana Law Review* 74/3 (2014).

Walker, M. D., "The New Uniform Digital Assets Law: Estate Planning and Administration in the Information Age," *Real Property, Trust and Estate Law Journal* 52 (2017).

Załucki, M., "Digital Content Left on-Line after Death of a User. On the Research that Needs to Be Conducted," *Legal and Administrative Studies* 19/1 (2020).

Załucki, M., "Contractual Limitations in the Mortis Causa Legal Succession on the Example of the Facebook Contract. The German Facebook Case," *Istorie, Cultura, Cetatenie in Uniunea Europeana* 13/1 (2021).

Załucki, M., "Digital Inheritance: Key Issues and Doubts. The Challenges of Succession Law in the Face of New Technologies," in *Future Law*, Vol. II, ed. F. da S. Veiga, P. de Brito, and Z. L. Pierdoná, Porto 2021.

Ewa Jędrzejewska

Division of joint property of spouses after termination of marital property: Selected practical problems

Abstract: Entering into marriage has a number of legal consequences, among which it is possible to distinguish the creation of marital property, covering property items acquired during its duration. The end of this joint ownership occurs as a result of the dissolution of the marriage (divorce or death of one of the spouses) or for reasons specified by the legislator (establishment of a contractual property regime, judicial establishment of compulsory regime of separate property for important reasons, incapacitation, or declaration of bankruptcy of one of the spouses, or separation). Termination of marital property involves the necessity to make a contractual or judicial division of joint property. Judicial proceedings for the division of joint property are non-litigious proceedings under Article 566–567 of Code of Civil Procedure. One of the features characterizing these proceedings and distinguishing them from procedural proceedings is the ex officio operation of the court. In the course of these proceedings, a number of practical problems often arise related to determining the composition and value of joint property, or the nature of these proceedings.

The purpose of this article is to discuss and characterize the proceedings for the division of joint property of spouses and selected practical problems related to these proceedings. The issue of determining the value of the mortgaged real estate to be divided as joint property of the spouses, the value of the subject of the appeal in cases for the division of joint property, or the admissibility of covering a consistent application for division of joint property with the actio Pauliana will be presented in detail.

Keywords: non-litigious proceedings, statutory marital property, joint property, judicial division of joint property

1. General remarks

The Polish legislator in the Family and Guardianship Code[1] distinguished three types of marital property regimes—contractual, statutory, and compulsory. The statutory marital regime is a property regime which arises between the spouses by operation of law upon entering into a marriage and covers property acquired

1 Act of February 25, 1964, Family and Guardianship Code (*Journal of Laws* of 2020, item 1359, hereinafter referred to as: FGC.

during the marriage by both spouses or by one of them (Art. 31 § 1 of FGC).[2] Spouses may regulate their property relations differently by concluding an appropriate marriage contract excluding the statutory regime.[3]

Statutory marital property, in turn, is terminated, in particular, when the marriage ends, that is, after divorce or when one of the spouses dies. During the life of the spouses, the statutory marital property may be terminated due to the establishment of a contractual property regime (conclusion of the so-called prenuptial agreement), judicial establishment of compulsory regime of separate property for important reasons, incapacitation, or declaration of bankruptcy of one of the spouses, or separation.[4] As a result of termination of marital property, it is necessary to divide the joint property accumulated by the spouses, which can be done as part of court proceedings or by agreement.[5]

In contentious situations, the division of property is conducted in court proceedings for the division of joint property. The subject of the division of joint property are items acquired for the purpose of marital property, so the only limitation determining the possibility of including a given item in the division of joint property is its acquisition for marital property. On the other hand, cases for the division of joint property after the termination of marital property are heard in non-contentious proceedings regulated in Article 566–567 of the Code of Civil Procedure.[6] One of the features characterizing these proceedings and distinguishing them from contentious proceedings is the *ex officio* operation of the court. The court determines *ex officio* the composition and value of the property covered by the division of joint property.[7]

Both in the doctrine and jurisprudence, it is uniformly assumed that in cases of division of joint property of spouses after the termination of statutory marital property, only assets are subject to division. However, the division does not

---

2 For more on marital property regime—see: D. Przewłocka, *Czynności prawne małżonków rozporządzające majątkiem wspólnym a ochrona wierzyciela przed czynnościami fraudacyjnymi*, Warsaw 2020, Legalis el.

3 A. Zieliński, *Postępowanie o podział majątku wspól*[ne]*go po ustaniu wspólności majątkowej małżeńskiej*, Warsaw 1992, p. 5.

4 J. Ignaczewski (ed.), *Małżeńskie prawo majątkowe*, 5th ed., Warsaw 2020, Legalis el.

5 A. Stempniak, *Autonomia i integracja postępowań działowych w prawie polskim*, 2017, Legalis el.

6 Act of November 17, 1964, Code of Civil Procedure (*Journal of Laws* of 2021, item 1805), hereinafter referred to as: CCP.

7 A. Zieliński, "Zwyczajne środki zaskarżenia (odwoławcze) w postępowaniu nieprocesowym," *Monitor Prawniczy* 2 (2002), Legalis el.

include liabilities (debts),[8] because, as indicated in the jurisprudence of the Supreme Court, despite the division of property, the debt incurred by both spouses continues to exist.[9] Such a view should be considered correct, as the adoption of a different concept could lead to a violation of the creditor's rights.

However, it is a different matter to determine the value of joint property to be divided in the proceedings. There is no doubt that the court in the course of property division proceedings is obliged to determine the composition and value of joint property. This is due to the appropriate application of the provisions on the division of inheritance to proceedings for the division of joint property (Art. 567 § 3 of CCP in connection with Art. 684 of CCP). In turn, the provisions on the termination of joint property apply accordingly to the proceedings for the division of inheritance (Art. 688 of CCP).

The composition of the joint property is determined, as a rule, according to the state existing on the date of termination of marital property,[10] however, it is assumed that the spouse may also demand that items that have been unreasonably disposed of, destroyed, or lost by the other spouse be taken into account.[11] On the other hand, the value of the joint property to be divided is determined according to the value at the time of the division of property.[12]

The above general remarks regarding the proceedings for the division of joint property are an introduction to further considerations, including selected problems appearing in court practice.

2. Selected practical problems

2.1. Determination of the value of mortgaged real estate

A particularly important issue for the entities participating in the proceedings for the division of joint property is, in the first place, the problem of determining

---

8 K. Skiepko, in *Komentarz do spraw o podział majątku wspólnego małżonków*, ed. J. Ignaczewski, Warsaw 2013, p. 216 et seq.

9 Decision of the panel of seven judges of the Supreme Court of December 5, 1978, III CRN 194/78, Legalis No. 21212; judgment of the Supreme Court of January 16, 2014, IV CSK 203/12, Legalis No. 1066928.

10 K. Skiepko, *op. cit.*, p. 78, A. Stempniak, "Ustalenie wartości przedmiotów majątkowych w postępowaniach działowych," *Iustitia* 4 (2011), pp. 198–199.

11 A. Stempniak, *op. cit.*, decision of the Supreme Court of November 4, 1999, II CKN 523/98, Legalis No. 344669.

12 K. Pietrzykowski, in *Kodeks rodzinny i opiekuńczy. Komentarz*, ed. K. Pietrzykowski, Warsaw 2020, p. 418.

the value of real estate included in the joint property, which is encumbered with a mortgage. This issue gave rise to many practical problems and discrepancies both in the doctrine and jurisprudence, which resulted in the development of divergent directions in the method of determining the value of mortgaged real estate subject to division as joint property of spouses.

According to the first view, a mortgage as an encumbrance of real estate affects its value, and determining the value of real estate is the duty of the court in property division proceedings. Supporters of this position referred to the principles of determining the value of real estate specified in the Regulation of the Council of Ministers on the valuation of real estate and preparation of appraisal reports[13] issued on the basis of statutory authorization contained in the Act on real estate management.[14] According to §38 paragraph 1 of the Regulation, when determining the value of real estate, the encumbrance of real estate with limited rights in rem is taken into account, if they affect this value. Therefore, if a property valuer determines the existence of a limited right in rem, such as an easement or a mortgage, the value of the property should be determined taking into account this encumbrance.[15] This view was additionally reinforced by the position that failure to take into account the amount that one of the parties repays as a mortgage debt when determining repayments may lead to a situation in which this party will repay a debt in which the other party will no longer participate due to the impossibility of pursuing claims under this title pursuant to Article 618 § 3 of CCP.[16] At the same time, the doctrine began to criticize such rules for determining the value of real estate, pointing to the fact that real estate traded on the market obtain similar values regardless of whether they are encumbered with a mortgage or not.[17] It was rightly noted that encumbering the real estate with

---

13 Regulation of the Council of Ministers of September 21, 2004, on the valuation of real estate and preparation of appraisal reports (*Journal of Laws* of 2021, item 555), hereinafter referred to as: the Regulation.

14 Act of August 21, 1997, on real estate management (*Journal of Laws* of 2023, item 344), hereinafter referred to as: hereinafter referred to as: REM.

15 M. Wolanin, *Opłaty, ceny, wartości i odszkodowania w gospodarce nieruchomościami*, 2nd ed., Warsaw 2021, Legalis el.

16 Such a view was expressed in the decision of the Supreme Court of October 5, 2000, II CKN 611/99, Legalis No. 48502, decision of the Supreme Court of September 29, 2004, II CK 538/03, Legalis No. 277052, resolution of the Supreme Court of June 25, 2008, III CZP 58/08, Legalis No. 100976, decision of the Supreme Court of January 21, 2010, I CSK 205/09, Legalis No. 338379.

17 M. Knotz, "Podział majątku wspólnego obciążonego hipoteką w orzecznictwie SN," *Iustitia* 3 (2011), p. 126 et seq.

a mortgage only results in a different regulation in the contract of the method of payment of the price by partial payment to the mortgagee. At the same time, some put forward a postulate of introducing the possibility of releasing from debt the party to court proceedings who, as a result of the division of property, will not receive ownership of real estate.[18]

At the same time, opposite views began to appear in jurisprudence, assuming that it is not possible to take into account the mortgage encumbrance when determining the value of the real estate to be divided in property division proceedings. The change in the direction of jurisprudence was undoubtedly influenced by the resolution of the panel of seven judges adopted by the Supreme Court on February 27, 2019, in which the view was expressed that "Article 618 § 3 of CCP does not exclude the pursuit of a claim between spouses for reimbursement of the amount of liability secured by a mortgage, repaid by one of them after the decision on the division of joint property became final and binding."[19] Adoption of the above position allows a spouse who has performed the obligation imposed on both spouses (or former spouses) after the decision on the division of joint property became final and enforceable, to claim from the other spouse part of the obligation attributable to this spouse. Thus, the only argument for taking into account the mortgage encumbrance when determining the value of real estate has lost its validity.

In subsequent rulings, the Supreme Court shared the position presented in the resolution of February 27, 2019, recognizing that in property division cases, the value of the mortgage encumbrance, as a rule, does not affect the value of the asset whose joint ownership is subject to termination. In the resolution of March 28, 2019, the Supreme Court expressed the thesis that "in cases for termination of joint ownership of a cooperative ownership right to a residential premises encumbered with a mortgage securing a bank loan and a loan granted to co-owners, the court—when granting this right to one of them—determines its value excluding the mortgage encumbrance, unless there are significant reasons for its inclusion."[20] In the resolution of July 25, 2019, the Supreme Court took a similar position, stating that "in a case for the division of joint property of

18 For example: A. Grajewski, "Podział majątku wspólnego a zwolnienie byłego małżonka z długu," *Palestra* 11 (2016), p. 20.

19 Resolution of the Supreme Court of February 27, 2019, III CZP 30/18, Legalis No. 1879403.

20 Resolution of the Supreme Court of March 28, 2019, III CZP 41/18, Legalis No. 1886370.

spouses, including real estate encumbered with a mortgage securing a bank loan granted to the spouses, the court—when granting this property to one of them—determines its value excluding the value of the mortgage encumbrance, unless there are significant reasons for its inclusion."[21] These views take into account the postulates expressed by the representatives of the doctrine.[22]

It should be noted that the views expressed by the Supreme Court, although firm, contain a general clause in the form of "significant reasons," enabling common courts to take into account the mortgage encumbrance when determining the value of the property subject to division.[23] Although some representatives of the doctrine point to the danger of correctly qualifying specific circumstances of the case as significant reasons,[24] undoubtedly the introduction of this general clause allows common courts to apply a different solution in a situation where, in specific circumstances, a typical solution would not lead to the achievement of the purpose of property division proceedings.

2.2. The value of the subject of the appeal in cases for the division of joint property

The value of the subject of the appeal is a concept derived from the value of the subject of the dispute. As a rule, this value may not exceed the value of the subject of the dispute, unless the claim has been extended or the court has ruled beyond the claim.[25] It is also often lower than the value of the subject of the dispute, in particular in the case of only partial acceptance of the party's demands.

The value of the subject of the appeal is important as it determines the amount of the court fee for the means of appeal, the admissibility of the cassation appeal, and also constitutes the basis for determining the amount of fees for attorney's or legal adviser's services. This institution also plays an important role in cases for the division of joint property after the termination of marital property, which are heard in non-contentious proceedings. In such cases, in accordance with Article

21 Resolution of the Supreme Court of July 25, 2019, IIIC CZP 14/19, Legalis No. 1977203.

22 M. Knotz, *op. cit.*, p. 129.

23 A. Stempniak, "Ocena kształtującej się linii orzecznictwa Sądu Najwyższego w zakresie ustalania w sprawach działowych wartości nieruchomości obciążonej hipoteką," *Monitor Polski* 12 (2020), p. 632.

24 *Op. cit.*, p. 632.

25 E. Czaplicka, "Dopuszczalność kasacji ze względu na wartość przedmiotu zaskarżenia," *Monitor Prawniczy* 10 (1999), Legalis el.

519^1 § 2 of CCP, it is possible to file a cassation appeal, unless the value of the subject of the appeal is lower than one hundred and fifty thousand zlotys.

Both in jurisprudence[26] and the doctrine,[27] it is commonly accepted that in cases of division of joint property, the value of the subject of the appeal is determined not by the value of the entire property subject to division, but by the value of a specific asset or claim whose division or settlement is questioned by the complainant. Therefore, as a rule, the value of the subject of the appeal in such cases may not exceed the value of the share held by the complaining party.

However, the principle indicated above is breached in a situation where a participant in the proceedings challenges the very principle of division, questioning, for example, the admissibility of the division of property. Then the value of the subject of the appeal may be higher than the value of the share attributable to the complainant.

Undoubtedly, the view regarding the determination of the value of the subject of the appeal in property division cases is already well-established both in the doctrine and jurisprudence, without giving rise to major interpretation doubts.

2.3. Admissibility of covering a consistent application for division of joint property with the *actio Pauliana*

A particularly important issue, having a significant impact on the security of trading, is the issue of the admissibility of making consistent procedural statements submitted by participants in property division proceedings the subject of a claim based on Article 527 § 1 of the Civil Code[28] (*actio Pauliana*).

Historically, two opposing views have developed in jurisprudence. The first of them assumed that it was inadmissible to include a consistent application for the division of joint property in a claim for recognition of the action as ineffective. This view was based on the position that the subject of the *actio Pauliana* is legal actions performed by the debtor to the detriment of creditors. Thus, while the division of the joint property of the spouses made by mutual agreement, belonging to the category of legal action, may be the subject of appeal with the *actio Pauliana*, the submission of a consistent application as to the method of division of

26 Decision of the Supreme Court of November 6, 2015, II CZ 76/15, Legalis No. 1361405; decision of the Supreme Court of October 26, 2018, V CSK 201/18, Legalis No. 1847260; decision of the Supreme Court of January 11, 2019, V CZ 87/18, Legalis No. 1861186.

27 A. Stempniak, *Autonomia*, *op. cit.*, Legalis el.

28 Act of April 23, 1964, Civil Code (*Journal of Laws* of 2022, item 1360), hereinafter referred to as: CC.

joint property in the course of property division proceedings is not such an action. In the judgment of October 19, 1995,[29] the Supreme Court emphasized that in a situation where the judgment is of a constitutive nature, the statements made by the parties are somehow consumed by the court's judgment, and therefore the intention to achieve certain effects is implemented through the court's judgment in accordance with the submitted statement. In addition, the court is not bound by the position of the parties as to the method of division of property, which, in the opinion of the Supreme Court, additionally strengthens the argument that it is not possible to cover a consistent application for division of joint property with the *actio Pauliana*.

This position has been criticized by the doctrine, in particular by Prof. M. Pyziak-Szafnicka.[30] She pointed out that there are no grounds for narrowing down the institution of *actio Pauliana*, which aims to protect the creditor, only to activities performed outside court proceedings. In addition to legal actions and procedural actions, she distinguished the so-called dispositional acts that express the will of the party to the proceedings as to the fate of the subject of the proceedings. As a consequence, M. Pyziak-Szafnicka took the position that dispositional acts may be subject to appeal against them by way of *actio Pauliana*, despite the fact that they were made in the course of court proceedings.

A position quite different from the view presented earlier is currently adopted in jurisprudence.[31] According to this position, pursuant to Article 527 § 1 of CC, the creditor may challenge the consistent application of the debtor and other participants in property division proceedings (i.e., proceedings for the division of joint property, division of inheritance, or termination of joint ownership), if, as a result of granting this application, the assets subject to division were acquired by participants in the proceedings who are not debtors.

The current view should be considered correct, taking into account the purpose of *actio Pauliana*, which is the protection of the creditor. This protection should also be guaranteed in a situation where the debtor chooses the court

29 Judgment of the Supreme Court of October 19, 1995, III CRN 40/95, Legalis No. 29580.

30 M. Pyziak-Szafnicka, "Glosa do wyroku SN z dnia 19 października 1995 r., III CRN 40/95," *OSP* 11 (1996), p. 211.

31 D. Przewłocka, *op. cit.*; resolution of the Supreme Court of October 8, 2015, III CZP 56/15, Legalis No. 1336447, judgment of the Supreme Court of September 29, 2017, V CSK 2/17, Legalis No. 1705319, judgment of the Supreme Court of January 17, 2017, IV CSK 194/16, Legalis No. 1569084, decision of the Supreme Court of October 24, 2013, IV CZ 84/13, Legalis No. 877735, resolution of the Supreme Court of June 17, 2010, III CZP 41/10, Legalis No. 226146.

procedure for the division of joint property and makes certain declarations in the course of it, which could have unfavorable consequences for the debtor's creditors. A different view would make it possible to use court proceedings as a way to act to the detriment of creditors, and to use the authority of the court making the division to sanction such behaviors.

3. Summary

To sum up, it should be stated that although in the Code of Civil Procedure the legislator provided for only two provisions directly referring to the procedure for the division of joint property (Articles 566 and 567 of CCP), the procedure for the division of joint property after the termination of marital property is a procedure involving a number of practical problems of significant social importance. In this respect, the activity of the legislator is sometimes necessary, although in most cases these problems result from a specific interpretation of the provisions and the activity of jurisprudence and the doctrine remains sufficient in this respect.

Bibliography

Czaplicka, E., "Dopuszczalność kasacji ze względu na wartość przedmiotu zaskarżenia," *Monitor Prawniczy* 10 (1999), Legalis el.

Ignaczewski, J. (ed.), *Małżeńskie prawo majątkowe.* Wyd.5, Warszawa 2020, Legalis el.

Knotz, M., "Podział majątku wspólnego obciążonego hipoteką w orzecznictwie SN," *Iustitia* 3 (2011).

Pietrzykowski, K., in *Kodeks rodzinny i opiekuńczy. Komentarz*, ed. K. Pietrzykowski, Warszawa 2020.

Przewłocka, D., *Czynności prawne małżonków rozporządzające majątkiem wspólnym a ochrona wierzyciela przed czynnościami fraudacyjnymi*, Warszawa 2020, Legalis el.

Pyziak-Szafnicka, M., "Glosa do wyroku SN z dnia 19 października 1995 r., III CRN 40/95," *OSP* 11 (1996), p. 211.

Skiepko, K., in *Komentarz do spraw o podział majątku wspólnego małżonków*, ed. J. Ignaczewski, Warszawa 2013.

Stempniak, A., *Autonomia i integracja postępowań działowych w prawie polskim*, 2017, Legalis el.

Stempniak, A., “Ocena kształtującej się linii orzecznictwa Sądu Najwyższego w zakresie ustalania w sprawach działowych wartości nieruchomości obciążonej hipoteką,” *Monitor Polski* 12 (2020).

Stempniak, A., “Ustalenie wartości przedmiotów majątkowych w postępowaniach działowych,” *Iustitia* 4 (2011).

Wolanin, M., *Opłaty, ceny, wartości i odszkodowania w gospodarce nieruchomościami*. Wyd. 2, Warszawa 2021, Legalis el.

Zieliński, A., *Postępowanie o podział majątku wspólnego po ustaniu wspólności majątkowej małżeńskiej*, Warszawa 1992, p. 5.

Zieliński, A., “Zwyczajne środki zaskarżenia (odwoławcze) w postępowaniu nieprocesowym,” *Monitor Prawniczy* 2 (2002), Legalis el.

Jurisprudence

Postanowienie składu 7 sędziów Sądu Najwyższego z 5.12.1978 r., III CRN 194/78, Legalis nr 21212.

Postanowienie SN z 04.11.1999 r., II CKN 523/98, Legalis nr 344669.

Postanowienie SN z 05.10.2000 r., II CKN 611/99, Legalis nr 48502.

Postanowienie SN z 29.09.2004 r., II CK 538/03, Legalis nr 277052.

Postanowienie SN z 21.01.2010 r., I CSK 205/09, Legalis nr 338379.

Postanowienie SN z 24.10.2013 r., IV CZ 84/13, Legalis nr 877735.

Postanowienie SN z 06.11.2015 r., II CZ 76/15, Legalis nr 1361405.

Postanowienie SN z 26.10.2018 r., V CSK 201/18, Legalis nr 1847260.

Postanowienie SN z 11.01.2019 r., V CZ 87/18, Legalis nr 1861186.

Uchwała SN z 25.06.2008 r., III CZP 58/08, Legalis nr 100976.

Uchwała SN z 17.06.2010 r., III CZP 41/10, Legalis nr 226146.

Uchwała SN 08.10.2015 r., III CZP 56/15, Legalis nr 1336447.

Uchwała SN z 27.02.2019 r., III CZP 30/18, Legalis nr 1879403.

Uchwała SN z 28.03.2019 r., III CZP 41/18, Legalis nr 1886370.

Uchwała SN z 25.07.2019 r., IIIC CZP 14/19, Legalis nr 1977203.

Wyrok SN z 19.10.1995 r., III CRN 40/95, Legalis nr 29580.

Wyrok SN z 16.01.2014 r., IV CSK 203/12, Legalis nr 1066928.

Wyrok SN z 17.01.2017 r., IV CSK 194/16, Legalis nr 1569084.

Wyrok SN z 29.09.2017 r., V CSK 2/17, Legalis nr 1705319.

Legal acts

Act of February 25, 1964, Family and Guardianship Code (*Journal of Laws* of 2020, item 1359).

Act of April 23, 1964, Civil Code (*Journal of Laws* of 2022, item 1360).

Act of November 17, 1964, Code of Civil Procedure (*Journal of Laws* of 2021, item 1805).

Act of August 21, 1997, on real estate management (*Journal of Laws* of 2023, item 344).

Regulation of the Council of Ministers of September 21, 2004, on the valuation of real estate and preparation of appraisal reports (*Journal of Laws* of 2021, item 555).

Elżbieta Zębek

European Union environmental policy toward society

Abstract: EU environmental policy is established on the basis of Art. 11 and 191–193 of the TFU. The role of this policy is to ensure ecological security and high quality of life for society. This policy is sustainable and is based on the principles of precaution, preventive action and treatment at source, as well as the "polluter pays" principle. Currently, the EU has The Eighth Environment Action Program until 2030, which is based on the objectives of the European Green Deal and other EU programs, that is, circular economy, Fit for 50, the strategy "Toward a sustainable Europe 2030" and "From the field to the table." This program establishes a framework of six priority goals for reducing greenhouse gas emissions and climate neutrality, adaptability to climate change, transition to a circular economy, zero pollution, protecting and restoring biodiversity, and reducing environmental and climate pressures related to production and consumption. The society plays an important role in shaping environmental policy, especially in environmental impact assessment procedures. All these activities with the participation of society should in the future contribute to the improvement of the quality of the environment and, consequently, the quality of their lives, as well as the implementation of the leading principle of sustainable development—leaving environmental resources to future generations.

Keywords: environmental law, EU policy, society, public participation, environmental impact assessment

1. Introduction

Environmental protection is of particular importance to the European Union, especially in the field of climate change, energy crisis and other worrying phenomena that undoubtedly affect the quality of life of society. For this reason, work and activities to improve the state of the environment have intensified in recent years, which is reflected in the EU's environmental policy. It should be noted that this policy is based on Articles 11 and 191–193 of the TFEU.[1] It is worth noting Article 191 of Title XX, entitled Environment, which states that the Union's policy on the environment shall contribute to the pursuit of the following objectives: (a) preserving, protecting and improving the quality of the

1 Treaty on the Functioning of the European Union (C 326/49 of 26.10.2012).

environment; (b) protecting human health; (c) prudent and rational utilization of natural resources; and (d) promoting measures at international level to deal with regional or worldwide environmental problems, and in particular combating climate change. Furthermore, the implementation of these objectives is based on the principles of environmental law, that is, sustainable development, prevention, precaution, rectification of damage at source and the polluter pays principle. The principle of sustainable development, as set out in the Rio de Janeiro Declaration, rests on three pillars that are important for the security of the world and the development of civilization: (1) international human rights law, (2) international environmental law, and (3) international economic law. The second principle says to prevent before you cure. It also requires that negative environmental impacts are addressed at the planning stage. The precautionary principle is based on the view that it is better to react early, before it is too late, than to wait for official confirmation of sinister suspicions. Even if the negative effects are not yet fully understood, all precautionary measures should be taken. The principle of rectifying environmental damage "at source" requires action to eliminate the effects of pollution where it occurs (applies to air and water). However, the polluter pays principle takes two forms: (1) the polluter is financially responsible for damage caused by his own activities, and (2) the polluter is financially responsible for non-compliance with the full range of standards established by law.[2]

The EU currently has the 8th Environmental Action Programme until 2030, which builds on the objectives of the European Green Deal and other EU programs, that is, the circular economy, "Fit for 55," the strategy "Toward a sustainable Europe 2030" and "A Farm to Fork Strategy." The primary objective of these programs is to improve the state of the environment and thus the quality of life of society through the reduction of greenhouse gas emissions, water pollution, zero waste, sustainable consumption and the protection of biodiversity. On the other hand, society also has an influence on environmental policy-making by implementing the principle of social participation in environmental programs and procedures, such as environmental impact assessments. The aim of this article is to identify the relationship between EU environmental policy and society. The research questions are: (1) How does EU environmental policy affect people's quality of life? and (2) What is public participation in EU environmental

2 See more: M. Roliński, "*Z problematyki zasad ochrony środowiska*," *Studia Iuridica Lublinensia* 21 (2014), pp. 145–155; E. Zębek, *Gospodarka odpadami w ujęciu prawnym i środowiskowym*, KPP Monografie, Olsztyn 2018, pp. 25–27.

policy-making? The article mainly uses the legal and dogmatic method, consisting in the analysis of EU environmental policies and programs, legal acts on public participation, as well as literature in this field.

2. EU environmental policies and programs

In the EU, the 8th Environment Action Programme until 2030 (EAP)[3] came into force on May 8, 2022. The EAP aims to ensure the effective implementation of the EU's climate and environmental legislation, which is the foundation for achieving the UN's 2030 Agenda and its Sustainable Development Goals (SDGs). The UN's 2030 Agenda[4] is a roadmap for people, planet and prosperity, with 17 SDGs aimed at achieving human rights for all, gender equality and the empowerment of all women and girls. They are integrated and indivisible, balancing the three dimensions of sustainable development: economic, social and environmental.[5] When analyzing the SDGs, the following goals are important for the relationship between environment and society: Goal 2. End hunger, achieve food security and improved nutrition, and promote sustainable agriculture; Goal 6. Ensure availability and sustainable management of water and sanitation for all; Goal 7: Ensure access to affordable, reliable, sustainable and modern energy for all; Goal 12. Ensure sustainable consumption and production patterns; Goal 13. Take urgent action to combat climate change and its effects; Goal 14. Conserve and sustainably use the oceans, seas and marine resources for sustainable development; Goal 15. Protect, restore and promote sustainable use of terrestrial ecosystems, manage forests sustainably, combat desertification, halt and reverse land degradation and halt biodiversity loss; and Goal 17. Strengthen the means of implementation and revitalize the global partnership for sustainable development. It follows from the above that environmental resources play an important role, both quantitatively and qualitatively, in the life and functioning of society, in areas such as food security, sustainable water management, renewable energy

3 Decision (EU) 2022/591 of the European Parliament and of the Council of April 6, 2022 on a General Union Environment Action Programme to 2030, PE/83/2021/REV/1 (OJ L 114 of 12.4.2022, pp. 22–36).

4 United Nations, Resolution No. A/RES/70/1 adopted by the General Assembly on September 25, 2015 Transforming our world: the 2030 Agenda for Sustainable Development.

5 United Nations, Department of Economic and Social Affairs Sustainable Development, Transforming our world: the 2030 Agenda for Sustainable Development, https://sdgs.un.org/2030agenda [accessed: 10.05.2023].

sources, sustainable food production and consumption, climate adaptation, sustainable use of biotic and abiotic resources of the seas and oceans, afforestation and restoration of biodiversity. The COVID-19 pandemic has severely altered the global economy, threatening the achievement of the SDGs on a large scale. In addition, the global economic downturn has not helped the climate change situation. In terms of identifying the main sustainability challenges for European countries, a key challenge is to make stronger and more comprehensive efforts to achieve specific environmental targets under SDG 2 (zero hunger and sustainable agriculture) and SDGs 12–15 (sustainable consumption and production, climate and biodiversity targets).[6]

In setting the direction of EU environmental policy for the period 2002–2012, four priority areas were identified for this period: climate change, nature and biodiversity, environment and health, and natural resources and waste. While progress has been made in each of these areas, there have also been significant setbacks and the EU's environment continues to deteriorate in many key areas.[7] Previous studies have already identified the environmental impact of EU consumption as a high-risk area in areas such as climate change and land use. This justifies the need to develop an updated EU environmental policy.[8] According to the 8th EAP, action to achieve the Union's environmental and climate change objectives must be coherent with the implementation of the European Pillar of Social Rights. This program sets out the priority objectives for 2030 and the conditions needed

---

6 A. Rydz-Żbikowska, "Implementing Sustainable Development Goals within the COVID-19 Pandemic Future Challenges for the 2030 Agenda," *Comparative Economic Research. Central and Eastern Europe* 25/4 (2022), pp. 135–160; Ch. Wamsler, G. Osberg, W. Osika, H. Herndersson, and L. Mundaca, "Linking Internal and External Transformation for Sustainability and Climate Action: Towards a New Research and Policy Agenda," *Global Environmental Change* 71 (2021), 102373, https://doi.org/10.1016/j.gloenvcha.2021.102373; A. B. Pedersen, T. Hickmann, O. Renn, N. Eckert, K. Jax, R. Lepenies, H.-Y. Liu, J. Lyytimaki, S. Reis, and G. Rusch, "SDGs at the Halfway Point: How the 17 Global Goals Address Risks and Wicked Problems," *Ambio* 52 (2023), p. 680.

7 S. Kingston, "I. Environment," *International & Comparative Law Quarterly* 59/4 (2010), p. 1132; E.-E. Halmaghi, "Environmental Action Programmes of the European Union—Programmes Supporting the Sustainable Development Strategy of the European Union," *Scientific Bulletin* XXI/2(42) (2016).

8 S. Sala, E. Crenna, M. Secchi, and E. Sanye-Mengual, "Environmental Sustainability of European Production and Consumption Assessed against Planetary Boundaries," *Journal of Environmental Management* 269 (2020), 110686, https://doi.org/10.1016/j.jenvman.2020.110686.

to achieve them. This program sets out a framework of six priority objectives: (1) Achieving the 2030 greenhouse gas emission reduction target and climate neutrality by 2050; (2) Increasing adaptive capacity, strengthening resilience and reducing vulnerability to climate change; (3) Moving toward a regenerative growth model, decoupling economic growth from resource use and environmental degradation and accelerating the transition to a circular economy; (4) Achieving zero emissions of pollutants, including air, water and soil pollutants, and protecting the health and well-being of Europeans; (5) Protect, conserve and restore biodiversity and develop natural capital, in particular air, water, soil and forest, freshwater, wetland and marine ecosystems; and (6) Reduce environmental and climate pressures related to production and consumption, in particular in the fields of energy, industrial development, housing and infrastructure, mobility and the food system (point 14).[9]

The 8th EAP is based on the European Green Deal. It aims to accelerate the transition to a climate-neutral, resource-efficient economy, recognizing that human well-being and prosperity depend on the health of ecosystems. It should accelerate the environmental transition toward a climate-neutral, sustainable, non-toxic, resource-efficient, renewable energy-based, resilient and competitive circular economy in a fair and socially inclusive manner (point 16). According to Article 3 of the EAP, in order to achieve environmental objectives it is necessary to (a) ensure the effective, efficient and full implementation of EU environment and climate change legislation and policies, in particular in the fight against environmental crime; (b) give priority to the enforcement of EU environmental law where implementation is lacking; (c) strengthen activities in the field of liability for environmental damage and the response to non-compliance with this law; (d) strengthen the integrated approach to policy development and implementation, in particular by integrating priority objectives and sustainable development into all policy areas; (e) strengthening environmental incentives and phasing out environmentally harmful subsidies, in particular fossil fuel subsidies; (f) addressing land degradation and ensuring soil protection and sustainable use; (g) transforming the EU food system so that it contributes, i.a. to the conservation and restoration of biodiversity; (h) fully recognizing the links between human health, animal health and the environment by integrating the One Health approach into policy-making; (i) seeking international recognition of the

9 European Commission, Environment action programme to 2030, https://environment.ec.europa.eu/strategy/environment-action-programme-2030_en [accessed: 18.03.2023].

right to a clean, healthy and sustainable environment; (j) making full use of ecosystem approaches and green infrastructure to protect biodiversity or reduce greenhouse gas emissions; and (k) contributing to supporting civil society in identifying climate and environmental risks.

The European Green Deal of 2019 (EGD)[10] is a growth strategy that aims to transform the EU into a fair and prosperous society with a modern, resource-efficient and competitive economy, achieving zero greenhouse gas emissions by 2050 and decoupling economic growth from the use of natural resources. Thus, the EGD has been proposed as a mission to make Europe the first neutral continent in the world by 2050 and to strengthen European cohesion through this mission. Both goals are challenging and can be transformed not only in terms of the environment, but also in terms of society and economic opportunities.[11] The EGD also aims to protect, conserve and enhance the EU's natural capital and to safeguard the health and well-being of citizens from environmental risks and negative impacts. This transition must be both equitable and inclusive. The transformation of the economy toward sustainable development is based on the following assumptions: (1) achieving climate neutrality by 2050—increasing to at least 50% and potentially up to 55% compared to 1990 levels, the EU's 2030 greenhouse gas emission reduction target; (2) providing clean, affordable and secure energy; (3) mobilizing the industrial sector toward a clean and circular economy; (4) building and renovating in a way that saves energy and resources; (5) accelerating the transition to sustainable and intelligent mobility; (6) creating a fair, healthy and friendly food system "A Farm to Fork": creating a fair, healthy and green food system; and (7) zero emissions for a non-toxic environment. The European Green Deal is thus a comprehensive strategic package aimed at transforming the EU into a climate-neutral and competitive economy by 2050. Environmental policy areas are not equally ambitious and equipped with legislative initiatives (setting out regulatory and economic instruments) to realize these ambitions. Taking these two aspects into account, climate and energy

---

10 EC, Communication from the Commission to the European Parliament, the European Council, the Council, the European Economic and Social Committee and the Committee of the Regions, The European Green Deal, COM(2019) 640 final, Brussels, 11.12.2019.

11 U. von der Leyen, A Union that strives for more—My agenda for Europe, European Commission, 2019, https://ec.europa.eu/commission/sites/beta-political/files/political-guidelines-next-commission_en.pdf [accessed: 4.05.2023]; S. Wolf, J. Teitge, J. Mielke, F. Schütze, and C. Jaeger, "The European Green Deal—More Than Climate Neutrality," *Intereconomics* 56 (2021), p. 102.

policies (including greenhouse gas emissions from transport) are emerging as the driving forces behind the EGD. In contrast, in the area of biodiversity policy, there is a clear gap between environmental objectives and legislative initiatives, which in the long term may jeopardize the achievement of all key EGD objectives, given their indivisibility.[12]

The "Fit for 55" program of July 14, 2021,[13] is one of the tools of the European Green Deal. It is a climate change regulatory package comprising 13 legislative acts. The regulations cover, for example, the entire energy sector, the management of forests and land use, road transport and the taxation of energy. The Fit 55 package aims to achieve the EU's more ambitious emissions reduction target for the benefit of all Europeans, creating opportunities to share in the change, helping those most in need and achieving higher overall emissions reductions. This package will also contribute to the greening of the EU economy in the wake of the pandemic, to the dissemination of the standard environment outside the EU and to the promotion of product innovation and future technologies. The main objective of this program is to reduce greenhouse gas emissions in Europe by up to 55% by 2030 (compared to 1990 levels) and to achieve climate neutrality by 2050. In order to achieve this level of greenhouse gas reduction, it is planned to strengthen all existing climate and energy legislation by revising its objectives, scope and structure. The proposed reforms cover the existing EU Emissions Trading Scheme, burden-sharing between Member States, energy taxation, energy efficiency and renewable energy.[14] There are plans to reform the EU Emissions Trading Scheme (EU ETS) by reducing the number of emission allowances. The increasing price of emission allowances and the annual reduction of the cap

---

12 S. Paleari, "The Impact of the European Green Deal on EU Environmental Policy," *The Journal of Environment & Development* 31/2 (2022), https://doi.org/10.1177/107049652210822; S. Schunz, "The 'European Green Deal'—a Paradigm Shift? Transformations in the European Union's Sustainability Meta-Discourse," *Political Research Exchange* 4 (2022), 2085121, https://doi.org/10.1080/2474736X.2022.2085121.

13 Communication from the Commission to the European Parliament, the Council, the European Economic and Social Committee and the Committee of the Regions, "Fit for 55": delivering the EU's 2030 Climate Target on the way to climate neutrality, COM/2021/550 final.

14 S. Schlacke, H. Wentzien, E-M. Thierjung, and M. Köster, "Implementing the EU Climate Law via the 'Fit for 55' package," *Oxford Open Energy* 1 (2022), oiab002, https://doi.org/10.1093/ooenergy/oiab002; A. Piebalgs and Ch. Jones, "The Commission's Proposal of a "Fit for 55" Legislative Package: What Impact Could It Have?," *Policy Briefs* 56 (2021), https://hdl.handle.net/1814/73249.

will encourage companies and institutions to use new, low-emission technological solutions. A revision of the Renewable Energy Directive is also planned, with the aim of increasing energy production from renewable sources to 40% by 2030 and using it in key economic sectors such as transport, industry, construction and HVAC systems. The EU also aims to remove CO_2 through natural sinks by planting 3 billion trees across Europe by 2030. Climate neutrality must also cover the agriculture, forestry and land-use sectors, and the tool for change is the reduction of emissions of gases other than CO_2 from the use of fertilizers and livestock, especially methane.[15]

The circular economy[16] is a program that supports the implementation of the objectives of the European Green Deal. The circular economy is a model of production and consumption that involves sharing, borrowing, reusing, repairing, refurbishing and recycling existing materials and products for as long as possible. This extends the life cycle of products. In practice, this means minimizing waste. At the end of a product's life cycle, its raw materials and waste should be kept in the economy through recycling. They can be successfully reused to create additional value. The main elements of the circular economy are:

1. Production. The circular economy starts at the very beginning of a product's life cycle. Both design and production have an impact on raw material extraction, resource use and waste generation throughout the product life cycle;
2. Product design. Better design can make products more durable or easier to repair, upgrade or regenerate. Better design can make it easier for users to recycle and disassemble products to recover valuable materials and components. Overall, it can save valuable resources;
3. Production processes. Even with intelligently designed products or materials, inefficient use of resources in production processes can result in lost business opportunities and generate significant amounts of waste. Primary raw materials, including renewable materials, will continue to play an important role in production processes, even in a circular economy. In this context, attention should be paid to the environmental and social impacts of production;

---

15 European Parliament, *Revision of the Renewable Energy Directive: Fit for 55 Package*, https://www.europarl.europa.eu/thinktank/pl/document/EPRS_BRI(2021)698781 [accessed: 10.05.2023].

16 Communication from the Commission to the European Parliament, the Council, the European Economic and Social Committee and the Committee of the Regions, Closing the loop—An EU action plan for the Circular Economy, COM(2015) 614 final, Brussels, 2.12.2015.

4. Consumption. Consumer choices can support or hinder the development of a circular economy. These choices depend on the information available to consumers, the range and price of products offered and the existing regulatory framework. This stage is also crucial for preventing and reducing the generation of household waste;
5. Waste management. Waste management plays an essential role in the circular economy: it defines how the waste hierarchy is applied in practice in the EU. The waste hierarchy establishes a priority order: from prevention, preparation for reuse, recycling and energy recovery to disposal, such as waste incineration. The aim is to encourage the use of options with the best overall environmental impact;
6. From waste to resource: promoting the reuse and market recovery of water. In a circular economy, materials that can be recycled are reintroduced into the economy as new raw materials, thereby increasing security of supply. These "secondary raw materials" can be sold or shipped, as can primary raw materials from traditional natural resources.

In addition, the circular economy is a regenerative system in which resource use and waste, energy emissions and leakage are minimized by slowing down, closing and narrowing material and energy loops. The aim is to reduce the amount of waste generated, reuse products and close production chains. This approach is suitable for achieving the environmental objectives.[17]

The next strategy is "Toward a sustainable Europe 2030." The aim of the strategy is to restore Europe's biodiversity by 2030 for the benefit of people, the climate and the planet. Biodiversity loss is a threat to the climate because the destruction and degradation of ecosystems and soils accelerates the process of global warming, while the restoration of natural resources mitigates the effects of climate change.[18] In the context of the expected post-COVID-19 situation,

17 A. Murray, K. Skene, and K. Haynes, "The Circular Economy: An Interdisciplinary Exploration of the Concept and Application in a Global Context," *Journal of Business Ethics* 140 (2015), p. 372; M. Geissdoerfer, P. Savaget, N. M. P. Bocken, and E. J. Hultink, "The Circular Economy—A New Sustainability Paradigm?," *Journal Clean Production* 143 (2017), p. 759; E. Zębek and J. Zięty, "Effect of Landfill Arson to a "Lax" System in a Circular Economy under the Current EU Energy Policy: Perspective Review in Waste Management Law," *Energies* 15 (2022), p. 8690. https://doi.org/10.3390/en15228690.

18 Komisja Europejska, Unijna strategia na rzecz bioróżnorodności 2030—Przywracanie przyrody do naszego życia, https://www.teraz-srodowisko.pl/media/pdf/aktualnosci/8708-unijna-strategia-bioroznorodnosc-2030.pdf.

the strategy aims to build the resilience of our societies to future threats such as the effects of climate change, forest fires, food insecurity and disease outbreaks, including through the protection of wildlife and the fight against illegal wildlife trade. The strategy includes the following specific commitments and actions to be implemented by 2030: (1) establishing a larger EU-wide network of terrestrial and marine protected areas—extending the EU's existing Natura 2000 sites, with strict protection for areas of very high biodiversity and climate value; (2) launching the EU Nature Recovery Plan—by introducing effective restoration measures to restore degraded ecosystems, particularly those with the greatest potential for carbon capture and storage, and to prevent and mitigate natural disasters; (3) taking action to enable the necessary transformative change—unblocking biodiversity finance and establishing a new, strengthened governance framework; and (4) taking action to address the global biodiversity challenge—the global biodiversity crisis, in particular working toward the successful adoption of an ambitious global biodiversity framework under the Convention on Biological Diversity.[19] This strategy also sets out commitments to protect biodiversity, including (1) overarching long-term goals for biodiversity in line with the United Nations vision of "living in harmony with nature" by 2050. By 2050, all the world's ecosystems should be restored, resilient and adequately protected; (2) more effective means of implementing the strategy in areas such as finance, skills, research, expertise and technology; (3) a much more rigorous implementation, monitoring and review process; and (4) fair and equitable sharing of the benefits arising from the use of genetic resources related to biodiversity.[20]

The most recent program analyzed is: "A Farm to Fork" (F2F) strategy presented by the European Commission in May 2020.[21] This strategy is part of the European Green Deal, which aims to make food systems fair, healthy and environmentally friendly. Although the EU has started to move toward sustainable systems in many areas, food systems remain one of the main drivers of climate change and environmental degradation. There is an urgent need to reduce

---

19 EC, Reflection Paper, Towards a Sustainable Europe by 2030, https://commission.europa.eu/system/files/2019-02/rp_sustainable_europe_30-01_en_web.pdf; EC. Biodiversity strategy for 2030, https://environment.ec.europa.eu/strategy/biodiversity-strategy-2030_en [accessed: 2.05.2023].

20 Komisja Europejska, "Unijna strategia na rzecz bioróżnorodności 2030," *op. cit.*

21 EC, Communication from the Commission to the European Parliament, the Council, the European Economic and Social Committee and the Committee of the Regions, A Farm to Fork Strategy for a fair, healthy and environmentally-friendly food system, COM(2020) 381 final, Brussels, 20.5.2020.

reliance on pesticides and inputs, reduce over-fertilization, enhance the environmental benefits of agriculture, improve animal welfare and reverse biodiversity loss. The EU's goal is to reduce the environmental and climate footprint of the EU system and strengthen its resilience, ensure security in the face of climate change and biodiversity loss, and lead the global transformation toward competitive sustainability from the field to the table, creating new opportunities. This means: (1) ensuring that the food chain, including the production, transport, distribution, marketing and consumption of food, has a neutral or positive impact on the environment by protecting and restoring the land, freshwater and marine resources on which the food system depends, contributing to climate change mitigation and adaptation, soil, water, air, plant and animal health and welfare, and halting the loss of biodiversity; (2) ensuring food security, nutrition and public health—ensuring that everyone has access to an adequate quantity of healthy and sustainable food that meets high standards of safety, quality, plant and animal health and welfare, while satisfying nutritional needs and preferences; and (3) keeping food affordable while generating fairer economic returns in the supply chain to ultimately the most sustainable food has also become the most affordable, supporting the competitiveness of the EU supply sector, supporting fair trade, creating new business opportunities, while ensuring the integrity of the internal market and safety and occupational hygiene. The main elements of this system are therefore: (a) ensuring food safety; (b) promoting sustainable practices in food processing, wholesale and retail trade, hotels and restaurants; (c) promoting sustainable food consumption and facilitating the transition to a healthy and balanced diet; (d) reducing food losses and waste; and (e) combating food fraud in the food supply chain. The F2F strategy therefore encompasses a number of policy objectives that affect agricultural production in the EU and beyond. The benefits of implementing this strategy include, for example, the impact on greenhouse gas emissions, biodiversity or landscape. The key quantitative targets of the F2F strategy to be achieved by 2030 are as follows: Reduce the use and risk of chemical pesticides and the use of more hazardous pesticides by 50%; Reduce nutrient losses by at least 50% while ensuring no loss of soil fertility; Reduce fertilizer use by at least 20%; Reduce sales of antimicrobials for livestock and aquaculture by 50%; Increase the total area under organic farming to 25%; Reduce per capita food waste at retail and consumer level by 50%; and Invest in food, bioeconomy, natural resources, agriculture, fisheries, aquaculture and the environment.[22]

---

22 J. Wesseler, "The EU's Farm-to-Fork Strategy: An Assessment from the Perspective of

3. Environmental impact assessment and public participation

An important legal instrument for the protection of environmental resources in the EU is the Environmental Impact Assessment (EIA) system. The importance of this instrument for environmental protection is twofold. On the one hand, EIA allows for the implementation of two principles of international environmental law, namely the right of access to information on the state and protection of the environment and the principle of social participation, which allows for the strengthening of the role of local communities in environmental protection and at the same time strengthens the human right to the environment. On the other hand, the use of EIA at the project planning stage allows the principle of prevention and precaution to be applied to environmental protection, by using this instrument as a preventive measure, even when the negative effects of the activity are not fully known. When analyzing the participation of society in environmental protection, the Aarhus Convention, adopted on June 25, 1998,[23] should be mentioned. This Convention was created to strengthen the role of citizens and civil society organizations in environmental matters and is based on the principles of participatory democracy. The Aarhus Convention establishes a number of rights for individuals and civil society organizations in relation to the environment. Parties to the Convention are required to take the necessary measures to ensure that public authorities at national, regional or local level contribute to the realization of these rights. The Århus Convention provides for (1) access to environmental information. The right of citizens to obtain environmental information held by public authorities; (2) public participation in environmental decision-making. The right of citizens to participate in the preparation of plans, programs, policies and legislation that may affect the environment; and (3) access to justice. The right of citizens to have access to review procedures when their rights to access to information or public participation have been violated. Ensuring these rights for citizens allows them to participate in environmental procedures, including environmental impact assessments.[24]

Agricultural Economics," *Applied Economic Perspectives and Policy* 44 (2022), https://doi.org/10.1002/aepp.13239.

23 Convention on access to information, public participation in decision-making and access to justice in environmental matters done at Aarhus, Denmark, on June 25, 1998 (*Journal of Laws* 1998, No. 78, item 706).

24 E. Zębek and R. Biedrzycki, "Regulations concerning dissemination of information about the condition and protection of natural environment in the light of legal acts in

In the EU, these issues are regulated by Directive 2011/92/EU,[25] which applies to the environmental impact assessment of public and private projects likely to have significant effects on the environment. Environmental effects should be taken into account at the earliest possible stage in all technical planning and decision-making processes. The principles of environmental impact assessment should be harmonized, in particular as regards the projects to be assessed, the basic obligations of developers and the content of the assessment. Environmental Impact Assessment means a process consisting of the preparation of an Environmental Impact Report by the developer and public consultation. The EIA shall identify, describe and assess, in an appropriate manner and on a case-by-case basis, the direct and indirect significant effects of a project on (a) population and human health; (b) biodiversity, paying particular attention to species and habitats protected under the Habitats Directive 92/43/EEC[26] and the Birds Directive 2009/147/EC[27]; (c) land, soil, water, air and climate; (d) material assets, cultural heritage and landscape; (e) the interaction between the factors referred to in points (a) to (d). Public consultation is therefore an integral part of the process. The purpose of carrying out an EIA is therefore to provide decision-makers, other stakeholders and the public with the necessary information on the environmental effects of a proposed plan, program or project. The purpose of the EIA process is to provide information on whether the environmental impacts of the investment have been optimally planned and whether the benefits of its implementation outweigh the environmental losses. An important element of the EIA is the environmental risk assessment, which is an assessment of the impact on human health and life and the environmental risk to the quality of surface water.[28] In relation to the European Green Deal, the Commission is committed

---

force," *Zeszyty Naukowe Wyższej Szkoły Finansów i Prawa w Bielsku-Białej, Scientific Journal WSFiP* 4 (2017), p. 51.

25 Directive 2011/92/EU of the European Parliament and of the Council of December 13, 2011 on the assessment of the effects of certain public and private projects on the environment (OJ L 26 of 28.1.2012, p. 1).

26 Council Directive 92/43/EEC of May 21, 1992 on the conservation of natural habitats and of wild fauna and flora (OJ L 206 of 22.7.1992, pp. 7–50).

27 Directive 2009/147/EC of the European Parliament and of the Council of November 30, 2009 on the conservation of wild birds (OJ L 20 of 26.1.2010, pp. 7–25).

28 J. Ciechanowicz-McLean, *The Lexicon of Environmental Protection*, Warsaw 2009, p. 192; M. Bar, J. Jendrośka, J. Lenart, *Environmental Impact Assessment in a Construction Project, Legal Procedure and Preparation of Reports in the Investment Process*, Warsaw 2011; E. Zębek, "Principle of Public Participation in EU Environmental Policy as the Public's Fundamental Right to Participate in the Implementation of Project Negatively

to assessing the consistency of all its future plans, programs and proposals with the objectives of the EGD. The reference to "impact assessments" in this context means a regulatory impact assessment based on the Better Regulation Guidelines. However, there is no mention of Strategic Environmental Assessment (SEA), which is undoubtedly much more effective in assessing the environmental sustainability of proposed strategic decisions than regulatory impact assessment.[29]

4. Conclusions

Analyzing the considerations made in this article, it can be concluded that the relationship between the environment and society is twofold. The environment is a common good and must be protected because the quality of life of society depends on the quality of environmental resources. The EU has also taken up this challenge, which was interrupted during the COVID-19 pandemic, and this is reflected in environmental policy, now in the Environment Action Programme until 2030 (EAP), based on the UN 2030 Agenda and its Sustainable Development Goals. Environmental policy is implemented through the implementation of EU programs. The most important is the European Green Deal, to which other programs are linked, that is, the circular economy, "Fit for 55," "Toward a sustainable Europe 2030" and "A Farm to Fork Strategy." When assessing the guidelines of the EU programs analyzed, it is important to recognize that they are comprehensive, that is, many aspects of activities that contribute to environmental degradation are taken into account and need to be addressed. The most pressing issue in this area is climate change caused by anthropogenic activities, in particular greenhouse gas emissions. The main challenge is to achieve a high level of mitigation and climate neutrality by 2050. In addition to reducing emissions of these gases, measures are being taken to adapt to climate change, also using natural methods, that is, the creation of green areas which, in addition to fulfilling many ecological functions—absorption of greenhouse gases, water retention—contribute to improving the value of the landscape. It is worth remembering that society initially pushed for the development of urbanization,

---

Impacting the Environment," in *Contemporary Problems of Human Rights: Selected Aspects*, ed. M. Mamiński and M. Rzewuski, Warsaw 2019, p. 361.

29 J. Jendrośka, M. Reese, and L. Squintani, "Towards a New Legal Framework for Sustainability under the European Green Deal," *The Opole Studies in Administration and Law* 19/2 (2021), p. 110.

industry and the extensive modification of the environment, and now, in order to improve its condition, it is returning to natural methods of pollution removal.

In addition to these measures to improve the quality of the environment, the first priority to reduce greenhouse gas emissions is the energy transition, which aims to increase the amount of energy produced, especially from renewable sources such as wind, solar, hydro and biomass. Unfortunately, the use of renewable energy is limited in some EU countries due to geographical conditions, for example, sunshine, wind speed, fast-flowing rivers. Here there seems to be potential in the form of biomass, particularly in the form of sewage sludge from treatment plants or landfill waste. It seems right to aim for zero emissions of air, water and soil pollutants and to decouple economic growth from resource use and environmental degradation by implementing a closed-loop economy that maximizes the use of raw materials and minimizes the generation of waste. In this case, by requiring the production of more durable products, in addition to environmental benefits, improvements in the quality of goods and responsible consumption can be achieved.

In particular, the "Toward a Sustainable Europe 2030" program shows a desire to protect and conserve biodiversity, which is so undervalued today. It should be noted that the greater the diversity, the more stable and resilient ecosystems are to anthropogenic influences. This is particularly important in agriculture, on which the food market is based. After all, the health of society depends on the quality of water, air and food. In addition to the practical aspects, the protection of biodiversity is also important for the preservation of our natural heritage. For this reason, we should strive to create new legally protected areas, especially at EU level, such as Natura 2000 sites, and treat them not as a form of restriction on economic activity, but as an environmental benefit, that is, the preservation of valuable and unique natural elements, while at the same time influencing the state of the environment, mitigating climate change, and providing opportunities for the development of tourism and organic farms producing healthy food. The EU has also taken up the challenge of healthy food production in the Farm to Fork Strategy program, which is based on food systems that are fair, healthy and environmentally friendly by ensuring food security, sustainable food processing practices, sustainable food consumption and reducing food loss and waste. In this way, the system has an impact on food quality by reducing the use of pesticides and fertilizers, as well as on greenhouse gas emissions, biodiversity or the landscape.

On the other hand, it is important to note that without public participation, the implementation of the above guidelines is difficult. By giving the public the right to participate in the development and shaping of environmental policy and strategic documents, it helps to identify its needs, but also to reduce the negative impact of economic activities on the environment. It should be noted that active public participation in this area of life is in the public's interest, as it influences the state of the environment in which it lives. An example of such a legal instrument is the Environmental Impact Assessment (EIA) system. In particular, the environmental impact of a project needs to be assessed at the planning stage, so that the most effective solutions can be found to protect environmental resources and, in the event of degradation, natural compensation can be planned. Public consultation is therefore an integral part of this process. In summary, the EU's environmental policy, particularly in the fields of combating and adapting to climate change and managing raw materials and waste, aims to improve the quality of life of society by improving the quality of air, water, soil and food. Society plays an important role in shaping environmental policy, in particular in environmental impact assessment procedures. Society has an influence on the implementation of projects that may have a negative impact on the environment and thus on the state and degradation of the environment. All these activities should contribute to improving the quality of the environment and thus the quality of life, as well as to implementing the guiding principle of sustainable development—leaving environmental resources for future generations.

Bibliography

Literature

Bar, M., Jendrośka, J., and Lenart, J., *Environmental Impact Assessment in a Construction Project, Legal Procedure and Preparation of Reports in the Investment Process*, Warsaw 2011.

Ciechanowicz-McLean, J., *Leksykon ochrony środowiska*, Warsaw 2009.

Geissdoerfer, M., Savaget, P., Bocken, N. M. P., and Hultink, E. J., "The Circular Economy—A New Sustainability Paradigm?," *Journal Clean Production* 143 (2017).

Halmaghi, E.-E., "Environmental Action Programmes of the European Union—Programmes Supporting the Sustainable Development Strategy of the European Union," *Scientific Bulletin* XXI/2(42) (2016).

Jendrośka, J., Reese, M., and Squintani, L., "Towards a New Legal Framework for Sustainability under the European Green Deal," *The Opole Studies in Administration and Law* 19/2 (2021).

Kingston, S., "I. Environment," *International & Comparative Law Quarterly* 59/4 (2010).

Murray, A., Skene, K., and Haynes, K., "The Circular Economy: An Interdisciplinary Exploration of the Concept and Application in a Global Context," *Journal of Business Ethics* 140 (2015).

Paleari, S., "The Impact of the European Green Deal on EU Environmental Policy," *The Journal of Environment & Development* 31/2 (2022), https://doi.org/10.1177/107049652210822.

Pedersen, A. B., Hickmann, T., Renn, O., Eckert, N., Jax, K., Lepenies, R., Liu, H.-Y., Lyytimaki, J., Piebalgs, A., and Jones Ch., "The Commission's Proposal of a 'Fit for 55' Legislative Package: What Impact Could It Have?," *Policy Briefs* 56 (2021), https://hdl.handle.net/1814/73249.

Reis, S., and Rusch, G., "SDGs at the Halfway Point: How the 17 Global Goals Address Risks and Wicked Problems," *Ambio* 52 (2023).

Roliński, M., "Z problematyki zasad ochrony środowiska," *Studia Iuridica Lublinensia* 21 (2014).

Rydz-Żbikowska, A., "Implementing Sustainable Development Goals within the COVID-19 Pandemic Future Challenges for the 2030 Agenda," *Comparative Economic Research. Central and Eastern Europe* 25/4 (2022).

Sala, S., Crenna, E., Secchi, M., and Sanye-Mengual, E., "Environmental Sustainability of European Production and Consumption Assessed against Planetary Boundaries," *Journal of Environmental Management* 269 (2020), 110686, https://doi.org/10.1016/j.jenvman.2020.110686.

Schlacke, S., Wentzien, H., Thierjung, E.-M., and Köster, M., "Implementing the EU Climate Law via the 'Fit for 55' Package," *Oxford Open Energy* 1 (2022), oiab002, https://doi.org/10.1093/ooenergy/oiab002.

Schunz, S., "The 'European Green Deal'—a Paradigm Shift? Transformations in the European Union's Sustainability Meta-discourse," *Political Research Exchange* 4 (2022), 2085121, https://doi.org/10.1080/2474736X.2022.2085121.

von der Leyen, U., *A Union that Strives for More—My Agenda for Europe*, European Commission, 2019, https://ec.europa.eu/commission/sites/beta-political/files/political-guidelines-next-commission_en.pdf.

Wamsler Ch., Osberg, G., Osika, W., Herndersson, H., and Mundaca, L., "Linking Internal and External Transformation for Sustainability and Climate Action: Towards a New Research and Policy Agenda," *Global Environmental Change* 71 (2021), 102373, https://doi.org/10.1016/j.gloenvcha.2021.102373.

Wolf, S., Teitge, J., Mielke, J., Schütze, F., and Jaeger, C., "The European Green Deal—More Than Climate Neutrality," *Intereconomics* 56 (2021).

Zębek, E., *Gospodarka odpadami w ujęciu prawnym i środowiskowym*, KPP Monografie, Olsztyn 2018.

Zębek, E., and Biedrzycki, R., "Regulations Concerning Dissemination of Information about the Condition and Protection of Natural Environment in the Light of Legal Acts in Force," *Zeszyty Naukowe Wyższej Szkoły Finansów i Prawa w Bielsku-Białej, Scientific Journal WSFiP* 4 (2017).

Zębek, E., "Principle of Public Participation in EU Environmental Policy as the Public's Fundamental Right to Participate in the Implementation of Project Negatively Impacting the Environment," in *Contemporary Problems of Human Rights: Selected Aspects*, ed. M. Mamiński and M. Rzewuski, Warsaw 2019.

Zębek, E., and Zięty, J., "Effect of Landfill Arson to a 'Lax' System in a Circular Economy under the Current EU Energy Policy: Perspective Review in Waste Management Law," *Energies* 15/8690 (2022), https://doi.org/10.3390/en15228690.

Legal acts

Communication from the Commission to the European Parliament, the Council, the European Economic and Social Committee and the Committee of the Regions, Closing the loop—An EU action plan for the Circular Economy, COM(2015) 614 final, Brussels, 2.12.2015.

Communication from the Commission to the European Parliament, the Council, the European Economic and Social Committee and the Committee of the Regions, "Fit for 55": Delivering the EU's 2030 Climate Target on the way to climate neutrality, COM/2021/550 final.

Council Directive 92/43/EEC of May 21, 1992, on the conservation of natural habitats and of wild fauna and flora (OJ L 206 of 22.7.1992, pp. 7–50).

Convention on access to information, public participation in decision-making and access to justice in environmental matters done at Aarhus, Denmark, on June 25, 1998 (Journal of Laws 1998, No. 78, item 706).

Decision (EU) 2022/591 of the European Parliament and of the Council of April 6, 2022, on a General Union Environment Action Programme to 2030, PE/83/2021/REV/1 (OJ L 114 of 12.4.2022, pp. 22–36).

Directive 2009/147/EC of the European Parliament and of the Council of November 30, 2009, on the conservation of wild birds (OJ L 20 of 26.1.2010, pp. 7–25).

Directive 2011/92/EU of the European Parliament and of the Council of December 13, 2011, on the assessment of the effects of certain public and private projects on the environment (OJ L 26 of 28.1.2012, p. 1).

EC, Communication from the Commission to the European Parliament, the European Council, the Council, the European Economic and Social Committee and the Committee of the Regions, The European Green Deal, COM(2019) 640 final, Brussels, 11.12.2019.

EC, Communication from the Commission to the European Parliament, the Council, the European Economic and Social Committee and the Committee of the Regions, A Farm to Fork Strategy for a fair, healthy and environmentally-friendly food system, COM(2020) 381 final, Brussels, 20.5.2020.

Treaty on the Functioning of the European Union (C 326/49 of 26.10.2012).

United Nations, Resolution No. A/RES/70/1 adopted by the General Assembly on September 25, 2015, Transforming our world: The 2030 Agenda for Sustainable Development.

Ius, Lex et Res Publica

Studies in Law, Philosophy and Political Cultures

Edited by

Anna Jaron

Vol. 1 Anna Jaron: Socio-Economic Constitutional Rights in Democratisation Processes. An Account of the Constitutional Dialogue Theory. 2012.

Vol. 2 Stanisław Filipowicz: Democracy – The Power of Illusion. 2013.

Vol. 3 Teresa Dukiet-Nagórska (ed.): The Postulates of Restorative Justice and the Continental Model of Criminal Law. As Illustrated by Polish Criminal Law 2014.

Vol. 4 Agnieszka Kupzok: Enforcement of Patents on Geographically Divisible Inventions. An Inquiry into the Standard of Substantive Patent Law Infringement in Cross-Border Constellations. 2015.

Vol. 5 Alicja Jagielska-Burduk / Wojciech Szafrański: Legal Issues in Cultural Heritage Management. A Polish Perspective. 2016.

Vol. 6 Maciej Mataczyński (ed.): The Takeover of Public Companies as a Mode of Exercising EU Treaty Freedoms. 2017.

Vol. 7 Maciej Barczewski (ed.): Value of Information. Intellectual Property, Privacy and Big Data. 2018.

Vol. 8 Pawel Smoleń, Marcin Burzec: Introduction to Polish Tax Law. 2018.

Vol. 9 Łukasz Pohl, Konrad Burdziak: Judicial Interpretation of the 1997 Criminal Code Provisions on Self-Defence. 2019.

Vol. 10 Adam Szot: Judicial Review of Administrative Discretion. The Influence of Court Decisions on Administrative Actions. 2019.

Vol. 11 Michał Peno / Konrad Burdziak (eds.): The Concept of Modern Law. Polish and Central European Tradition. 2019.

Vol. 12 Leszek Leszczyński / Bartosz Liżewski / Adam Szot (eds.): Potential of Precedent in the Statutory Legal Order. 2010.

Vol. 13 Łukasz Bolesta: In Search of a Model for the Legal Protection of a Whistleblower in the Workplace in Poland. A legal and comparative study. 2020.

Vol. 14 Paweł Chmielnicki / Adam Sulikowski (eds.): New Perspectives on Legislation. A Comparative Approach. 2020.

Vol. 15 Marcin Burzec / Beata Kucia-Guściora / Paweł Smoleń: Agricultural Activity in Poland: A Fiscal and Legal Study. 2020.

Vol. 16 Magdalena Półtorak / Ilona Topa (eds.): Women, Children and (Other) Vulnerable Groups. Standards of Protection and Challenges for International Law. 2021.

Vol. 17 Josef Albert Fox: Die polnische Verfassung vom 3. Mai 1791. Hintergründe der Entstehung und der Außerkraftsetzung. Stellung Polens im Zeitalter der Aufklärung. 2021.

Vol. 18 Barbara Janusz-Pohl (ed.): Juvenile Justice Systems: Poland-Brazil-Portugal. 2021.

Vol. 19 Leszek Leszczyński: General Reference Clauses in the Judicial Process. Context of Legislative Intentions Interpretative Discretion. 2021.

Vol. 20 Francisco J. Campos Zamora: Das Problem der Begründung richterlicher Entscheidungen. Eine Analyse auf der Grundlage der Theorie der juristischen Argumentation. 2021.

Ius, Lex et Res Publica

Studies in Law, Philosophy and Political Cultures

Edited by

Barbara Janusz-Pohl and Anna Jaron

Vol. 21 Aneta Skorupa-Wulczyńska: Language Rights of the Citizen of the European Union. 2022.

Vol. 22 Mateusz Osiecki: International Legal Aspects of Aerial Terrorism. Methods of Law Enforcement in Avia-tion. 2022.

Vol. 23 Vladimír Sharp / Gabriela Blahoudková / Jakub Handrlica (eds.): Law, Pandemics and Ownership Restrictions. 2022.

Vol. 24 Piotr Kasprzyk / Anna Konert: Drones – Future of Aviation Law? Interference of Public Law in Private Law. 2023.

Vol. 25 Szymon Pawelec (ed.): Consensual Procedures in Criminal Law – Comparative Perspective. 2023.

Vol. 26 Dorota Pudzianowska: The Statelessness in Public Law. 2023.

Vol. 27 Bogusław Przywora / Aleksander Wróbel: Formalised Access to Pre-jurisdictional Free Legal Aid. Analysis based on Example of Ukraine, Poland, Great Britain and Sweden. 2023.

Vol. 28 Ewa Dawidziuk / Patricia Panero / Anna Tarwacka (eds.): Family, Law, and Society: from Roman Law to the Present Day. 2023.

www.peterlang.com

www.ingramcontent.com/pod-product-compliance
Ingram Content Group UK Ltd.
Pitfield, Milton Keynes, MK11 3LW, UK
UKHW041447071026
15587UKWH00010B/503

9 783631 910108